Field Theory

as Human-Science

Field Theory

as Human-Science

CONTRIBUTIONS OF LEWIN'S BERLIN GROUP

COMPILED WITH COMMENTARY BY

JOSEPH DE RIVERA
Clark University

GARDNER PRESS, INC., New York

Distributed by Halsted Press Division of John Wiley & Sons, Inc.

NEW YORK • TORONTO • LONDON • SYDNEY

GARDNER PRESS, INC.
32 Washington Square West
New York, New York 10011

Distributed solely by the Halstead Press Division of John Wiley & Sons, Inc., New York

Library of Congress Cataloging in Publication Data
Main entry under title:

Field theory as human-science.

"Translation . . . of some of the early papers by
Lewin and his students."
Includes index.
1. Lewin, Kurt, 1890-1947–Addresses, essays,
lectures. 2. Field theory (Social psychology)–Ad-
dresses, essays, lectures. 3. Society for the
Psychological Study of Social Issues. I. Lewin,
Kurt, 1890-1947. II. De Rivera, Joseph.
HM251.F49   301.1   75-35530
ISBN 0-470-20368-4

27, 634

PRINTED IN THE UNITED STATES OF AMERICA
1 2 3 4 5 6 7 8 9

PREFACE

KURT Lewin was one of the founding members of the Society for the Psychological Study of Social Issues (SPSSI), a group of some 3,000 persons with a truly democratic structure and set of ideals. In 1963, the Council of the Society decided to use the Kurt Lewin Memorial Fund to facilitate the translation and publication of some of the early papers by Lewin and his students, and accepted my proposal to give priority to the many doctoral dissertations that were supervised by Lewin and formed the empirical background for the development of field theory. While I believe that this was the best course of action, it does mean that the bulk of Lewin's own early work still remains to be translated. A listing of this work may be found in Alfred Marrow's biography, *The Practical Theorist,* and some of the royalties from this present book will be returned to the Lewin Memorial Fund and eventually used to insure the translation of these earlier studies.

Initially, I had simply intended to gather together some translations that had already been made by Sibylle Escalona, to arrange for the translation of the remaining studies, and to make the series of dissertations available on microfilm. And even this modest project took a good deal of energy. It was hard to locate some of the translations and difficult to find a reasonably priced translator who could put into good English the technical vocabulary of scientific German that was frequently written by a student whose first language had been Russian!

Fortunately, in 1965 I finally met Dr. Hedda Korsch, whose intelligence, wit, and determination were much stronger than her aging eyes were weak. In fact, Dr. Korsch had only one "good" eye (she had a sort of lens that she used to peer through at the print she was translating). Finally, that eye gave up, too, but Dr. Korsch didn't. She simply had the German read to her and "dictated" the English right into the typewriter. I also discovered a young librarian who was a skillful translator. Marsha Horwitz had the gift of taking pleasure in simple things (as when I immediately spelled her name with one "o"), and was able to cope with some of the longest technical passages that I hope have ever been invented.

By the fall of 1967, there was enough material available for me to give a seminar at New York University, where I was teaching, and for the first time I became aware of the full scope and breadth of the series of dissertations. It was rather overwhelming, and as I was in the middle of another book, I simply took notes and let the material simmer in the back of my mind. However, when SPSSI Council proposed that the studies be somehow made into a book, it was clear to me that the idea was sound and should be executed.

The translations were completed by the winter of 1968, and when I discovered that Susan Goodman (then a graduate student at N.Y.U.) had editorial experience, I asked her if she would be willing to spend the summer reading over some of the material and smoothing out the translations. I am very glad that she did so. I also want to mention that throughout all this time I felt sustained by the quiet presence of letters from Caroline Weichlein, SPSSI's excellent executive secretary.

My first proposal for a book based on the translations was titled *Gestalt Contributions to the Dynamics of Behavior.* It suggested a format of seven of the most original dissertations, together with commentary by five contemporary psychologists who came from a general gestalt tradition. I believe it would have been an interesting book; but during 1969 and 1970 neither I nor a number of SPSSI representatives were able to interest any of the commercial publishers who felt that the material was too specific to have much sales value. Consequently, in 1971, I proposed a more modest book, *The Dynamics of Intention,* that contained only an introduction and the translations, and emphasized the applicability of the studies to current problems in motivational theory. Some interest was expressed in this proposal, and, encouraged, I began to write an introduction during the summer of 1971.

This was the first time I had really had the opportunity to become fully immersed in the material of the dissertations and Lewin's thought. I had believed it would be easy to write an introduction during the summer; but as I read, it became clear that the data were so rich and the ideas so complex that the job of mastering the material was much larger than I had anticipated. Further, I discovered that my own approach to the material led to a reinterpretation of many of the ideas, and would require some commentary after each of the studies. Each summer I returned to work on the manuscript, and by the fall of 1973 I had enough written to base a seminar at Clark University on the material. The manuscript was slowly becoming *Field Theory as Human Science.*

The late winter of 1974 was a critical period. I had two months that were free of teaching, and somehow the separate batches of notes and ideas had to be made to cohere into a book. Finally, I isolated myself in a small cabin on a Maine island and wrote continually for two weeks, stopping only to cut wood and cook meals. Margaret, my wife, gave me a white turtlenecked sweater and Eric loaned me his coat. They kept me warm and made me feel cared for.

How good it is to have a really good secretary. When I returned, Becky Clark quickly typed up my manuscript and mailed chapters off to a number of friends and colleagues. As a result, Solomon Asch, Dorwin Cartwright, Don Campbell, Mary Henle, Jacqueline Goodchilds, Susan Goodman, Frederica

Parlett, Al Pepitone, and Eva Wong were kind enough to share their ideas and criticisms with me. I went to see Fritz and Grace Heider and enjoyed their hospitality, challenging ideas, and thoughtful comments. And at Clark, Donna Apter, Joel Funk, Jim Laird, John Lau, Jan Lindsay, Gary Overvold, Neil Rankin, John Teske, Ina Uzgiris, Seymour Wapner, and Mort Weiner read sections of the book and gave me important suggestions.

As a result of all this help, I spent the summer and fall of 1974 rewriting the manuscript and attempting to respond to the comments that I had received. I would like to thank all of the persons I have mentioned above, as well as a number of unnamed students whose questions and comments in the classroom stimulated my thinking.

I especially want to thank Isidor Chein, Tamara Dembo, and Margaret de Rivera for both their recent comments, suggestions, and criticisms, and their continuous intellectual stimulation over the years.

Finally, I want to thank my son, Eric, for doing the drawings in this book, Alice for trying to combine being human with being a premed student, Freda for representing our family in the struggles of the Worcester Food Coop and the United Farmworkers, and Lucinda for being so patient when her Daddy was so preoccupied with writing that he could not tell stories or give piggybacks.

It has been over ten years since this project was begun, I find that what stays in my mind after so long a history are not the objective historical facts, which are clear from the inch-deep pile of letters that I have just reread, but a few strange details that seemed, at least at first, to be of rather trivial importance —things like Dr. Korsch's lens, Horwitz spelled with one "o," and my white turtleneck sweater. Behind the flow of activities, situations, and ideas, there is always the be-ing of persons.

CONTENTS

I (have) tried to communicate an impression I get whenever I try to understand Lewin's basic notions, and that is, that they are, so to speak, visions, not at all completely formulated and explicated; that they have a wealth of implicit meaning which has not yet been exhausted, and that they therefore are still full of promise of further development.—FRITZ HEIDER

Chapter I

INTRODUCTION

WE, and the persons about us, are continually engaged in a myriad of activity. You are reading, I am writing, my daughter is doing a puzzle. Throughout the day, our everyday life is filled with conversations, makings, playings, and eatings until, finally, we engage in a sleeping.

Persons appear to move in and out of these activities as they become involved, are interrupted, forget to make a phone call, become satiated and set their task aside. And if we look more closely at this ebb and flow of involvement, it becomes apparent that each of ourselves is in an emotional relationship with whatever activity we are embracing or casting away. This relationship is not a static one. Whenever we are involved, the activity that is our partner is ceaselessly changing, progressing, carrying us towards new horizons until it expands into a new activity or breaks into pieces and frees us for the next plunge.

While these activities may be isolated entities, usually they are embedded in larger activities, and are themselves the source of actions that are more molecular. Our reading and writing is part of a larger activity—the advancement of our knowledge—and in turn, our reading and writing contains within it the activity of mastering each sentence, of occasionally turning to a dictionary, of side conversations about the merit of some idea. We may, therefore, study the organization of all this activity, may even define ourselves in terms of the complicated structure of activities to which we are committed.

All of this activity between ourselves and the numerous objects of our environment always occurs in the context of some situation in which we are embedded, and is often accompanied by the emotion which occurs when the situation changes. Thus, an action may occur in a situation which imposes a barrier between the person and his goal, and we may see him suddenly explode with anger or retreat into unreality as he finds himself trapped in a frustrating situation. Consequently, while we may view a person as engaged in a stream of activity, we must always see this activity as subject to the vicissitudes of the surrounding situation. This situation may control the person's activity through rewards or through punishments; it may be so unstructured that the person becomes anxious and activities disintegrate; or it may be "open" so that activities develop in a way that expresses the person's full potential. Situational events such as success or failure have an emotional impact on activity, often affecting a person's sense of worth, and almost inevitably influencing his choice of goals for the future. Such choices are part of the person's flow of activity and may be regarded from two quite different perspectives. On the one hand they may be seen as completely determined by the situation which the person confronts; on the other they may be regarded as an activity that is the complete responsibility of a person who is free to choose the situation that he will create.

This sort of material—the flow of activity within situations, the acts of choice, and the eddies of emotion—is the subject matter of this book. It is a book that is based on the studies of Kurt Lewin and his students at the University of Berlin in the 1920's, studies which were inspired by Carl Stumpf's challenge to bring will and emotion into the laboratory. The resulting dissertations and papers were initially published in *Psychologisch Forschung* as a score of monographs under the series title *Untersuchungen zur Handlungens und Affektpsychologie—Investigations in the Psychology of Action and Emotion.* While Lewin (1) wrote a chapter which briefly surveyed these studies, the length of the original monographs hindered their complete translation and publication, and, until now, only the first two investigations (Lewin's theoretical introduction to the experimental work), and an abridged version of Zeigarnik's work have been published in English (2). Because of their contemporary importance, I have arranged for the translation of all the original papers—perhaps the most brilliant series of experiments ever performed in psychology —and propose to re-examine their content, their method, and the conceptualization of behavior to which they lead.

We have already noted that the *content* of the investigations concerns the activity and emotion of everyday life. Although the experiments are quite simple in design and require a minimum of apparatus, each proves a rich source of data of fundamental relevance to contemporary theories of human motivation.

I shall attempt to show the threads that connect these early investigations of Lewin and his students to the later studies in group dynamics and action research; but the later work really constitutes a relatively separate phase of the Lewinian group that deserves a book in its own right. However, it would be a mistake to think of the earlier work as "academic" and the later as "applied." Although the studies that we shall consider all fall under the heading of "basic" rather than "issue-relevant" research, because they are truly basic rather than trivial they turn out to be quite relevant to those of us who are concerned with creating a society that is more responsive to human needs. In particular, they prove to have a relevance for democratic education; and in this regard, they furnish important arguments for the desirability of programs of open education, together with insights into some of the fundamental processes necessary for the success of such programs.

I mention the *method* of the studies, because it should be realized that Lewin's early method of investigation is somewhat different from that in current use in American psychology; the richness of content which it produced leads me to believe that it should be rediscovered and considered for use in further investigations. In many ways, Lewin's method is similar to that of Piaget or Tinbergen. That is, there is a stress on the careful observation of individual cases; and the experimenter feels free to vary his experimental conditions and conduct a number of different manipulations in order to investigate the state of different subjects. Some American psychologists appear to regard such experimentation as "sloppy," without realizing that a careful experimental strategy is, in fact, being utilized. Shortly, we shall discuss this strategy in detail. Because of its descriptive emphasis, and its sensitivity to what the experimental situation means to the subject, I shall call Lewin's method "experimental phenomenology" and constrast it with the "statistical experimentation" in more common use.

If only the content of these historic studies were of interest, considerations of space and of the reader's time, would lead me to present detailed summaries of the material. However, one can only acquire an understanding of their methodology by examining the rather lengthy original studies. Therefore, I have decided to use five of the original studies in an almost unabridged form as the basis for this book. In deciding which studies to select, I attempted to choose those that seemed most basic, in the sense that they provided a conceptual basis for understanding the other studies in the series. The latter will be summarized and discussed, and the reader interested in more detail may obtain the complete translations from Xerox: University Microfilms (3).

The *conceptualization* of behavior that Lewin formulated with his students as they produced the experiments we shall examine, eventually became known as "field theory." Basically, field theory is an attempt to describe the essential here-and-now situation (field) in which a person participates. It assumes that if one fully understood a person's "situation" (in the broadest meaning of this term), one would fully understand his behavior. Hence, the goal of field theory is to be able to describe fields with systematic concepts in such a precise way that a given person's behavior follows logically from the relationship between the person and the dynamics and structure of his concrete situation.

Field theory has a systematic elegance, and is one of a handful of basic approaches to understanding human behavior and experience. Further, it has been an important factor in spawning the fields of group dynamics, action research, and psychological ecology, and in dealing with socio-emotional relations in rehabilitation psychology. Nevertheless, in spite of its scope and fertility, it is clear that the specific field theory proposed by Lewin has a number of unresolved problems. These include internal problems, such as inconsistencies and limitations on what can be represented in the field; some difficulties in integrating the theory with classical gestalt psychology; and the current rigidification of the system so that it is no longer stimulating much research.

Yet it is important to realize that field theory should not be considered as a closed system of completed conceptualizations that has merely to be applied to the complete range of psychological problems. Rather, it is a way of looking at psychological events as determined by contemporary structures and forces.

Lewin himself did not see field theory as a limited system with a given psychological content, but aspired to develop a systematic language that was independent of schools of thought, and would help in the task of unifying psychology. He viewed field "theory" more as an *approach* to conceptualization, the beginning of a set of concepts that could be used to represent fundamental psychological processes and reality.

Because field theory is more an approach than a specific set of principles, when we return to the original studies we need not be bound to the particular conceptualizations developed by Lewin. Fortunately, Lewin's method insures the detailed presentation of the original data, and from our privileged position —viewing each study from a distance and the entire series in perspective—we may find conceptualizations that seem to provide a more useful and systematic interpretation of the findings than those theoretical metaphors which provoked them. If so, then we may be able to extend field theory and revitalize its power to stimulate research.

In order to preserve the integrity of the original material and still present my own commentary and interpretation of the results, this book is arranged in a series of alternating chapters. After each of the five original studies, there is a chapter of my own which summarizes other studies by Lewin's students and some closely related theoretical work by other psychologists. In these latter chapters I shall attempt to faithfully report Lewin's own theoretical conceptions, but my own comments will, at times, be directed towards a reinterpretation of the data and a reformulation of some of the concepts of field theory. While I believe that Lewin would welcome such a re-examination of field theory, the reader who wishes to experience the full impact of Lewin's own thinking in a pure form may easily read the five original studies consecutively, together with Lewin's theoretical introduction to the experiments (4). Or he may do this and then re-read each of the studies together with my commentary. However, each of the commentary chapters presuppose some knowledge of the original study to which they refer.

In the remaining sections of this introductory chapter I will discuss: 1) the social conditions that permitted such an unusual series of investigations to be conducted; 2) the methodology used by the Lewin group—and that I hope will be used again by contemporary psychologists; and 3) the conceptual issues that lie between the field theoretic approach as it is currently formulated and the "human-science" approach of my own commentary.

SOCIAL CONDITIONS FOR THE STUDIES

Most of the studies we shall be examining were doctoral dissertations. Yet, in contrast to many contemporary dissertations, one senses artisans at work. Instead of students who are methodically stamping out required variations— dutiful thought machines—one has the impression of thinking human beings who are genuinely trying to find something out. There is a good deal of bumbling about and some mistakes, but there is someone there asking a real question, someone who is not afraid to say, "I don't know," who is willing to be wrong. Consequently, there is the excitement, the aliveness, of a person working on meaningful material.

So we wonder what sort of social conditions made these creative dissertations possible. What kind of soil led to the growth of numerous live doctoral dissertations? What was the atmosphere of the Psychological Institute at Berlin, and what sort of person was Kurt Lewin? How large was the group at the lab? did students say, "Herr Professor?" and how were they supported? How competitive were the students with one another, how frightened of being wrong, did they talk to each other about their work? Were the dissertations assigned, how long did it take to get a degree?*

First, we must note a number of cultural differences which provide an important background against which the figure of the Institute must be placed. The handful of universities in Germany during the twenties was part of a state system subject to various social and political forces that limited career opportunities. For example, it was much more difficult for a woman, a foreigner, or a Jew to obtain one of the limited tenured positions in a German university. Most students did not even aspire to such a position. On the other hand, admission was open to anyone who had completed the Gymnasium. Tuition was low and the living expenses of many of the students were met by their families.

There was a different feeling about *time*—which was less important than it is today in the United States. Everything was more relaxed, more leisurely, without the press of having to be somewhere at some exact time. A person did not "waste" time if he sat around after lunch and discussed psychology. This

---

*In attempting to answer these questions, the writer is indebted to the recollections of Tamara Dembo and Fritz Heider.

atmosphere of relaxed time is reflected in the long journal articles, the way experiments were run—sometimes for days at a time—the length of time spent in studying for a doctorate. (Since the universities had no dormitories and did not attempt to be "parents" to the students, the role of the student was an accepted *adult* role.)

Finally, as Lewin (5) himself described in his article contrasting German and American character structure, there was a greater degree of social formality. For example, most persons were addressed by their last name, regardless of status or length of acquaintance. The only exceptions involved very close friends. The boundary between what was public and what was private was placed further out from a person's center. Financial affairs were private and not discussed with most fellow students.

At the university, there were few prescriptions and no grades. The only examinations, which were given after the thesis had been accepted, were extensive oral exams on the content of one's major discipline (*e.g.*, philosophy, of which psychology was a part), and two minor disciplines (*e.g.*, economics and physics). While occasionally a student would fail (in which case he could twice retake the exam), the major selection process seems to have involved the person's own decision to go to the university in the first place. With few external motivations and with a Ph.D. program that was clearly oriented toward encouraging thinkers rather than technicians, a major reason to attend was intellectual curiosity. In any case, as will become evident, the faculty had ample opportunity to become thoroughly acquainted with each student. Throughout the university, lectures were an important institution, much more so than they are in the contemporary American university. A student or fellow might often retake a course, or go year after year to hear a person such as Köhler give his lecture series on psychology. And a popular lecturer might earn more from the modest fees which students paid to attend lectures than from his basic university salary.

The Psychological Institute was housed in quite a large space (a wing of the old Imperial Palace). There were three floors, each with numerous rooms so that a student who needed space for a study was easily accommodated. However, in terms of personnel the Institute was quite small by today's standards. In the late twenties, there were only a half dozen faculty members (including Köhler, Lewin, and Wertheimer), a few postdoctoral scholars, and about a dozen graduate students who were active at any one time. Thus, when a student joined the Institute, he became a member of a small group.

I say a student "joined" the Institute, but in fact the boundary lines were not formal or as sharp as those we are accustomed to. Thus, while a person was admitted to the university, he was not admitted to the department of philosophy or the Psychological Institute. Rather, he simply began to attend the classes offered at the Institute, or to join the group eating lunch there, or to begin going to the Institute colloquiums chaired by its Director. Yet this informal group appears to have become one of those unique collectives which persons can occasionally create, a breath of freshness in an often stale university atmosphere, a source of inspiration for all who come into contact with it.

Perhaps the most important characteristic of this group was an enthusiasm for ideas and research, an enthusiasm which was bound up with the feeling that one was at the very edge of discovery, a pathfinder in new realms of knowledge. Consequently, a student felt that he or she was doing *important* work. The atmosphere was fundamentally a cooperative one, with faculty and students helping one another think through and set up experiments. To be a subject for an experiment was as much a part of one's profession as reading a book, and hence there was a self-understood participation and cooperation. We will see that the method of experimental phenomenology encourages a partnership between subject and experimenter—a basically helping attitude. The extent of this mutual helping was far beyond what is typical today—students and faculty were often subjects for one another, occasionally for as much as four or five hours during the day.

The fact that an important part of one's professional work involved being the subject in experiments speaks to one of the ethical issues which confronts us today. Lewin's studies, like many experiments today, occasionally involved minor "casualties." These occurred when something in the experiment accidentally touched on the rest of the subject's life. A subject in Karsten's study of satiation, to whom poetry was particularly meaningful, repeats poems that were close to her and loses her taste for poetry for several months. A subject in Dembo's experiment on frustration becomes upset and reveals thoughts which would otherwise have been kept private. A subject in Hoppe's experiment on the effects of failure loses his self-confidence for several weeks after the experiment. In spite of the best safeguards, we believe that such mishaps are perhaps inevitable consequences of meaningful experimentation where the subject is not simply playing the game of being a subject. While these chance mishaps do not leave permanent effects, we hardly have the right to run these risks with persons who cannot fully realize what they are getting into. However, professionals *can* take these risks themselves.

The students had great respect for the faculty, each of whom was considered a leader in the advancement of psychological knowledge. In asking to work with a particular faculty member, students carefully considered the professional interests of the faculty (they were well aware of these through lectures and through serving as subjects), and were eager to be taken on by the person they felt they could do creative work with. In turn, the faculty listened closely to the ideas of the students and took these ideas seriously. Accordingly, there was a sense of mutual going-forward in the exploration of new knowledge. Several years after the rise of Nazism had forced this group to disband, Lewin wrote (6):

> . . . collectives have had and will, I think, always have their place in scientific work. The group which was called the Psychological Institute of Berlin has been, I think, such a collective of friends, working together for many years, interested in all fields of psychology, and concerned as much as with experiments as with theories. Whether it was valuable, history will show; but at least it was happy and lively.

After a few years at the Institute, when a student had learned the interests of each of the faculty, the student would go to some member of the faculty and ask to do a dissertation with him. The faculty member might suggest a dissertation topic or one might emerge from conversations. It did not matter if one had previously worked with some other faculty member, since all students viewed themselves as fellow students of the Institute as a whole. Thus, a student who had worked with Lewin might do his dissertation with Köhler, or one who had started with Wertheimer might finish with Lewin because of a change in interests. While there was a definite feeling of working with a particular person, this was in the context of being a member of the Institute. On the other hand, there was no dissertation committee at the Institute; a student did his dissertation with one professor. The standards were quite simple—the dissertation should be publishable—and since all of one's colleagues became familiar with each other's experiments, it was easy to appreciate what this meant.

Within the Institute a group of persons centered about Lewin himself, who generated a particularly healthy atmosphere. There was relatively little rivalry and concern with the ownership of ideas, no constant comparison of one student against another, and no ridicule if one said something that was uninformed. If a student said something that proved to be uninformed, he felt badly but not as though he were being laughed at. In line with this, Lewin's students felt a norm that it was inappropriate—in bad taste—to descend to a personal level and belittle or joke about a psychologist at some other university. In his biography, Marrow has portrayed Lewin by presenting the views of his different students as well as showing the scope of his work and influence (7). From these views one might make the following sketch: Lewin was a person who was tremendously involved with ideas and spread his excitement to those around him. He wanted to see persons in their own right, to understand them and how they saw the world. His talks with students were extremely intense and stimulating sessions which could go on for hours with complete disregard for time

and place. These talks were task-oriented—focused on ideas and phenomena
—so that there was little chance for ego-oriented tensions, such as personal
ambition, competition, and test anxiety, to enter the picture. Clearly Lewin did
not have feelings of superiority. He treated students as peers—co-workers who
were also interested in ideas. He valued their ideas as much as his own.
Further, he could nondefensively hear what the other person was saying,
responding to criticism and searching for ways to fit other ideas with his own
so that there was a real interchange. He was a person who thought most
productively with others, was stimulated by the interplay of ideas, and indeed
needed this sort of interchange. He was not a solitary person, who did his best
thinking in isolation.

Nor was Lewin a person with a cause. His ideas did not have the sort of
moral component that Freud's or Wertheimer's had. Consequently, he was
very tolerant of disagreements and did not require agreement or loyalty. On
the other hand, he was a person with a very definite direction. He was going
somewhere with his project, and was interested in cooperatively developing his
ideas and assimilating those of others. His only fault appears to have been that
his sense of urgency often led him to try to do too much.

Lewin's personality was a stimulus for the formation of enthusiastic groups.
At Berlin the group that formed was called the *Quasselstrippe* ("rambling-
string"). Marrow quotes from one student as follows:

> On a particular day the group might range in number from four or five to as many
> —though rarely—as ten. It's literally true that at the end of one of these discus-
> sions, which might go on for two, three, or even more hours, often with shifting
> membership as people came and went, no one could say who was the source of
> a given idea, even of a very productive and ultimately influential one. The
> discussion might take off from a more or less casual question or notion, be
> changed over in this corner, qualified in that, re-oriented in another, and catch
> fire in still another. Then someone might see a possibility of broader application
> or relevance to problems not under discussion so far—and after more tinkering
> and batting about, it might emerge as something only remotely related to the
> remark that had set off the whole *causerie* in the first place—but of real impor-
> tance. Kurt was right in imputing creativity to the collective . . . There was no
> doubt in anyone's mind that Lewin was the indispensable member. He neither
> dominated nor overwhelmed, but his willingness to grant an enthusiastic hearing
> to even the most adventurous speculation supplied the ferment that made each
> participant rise above himself (8).

Finally, there were the students themselves. Aside from the fact that they
were obviously intelligent and well educated, one other fact may be of considerable importance. No less than six of Lewin's students were from Russia. All
of these were women, and most, perhaps all, had been exposed to the study

of literature in the Russian high schools. This study was oriented in a psychological direction in many interesting ways—for example, a student might be asked to compare the psychology of Molière's miser with the psychology of Pushkin's miserly knight. In the case of many of these students, their initial interest in psychology stemmed from this training, and it was searching for this sort of psychology that brought them to the exciting new developments at the Institute of Psychology.

The gestalt formed out of the above parts—aspects of the German culture, the uniquely creative and supportive atmosphere of the Institute, the method of experimental phenomenology, the stimulation of Lewin, the interests of his students—was the ground which nourished the studies we are to examine.

EXPERIMENTAL METHOD

In many ways, Lewin's method is similar to that in current use: the experimenter designs experimental conditions, and manipulates variables in order to establish the nature of psychological reality. It would be easy to make the error of assimilating Lewin's method by thinking that his procedures are ingenious, but a bit sloppy. In deciding to contrast Lewin's method with that in current use, I may be making a contrast error that is as great as the assimilation error that has exited until now, because, in one sense, Lewin's procedures differ more in degree than in kind. However, differences in degree that are so large may amount to a qualitative difference, and since I believe that a clear contrast will facilitate the presentation of Lewin's method, I shall briefly describe and criticize our current method, and then contrast it with that used by Lewin and his students.

Statistical Experimentation

The experimental method that is most used in the United States today is a method of statistical experimentation. The experimenter places a sizable number of subjects in each of two or more conditions that are designed to manipulate whatever variable is of theoretical interest (anxiety, dissonance, esteem). These conditions are kept objectively constant—externally they are the same for each subject. The experimenter, who has made a theoretical prediction about a differential outcome, calculates the *average* results and sees whether or not his prediction is borne out. While he may have purposively varied sex, age, social class, or some personality variable, and predicted differential outcomes, or interactions, he is still dealing with the average response of males, females, and so on. He then runs a statistical test to establish the likelihood of the results being due to chance. If this likelihood is small, he concludes his theory is supported. The argument for this method is that it supposedly provides a clear test of the experimenter's hypothesis, and should be easy to replicate.

The disadvantage of the method is that for any given subject one has no idea as to the meaning of the condition for that subject. Even when a sophisticated experimenter tests to see if each condition has the meaning which he intended, he usually establishes this for the average subject. And even if the experimenter then uses only those subjects who responded in the way that was hoped, the investigator still looks at the average response, and hence has no idea what different sorts of psychological processes may be accounting for these responses. Further, even this degree of selection tends to be viewed dubiously, because it seems less "objective" and the experimenter is afraid he will be criticized for "throwing out subjects."

The effect of this focusing on averages rather than individuals is that the experimenter makes the objective conditions the "subject" of the experiment, rather than his subjects. It is presumed that a particular experimental situation has the same meaning for each subject (or each subject within some designated class). Since, in fact, different subjects may give an objective situation quite different meanings, and since apparently similar responses may also have different meanings, it is evident that different processes may be occurring in different subjects. Consequently, there are many different possible interpretations of the results, and one is not sure of their theoretical significance. After wading through the resulting statistics (often weighing the effects of another significant three-way interaction), the reader has learned a lot about management of conditions, but very little psychology; the results are of more technical than theoretical relevance.

Now of course, there is a place for testing a statistical hypothesis, and in principle statistical tests can help us to maintain our objectivity. My point is that, in practice, the statistical tail (one or both of them) is wagging the psychological dog. Since most journal articles report only average results, many interesting phenomena are completely masked; what may be completely different processes are clumped together, and the studies leave one completely uninformed as to what really happened. Such a format encourages the investigator to have a mechanical approach that is insensitive to the experience of the individual subjects.

While it is sometimes argued that the paucity of interesting results in contemporary studies is necessarily true of the experimental method, that all the chaff is necessary for the few grains of wheat that occasionally emerge, I suspect that the problem is caused by the specific experimental method we are using.

There are two other unfortunate outcomes of the method of statistical experimentation. First, it emphasizes the experimenter's hypothesis rather than his curiosity. (One only learns something by "testing" a hypothesis.) This emphasis establishes precisely the sort of situation in which an experimenter's hypotheses are likely to affect his results. Rosenthal (9) has repeatedly demonstrated how this occurs. (Note, however, that Rosenthal himself is in the same trap since the biasing of experiments by hypotheses is *his* hypothesis, and he is using the same research method.)

Second, since the subject is being manipulated and usually does not feel himself to be in any way a partner in the research, there are various ethical and methodological problems. Kelman (10) has explicated these. Among them are the dehumanization of the subject, and the fact that the subject is placed in a position where he is likely to do what he thinks the experimenter wants him to do. (How this influences the meaning of the condition in which the subject finds himself is buried in the averages.)

I believe that many of my colleagues are fully aware of the problems that have been very briefly sketched above. However, they do not see an alternative that could be systematically used to advance psychological knowledge. It seems to me that the method used by the Lewin group constitutes one such alternative.

Experimental Phenomenology

In contrast to the method of statistical experimentation, Lewin's group often uses relatively few subjects in a relatively large number of experimental conditions. The investigator often focuses on the individual subject, and feels at ease in having the objective conditions vary as long as he knows what the condition means for the subject. While the studies would undoubtedly make more use of statistics if they were performed today, it is clear that the place of averages and the statistical test is subordinate to the description of the behavior of individual subjects. Exceptions to predicted results are eagerly examined for clues as to possible new processes, and the investigator is careful to examine how his subjects experienced the experiment so that both behavior and experience are used to establish the underlying meaning of the experimental conditions and the subject's response. The subject's reports could be trusted because the subject himself was often a colleague, who usually saw himself as a partner in the over-all research enterprise of gathering new knowledge about psychological processes.

It is difficult to give a precise and concise description of Lewin's experimental methodology because, as the reader will see, it is extremely flexible and varied. In the first study we shall examine, Ovsiankina works with a classical hypothesis-testing paradigm, using a series of control experiments to eliminate possible alternative explanations of her data. However, the major part of Karsten's work does not include any hypothesis testing. Rather, the experimenter focuses on the description of a progressive series of phenomena that inevitably happen with each of her subjects. The third study hinges on the experimental production of predicted behavior, but uses only a few subjects and extensive self-observation; the fourth is mainly a conceptual elaboration of common behavior that is observed in the experimental situation; and the fifth concentrates on the description of differences in the behavior of various subjects.

At first glance, the only common elements in the method involve the production of some phenomenon in the laboratory, and the meticulous observation and description of the behavior and experience of the subjects (often revealed by a whole series of experimental manipulations). We shall soon see that these descriptions are one pole of a dialectic. Nevertheless, they are sometimes so meticulous that the American reader, who is apt to be unfamiliar with detailed observations, may find himself quickly becoming satiated. However, if he perseveres, he will soon learn how to read this sort of material, and will begin to find that his own powers of observation increase so that he starts to notice many details of behavior that had previously been completely overlooked. The greater use of description in German psychology, and the important role which it can play in psychological research, has been noted by Koffka (11):

> One can read many American books and articles on psychology without finding any such or similar description, whereas in German works one will meet with them quite frequently. This difference is not superficial, but reveals a thoroughgoing difference in the character of American and German work. Americans will call the German psychology speculative and hairsplitting; Germans will call the American branch superficial. The Americans are justified, when they find an author introducing such descriptions, refining them, playing with them, without really doing anything to them. The Germans are right, because American psychology all too often makes no attempt to look naively, without bias, at the facts of direct experience, with the result that American experiments quite often are futile. In reality experimenting *and* observing must go hand in hand. A good description of a phenomenon may by itself rule out a number of theories and indicate definite features which a true theory must possess. We call this kind of observation "phenomenology," a word which has several other meanings which must not be confused with ours. For us phenomenology means as naive and full a description of direct experience as possible.

The method of "experimental phenomenology" has its historic roots in the work of men like Herring and Stumpf. Thus, Boring observes that Herring's experimental color equipment, like the later illustrations used by the gestalt psychologists, was designed to provide the viewer with, "the immediate experience which constitutes the evidence" (12). And Stumpf, who was a student of Brentano's (both taught Husserl), and began the Psychological Institute at

Berlin where Koffka, Köhler, and Lewin were trained, designed experiments that provided auditory experiences that empirically demonstrated various conceptual distinctions.

Later, we shall see that "experience" (and, hence, "phenomenology") has a somewhat different meaning for Stumpf's Berlin group than for Husserl and contemporary phenomenologists. Yet Spiegelberg, the historian of the phenomenological movement, observes:

> It is . . . important to pay attention to the motive and purpose of Stumpf's experiments. Their primary purpose was not the statistical establishment of correlations between physical stimuli and psychological responses, but the discriminating and controlled exploration of the subjective phenomena, such as overtones, fusions, etc., in a way which makes their reproduction and checking possible even on an intersubjective basis. The means for such a systematic exploration was the experimental variation of the stimuli. (13)

As a result of his work, which provides an example of the free and unbiased description of experience, Boring notes that Stumpf's students began, "an experimental phenomenology that formed the basis for the new *gestalt psychology*" (14).

While gestalt psychology originated with Wertheimer's experiments on visual experience (he, Köhler, and Koffka were the subjects), Lewin began his own experimental work on the experience of the will. We shall see how this work led him more and more into the investigation of behavior and its control by various field forces. However, it is important to realize that although Lewin's subject matter began to be behavior as well as experience, his "behaviorism" is grounded in the phenomenological enterprise of understanding, rather than the pragmatic enterprise of prediction and control. Consequently, Lewin and his students carefully attend to the meaning which the situation has for each subject and make a close observation and careful description of the details of the psychological processes that are involved.

It is interesting to note both the similarities and the differences between Lewin and the "classical" gestalt psychologists. For many purposes Lewin may be regarded as a gestalt psychologist who focused on problems of action rather than problems of perception and thinking and, as we shall see, he makes good use of many gestalt principles. However, Lewin's thought—like that of his colleagues—is extensively grounded in philosophy and here he differs from the classic gestaltists on two counts: First, he does not share their hope that the study of organization will serve to unify the physical, biological, and psychological sciences. We shall see that, for Lewin, living systems have peculiar properties that cannot be related to physics by isomorphism. Second, the principle of *Prägnanz*—the tendency towards the formation of the best possible organization—that is used so extensively in gestalt theory, does not play an important role in Lewin's thinking.

It would be wrong to think of either the classical gestalt psychologists or Lewin as being interested in simply experience and behavior. Rather, they were also interested in a set of essential processes that are conceived to underlie experience and behavior. For Wertheimer, Köhler, and Koffka these were processes that were, necessarily, also found in physics and physiology. For Lewin, these processes were peculiar to psychology (or biology). In any case, the subject matter of psychology is the essential processes that underlies both experience and behavior, as well as the concrete experience and behavior of an individual person.

The central core of Lewin's method is the tension between the abstract conceptualization of essential underlying processes and the concrete facts of the individual case. The conceptualization strives for breadth and elegant simplicity, the theorist attempting to relate his concepts to each other with mathematical precision. But at the same time, the raw facts of each existent individual case demand accountability for every detail of their case.

It is important to realize that these are not, cannot be, separate endeavors. They *cannot* be, for they are simply the two poles of one dynamic whole. The facts have no meaning without the conceptualization, the theory has no substance without the facts. The tension of this dialectic must be embodied in the investigator. Lewin asserts that the investigator faces, "The abyss between the apparently abstract theory and the earthbound reality of the experimental procedures . . ." and must ". . . build a bridge from the theory to the full reality of the individual case . . ." (15).

On the concrete side of this abyss Lewin is always interested in the phenomenon for its own sake. In this aspect of his work he is close to the approach advocated by Luchins in his intensive study of rigid behavior,

> In contrast to (the) contemporary theory-centered orientation, ours is more of an empirical, phenomenon-centered or phenomenological orientation. We are interested in the selected case of rigid behavior for its own sake and not for the sake of defending or refuting a theory. We do not start with a theory or a hypothesis suggested by a theory; rather, we first look at the phenomenon for clues concerning its structure and dynamics, the phenomenon is allowed to speak for itself (16).

Likewise, Lewin and his students are always close to the raw data, taking care with each subject, seeking the raw phenomena without the lenses of abstract assumptions.

However, on the conceptual side of the abyss, Lewin is interested in a highly abstract conceptualization. He clearly distinguishes between "mere description" (that is, correctly naming whatever is occurring), or providing some physical or physiological analogy to what is occurring, and his own interest in "systematic conceptualization." The latter involves coordinating the raw phenomenon to an abstract concept *which has necessary relations with other concepts* (that is, is defined in terms of a system of concepts—as in mathematics).

In contrast to simple description, systematic conceptualization has implications for what other phenomena will occur. In contrast to an analogy, one must acknowledge *all* the consequences of a systematic conceptualization and cannot discard it at some arbitrary point where it is no longer applicable. Lewin states that while analogies may have heuristic value, they often create the illusion of possessing a greater degree of reality without really advancing the conceptual determination of what must necessarily occur (17).

As an example of systematic conceptualization, we may consider Lewin's definition of psychological "force." The conceptual properties of a force are its direction, its strength, and its point of application. The coordinating definition of a force (which lets us relate the concept to the description of behavior) is that whenever the resultant of the forces acting on a given region is greater than zero, there will be a change in the structure of the situation in the direction of the resultant force. (Often this change will be the movement of a person towards a goal.) We may then discover empirically that as the distance between a person and a goal decreases, the force relative to the goal increases.

In some respects, Lewin's approach to theory is quite similar to Freud's. Both men were careful observers of behavior and experience, and both constructed abstract conceptualizations that helped account for these observations and led the investigation into new directions. There is always a danger that a theorist may become blinded by his own theory, and I would say that, at times, both Lewin and Freud became so attached to their conceptualization that they overlooked points where it did not fit their own data. On the other hand, both men were such honest observers that they seem to always report the data correctly, even when it is apparent to an outsider that the data does not really fit the conceptualization.

In relating the concrete to the conceptual, Lewin assumed that all existents (concrete instances of experience or behavior) reflect essential structures. He believed that all sciences dealt with these realities that underlay superficial observations, but that each different science had to construct its own underlying essentials. This view of science was greatly influenced by Ernst Cassirer, who showed that a scientific concept (actually, *any* concept) is not an abstraction of something that is substantially common to each of the cases to which the concept may be applied. Instead, each concept is a construction in its own right, a relational construction that is separate from each case, yet can generate each unique concrete instance (18). Because of his concern for these relational concepts which captured the *essential* meaning of an experience or a behavior, Lewin distinguished between superficial experiential or behavioral similarities ("phenotypes"), and underlying identities ("genotypes"). Thus, just as the same species of a plant may look quite different at different altitudes, the insecurity provoked in a child by a stranger may be reflected in either overly shy behavior or overly boisterous behavior—depending on the distance of the stranger. An action that appears calm may reflect true calmness, or it may be a well-controlled affective outburst. A heartfelt intention to do something may be experienced quite strongly, and yet have less dynamic weight and influence on behavior than a mere thought that the person barely notices.

In order to arrive at essential genetic concepts that account for both superficial behavior and experience—and grasp what we may call, the "meaning" of the behavior or experience—the investigator must consider the subject's behavior in the context of the situation. Lewin is careful to note, "The observation of external behavior may yield valuable information concerning the specific structure of psychic events, but decisive information concerning the actual processes often comes only from self-observation" (19). Thus, the experimenter and the subject must form a partnership to interpret the actual meaning (essence, "genetic structure") of the behavior and experience.

Whereas the method of statistical experimentation relies heavily on the description and manipulation of objective situations, Lewin argued that psychologists should focus on describing and affecting the individual's life-space. Lewin was very conscious of the different meanings which an objectively constant situation could have for different subjects, or for the same subject at different times. In a perception experiment the background of a stimulus will influence the figure which the subject perceives. Likewise, Lewin notes that in a behavioral experiment the total situation of the subject is a background that is important in determining the meaning of his behavior. In the same external experimental set-up, the behavior of one subject may be directed at pleasing the experimenter, while another can be intent on proving himself, and a third completely immersed in the task given by the experimenter.

To understand a piece of behavior it is essential to place it in its context— in the "surrounding field"—for its meaning will depend on the whole of which it is a part. Thus, the activity of "writing" if one is engaged in calligraphy is quite different from "writing" if one is writing a letter. It is a major error to assume the behaviors are the same because they are both called "writing." The experimenter must be on constant guard against seeing behavior in terms of "achievement concepts" such as writing, loving, eating, and so on. These lump together what may be quite different processes. Thus, a beginner's typing is essentially a search process, which is a completely different psychological activity from that of a skilled typist. Lewin repeatedly warned against the overuse of statistics because it is so easy to combine cases that are psychologically quite different into a single group.

At the conclusion of the study by Schwarz we shall see a particularly clear example of Lewin's point. Schwarz discovers two qualitatively different types of negative transfer that have been viewed as identical in all the behavioral experiments with which I am familiar. In all of the studies we shall examine, there is an emphasis on *qualitative* analysis that continually produces interesting effects.

In many respects Lewin is an example of the type of behavioral scientist that Chein calls a "clinicalist." Thus, Chein notes, "The key to clinicalism is its urge to be able to comprehend every instance in a domain of inquiry in all of its particularity and unique individuality" (20). Therefore, the clinicalist is interested in the formulation of "looking rules" that lead to keener observation in the future, rather than a precise summary of what he has learned in the past. However, unlike the pure clinicalist, who "tends to be suspicious of any fixed scheme of classification, preferring to pick the concepts that best fit the case, and hence to select from a nonsystematic array of concepts," Lewin was also interested in the development of systematic conceptualization. Thus, while Lewin was very sensitive to the range of meanings of each situation, and of each behavior in different individuals, this did not cause him to abandon the systematic aspects of the scientific enterprise. On the contrary, he asserted that if one had real confidence in the lawfulness of behavior, one should be able to account for each *individual* instance of behavior.

Because of the unique situation of every subject, he argued for the study of each individual case. In support of this position he asserted that this was inherent in the method of experimentation introduced by Galileo. He points out that Galileo did not roll lots of stones down a hill and take the average of their velocity. Rather, abstractly conceiving of an ideal sphere on an ideal plane, he approximated these conditions in the laboratory, and demonstrated that the behavior of each individual ball depended on the essential properties of the situation (the slope of the plane). Although the law is idealized, rather than dealing with an abstract average, he deals with the individual case in the "full concreteness of the particular situation." As Lewin notes,

> The accidents of historical processes [*i.e.,* chance differences between how subjects react to a situation] are not overcome by excluding the changing situations from systematic consideration, but only by taking the fullest account of the individual nature of the concrete case. *It depends upon keeping in mind that general validity of the law and concreteness of the individual case are not antitheses, and that reference to the totality of the concrete whole situation must take*

the place of reference to the largest possible historical collection of frequent repetitions" (the material in brackets is mine, the italics are Lewin's) (21).

In short, numbers are no substitute for knowledge of each subject.

Now, some of my colleagues may argue that statistics can be of aid in isolating the vagaries of chance occurrences from the effects of ideal laws. They assert that all these chance deviations are due to irrelevant or unidentified variables causing subjects to see and behave in different ways. What Lewin is saying is that there are no irrelevant variables, and that there is more payoff in examining each individual case in order to identify what is happening than there is in grouping cases and simply examining one major variable of theoretical concern. Thus, he notes, "Single concrete experiments, which statistical treatment considers identical, must be treated not statistically, but as full realities. . . . Instead of the massing of *identical* cases, the concrete specificity of the single experiment should be taken into consideration, even in forming theories" (22).

Lewin believed that psychology tended to be caught in pre-Galilean thinking. This is shown whenever psychologists take frequency of recurrence to be the criterion for lawfulness and a requirement for experiments. It is also revealed by their attitude towards particular phenomena. He observes, "If, for example, one shows a film of a concrete incident in the behavior of a certain child, the first question of the psychologist normally is: 'Do all children do that . . . ?' " (23).

If the investigator really believes in the lawfulness of psychological phenomena, then, says Lewin, he must be open to "considering contradictory examples from the whole field of psychic life." If the structure of a case is established, a *single* case may prove or refute a proposition. Thus, he wryly observes that, "According to the old law that 'the exception proves the rule,' *psychology does not regard exceptions as counterarguments so long as their frequency is not too great"* (24). Not only does this attitude lead to meaningless "laws," it places a limitation on research in the area of will and emotion where reoccurrences of the same event are not to be expected. "It makes it appear hopeless to try to understand the real, unique course of an emotion or the actual structure of a particular individual's personality. It thus reduces one to a treatment of these problems in terms of mere averages, as exemplified by tests and questionnaires" (25).

In the studies that follow, the reader may see how Lewin and his students created controlled experimental situations, but then were very careful to note the meanings which these had for their subjects, and the different meanings of behaviors which were sometimes superficially similar.

Because of this attention to the experience of the individual and the nuances of his behavior, Lewin and his students appear to be more in touch with psychological reality and more able to reveal it to us. Indeed, it is the *attitude* towards data that is the heart of the method of experimental phenomenology; and in attempting to convey this attitude I can do no better than to quote Wertheimer's tribute to Stumpf:

> There are some who approach nature as an enemy. They set up traps and try to defeat her or they are like sportsmen who want to show off their own skill and strength. How different are you? . . . With one African tribe there exists the following custom: when they want to show a guest that they trust him, a mother puts a baby into his arms and says, 'Hold the child.' That is how you hold the facts in your hands, and that you have taught us, reverence for reality (26).

CONCEPTUAL ISSUES

The studies that we shall be examining deal with so many different aspects of personal action and emotion that we will become lost in a forest of interesting detail unless there is some conceptual path to guide us. Lewin's field theory can partially serve this function, but I believe that an examination of the original studies reveals that the conceptual problems and theoretical ideas that stimulated the Lewinian group are somewhat different from a conceptualization that seems fully adequate when we view the whole series of studies from a contemporary perspective.

It seems important to present both how the studies were conceptualized by the Lewinian group and how they might be interpreted today. Then the reader has the best of both possible worlds. Unfortunately this necessitates a presentation of two different conceptual paths, and in order to avoid confusion, the outline of these two systems must be clearly delineated before we become immersed in the original studies and the different interpretations of their data. Therefore, in this section I will attempt to provide a brief overview of how the studies are conceptualized within Lewin's field theory, and how they may be interpreted somewhat differently from the perspective of a contemporary human-science approach. While such an overview may seem too abstract before the reader encounters the concrete substance of the studies, it will provide an initial orientation; and one may always reread this section after he has acquired a knowledge of the concrete substances of the investigations.

Lewin's Field Theoretic Approach
Empirical Background. One of Lewin's first publications contrasts the landscape as seen by a civilian in peacetime with the warscape seen by a soldier in danger (27). Describing his own experience during the First World War, he

notes that away from the front the horizon spreads out equally in all directions, and he notices the presence of homes. However, as he approaches the line of battle the scenery takes on a "directedness." The horizon ends abruptly at the front, and instead of homes, he notices shelters from enemy fire. Within these shelters he sees "firewood" rather than the "furniture" he sees in homes. There is a corresponding change in behavior. It is not possible to march as rapidly toward the front as toward a distant horizon; it is possible to destroy a shelter, whereas it is impossible to treat a home in such a callous way.

In a later article, Lewin suggests that we always respond to an environment that is affected by our needs and calls upon us to perform specific actions (28). Thus, the hungry person sees an apple that entices him to eat, the tired man sees a chair that invites him to sit, the ambitious person sees a desk that calls him to work. This property of objects that is related to needs became known as "valence"; and a person's behavior is seen as directed by the environmental forces that arise from valenced objects.

It is important to realize that while we are describing the environment that exists for a given individual at a particular moment of time, this environment and the forces it exerts are *objective* in the sense that an independent observer can construct the field of forces that is playing upon the person. Lewin made a number of early movies (29) that demonstrate how behavior can be understood in terms of such a field of forces. In one of these a child is separated from a desired toy by a circular barrier. Either the child or the toy may be placed within the barrier. When the child is placed within, he stays pressed against the region of the barrier that is closest to the toy. However, when the toy is placed within, the child runs repeatedly around the outside of the circular barrier, his restless behavior held in orbit by the attractiveness of the toy and the constraining force of the barrier.

This sort of objective yet personal field later became conceptualized as the "life space." Lewin's field theory asserts that a person's behavior is best comprehended in terms of the structure and dynamics of this field. A scientific observer can construct an abstraction of this field by representing within it everything that affects the person's current behavior.

Lewin's naturalistic observations of perception and behavior suggest that the behavior of a person should be understood in terms of his environmental situation, and that this situation is correlated with personal needs. Lewin's first laboratory experiments demonstrate a related point: the subject's behavior is not determined by mechanical associations to impersonal stimuli but by perceptions that are influenced by his intentions (30). Thus, if a subject is asked to respond with the nonsense syllable "lub" whenever he is presented with the syllable "bak," the subject does not see an impersonal nonsense syllable "bak" that mechanically causes him to say "lub." Rather his intention to reproduce "lub" leads him to see a "bak-that-commands-me-to-say-lub." Lewin goes on to postulate that intentions (acts of will) affect one's environment just as needs do (31). That is, they determine our behavior by affecting how we perceive. For example, when we intend to mail a letter, we essentially establish a quasi-need that will lead us to perceive in our environment a mailbox-that-directs-us-to-deposit-our-letter.

A number of the experiments performed by Lewin's students are directed toward demonstrating the fruitfulness of conceiving of intentions as establishing quasi-needs. Thus, Ovsiankina's study (Chapter III) shows that once a person intends to perform an activity, the performance of the activity is not instigated by the presence of impersonal stimuli. Rather there is a real need to complete the activity, a need that leads the person to actively search out the required objects. And Karsten's experiment (Chapter V) shows that an intention to perform an activity (such as reciting a poem) appears to satiate with repeated recitations in the same manner as a need such as hunger satiates with repeated eating.

The implication of Lewin's position is that behavior is always motivated by needs (including intentions) rather than by habits. How then can we explain the fact that a person may do exactly the opposite of what he apparently intends to do—as when we catch ourselves reaching habitually for something where it *used* to be kept? Schwarz (Chapter VIII) succeeds in producing such "relapses" in the laboratory, and in demonstrating that such unintentional behavior is actually motivated by the very intention that it appears to deny.

Impressed by the fact that intentions and needs seem to continually affect how the environment is perceived and lead the person to actively search for sources of satisfaction, Lewin argues that the energizing source of behavior lies in a person's needs or intentions rather than in associations between stimuli and responses. On the conceptual level, he decided to conceive of these sources of energy as "tension-systems", to treat the idea of tension as having as much psychological reality as the idea of force, and to conceive of a tension-system as a region in the person that is under pressure. Until such a tension-system was released—on the descriptive level this corresponds to having one's need or intention fulfilled—its pressure exerts influences on other regions within the person.

We have already seen that needs and intentions affect the valences of the personal environment, and thus indirectly the forces that lead a person to interact with objects in the environment. Ordinarily such forces would lead the person to perform behaviors that would fulfill his need or intention (on the conceptual level, the tension-system would be discharged); but what would happen if circumstances prevented such behavior? Lewin and his students argued that the tension-system must continue to exert pressure that must affect the total field, and hence influence behavior.

What could these influences be? In Zeigarnik's experiment (see Chapter IV), we shall see that unresolved intentions affect one's memory so that it is easier for persons to recall uncompleted activities. Then in the experiments of Lissner, Mahler, and Sliosberg (Chapters VI and XI), we shall see that unresolved intentions may also lead to substitute activity. On the conceptual level, the pressure from the unresolved tension-system spreads to the surrounding regions of the person, and this influences the valences of the environment. Speaking concretely, a person's needs are extended and a wider range of objects become appealing (or repelling). Thus, as hunger increases, the range of objects that are appetizing increases. Finally, the person may engage in a substitute activity that he would initially find completely unappealing. The successful completion of this substitute activity leads to a lowering of pressure in the region that had been under tension. (We shall, of course, examine these ideas in much more detail as we proceed in this book.)

The idea that tension may spread from one region to another suggests the importance of investigating the organization of such regions within the person. Obviously some regions of activity may be close and mutually interdependent, while others may be relatively isolated. Such organizational factors are shown to affect the extent to which one activity can substitute for another, and the extent to which satiation in one region will spread to another. Further, we shall see that Birenbaum's experiments (Chapter IX) show that the forgetting of an intention may often be understood in terms of organizational factors, such as whether or not the intention is a part of another intention system, rather than in terms of the intention's strength or the existence of counter intentions.

The experiments mentioned thus far have been concerned with a person's *activity*—with how his needs and intentions (his will) affect behavior by influencing the perception of the environment, indirectly organizing the field of forces which determine his behavior. This material is the subject matter of the first half of this book. However, Lewin and his students were equally sensitive to the fact that many psychological events are happenings rather than activities. Thus, a person's activity may happen to meet with frustration, or may succeed, or may fail. Such events, often beyond the control of the person, may have a profound influence on the person's situation, and hence on his subsequent behavior.

The first experimental study which focuses on the person's situation rather than on his activity is Dembo's investigation of anger (Chapter XI). Dembo places her subjects in what we might call an impossible situation: the subject is asked to solve a problem which has no solution, and when he finally attempts to leave the experimenter insists that he remain and try again. On the conceptual level, Dembo describes how some forces push the person toward the goal (a solution); how the barrier to the goal gradually acquires a negative valence that pushes the person away; and how the insistence of the experimenter creates an outer barrier that prevents the person from leaving. As the person oscillates between these barriers, the forces mount until there is no place in the field where the subject is not subjected to the tension created by the conflicting forces upon the person. (Note that this tension is *not* equivalent to the previously mentioned tension-system within a person.) The person may attempt to escape the field by entering a level of unreality (for example, by daydreaming), but finds that eventually he must return to reality. Finally, the tension becomes so great that boundaries within the field (for example, the boundary between the person and his environment) begin to disintegrate, the person loses his self-control, and there is a general primitivization of the field that ultimately leads to behavior that is quite irrational.

Subsequent studies by Fajans (Chapter XIII) demonstrate the tremendous impact that success or failure has on a person's emotional behavior. Hoppe (Chapter XII) shows how the occurrence of success or failure affects a person's intentions by influencing his goal setting behavior (his level of aspiration), and Jucknat (Chapter XIII) establishes that such an influence transfers to other tasks. In all of these studies, we see how a person's behavior may be understood as an outcome of the situation in which he is placed.

It may be observed that the theoretical ideas of Lewin's group were in a constant interplay with the observations and experiments that were performed, and that there are a number of different strands of thought and data with which the group was involved. Thus, we have the idea that behavior is the result of field forces, that intentional activity works by influencing field forces and may be conceptualized as tension-systems within the person, and that what happens to a person may be described in terms of his position in a situation. When it came time to collect these strands together, Lewin was more interested in asserting a general approach toward generating theory than a specific theory; and thus, in a real sense, his "field theory" may be better understood as a "field approach." The details of this approach have been well explicated by Lewin (32), critically examined by Leeper (33), and by Cartwright (34), and systematically summarized and related to subsequent research by Deutsch (35). Here I shall simply give a brief sketch of the major characteristics of Lewin's approach, so that it can be related to the observations and experiments and contrasted with my own thought.

Philosophical perspectives. To begin, it is important to realize that Lewin saw psychology as a part of biology and believed that psychobiology should develop as a science in its own right, independent of the physical sciences. In an early work, he argued that living organisms have a fundamentally different sort of identity than physical entities (36). Whereas any object studied by the physical sciences becomes a different object with different properties if it changes its physical or chemical composition, living systems continually change and yet maintain their identity. They persist in spite of change (or by means of change) by maintaining a dynamic equilibrium with their environment. Whenever this equilibrium is upset, forces arise that create changes which restore a balance with the environment, so that the organization as a whole persists in its identity. Such an analysis suggests that the proper unit of study for a psychologist is not a body (a physical entity), but rather a person-in-relation-to-his-environment. It was this organization that Lewin called a "life-space"; and the object of his study is not the behavior of a body, but the behavior of a life-space.

We may divide the life-space into two parts, a person and an environment, but it makes no sense for us as psychologists to speak of the behavior of a person unless we mean a behavior-related-to-the-person's-environment. Conversely, we are not interested in the environment as it might be described by a physical scientist, but the environment-that-affects-a-person's-behavior. Hence, the two parts are interdependent parts of one whole.

The complete interdependency of person and environment from a biological point of view is convincingly described by Angyal, who called the whole a "biosphere." Since Angyal was more interested in an historical account of the development of the biosphere and the directions of its growth, his descriptions have never been integrated with Lewin's ahistorical descriptions of the momentary dynamics of the life-space (37). To attempt such an integration would be highly worth while.

The task of theory. Lewin himself was primarily interested in accounting for present behavior, although we shall consider his developmental analysis in Chapter IX. And, as we have seen, he believed that current behavior was best comprehended in terms of the current distribution of forces within the life-space. However, Lewin hoped that his framework would include all branches of psychology. His intent was to create a psychological language—a system of concepts—that would be independent of schools of thought, and useful in unifying fields as diverse as animal, child, clinical, perception, personality, and social psychology (38). Thus, his ambition was not to create a new psychological theory that pertains to a given content area but a tool—a general means of representing psychological reality (39). In order to accomplish this, he wanted to make no more assumptions than were required and to proceed by a method of successive approximation. He wanted, ". . . to proceed slowly by tentative steps, to make decisions rather reluctantly, to keep in view always the whole field of psychology, and to stay in closest contact with the actual work of psychological research" (40).

As a consequence, when it came to defining the life-space, Lewin was quite cautious. Clearly, the space must include more than what a person is conscious of—a child behaves quite differently when his mother is present than when she is absent, even when he is not conscious of her presence. It would be more possible to define the life-space in terms of what is experienced—the child must experience the environment differently in the two cases, even if his mother is absent. However, we may wish to include factors that affect our behavior without being experienced in any way—for example, the fact that it takes longer to saw a piece of maple than a piece of pine. Hence, Lewin decided to include in the life-space everything that affects a person's current behavior. Of course, this still leaves much outside the space, since many events have no effect whatsoever on a person's current behavior. However, events in the future may enter the life-space without the person having any control—as when a heatwave affects the environment, or a fever affects the person, with subsequent consequences for behavior.

As noted when we discussed methodology, Lewin distinguished between a surface description of the life-space—the apparent facts of a person's circumstance and behavior—and a deeper, more conceptual, "dynamic" description that captures the underlying essential reality of the case. Both the apparent and the dynamic properties of an event are properties of the same psychological event, and the situation must in either case be described as it affects the individual in question, rather than as it affects the experimenter or in the way the experimenter would like it to affect the subject. However, the investigator attempts to go behind the apparent surface description to discover invariable relationships between the facts. He attempts to construct a conceptual system that will on the one hand be coordinated to a surface description of the concrete special properties of a given individual life-space at a given moment, and on the other, make use of a systematic set of concepts that are related to each other in a logically consistent way. Ultimately, Lewin states, ". . . the task of a dynamic psychology is to derive univocally the behavior of a given individual from the totality of the psychobiological facts that exist in the life-space at a given moment" (41).

The system of concepts and some problems. Each of the studies we shall examine illustrates a field approach, in that each attempts to coordinate the concrete behavior of an individual at a moment of time to concepts that reveal the general dynamics that underlie the particular case. And in this sense, it seems to me that they provide convincing evidence for the fruitfulness of the method of experimental phenomenology, and for Lewin's general field approach. However, the ultimate goal of the field approach is to unify psychology; and to accomplish this, Lewin asserts (42):

Theoretical psychology in its present state must try to develop a system of concepts which shows all the characteristics of a gestalt, in which any part depends upon every other part.

I take this to mean that Lewin had among his concerns a desire to formulate a coherent set of concepts that are related to each other in a systematic way. There are a number of possible ways to attempt this. Lewin tried using a few powerful mathematical concepts, and I believe that in the process he sometimes sacrificed contact with his descriptive data. Unfortunately, the resulting conceptual system has become somewhat rigidified into what is known as "field theory." While this system has many meritorious features, I believe that it is no longer stimulating new ideas and has ceased developing into a unified system of concepts for psychology.

We may make a distinction between a closed system of concepts, such as Hull's system or any mathematical model, where the network of concepts is systematically defined and then applied to future data; and an open system, such as Lewin's, where separate conceptualizations develop in response to new data and are only gradually related to one another. Thus, it is incorrect to treat field theory as though it were a finished conceptualization that has only to be evaluated for consistency and applied to new data. However, it seems to me that if we accept Lewin's goal of a unified system of concepts, each part of the system—even though it is an open system—must be consistent with, and ultimately related to other parts. Therefore, one aspect of our evaluation of any concept must be whether or not it can be systematically related to other concepts. Indeed, this kind of evaluation is necessary to insure the adequate development of the conceptualization. It may be helpful to take a brief look at Lewin's system of concepts in order to appreciate its merits and rate its problems.

In his formal conceptualizations, Lewin uses the topological concept of a *region* (which can be included in, connected to, share a boundary with, other regions) to correspond to the life-space and parts within it. These parts may represent different aspects of time (one's future, past, and present) or levels of reality, so that it is possible to represent the person's view of the future, his position in fantasy, and so forth. Within the environmental part of the life-space, regions can be used to represent anything that a person can be inside or outside of—physical space, social groups, activities. The adjacency of regions with a shared boundary can represent the fact that a person may move directly from one region into another, whereas he cannot go directly between regions that lack a common boundary. For example, one can go directly from high school to college, whereas one has to pass through college to go to medical school. The position of the person within the network of regions in his environment can be used to represent one of the most important properties of his particular life-space—what is possible and what is impossible for him to do. Within this environment there are goals (regions with positive or negative valence), barriers (whose restraining force prevents access to a region), and paths (that lead from one region to another).

Within the person part of the life-space, regions can be used to represent different tension-systems. Here, however, the adjacency of regions represents the fact that the tension in one region may spread into or influence the next region, if there is a pressure differential that exceeds the strength of the regional boundaries.

Now, there are two types of behavior that can occur within the life-space: the person may move from one region in the environment to another, thus changing his position in the life-space; or a restructuring of the life-space may occur, as when a person sees that a region which appeared to lead nowhere is actually a path toward his goal. Lewin uses the concept of *force* (with its properties of magnitude, direction, and point of application) to account for this behavior. He assumes that all behavior is the result of the constellation of forces within the life-space.

In turn, any given force is determined by the state of the person, the nature of the environment, and the person's position in his environment. It will be recalled that a tension within the person part of the life-space is implied whenever there is a valence in some region in the environment. The magnitude of a force is directly related to the strength of this valence and inversely related to the distance between the valence and the person. The direction of a force is related to the relative position of the person and the valenced region in such a manner that it directs the person toward the path which leads him toward a positively valenced region, or away from a negatively valenced region. Thus, the forces of the life-space lead to behavior that will restore equilibrium to the person-environment relationship that is the life-space.

In some ways, Lewin's formal conceptualization is a successful demonstration of his approach. With a very few precise concepts he can elegantly capture an enormous number of important psychological relationships, many more than we have reviewed here. However, there are a number of unfinished tasks: at the conceptual level it has not yet proved possible to rigorously relate forces to topological (or hodological) concepts; on the descriptive level, it has proved difficult to represent the sufficient (as opposed to the necessary) conditions for an event.

Most important, I believe there is a fundamental schism in the network of concepts themselves: the conceptualization of tension-system, which serves so well to unite the studies on personal activity, cannot be logically related to the conceptualization of a force field that serves to unite the observations, and studies that demonstrate how a person's situation determines his behavior. On a descriptive level, the connection between intentional activity and situational force is clear—personal intentions affect environmental valences, and hence the field of forces which play upon us. But on the conceptual, dynamic level, the connection is not achieved. How can an undirected tension-system in a region within the person part of the life-space correlate with the very specific valence of a region in the environmental part of the space? It appears impossible to relate the two parts of Lewin's system. Actually, I believe that this conceptual dilemma reflects a more fundamental problem to which we may now turn.

The Human-Science Approach

Lewin's conceptual net is widely cast in an attempt to include everything that could interest a psychologist, and it will become apparent that his field approach may successfully encompass the psychological discoveries of investigators as diverse as Freud, Hull, Piaget, and Tinbergen. Yet, as I read over the descriptions of the original studies, I find myself repeatedly outside of its conceptual folds. The descriptions seem to require another dimension of conceptualization. What is missing?

When we return to the original studies performed by the Lewin group, the meticulous descriptions clearly reveal subjects who *act* to make intentions and form new organizations. Yet the conceptualizations of the Lewinian group capture only the *products* of these acts—the objective tension-systems and regional connections that are then said to determine behavior. The conceptualization of an objective life-space that determines the person's behavior by tension-systems and fields of force is useful from an objective perspective, but ignores the equally valid perspective that it is the person as a subject who participates in the formation of the very field that determines his behavior. When we are discussing the field of forces and the situation that the subject happens to be in, the essentially passive conceptualizations of Lewin's group fits the descriptive data. When we examine personal activity, a passive conceptualization such as a tension-system does not do justice to the description of a person as an intending, creative being. This flaw must be related to the conceptual weakness we discussed before—that there is no logical way for the tension-systems within the person to relate to the valences of the environment.

To balance a field approach that is entirely from an objective perspective (describing experience and behavior as determined by a set of objective psychobiological conditions), we may take a subjective perspective that views the life-space as determined by how a person acts to organize his relations with his environment.

Note that such a perspective is not contrary to Lewin's analysis of behavior in terms of the situation that the person is in. Lewin elegantly captures the fact that if a person is engaged in an activity, he must have certain needs, the environment must have correlative properties, and a given set of forces must be acting upon the person. Indeed, if we were simply dealing with animal behavior, the conceptualization might stop here. However, Lewin himself describes how the act of intending establishes an organization (a tension-system) that is part of the life-space (43). He describes the act, but conceptualizes only the result of the act. We must insist that an adequate conceptualization must also capture the descriptive fact that the situation we are in is influenced by our own intentions. That is, the person influences the meaning of his situation (the life-space) just as surely as his situation determines the person's behavior. The life-space is as much the consequence of an act that organized it as it is the determiner of our activity.

It might be objected that Lewin captures these facts when he says that behavior affects the life-space by the person's movements in it and by its restructuring. Is not the making of a decision and the forming of an intention an activity that takes place within the life-space? and does not this activity then establish the situation the person is in (the state of his needs and the valence of his environment)? Certainly. But these behaviors are all the resultants of forces in the life-space. I insist that the person is also an actor who is responsible for the very organization that then determines the forces upon him. The person and the environment described by Lewin may then be seen as the results of a person's organization. From a subjective perspective, the person creates organizations, and may even be said to participate in the creation of himself. Such a person can hardly be represented as a region of tensions within the life-space.

This perspective of the person as actor rather than as acted upon, stresses the responsibility which the person bears in determining the meaning of his life in the world. However, it should be clear that it in no way denies the legitimacy of the complementary perspective—that there is a set of objective conditions that determines our behavior. As Merleau-Ponty puts it, "Consciousness holds itself responsible for everything . . . but it has nothing of its own and makes its life in the world" (44). The person organizes the life-space, but the constitution of the life-space determines his behavior, and together with external circumstances provides the material out of which the person must organize a new life-space.

In fact, it is the integration of the two perspectives—the objective and the subjective—that is the main theme of the human-science approach that has been articulated by Giorgi (45), and productively advanced by the work both of behaviorists like Chein (46) and phenomenologists such as Gurwitsch (47), Merleau-Ponty (48), Ricoeur (49), and Schutz (50). In fact, as Fischer has described, the co-existence of both perspectives has been implicit in works throughout the history of psychology (51).

Earlier, we noted that *experience* has a somewhat different meaning for contemporary phenomenologists than it did for Lewin or the classical gestalt psychologists. For the latter, experience, like behavior, was simply one aspect of nature that had to be described and accounted for by psychology. There is a division between a reality that is external to the life-space, and a reality that is inside the life-space. (For the gestaltists there is a corresponding division between physiological and psychological reality.) For the contemporary phenomenology that stems from Husserl, "experience" always has both a personal and an objective reference. Hence, on the one hand experience is not "in" the person, and on the other hand, there is nothing "outside" the person. All we can speak of is our-experience-of-the-world. We cannot really speak of an experience separate from the world, or a world separate from our experience. Furthermore, the person is always both responsible for his-experience-of-the-world and subject to the-world-as-he-experiences-it. Parenthetically, I believe that in spite of this important philosophical difference between Lewin and Husserl, there is a methodological relationship between Lewin's search for "conditional-genetic" conceptualizations that underlie the surface description of experience and behavior, and Husserl's search for the essences of experience.

When we return to the original studies with the addition of a subjective perspective, viewing the person as actor as well as acted upon, we see phenomena somewhat differently. My commentary will reflect these differences, especially when the activity of the person is considered, and will suggest a different conceptualization of the descriptive facts. The general outline of my thought may be summarized as follows:

1. On the conceptual level, the formation of an intention is equivalent to a person becoming *involved* in an activity. That is, he and the activity become joined together as one unit so that the activity is a part of the person, and the person a part of the activity. This new organization, which I shall call an "intention-system," motivates behavior by influencing our perceptions of the environment in the way that Lewin describes. However, unlike a tension-system, it has a basic directionality and a tendency towards closure rather than discharge. Borrowing from Ricoeur's analysis of will, I suggest that an intention-system is a whole that consists of three parts: a project of action, the reasons (motives) for the action, and the person's responsibility for the action.

It should be noted that while such an organization is attributed to the person, and in this sense could be said to be "in" the person part of the life-space, it contains an inherent reference to the environment. Most importantly, while systems are motivated (often by other intention-systems), the person is responsible for their formation in a way that he is not responsible for a need. I shall show how the investigations of Ovsiankina and Zeigarnik may be understood in terms of a subject becoming involved in the activities of the experiments and forming an organization with the properties of an intention-system.

2. When an intention-system is not fulfilled, it may become a motive for a new intention-system. In such a case, the new system is organized in a way that includes the old intention. Note, however, that the new intention-system is not caused by the old one. Rather, the new system is formed autochtho-nously, and organized to encompass the old system. Thus, the person is in-volved in a completely new activity. I argue that such dynamics are involved in the studies on substitution by Lissner, Mahler, and Sliosberg, and may account for the transformation of motives in personality development.

3. Persons are continually organizing and transforming intention-systems. In fact, one fundamental property of human behavior is that an intention-system cannot be repeated. If the situation requires a person to repeat some activity, the person will be unable to reform the old intention-system, but must form a different organization with a slightly different project of action. If circumstances force an attempt at exact replication of the activity, the organi-zation of the person's action will disintegrate into meaningless fragments. There is one partial exception to this law—it is possible to repeat an activity that is simply a means to an end. Note that in such cases the person is "involved" in the end and not the means. All of these dynamics are illustrated in Karsten's study of satiation.

4. Intention-systems may themselves become organized into larger organiza-tions—more comprehensive intention-systems. As a consequence, two inten-tions may become part of the same organization, or may become isolated from one another. The former case is examined in Schwarz's study of "uninten-tional" consequences, the latter in Birenbaum's study on the forgetting of intentions. Schwarz shows that habits may be conceived of as organizations rather than associations. A complex habitual organization is formed when a number of lesser intention-systems are the means for an end. When a person intends this end, he evokes the entire organizational means. Thus, if a part of the organization is no longer functional, the person's activity will provoke "unintended" consequences until he uses conscious attention to break apart the organization. On the other hand, Birenbaum's study illustrates how inten-tions are forgotten when they become isolated from the intention-system that is affecting current behavior.

The possibility of describing the detailed organization of intention-systems suggests that the development and structure of personality may be fruitfully described in terms of the organization of intention-systems.

5. While Dembo's study shows that a person's circumstances may lead to

tension throughout the field and provoke a disintegration of behavior, I argue that emotions themselves are organizations which relate person and environment. The organization of an emotion differs from that of an intention-system in that it is "between" the person and the environmental part of the life-space, rather than "within" the person part of the space.

6. While a person's behavior may be determined by his situation, it is also true that he is capable of making choices that determine the meaning of the situation he is in. In the studies of Hoppe and Dembo we see that he can create goals and decide whether or not to believe something is true. Therefore, a person always has the possibility of either taking the responsibility to assert his own meaning and accept the consequences, or passively allowing someone else to determine the meaning of his situation.

FOOTNOTES

1. Cf. "A Brief Survey of the Experimental Work," in Kurt Lewin, *A Dynamic Theory of Personality* (New York: McGraw-Hill, 1935).

2. Most of a translation of Lewin's theoretical introduction is published as chapters four and five in David Rapaport (Ed.), *Organization and Pathology of Thought* (New York: Columbia University Press, 1951). However, a translation of the second part of the first article is published under the title, "On the Structure of the Mind," as chapter two of *A Dynamic Theory of Personality*. The abridged translation of Zeigarnik's study may be found in Willis E. Ellis (Ed.), *A Source Book of Gestalt Psychology* (London: Routledge and Kegan Paul, Ltd., 1938). This is reprinted as Bobbs-Merrill reprint P-375.

3. All translations, which will be referenced as we proceed, have been deposited with Xerox: University Microfilms, 300 North Zeeb Road, Ann Arbor, Michigan 48106.

4. Cf. reference 2 above.

5. Kurt Lewin, "Social-Psychological Differences Between the United States and Germany," in *Resolving Social Conflicts* (New York: Harper, 1948).

6. Kurt Lewin, *Principles of Topological Psychology* (New York: McGraw-Hill, 1936), viii.

7. Alfred J. Marrow, *The Practical Theorist* (New York: Basic Books, 1969).

8. Ibid., 26–27.

9. Robert Rosenthal, "On the Social Psychology of the Psychological Experiment: The Experimenter's Hypothesis as Unintended Determinant of Experimental Results," *American Scientist* 51(1963), 268–283.

10. Herbert C. Kelman, "Human Use of Human Subjects: The Problem of Deception in Social Psychological Experiments," *Psychological Bulletin* 67(1967), 1–11.

11. Kurt Koffka, *Principles of Gestalt Psychology* (New York: Harcourt, Brace and World, 1935), 73.

12. Edwin G. Boring, *A History of Experimental Psychology,* 2nd ed. (New York: Appleton-Century-Crofts, Inc., 1950), 602.

13. Herbert Spiegelberg, *Phenomenology in Psychology and Psychiatry* (Evanston, Illinois: Northwestern University Press, 1972), 6.

14. Boring, *A History of Experimental Psychology,* 369.

15. Kurt Lewin, "Comments Concerning Psychological Forces and Energies and the Structure of the Psyche," in David Rapaport (Ed.), *Organization and Pathology of Thought* (New York: Columbia University Press, 1951), 77–78.

16. Abraham S. Luchins and Edith Hirsch Luchins, *Rigidity of Behavior* (Eugene, Oregon: University of Oregon Press, 1959), 3.

17. Cf. Lewin, *Principles of Topological Psychology.*

18.   Cf. Ernst Cassirer, *Substance and Function* (New York: Dover, 1953, original, 1910).

19.   Lewin, "Comments Concerning Psychological Forces and Energies and the Structure of the Psyche," 93.

20.   Isidor Chein, *The Science of Behavior and the Image of Man* (New York: Basic Books, 1972), 310.

21.   Lewin, *A Dynamic Theory of Personality*, 41–42.

22.   Ibid., 88.

23.   Lewin, *Principles of Topological Psychology*, 13.

24.   Ibid., 19.

25.   Ibid., 18.

26.   These remarks, from a typed account of the celebration of Stumpf's 70th birthday in 1918, have been published by Fritz Heider, "Gestalt Theory: Early History and Reminiscences," *Journal of Historical Behavioral Science* 6(1970), 131–139.

27.   Kurt Lewin, "Kriegslandschaft," *Zeit. Angewandte Psychol.* 12(1917), 440–447. A translation, "Warscape," may be obtained from Xerox: University Microfilms.

28.   Kurt Lewin, "Intention, Will and Need," in David Rapaport (Ed.), *Organization and Pathology of Thought* (New York: Columbia University Press, 1951).

29.   These may be obtained from Calvin Communications Inc., 215 West Pershing Road, Kansas City, Missouri.

30.   Cf. Kurt Lewin, "Das Problem der Willensmessung und der Assoziation," *Psychol. Forsch.* 1(1922), 191–302, 2(1922), 65–140.

31.   Lewin, "Intention, Will and Need."

32.   Cf. Lewin, *Principles of Topological Psychology*, and "Behavior and Development as a Function of the Total Situation," in Dorwin Cartwright (Ed.), *Field Theory in Social Science* (New York: Harper and Row, 1951).

33.   Robert W. Leeper, *Lewin's Topological and Vector Psychology* (Eugene, Oregon: University of Oregon Press, 1943).

34.   Dorwin Cartwright, "Lewinian Theory as a Contemporary Systematic Framework," in S. Koch (Ed.), *Psychology: A Study of a Science,* vol. II (New York: McGraw-Hill, 1959).

35.   Morton Deutsch, "Field Theory in Social Psychology," in Gardner Lindzey and Elliot Aronson (Eds.), *The Handbook of Social Psychology,* 2nd ed., vol. I (Reading, Massachusetts: Addison-Wesley, 1968).

36.   Kurt Lewin, *Der Begriff der Genese in Physik, Biologie und Entwicklungsgeschichte* (Berlin: Gebrüder Borntraeger, 1922).

37.   See, however, Isidor Chein, "The Genetic Factor in Ahistorical Psychology," *Journal of General Psychology* 36(1947), 151–172.

38.   Cf. Lewin, *Principles of Topological Psychology*, viii.

39.   Ibid., 6.

40.   Ibid., viii.

41.   Ibid., 74.

42.   Ibid., viii.

43.   Lewin, "Intention, Will and Need."

44.   Maurice Merleau-Ponty, Phenomenology of Perception (London: Routledge and Kegan Paul, Ltd., 1962), 453.

45.   A. Giorgi, *Psychology as a Human Science: A Phenomenologically Based Approach* (New York: Harper and Row, 1970).

46.   Chein, *The Science of Behavior and the Image of Man.*

47.   Aron Gurwitsch, *The Field of Consciousness* (Pittsburgh, Pennsylvania: Duquesne University Press, 1964).

48.   Merleau-Ponty, *Phenomenology of Perception.*

49.   Paul, Ricoeur, *Freedom and Nature: The Voluntary and the Involuntary* (Evanston, Illinois: Northwestern University Press, 1966).

50.   Alfred Schutz, *Reflections on the Problems of Relevance* (New Haven, Connecticut: Yale University Press, 1970).

51.   Constance Fischer, "Historical Relations of Psychology as an Object-Science and a Subject-Science: Toward Psychology as a Human-Science," paper presented at the annual meetings of the American Psychological Association, 1974.

PART ONE:

THE DYNAMICS
AND STRUCTURE
OF ACTIVITY

Chapter II

THE FORCES OF HABIT AND WILL

THE first three studies we shall be examining in this book grew out of the attempt to bring the act of will into the laboratory, to describe its properties, and measure its force. In order to appreciate the range of phenomena at stake and the work done in field theory by the concept of "tension-system," we must note the basic psychological facts which Lewin and others were trying to explain.

ACH'S STUDY OF WILL

In the early 1900's there were a number of attempts to measure the speed of thought. Investigators compared the time it took a subject to respond to a simple stimulus with the subject's reaction time when different stimuli required different responses. They reasoned that in the latter case the subject would have to "think" what to do. Then the speed of this thinking could be calculated by subtracting the simple reaction time to a single stimulus from the longer reaction time to the different stimuli which required thinking (1). At first, this method seemed quite promising; but then, at Külpe's laboratory in Würzburg, the subjects of such experiments were asked to reflect upon their experience while their reaction times were being obtained.

This method, a type of experimental phenomenology, was elaborated by Ach, who called it "experimental self-observation" (2). It involved having a subject carefully describe his experience directly after it had been induced by experimental means. This technique prevented the act of observation from interfering with the experience that was being observed; it was made possible by the fact that the experience "persevered" for a while after it had been induced. (This perseveration is not a "memory" of the experience, in that it is not a reconstruction and has the clearness of details and "giveness" that a perception has. A number of investigators measured time of perseveration and showed that it has a positive dependence on the subject's intention to describe the experience, the intensity of focused attention, and the number of repetitions. The perseveration can last from a few seconds to several minutes.)

Ach used one signal to prepare the subjects for an experience and another signal to have them reflect upon the experience. After this observation, the experimenter questioned the subject to bring out additional detail. Ach notes how this technique involves a constant close communication between subject and experimenter. He also discusses the importance of obtaining a complete description that is unbiased by expectancies from either the subject or the experimenter, and shows how such a description may be obtained by using repeated observations from each of a number of subjects.

Using "self-observation," Watts and Ach found that the attempt to measure the speed of thought by comparing reaction times was basically invalid. It was invalid in that subjects did not report thinking after the stimulus was presented —rather, they reacted "automatically," even when different stimuli called for different responses. On the other hand, the investigators found that the subjects reported that a considerable amount of effort went into preparing themselves for the stimulus, as they determined to react quickly and set themselves to give the correct response to the right stimulus. Their response was steered by this "determining tendency" which, because of its directionality, and the feelings of effort and determination, seemed to be a manifestation of "will."

To study the act of will, Ach created a number of different experimental arrangements which required his subjects to "exercise will" (3). For example, he asked them to release a button at the exact instant when a specific stimulus appeared. (There were numerous variations of this arrangement over a period of several days.) He concluded that the experience of willing could not be reduced to cognitive, sensory, or emotional elements, but had to be described as a whole with four dependent parts. These aspects of will were: sensations of tension (often in the face); an "inner dialogue" about the projected act and how to accomplish it; sensations of effort; and, most important, an act of decision—an "I *can* do it and I *really will* do it." During the act of willing, the *I* becomes salient, so that the person is aware of the dependence of the action on himself. (The *I* who has chosen is part of the immediate experience and is not inferred.) The activity of willing functions by excluding all other possible actions, making the projected action a present reality. Ach demonstrates that when the activity of willing is "actual" and not simply "in awareness," it determines behavior. Further, its effectiveness is strengthened by prior successes and weakened by previous failures (4).

Having established the independent existence of willing as an activity, Ach argued that it might have effects which had previously been attributed only to associations. It had been assumed that a stimulus which had been repeatedly associated with a response acquired the power to exert a force that would elicit that response. This was the "force of habit." Ach reasoned that a second way in which a stimulus might acquire such a power was through an act of will. Rather than having repeated associations establish a connection between the stimulus and the required response, an act of will might establish a connection so that the presentation of the stimulus would elicit the response. The subject who set himself to release a button upon the presentation of a stimulus might be said to have established such a connection between the stimulus and the response of releasing the button. Ach did several experiments with post-hypnotic suggestions to demonstrate this point.

In order to firmly establish the existence of will as a causal connector, Ach designed some experiments in which he could actually measure the strength of will by pitting the force of association-established connections against the force of will-established connections. In these experiments he had subjects learn pairs of nonsense syllables until there was a firmly established connection or association between the stimulus syllable and the required response syllable.

In one experiment, the first series of syllables consisted of rhymes (e.g., rik-tik), while another series consisted of inversions (e.g., kep-pek). In the second part of the experiment the subject was given a mixed list of stimulus syllables which he was sometimes asked to rhyme and sometimes to invert. Ach showed that reaction times were faster when the instructions agreed with the previously established habit. When the subject had to rhyme to a stimulus syllable that had previously called for an inversion, or vice versa, the subjects were placed in conflict and their reactions took longer. Ach believed that these results demonstrated the existence of will (e.g., the subjects trying to rhyme) pitted against the strength of habit (e.g., the subjects' prior association to the stimulus syllable). The reader may easily experiment with this type of conflict by making a list of color-names written with different colored pencils or crayons (5). It is helpful to write the first few color-names in colors that are the same as the name, but the remainder should be written in colors that are different from the names that are spelled (for instance, red written in blue pencil). If one now attempts to read off the colors in which the words are written, some difficulty will be experienced as soon as the colors conflict with the color-names. The will to read off the colors in which the names are printed is thwarted by the habit of reading the names of the colors as soon as the two are in conflict.

Working with nonsense syllables, Ach attempted to get a precise measure of strength of will by equating the degree of will with the strength of the association that blocked it. In doing this, he assumed that the strength of association was controlled by the number of repetitions of stimulus-response pairing that the subjects had experienced. Unfortunately, a number of ir-regularities in the data prevented the fulfillment of this promising plan.

LEWIN'S FIRST EXPERIMENTS

Inspired by Stumpf's hope that will could be successfully experimented upon, Lewin's first experimental work (6) was an attempt to refine Ach's methods in order to be able to measure the strength of will with more precision (7). However, he found that his data did not support one important feature of Ach's reasoning. It was not that Ach was wrong in introducing the concept of will or conceiving of it as exerting a force. Rather, Lewin found that he was incorrect in supposing that associations had independent force of their own that could be opposed to the force of will. Lewin performed a number of experiments with nonsense syllables which showed that connections or habits did *not* automatically lead to the behavior which should have occurred if mere association was a cause of behavior. For example, after subjects had learned pairs of nonsense syllables, some of which were rhymes and others inversions, Lewin asked his subjects to simply read a list of nonsense syllables in which previous stimulus words were embedded. Subjects had no difficulty in doing this and did not experience any tendency to give the previously learned responses. In some cases they did not even recognize the stimulus syllables. Again, if subjects were asked to change the middle letter of the syllables, they usually experienced no difficulty, even when prior stimulus syllables were inserted in the list.

On the other hand, Lewin showed that these same subjects showed the conflict which Ach had previously demonstrated if they attempted to rhyme to syllables which had previously called for an inversion and vice versa. To explain this conflict, Lewin argued that the force of habit really stemmed from an underlying intention or act of will. He asserted that when subjects were ostensibly trying to rhyme to a syllable, they were actually engaged in the activity of reproducing the response which they had previously learned. Hence, they were really in a conflict between the conscious intention to rhyme and an underlying intention to reproduce.

Lewin argued that in his first set of experiments there was no conflict between the previously learned response and the new response because the subject had no intention to reproduce the old response. The new intention— to simply read the syllables or to change a letter—was so different from the old intention that the subject was not placed in any conflict. On the other hand, an instruction to rhyme to the old syllable could be acted upon as though it were an instruction to reproduce what had been learned before, and the subject was thus caught between obeying two conflicting intentions. Thus, Lewin asserted that Ach was not really dealing with a conflict between the force of habit and the force of intention (act of will), but with a conflict between two different intentions—the will to reproduce and the will to rhyme—which were both activated by the instructions given to the subjects. If a stimulus caused a response, it was not simply because the response was connected to the stimulus by past associations, but because some intention was present which, together with the connection, led to the response.

If the reader experiments with color names, he may grasp Lewin's point by returning to the colors that are difficult to read (because they conflict with the color-names), and attempting to count the letters in each name. The fact that he experiences no difficulty shows that the words themselves do not really automatically force one to read them. Thus, the conflict he had initially must have been caused by some intention to read the words. Such an intention seems to be invoked by the use of a list of words, and the attempt to "read" the color in which the word is written.

The feature of Lewin's argument which may be most difficult to grasp is the idea that what we ordinarily think of as a habit is, in fact, intended. Clearly, one does not experience oneself as trying to reproduce an old response (or read a word); rather, one tries to rhyme (or name a color) and has to fight against an automatic and unwanted force. Lewin is not denying this experience. But he insists that the energy for this unwanted force comes from the person, rather than the stimulus. Thus, the force does not stem from the fact that a physical stimulus (*e.g.*, TUR) has been paired 20 times with a response (*e.g.*, POF), but from the person's own intention to reproduce the learned response. While Lewin did not deny the existence of some connection between stimulus and response he felt it had to be activated by an intention.

Lewin reasoned that connections themselves could not be sufficient causes of behavior. He argued that dynamic factors—forces—must be present in order for behavior to occur. The mere existence of a prior association between a stimulus syllable and a response syllable could not account for the force exerted by the stimulus syllable, and hence the conflict Ach had demonstrated. Some force of will, some intention, must also be present in order for the association to lead to the old response, and hence conflict with the subject's current intention.

It should be observed that according to Lewin's analysis, the physical stimulus—the printed word—has no effect on behavior that is independent from the behaver. The word has no meaning unless it is read, and hence the meaning of the word resides neither in the word, nor in the reader, but in the word-as-read. It might be noted that such an analysis is completely congruent with the position taken by most phenomenologists. Indeed, Gurwitsch argues that the analysis of Gestalt psychology implicitly involves a phenomenological reduction (8).

As a result of his discovery that subjects who were consciously intending to rhyme were actually engaged in the intentional activity of reproducing a previously learned response, Lewin shifted his attention from the "pure" experience of conscious intention to intentional behavior—activities—and, in my own analysis, the experience of intended behavior. The very pervasiveness of will led him to believe that its essential characteristics were more apt to be revealed by an examination of a broad spectrum of behavior, rather than of isolated experiences of conscious acts of willing.

In order to test his hypothesis and reveal various aspects of will, Lewin subjected behavior to a number of different interventions. Consider the first three studies that we shall be examining. In the first study, Ovsiankina *interrupts* activity and observes the forces that lead the subject to resume it—as when we resume reading a book interrupted by a phone call. In the second study, Karsten has her subjects *repeatedly perform* activities until the subject is "satiated" and faced with forces that prevent continuation. This, of course, happens to us whenever we continue to play a musical instrument, or write —we finally want to stop the activity. Finally, Schwarz introduces a *change* in a behavior, and investigates the forces that lead the behavior to "relapse" into the old, unwanted pattern. This sort of thing happens to us when we change where we keep our pencils, or wastebasket, or chair, and find ourselves repeatedly starting to reach for, throw at, or go to where the object used to be.

It may be observed that in these studies the investigation of the pure experience of *will* becomes transformed into the investigation of the experience of behavior as influenced by *forces*. While this transformation highlights many motivational aspects of will that would otherwise be overlooked, there are other features—often involving choice and freedom—which are rather ignored. In the commentary chapters, I shall attempt to restore these ignored dimensions of will by describing the structure of behavior from a subjective viewpoint.

LEWIN'S THEORY OF INTENTION

The first three studies deal with concrete phenomena that are in a dialectic relation to Lewin's abstract conceptualization of "intention." Lewin is not using *intention* in its technical phenomenological sense (that is, "intending" as a giving of meaning), but in its everyday usage as an "intention" to do something. Taking such intentions as examples of willing, he asks when we make intentions and how they function. Since his answers depend on an understanding of the phenomena of "valence" and "field forces," we shall begin by examining these concepts in some detail.

Lewin first became aware of valences in his experiments on the relationship between will and habit, which we reviewed above. He found that even when a subject had an intention to rhyme and was engaged in the activity of rhyming, rather than reproducing, occasionally the subject would respond by reproducing a previously learned response. Lewin believed that in these cases the syllable as perceived by the subject had taken on a will of its own and was commanding the subject to give the previously learned response. The prior intention to reproduce had become "fixated" on the syllable.

He points out that an experimenter gives instructions to his subject by means of imperative sentences which are commands—for example, "When a nonsense syllable appears, I want you to create a rhyme for it." But these verbal commands do not have to be repeated when the same task is repeated a few minutes later. Merely being led to his seat and witnessing the start of the machine that presents the nonsense syllables is enough to get the subject to perform. The environment, then, has acquired the meaning initially given by the verbal command. Now, this command meaning can also be transferred to a given nonsense syllable, so that if the syllable *tuk* has been used in a task which calls for the inversion of the syllable, the presentation of *tuk* does not simply mean "a nonsense syllable"; rather, it means "form the inversion of *tuk*." Hence, an object in the environment, such as a nonsense syllable may, under certain conditions, acquire a command character *(Befehlscharaktere)*. Lewin later used the term *Aufforderungscharakter* ("invitation" character), as the concept began to include the idea of a request, or even an enticement. Edward Tolman had a similar concept which he termed "demand value"; and after Donald K. Adams used *valence* as a translation for *Aufforderungscharakter,* the two men agreed to use valence as a common term to denote the "will" we meet from certain objects or events in our environment.

To paraphrase Lewin: Our psychological environment consists of objects and events. These affect our behavior, not only by facilitating or obstructing our actions, but by confronting us "with a will of their own" and challenging us to specific actions. Good weather may entice us to walk, small crumbs to pick them up, and dogs to pet them; a piece of cake wants to be eaten, a book to be read, and a confused situation calls for decisive action. The intensity of these challenges or demands varies from an irresistible to a very weak force; these valences may be positive and press us to approach, or negative and press us to retreat. But the crucial feature of valences is that they press for certain definite actions, the range of which may be broad or narrow (9).

The valence of an object or event is as much a part of it as is its figural form, and is not a separate psychic structure. Hence, one should not speak of changes of the valence of an object, but rather of different objects which are only externally identical (10). Psychologically, a structure whose valence has changed because of a change in one's situation is a different structure. Thus, a mailbox is not the same object before we mail a letter, when it calls to us to deposit the letter, as it is after we mail the letter.

Valences depend, of course, on the situation of a person. They may directly reflect a means of need satisfaction, as when a concert attracts one who enjoys music, or they may be derivative, as when the home of a loved one acquires a positive valence. They undergo transformations which depend on the action which the person is engaged in, as when all objects near the front line of battle lose their ordinary meanings and are seen only as relevant to survival, or when formerly unnoticed things become interesting on a vacation, or after a change of occupation. Changes of valence are often the first indication of changes in one's internal situation, as in shifts in love or in fundamental decisions about one's occupation. Considerations such as these led Lewin to believe that changes in valence corresponded to changes in needs and inclinations, and he postulated, "the proposition that 'such-and-such a need exists' is to a certain extent equivalent to the proposition that 'such-and-such a region of structures has a valence for such-and-such actions' " (italics omitted) (11). It should be noted, however, that valences do not only stem from one's own needs, but may also be induced by the will (needs) of another—a subject that I shall discuss in more detail in chapters four and twelve.

Lewin made a distinction between behavior that is directly determined by the field forces of valences—field action—and behavior that is "controlled action." For example, a child who is going home but takes a long detour past a mean-looking dog is exhibiting field action, whereas if the child forced himself to walk directly past the dog he is showing "controlled action." Lewin notes that an act of intention—a resolution to do something—is often itself a controlled act. However, the same intention is often executed as a field action. The subject may intend to press a lever when a buzzer sounds, but this leads the subject to abandon himself to the field so that when the buzzer sounds he involuntarily presses the lever—a field action of responding to the valence of the buzzer which "says," "Push the lever" (12).

This idea, that an intention, like a need, can act to create a valence in the experienced environment, and that this valence exerts a force on the person's activity, is basic to Lewin's theoretical analysis of intention. This analysis may now be summarized as follows (13):

1. Acts of intention occur when the subject's needs lead him to forsee a situation in which he desires to act in a certain way, but knows that the situation will not automatically bring about the desired action. That is, he anticipates that the field of forces to which he will be subjected will not lead to the desired action.

2. When successful, the subject's act of intention functions to transform the future psychological field so that he can abandon himself to the valences of the field with the assurance that the desired behavior will result.

3. This is accomplished by the act of intention creating a tension state which functions exactly as a real need would function. Such a quasi-need is embedded in a specific psychic region which is influenced by the subject's real needs (drives and general goals of will). The intensity of the quasi-need depends on the intensity and centrality of these needs, which may be different from those which led to the act of intention in the first place. It is these real needs which govern whether or not the intention will be successful in affecting future fields.

4. Like a real need, a quasi-need—the tension-system—is associated with a region of objects and events that have a valence which leads the person to perform actions that satisfy the need and discharge the tension. As with real needs, the extent of this region depends on the strength of the need. Also, the need tension causes occasions to be sought out, and any interrupted actions to be resumed or better retained in memory. As with real needs, when the quasi-need is satiated, the valences disappear. As with real needs, genuine consummation may be replaced by substitute consummation.

5. A good deal of our volitional behavior is not preceded by conscious acts of intention. For example, in a conversation, we do not always intend—resolve —what to say next. Thus, an act of conscious intention is only one type of volitional behavior, and is not the prototype of all willed action. On the other hand, an act, such as accepting an instruction, or a thought, such as "it could be done in such a way," may dynamically be an intention—that is, reflect the establishment of a tension-system—although such thoughts are hardly distinguishable phenomenally from mere understandings.

6. In contrast to an intention, which operates by creating a tension-system, with resultant valences that influence field forces, a decision affects behavior by creating an access to the motor region for a tension-system that already exists, but was in competition with other tensions for control of action. (Such decisions and other possible acts of will are not treated in detail by Lewin.)

To recapitulate: While Ach proposed that an intention (an act of will) established a connection between the desired response and some stimulus, Lewin asserted that an intention operated like a need corresponding to a tension-system that actively sought fulfillment and influenced the organization of the environment so that the response could occur. If Ach was correct, the occurrence of the intended response should be dependent upon the occurrence of the stimulus. In order to demonstrate that this was not so, Lewin and one of his students, Maria Ovsiankina, designed the experiment we shall now examine.

1. Cf. the account in Edwin G. Boring, *A History of Experimental Psychology,* 2nd ed. (New York: Appleton-Century-Crofts, 1950), 147–149.

2. N. Ach, *Über die Willenstaetigkelt und das Denken* (Goettingen: Vandenhoeck und Ruprecht, 1905).

3. N. Ach, *Über den Willensakt und das Temperament* (Leipzig: Quelle and Meyer, 1910).

4. Subsequently, Honoria Wells, replicating an early experiment by Michotte and Prum, had subjects reflect on the act of choice and found similar descriptions of experience. *Cf.* "Phenomenology of Acts of Choice," *British Journal of Psychology* (1927), no. 4, monograph supplement.

5. A number of investigations have used such an arrangement of colored words. See, for example, George Rand, Seymour Wapner, Heinz Werner, and Joseph H. McFarland, "Age Differences in Performance on the Stroop Color-Word Test," *Journal of Personality* 31 (1963), 534–558.

6. However, it should be noted that his first published work was a phenomenological study of how a soldier's experience of his environment changes as he approaches the line of battle. Cf. Kurt Lewin, "Kriegslandschaft," *Zert. Psychol.* 12 (1917), 440–447.

7. Kurt Lewin, "Das Problem der Willenmessung und der Assoziation," *Psychol. Forsch.* 1 (1922), 191–302 and 2, 65–140.

8. The argument that the dismissal of the "constancy hypothesis" (the assumption that experience is governed by physical stimuli) constitutes an implicit phenomenological reduction is made in detail by Aron Gurwitsch, *The Field of Consciousness* (Pittsburgh, Pennsylvania: Duquesne University Press, 1964).

9. Kurt Lewin, "Intention, Will and Need," in David Rapaport (Ed.), *Organization and Pathology of Thought* (New York: Columbia University Press, 1951), 117–118.

10. Ibid., 130.

11. Ibid., 122.

12. Ibid., 148.

13. Ibid., 151–153. I am almost paraphrasing Lewin.

Chapter III

THE RESUMPTION OF INTERRUPTED ACTIVITIES*

Maria Rickers-Ovsiankina

*Translated by Dr. Hedda Korsch. The original article, "Die Wiederaufnahme unterbrockener Handlungen," was published in *Psychologische Forschung,* vol. 11(1928), pp. 302–379. Permission to publish this translation was generously granted by Springer-Verlag.

INTRODUCTION

Experimental exploration of the processes involved in volition have resulted in the postulation of determining tendencies. According to Ach, these are the aftereffects of volition that are involved in intention and planning, etc. (1). They are aspects of psychic functioning which are not based on associations, but rather are goal-directed. This approach is in accord with the general tendency to emphasize the goal-directedness of life processes.

Goal-directedness in general is treated rather vaguely by the neovitalists. In like fashion, the psychological goal-directedness involved in the concepts of drive and determining tendencies is not clearly defined. It is envisaged as an indivisible fundamental which is unsuited for further analysis.

In this study we do not intend to discuss the abstract question of whether or not goal-directedness is a basic force of life. Rather, we use concrete experiments to try to determine the dynamic factors at work in the execution of intended activities.

Based on experiences in everyday life, we *interrupt* our subjects in the midst of activities. We then keep them otherwise occupied in order to see under what conditions they will *return to their original activity.* Suppose that, at the moment of forming an intention to carry out a certain activity, what occurs is a coupling (association) between the image of what one wishes to do, and the image of the occasion for the action, and this coupling provides the essential reason for the execution of the intention when the occasion occurs. Then it would follow that the activity would come to a complete stop if it were interrupted. Continuation or resumption of the activity would only occur if the person in question again experienced the same, or a similar, image of the occasion for action. On the other hand, if Lewin's theory is correct and the process underlying the execution of intended activities is not a coupling but a system of tensions, then we might expect a resumption of the activity (2). This is the same problem which Zeigarnik investigated by her indirect method (3).

In addition to the above question, we hoped that the interruption experiments would help us find out what determines the strength of the forces underlying the performance of an intended activity, and the nature of the connection of these forces with other factors in the inner psychic situation.

I. EXPERIMENTAL PROCEDURE

The experiments were carried out from 1924 to 1926 with 124 subjects (Ss). 108 were adults, mostly university students, 16 were children from 3 to 16 years of age.

The subjects had to carry out a number of activities which were *interrupted* by the experimenter (E) during their execution. In each experimental session, 3 to 11 activities took place. In addition, several "decoy experiments" were introduced; they were non-interrupted activities, intended to deceive the subjects about the real purpose of the experiments. In spite of this, it should be noted that after repeated interruptions, fear of new interruptions sometimes appeared. One to two hours were spent with every subject. Subjects were kept strictly in ignorance of the aims of the experiments.

We supplemented the experimental activity with self-observations on the part of the subjects, since many questions could not be clarified by mere observation of the subjects' behavior.

The subjects' statements sometimes occurred spontaneously, but usually required a few questions from the experimenter.

The Activities

Fifteen activities of a widely divergent character were used in the experiments.

1. Kind and structure of activities* The main activities the subjects were asked to perform were:

1. Solving a steel ring puzzle in which the rings must be detached from one another
2. Solving a braintwister in which:
    a) 5 small chains were to be combined into one large chain by opening only 3 links.
    b) 4 dots were to be removed from a picture frame so as to leave 12 dots on each side of the frame.
3. Assembling a square from its parts
4. Assembling a mosaic picture from colored tiles according to a model
5. Unraveling a complicated tangle of yarn.
6. Copying a correlation schema
7. Sorting and putting away chips
8. Hatching checkered patterns

* (The original contains illustrations of most of these tasks—Editor.)

9. Stringing various numbers of beads
10. Making a paper chain
11. Modeling something from plasticine
12. Building a tower of blocks, to own design
13. Drawing without a model
14. Reassembling a cut-up picture postcard
15. Folding paper figures

According to their inner structure, we make a distinction between finite and continuous activities (4). Typical *finite activities* consist of a completed task, accomplished in a brief time-span, whose single steps derive meaning and cohesion from a more or less fixed goal. Typical *continuous activities,* on the other hand, do not have a natural conclusion in themselves; the individual steps of the task are not related to a fixed goal, and are essentially of equal value.

Of the activities listed above, Nos. 1–4 are typically finite. 8–10 can be regarded as typically continuous if no clear-cut limits are set either by the instructions or by the material. A limit will be set, for example, if only two tape rolls are handed out for the paper chain. Typically continuous activities, however, can figure as weak finite activities, if, for example, the subject has to fill in a checkerboard of only 16 squares, or if he is instructed to hatch only half of the squares within a chessboard pattern of 32 squares. Activities 5–7 are finite, but less typically so than the first four. Activities 11–13 are also finite, but somewhat unpredictable, since their aim is not delineated by a model or precise instruction, but presented only in a rather general way (*e.g.,* to model an animal). Activities 14–15 are used only as decoy or disturbing activities.

Even with identical instructions and identical materials, an activity may appear as more or less finite or continuous to different subjects, depending upon their individual approach to the material.

Most experiments were carried out with finite activities.

2. Pleasant and unpleasant activities We wanted to take into account the degree of pleasantness or unpleasantness involved in the various activities. This factor, however, was not easily predictable. We found that, apart from gross physiological revulsion, under laboratory conditions there were hardly any activities that appeared pleasant or unpleasant to everybody alike. Activities rejected emphatically by one subject were carried out with pleasure by others, and vice-versa.

For this reason, the classification of activities as "pleasant" or "unpleasant" could not be made until the records of the subjects' self-observations were completed. Similar results, and consequently the same method of evaluation, were obtained by Karsten (5) and, more recently, by Lindworsky (6).

Kinds of Interruption

1. Interruption by disturbing activities Disturbance interruptions are made by assigning another task (disturbing activity) to a subject who is occupied with a first (main) activity, and insisting that the second task be tackled immediately. The subject, for example, may be constructing something from building blocks. While he is busy in this way, the experimenter hands him a ring puzzle and requests that he take it apart right away. As far as possible, the experimenter refrains from mentioning the first activity, because he does not want to influence the subject's future attitude towards it.

2. Interruption by expressly prohibiting completion During his first activity, the subject is suddenly instructed to put his unfinished work aside for good. This interruption, expressly prohibiting completion, is of the same type as interruption by disturbing activity, but is of a heightened form. In an interruption by disturbing activity, continuation of the main activity remains possible, but here it is definitely forbidden.

Besides these two kinds of interruption, we used a number of less drastic types for purposes of comparison:

3. Interruption by "chance" These interruptions were intended to appear to the subject as if they were caused by chance occurrences, rather than by the experimenter.

Some chance interruptions which we used were:

a) The experimenter drops a box filled with many small objects (thumb tacks, paper clips, etc.) to the floor. The subject, probably spontaneously, helps the experimenter to pick up the scattered objects. If this does not occur, the subject is asked to help with the excuse that he must not work at the table unobserved. The disadvantage of this kind of interruption is that it can hardly be extended over a considerable time. Its duration is about 1/2–3 minutes.

b) The subject is placed at the table in such a way as to sit directly in front of the desk drawer. The experimenter pretends that he needs something from the drawer. The subject has to stand up, thus interrupting his work. He believes that this is an occurrence that has arisen "naturally" from the situation, and does not realize it was engineered by the experimenter. It is easy to start a conversation during the disturbance in order to lengthen the interruption. This will divert the subject's attention. Additional distraction from the work can be added if the experimenter remains seated in the subject's chair during the conversation. Average duration of this kind of interruption is from 2–8 minutes; the maximum is 15 minutes.

c) An electric bell, invisible to the subject, is installed at the experimenter's place. By ringing it, the experimenter can summon another member of the Institute. The newcomer then asks subject and experimenter to assist him in the adjoining room. An advantage of this arrangement is that it prevents even suspicious subjects from surmising a secret intention behind the chance interruption, as had occasionally occurred with the other methods. Moreover, the interruption could be extended *ad libitum;* occasionally it was stretched to 30 minutes. (To gauge the effect of duration, both longer and shorter times of interruption were used.) Finally, the subject was effectively removed from the experimental situation and especially from the special environment of the interrupted activity.

These chance interruptions were used with equal frequency, and represent, by and large, a graduated series of interruptions of varied intensity.

d) Initially a fourth kind of chance interruption was used, but it did not give very satisfactory results, and we mention it mainly in order to point out the significance of different factors in such interruptions. By means of a hidden switch the experimenter shut off the electric current and caused the lights to go out. Then he busied himself trying to "fix" the lights for the length of time allotted to the interruption. In this case, the subject stayed in his seat with nothing to divert him; often he even kept his hands on whatever he was doing. Such proximity to the task considerably increased the probability of resumption, a circumstance that diminished the value of this method for our purposes.

4. Interruption by reports on self-observations If self-observations were used for the purpose of interruption, and if they referred directly to the interrupted activity, they would not really detach the subject from what he had been doing. As mentioned before, usually self-observations immediately followed each activity. This rule was broken for activities preceding those designated for this type of interruption. The procedure was: When the subject was busy performing the next task, the experimenter suddenly remembered that he forgot to ask for self-observations about the preceding task. He then asked the subject to make up for the omission. If the subject tried to continue work on his current task at the same time, he was requested to discontinue it, in order to "concentrate better."

This type of interruption has a position between the two first kinds. On the one hand, nothing requires a complete abandonment of the unfinished work (as possibly happens with interruptions by disturbing activities); on the other hand, it lacks a chance character, since the experimenter insists explicitly on the performance of the different task of narrating self-observations. In this regard, it is similar to interruption by disturbing activities, but it differs from the former inasmuch as it seems to come about naturally and not as a disturbance manufactured by the experimenter.

5. *Interruption by distracting conversation* An even weaker type of interruption consisted of occasional questions put to the subject by the experimenter during the activities. These appeared to be chance interruptions. If, however, such questions were extended into a conversation, the interruption approximated the character of a disturbing activity. The length of the conversation distracted the subject and gave him the impression that the experimenter was no longer interested in the completion of the activity. Resumption of an activity after interruption would not seem remarkable if the situation resembled that of a slight disturbance by a noise which distracts the subject momentarily, but did not actually bring his work to a stop. In our experiments, however, even the weak interruptions were never so negligible. An interruption of 1–2 minutes, let alone longer ones, forced the subject really to enter into the new situation. If, afterwards, the subject returned spontaneously to the previous task, we were faced with a genuine resumption of his former activity, not only in terms of his behavior, but also psychologically. Even in cases of lasting phenomenal perseveration, the character of the return to the first activity was unmistakably experienced as resumption.

II. QUALITATIVE DESCRIPTION OF THE BEHAVIOR AND EXPERIENCE OF THE SUBJECTS

Since qualitative characterization is the necessary precondition of every quantitative evaluation, we will now proceed to give a description of the subjects' behavior and of the course of their subjective experiences from the moment of interruption, through the intervening time, to the eventual resumption of the main activity.

We shall start by relating an individual case and shall go on to present a systematic survey of the typical phenomena occurring in our experiments.

An Example

For this concrete example, we selected a case in which the act of resumption does not appear as markedly as in some others, but which does illustrate some of the finer shades and secondary phenomena that appear in one form or another in most cases. Besides, this subject had been filmed without his knowledge during the experiment, so that we are able to illustrate our presentation by film shots.*

Because of the filming, the experiment took place in a garden. This circumstance made for a relaxed, loosely structured situation, not very favorable to resumption. We shall describe the course of the experiment as it appears on the film.

* *Ten pictures have been omitted which may be found in the original—Editor.*

Subject begins with work on the puzzle game. At first he is uninterested, but soon becomes rather keen; on account of the difficulty, he is insecure and nervous, pushing his hands under the table.

While he is working busily, the experimenter interrupts the subject with the new task of hatching. The new instruction is given without any explanation or comment about the first activity.

At first the subject does not react to this interference at all, although the experimenter pushes the checkerboard towards him energetically, urging him to take it. Not until 40 frames later (16 frames in one second) is the subject seen to approach the new task, half surprised, half embarrassed. Even then, another 10 frames go by before the subject, urged on by the experimenter, draws the first line of hatching.

Nonetheless, it can be said that, in this case, the subject adapted rather quickly to the new situation (within 10 seconds). He turns to the new activity, enters into it wholeheartedly, and feels again on solid ground. He is hatching with intense concentration.

What is now the subject's feeling towards the former activity? The subject reports: "As long as I was hatching, the rings were completely out of my mind." Phenomenologically, the new occupation has taken the place of the old one; it has become the sole action, dominating the field.

When the disturbing action is terminated, the subject sits inactive while the experimenter is "busy taking notes" in order not to influence the subject during the short intervening pause. Later, the subject reports about this outwardly dead time-span: "I waited until you (experimenter) would finish writing so that I could ask you about the solution (of the puzzle)." The subject, then, after completing the disturbing activity, had inwardly so completely reverted to the first task that he did not even mention whether his question referred to the first or the second task. For the subject, the first task had again become the only one, not just in the sense of being a given fact, but in the sense of a task driving towards completion.

When the subject is asked by the experimenter to narrate his experiences with the first activity (ring puzzle), he picks up the rings, holding them loosely without any serious attempt to find the solution. The subject pushes the rings around, twisting them, his head inclined to one side with a slight smile during his report on his self-observations.

We have here an example of "playful" resumption which is usually encountered when the tendency to genuine resumption is met by obstacles. In this case, the obstacle consists of the subject's doubt about whether resumption is permitted or not.

Gradually the playfulness assumes the character of more serious handling —again below the table—although it never turns into a completely serious resumption of the work.

After this, the experiment goes on to a new activity and an additional disturbance which we shall not discuss here in detail. When the experimenter finally leaves, the subject immediately picks up the rings again, evidently intending to finish the task. The official situation of "being a subject" is over; the need to complete the interrupted activity can assert itself without restraint, and is now leading to a genuine resumption.

The experimenter returns and hands the subject another task of the same kind (ring puzzle II). Again a disturbing action is introduced. This time, immediately after the end of the disturbing activity, the subject returns to the rings that are still lying on the table. When he sees that the experimenter is about to definitely terminate the experiment, he quickly picks up the rings, holds them out to the experimenter, and begs to be shown the solution.

Experimenter refuses, but without preventing the subject from working further on the rings. The need for completion breaks through, and results in intensive continuation of work on the task. Soon the subject is deeply involved and carries out the task to its correct termination.

A Survey of the Phenomena

Following this example of the course of an individual experiment, we present a systematic survey of the principal phenomena and their typical variants which we observed during the different phases of our experiments. Which phenomena occur in the course of the same individual experiment can be seen below in Section IX.

1. Phase of interruption As a rule, interruption of the first activity did not take place without incident. It met difficulties and resistance of various kinds and various degrees. At first, the subject was often baffled. S 35 for example, looks up at the E (experimenter) in a confused way: "Now, what is to become of *this* stuff (the old task)?"

The majority of subjects were annoyed and unwilling; many expressed direct anger; only few of them showed no signs of annoyance: "I was irritated by the intrusion of something new before the old task was finished" (S 42). "The interruption annoyed me intensely and my irritation lasted through all of the new activity," (S 39).

Frequently, the annoyance at being interrupted was colored by frustrated ambition. This led to open protests against the disturbance. For example, S 74, highly irritated, exclaimed: "No, I won't do it! The same thing all over again." (The S had already been repeatedly interrupted.) "This time I shall finish first." When the E insisted on the interruption: "No! Do I *have* to obey you?" At the first interruption S 73 blushed hotly, looking up in amazement. At the second, he gripped the E's hand in order to prevent the disturbance. He said: "I won't let myself be fooled again!"

Children, too, often resisted interruption energetically. Not infrequently, excuses were found to support the subject's resistance against the disturbance. For example, when S 45 was told to tidy up various objects at another table, he looked, slightly irritated, across from his own seat and snapped: "But it *is* all tidy." He went on working quietly. Subjects 74 and 4 acted the same way. If the experimenter forced the interruption by making the subject leave his seat, many subjects took their incomplete work with them to finish, as well as possible, elsewhere.

When a subject, after experiencing several interruptions, expected to be interrupted again, he often took preventive action in the form of a pro forma execution or a kind of short-circuit action. For example, when S 45 was presented with the schema of a checkerboard for hatching, he immediately drew a doodle in each square to be shaded and said before beginning with the proper task (hatching): "All right, now you can interrupt me as much as you like! I have anticipated all that is important to me."

Manual activity on the first task was stopped abruptly by some subjects. Most, however, tried to carry on a little longer in order to achieve at least partial completion. This occurred primarily with activities that structurally consisted of comparatively finite subactivities. It also occurred with other kinds of activities. Most subjects had to be admonished repeatedly before they would change over to the next task.

This unwillingness to let go of the old job was a typical phenomenon. The subject abandoned the first activity only reluctantly, and frequently returned to it later. Even subjects of a normally calm and equable disposition often had to be urged repeatedly before they released the first task.

While continuing work on a task against the experimenter's will, a subject said, for example, "Just a moment, I've almost got it" (S 44); "No, wait a minute" (S 35); or, half defensively or half evasively "O.K., O.K.!" Sometimes, they simply went on working silently.

Even in cases when work on the old activity had already been stopped outwardly, or when the subject was already busy with the next task, the subject was still with the old task inwardly. This state of mind was described as "oscillating," "unable to pry myself loose," "tearing myself away," or "difficult to change around."

The difficulty of prying oneself loose from the old work was usually associated with undisguised anger. However, there were cases, though few, when in spite of emotional neutrality, the subject clung to the first activity and needed a special act of will to make the inner transition to the second. In some cases it was true that, in spite of some reluctance, abandoning the task presented no difficulties. Based on the total number of experiments that yielded statements on this point, the subjective experiential quality that the transition was difficult occurred three times as frequently (50:16).

Most subjects left the interrupted activity with a feeling of incompleteness. Many subjects felt a *desire* to complete the task at some future time, some of them even formed an immediate corresponding intention. Those subjects often also protested vigorously against the interruption. For example, S 7 reported: "I was really angry and said to myself: Of course, I'll finish it later by myself."

All the phenomena discussed indicate that the psychic situation of the subject at the moment of interruption is determined by quite definite field forces. The topology and field forces of the situation are essentially like those characterized in Figure 1. It is self-evident that such illustrations can show only one typical single variant out of the many that actually occur, and that only at one specific moment. The graphic schemata are introduced here not only for purposes of illustration, but also because, in our opinion, they aid in formulating theories with greater accuracy. This is not the place to enter into a discussion of the basic problems of our theoretical conceptions, particularly the justification for the use of the field concept. We will only mention that field-forces are to be understood specifically as mathematical vectors. Their directions are defined as purely psychological tendencies directed towards definite actions which can only be represented partially by directions within physical space.

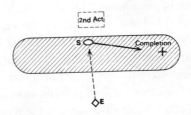

FIGURE 1. Topology and Field of Forces at the Moment of Interruption.
/// The first activities field of work. The narrowness of the hatching roughly illustrates the degree to which the subject is involved in the activity.
+ Positive valence.
The dashed line indicates that the subject experiences the pressure towards the second activity as coming from the experimenter.

In Figure i, we see the subject as inside the work space of activity i. The experimenter tries to approach him with a second activity. The second activity, still somewhat in the future, is drawn here in dotted lines. The experimenter puts pressure on the subject, in the direction of the dotted arrow. The subject tries to resist that pressure. In opposition to the danger of being pushed out of the work field, a strong counterpressure is experienced corresponding to a vector in the direction of the positive valence: completion of the task.

The results of this constellation are: holding on to the work while being pushed out of the work space, protest, anger, resistance, the need of repeated admonitions by the experimenter, and serious difficulties in "tearing oneself away."

2. *Phase of performing the disturbing activity* Once the subject has gone on to the next task, he may have forgotten all about the interrupted activity, or he may have been unable to stop thinking about it. In the latter case, the interrupted activity remains alive and effective both in the experience and in the outward behavior of the subject.

Survival of the first activity in its weakest form occurred as just a fleeting thought, especially in cases when the subject's affective attitude towards the interruption was fairly neutral.

The strongest form of the phenomenon consisted in the direct continuation of the first activity even though sometimes this was not openly done. For example, S 28 reported: "During the interruption I carried on the first activity in my mind." While sorting out chips, S 97 was presented with a braintwister to solve. He quickly put in place some more chips of the same color and even reached for another color, but was prevented by the experimenter from continuing. He then turned to the braintwister. But almost immediately he went back to sorting out chips, provisionally on the table, but without giving them his full attention. He seemed to do this almost unconsciously. Simultaneously he continued with the braintwister. Two minutes later he put his hand back on his arrangement of chips, lifted them up, put them back on the table, and ended up by placing them in the box after all.

Apart from these comparatively rare extremes, the phenomenal existence of the first activity was usually described as an undefined, vague, but very uncomfortable feeling: "It demanded something of me, haunted me" (S 39); "I felt a constant pull backward" (S 58). "The feeling persisted that back there I left something behind that still has to be done" (S 57).

For the most part, the interrupted activity was experienced as the real main activity: "I did not think directly of the interrupted activity, but I kept feeling that the one really most important thing is the main job that has still to be done" (S 39). "The new activity went on quite peripherally" (S 45).

Sometimes the phenomenal perseveration of the interrupted activity continued to decline steadily; at other times, it alternated between a close, lively insistence and a dim, rather unreal distance; occasionally it emerged at odd moments only.

Phenomenal perseveration of interrupted actions occurred most markedly with the chance interruptions. Then, the interrupted activity retained the character of main activity to the degree that the interruption was considered just a momentary interference.

"Forgetting" the first activity, on the other hand, coincided mostly with the cases in which the subject had partially completed the task before the interruption. Later on, we shall see that termination of a subunit, as a *pars pro toto* completion, affects temporary release of tension.

In our experiments, cases of experiential disappearance and cases of at least temporary perseveration of the interrupted activity occurred in about equal numbers. A detailed description of all variants will be found in Section IX.

Pressure generated by the need for completion manifests itself in *how the new activity is performed*. It was most evident in cases of experiential perseveration of the first activity, but occurred also in the others. Many subjects approached the new task with obvious reluctance; they did not even want to look at it. Under pressure from the need to finish the old task, the emerging affect was negative. "I regarded the new occupation as an obnoxious disturbance, a feeling of discomfort accompanied its whole performance" (S 49).

Consequently, the new activity was carried out in haste ". . . to get it over with as soon as possible, to get it out of the way so as to return to the interrupted work" (S 39). Without authorization, S 99 cut the disturbing activity short, returning immediately to the old one. The urge to get away from the interrupting task was especially strong in the case of disturbing conversations. The subject entered into conversation only with great reluctance, evidently waiting only for the moment when he could return to his task without seeming to be rude. Being asked for self-observations had a similar effect: the subject was monosyllabic and uncommunicative. After a few casual and perfunctory words, S 72 returned to his previous occupation. Asked by the experimenter to be a little more specific, he retorted: "I don't know more than that," and continued intensive work on the old task, S 99 and S 97 behaved in an analogous fashion.

If the subject's defense against the disturbance was unsuccessful, an uncomfortable, tense state of conflict arose in which the subject wanted to return to his former occupation, but was prevented by courtesy or similar reasons from breaking off the conversation with the experimenter.

Frequently this situation of wanting to go back, but not being able to do so, led to outbreaks of affect or an aggressive attitude towards the experimenter. S 40, for example, exclaimed with irritation: "My goodness, you are a restless experimenter!"

It is interesting to observe how differently the subjects reacted when an activity that had been introduced as a disturbing activity was interrupted in its turn. The frequent cases in which a subject welcomed interruption of the disturbing activity can best be explained by the hope that this interruption might open the way to resumption of the old activity. "When I was interrupted I had no desire whatsoever to go on, I was back with the first one right away" (S 67). This phenomenon can also be observed with children. Apparently, the subjects have a real desire to get away from the new activity (negative valence).

It is true that, later on, a tendency to finish the second activity as well may appear, but, as a rule, it is only a weak one. This indicates that no strong system of tensions can develop in connection with the second activity during the perseveration of an unsatisfied need for completion of the first activity. The arrangement of the experiments excluded the possibility that the particular kind of activity might be responsible for this.

Of course, the situations are not always identical. At times, the interrupting activity, which at first was resented, gradually became absorbing to the subject and occasionally took the place of the interrupted one, so much so that no resumption of the first activity was attempted.

Once the disturbing activity was completed, it was absolutely finished for the subject. Phenomenally, it ceased to exist without causing satisfaction or any other clear-cut experience. S 39 reported: "When the drawing (disturbing activity) was finished, it disappeared. Right away I was back with the modeling

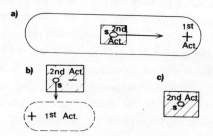

FIGURE 2. Topology and Field-forces During the Performance of the Interrupting Task.

(main activity)." S 57 said: "Not for a moment did I think of your interruption (disturbing activity)."

Such an immediate complete disappearance of the disturbing activity was most striking when the first activity retained the character of main task even during the interrupting activity. This was particularly the case with the brief chance interruptions. Afterwards, when asked for self-observations, the subjects remembered the disturbance only with an effort, or not at all.

During the phase of execution of the disturbing activity, the topology and field-forces of the situation are illustrated in Figure 2.

Permanently or temporarily the second activity is in the position of an island within the first, (Figure 2a), or else the subject really crosses over from the work space of the first activity to the work space of the new one, but the first activity somehow lingers in the background of the experiential situation (Figure 2b). Finally, the first work-space may be completely forgotten during the execution of the second activity,—that is, experientially it disappears completely (Figure 2c).

The experiments demonstrate that, especially in cases shown in Figure 2a and b, the second activity retains a negative valence. This finds expression in affective resistance to the second activity, as well as in the tendency to its hasty termination and the total lack of a tendency toward its eventual resumption. If, as in the case of Figure 2b, the first and second activity are about equally alive, the subject may get stuck on the borderline between the first and the second activity, whereupon the situation becomes one of conflict. The topology and the vectors in the situation also clarify why the subject, if the first activity has sustained the character of main activity throughout, is back in the field of that first activity immediately upon completing the disturbing activity.

3. Phase of resuming the original activity In most cases, concern with the first activity actually resumed either during the termination of the disturbing activity, or else immediately after that, possibly after a brief latency period. Even in cases when the subject never got completely away from the main task during the period of interruption, the main task regained genuine actuality only at this point. Cases where no resumption occurred were comparatively rare.

After the actual revival of the need for completion, the direction of the need was not always immediately apparent. Experientially, it often started as a vague urge towards resumption which lacked a well-defined direction. For example, S 42 recalled: "Immediately after solving the riddle I had the feeling that something was left undone. But what? I didn't realize that right away, only later." S 80 reported: "After solving the ring puzzle I was aware of something else to be done, yet I did not know what it was, I even turned to something different first. The feeling was, as it were, knocking on my conscience." Evidently there was a readiness for action, a tendency to do something, but without a clear awareness of direction (7).

The frequency of such a diffuse urge towards action indicates that, dynamically, we are not faced right away with a definitely directed vector, but with a system of tensions. It further indicates that there is no possibility that a coupling of two definite ideas is the cause of the resumption.

If the subject was not otherwise occupied, the diffuse urge did not last longer than a few seconds. It became transformed into an unmistakable tendency towards completion of the one special activity. In most cases, this led to resumption and completion of the original task. In a few cases, it stopped at a tendency towards completion which was not realized.

The stopping short of realization was caused by outer or inner inhibitions, e.g., by "being a subject." The following example, however, may show how strong the readiness can be even in such cases: when S 74 did not seem to resume the first activity spontaneously, the experimenter was on the point of proceeding to a new activity. The experimenter said, "Well, now . . ." and this slight push, meant to switch the direction of the experiment, sufficed to produce instant resumption of the first task.

In their self-observations about the phase of resumption, the subjects mentioned two kinds of experience with about equal frequency: a) a spontaneous desire, an inner urge, that preceded seeing the unfinished work; b) attraction occasioned by the sight of the unfinished work, which had caught their eye by chance and had not been searched out in response to a previous urge. The inner urge emerged most frequently when the subject reacted to the interruption with affectual protest and with a decision to complete the task in the belief that such resumption would go against the experimenter's wishes.

A sense of compulsion or being driven prevailed at times even against the subject's own conscious will. S 100, for example, complained that he had not wanted to spend any more time on the braintwister, but had not been able to get away from it and had caught himself repeatedly returning to it.

Even when a subject considered resumption "as nonsense," it did not necessarily mean that his sense of compulsion was relieved. S 17, for instance, said: "Basically I don't give a hoot, but I have to finish it anyway."

The irrational, compulsive character of the resumption also explains why the subjects often reacted to the option of completion with embarrassment and excuses. They, themselves, felt the discrepancy between the urge to resume and the lack of real, rational interest in the task.

In their self-observations, the subjects sometimes reported that they were not interested in resumption, and then, suddenly, corrected their statements soon afterwards: S 56, for example, said: "It is not true that I was free of it (the uncompleted work). The thought that I left a problem unsolved haunts me."

In almost as many cases, resumption was not based experientially on an inner urge that preceded the sight of the unfinished work, but rather on the positive valence of the perceived unfinished object. Not infrequently an aesthetic component entered into the situation. S 41, for instance, said: "The unfinished picture was ugly, it offended my sense of beauty."

In order to prevent misunderstandings, we emphasize: even when, experientially, an attraction from without appears to be the motivating factor, that does not prove that a real psychical system of tensions, stemming from the uncompleted activity, is absent. On the contrary, impressive evidence, which will be mentioned later, indicates that the positive valence in these cases has to be evaluated fundamentally as an experiential symptom of such a tension system.

In these cases, too, the subject experienced the resumption as a result of his own inner need. For example, S 61 said: "When I saw the rings, I thought, Aha, here they are, let's have a quick stab at them! . . . I thought that you (experimenter) had considered only the beginning important."

Up to now, we have discussed cases in which the actual resumption was preceded by a short phase in which the need for resumption was experienced in one form or another. Occasionally, and not infrequently, however, resumption of the interrupted work occurred immediately without any consciousness of a need whatsoever. It happened without any premeditation, as it were, without any awareness on the part of the subject. Even in cases when the subject made statements about a need for completion, he often realized its existence only in retrospect. In such cases, the act of resumption occurred so suddenly, action was taken so immediately, that there was no time for motivations or inhibitions. S 72 reported, "I really don't know myself how it occurred"; and S 49 said, "I did it the way one scratches when it itches."

These cases demonstrate clearly that the occurrence of resumption is accounted for by the existence of need-like tensions, regardless of whether these tensions rise to the surface of consciousness.

Another observation concerns the final completion of the first activity after its resumption: neither immediate nor delayed resumption entailed any kind of reorientation comparable to the first orientation phase in the initial work on the task. For example, S 93 recalled: "Straight way, I was right back with the old activity." The interruption had radically changed the subject's attitude towards the first activity and the original nature of the activity. An activity that was previously considered indifferent or boring was now viewed as painfully interrupted. The interruption itself seems to bring the work closer to the subject, to make him regard it as "my job." Evidently, the interruption appreciably strengthens the relation between the work and the subject's ego, maybe even brings the relation into being. The performance of the remaining work changes, too. The subject puts on additional speed and works with heightened intensity, as if he feared he might be disturbed again. S 25, for instance, in some experiments tried to stay as far away as he could from the experimenter until he could put the completed work down on the table.

Many subjects reported a feeling of joy or relief connected with the resumption of the task. Such feelings also point to the existence of a system of need-like tensions as primary cause of resumption. Once the action is performed and the subject is satisfied, tensions disappear. The release can go so far that an activity which the subject was eager to complete a moment ago, now seems indifferent or meaningless to him. S 26, for example, said, "Now the activity is pointless, but it would have bothered me very much to leave it unfinished." S 23 was given an option to finish the task, and he took it up. After completion, he gave a sigh of relief: "Thank God, I've finished," and lapsed into a state of complete passivity and apathy.

In spite of the surprising strength of the need for resumption, then, and in spite of its manifold experiential effects, the subjects evidently did not take a deep-seated interest in the activity as such. Essentially, they only experienced a quasi-need directed towards completion of an initiated activity.

As already mentioned, the subject's attitude towards his work is fundamentally changed by the interruption. Nevertheless, he definitely experiences the phase of work after interruption as a continuation, as a second phase of the original activity. This complete unity, the way in which two chronologically separated phases of activity belonged to a single total action, was dramatically manifested in the fact that subjects hardly ever spontaneously mentioned the gap in the performance of the original task caused by the interruption when they reported on the course of events. If the experimenter wanted the interruption mentioned, he had to ask direct questions. When asked specifically, subjects even found it surprisingly difficult to recall at will the exact time of the interruption. This indicates the degree to which work on the first task acquired, in retrospect, the character of one coherent, continuous event!

S 42, for example, was interrupted while kneading plasticine; the experimenter called him away from his seat to arrange some objects on another table. When the subject, later reporting on self-observations, did not mention any kind of disturbance, he was asked by the experimenter: "Did anything interfere with your kneading?" "No." "Don't you remember that you did some arranging? "Well, that must have been after the plasticine work—yes, I remember having done it, but I cannot pinpoint the time."

III. QUANTITATIVE ANALYSIS OF THE TENDENCY TOWARDS RESUMPTION

Experimental arrangement I was primarily aimed at establishing the existence or nonexistence of a tendency towards resumption, and its strength. It also yields answers to questions about the significance of various factors, which shall now be discussed.

Comparison of Interruption by Chance and by the Experimenter

Technique of experiments The two experimental sessions comprised 4–6 activities each. Of these, a total of 6–8 activities were interrupted, partly by chance interruptions, and partly by disturbing activities. There are also the disturbing activities themselves, and the activities created by chance. Since all of those activities are completed, they, like the decoy activities, counteract the impression of being constantly interrupted. Different sorts of interruptions alternated irregularly; a point was made of using the different sorts of interruption of the same activity with different subjects. 28 subjects were used; the total number of interruptions was 141. Of these, 47 were chance interruptions, and 94 were interruptions by disturbing activity.

Results Resumption and completion of the first activity occurred in 115 out of 141 cases. In general, the subjects returned to the original activity at the first opportunity. Usually, they did so as soon as they felt themselves free, as a rule immediately after terminating the disturbing activity. Besides genuine resumption (R) and nonresumption (N), we also encountered intermediate cases.

A mere tendency towards resumption (TR), manifested somewhat in the subjects' behavior, but primarily in his verbal statements. In such cases, the psychic pressure towards resumption existed, but the physical action did not materialize—not so much because the tendency was not strong enough, but rather because the situation itself presented obstacles to the act of completion.

Doubtful resumption (R?): in a number of cases the subject returned to his earlier activity by reaching out towards it, by playful handling, or similar vague gestures, without actually completing the task. To avoid undue biasing of our results, we classified these cases not as R, but as a special group, R?; in rough evaluations, we counted them as 1/2 R, 1/2N.

We counted as a special group those cases when the subjects rebelled at the moment of being interrupted, refusing to give up the first activity and continuing to work unauthorized (C). C is in contrast to R, which signifies resumption of the unfinished task after completion of the disturbing activity.

The main findings are represented in Table I by percentage of frequency of resumption. The percentage of resumption, together with the percentage of cases with a tendency towards resumption, are also listed. Cases of C are not included in these figures, since they did not involve any unfinished activities.

TABLE 1

Extent of Resumption as a Function of Duration of Interruption

Duration of interruption in min.	Chance Interruptions						Disturbing Activities						
	C	TR	R	R?	N	R in %	C	TR	R	R?	N	R in %	R+TR in %
0–2	3	—	18	—	—	100	3	—	15	—	—	100	100
2–4	—	—	14	—	—	100	—	—	19	—	1	95	95
4–8	—	—	8	—	—	100	—	1	17	—	5	74	78
8–20	—	—	3	—	—	100	—	—	13	—	4	74	78
20–40	—	—	1	—	—	100	—	—	5	1	—	92	92
above 40	—	—	—	—	—	—	—	—	2	1	—	83	83
not timed	—	—	—	—	—	—	1	—	—	—	5	—	—
	3	—	44	—	—	100	3	3	71	2	15	79	82

Table I demonstrates that chance interruptions were followed by resumption in 100 per cent of cases, without exception; disturbance interruptions were followed by resumption in 79 per cent of all cases. On the whole, this represents a remarkably high percentage of resumptions.

The tendency towards resumption appears even more striking in the light of the following considerations: most cases of nonresumption can be traced to 3 out of the 28 subjects, and one out of 8 activities (the unwinding of a ball of yarn). If the experiments with the 3 subjects in question and those involving the ball of yarn are eliminated, the percentage of resumptions after disturbing activities is 88 per cent (R + TR = 92 per cent).*

Significance of the Duration of Interruption

The majority of chance interruptions lasted from 0–4 minutes, since such interruptions could not be extended easily over a longer period. However, occasionally they lasted up to 30 minutes.

The resumption after chance interruptions occurred unfailingly, even after prolonged interruptions when the subject had completely lost touch with the first activity. In one case, even after having left the room for a lengthy period of time, the subject returned spontaneously to the work in the first room.

*Table omitted—Editor.

If the intervals were brief (0–2 minutes), the experiments with disturbing activities all resulted in 100 per cent resumption. The percentage falls with increased duration of the interruption (minimum $R+TR=78$ per cent). Evidently, the length of interruption had a certain influence, yet this influence was not nearly as strong as might have been expected. Moreover, the percentage of resumptions did not decline steadily as the length of interruption increased. In our experiments, when the time interval lengthened to 20–40 minutes, the percentage rose again to 92 per cent. (There were, it is true, only six such experiments.)

When we checked on these results by tabulating the findings from all of our experimental arrangements that involved disturbing activities, we found full confirmation of the above results (Table 2).*

TABLE 2

Resumption as a Function of Duration of Interruption: Over-all Data

Duration of interruption in min.	C	TR	R	R?	N	R in %	R+TR in %
0–2	11	—	32	—	1	97	97
2–4	—	5	50	2	4	84	92
4–8	—	6	49	2	12	72	81
8–20	—	4	39	2	11	71	79
20–40	—	4	14	1	1	73	93
above 40	—	—	2	1	—	83	83
not timed	1	8	38	3	18	—	—
	12	27	224	11	47	74	83

Table 2 demonstrates that here, too, the percentage of resumptions after disturbance interruptions at first falls from 97 per cent to 79 per cent with interruptions of 8–20 minutes, only to rise again to 93 per cent with interruptions of 20–40 minutes. The percentage of resumptions after such long-lasting interruptions is equal to that after interruptions of 2–4 minutes. If the duration of interruptions was increased further, the percentage of resumptions decreased slightly. Not infrequently, we ran into cases of resumption after 1 hour, 10 hours, or 3 days. Many subjects also reported that the unfinished tasks annoyed them much later, when they were already at home.

The high percentage of resumptions, in accordance with our qualitative

*Figure omitted that graphs this result—Editor.

findings, furnishes quantitative proof of the existence of a strong tendency towards resumption of unfinished activities. Resumption occurs spontaneously. The tendency towards completion stems from inner tensions arising from quasi-needs that persist in the subject, and survive even prolonged interruptions. Consideration of the duration of the interval shows that the time spans in question did not weaken the need for completion by an appreciable degree.

Significance of the Moment of Interruption within the Activity

The strength of the system of tensions persevering after interruptions is probably linked to the moment of interruption—whether the interruption occurs near the start of an activity, halfway in the middle of the work, or else close to its completion.

In experimental arrangement I, we placed the interruptions at different phases of the activities, timed as follows:

1. Interruption *b.a.* *before* the actual start of the *activity,* after instructions were given
2.   "   *st.* *right after start* of activity
3.   "   *m.* *midway through* the activity
4.   "   *m.e.* *Between middle and end* of activity, with about 3/4 of task completed
5.   "   *e.* immediately before end of activity.

Obviously, the placing of the interruptions cannot simply be allocated according to the time already spent on an activity by the subject. Instead, if the interruption was to occur at the desired phase of the activity, the experimenter had to break off each particular task at different times according to its individual nature. When the progress of a task was outwardly visible, it was comparatively easy to determine the phase of work with which the subjects were busy. In other cases, such as the solution of a braintwister, the experimenter had to rely mostly on the subject's facial expressions. In such cases, and in others that were equally hard to determine, the later self-observations, as a rule, permitted the classification of each interruption in one of the 5 groups with sufficient accuracy.

The results are shown in Table 3, which may be read in the same way as Table 1. The only difference is that the first vertical column gives the symbols for the moment of interruption rather than the duration of the interruptions.

Table 3 shows a decline in percentage of resumption after disturbance interruptions from 100 per cent right after the start of an activity, to 63 towards

TABLE 3
Resumption as a Function of Moment of Interruption

Moment of interruption	Chance Interruptions						Disturbing Activities						R+TR in %
	C	TR	R	R?	N	R in %	C	TR	R	R?	N	R in %	
b.a.	—	—	—	—	—	—	—	—	—	1	—	—	100	100
st.	—	—	—	—	—	—	—	—	1	1	—	—	100	100
m.	2	—	28	—	—	100	1	2	32	—	4	84	89
m.-e.	—	—	8	—	—	100	1	—	14	1	8	63	63
e.	1	—	8	—	—	100	1	—	23	1	3	87	87
	3	—	44	—	—	100	3	3	71	2	15	79	82

the end. However, at the very end of the activity resumptions rise again to 87 per cent.

As before, we may check these results by tabulating the data from all the different experimental arrangements. Table 4 shows a confirmation of our results.*

TABLE 4
Resumption as a Function of Moment of Interruption: Overall Data

Moment of interruption	C	TR	R	R?	N	R in %	R+TR in %
b.a.	—	—	5	—	—	100	100
st.	2	3	23	3	1	82	92
m.	4	14	100	5	19	74	84
m.-e.	1	3	28	1	12	65	72
e.	5	7	68	2	15	75	83
	12	27	224	11	47	74	83

Tabulation of all experiments in Table 4 confirms our results. Interruption shortly after the middle of the activity (m.-e.) once again proves most

* *Figure omitted which graphs this result—Editor.*

unfavorable to resumption, (although the 100 per cent resumption after chance interruptions must be remembered). The explanation may be that the need to reach the goal is strongest at the start, thus producing an especially high percentage of resumptions. Progress on the task, accompanied by a degree of satisfaction, results in a relaxation of the need which, in turn, entails a decrease of the tendency towards resumption. Shortly before termination, the proximity of the goal again reinforces existing needs. Such impulses in the final spurt are a familiar phenomenon in many sorts of long-term efforts (8).

The gradual relaxation of tension was also mentioned in the self-observations, especially in connection with the moment when the subject felt that he was out of the woods. It remains surprising that the percentage of resumptions is as high as it is when interruption is quite close to the start of the activity. While the results cannot be regarded as conclusions because of the low number of cases, we will see later that entering into the activity plays an important role in resumption.

Significance of the Structure of the Interrupted Activities

Apart from the amount of progress into the activity, the activity's particular individual structure plays an important role. If the structure is not homogeneous, but consists of relatively independent subunits, then whether the interruption intervenes in the middle of such a subunit or after its completion must be taken into account. If the interruption cut through a subunit, it produced a very strong tendency towards resumption. More often than not, in such cases, the subject simply resisted interruption by trying at least to quickly complete the subunit.

For example, with the hatching on the checkerboard, at least one of the squares on which the subject was at work was always finished, and occasionally a whole row of squares was completed. In copying the correlation schema, usually at least the missing lines of a section were drawn; in bead-stringing, the planned pattern was completed. Sorting out chips produced a strong tendency to put away at least all the chips of one kind. Seventeen minutes after the interruption, S 80 emphasized that he was still bothered by two left-over chips of the same kind.

In agreement with the studies by Karsten (9) and Zeigarnik (10), our investigation proves that the division of an activity into subunits is not only a phenomenal structure which is visible to the observer, but that it is also of dynamic significance for the course of the activity. The tendency towards completion, as manifested in resumption of an interrupted total activity, prevailed also with respect to the smaller subunits. This proves the existence of comparatively self-contained subsystems of tension contained within the total system and corresponding to the subunits of the activity in question. The fact that tension is strongest shortly before reaching a goal is evident as well in relation to the subunits.

IV. ALTERNATIVE EXPLANATIONS FOR THE TENDENCY TOWARDS RESUMPTION

The frequency of resumption even after prolonged interruption, the connection of the tendency towards resumption both with the structure of the activity and with the moment chosen for interruption, as well as the self-observations of subjects, have all furnished evidence of the fact that a system of tensions will push towards resumption of the original activity after it has been interrupted. The problem remains as to exactly what generates that pressure.

Before concluding that resumption is really based on a need stemming from the old activity, two possible objections have to be considered. First, it is conceivable that inactivity after interruption is conducive to boredom, and that boredom would lead to resumption of the former occupation. Second, it is possible that the subjects resumed the interrupted activity because they thought the experimenter desired completion of the task.

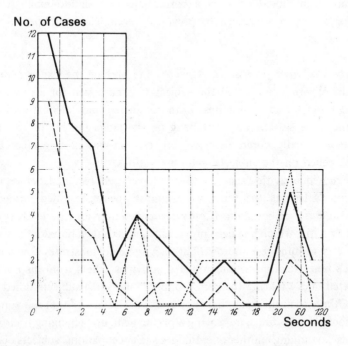

FIGURE 3. Interval Between End of Disturbing Activity and Resumption of Main Activity.
_____ curve 1, ------- curve 2, ... curve 3.

Boredom

Interval between disturbing activity and resumption In our experiments, boredom as cause of resumption is out of the question, at least as a factor of any quantitative significance. We prevented the outbreak of boredom by seeing to it that the subjects were not allowed to wait more than 15–20 seconds after the end of the interruption. If they had not returned to their old activity during that brief interval, we went on to the next experiment.

For some of the experiments (n = 50), we timed the interval of rest between the end of the disturbing activity and the start of resumption with a stopwatch and obtained the curve in Figure 3, Curve 1. Curves 2 and 3 will be discussed later.

It appears that resumption occurred immediately in 24 per cent of the cases, while 86 per cent of the cases show resumption after an interval of less than 20 seconds.

The self-observations confirmed that during the 20-second interval there was absolutely no question of boredom.

In some experiments, we intentionally attempted to create a situation of boredom. If, in the preceding experiments, there had been no genuine tendency towards the resumption of interrupted activities, but only a tendency to escape from boredom, then a boring situation should make it just as easy for a subject to return to previously completed activities as to uncompleted ones.

Experimental Arrangement II Towards the end of the experimental session, the experimenter asked the subject to excuse him for a moment and left the room for 10–15 minutes. Both completed and uncompleted objects from the same session were left lying on the table. On his return, the experimenter usually could perceive any resumptions at a glance. Beyond that, he relied on the subjects' self-observations.

Interrupted activities that could not have been resumed before the experimenter's leaving the room were almost always resumed immediately, before the onset of boredom. If only completed activities were left (or interrupted activities which had been previously ignored) then boredom ensued, but hardly ever genuine resumption. (This fact alone demonstrates how much the subject's inner relation to uncompleted activities differs from his relation to completed ones.) During the period of boredom, some subjects tidied up the table. Others took up tasks that they had liked before or that left something to be done—for instance, improving a plasticine figure, changing it into something else, or adding another one. Besides such occupations, subjects occasionally also picked up unfinished work which they had failed to resume on previous occasions. Such resumptions, however, lacked a characteristic quality of having a purposeful and clear direction; they were hardly ever carried through to completion.

This re-occupation with a task that is in part occasioned by boredom typically presents a very different picture from genuine resumption. The divergence between uncompleted and completed tasks also gives clear evidence that perseveration as such, considered as a universal force towards further occupation with previous activities without respect to their state of completion, is not a factor of consequence in our results.

In this connection, we may also point out that the attempt to use indirect motives for continued activity as an explanation fails for the same reasons. By and large, in fact, indirect motives for continued activity should not be less with completed activities, seeing that the work is left in full view on the table, than with uncompleted ones.

All in all, we have established that in our experiments, boredom was of no essential importance, if only because of the short time between tasks and because of the fact that resumption usually occurred at the first opportunity. If boredom was allowed to develop sufficiently, it was conducive to a certain re-occupation with previous tasks. However, the difference between such re-occupation and genuine resumption revealed that genuine resumption was caused by a need-like tension directed towards a specific activity, rather than by a pressure occasioned by the environmental situation and directed towards the creation of just any kind of occupation.

Pleasing the Experimenter

A second, rather obvious, hypothesis concerning the source of the tendency towards resumption is as follows: the subject resumes the interrupted activity because he thinks that it is a part of the experiment to do so, and that the experimenter desires completion of the task even if he does not say this in so many words.

Experimental arrangements III and IV were designed to clarify this point.

Experimental arrangement III: Interruption where the experimenter expressly prohibits completion In arrangement I the new activity was initiated after interruption, without the experimenter's referring to the original activity in any way. To direct questions by the subject, the experimenter reacted as passively and evasively as possible: He did not hear such questions, or he acted deaf and dumb, going on to something else. In arrangement III, the experimenter stated clearly that the first activity was definitely not to be continued: "No, you will not work on that any more," "Leave it be, now," "We are giving that one up." The tone of these instructions was forceful and unequivocal, and, as evidenced by their self-observations, was correctly understood by the subjects.

The data show* that the percentage of resumptions plus tendency towards resumption (R+TR) is not smaller than in the preceding experiments, and even somewhat higher than in experimental arrangement I (89 percent as against 82 per cent). What has changed is only the proportion of TR to R: TR increases, to the detriment of R. R occurs here in 65 per cent of the cases, compared to 79 per cent in arrangement I. This means that the tension towards completion of a task remained in force after the prohibition, but, due to extraneous obstacles, it did not quite so often materialize in actual completion.

Subjects normally resented the interruption coupled with prohibitive instructions as a particularly harsh interference with the course of events. In 37 out of 41 cases, the subjects attempted to finish the activity quickly anyway, or to persuade the experimenter to agree to the completion. Only 2 subjects broke off the first activity without any resistance. This finds expression in the higher percentage of C: 12 per cent as against 3.5 per cent.

Furtive Resumption against the will of the experimenter In some other situations, there was an inner effect similar to that of prohibitive instructions (Experimental Arrangement III): The experimenter, when interrupting, did not directly use prohibitive expressions, but his meaning was interpreted in that way by the subjects, as their self-observations witness. Many subjects reported their impression that the experimenter considered the first task to be terminated. Nonetheless, they returned to the tasks, often feeling that they were acting against the experimenter's wishes.

This conflict was blatantly apparent in cases of what might be called furtive resumption. While the experimenter was writing, not looking at the subject, the latter quickly reached out for the first task and tried to complete it unnoticed, with silent and inconspicuous movements. If the experimenter looked up, the subject desisted immediately as if he were caught doing something forbidden.

Our filmed subject (no. 118) shows such a timid, slightly furtive attempt at completion of the task with a hasty withdrawal of the hand. The very look towards the experimenter is characteristic. The subject pretended that his preparatory sorting of chips was "not real." He put them in place with small, cautious movements. It was a drastic departure from the intensive, undisguised manipulation with both hands characteristic of his natural, uninhibited work on this task before the interruption. (The film shows this difference very strikingly.)

Table omitted—Editor.

Here two conflicting forces were at work. On the one hand, the quasi-need pushed the subject towards completion of the unfinished task. On the other hand, the wish to comply with the experimenter's instructions and also to keep his own impulses under control kept him back.

Optional resumption As mentioned before, in arrangement I after terminating the disturbing activity the subjects often asked the experimenter what was going to happen to the first task; the experimenter was then as evasive as possible. If he could not bring that off well, he said that he did not care, it was sufficient for him as it was. The correct formulation here was not without difficulties, and occasionally there were misinterpretations. The experimenter's remark was typically followed by a moment of hesitation and of embarrassed smiles, ending usually in resumption.

If these cases are considered by themselves, they yield about the same percentage of resumptions as the average of all cases.

It is noteworthy that in the conditions mentioned above, most subjects were inclined to proffer some kind of excuse for resumption: "You cannot leave everything lying around like that" (while sorting chips into a box); "Since I've got the time" (experimenter is writing); another frequent remark: "I may as well finish it."

The character of irrational compulsion in the urge for completion mentioned earlier, may have had a puzzling effect on the subjects and may have been one reason for the frequent first refusal when resumption was left open to him.

During a pause, subject 80 pulled out the half-covered, unfinished correlation scheme and asked whether it should be completed. "Just as you like." "Well, then I won't. I am not very interested in it." Experimenter did not answer. Subject looked at the drawing for a little while and suddenly blurted, "There is really not much left to do," whereupon he completed the task.

In some cases, though not many, the expressed permission to resume the task led to its omission. This often occurred in cases when the subject tried to be a good subject who suppressed his own inclinations.

The high percentage of resumptions seems to indicate that the subject's spontaneous question concerning his right or his duty to complete the old task was in itself a result of pressure, even though somewhat diffuse in its direction.

Experimental arrangement IV: Weakened intructions It seems reasonable to ask whether a contributing factor in the resumption of the task might be the fact that, at the beginning of the experiment, the given instruction implied completion. In order to clarify this question we changed the instruction, weakening it as follows: The subject was to start an activity, the experimenter did not yet know if it could be finished.

This arrangement was carried out with 6 subjects. Two of them were even interrupted twice during the same activity. With one subject, explicit prohibition of completion emphasized the experimenter's intention not to let the task be finished.

Nonetheless, all the tasks were resumed. Resistance to interruption was no weaker than usual.

These facts demonstrate that the influence of the instructions given at the start of an activity was almost negligible.

Summary

The experiments made with "explicit veto of completion," with "optional completion," and "weakened instructions," combined with the phenomenon of "furtive resumption," all provide evidence that resumption of interrupted activities was not based on the subjects' belief that they were acting in accordance with the experimenter's wishes. Quantitative results of the various experimental arrangements confirm the experiential finding that the subjects were motivated by a spontaneous need for resumption. This statement does not mean that a subject returned to the task because he felt committed by an originally formed intention to which he stubbornly clung. Instead, the subjects often spoke of their "duty" or of "compulsion." That is to say, neither the experimenter's will nor the subject's own determination was perceived as the source of resumption: the subject experienced the driving force as an impersonal "it" dominating his personal "I." In other words, at the time of resumption, the quasi-need under discussion formed a relatively independent, self-contained system of tensions.

V. EFFECT OF AN ACTIVITY'S PLEASANTNESS OR UNPLEASANTNESS ON RESUMPTION

So far our findings might be explained by the hypothesis that it is not the incompleteness of the interrupted task that accounts for its resumption, but rather the subject's experience of the task as interesting or pleasurable in itself.

Without examining in general terms to what extent interest or pleasure can ever motivate the spontaneous execution of any activity, we limit ourselves here to the question of the importance of these factors in our particular experiments.

Resumption of unpleasant activities As mentioned above, there were frequent cases when the subject resumed an activity to which he felt downright aversion: "I dislike doing it, but I cannot just leave it there" (S 34). "I will not give it up, in spite of my aversion against it" (S 29). "The activity was uninteresting, especially when you offered a far nicer occupation (the disturbing activity), but still I have to finish it, get rid of the burdensome duty" (S 62).

A quantitative tabulation of resumptions comparing pleasant or interesting tasks with neutral or unpleasant ones is difficult because in our experiments, it was rarely possible to classify any single activity unequivocally according to these categories. Frequently, enjoyment of an activity and interest in it changed drastically even during its execution. If cases with marked temporary changes were counted as neutral, most of our experiments would have to be so classified.

The high percentage of resumptions, in itself, indicates that in our experiments pleasure was only a very minor determining factor.

Repetition of a pleasurable activity, completed once before If, rather than their incompleteness, an inherent positive quality of the task was the real cause of resumption, then one could have expected that, during the free interval, the subjects occasionally would have returned to an activity they previously had completed. For without a doubt, there were often more enjoyable and interesting activities among the completed tasks than among the uncompleted ones. In addition, situational factors did not interfere: the finished tasks spread out openly on the table provided an opportunity to resume either the completed or the uncompleted activities.

Actually, only the ring puzzle provoked repetition of a completed activity. If, for reasons to be explained, we do not consider the ring puzzle in our calculations, we find that out of more than 1000 completed activities (445 interruptions), only 6 were repeated by the subject. That is a negligible number. These findings are all the more conclusive because the situation was loosely structured, and the subjects had ample opportunity to resume any activity they desired, even in periods other than the official free intervals.

The six exceptions were essentially provided by the mosaic picture and the plasticine work. In these activities, and even more so with the ring puzzle, the subjects aimed at mastering the activity, at finding the solution or getting the trick. This need could not be satisfied by just one solution as success could well be due wholly or in part to chance (11).

Sometimes a subject separated the rings by a lucky push or twist. Or else, the first solution gave him some insight into the principle of the task, but not a clear grasp of all necessary manipulations. Thus, the relative frequency of spontaneous repetition was accounted for by the fact that the original solution did not bring full satisfaction; it was only one step on the way to complete mastery of the task.

In like fashion, the repetition of the mosaic picture or the plasticine shape consisted without exception in variations or improvements on the original solution.

As a matter of fact, then, occasional resumption of completed activities did not constitute genuine repetition of a finished task, but rather resumption of a psychologically unfinished activity. In this connection, Zeigarnik has made the point that a task may be outwardly completed but inwardly incomplete (12).

The cases counted here as repetitions of a completed task are not numerous. Most of them are based on pressure in the direction of a definite goal, regardless of the pleasantness or unpleasantness of the task.

If the activity was completed both outwardly and inwardly, it was, as a rule, followed by an astonishing degree of passivity and indifference even in cases when tension was very intense at the moment of resumption. The attraction of the activity was obviously linked throughout to the existence of a quasi-need.

Experimental arrangement V: Spontaneous approach to interesting new activities Finally, we attempted to interest the subject in an activity that he had not performed before by showing and explaining it to him without setting it out as a task. For this purpose, we used activities that had produced resumption in the interruption experiments, such as the rings and the mosaic picture.

With two exceptions (10 per cent) out of 19 experiments, no resumption took place, although the subjects showed lively interest in the demonstrations. Later on, when they had time on their hands and the objects were lying available on the table, the subjects looked at them with complete indifference: no indications of a desire to tackle the activities could be observed.

These cases, it should be remembered, differ from cases of resumption after interruption inasmuch as they did not include tasks on which the subject had worked before.

We do not intend to postulate that it is impossible to motivate a subject by demonstration sufficiently to make him enter into somebody else's task as if it were his own. Yet, we have shown that interest in a certain activity was, in itself, not enough to have it inwardly adopted as the subjects' own concern.

Many unpleasant activities were resumed after interruption, while completed activities of a pleasant or interesting nature were never repeated. These findings show that, on our experiments, resumption was not contingent on any positive, attractive properties of the activities but only on the factor of their noncompletion.

VI. IMPORTANCE OF EXTERNAL STIMULI (SIGHT OF THE UNFINISHED TASK)

The Part Played in Resumption by Positive or Negative Valences

As discussed in Section V, the tendency towards resumption is based essentially on a system of need-like tensions. The question remains whether and to what degree external stimuli contribute to that tendency. It could, for instance, be supposed that for the subject the unfinished task constitutes a positive valence towards completion.

More exactly, there are two questions: 1. How much is the tendency towards resumption dependent upon perception of the uncompleted task and on a possible attraction emanating from it? 2. Is the hypothetical positive valence a property of the unfinished object which would create a system of psychic tensions, or, conversely, is the positive valence of the outwardly perceived object only a symptom, an effect, of the quasi-need already in existence?

Phenomenological data Resumption after sight of the unfinished work. The assumption that sight of the uncompleted work might be a prerequisite for generating the desire to complete it appears strengthened by cases like the following: "In the meantime I did not give this matter a thought, nor had I planned to finish it eventually. But then I saw it lying before me, almost finished, and I began to wonder what the completed picture would be like" (S 13). (Resumption follows.) S 7 picked up a sheet of paper with the uncompleted correlation scheme on it for a different purpose; he saw the unfinished scheme, and said, "You will not mind this one line," and proceeded to draw the one missing line of a bundle of rays.

Very frequently, the subjects claimed that they were "seduced" by the task, and therefore picked it up again. In this context, it may be justifiable to speak of a certain positive valence of the uncompleted objects. They demand from the subjects a finishing touch, an addition that would complete them.

Resumption without sight of the unfinished work. In many cases, on the other hand, the subject expressed his intention to resume the unfinished work without having seen the task. We know this through our own observations and from the subjects' self-observations, as well as through the device of concealing the task in order to find out whether the subject would look or ask for it spontaneously. In addition, some subjects voiced their intention to resume the work when they had already left the room after the experiment.

For example, S 35, from whom the rings had been taken away and hidden, said, when presented with a new task after the disturbing activity: "Could I not first try the rings once more?" He searched for them. S 31 reported: "On entering the room before seeing the work I had started earlier, I thought, here is that unfinished business which I have to complete. . . ." (It should be remembered that psychologically an object can be present whether it is seen or not.)

With children, too, this type of resumption was not infrequent. S 115, five years old, returned to the unfinished activity after 7 minutes without having seen the object. S 112, ten years old, asked after a disturbing task of 10 minutes' duration: "Now where is my drawing?" (The experimenter had hidden the drawing during the interruption.) Similar behavior by a five-year-old subject, after 7 minutes, and by an eleven-year-old, after 17 minutes, was observed.

It is evident that, in cases of this kind, the need for resumption asserted itself spontaneously, in spite of the fact that the subjects did not see the task.

Transitional cases. Often it was difficult to determine to what extent visual perception of the unfinished task influenced resumption. Many subjects did mention the external stimulus, but did not ascribe a major role to it. Moreover, it should be remembered that often the unfinished object was in full view of the subject during the interval of the interruption, but without having any effect on him. It was only after termination of the interrupting activity that the urge to complete the first task became active again, and the unfinished object acquired a positive valence.

Sometimes, the urge for completion seemed to exist all along and the positive valence only enhanced its liveliness.

S 29: "My desire to complete it was not very strong. When I looked at the unfinished chessboard, I saw it finished in my imagination. That pleased me aesthetically, and the emergence of that aesthetic element moved me to complete the task." A general statement can be made that resumptions motivated by positive valence often include an aesthetic component.

Talking about an unfinished task had the same effect as looking at it, since it also led a subject back into the old field of activity. It often happened that in the course of reporting his self-observations about several successive tasks, a subject stopped to resume an uncompleted activity when his narrative reached it.

Quantitative Results Extreme cases on both ends of the scale, as well as the transitions between them, can be observed in the subjects' behavior and in their self-observations. Sorting of the cases in all our experimental arrangements that permitted frequency counts revealed that in 77 instances the interrupted work was sought out without having been seen again, while in 50 cases resumption of the work was preceded by its visual perception.* These 50 cases include those in which sight of the object evoked the urge for resumption or at least reinforced it. The results show that cases in which a primary inner urge towards resumption was felt were considerably more frequent than the two other types.

If, after eliminating all doubtful cases, the strength of the need for resumption is measured by percentage of actual resumptions, the result may seem slightly paradoxical: the percentage of resumptions after sight is smaller (63 per cent) than that of resumptions without sight (91 per cent).*

The finding that sight of the unfinished object actually seems to lessen the need for resumption could be an artifact if particularly long-lasting interruptions were involved in the cases with sight. Table 5, however, shows that this factor was immaterial. In fact, two experiments in which resumption occurred without sight of the object included the unusually long time intervals of 10 hours and 2 days, respectively.

TABLE 5

Resumption with and without Sight of the Unfinished Task

Duration of interruption in minutes	S			O			S?		
	R	N		R	N		R	N	
0–2	5	1	6	14	—	14	13	—	13
2–4	15	3	18	20	—	20	16	2	18
4–8	7	8	15	23	1	24	20	4	24
8–20	10.5	5.5	16	15.5	1.5	17	14	5	19
20–40	7.5	0.5	8	3	—	3	4	1	5
above 40	1	—	1	0.5	0.5	1	1	—	1
not measured	4	4	8	1	—	1	34.5	15.5	50
	50	22	72	77	3	80	102.5	27.5	130

It is also a fact that the no-sight cases did not especially involve those activities which evoked a particularly strong need for resumption.

These results seem to be paradoxical, and also to go against our subjective impressions. Yet, they are there. They could be explained as follows: when the tendency towards resumption is so strong that it demonstrates a dynamically significant quasi-need, then the subject goes actively in search of the interrupted activity. Resumption takes place without previous sight. In cases, however, when the quasi-need by itself is not strong enough to bring about resumption, the circumstances of the experimental arrangement will bring the unfinished object into view of the subject sooner or later. If the need is quite weak, even that sight may have no effect.

If this interpretation is correct, the no-sight resumptions should belong to those cases when the subject attempted resumption very soon after termination of the disturbing activity, whereas resumption in sight cases would be expected

* Table omitted—Editor.

to occur after a longer free interval. In fact, the average free interval lasted 2 seconds in (no sight) cases and 15 seconds in sight cases.* Curves 2 and 3 of Figure 3 illustrate the duration of the interval for sight and for no-sight cases (corrected values make comparison possible).

Our findings indicate that the unfinished objects in our experiments were only invested with a positive valence towards completion if and when a clearly marked tension system in the same direction already existed before sight of the unfinished object. Thus, the cases in which tendency towards completion appeared only after sight of the object must be understood dynamically. That is to say, the positive valence of the object must be viewed as a symptom of an already existing system of tensions. The quasi-need was not developed solely through the renewed sight of the object.

The Valence of the Unfinished Objects of Others

Up to this point, all the findings indicate that resumption is essentially determined by unsatisfied quasi-needs developed in the period before interruption. If such is the case, then no tendency towards resumption should occur if the subject is offered unfinished tasks of the type he has been carrying out, but which were not produced by him but were the work of others. We examined this problem by means of some experiments.

Experimental Arrangements VI and VIa Before the first experiment started, several unfinished tasks left by other people were placed on the table. We used a three-quarters finished chessboard and the cutup postcard, partly reassembled. The objects remained on the table during the whole experimental session.

A tendency toward completion occurred only in a few cases.* While in the interruption experiments the percentage of resumptions of these same activities was 79 per cent, here resumption occurred in only 3 out of 11 cases. Moreover, 2 of these resumptions were due to the chance of persons who entered the experimental room out of curiosity. In the experiments proper, an unfinished object left by someone else was completed in only one case, and in that case only after a forty-minute interval.

These findings could be accounted for by the fact that the tasks were strange to the subject. Therefore, in a parallel experimental arrangement (VIa), the subject was presented with an unfinished task of a kind that he himself had already worked on, but where the individual object was not produced by himself.

The technique was the same as in arrangement VI. The material was supplemented by a three-quarters finished mosaic picture (R in the interruption experiment = 82 per cent).

Table omitted—Editor.

The behavior of subjects also showed a very marked contrast between the experiments in arrangement VI and VIa and the interruption experiments.* In his first experimental session, S 62 relinquished the mosaic. In his next experimental session, he found an unfinished mosaic started by another subject, but did not show the slightest interest. When asked directly by the experimenter whether he felt like working on it, he replied: "No, today I have to start on that old picture all over again." It never occurred to him to complete a stranger's work. S 61 reacted in the same way.

These experiments were, in part, convincing *a fortiori* because the subject's own handiwork had not always been completed, so that a certain tension might have persevered.

In both arrangements, a longer period of inactivity favored the tendency towards completion of the first task. In contrast to all our other experiments, the subject never began completion immediately after the end of the interruption.

The observations of qualitative behavior, the quantitative results on resumption with and without sight, the experiments on completion of strangers' work, all lead to the same conclusion: the presentation of an unfinished object can evoke the tendency to completion. In our experiments, however, this tendency was extremely weak compared to the forces pushing towards resumption that were rooted in a quasi-need originated by interruption of work in progress. In our experiments, it was the existence of a system of inner tensions that determined the tendency towards resumption.

Such inner tension was not generated by sight of a stranger's unfinished work, but only by a special personal relation between the subject and his work. This could be developed by means of the instructions or by a concentration on the activity which made the task into the subject's own job.

VII. ABNORMAL RESUMPTION AND FAILURE TO RESUME

Besides definite resumptions aimed at actual completion (R), tendencies in the same direction (TR), and complete nonresumption (N), we encountered a number of cases of weakened, not genuine resumption. The subjects turned to unfinished tasks and handled them in a way that made it difficult to decide whether it was or was not genuine resumption. Such cases were not numerous, but they permit so much insight into the psychological subtleties of the process that they shall be discussed here in comparative detail.

In the quantitative tabulations, these cases are mostly counted as R?; in percentage terms, they are grouped half with R, half with N.

* Table omitted—Editor.

For the moment, we will not examine whether in each given case such questionable resumptions were due to inhibitions of the existing tendency towards resumption or to insufficient strength of the quasi-need itself.

In some cases of nonresumption, we can point out certain factors that either suppressed an established need for resumption or prevented it from developing at all. These factors will be discussed at this point because, dynamically, they are related to the cases mentioned above.

Substitute Satisfaction

1. Incomplete performance When a task made certain intellectual demands on a subject, it often happened that, under unfavorable conditions, the subject contented himself with an inner solution to the task, but dispensed with outward execution—a psychologically completed, but physically uncompleted activity.

S 55 showed a tendency towards completion but did not go through with it. He explained: "The intellectual part was all finished before the interruption. All that was left was the manual job."

Nonetheless, in this case and in similar ones, the subject was not altogether indifferent towards the practical performance. Given enough time, for example, the reassembling of a square from its parts was finally carried out in each case. It was just that the main weight of the need did not lie there. Consequently the subject, upon encountering environmental obstacles, was satisfied with mental completion or, as sometimes happened in cases of covert resumption, with only sketching the solution into the blank.

Even more drastic were cases in which the subject limited himself to preparatory moves or in other ways failed to go through with the task.

Although the experimenter forbade completion, S 73 went on sorting out the chips. Prevented forcibly by experimenter, he grouped the remaining chips on the table in small piles just as he would have distributed them in the compartments of the box, S 118, filmed, did the same.

If the subject felt inhibited, covert completion sometimes occurred: outwardly it did not look completed, but it gave some subjective satisfaction.

S 120, for instance, put only some pieces of the cut-up picture in their correct place; he indicated the place of the others roughly, leaving large gaps. It is interesting to note that if the urge for completion were based entirely on positive valence, the pressure towards complete filling-in of the picture in this case ought to have been particularly strong.

Occasionally the inhibiting situation during resumption led to short-circuit actions similar to the pro-forma executions that occurred out of fear of more interruption (13). S 57, for example, interrupted for the second time, attempted to complete his unfinished hatching task by means of a few long, hasty lines. Subjects 38 and 62 did the same.*

2. *Goal Diffusion* In the cases discussed above, the work was not really carried to completion, but on the whole it retained the character of a serious endeavor in the direction of the original goal. On occasion, however, the resumption activity revealed considerable slackening in goal direction or in the seriousness of intent, even switching to mere playfulness. (The cases mentioned above were somewhat relaxed in the same way.)

S 22, like S 58, resumed work on the interrupted mosaic picture, but did not try any longer to copy the model with exactitude. He just used up the remaining pieces arbitrarily and haphazardly, yet not completely senselessly, so that the basic structure of the figure emerged in an approximately correct, though crude form.*

While S 70 was interrupted in his chessboard hatching, the experimenter dropped an ink spot on his work (an experimental arrangement we shall discuss later), whereupon the subject began to smear the ink around playfully with his pencil. Yet, again the play was not completely arbitrary; it clearly showed the tendency to continue hatching, although in a slightly caricatured form.*

In spite of changes in the process of the above resumption activities, they unquestionably show a certain amount of goal-directedness. In other cases, which we label "playful resumptions," no attempts at all were made to work in any definite direction. Serious activity (the experimental task) had turned into a game that did not aim at a definite goal but provided a pleasant pastime.

These actions cannot simply be considered as equivalent to random activity resulting from boredom or motoric restlessness. In that case, it would then be inexplicable why a subject, facing a table cluttered with all kinds of things, should have selected that one special object to play with. Evidently in these cases, the tendency to act was related to the unsatisfied quasi-needs.

Not infrequently, as in the filmed experiment, a playful resumption gradually turned more and more into serious handling and finally led to normal resumption and to completion of the unfinished task. Here, playful occupation with the object reactivated the task for the subject, and the need for completion pushed through into action.

The weakest form of resumption was represented by cases which appeared outwardly intact in direction and in seriousness, but occurred only in a momentary flash without perseverance (ephemeral resumption).

Figure omitted—Editor.

Frequently, a mentally unoccupied subject also added further improvements to the completed part of an unfinished task.

3. Transfer to the Experimenter Sometimes a subject, prevented from completing a task, asked the experimenter, at least, to finish it in his stead. This occurred mostly with intellectual tasks. Relinquishing his own solution, the subject requested the experimenter to show him how it was done (subjects 55, 65, 72, and, on film, 118).

When this request was refused and the experimenter kept holding the object in his hand, the subject often could not be persuaded to turn to a new activity. By various remarks about the task or by direct request, he tried to make the experimenter produce the solution. Sometimes a subject emphasized that, although this would not give them full satisfaction, he would be willing to settle for it. Unfortunately, one cannot examine here the important problem of the interplay of objective and personal factors.

The common element in some of the cases discussed above and in this willingness of the subject to leave completion to the experimenter, was that the subject settled for less. Information about such changes in the level of aspiration will be found in a study by Hoppe (14).

Similar to these cases, although differently structured, were the cases in which the subject tried to shift responsibility for continuing or breaking off from himself onto the experimenter.

As mentioned before, when the subjects were interrupted they often asked with great perseverance about the fate of the unfinished task. Often the questions assumed the character of a demand: the experimenter should declare unequivocally that the activity was closed. It seemed to matter to these subjects that once they were denied completion, and its concomitant finality, at least the experimenter should give the episode a formal conclusion.

The facts can also be interpreted differently, as follows: the subject tried to bring about a change of meaning which would bestow on the events a character of finality—for example, the experiment had given sufficient evidence to the experimenter; it therefore had served its purpose.

The situation is theoretically interesting, since it seems to indicate that inner tension of a subject can be removed or at least considerably weakened by the experimenter's pronouncement that "The job is finished." On the other hand, it was observed that tension was in no way removed or appreciably lessened when completion was forbidden at the time of interruption. An explanation for the difference might be that prohibition at the time of interruption was experienced as related to the self, whereas the subjects desired an objective pronouncement of conclusion by the experimenter that would give a different twist to the original meaning of the activity.

4. Destruction of Work The following case has a somewhat similar character: S 54 would not let himself be interrupted while building a tower. When the tower collapsed, however, he said: "I'm glad. Now I have the right to turn to something else, for I would never have stopped spontaneously."

Some subjects, when inquiring about eventual completion of an unfinished task, asked immediately: "Or should I destroy it?" (S 68). Some actually destroyed the unfinished work as soon as they were interrupted, although there was no visible reason for doing so; the table had room enough for the old and the new activity. They did not like to leave things half done, and by destroying them they reached a kind of conclusion, even if it was not the one they originally intended.

5. Summary In all of the above cases, the original need had been obstructed in its natural satisfaction and was therefore discharged by an inexact fulfillment in the direction of the goal (15).

We did not enter into an experimental investigation of whether and to what degree substitute satisfaction brought with it a relaxation of tension in the underlying psychic system. We can state, anyway, that at least in some of the cases, tension was relaxed considerably. Even in cases when an anticipatory completion did not quite prevent the proper resumption activity (careful hatching was performed later), the subject was already almost satisfied. This was proved by the acceptance of further interruption without any resistance on the part of the subject.

Some forms of substitute satisfaction, especially playful resumption, are theoretically very significant: they show that the underlying forces, in spite of the goal-directedness of the process, must not be interpreted in the sense of *causa finalis*. The existing tensions, if the way directly towards the original goal is blocked, can create effects in different directions in the sense of a *causa efficiens*.

Disappearance of the Need for Resumption

What are the conditions that cause disappearance of goal-directed pressure? Execution of an activity to its natural completion relaxes tension automatically. As we have seen, inexact completion can have the same, or a slightly weakened, effect. There were, however, a small number of cases when the need disappeared altogether without any tangible completing activity (in our summation these cases comprise about 7 per cent of our experiments). Theoretically, it must be assumed that for some reason the systems of quasi-needs in these cases were discharged very rapidly in a diffuse way (16).

1. Subjects who are "all subject" Some subjects tried to be completely submissive to the experimenter, suppressing their own desires altogether. On the whole, they experienced the need to complete the work; but when interrupted by the experimenter, the dominating tendency to be an obedient subject throughout the experiment counteracted the need for completion. This over-all goal was so dominant that it prevented not only resumption but even the urge towards it.

Here the tendency towards resumption manifested itself only as a subordinate part of a more comprehensive goal and lasted only as long as it was compatible with it.

2. *Fear of failure or embarrassment*   If a subject encounters unusually serious difficulties, or if he feels that failure would put him in a highly embarrassing situation, the need for completion may cease altogether even if it was clearly evident at first. Similarly, continuous lack of success may finally induce the subject to give up.

S 58 was interrupted while building a tower at the exact moment when the still-unfinished tower collapsed of its own accord. The urge for resumption was so strong that after two minutes the subject, busy with his new task, broke off suddenly in order to return to the tower. Three times the tower collapsed, and three times the subject started over again spontaneously. Then, at the fourth start, the subject suddenly said emphatically: "Well, now we'll forget about it," and put away the blocks without even asking the experimenter.

3. *Giving up because of hurt feelings*   There were subjects who experienced the interruptions, especially when they accumulated, as a personal injury. This feeling could destroy the need for completion, even if it was of considerable strength.

S 74, for example, protested against each successive interruption, trying to resist it. When the experimenter insisted, the subject stopped work abruptly, saying in an emotional tone: "Well, all right, there's another fragment for you!" He was now through with the task. Tension had been stopped abruptly by the act of giving up (17), unless we assume that it had found discharge in affect. It could not be determined whether in this process the activities had changed meaning for the subject—perhaps in the direction of seeing the whole course of events as a task of "producing fragments."

A similar effect was produced by laughing at the subject's work. S 66, busily molded a plasticine shape. When the experimenter, after interrupting, looked at the half-finished shape and laughed at it, the subject declared that he no longer felt like working in plasticine. He turned away from the task without returning to it later, although before that, a need for completion was clearly in evidence.

To characterize the relationship between action and affect, we might mention here a case that does not quite belong in this context: S 72 was interrupted while assembling the mosaic picture. His immediate reaction was to scramble the pieces about in an angry manner. Very soon, however, he stopped, hesitated for a few seconds, and then started to mend the spoiled picture. Here the affective discharge of anger pushed in the opposite direction from the need for completion, which resulted in a conflict of the two tendencies.

4. Haste If, on the day of experiments, the subject was in a great hurry, his main goal, even during execution of the activities, became to get the experiment over with as fast as possible. In that case, the needs generated by the various unfinished activities did not develop at all or reached only a very low degree of intensity. Partly this was a consequence of the interaction of the desire to leave and the desire to complete. Even when a tendency towards completion was clearly evident, it often petered out under pressure of the subject's predominant main goal.

VIII. THE CONDITIONS FOR THE DEVELOPMENT OF TENSION

We now come to the question about the conditions prerequisite for the development of the tensions effective in our experiments.

Significance of Kind of Activity

Rank Order According to Percentage of Resumptions What role was played by the kinds of interrupted activities? The 12 different activities mainly used in our experiments yielded resumption tendencies of different strengths.

Table 6 shows the activities ranked according to the percentage of resumption (including resumption tendency). Columns also give the raw numbers of resumption tendency plus resumption on the one hand, and nonresumption on the other.

The percentage of frequency of resumption of the individual activities varies, as a rule, from 88.5 per cent to 79 per cent, that is to say, very little. Since the values of N are often very small, minor differences need no particular consideration. Two extreme values—plasticine kneading with 93 per cent and disentangling of yarn with 64.7 per cent—show marked divergence from the median.

It would take a special study to establish the relationship between the individual structure of an activityand the strength of the need for resumption. Here we have to confine ourselves to a more detailed examination of activities ranking at the top and at the bottom of the scale.

With plasticine kneading the "creative" character of the activity was most conspicuous. The subject did not feel forced to complete a set task, but ex-

TABLE 6
Rank of Activities According to Percentage of Resumptions

Rank	Activity	R+TR	N	R+TR in % of all cases
1	Plasticine	26	2	93
2	Assembling of square	23	3	88.5
3	Braintwister	15	2	88
4	Drawing	16.5	2.5	87
5	Stringing beads	13	2	86.7
6	Building tower of blocks	17	3	85
7	Copying correlation scheme	22	4	84.6
8.5	Mosaic picture	55	12	82
8.5	Ring puzzle	41	9	82
10.5	Hatching	36.5	9.5	79
10.5	Fast sorting out of chips	19	5	79
12	Unraveling ball of yarn	11	6	64.7

perienced the activity as a creative product of his inner self. He could express himself, his own personality. With some subjects the desire to test their own capabilities, maybe to demonstrate them, was in the foreground. According to their self-observations, many subjects feel challenged by the thought, "Let's see what I can do in this field." At any rate, working with plasticine was not an indifferent matter; the square and the braintwisters revealed a similar situation. The paradoxical character of the braintwisters was especially intriguing. Here, too, the subjects were normally intent on testing or demonstrating their own performance. The task was essentially an intellectual one, less creative than the plasticine work. The ambition to match or to excel other subjects' achievement, however, was especially strong. If the subjects felt doubts about their ability, it hurt their self-esteem all the more, since most of them were students.

Evidently not only the top-ranking activity, but also the activities that take second and third place, generated genuine needs, affecting central layers of the subject's personality.

Among the activities ranking last, the sorting of chips takes a special place. In some subjects it awakened a particularly strong urge for completion. In general, however, interruption here led to a peculiar change of attitude in the subject. The subject was told to put away the chips as fast as possible and was timed by a stopwatch. As a rule, the work was carried out with great intensity.

When it was approximately 75 per cent finished, the experimenter interrupted abruptly, saying: "Stop. Time is up." The subject was surprised and startled. It should be kept in mind that this kind of task loses its meaning when interrupted, or at least its character is radically changed. The original goal to sort out the chips as fast as possible can no longer be reached. In the strict sense of the word, "completion" of this activity is no longer possible, since its duration can no longer be measured.

This is the reason why sorting of chips is towards the bottom of the scale. It was not weakness of the original tension, but the fact that resumption could only result in an entirely different activity psychologically. It is remarkable that, nevertheless, resumption or tendency toward resumption occurred in 79 per cent of these cases. The original force of entering into the activity had created so much tension that it took effect even after the interruption though with a minor intensity, as could be especially noticed in the changed speed of working.

Conditions were different with hatching and unravelling yarn. These are homogeneous, somewhat monotonous activities with few problems. They did not affect the subject much nor did they produce tensions towards a well-defined goal: "You know anyway how it will come out"; "You can do it without giving it a thought." If these activities had any positive attraction, it seemed to lie in the occupation as such.

The unravelling of yarn frequently produced temporary, playful resumption without a strong urge towards completion. However, individual differences were especially conspicuous with unravelling of yarn, as they also were with hatching and threading beads.

Continuous and finite activities: Experimental arrangement VII With hatching and unravelling of yarn, as mentioned earlier, the goal was not emphasized much. This brought these activities close to being continuous ones which lack a definite goal.

Our assumption is that this kind of structure is partly responsible for the low-ranking position of these activities. If that is correct, the urge for resumption would have to be even smaller if the interruption cut off definitely continuous activities. Arrangement VI was designed to test this problem. Due to the relatively small number of subjects (15), it can serve only as a crude orientation.

The tasks of threading beads, hatching, and making a paper chain were given in three variations, representing a progression from moderately goal-directed to entirely continuous activities. Of course, such character could not be definitely established by instructions and the environmental situation. In the first group, the activity was limited as to its goal by limiting the material—a short thread and thirty beads handed out with the instruction to thread all

of them. In the second group, a definite goal was established only by instruction—subjects were told to thread thirty beads, but a whole ball of yarn and
about 200 beads were handed out. The subjects in the third group were given
the same materials as the second group, but without any limiting instructions.

There is a distinct drop between the 70 per cent resumption in the group
of relatively finite character (Group 1) and the 45 per cent resumption in the
other two groups.* There is no disparity between groups 2 and 3. Furthermore,
in this experimental arrangement, the 70 per cent resumption of the comparatively finite activities shows a lesser need for resumption than the same activities in Table 6, where the median = 83 per cent. This is in keeping with their
weaker accent on finiteness.

The structure of continuous activities did not lead to a well-defined goal,
consequently there were fewer resumptions: "You regard it as finished whenever you please" (S 34 and S 44).

An activity with a more finite character, then, results by and large in a
stronger urge for resumption.

The finiteness of the goal, however, could not always be clearly established
by environmental influence. It sometimes happened that a subject, in the face
of unlimited material, set a quite definite goal for himself; for example, using
the beads to compose the colors of all national flags of countries known to him.
Here, the subject's intention changed a continuous activity into a definite finite
one. The result was—even in cases within Group 3—a stronger urge for
resumption than is usual for continuous activities.

It is striking to observe the relatively strong urge for the continuation of
continuous activities at the moment of interruption: in group 2, C = 30 per
cent, and in Group 3, C = 13 per cent, as compared with the total average of
C = 3.5 per cent.

In spite of the strong tendency towards continuation in these situation, the
need for resumption was small. It was difficult to break away from the manual
occupation, but there was no genuine tension towards a goal characteristic for
the urge for resumption. S 97, after protesting strongly against the interruption, had completely forgotten the task when a break was made three minutes
later. S 100 would absolutely not part with his paper chain when interrupted;
he even grabbed it back from the experimenter's hand. During a break, ten
minutes later, he nevertheless did not return to the work still before him on
the table. Not until the experimenter asked for his self-observations did he say,
"Oh, yes" and reach for the paper chain, only to put it away again almost
immediately. "It is only finger play," he remarked. Evidently, it was difficult
to break off such fluid motor activities abruptly (18).

* Table omitted—Editor.

The strength of the need for resumption, then, depended upon the kind of activity: whether it had a goal-directed, finite structure or a labile one not geared to a definite end. However, this could not always be observed from the outside by watching the activities; it differed according to the activity's meaning for the subject.

Significance of Attitude and Type of Subject

An analysis of the individual subject's attitude towards the activities results in the establishing of factors similar to those above.

Subject's inner attitude towards the activity Roughly, the subjects can be divided into two groups: those that were completely dominated by the experimental situation, and those that behaved in an essentially natural and relaxed manner, more or less as they would behave if faced by similar activities in everyday life.

The second group, whose behavior was, by and large, "natural," that is, corresponding to the desires of the subjects, comprised 72 per cent of the subjects (a large majority). However, within this group we may distinguish three groups: Subjects who have involvement in the task; subjects who have involvement in their own achievement; and subjects who have an absence of any inner involvement. The establishment of these groups and the classification of individual subjects into each was essentially based on general characteristics

Table 7
Importance of the Ss' inner attitude towards the activity

S's inner attitude	No. of Ss	R	TR	R?	N	R in %	R+TR in %
1. Involvement in task	47	110	19	11	15	75	87
2. Involvement with own achievement	13	35	3	3	8	74	81
3. Ss without inner relationship to the activities	12	16	2	1	17	46	51
4. Ss that are "all subject"	12	13	6	4	11	44	62
5. Intermediate types	16	22	8	8	9	55	72
Total	100	—	—	—	—	—	—
Children	16	18	—	—	3	86	86

of the subjects' behavior and of their depositions. In most cases, it was difficult to gain a reliable picture of the subjects' attitude. However, only 8 cases out of 105 were so doubtful that the subjects in question could not be included in the classification.

It is noteworthy that the actual need for resumption was not considered at all when the classification of individuals was made. Nonetheless, a good, meaningful, and regular shift in the percentage of actual resumptions was found later—an objective finding that can be regarded as a gratifying confirmation of the correctness of our groupings. The data is shown in Table 7.

1. *Involvement in the task.* This group of subjects, comprising 47 per cent of subjects, behaved in very different ways, according to the type of activity and to the subject's personal attitude towards it. They enjoyed some activities and were annoyed or bored by others. Each activity was carried out for its own sake; it was an end in itself. The personalities within this group differed greatly: some were vivacious and impulsive, others more balanced and stable. The former regarded the whole matter as a kind of game; the latter took the task more seriously. Both types entered into the task for its own sake, and both consequently developed a distinct relationship to their activity. The corresponding high percentage of resumption is not surprising (R + TR = 87 per cent).

2. *Involvement in own achievement.* With this group, comprising 13 per cent of our subjects, the inner situation was somewhat different, although their behavior was still natural. They did not devote themselves to the special peculiarities of the current activity as directly and completely as the preceding group did, but looked upon the activities as an expression of their own achievement. They saw it as a test of their abilities, skills, and intelligence. In this way, all the tasks were seen in more or less the same perspective, subordinated to one single goal. If the activity could not be experienced as a genuine achievement, the subject remained uninterested. Involvement of this sort with one's own achievement was, however, not always identical with ambition.

While, in the first group, the various activities called forth quite various needs, the second group related all activities to just one need: demonstrating one's own capability to oneself and to others. The first group was, on the whole, dominated by objects; the second group by the encompassing need to prove the subject's abilities. This need may have been to a certain degree due to the experimental situation. Mostly, however, it occurred with persons who showed similar tendencies in everyday life. In any case, a close personal relationship to the tasks was also created in the second group, although less directly. The need for completion was still very strong (81 per cent), almost as strong as in the first group.

3. *Absence of inner relationship to the activities.* In contrast to the preceding,

some subjects did not get genuinely involved in the activities, not because of a momentary attitude on their part, but because of their own inborn individuality. It went against the grain of those subjects, was alien to their personality and philosophy of life, to give attention to such "useless" matters.

Some of these subjects considered it beneath their dignity to harbor such desires.

S 36, for example, resumed an interrupted task and completed it. Although resumption had expressly been made optional, he declared that he did not do it out of his own desire, but only out of politeness: "You (experimenter) seem to need it." Originally the activity had not been set as an experimental task, but as a favor to the experimenter. Nevertheless, the rationalization seemed to be only an excuse, because the subject considered it ridiculous to go through with such meaningless tomfoolery. Ten minutes later, however, he picked the task up again to add some finishing touches, not without repeating that he did so "only out of politeness, not from any inner need."

Besides those subjects who considered the tasks contemptible, we encountered those who were really indifferent. Subjects 75 and 85 did not return to anything but the braintwister because, in their view, that task offered a certain intellectual challenge that one could not "remain wholly detached from." These two subjects were ministers; other members of this group were a third minister and a highly intellectual and abstraction-minded student.

The same situation often occurred with quiet, relaxed, or even phlegmatic subjects. We leave open the question whether tension developed rarely in such subjects or whether they did not express it—or both.

None of the subjects who lacked an inner relationship to the activity really entered the activity; consequently, they often did not feel a desire for completion. This group, which comprises 12 per cent of our subjects, shares, in fact, the lowest percentage of resumptions. Nonetheless, even here R + TR equals 51 per cent.

4. *Subjects that are all subject.* The group of subjects discussed so far have one factor in common: they behaved in an essentially natural way. On the other hand, there were subjects (12 per cent) who were strongly dominated by the experimental situation, being "all subject." These subjects tried to subordinate their own will entirely to the will of the experimenter. S 30: "My aim was, not to allow personal wishes to influence me." S 38: "I tried hard to do only what I was supposed to, the way I was supposed to do it." S 101: "After all, I came here for *your* sake, not for my own."

These subjects, then, hardly made the tasks their own; therefore, no appreciable need tension was generated. For them, the meaning of the activities was to do what the experimenter wanted. That is why, for them, in contrast to the subjects in groups 1 and 2, the interruption frequently meant a genuine end to the task. Since the experimenter considered the matter closed, the same went for the subject. S 63: "If you interrupted me, that indicates that you are satisfied with what I have done; the activity must have served its purpose." S 14: "If it is enough for you, it is finished for me, too."

However, if the activity created suspense, or if it had a strong natural affinity to the person, even subjects with this attitude developed more or less tangible quasi-needs. Yet, they were seldom followed by actual resumption, since the subject considered such action unwelcome to the experimenter.

In keeping with the subjects' inner attitude towards the tasks, the percentage of need for resumption was comparatively low (R + TR = 65 per cent; R alone = 44 per cent). Due to the strong inhibition here, the difference between R and TR was relatively great.

Children Children, and particularly school children, belonged as a rule to the group of subjects who were "all subject." Their situation, however, was slightly different, so that we did not include these experiments in this analysis.

In general, the children were more dominated by the situation and more dependent on the authority of the adult experimenter. A number of the younger children behaved rather naturally, anyway. However, a group of 9–11 year-old children taken to the Psychological Institute by their school brought with them an examination attitude which was not easily overcome. They asked, for example, "Will we get grades here?"

The average resumption percentage of the children was rather high (86 per cent). Still, we could never be certain that a child was acting spontaneously. If the experimenter called a child away from a task and gave him an occupation in another place, he stayed there until the experimenter left that place to return to the first location. The child, then, also returned to the first place, and in most cases resumed the interrupted work. If the experimenter did not approach the table again, the child did not return to it either. Probably, he wanted to be "good," by not doing anything against the experimenter's will. That assumption is reinforced by the fact that the children usually looked for the unfinished work if the experimenter hid it from view. The results of Zeigarnik's study indicate that children develop a relatively strong need for completion (19). However, in our experiments it was hard to decide how much it was due to pressure from the experimenter.

5. *Intermediate Types.* A number of subjects occupy an intermediate position between the subjects that behaved naturally and those who were all subject. 16 per cent of our subjects belong to this group. Table 7 shows, in fact, that the percentage of resumptions of the group lies between groups 2 and 4.

The grouping of subjects according to their attitude towards the tasks demonstrates that the need for resumption corresponds with the degree to which the subject entered into the task and made contact with it.

The fact that inner contact determined the need for resumption is confirmed by the following: sometimes an opportunity to interrupt a person at work occurred in daily life. After an interruption of an activity with an autonomous goal, the tendency towards resumption was extremely strong. Similar findings were noted with occasional experiments outside the laboratory situation, *e.g.*, with activities carried on before or after the official experimental session. For example, the experimenter was "busy," but asked the subject meanwhile to do something for him "as a favor"—like unravel a ball of yarn, or draw a checker-board schema—since the experimenter "needed it for experiments with other subjects." In such cases, resumption occurred even after a lengthy interruption.

In occasional experiments or courtesy activities, the task was not set before the subject as an experimental task: consequently, he felt completely free in the matter. Granting the request was from the start an action of a more central part of the ego, so that a more personal relationship with the request prevailed. When doing a favor, the subject was not an object of an experiment, under conditions that were more or less constraining. He was a companion requested to give some help to the experimenter so that, perhaps, they could leave together afterwards.

In such cases, the task was not only in close internal contact with the subject, but it was also advanced by plans for the future. However, this did not hold true for the following example: S II was to translate something from an English book. He was studying English and anxious to ascertain how well he was doing. He was not a subject busy with an externally imposed task; he was, in the first place, a student of English. This fact brought the activity closer to his inner self, appealed to more central sources of will power.

Classification of a subject under a certain groupheading does not mean that he shares particular personality traits with all the others. By changing the experimental situation, the experimenter could easily increase or decrease the number of people in each group—for instance, by being more or less authoritarian in his manner and behavior. By strict discipline, subjects who, left to themselves, would tend towards natural behavior could rather easily be moved to act like members of the intermediate type. On the other hand, subjects who at first were "all subject" could be turned towards a more natural behavior, if the experimenter's attitude was very free and easy or, conversely, startling. It would, therefore, be improper to draw conclusions about a subject's personality from his experimental behavior. However, if the situation remains constant, differences in behavior are indeed based on differences of character.

Importance of individual character traits Certain general personality traits made themselves felt in the strength of the need for resumption, even in subjects who had the same attitude towards the situation. Out of the wealth of such elements we selected only two for more detailed study—ambition and fidgety behavior:

Ambition. A subject's ambition could favor resumption, but it could also counteract it. The behavior of ambitious subjects during the experiments was, as a rule, quite egocentric. The tasks were interpreted by them as a test of their own capability. Did the tasks threaten their ambition, or did they promise success? In the latter case, the subjects entered into the activities and resumed them very frequently after interruption. The other tasks, however, were regarded as a painful experience from which they wanted to get away quickly, and so they were disinclined to resume the activity after interruption. Nonetheless, the uncompleted task frequently remained psychically unfinished. One subject reported that a desire for completion was felt, but said, "I can't do it anyway." This carried the implication: "Rather than make a fool of myself, I'll stay away from it."

Often, such cases of nonresumption based on fear of failure were hard to diagnose. It was difficult to judge whether the subjects were disguising their ambition, or whether they really were as unconcerned with success as they seemed.

However, all in all, ambition was conducive to resumption, unless it was counteracted by fear of failure and exposure. This was confirmed by the special character acquired by activities that appealed directly to the subject's ambition, such as competitive tasks or braintwisters.

The experimenter could stimulate the subject's ambition, for instance, by showing him especially good plasticine models made by other subjects, or by saying of a braintwister, "This is quite easy." The subjects would then react noticeably in direction of resumption.

All groups of subjects classified under 1 include a certain number of ambitious subjects. Out of the 20 (from 100) subjects, whose behavior was markedly ambitious, 35 per cent belonged to the group of subjects focusing on achievement. This high percentage is easily understandable. Quantitative assessment of the percentage of resumptions, in agreement with the qualitative findings, reveals a rather strong need for resumption, though not essentially above the average (87 per cent). This last feat may be due to the inhibitive forces also inherent in ambition.

Fidgeting. One type of subject can be best described as "fidgety." Subjects of this sort entered into the activities forcefully, but did not combine their intensity with corresponding firmness or perseverance. There was a tendency towards unrest and change of occupation. Behavior was jerky and impulsive. They showed more excitation than intensity, messed around with the objects, were easily enthusiastic, but also irritable. Sometimes a kinship with certain psychopathic types was evident.

We observed this type in 10 per cent of our subjects. Their inner attitude towards the tasks placed them almost exclusively within the group, Involvement in the task. (The other subjects in that group behaved much more calmly.)

Fidgety subjects appeared temporarily engrossed in their activities, often protested the interruption vehemently, then forgot the interrupted activity abruptly, only to resume it later. This style of resumption was largely influenced by the positive valence of the unfinished object. Resumption itself started suddenly and impulsively, and was often not finished in a disciplined way. Resumption without completion occurred frequently, as did completion in installments with breaks in between. Subjects also produced self-interruptions, (often repeatedly) in which, without action by the experimenter, the subject would suddenly stop work spontaneously, sit idle, or turn to something else. Usually, however, they later returned to the activity.

The fidgety subject's behavior resembles, in many ways that of a busy child who lives in relatively brief spans of time. A child cannot stay long with one thing; he soon switches to something else, especially when his eyes are caught by it. Children, too, will often return to an abandoned activity after a short while.

IX. DIFFERENT WAYS OF RELEASING TENSION

As we have seen, the quasi-needs developed under our conditions can produce different effects, such as genuine resumption, substitute satisfaction, and so forth. The total course of events in which the discharge of the quasi-needs materializes is structured in different ways.

The subjects' behavior during the phase of resumption must, of course, not be seen as an isolated component, but as a dependent part of the total dynamic process of the tension-system. This process also encompasses behavior during the interruption, and during the interval between interruption and resumption.

In the following, the initial phase before interruption is elaborated only occasionally. This is partly for practical reasons (few significant self-observations), and partly because only the structure of the work itself and the subject's inner attitude toward the work at the moment of interruption are essential for what follows later. The detailed course of events before that period is less important.

Our classification of experiments according to typical courses of events is based on 191 experiments, carried out with 78 subjects. We first scrutinized behavior during interruption (phase I) and behavior during resumption (phase

3) separately. (With both, the interval between interruption and resumption —phase 2—was also taken into account.) It turned out that a certain type of interruption tended to create a corresponding type of resumption. Exceptions could usually be explained by peculiarities of the individual case. The over-all result gave an impression of solid regularity. It confirms the assumption that the single phenomena described above are expressions of typical states, characteristic for certain inner situations of interrupted activity.

We shall describe the various types according to their behavior during the various phases. Characterization will follows the same guidelines as in Section II. Whenever classification of an individual case was problematic, it was not decided by isolated observation of a specific phase, but on the basis of the total picture.

Four Typical Courses of Events

Type 1. The first type is characterized by a particularly strong and unequivocal need for completion. Reaction to the interruption is quite affective, mostly in the form of displeasure or downright anger. Separation from the old activity and a transition to the new one are difficult; they are made with an effort and often without complete success.

During the disturbing activity, the interrupted activity persists in some way or other. This type is characterized by the phenomenon of intermitting continuation described in Section II: fleeting thoughts referring back to the interrupted activity; a permanent, disturbing feeling of something unfinished; the presence of the interrupted task as the main activity.

Mostly, the disturbing activity is expressly rejected. Even when the disturbing activity is more pleasant and interesting, the subject is left with an uneasy feeling which prevents him from getting fully absorbed in the new activity. He experiences the disturbing activity as something nonessential, to be gotten rid of. As a rule, the need for resumption is experienced as compulsive. The other events, too, are rather compulsive with this type of person.

Resumption itself grows mostly from a strong inner need, pushing unwaveringly towards discharge. Consideration, decision, or reflection does not precede it (20). Usually, the urge for completion is so strong that it prevails directly and spontaneously without exterior stimulation (positive valence of objects).

The percentage of resumptions in Type 1 (the most frequent type, including 65 cases) is very high: R + TR = 98 per cent. R alone = 87 per cent, TR = 11 per cent.

We may succinctly characterize Type 1 by the phenomenal survival of the interrupted activity during the disturbing activity.

Type 2. Type 2 is not quite as homogeneous as Type 1. While the need for resumption is also very strong, its quality differs greatly. Quantitatively there is only a slight difference.

During the phase of interruption, it is striking to observe how often the subjects were at first taken aback, mostly with an expression of displeasure and discomfort. Often they protested expressly against the interruption. The switch to the new occupation was described by the subjects as difficult. Many times, however, subjects of this type changed over to the new activity smoothly and easily, even in spite of overt revulsion at the first moment of interruption.

Once the Type 2 subjects had turned to the new activity, a marked change was shown, which is what differentiates them essentially from Type 1: the first activity was forgotten; experientially it had, as it were, disappeared. However, this is true only for the time of absorption in the new activity, as is evident from the high percentage of resumptions (R = 73 per cent, N = 7 per cent).

Just as with Type 1, resumption occurred in part as an outcome of a direct inner urge, without external prompting. Mostly, however, the positive valence of the unfinished object acted as a stimulus or reinforcement. Not infrequently the desire for resumption was accompanied by fear that the experimenter might prevent it. In that case the intention to disobey the experimenter was frequently formed. As a rule, this happened in the same cases in which interruption produced a reaction of protest by persevering, and the desire for completion preceded the sight of the unfinished object.

In some cases, resumption assumed a more playful character. Sometimes vacillation between the wish for resumption and the inhibition of that wish was clearly observable, followed by actual resumption in only 50 per cent of cases. Furthermore, this type produced a few cases in which the activity was actually resumed even in the absence of a genuine desire for resumption.

That situation is so particular and so characteristic of the "subconscious" quality of the quasi-need that we offer an example: S. 74 resented interruption and was unable to give up his work immediately, wishing to complete it anyway. Asked later whether that desire persisted even at the present moment, he answered: "No, I don't care about it any more," adding immediately, "but, then, why am I now completing it?" As a matter of fact, the subject had already resumed his activity while denying the desire for it, but became conscious of this only when he had already placed the last chip into the box.)

Type 2 occurs almost as often as Type 1 (60 cases). R is somewhat less high; it equals 73 per cent; TR = 13 per cent, N = 7 per cent. The remaining 7 per cent is divided between resumption without completion, and obstinate continuing at the moment of interruption.

We characterize the course of events in Type 2 briefly by the fact that the interrupted activity is forgotten during execution of the disturbing activity.

Type 3. Type 3 comprises a group of cases with only a slight urge for resumption. Although this group contains relatively few cases (32), it showed such definite variations of detail that we subdivided this type into three groups.

Type 3a. The subjects all emphasized that they resented the interruption, wishing at first to complete the activity, but that this wish had subsided very quickly. Actual resumption occurred only with 6 subjects (31 per cent); TR = 10 per cent. S.83 for instance, reported that he had no desire to complete the unfinished task, but nonetheless something of it had stayed with him; it did not seem done with after all.

Frequently (in 42 per cent of the cases), the interrupted activity was completely finished and done with. The quick subsiding of the need for resumption is partly explained by the slight contact of the subject with the task from the beginning and partly by strong interest in the disturbing activity. Type 3a comprises 19 cases.

Type 3b. Contact of the subject with the interrupted task showed only in the subject's slight dissatisfaction and displeasure at the moment of interruption. They mentioned this fact as a particular experience. After that, the subjects abandoned the task in their minds before tackling the next one.

After completion of the disturbing activity, 3 out of the 6 cases revealed weak effects of the need for resumption. 1 playful resumption; 1 tendency to make the experimenter complete the task; 1 uncompleted resumption. In the remaining 3 cases, the first activity did not reappear in even so minor a form.

Type 3c. In this group (7 cases), the last vestige of attachment to the interrupted activity has disappeared. The interruption was accepted with complete indifference. Detachment from the old occupation, considered as finished and immediately forgotten, proceeded smoothly. S. 59 said, "The interruption was completely indifferent to me. I considered it (interrupted task) finished and did not give it another thought."

Only one subject attempted resumption, stressing expressly that he did so only because he believed it to be part of the experiment. The other subjects did not return to the old task in any way.

Type 3 is characterized, though not always exhaustively, by the rapid subsiding of the need for resumption.

Type 4. Types 1 through 3 represent a gradual scale of subsiding contact between the subject and the activity. There remains a considerable number of subjects (34) who could not be easily classified in one of these groups. They show behaviors of a more complicated structure. The formal characteristic of this structure is contradiction, a conflict in the subject's behavior. The discrepancy is partly based on contradictory behaviors at the moments of interruption and resumption. In part, the dichotomy is already evident at the moment of interruption. S. 63 said: "Thank heaven, that is over. I was glad to get rid of the puzzle. I could not solve it anyway. Still, I was not altogether indifferent, a feeling of something unresolved remained in the background.

If the subject enjoyed the disturbing activity and found it interesting, or if he disliked the main activity or found it hopelessly difficult, the result is a conflict of two tendencies at the moment of interruption. "On the one hand, I'm keen on the solution, on the other hand, I'm resigned—I cannot do it anyway" (S 34).

This type includes those subjects who suppressed their own wishes in the interest of the experiment, or who went back to the task but tried to conceal the significance of their behavior from the experimenter, emphasizing repeatedly that they resumed the activity only out of politeness.

It is noteworthy that it was usually the need for resumption that prevailed in the conflict of tendencies (R = 71 per cent, TR = 6 per cent, N = 21 per cent).

The course of events of Type 4, is briefly characterized by its state of conflict.

These various types of events throw light on the dynamic structure of the effects of need-like tension systems. A strong and lasting system of tensions (Type 1) can produce a persisting, unequivocally goal-directed process. Intervening disturbances do not stop experiential persistence of the pressure in the original direction in one form or another. The course of events is forceful and straight to the point.

However, a need-like system, even one of possibly the same intensity, can be completely wiped out of consciousness by the disturbance (Type 2). Nonetheless, in its subterranean existence it need not suffer any essential loss of tension, but can often re-emerge intensively, especially if prompted by some slight external stimulation (positive valence). The whole structure of the course of events seems to proceed in a somewhat jerky manner, easily aroused, but calming down just as easily. It seems that in such cases considerable tension is formed. It, however, can never dominate the dynamic field for a period of time, but breaks through primarily in occasional impulses. The mutual relationship of the individual tension systems does not seem to be very stable. At a given moment, though, only one system or the other is responsible for the motoric events.

Type 3 deals with a tension system that is either weak from the start, or of a fleeting nature, and whose pressure can take effect only in the direction of least resistance.

Type 4 shows, as a rule, a fairly strong quasi-need in the direction of completion. However, different inner needs, or counter forces in the momentary field, produce a conflict—usually, it is true, without preventing resumption.

The question might be asked: What is the basis of the different types of events? Are they, for example, distributed evenly between all types of subjects, or are certain types of events characteristic of certain individuals? We examined this question, an important one also for the general problems of behavioral style, with the aid of our material, and found marked relationships between certain courses of events and certain structures of tasks on the one hand, and with certain personality types on the other hand.

Relation of Courses of Events to Type of Activity and Type of Subject

[In this section, the author relates the frequency of each of the four courses of events to the type of activity and the type of subject that was involved. The highlights of the data are summarized below. The reader who wishes more detail may obtain the tables of data from University Microfilms.

The first course of events, survival of the interrupting activity during the disturbing activity, occurs most frequently with the plasticine and square assembling tasks, and in general with those activities that must involve the subject and are most often resumed (See Table 6).

The second course of events, where the interrupted activity is forgotten but easily emerges at the end of the interruption, occurs most frequently with tasks that are continuous or semi-continuous, such as stringing beads, hatching, and sorting chips.

The third course of events, with its slight urge for resumption, occurred infrequently. When it did occur the majority of cases were with the mosaic, the chip sorting, copying correlation scheme, and hatching tasks—all tasks where the subject could construe the task to be finished.

The fourth course of events, state of conflict, occurred primarily with the braintwister, and, to some extent, with the ring puzzle—where failing a test is a possibility.

Turning to the influence of the type of subject, the first course of events occurs most frequently with subjects who have either a high achievement or task involvement, provided that they are of the balanced rather than fidgeting type. The second pattern tends to occur with subjects who are fidgety, or who have an intermediate type of involvement. The third pattern occurs more with subjects who are "all subjects" or with those who have no inner contact with the task. The fourth pattern occurs with about equal frequency across all subjects, except that it seems less frequent with either fidgety or no contact subjects.

Thus, the course of events is influenced by both the character of the activity and the type of subject—each influencing the extent of contact with the interrupted task—Editor.]

X. APPENDIX

Beyond the basic problems of resumption discussed above, interruption of activities can be utilized many ways for investigating the dynamic structure and the laws of psychological processes. In conclusion, we wish to mention the results of a few such experiments which, however, are only of an explorative nature and demand further checking for confirmation.

Interruption of activities that had been previously carried out. Some subjects claimed that they resumed a task only to see what the finished work would look like. In order to examine the importance of an experience being the first one, the subject was instructed to repeat a task previously completed (on the same or on the preceding day), and was interrupted this second time. During their first execution, some of those activities had been carried out without a break; some had been interrupted.

Even with repetition, the percentage of resumptions turned out to be very high ($R = 77$ per cent n $= 29$), which demonstrates that the corresponding need is relatively high even when the subject already knows how the work is to be done and what it will look like when finished. However, it is smaller than with interrupted first-time activities ($R = 87$ per cent, n $= 21$). Possibly this weakening of the need for resumption is based on psychic satiation (21).

Repeated interruptions during one activity. If a subject, having resumed an activity after interruption, is interrupted again before completion, renewed resumption occurs in 71 per cent of cases (n $= 12$). In this case, by definition, the percentage of first resumption was 100 per cent. The strength of the need after repeated interruption lies clearly, but not very far, below our average.

The negative cases might be accounted for in part by the fact that fragmentation of the activity through repeated interruption weakens the need for completion; or else perhaps the subject abandons the work as hopeless.

Resumption of ruined tasks. Theoretically, it is essential to find out how a subject behaves when his wish cannot be fulfilled by completion of the unfinished task, but instead he has to start all over again. In order to examine this question, we ruined the work. We employed the following variants on this procedure:

The product (*e.g.,* tower built with blocks) collapses "spontaneously." Simultaneously the experimenter puts a new task before the subject.

The experimenter destroys the subject's product without giving instructions to stop work.

While the subject is occupied with the disturbing activity, the experimenter destroys the unfinished product of the main activity.

The finished work is destroyed by the experimenter shortly after the beginning of a new activity.

Result: Surprisingly, all the subjects with one exception (see below) restored the ruined work (R = 95 per cent). This fact stands in direct contrast to the hypothesis that the sight of an unfinished object is needed for completion. It is especially striking that even a fully completed product was restored after its destruction. This complex of problems in this area needs to be investigated thoroughly.

Simultaneous presence of several interrupted and finished tasks. Apart from the primary and decisive fact of incompleteness, several other factors play a role in the resumption of activities, such as their chronological place in the order of experimental tasks and their concurrent vitality and actuality. These factors were elucidated by observing situations in which a longer than usual break was made, and during which a number of both finished and unfinished products were in view of the subject.

The findings were:

When 2 unfinished products were seen, the last one worked on showed a higher percentage of resumption than the first (86 per cent; 71 per cent; n = 7).

Upon sight of 2 finished products, a certain tendency towards the last one could be observed in 37 per cent of cases. Only 14 per cent of the subjects turned towards the chronologically earlier task (n = 8).

If the sequence of activities was finished-unfinished, the incompleteness of the last task could dominate the psychic field undisturbed so that resumption of the unfinished activities was 100 per cent. In this constellation, on the other hand, finished activities were never resumed or even turned to (n = 8).

If the sequence was unfinished-finished, however, interest in the finished task, now the last one, was shown in 12 per cent of the cases. Here, the percentage of resumptions of uncompleted tasks was 81 per cent (n = 24).

Thus, in all cases the last, more recent one, was favored as to resumption.

When both activities were resumed, the chronological sequence of such resumptions usually paralleled the original sequence, so that the older task was resumed first. It seems that the second activity, all things being equal, produced a weaker system of tensions; on the other hand, it is still more alive and in some ways in the psychic foreground.

Full satisfaction. As mentioned earlier, the subjects sometimes were satisfied if the experimenter completed a task. However, a special arrangement in which the experimenter himself regularly finished the interrupted work found all subjects, without exception, declaring that "a certain feeling of unfulfilment" remained. In other cases, too, many subjects often expressed the strong wish to finish the job themselves. This indicates that satisfaction with completion by the experimenter was experienced only as second-best and not fully satisfying.

Satisfaction with the resumption of record-speed experiments was less complete, since completion can only reach a goal inferior to the original one. In fact, this activity takes next-to-last place in our rank order (see Table 6). It was not carried out with the usual energy.

The aim of resumption, then, is complete satisfaction of the original need by reaching the first goal correctly by the subject's own unaided activity.

It would be wrong, though, to conclude from these findings that the intended goals in our experiments are rigidly fixed. This is disproved by the very fact of substitute satisfaction. Furthermore, it should be noted that subjects complied easily and willingly if the experimenter changed the instructions during the course of the activity. He may have requested that the drawing be completed with crayons rather than pencil, or that the hatching be performed with a different technique, a larger surface, etc. Sometimes the change required a moment of hesitation. Of course, the task has to remain within approximately the same framework. If the new instruction is too divergent, it may lead to resistance, similar to that evoked by the first interruption.

The quasi-need, then, is neither rigidly fixed nor can it be arbitrarily transformed.

[*I have omitted a final section which summarizes the results of the entire study. We will consider these results in Chapter IV—Editor.*]

1. N. Ach, *Ueber den Willensakt und das Temperament.* (Leipzig, Quelle and Meyer, 1910), 4.

2. K. Lewin, "Vorsatz, Willie and Beduerfnis," *Psychol. Forsch.,* 7 (1926), 330–385.

3. B. Zeigarnik, "Ueber das Behalten von erledigten und unerledigten Handlungen," *Psychol. Forsch.,* 9 (1927), 1–85.

4. Cf. B. Zeigarnik, 54.

5. A. Karsten, "Psychische Sättigung," *Psychol. Forsch.,* 10 (1928), 142–254.

6. Lindworsky, "Orientierende Untersuchungen ueber höhere Gefühle," *Arch. f. Psychol.,* 61 1/2 (1928), 255.

7. Cf. N. Ach, *Ueber die Willenstaetigkeit und das Denken.* (Goettingen, Vandenhoeck und Ruprecht, 1905), 188.

8. P. Kraepelin, "Gedanken über die Arbeitskurve. "*Psychol. Arb.,* 7 (1922), 545.

9. A. Karsten, "Psychische Sättigung," 164.

10. B. Zeigarnik, "Ueber das Behalten von erledigten und unerledigten Handlungen," 53.

11. W. Köhler, *Intelligenzprüfungen an Menschenoffen,* 14.

12. B. Zeigarnik, 40 ff.

13. Cf. A. Karsten, "Psychische Sättigung," 156.

14. F. Hoppe, "Erfolg und Misserfolg," *Psychol. Forsch.,* 14 (1931), 1–62.

15. Cf. Michotte and Prüm, Etude expérimentale sur le choix volontaire et ses antécédants immédiats, 1910. Mere reacting may serve as a substitute for execution of the original intention—in this case, arithmetic problems.

16. Cf. B. Zeigarnik, 71 ff.

17. Cf. B. Zeigarnik, 47.

18. Cf. K. Goldstein, "Über den Einfluss motoriecher Störungen auf die Psyche," *Allg. Z. f. Psychiatr.,* 82 (1925), 164. Goldstein uses the technical term "momentum".

19. B. Zeigarnik, 79.

20. Cf. A Kronfeld, "Zur Phänomenologie des Triebhaften," *Z. Neur. B.,* XCII, Heft 3/4/, 394.

21. Cf. A Karsten, "Psychische Sättigung."

Chapter IV

THE DYNAMICS OF INVOLVEMENT

WE shall begin by considering a different way of conceptualizing Ovsiankina's results, a way that is opened by phenomenological considerations of the nature of involvement, and that will lead us back to classical gestalt theory and the possibility that tension-systems are actually gestalts. These ideas will then lead us to consider the dynamics of a person becoming part of, or separating from, a gestalt, and the strong compulsions and preoccupations that inevitably result from this involvement. Finally, we shall examine Zeigarnik's well-known experiment and a number of important issues that her experiment raises about different types of involvement.

TENSION-SYSTEMS AS GESTALTS

The central phenomenon described by Ovsiankina—the strong need to return to an uncompleted task—is a robust phenomenon that may easily be observed in everyday life and easily replicated in the laboratory. One interesting replication, performed by Evelyn Katz (1), used children who were from four to five years old, thus avoiding the tendency of school-aged children to be compliant subjects. Katz interrupted one activity and then observed whether the child went back to that activity or to an equally interesting activity which was placed nearby. Working with 177 different children and a total of 484 interruptions, she found unambiguous direct resumption of the activity in 88 per cent of the instances and, at least once, in 173 of the children. The phenomenon is demonstrated with particular clarity when a child who initially wants to work on one activity is started on another activity that does not appear as attractive. After being interrupted, the child usually returns to the less attractive with a remark such as "I'll finish this one first," or "I *have* to get to this one." Katz also shows that the phenomenon is not dependent on intelligence (at least between I.Q.s of 80 and 150) or social class, underprivileged children from settlement houses having the same rate of resumption as those from well-to-do suburbs.

It seems clear that this phenomenon cannot be accounted for by a stimulus-response theory, or by the idea that an intention simply establishes a connection so that some specifiable stimulus will trigger some specifiable response. Rather, Lewin is correct in asserting that the intention has established a need, and that the subject fulfills his intention to perform the activity by searching out the activity and ways to perform it. Further, it seems acceptable to coordinate such a need with the concept of a system that is under tension.

Lewin elected to view this tension system as a region within the person that was under tension or pressure. He was then able to relate this concept to a whole set of ideas: tension could spread to other regions—but this could only happen if the other regions were proximal and if the boundaries between regions were relatively permeable; regions could be more or less differential; and the material of the region could be varying degrees of fluidity. And, in the succeeding chapters, we will see how these concepts may be coordinated with phenomena such as substitute satisfaction, the spread of satiation, and degrees of rigidity. Thus, a strong argument for Lewin's conceptualization is that it provides a single set of logically coherent concepts that can be coordinated to a wide array of phenomena.

However, we have seen that at the same time that Lewin was working with the above conceptualization of tension-system, he was also working with the idea of a person as a point in a field of forces. This environmental field governed the movement of the person within it, and Lewin's movies convincingly demonstrate how the behavior of young children is governed by the surrounding force field. In Chapter X, we shall see how this type of analysis is used by Dembo to account for the dynamics of frustration and anger.

As Lewin's over-all theory developed, he saw the necessity of integrating these two different conceptualizations: tension systems as regions within the person that influenced the perception of the environment, and the person as a point in a field of environmental forces. He attempted to achieve this integration by conceiving of the person as a differential region within an environmental field of forces—this whole being the life-space. Thus, an intention (such as mailing a letter), or a need (such as hunger) was coordinated with the concept of a "tensed" region within the person part of the life-space (2). (I shall discuss the organization of these regions in Chapter IX.) The tension within such a region, like pressure in a container, was a scalar variable, having magnitude but no directionality. Its strength corresponded to the strength of a need or an intention, and it exerted pressure on the boundaries of the region, thus influencing surrounding regions that were coordinated to related needs and intentions. However, it did not directly influence the person's movements relative to the environment. Rather, it functioned to establish valences— positive or negative regions in the environmental part of the life-space. These regions were coordinated to activities with objects—such as perceiving a mailbox that called for a letter, or eating a delicious looking piece of cake. Such valences, in turn, exerted forces on the person who was attracted towards or repelled by the valenced object. These forces were vectors whose magnitude depended on the strength of the valence and (inversely) on the distance between the person and object, and whose direction depended on the sign of the valence and its relative position. The locomotion of the person was a resultant of all the forces playing upon him.

This ingenious theory succeeds in relating two important conceptualizations, and is attractive in a number of respects. First, intentions and needs do appear to "push themselves up in our minds," and valences do tend to wax and wane as if an underlying system was being filled with pressure or relaxed. Second, when a person has unmet needs, he often feels tense. Third, such intentions, needs, and tensions do seem to be in the person rather than in the environment. However, the theory has one serious problem: if needs and intentions are coordinated to a directionless variable, such as the pressure in a region within the person, how can they endow specific activities and objects in the environment with valence? The connection between regions under tension and regions in the environment appears to be totally arbitrary.

In fact, Lewin (3) himself clearly describes an intention as creating, "an internal pressure *of a definite direction,* an internal tension-state which presses to carry out the intention even if no predetermined occasion invites the action" (my italics). However, he later conceptualizes this tension-state as a pressurized region within the person—as a system of energy without direction. Clearly he wants to make it possible for the actual direction—the force—of the intention to come from the environment. But we are left with the problem of how a directionless energy state can establish specific valences in the environment. Clearly, the internal tension-state must have some directionality.

This problem is probably related to an apparent inconsistency in the usage of the concept of regions. Suppose we let different regions in the life-space represent different activities. Then in the environmental part of the life-space, adjacency of regions means that a person can directly proceed from one activity to another in a means-end relation. However, Heider observes that within the person part of the life-space, the adjacency of regions reflects the fact that the activities are similar so that tension can spread from one activity to another (4).

If one is interested in a universal language for psychology, Lewin's theory of tension-systems presents another problem. While most of Lewin's field theory is completely consistent with gestalt theory, Heider has pointed out that the theory of tension-systems is substantially different from the motivational theory of classical gestalt psychology (5). This difference stems from the different problems that gave rise to the theories. Wertheimer, focusing on the problem of perceptual organization, found that he could best account for the organization of perceptual gestalts by postulating that the perceptual field is always organized into the "best" (most balanced and stable) organization that is possible (the principle of Prägnanz). Thus, the forces for organization stem from a tension for coherence in the structure of the whole field. Applied to a person in a situation, this principle suggests that there is a tension for a balanced and stable configuration of the person within his environment.

On the other hand, we have seen that Lewin began his work by focusing on the problem of will. This led him to view the intentions of the person as the source of tension that organizes the field. Hence, whereas classical gestalt theory (or balance theory) derives forces from the structure of the situation, Lewin's theory derives forces from tension-systems within the person. Thus, MacColl observes that in gestalt theory, field forces function as a whole—as they do in an electrodynamic field—while in Lewin's theory, tension is a property of a region within the ego and spreads in a mechanical way (6).

This fundamental difference in accounting for the dynamics of the field poses a serious problem for anyone interested in a unified theory. As Gibson notes:

> . . . (the) distinction between the forces of attitude or set, on the one hand and the forces of sensory organization on the other, has proved just as embarrassing to gestalt psychologists as the distinction between attitude and habit has proved to be to American functionalists. The ego attitudes (vectors) of Lewin and the sensory organization of Koffka and Köhler are not easily reconciled. (7).

Finally, I believe there is a problem involved in coordinating both intentions and needs to the same construct of tension-system. Experientially there is one major difference between intention and need; we accept responsibility for the former, but not the latter; and it is difficult to see how Lewin can account for such a fundamental distinction stemming from the same construct. In any case, the three problems I have mentioned led me to go back to the original data in order to search for an alternative conceptualization that may preserve the theoretical advantages of Lewin's formulation without incurring the above costs.

When I go back to Ovsiankina's data without theoretical preconceptions, what I find are not so much needs or tension-systems that are pressing for satisfaction, but rather, a need to unify oneself with an activity to which one is committed. I submit that, in fact, intentions and activities are always intimately related to objects, and that therefore the system that is tensed cannot be simply considered as a formless region that is under pressure. Rather the system itself must be organized, must have a definite structure that includes the person, the activity, and the relevant objects.

I find that we may preserve the rest of Lewin's conceptualization without coordinating needs to a system that is conceived as a region—a space within the person—in tension, like a container filled with pressure. Instead, it seems more desirable to view such a system as a relationship between the person and the activity in which he is engaged. In fact, when I consider many of the phenomena which Ovsiankina describes, I can only make sense of them by supposing that the person has entered into a unit with the activity.

By a "unit" I mean that the person and the activity are joined, so that it is *his* activity—the activity is part of his self. This formulation has the advantage of stressing the act of the subject in becoming involved with the activity. While Lewin is not clear as to how an act of intention would establish a region filled with tension, it seems evident that one can act to become involved in an activity—to join one's self and the activity—and can act to separate one's self from the activity when it is abandoned or finished. Ovsiankina notes the little touches which a subject makes to "round off" the activity and complete it. I believe that these do not simply serve to complete the activity as a unit, but also have the function of separating the activity from the self so that the activity no longer "belongs" to the person—is no longer a part of the self. Thus, in my view, an intention is the formation of a unit between person and activity, rather than the filling of a region with tension.

This unit between a person and a projected activity is a true system, a gestalt or organized whole with interdependent parts. I shall call it an "intention-system," in order to distinguish it from the tension-system to which it is conceptually related. Part of the tension of this system stems from the various motives involved in its formation, an aspect we shall consider below. However, there is some tension in the system simply because there is a lack of closure to the form. That is, the person has not yet completed the project to which he is committed, and, the principle of Prägnanz operating, the system moves towards the better form of a completed commitment. Note that it is not the unfinished task *per se* which is the source of tension but, rather, the unfinished commitment to perform the task. The tension of the system is not analogous to pressure. Rather, it is a constant searching for opportunities to fulfill the project of action.

I have noted that the intention-system is formed when a person enters into a unit—involves himself—with the task. In fact, we may take the need to return to an activity as part of the essence of the meaning of involvement. Thus, if a person is involved in an activity, and if he is removed from the activity, then he will return to the activity. I take this to be an essential structure. It seems clear from Rickers-Ovsiankina's reports, that subjects who did not return to an activity were either not involved in it to begin with, or else gave up their involvement after being interrupted. Thus, "involvement" indicates the internal tension of a unit between person and activity that resists separation.

Note that as long as there is no force taking the subject away from the activity, there can be no need evidenced in the phenomenon of having to return to the task. The need to complete the task is not experienced as a need if one is involved in the task—it only occurs as a phenomenon of separation.

When persons are not separated from tasks, their involvement is shown in the fact that they transform the activity in which they are engaged. Thus, we cannot assume that the activity initially described by the experimenter is an adequate description of the activity as experienced by the involved subject. Henle and Aull have clearly documented this transformation (8). In one of their experiments, they gave five- to six-year-old children a small cardboard house with a wooden pegboard and colored pegs. The children were given the task of making a "fence" and a "garden" for the house. They observed how the children began to transform the activity in numerous ways. Some made up stories around the activity. For example, one child began a fantasy about a dog who lived at the house and would run out of the yard if the fence wasn't finished. Others made up a plan of action—for example, putting trees across the front of the lawn and planting a garden. Henle notes, ". . . the task is no longer the task as it was set by the experimenter. It is not just a matter of building a fence around a house; rather, the Great Dane must be prevented from running away or the flowers must be protected against children, or else a house must be made suitable for sale" (9).

Whenever a person is involved in a task, the activity part of the whole intention-system is colored by the personality, emotions, and motives of the self part of the unit.

Conversely, since the parts of a gestalt are always interdependent, the character of the task affects the involvement of the person and whether or not an intention-system fully develops. This is neatly demonstrated by an experiment of Torrey's (10). The character of the activity was manipulated through the use of three pairs of tasks that were similar in every way, except for the goodness of the task structure. Thus, the activity might be bead stringing—with a color pattern or without one; or snapping fasteners through holes in a card—with the holes arranged in a circle or scattered randomly; or cutting paper with scissors—with a design that turned into a large ring when completed, or simply a series of separate strips. Torrey interrupted the subject on all of these tasks (other activities were allowed to go to completion), and then observed which tasks the subjects resumed. While only eighteen of the thirty-three subjects resumed at least one of the six tasks (probably an indication of the relatively low amount of involvement), twelve of these eighteen subjects resumed more of the tasks which had good form (five resumed an equal number, one more of the formless tasks), and sixteen of the eighteen subjects initially resumed one of the tasks with good form, rather than one of the formless tasks. Evidently, it is easier for a person to become involved in a task with good form, and hence a clear need for closure, than to become involved in a task with poor form, where there is no "need" in the object. Similarly, Ovsiankina's results with continuous tasks, such as stringing beads, suggest that the person is less likely to continue in a unit with an interrupted task whose goal is not well defined.

By conceiving of an intention as a gestalt, we give recognition to the intimate interrelations between ego and activity. Further, since an activity always involves objects, the intention, which is conceived as inside the person, contains a reference to something outside the person via the activity that is between the ego and the objects involved in the activity. Thus, we have no problem in understanding why an intention endows specific environmental objects with valence.

The conception of an intention as a gestalt rather than a tensed region also has the advantage of being compatible with the rest of gestalt theory. If we conceive of an intention (set, act of will) as a tensed region, we introduce another dynamic element into gestalt psychology. This element then becomes another one of the determinants of organization—like proximity or similarity. Instead, we conceive of the intention as a system of involvement between person and activity, whose tension towards closure obeys the law of Prägnanz. By conceiving of an intention or set as a form of organization in its own right, we maintain the primacy of Prägnanz and preserve parsimony. In fact, the proposed intention-system is quite similar to the bipolar organizations that Köhler describes as existing between persons and the objects towards which they direct actions (11). Of course, this gain in parsimony will only be realized if the concept of an intention as a unit relation can also explain substitute satisfaction and the other phenomenon that the concept of tension-system can handle. In Chapters VI and VIII, I shall attempt to show that this is indeed possible.

Further, the concept of an intention as a gestalt makes a distinction between this unit between person and activity—for which the person is responsible—and needs for which the person is not responsible and that may possibly be conceived of as tensed regions. To understand how the distinction may be drawn we must discuss how a person forms a unit between himself and an activity. Consideration of these dynamics leads us to recognize a third part of the gestalt—the motives that underlie the formation of an intention-system. To understand how such an intention-system is organized and to account for the relationship between the person-activity unit and the person's needs, we may turn to Ricoeur's phenomenological analysis of will, an analysis that is concerned with uniting the voluntary and the involuntary as parts of one whole (12). We have stated that a person acts to form the dynamic unit between himself and the activity in which he becomes involved; but just how is such an intention-system organized? According to Ricoeur, such willed action involves three essential components; we may view these components as parts of the whole that we call an intention-gestalt. In all willed action there is: (1) a projection of future action that creates new possibilities in the world, events that would not occur without the person's own participation and his power to bring these events about; (2) an attribution of the action to oneself as the responsible agent; (3) a relating of the action to one's motives and body as the reasons (not causes) of the action.

The projection of the action refers, of course, to the task to which the person commits himself, and the attribution of responsibility to the self refers to the person part of the unit between person and action. However, we have not yet discussed the reasons why the person becomes involved in the activity, and how these motives are part of the unit between person and activity. Lewin, and Ovsiankina, observe that a subject may be motivated to accept a task by ambition, or by a desire to please the experimenter. And Chein has pointed out that such motives usually are themselves uncompleted projects of action (13). Often, these are projects which are "perpetuated"— projects that can by their very nature never be completed. For example, if a person commits himself to being a caring person, this project may never be completely fulfilled and may motivate countless other projects. Since these projects are important aspects of the person, and are the reasons why he commits himself to an activity, they too are involved in the unit between the self and the activity.

However, it should be observed that such motives are not really the "causes" of the activity. Rather, they are a part of the organized system that I have termed an intention-gestalt. The person himself organizes this unit when he commits himself to some project of action in order to fulfill some of his needs (which are often prior projects). In organizing his project of action the person selects which needs he will respond to (14). *Then* these needs or prior projects motivate the commitment. It should also be remembered that the motivational forces for the completion of the project of action do not only stem from the original motives, but also from the lack of closure inherent in the person's commitment to the as-yet-unfinished project. The resultant tension of the intention-system motivates a search for, or responsiveness to, ways to complete the project.

There may also be unorganized needs—that is, needs which have not yet become part of an intention-system, whose objects have not yet been discovered. While such needs might be represented as unorganized regions that are filled with tension, they could not automatically endow objects with valence, and would not constitute the major portion of a person's needs.

It should be noted that the organized needs—intention-systems—that we are proposing, function as Lewin's tensed regions function. That is, they are experienced as belonging to the person part of the life-space, and, whenever it is possible, they create valenced objects in the environmental part of the life-space. The intention to eat is conceived as "in" the person, while the real object at which the intention is directed (*e.g.,* a piece of cake) is experienced as in the environment rather than in the person. Thus, when an intention-system is actualized, the person's behavior is guided by attractions or repulsions to objects in the environment, and we are simply asserting that an intention is best conceived as a gestalt, formed when the person commits himself to some project of action in order to fulfill other intentions or needs.

By viewing an intention as a gestalt, we deduce its tension—its need for completion—from the rule of *Prägnanz,* and we give recognition to the interdependences between the various parts of the intention-system. The force of closure is inherent in the structure of an intention. Thus, Schutz (15) observes that an intention implies a fantasy of the future in which one looks back at the completed act. That is, the projected action is actually in the future perfect tense—it will have been done—and this is an inherent part of an intention's organization. The various interdependences of the intention-system are also inherent in its organization. Thus, the person is responsible for the action and transforms the meaning of the activity, but the action determines the identity of the person; the action is taken to satisfy prior needs, but these needs only become motives once they are incorporated into the project of action; the person selects which motives to actualize but the network of motives is part of the person. The meaning of the person (his identity), the meaning of the action, and the meaning of his motives are all dependent on the meaning of the whole—the intention-system.

Such a conception gives us an interesting perspective that leads us to look for certain effects that might otherwise be ignored. Since involvement is a relationship, we begin thinking in terms of interactions; whenever one term of the relationship is altered, we expect effects on the other terms of the relationship. For example, when a person abandons an activity, this act must have implications for either himself or for the activity. The person may conclude, for instance, that he lacks some ability or that the activity is an uninteresting one. In the following sections we shall observe many examples of these effects.

It may be seen that the need to complete an unfinished activity, so simple at first glance, has enormous implications, for it suggests that all action has an inherently emotional core. To will, to act, we must involve ourself in an activity. To do this we become a part of a gestalt larger than ourselves, and once we are thus bound to an activity, we are no longer the master of our fate. Once formed, each intention-system is a motive in its own right, inexorably moving towards closure, ceaselessly seeking for ways of fulfillment in spite of obstacles and even our own personal preference.

POSSESSION DYNAMICS

One of the advantages of conceiving of an intention as a unit among person, activity, and motives is that we are reminded that the act of will essentially involves forming or destroying this gestalt—the person entering into or abandoning a unit with the activity.

If we consider the question of how a person becomes involved in an activity, we raise the issue of what might be called "possession dynamics"—the dynamics of a person forming a unit with some activity or other person. It appears as though the person may do this in two ways: either by actively taking on the activity, or by receptively opening himself to the activity. That is, he may possess the activity, or allow himself to be possessed by it. Perhaps, in a sense, both of these processes always occur for as the person becomes involved so that the activity is "his," it is equally true that he is "possessed" by it and subject to what Anatol Rapoport (16) has termed the "blindness of involvement." That is, he becomes unable to see the possibilities of other commitments.

Conversely, when a person separates himself from a task, either by abandoning it—because of repeated failure, or being laughed at, or in disgust at repeated interruptions—or by finishing it—exhausting its possibilities—he takes himself back so that he is no longer preoccupied and is available to enter into some other activity. We shall consider this issue of availability in more detail in the following section on preoccupation, and in Chapter VI when we consider the dynamics of satiation. Here we simply want to point out that once a person is involved in an activity, he must somehow separate himself from it if he wishes to become involved in some other activity. Those subjects of Ovsiankina's who became involved had to try and separate themselves from the task when the experimenter forced them to interrupt it and engage in a different activity.

It appears that different subjects use different ways to try to separate themselves from a task which has to be interrupted. The way which they use may, in turn, affect how they return to the task.

One of the major contributions of Ovsiankina's study is the demonstration that an intention-system can manifest itself in a number of different phenomenal experiences. Thus, the need to complete an activity might, in one subject, be directly experienced as an inner urge, whereas it could be reflected in another subject by an experience of a positive valence—the sight of the unfinished activity calling to him for completion—and only indirectly inferred by some subject who finds himself performing the activity. While we might view these different experiences as phenotypic variations of the genotype tension-system, Ovsiankina notes that these different experiences reflect different dynamic relations between the person and the interrupted task.

There are at least three such relations. First, the person may remain emotionally attached to the task, separating himself only enough to give the interrupting activity some perfunctory attention while he really remains engaged with the first activity. In this case he will go through the motions of performing the second task, but will never really leave the uncompleted task. It is this subject, still preoccupied with the first task and not really involved with the second, who experiences the inner urge for completion of the first task.

Second, the person may separate himself by erecting a boundary between himself and the unfinished task. Probably this is often accomplished by making an intention to return to the task. We may speculate that this act is inevitably accompanied by the organization of valences. If we are correct, whenever a person maintains involvement, but acts to create a boundary that will free his attention, he does so with the understanding that the activity, event, or person will command him to act when it appears in the future under more favorable circumstances. Thus, the expression of the involvement with the task, which was a force in the present, becomes translated into the valence of the future. In this connection it is interesting to note that Freud made the following observation (17).

> If I go walking and take a letter with me to be posted, it is not at all necessary that I, as a normal, not nervous individual, should carry it in my hand and continually look for a letterbox. As a matter of fact, I am accustomed to put it in my pocket and give my thoughts free rein on my way, feeling confident that the first letterbox will attract my attention and cause me to put my hand in my pocket and draw out the letter.

In other words, when the subject keeps his relationship of involvement with the task but puts the task aside so that he can attend to other activities—thus affecting this relationship—the change alters his relationship with the objective task so that the task acquires valence. When he resumes work on the task, the valence will disappear.

Third, a person may separate himself from an activity by isolating it. That is, he may use counterforces to create a barrier, rather than simply a boundary, between himself and the activity. In this case, he completely forgets the activity and the activity does not acquire valence. However, when the interrupting task is completed and an opportunity arises, the first intention may escape from behind the barrier and lead him to work on the task without becoming aware of what he is doing.

The character of the task evidently may influence how a person separates from it. Thus, Ovsiankina notes that continuous tasks were harder to set aside, probably because there was no stopping point, and yet often lacked a resumptive urge. We might speculate that the absence of an intention-system in these cases is due to the way in which the activity was set aside. It seems possible that instead of creating either a barrier or a boundary, the subjects withdrew their involvement by declaring the task to be finished.

To some extent the withdrawal of involvement may be encouraged by external events. For example, while the experimenter cannot affect the subject's motive system directly, either by telling him not to want to finish the interrupted task or by prohibiting him from finishing, he can declare that the task is finished. In at least some cases, the subject accepts this and the motive is satisfied. Thus, while the experimenter cannot directly influence the subject's involvement, he can influence the involvement by dealing with the objective structure and by making the task finished.

Release may also occur when the task product is destroyed. This ends the task, removing the obligation and freeing the subject. This probably occurs more frequently when the motive system is compulsive or obligatory. The fact that release may occur under these circumstances, and that this may be the only way to obtain release under certain circumstances, suggests the interesting possibility that some destructive behavior may be aimed at freeing the destroyer from compulsive or obligatory motivation requirements.

It should be noted that Ovsiankina's method may easily be applied in naturalistic investigations. We, and the persons surrounding us, are continually immersed in activities of various sorts, and these are often interrupted with easily observable effects. If we wish, we may create interruptions of various sorts in order to verify Ovsiankina's observations and make new ones which extend the analysis. For example, while working on this material I observed my three-year-old daughter become involved in carefully picking up individual peas and eating them. I showed her a "tiny broom" (a plastic whisk to butter corn), and after sweeping the table with it, I offered it for her to play with. Her face lit up with interest; she took the broom, made a few sweeps, and then put it down and quickly returned to picking up peas! The intention-system of the first activity had asserted its supremacy over an interrupting activity that would ordinarily have had sufficient interest to capture prolonged attention— it probably would have evolved into a game with a considerable intention-system in its own right. One can imagine a number of experiments which might clarify the issues of how one gets involved in an activity, how the resultant intention-system competes with other systems, how one manages to relinquish an activity, and the price one pays for such a decision.

Before leaving this general topic, my own need for completion compels me to note one additional problem—the relationship between activity and energy expenditure. Experientially, exertions of will require the expenditure of energy. That is, the person feels that he has worked and that there has been a drain on his resources. This feeling of energy output may be contrasted to the experience of energy input—as when a person relaxes and is restored. It may also be contrasted to the experience of energy being released—as when a person hears good news or becomes excited, and engages in activity without expending effort. Such feelings involve psychological energy, and are probably unrelated to the quantity of physical energy involved in the activity. For example, a person who is loading a truck in a routine way exerts much more physical energy than a person deciding he had better make an important phone call; yet, the latter may feel that he has expended much more energy. Nevertheless, psychological energy may possible follow laws that are analogous to physical energy, such as conservation. In general, restructuring a system of activity requires psychological energy, while merely continuing it does not. Thus, a person who is out for a walk may actually walk around a log rather than step over it because it seems less effortful.

Observations from everyday life suggest that the engagement of motive systems that have been placed behind boundaries sometimes require an expenditure of psychic energy—that is, they "take something out of a person." For example, a mother whose attention is occupied with a book is interrupted by a child. She attempts to maintain her engagement with the book by absentmindedly meeting the child's demands to tie his shoe laces, give him a cookie, and so on. However, since the child's real need is to have the mother's undivided attention, thus assuring himself of her involvement, he continues his demands until the mother is forced to give up her book, by creating some sort of boundary, and pay her full attention to the child. The minute this occurs, the child may be satisfied and go off to play. But the mother cannot seem to get back to the book. Instead of the book's acquiring a positive valence, it may take an act of will and an expenditure of energy for her to cross the boundary and re-engage the book.

On the other hand, the abandonment of a motive system may release considerable quantities of energy for the person to become involved in other activities. Of course, this is particularly true when unfruitful central concerns are abandoned. Thus, as William James points out, the giving up of pretenses may free a person to live a much more satisfying life (18).

I hope that the above notes will convince the reader that we need more experiments on interrupted tasks. However, we do not need studies that focus on the quantification of general trends. Rather, we need experimental observations that pay meticulous attention to the acts of individual subjects and the psychological consequences which ensue.

THE COMPULSIVE NATURE OF THE PHENOMENON

In considering the central phenomenon to be the strong need to return to an uncompleted task, we set aside an important distinction that we must now make. It is important to note that in the conditions of Ovsiankina's experiment (or Katz's), what subjects report is a diffuse urge toward resumption and a feeling of incompleteness, rather than a wanting to return to the interrupted activity. They feel "compelled" to, or "obligated" to, that it is their "duty," that they do not have the "right" to stop. In line with this, completion of the task brings relief, but not the experience of pleasure. In general, it seems clear that the average subject's involvement was fundamentally of the nature of a "have to" rather than a "want to."

Of course, having to do something may mean different things. For example, we have to do something which we do not want to do, but which will get us something we want. Thus, a person may have to sweep the floor in order to get the clean house he wants. However, there may be no urge to perform such an act. Often, in fact, we must use our will to perform the activity. We may also use the term *have to* in describing the autonomous nature of what we really want to do. Thus, a novelist may speak of having to write when he is describing the spontaneous urgency of the writing he actually wants to do. In the present case, however, we are using "have to" in the sense of there being a force which makes us perform an activity, or causes us to be preoccupied with an activity which we do not want to do and would not otherwise do. While such forces are not as alien to the ego as are compulsive id forces, they do have some of the same external quality. In Lewin's terms, the forces involved seem to be induced by a will other than the person's own. And this is true in spite of the fact that the person allowed himself to become involved in the activity that was presented by the experimenter.

We must ask why subjects experience having to return to the activity, rather than wanting to. In part, this feeling of compulsion or duty may be a defense against assuming the responsibility of admitting the strong and irrational desire to return to the activity, for when a person has to do something he need not admit that he wants to. In support of this explanation is Ovsiankina's observation that feelings of compulsion occurred most frequently in subjects who thought that the experimenter would be opposed to their resuming the task.

In part, too, some subjects probably had obsessive personality characteristics. The influence of such a factor is suggested by Kendig's study of compulsive perseveration (19). She had ninety subjects engage in the task of thinking of words starting with "c". A review of her data suggests that when the task was taken as a test of ability, those subjects with obsessive traits on the Bernrenter Personality Inventory tended to perseverate in the activity for several days after they left the laboratory. It is interesting to note that this effect only occurred when there was a short interval of free time after the task was ended. Although the perseveration only occurred when the activity was a test, I do not believe that the effect depends on whether the test was passed or failed.

The feelings of compulsion may also partly stem from the interruption technique itself. The experimenter exerts a force on the subject to get him to leave the task he is involved with and begin another. The subject meets this with a counterforce to fight the interruption. Ovsiankina and Lewin believed that the exertion of this counterforce might bring the task closer to the subject and help make it his own. It might also contribute to the compulsivity of the desire to return to the task. A rather different explanation would be generated by Festinger's theory of cognitive dissonance (20). This approach would predict that a subject who finds himself fighting to complete an assigned task might justify his behavior by increasing his attachment to the task. Such an attachment might well take on a compulsive character. Yet another explanation was proposed by Rank to account for the compulsivity of the patient's "love" for the psychotherapist. He observes, ". . . libido fixation in the transference . . . is not 'pure love,' but rather a phenomenon of resistance. As such it is nothing more than a disguised will assertion of the patient, who wishes to have that which is denied him just because it is denied" (21).

While these explanations may account for aspects of the compulsivity of particular subjects, the experience of everyday life suggests that the general feeling of having to do something is not simply due to being interrupted. We must, therefore, continue to ask why this was the general feeling of all of the subjects. Why didn't they experience a desire to return to the activity? Instead of compulsion and duty, why did they not spontaneously return to the activity and experience pleasure? It is not that the subjects were doing something against their will, or that they were not personally involved. Clearly, the subjects who experienced the phenomenon freely committed themselves to the activity. And those activities which gave the most room for personal expression, such as molding a figure, were the most personally involving and gave the clearest examples of the phenomenon.

There are instances in our lives when we spontaneously want to return to an activity. We may want to return to studying about an idea, building a piece of furniture, or even mending a shirt. What is the difference between these activities and Ovsiankina's? The only evident difference is that Ovsiankina chose the activities and assigned them to her subjects, whereas in cases of wanting to complete an activity the person himself freely chooses the activity in which to be involved. This, in some sense, Ovsiankina is dealing with induced, rather than own, forces.

In spite of the apparent straightforwardness of the above explanation, it actually raises a number of interesting questions about the nature of choice. For as we have noted, the subjects freely chose to participate in the experiment and chose to involve themselves in the activities. Further, there seems little doubt that if the experimenter had offered them a choice between several activities and then interrupted the chosen one, the subjects would still have felt that they had to complete the activity—rather than wanting to complete it. In fact the nature of choice in experiments on cognitive dissonance and self-attribution has the same quality of somehow leading to induced force. It seems evident that simply because the subject has a "choice" does not mean that we are dealing with own forces.

How, then, can we specify what own forces are? Evidently, we must look at the larger situation in which the choice is embedded. In fact, it appears that by agreeing to be a subject in an experiment, the person has surrendered his will to the experimenter, agreeing (within certain limits) to become engaged in whatever the experimenter chooses. (In Chapter XIII we shall examine this assertion in more detail when we deal with issues of will and freedom). Under such conditions, when the experimenter gives the subject a choice, the choice may be too limited to encompass any of the activities that the subject would have chosen on his own had he not been in an experimental situation. When this is the case, the subject really engages in the activity for the experimenter rather than for himself. Evidently, even when he then becomes involved in the activity, there is still a feeling of having to complete it, rather than wanting to.

Since Ovsiankina, and subsequent experimenters, have interrupted assigned tasks, rather than more natural activities, we may wonder if the tension to complete an activity is somewhat dependent on compulsive forces, and might not occur if a person's own activities were interrupted. In the next section, we shall see that this is not the case. The tension to complete an activity is actually a more general phenomenon which appears to apply to all activities in which a person is involved.

PREOCCUPATION

Once established, an intention-system is capable of exerting powerful forces on the person. These may work towards insuring the execution of the intention regardless of whether or not the situation is favorable for this execution. When the person continues to be involved with the activity and does not separate himself by creating boundaries, the intention-system leads to a preoccupation which prevents the formation of other intention-systems, and hence an involvement in other activities. This appears to be the major cause of regression in the well known frustration-regression experiment.

The Frustration-Regression Experiment

Lewin's conceptualization of development (which we shall examine in more detail in Chapter VI), includes the idea that more developed activities will show both greater differentiation and greater hierarchical integration. Thus, while a simple activity might consist of one homogeneous unit (*e.g.,* a child rolling a truck back and forth), a more complex activity will show mean-end relationships (*e.g.,* rolling the truck over to pick up a block), and a well-developed activity will consist of numerous units of activity organized into subgoals which are, in turn, governed by an over-all plan of behavior (*e.g.,* using the truck to pick up a block, to be used in building a fort, that will be defended against a forthcoming attack). By recording the units of action that occur in a given interval of time, and noting the presence or absence of more inclusive units of activity, it is possible to devise a scale that measures the level of development shown in different episodes of behavior. This development level can then be compared under different psychological conditions to see if a person's behavior shows a greater level of development or a lesser level—a regression.

In the late 1930's, at Iowa, Barker, Dembo, and Lewin (22) investigated the effect which the condition of frustration would have on developmental level. The design was as follows. First, a child (there were thirty children whose ages ranged from two to five) was allowed to play with ordinary sorts of toys, such as blocks and coloring books, and the constructiveness (developmental level) of the play was measured.

On a following day a partition, which had concealed half of the room, was opened, and the children were allowed to play with a set of particularly entrancing toys that were revealed. There was a full-sized doll's house with electric lights, a pond with water and boats, a table prepared for a party, and other fascinating play things. After the children were fully involved with these toys, the investigator told the children, "Now let's play at the other end"; drawing a wire partition, through which the toys could still be seen, he left them to play with the ordinary toys in the other half of the room. The childrens' desire to play with the entrancing toys having been frustrated, the investigators observed their subsequent play with the ordinary toys to see whether the level of development increased or regressed. (At the conclusion of the experiment, the children were again allowed to play with the enchanting toys in order to insure that they would be fully restored.)

In almost every case, measures of the childrens' total play showed less constructiveness. However, the investigators noted that this might well be due to the fact that the children were overtly distracted by the entrancing toys, and spent a certain amount of time hovering around the barrier or trying to get the experimenter to let them in. They therefore devised measures to eliminate this contamination. For example, they measured and compared the maximum constructiveness of play when the child was physically occupied with the ordinary toys for a sizable interval of time. The average child still showed less constructive behavior (seventeen decreased, eight stayed the same, five increased). Furthermore, the stronger the level of frustration (as measured by time spent at the barrier and in trying to escape the situation), the less constructive the play (during the periods when the child was actually engaged with the ordinary toys for at least thirty seconds).

The investigators point out that the frustrating situation could have caused the regression for at least three different reasons:

First, since the experimenter had arbitrarily removed the child from an enjoyable play situation, the child might suffer a loss of security. This could well cause a loss in time perspective and hinder his ability to develop plans for his activity, or make him less free to express himself, either of which effects would lower the constructiveness of his play.

Second, if the child felt trapped in the frustrating situation, his emotional tension would increase. This, in turn, would lead to a de-differentiation and disorganization of regions within the person, and hence to a primitivization of behavior. In Chapter X, we shall see this sort of effect occurring in Dembo's experiment.

Third, to the extent that the child was preoccupied with the entrancing toys, he would be unable to get fully involved with the ordinary toys, and hence the constructiveness of his play would decrease. In fact, this seems to have been the major effect in the experiment. Most children were so preoccupied with their interrupted involvement with the entrancing toys that they were unable to become involved with the ordinary toys the way they had been previously, and the developmental level of their activity showed a considerable regression. This effect demonstrates the detrimental consequences of task interruption on creative activity. Further, since it seems safe to surmise that the children wanted to return to the entrancing toys and did not simply feel they had to, the experiment shows that the "Ovsiankina effect" is just as strong in the noncompulsive form generated by children choosing what activities they wished to become involved with.

It is interesting to note how Lewin handles these results theoretically. He assumes that the constructiveness of an activity will increase with the degree of a person's involvement in the activity. If we conceive of the person as a region within the life-space that is subdivided into numerous subregions or cells, then we can represent the person's degree of involvement by indicating how many of these cells are involved in the activity. Now we may think of the children as being in two overlapping situations at the same time. On the one hand, they are in the situation of playing with the ordinary toys. On the other, they are "somewhere else"—still somewhat in the situation of playing with the entrancing toys. Hence, each child will have a number of subregions—a part of its self—engaged in each of the situations. The more potent the situation with the entrancing toys, the more involved the child in that activity—the greater the number of cells engaged—and the fewer cells available for the situation with the ordinary toys.

There were only two children who showed a significant increase in constructiveness after being prevented from playing with the entrancing toys. One appeared to not really be in overlapping situations, but rather to be in a succession of separate situations. The other, initially passive and lethargic, was apparently energized by the experience so that he became involved for the first time, and his play became more organized.

The Personality Structure of Schizophrenics

The fact that preoccupation in one activity may prevent involvement in another suggests that some of the symptoms of schizophrenia may actually be due to powerful preoccupations. In 1935, Ovsiankina performed a study which bears on this issue (23).

First, subjects were placed in a free situation—simply asked to wait in a room until the investigator became available. On the table at which the subject was seated, there were twelve potentially attractive objects (a kaleidoscope, a puzzle, a small xylophone), and the investigator carefully noted the extent to which the subjects became involved with any or all of the objects. The reactions of 125 patients who were diagnosed as schizophrenics were compared with 75 control subjects who had comparable ages, educational levels, and social backgrounds, and in the majority of cases were also institutionalized for chronic illness or destitution.

During the half-hour in which they waited, the schizophrenics actually spent almost as much time with the objects as the control group (paranoids more, catatonics less). However, their time tended to be spent in more superficial responses such as merely touching or regarding an object (with the exception of paranoids). Further, rather than becoming involved in directed activities with definite goals (e.g., solving a puzzle, playing a tune), schizophrenics (including paranoids) tended to become engaged in undirected activity (e.g., rotating a sparkler, simply striking the xylophone). In general they showed much less involvement in the activities, forming less of a real relationship between themselves and the objects.

Following this period of free time, the experimenter gave each of the sixty-one schizophrenics (individually) a series of tasks to perform, occasionally interrupting one of the tasks (24). Unlike normal subjects, schizophrenics often interrupted themselves to be engaged in undirected activity, showed indifference towards the tasks—sometimes not completing them—and had much less tendency to resume a task once it had been interrupted. Nevertheless, although resumption was quite casual, appearing almost accidental, it occurred 42.9 per cent of the time! Over-all, their performance was much less goal-directed than in the case of normals—subjects failing to definitely enter into or leave a unit with the activity. Subjects who did tend to complete interrupted tasks also tended to be the subjects who showed directed activity during the period of free time, and to show signs of self-initiated activity in the hospital (e.g., playing a card game).

There are two possible explanations for the difficulty which schizophrenics have in becoming involved in a task. Ovsiankina suggests that there may be a general impairment of the ability to form and maintain segregated tension-systems in the peripheral personality layers. This explanation would account for the problem, which schizophrenics often have, of pursuing an idea without having other thoughts intrude upon them. However, as Ovsiankina herself observes, there are many schizophrenics who show signs of central preoccupations which reflect very strong and segregated tension-systems. In the light of the frustration-regression experiment, I believe that in all cases there may simply be strong central preoccupations which prevent schizophrenics from becoming involved in superficial activities. At least this must be true in some cases, and may be a profitable way for us to relate schizophrenia to more normal experiences.

I should also note that Pierre Janet (25), whose treatment and case histories of various neurotic disorders precedes Freud's work, and in some aspects go beyond it, accounted for many disorders by pointing out that the person was unable to separate himself from a traumatic event, and was therefore continually preoccupied by it. He sees his patients as attached to their former situation, so that they cannot control their activity either by triumph or liquidation, but remain bound to it, losing their freedom to detach themselves and proceed to other activity. Of course, traumatic memories and repetition compulsion may be accounted for in this way, and Chein has pointed out that the dynamics of all neurotic symptoms may be related to Ovsiankina's findings and reflect "unfinished business" (26).

Social Implications

The need to complete activities in which we become involved is so pervasive in our everyday lives that it has important consequences for the conduct of education, work, and family life. In education, a major problem is the establishment of conditions which will encourage the development of intrinsic motivation. Yet we find that many educational programs for children have rigid structures that constantly interrupt the child and take him away from activities in which he is engaged. This not only creates tension and preoccupation problems, it leads to a situation where many children defend themselves against involvement out of a fear of being interrupted. The child may dutifully comply with a teacher's request for him to perform an activity, but refuses to consider the activity his own so that he will not become involved and suffer the pain of continual interruption. One of the advantages of an open education program is its relative freedom for individual activity, so that it is not necessary to interrupt a child's activity so frequently.

In industry, there is an identical problem for any management that desires worker involvement. In most enterprises there are natural units of work, and general morale is seriously lowered when workers are constantly interrupted in the middle of these units. On the other hand, Maier (27) has observed that it is often possible to create artificial units of work that provide completion experiences. Thus, a repetitive task can be divided into units by artificially grouping a given number of elements into units with different colors, or a long, involved task can be broken down into meaningful subunits. In either case, the worker achieves a sense of progress in the meaningful completion of work. One of the reasons for the increased meaningfulness of work under conditions of worker control, is that the workers themselves can organize their work into meaningful units that do not get interrupted.

With regard to family life, the mother role may almost be characterized as a continuous series of interruptions. The duties of caring for small children effectively prevent extensive involvement in other activities, which will inevitably be interrupted. Consequently, persons who wish to be involved in activities in addition to mothering have a need for day-care programs or various types of extended families.

Sources of Tension

While intention-systems control a great deal of human behavior, they may be only one of the sources of tension which induce action. In his *Principles of Gestalt Psychology* (28), Koffka argues that there are three such sources of tensions: intentions (which are experienced as stemming completely from the ego), field stresses (which stem completely from the environment—*e.g.*, the forces involved in visual accommodation), and emotional stresses (which appear to be between the ego and some object in the environment—as in flight from danger).

Koffka asserts that any of the three types of stresses may control action. Further, he makes an important distinction between two types of valences— demand character, and physiognomic character. In the case of demand charac- ter, Koffka agrees with Lewin: stresses within the ego, such as intention, endow the object with valence—for example, the intention to mail a letter makes one notice a mailbox which commands "Put the letter in me." However, even in these cases, the specific character of the object has an influence of its own on the strength and type of valence that occurs. Thus, as we have seen, a task with form can more readily become part of an intention-system, and some objects lend themselves to specific valences much more readily than others. If a person intends to paint some wood, old paint that is peeling can command "Scrape me" much more easily than paint that is only cracked.

In the case of the physiognomic character of objects—a majestic mountain, a mean-looking face—Koffka argues that the valence does not depend on intra-ego stresses, such as intentions, but instead involves stresses between the object and the ego. (Note that the positive or negative character of the valence seems more pronounced in the case of physiognomic character, while the specific command quality is more pronounced in the case of demand charac- ter.) Later, in Chapter XI, when we deal with emotions, we shall return to these points.

There may be yet a third type of valence, perhaps related to Koffka's field stresses. We have noted that Lewin suggested that the field forces of valences are always related to needs (tension-systems) within the person. Thus, the piece of cake that says "Eat me" is related to hunger. However, there are times when events in the environment appear to be the need that motivates an action. This is particularly evident when another person is in need,—for example, if some- one else is about to step in front of a car, and we shout "Look out!" In the next section, and in Chapter XIII, we shall see that impersonal needs that are external to us are often experienced whenever we are task-involved in an activity. In both cases the field forces or demand character does not appear to be related to our own needs in the way Lewin's valences are. Hence, I shall call this quality of events or objects their "external need character."

This does not mean that an intention-system is not involved in such cases. It may well be that the person has previously established an intention-system of the perpetuated sort—for example, an intention to protect persons from harm. However, a primary motive for this intention is the need of another, rather than the need of the self. Thus the sight of another in danger is not simply the occasion for the intention to be actualized, but also the reason for the actualization.

We know from Ovsiankina's work that the mere sight of someone else's unfinished work does not usually motivate a person to complete the work—the person simply does not become involved in the activity. However, Mary Henle and her students have been successful in indirectly producing subject involvement (29). Their technique is to have a person observe another subject whose activities are interrupted. Some of the observers show a definite tendency to want to complete the interrupted tasks. It is not clear whether this effect is due to the development of the external need character of the incompleted tasks, or whether the observers became involved with the task via an identification with the subjects who were interrupted.

We might expect that the strength of the external need character of an incomplete object or task would increase with the degree of completeness of the object or task. Hornstein has reported a series of investigations that bear on this issue (30). He and his colleagues have studied the response of persons who find "lost" wallets or envelopes that are placed on the sidewalk. When envelopes are used, they are unsealed but addressed, and presumably were lost before being mailed. By varying the content of the envelopes, the investigators could vary whether the loser would be liked or disliked. The loser had, apparently, been involved in soliciting ten contributions for a medical research fund. By varying the number of contributions collected, the investigators could vary whether the loser's task was more or less completed. The results show that when the loser is liked, the probability that a finder will mail in the contribution for the loser is .87 when the loser is close to his goal, and only .53 when the loser is far from his goal. There is no significant difference when the loser is disliked. Of course, in such studies we are also dealing with issues of importance, empathy, conscience, and "we-feeling"; but the results clearly suggest that the strength of the promotive tension may increase with the degree of task completion.

EFFECTS ON MEMORY—ZEIGARNIK'S WORK

Ovsiankina shows that a tension-system affects overt behavior, compelling her subjects to seek out the interrupted activity in order to complete it. She also demonstrates that the system affects the the subjects' perception; if the unfinished task was in the room, a subject who was not consciously thinking of the task would notice the task and would give the task a positive valence that would entice him to resume its activity. Now we shall consider Zeigarnik's classic experiment which, because of space limitations, we have deposited with University Microfilms (31). Zeigarnik's thesis is that a system of tensions should also affect a person's memory. She argues that if tension-systems exist, they should lead the subject to have a better recall for unfinished activities. In addition, her work leads to further elaboration of the nature of intention-systems and involvement.

In Zeigarnik's experiment, subjects were given from eighteen to twenty-two diverse tasks. These included activities such as writing down a poem liked by the subject, drawing a vase of flowers, drawing the subject's initials, filling a sheet of paper with crosses, stringing beads, forming a sentence containing given words, solving various problems, and making a cardboard box with a lid. Half of these tasks were interrupted at the very point when the experimenter felt the subject was most deeply involved with the task. This point of strongest contact generally occurred near the end of the task. The other half were allowed to be completed. At the end of the tasks the experimenter unexpectedly asked the subject to recall what the various tasks were. The subjects would usually respond with names or descriptions for various tasks and then pause, unable to recall more. After a lapse of time the subject might recall others, but only those tasks recalled without difficulty, i.e., before the pause, were scored. Zeigarnik found that the average subject recalled the uncompleted tasks 90 per cent more frequently than the completed tasks (about half of the tasks were recalled). Of the thirty-two subjects, twenty-six remembered more uncompleted tasks; of the twenty-two tasks, some seventeen were remembered better when they were uncompleted. The experiment was successfully replicated with another sample of fourteen individuals, with a group of forty-seven new subjects, and successfully repeated again with a group of forty-five children aged thirteen to fourteen. In the group experiments, the tasks were interrupted when about half the subjects were finished with a task.

To account for the above results, Zeigarnik asserts that memory is influenced by forces which exist at the moment of recall, rather than by the subject's experience at the moment a task is interrupted. In the latter regard, she shows that the superior recall of the uncompleted tasks cannot be due to the shock of interruption (interrupted tasks which are completed later are not better remembered), or to subjects trying to remember the interrupted tasks because they think they will be repeated. (Telling the subjects that interrupted tasks will reoccur or will not reoccur makes no difference.) Zeigarnik argues that there are two sets of forces at the moment of recall: forces exerted by the tension-systems of each uncompleted task, and the force exerted by the experimenter's request to recall all of the tasks. The final tension which favors the recall of the uncompleted tasks obviously depends on the relative strengths of these two sets of forces, with the relative advantage of unfinished tasks declining if the tension to recall all the tasks is very strong. Hence, when the experimenter asks subjects to recall the tasks, those who suddenly construe the experiment as a test of memory try very hard to recall all the tasks, with the result that the average subject remembers only 50 per cent more uncompleted tasks than completed tasks. On the other hand, subjects who simply regard the experimenter as requesting a telling of what happened, show a 180 per cent advantage for the uncompleted tasks. These subjects react as though the experimenter's request is a demand with which one can comply but is somewhat inappropriate—like being asked to dance in public.

While Zeigarnik's general line of reasoning is clear, it is not evident why the system of tension dealing with the uncompleted task should necessarily exert a force on memory for the task. A somewhat different interpretation of the results, one that appears to solve this problem, is offered by Koffka (32). Referring to Harrower's studies, which show that uncompleted jokes are retained more than completed ones, he argues that the structure of an activity is kept well articulated by the tension in a system involving an uncompleted task. Since forms which are well articulated are easier to remember, the uncompleted tasks have an advantage.

Still another possible explanation is suggested by Janet's distinction between the reaction to an event and the memory of an event as a "story" told after the event (33). Janet's point is that in so-called cases of "traumatic memory," the patient is not repressing a memory of the event. He is still reacting to the event, rather than remembering it. His analysis suggest that Zeigarnik's subject may also be still engaged in the unfinished tasks, rather than remembering them. Such an explanation would be quite compatible with the idea that the system in tension is an intention-gestalt among person, task, and motives.

Regardless of whether an unfulfilled intention-system presses towards being remembered, is preserved as a more articulate form, or keeps the person engaged in it, it is clear that most tasks are more apt to be recalled when they are not completed. In accord with the method of experimental phenomenology, Zeigarnik was careful to examine all the exceptions to this rule. Most of the exceptions proved to be due to a discrepancy between objective and psychological completion. For example, the subject may appear to have finished a task when psychologically he is still dissatisfied with the results, or is working on a second alternative solution, or is not convinced that he could do it again and hence is still involved in the task. Zeigarnik shows that some tasks are more susceptable to this than others, and accordingly are remembered even when they are objectively completed. Conversely, a subject may appear not to be finished but may be psychologically through, as when the problem of how to do a task is solved, and this solution constitutes the task as far as the subject is concerned. Such problems are, of course, forgotten, although objectively they are incomplete.

A different type of exception occurs if a subject becomes convinced that he cannot do a particular task and gives it up so that no tension-system remains. (This often happens when a task is accidentally destroyed.)

Finally, uncompleted continuous tasks are not remembered as often as uncompleted discrete tasks. As Ovsiankina also notes, persons found it more difficult to maintain a unit with an interrupted continuous task. Zeigarnik is able to elucidate the differences between continuous and finished tasks. She notes that the following characteristic differences exist:

1. The subject engaged in a finite task has a fixed goal; continuous tasks have no goal that governs the activity.

2. The actor is attracted to the goal of a finite task; he is carried along by the preceding phase of a continuous task (rhythm is clearly important here).

3. Finite tasks are broken into subunits with subgoals, and demonstrate an organic development; the phases of a continuous task are only a consecutive series.

4. A finite task leads the subject to estimate the amount of work, and to create relatively independent systems for each task; in continuous tasks the subject must tap the sources of energy again and again.

5. With finite tasks, a definitely demarcated tension-system, corresponding to the structure of the task, is found during execution of the task. This system can persevere after interruption; in continuous tasks the only anticipation is the same step that has gone before and no system can persevere once the task has been interrupted.

Notice that Zeigarnik's description of finite and continuous tasks implies the unit between person and activity which we have advanced as essential to an intention-system. In the case of finite tasks, this unit is reflected in the subject's attraction to the task's goal. In the case of continuous tasks, the unit is established by the subject being caught up in the rhythm of the task. Since the latter unit is broken by the interruption, there is less tendency to remember the task.

The fact of a unit is also indicated by Zeigarnik's observation that subjects often terminate tasks by marking the end with some sign of finality. Evidently, disengagement, separation from the unit, is facilitated by a final gesture, such as the pressure put on a final period, a knot after beads are threaded, a final push of the product towards the experimenter, and so on. When a subject is interrupted in the midst of a continuous activity, he will try to end by such a gesture, for example, making the beads into a necklace.

There are occasional instances of a subject being bound so strongly by the flow of a continuous task that he wants to keep on, and resists any final gesture or search for a way to transform the task into a finite unit. In everyday life this may occur in states of fatigue or brooding. Again, note the obvious unit between person and activity, a unit which continues until some external force disrupts it and ends its power.

In a separate series of experiments, Zeigarnik shows that fatigued subjects are more apt to recall completed activities. This effect occurs when the subject is fatigued as he performs the tasks, rather than when he recalls them. It is postulated that the lower recall for incompleted tasks is due to the fact that the tension-systems cannot be maintained in the fluid medium of the fatigued psychic state. From our perspective, the subjects cannot maintain their involvement because of the fatigue. Since the completed tasks are remembered as well as before, it is supposed that these tasks are recalled because their articulation remains unchanged—each task having a fixed shape in spite of its absence of tension.

In the course of investigating the effect of fatigue, Zeigarnik finds that the recall advantage of unfinished tasks tends to disappear with time. (It is not clear why the effect is less stable than the tendency to return to the task.) The loss of recall is probably not due to a simple time lapse. Zeigarnik shows that similar loss of recall occurs immediately if a subject who has been interrupted from a number of tasks is suddenly subjected to an exciting event. Either the consequent state of high tension overwhelms the tension-systems of the incompleted tasks; or, similar to fatigue, it changes the psychic fabric so that the systems are not maintained.

On the other hand, when subjects who have completed some tasks and been interrupted from others, are suddenly placed in a different (but not particularly exciting) psychological situation (e.g., the experimenter involves them in talking about a subject which she knows is of interest to them), the effect on the recall of uncompleted tasks depends on how the subject adjusts to the new situation. Subjects who find it easy to push the tasks out of their mind and attend to the new topic of conversation, often find it easy to retrieve the tasks, and show a recall advantage for the interrupted tasks. Subjects who find it difficult to forget the tasks and adjust to the new situation may also find it hard to re-enter the region of the tasks when they are asked to recall them. Like those subjects who were shaken up with excitement, they find it easier to recall the completed tasks. The reader who is interested in these effects should, of course, consult the original text. We find them intriguing and probably relevant to the possession dynamics briefly discussed above. To our knowledge, no investigator has followed up these promising leads.

That Zeigarnik's major finding—the superior recall of uncompleted tasks—is not peculiar to the German culture is shown by successful replications by Pachauri (34) in England and Marrow (35) in the United States. Additional generality is furnished by a further experiment by Marrow (36) in which he introduced the interesting variation of having the interrupted tasks be experienced as completed and the finished tasks as incomplete. This was accomplished by telling the subjects, "On such tasks as you indicate to me by your manner of handling and by the speed with which you work that you have sufficient mastery of the task, it will not be necessary for you to finish that task." Thus, an objective incompletion was experienced as a completion. In spite of the test-taking atmosphere of this study (and of Marrow's first study), the tasks that were experienced as incomplete (in this case objectively complete) were significantly better remembered. (Note that this was true in spite of the fact that such tasks were defined as failures.) In yet another variation, Marrow provided intense competitive pressure by comparing the "test" scores with "German averages" and increased the superiority of memory for incompleted tasks. This result held regardless of whether the subject succeeded or failed in his competitive effort. In comprehending these results it is important to realize that although the subjects were very involved in a competitive way —and experiencing failure with incompletions—the subjects were still *task* involved. They were simply engaged in a competitive task.

The Zeigarnik effect is a sensitive phenomenon, rather than a robust one like the Ovsiankina effect of having to complete a task. Recently, Van Bergen (37) has reviewed the extensive literature (160 studies) on memory for incomplete tasks, and concluded that the findings are so confusing, and the interruption technique is such a poor one, that it cannot lead to valid replications. We do not subscribe to this conclusion. An alternative possibility is that some experimenters have not been careful enough in creating the conditions which produce the phenomena.

We see no reason to doubt the validity of Zeigarnik's results. She is careful to describe a number of factors which contributed to these results, and it seems quite clear to us that in many cases subsequent investigators, who have not followed the method of experimental phenomenology, have not attempted to see if these factors obtain. Because a number of investigators have not obtained similar results, it is crucial to pay careful attention to these factors. Many experiments on the memory for uncompleted tasks have simply failed to meet the conditions which Zeigarnik describes quite precisely. I hope that future investigators will note these, and now that a complete translation is available, consult the original article.

The Importance of Real Involvement—Brown's Experiment

First, Zeigarnik notes that better memory for tasks which are incomplete occurs only when the subject is involved in the tasks. She considers this factor in the context of attempting to account for the fact that subjects are in maximal contact with the task, and show the most tension, towards the end of the task. Since a tension-system for a task is created at the beginning of the task, one might expect more tension to be available at the beginning than at the end. There are two considerations which are opposed to this. The first has to do with the observation that the force exerted by the valence of an object increases as the psychological distance decreases. Hence, the attractiveness of the goal of a task increases as a person approaches the end of the task. This would, of course, increase the degree of tension. The second consideration is that a person gradually becomes more and more involved in a task, getting drawn into it until it increasingly becomes his task, and involves more of his personal needs.

Such involvement may entail the arousal of needs to achieve, or to compete, or to test one's competence. The average subject may have such needs aroused by particularly challenging tasks, such as interesting puzzles or riddles; and later we shall see that such arousal is particularly apt to occur in the case of ambitious subjects. However, involvement often occurs simply by the subject's allowing himself to get lost in the task for its own sake. Zeigarnik notes that children are more apt to do this than adults. The tasks are more important to them, and they accept the tasks more seriously and with more naturalness, abandoning themselves to each individual task and becoming immersed in its particular characteristics. Zeigarnik notes that this involvement is not the same as being "interested" in a particular task. This is likely to simply result in the recall of a task that was particularly interesting—whether or not the task was completed.

The average child shows a 150 per cent recall advantage for interrupted tasks, compared to the average adult's 95 per cent advantage. In noting how children develop a genuine need to complete whatever task they are involved in, Zeigarnik states:

> . . . children experience everyday play not as an "interesting" way of passing the time; it is for them a serious, vitally important affair. It is fundamentally wrong to regard play in a child's life as second to washing, meals, etc. Saying to a child, "You can put your teddy bear to bed later" is equivalent to saying to a mathematician "You can finish your calculation later" (38).

Zeigarnik observes that those adults who are more childlike and spontaneous let themselves become involved in the tasks; whereas adults who are very grown-up may consider it beneath their dignity.

One might expect that the tasks which Zeigarnik used might be perceived as more play than real by many adults. At least this dimension of how real —that is, how serious, or important the activity is perceived to be—would seem an important factor to consider in predicting involvement, and hence later memory. Another student who worked with Lewin at Berlin, an American—J.F. Brown—performed an experiment which bears on this issue (39). The complete translation may be obtained from University Microfilms.

Brown told his subjects that they were taking an intelligence test which consisted of ten problems. After each problem there was a short "rest period" which was filled by working on an "activity" Actually these ten activities were ten equally difficult problems. Whereas the test problems were neatly typed on separate pages, the rest activities were given orally, done on yellow scrap paper, and later thrown in the wastebasket by the experimenter! (Brown notes the experiment was very successful technically.) The problems themselves were quite varied, and included mathematical problems, the writing of poetry, word meanings, sketches, historical questions, translations, and physical formulas. (Reading them makes me feel rather uneducated.) Subjects were told that all of the problems were designed so that "only a genius" could finish in time, scores being computed on the basis of part answers. In this way, all the problems could be interrupted without creating any sense of failure.

After the subjects has completed all twenty problems, they were asked to recall what the problems were. Some subjects were asked in the same room only five minutes after completing the problems, others were asked in a different room in thirty minutes, or after twenty-four to forty-eight hours, or after a week. The crucial question, of course, concerns whether or not the problems with high reality (the test problems) were remembered better than the problems with low reality (the time fillers). Remember that all of the problems were interrupted. Brown shows that the real problems are remembered with 30 per cent more frequency after five minutes, 70 per cent more after thirty minutes, 150 per cent after twenty-four to forty-eight hours, and 280 per cent more frequently after one week. (The major factor here is the forgetting of the low reality problems.) We may therefore, conclude that a subject is much more likely to remember a task in which he has been really involved.

We must note that there appear to be two somewhat different definitions of *reality* in the Lewin studies. Zeigarnik, Ovsiankina, and Brown use it to mean "serious" or "important," whereas Mahler, Lissner, and Dembo use it to mean "solid" rather than "fluid"—that is, limited by environmental requirements as opposed to the fluidity of imagination. Both Brown and Mahler evidently believed that these two meanings were related, but there is no conceptual or experimental evidence for this conjecture. In Chapter XI we shall examine this issue more closely.

Zeigarnik notes a number of circumstances under which subjects will not get involved in the tasks. One set of subjects who failed to get involved were those persons who approached the experiment determined to "learn something"; to gain insight into themselves; to try and find out what happened in a psychology laboratory; or to constantly try to find out the meaning of the experiment. Such subjects were preoccupied with their particular individual tasks, and hence failed to recall the interrupted tasks more frequently.

In accounting for this failure, Zeigarnik makes another important point—

that having an over-all goal makes the individual tasks lose their special character and separateness. The different tasks become molded into one continuous activity guided by the experimenter. Under these conditions, individual tension-systems are not formed, because the boundaries between the tasks are so unsubstantial that interrupted tasks do not maintain any tension and are not recalled more frequently. Zeigarnik performed a separate experiment to show this effect. At the start of this experiment she told the subjects the whole series of tasks they were to perform. This created a relatively undifferentiated series, and succeeded in abolishing superior recall for the interrupted tasks in the series.

Some experiments which have replicated features of Zeigarnik's study have ignored this factor. For example, the problems given to the subjects are all of one type, and are probably perceived more as a series than as discrete entities. In these cases, it is not surprising that there are no significant differences in recall for incompleted as opposed to completed problems.

Yet another circumstance in which the subjects failed to get involved may be of particular importance because of contemporary subject pools. Zeigarnik notes that once a group of high-school students visited the psychology laboratory on the suggestion of their teacher. These students had no spontaneous interest in the task, and felt they had no choice other than to obey the experimenter. They acted like students working for grades or soldiers under orders, suppressing their own wishes, and hence not getting involved in the tasks. They did not care when the tasks were interrupted. This group of students, like those individual subjects who tried too much to please the experimenter, failed to show superior recall for the interrupted tasks.

Types of Involvement—Task vs. Ego Involvement

The second factor which is clearly relevant to Zeigarnik's results concerns *how* her subjects were involved. Zeigarnik notes that a subject might come to the experiment and approach the tasks with one of three fundamentally different attitudes: (a) obligated to the experimenter—trying to give an honest performance, trying his best to meet the experimenter's wishes; (b) ambitious —trying to prove himself to the experimenter, or to test how well he could do. (Frequently, these subjects believed the tasks constituted a sort of aptitude test) (c) task-involved—interested in the inherent task. Here the activity itself attracted the subject and demanded adequate performance—for example, to make a circle as round as possible. The example is given of one subject who molded a dog saying "This dachshund must not have such a long tail. Not that I care what the experimenter would think . . . but the dog itself would feel offended (40).

Methodologically, it is important to note that as an experimenter Zeigarnik varied her behavior to complement the attitude brought by the subject. With the conscientious subjects of the first type, she actively expressed wishes—"Yes, I prefer the green beads." With ambitious subjects, she presented an "examiner's face"; and with subjects stimulated by the task itself, she remained passive.

Zeigarnik found that her ambitious subjects were the most likely to remember the uncompleted tasks, and that the task-involved subjects were a close second. The average ambitious subject remembered unfinished tasks with 175 per cent more frequency than completed tasks, as opposed to the over-all average of 90 per cent more frequency. Zeigarnik notes one important qualification to this general tendency. If a subject finds a task is too difficult to perform, and concludes that his abilities are inferior, he is less likely to remember that particular uncompleted task. In forty such instances, only thirteen were remembered—less than half as many as should have been remembered on the average. When the task was crocheting a braid, boys remembered the task even when they could not complete it, but girls who could not crochet experienced some shame and were less likely to remember the task. Zeigarnik believed that repressive forces were operating in such failure experiences, with the subject encapsulating the tension-system of the failed activity so that it was not accessible.

A subsequent experiment by Rosenzweig (41) has reproduced this last effect. Rosenzweig showed that when subjects were exposed to a test situation in which incompletion was experienced as personal failure, the completed tasks were remembered with more frequency. In comparing these results with Zeigarnik's general findings, it is important to note that Zeigarnik's situation was purposely ambiguous and relatively nonthreatening. Only about a third of her subjects interpreted it to be a test situation, and even these subjects remembered the unfinished tasks better—evidently because they did not experience the average interruption as a personal failure.

To summarize: Zeigarnik found that incompleted tasks were remembered more frequently only if the subjects were involved in the tasks. This involvement could occur either by becoming involved in the task for its own sake, or by becoming involved via one's ambitions. The latter type of involvement results in the most frequent recall of incompleted tasks unless the situation is such that the subject experiences interruption as a personal failure.

It is this last qualification that has produced many of the discrepant results in the literature. Some investigators, such as Glixman (42), have purposely attempted to get greater recall for completed tasks by creating a setting in which incompletion would mean personal failure. A typical manipulation is to have a prestigious experimenter tell some subjects that they are "being tested," while a low-prestige experimenter simply asks other subjects to "help the experimenter" decide which items are good. It is postulated that in the first condition, not completing an item will mean failure. The problems of statistical experimentation are evident in the typical experiment of this kind. What subjects are actually experiencing is often completely unclear, and we agree with Sear's judgment (43) that the incompletion technique is an unfortunate way of trying to experimentally provoke feelings of failure.

Since subjects who interpret interruption as a personal failure must have let their ego become involved in the activity, Alper (44) has suggested that the Zeigarnik effect holds when a subject is task involved, but that memory for the completed tasks is better when a subject is ego involved. She has also tried to straighten out the confusing mass of contradictory results by distinguishing between ego and task orientation (45)—whether the experimenter has attempted to establish a condition that will orient the subject towards ego feelings or towards an interest in the task—and ego and task involvement— whether the subject is actually more concerned with ego or task needs.

Alper (46) notes that most investigators (herself included) have produced ego involvement by threatening self-esteem, making the subject feel in danger of being shown up by questioning his capacities or personality, or by threatening the good opinion he has of himself or feels that others have of him. In fact, she suggests that a more accurate term might be "self-esteem involvement." It seems probable that an investigator could also provoke self-esteem involvement by flattery, or getting the subject to show off to the experimenter. In any case, when there is self-esteem involvement, we would expect a better recall for completed tasks.

It is clear that a genuine task involvement will lead to a Zeigarnik effect, that a self-esteem involvement will lead to the reverse effect, and that self-esteem involvement is one type of ego involvement. What is not clear is how other types of ego involvement will affect the recall of tasks. It must be recalled that Zeigarnik's ambitious subjects and Marrow's competitive testing conditions still produced a better recall for the uncompleted tasks. Yet these subjects were hardly interested in the task for its own sake. Therefore, we must return to the complex question of the nature of ego involvement.

Perhaps the clearest distinction between ego and task involvement is the one drawn by Helen Block Lewis (47) in terms of whether or not the ego is in the foreground or background of an activity. When the ego is the focus (the theme) of the activity, the person may be primarily seeking approval or fearing failure. However, when the objective world demands the person's attention, his ego recedes into the background of the activity. As an illustration, Lewis contrasts a child constructing a toy house with continual glances at his parent or teacher with a child "completely and selflessly involved" in an activity. Of course, these activities are experientially quite different activities. Viewed in this way, probably most of Zeigarnik's subjects were not ego involved, although a third of them (and probably all of Marrow's) were motivated by ambition and a competitive spirit.

Lewis points out that a person's needs are much wider than the ego needs of achieving pleasure, reward, status, etc., for the self. These are only some of the needs which a person has. Thus, hedonistic theories of motivation, where a person performs a task to gain reward or avoid punishment—a child reading in order to get a gold star—describe only one possible relationship between person and task. An alternative where the ego is in the background is a child striving to complete a task because he is interested in the task. On still other occasions, a person enters an activity in order to help others or to achieve an ideal. Ego needs may be pushed aside in the interest of the needs of the other or of the ideal—which are included in the person's needs. Thus, a person will often become involved in an activity because of the intrinsic properties of the objective situation which he confronts, rather than because of the needs of his ego.

We are in complete agreement with Lewis on the above points and would only add that part of the objective situation is the be-ing of the individual person. Thus, in addition to ego needs, needs of the task, of others, and of ideals, part of a person's needs are what we might call "own" needs, such as the need to express oneself in one's work.

In fact, as Asch (48) points out, some persons appear task oriented when they are actually engaged in escaping from a genuine challenge that concerns themselves. This would, of course, actually be an ego orientation at the expense of own needs. We believe that such pseudo task-orientation evidences itself both in experience and behavior.

The needs of the ego, as opposed to other needs, is, of course, of great interest in any theory which deals with the functioning of society. Although this takes us beyond the scope of this book, the interested reader may wish to examine Asch's treatment of this problem (49). In passing, we note his view that acute ego centeredness (in Lewis' sense) is not an inherent feature of being a person, but is, rather, a response to the thwarting of needs to be part of a group, to be needed by others, and to know that larger issues unite oneself with others.

When Lewin began to deal with groups and to demonstrate that a group could be studied as a whole in its own right, with many gestalt properties, he and his students showed that many of the dynamic processes observed in individual persons have an important extension to the study of groups. For example, groups get involved in tasks. That is, the members of a group may agree that their group should undertake a task, and this consensus establishes a group goal. Horwitz (50) has shown that when such a task is interrupted, the members of the group will be more apt to remember the task than a task that has been completed. Further, if the group votes to abandon the task, then this affects the individual members so that such tasks are no longer remembered so well. Such effects indicate that an individual's intention-systems may be oriented towards common goals so that cooperative group behavior occurs.

Lewis notes that in order for cooperative behavior to occur, the ego must recede into the background. While an individualist may be highly task involved, and hence able to cooperate in some joint endeavor, individualistic competition puts the ego in the foreground and prevents cooperation. Deutsch's work on the conditions necessary for cooperation gives support for this line of reasoning, and suggests that a member of a cooperative group will accept the action of another group member as substitutable for his own (51). In fact, the observation of Chinese schoolchildren by American psychologists suggest that a culture that encourages cooperation and ego recession can achieve a degree of cooperation and substitutability that is far greater than most individualistic Westerners have imagined possible (52).

In order to demonstrate her points, Lewis created three different conditions for subjects (53). In the first condition, the subjects were ill at ease and concerned about their success (the ego in the foreground). They showed a better memory for completed tasks, which Lewis believes reflected a tendency for ego enhancement, rather than repression of the uncompleted tasks. In the second condition, the subject worked side by side with another subject in a relaxed situation where the experimenter was "finding out something about these materials" that were to be used in a future experiment. Half the tasks were interrupted, and as expected, the Zeigarnik effect was obtained—the interrupted tasks being significantly better remembered.

Finally, in a third condition, Lewis had the subject help another student who was engaged in completing a series of tasks. All the tasks were begun jointly, but in half of them the subject was interrupted by the student, who completed the task herself. In the other half, the student withdrew and let the subject complete the task. In this condition, there was no Zeigarnik effect. The reason is clear—the subjects did not consider the tasks to be uncompleted because it made no difference to them who finished the task. With their ego in the background, they often would not even remember who had completed the work. Notice that in this condition the subject is still involved with the tasks; it is simply that his motivations are such that closure is obtained when the other completes the task.

The only exceptions to the finding that the partner's work could substitute for one's own occurred with tasks which lent themselves to individualistic interpretations. These were tasks where the other person could not really fully complete the task as envisaged by the subject—an example of what we mean by an own as opposed to an ego need.

While Lewis' analysis clarifies the nature of ego involvement, it is still not possible to specify all the conditions under which a subject's desire for ego enhancement will lead to ego involvement and a superior recall for the completed tasks. Certainly this occurs when self-esteem is threatened. On the other hand, there was a superior recall for uncompleted tasks in the case of Zeigarnik's ambitious subjects and in the case of subjects in Marrow's competitive conditions. Possibly these subjects actually became task involved. That is, in spite of the fact that such subjects initially became involved through the ego motives implicit in ambition, competition, need to achieve, and competence testing, the activities may have been performed in such a way that the subject's ego receded to the background. It seems clear that this is an important issue for future investigations.

In spite of the above ambiguity, it is clear that in order to really replicate Zeigarnik's experiment, one must have subjects who come of their own will, are provided with a distinctive set of tasks, and who are in an atmosphere that is involving—but where the task, rather than the ego, will become the focus of attention. Finally, in asking them to recall the tasks, one must encourage an easy narration without getting the subjects involved in an attempt to master a memory test.

Unfortunately, in today's climate it may be difficult to produce these conditions. There is some evidence to suggest that recall for incomplete tasks is less strong in our contemporary Western culture than in the 1920s and 30s (54). If this is so, a possible reason may lie not only in current norms against ambition, but in the more serious malaise of noninvolvement. Certainly many persons today seem to have difficulty in getting involved, and if this is true, it should undoubtedly be reflected in a decline of the Zeigarnik effect.

The issues raised here, the difference between involvement and noninvolvement, and the distinctions between the various types of ego and task involvement, are complex issues which are subtle, and of the utmost importance. It seems clear that in order to produce the Zeigarnik effect, one must be able to create conditions under which subjects as persons are involved and yet as egos are detached. In our contemporary situation, this may be the equivalent of uniting the personal involvement of which the West is justly proud with the ego detachment that has been cultivated by the East.

FOOTNOTES

1. Evelyn Katz, "Some Factors Affecting Resumption of Interrupted Activities by School Children," *Institute of Child Welfare Monogram Series,* No. 16 (University of Minnesota Press, 1938).

2. Kurt Lewin, "The Conceptual Representation and Measurement of Psychological Forces," *Contributions to Psychological Theory* 1 (1938), No. 4.

3. Kurt Lewin, "Intention, Will and Need," in David Rapaport (Ed.), *Organization and Pathology of Thought* (New York: Columbia University Press, 1951), 114.

4. Fritz Heider, "The Gestalt Theory of Motivation," in Marshall R. Jones (Ed.), *Nebraska Symposium on Motivation* (Lincoln, Nebraska: University of Nebraska Press, 1960), 160–161.

5. Ibid., 168–170.

6. Sylvia H. MacColl, "A Comparative Study of the Systems of Lewin and Koffka with Special Reference to Memory Phenomena," *Contributions to Psychological Theory* 2 (1939), 160 ff.

7. James J. Gibson, "A Critical Review of the Concept of Set in Contemporary Experimental Psychology," *Psychological Bulletin* 38 (1941), 781–817, 791. In fact, even within Lewin's particular field theory we can see both types of motivation, and this results in two different uses of the concept of "tension." In his systematic presentations of field theory, Lewin uses tension within the person to induce organization in the environment (*e.g.,* valences), which then places forces (goal directedness) on the person. However, at other times Lewin speaks of tension within the situation, as in his paper on reward and punishment, or as in Dembo's study (Chapter XI). Here the tension stems from opposing forces and is related to structure and structural changes. This perspective is analogous to the organizational tensions of classical gestalt theory, but is theoretically inconsistent with Lewin's main usage.

   It is interesting to note that Alfred Schutz asserts that we have two different ways of understanding our behavior in *The Phenomenology of the Social World* (Evanston, Illinois: Northwestern University Press, 1967). We may say that a person did something in order to accomplish some project—an active dynamic —or we may say that he did something because of some past set of conditions —a passive dynamic. It seems to us that in focusing on conscious intention, Lewin is dealing with the in-order-to motives involved in the projection of future acts. On the other hand, by focusing on how perception is organized, classical gestalt theory is involved with because motivation. Unfortunately, the active character of Lewin's theory is somewhat masked by his use of the mechanical concept tension-system. One of the advantages of treating field theory in a phenomenological way is that this approach reveals the essential active nature of the theory, and ultimately provides a better basis for integration with gestalt theory.

8.   Mary Henle and Gertrud Aull, "Factors Decisive for Resumption of Inter-
      rupted Activities: The Question Reopened," *Psychological Review* 60 (1953),
      81–88.

9.   Ibid., 86.

10.   Jane W. Torrey, "Task Completion as a Function of Organizational Factors,"
      Journal of Personality 18 (1949), 192–205.

11.   Wolfgang Köhler, *Gestalt Psychology* (New York: New American Library,
      1947), 176.

12.   Paul Ricoeur, *Freedom and Nature: The Voluntary and the Involuntary* (Evan-
      ston, Illinois: Northwestern University Press, 1966), 227.

13.   Isidor Chein, *The Science of Behavior and the Image of Man* (New York: Basic
      Books, 1972).

14.   Cf. the analysis of decision-making in Joseph de Rivera, *The Psychological
      Dimension of Foreign Policy* (Columbus, Ohio: Charles E. Merrill, 1968), Chap-
      ter 4.

15.   Alfred Schütz, *Reflections on the Problem of Relevance* (New Haven: Yale
      University Press, 1970).

16.   Anatol Rapoport, *Fights, Games and Debates* (Ann Arbor: University of Mich-
      igan Press, 1960), 259–272.

17.   Sigmund Freud, "Psychopathology of Everyday Life," *The Basic Writings*
      (New York: MOdern Library, 1938), 107.

18.   William James, *The Principles of Psychology* (Dover, 1950) original, 1890, 311.

19.   Isabel Kendig, "Studies in Perseveration: II. Determining Factors in the Devel-
      opment of Compulsive Activity," *Journal of Psychology*, 3(1936), 231–246, data
      on 241.

20.   Leon Festinger, *A Theory of Cognitive Dissonance* (Evanston, Illinois: Row,
      Peterson, 1957).

21.   O. Rank, *Will Therapy and Truth and Reality* (New York: Alfred A. Knopf,
      1945), 21.

22.   Roger Barker, Tamara Dembo, and Kurt Lewin, "Frustration and Regression:
      An Experiment with Young Children," *University of Iowa Studies of Child
      Welfare*, 18 (1941), No. 1. For Lewin's conceptualization of involvement, see
      212–215.

23.   Maria Rickers-Ovsiankina, "Studies on the Personality Structure of Schizo-
      phrenic Individuals: 1. The Accessibility of Schizophrenics to Environment
      Influences," *Journal of General Psychology* (1935), 153–178.

24.   Maria Rickers-Ovsiankina, "Studies on the Personality Structure of Schizo-
      phrenic Individuals: II. Reaction to Interrupted Tasks," *Journal of General
      Psychology* (1935), 179–196.

25.   Pierre Janet, *Psychological Healing* (New York: Macmillan, 1925), I, 660–669.

26.   Chein, *The Science of Behavior and the Image of Man*, 244–249.

27. Norman R. F. Maier, *Psychology in Industry,* 3rd ed. (Boston: Houghton Mifflin, 1965).

28. Kurt Koffka, *Principles of Gestalt Psychology* (New York: Harcourt, Brace and World, 1935), 342–367.

29. Mary Henle, "On Field Forces," *Journal of Psychology* 43 (1957), 239–249, and Gertrude Baltimore *et al.,* "Some Cognitive Aspects of a Motivational Field," Unpublished Masters Thesis (New York: New School for Social Research, 1953).

30. Harvey A. Hornstein, "Promotive Tension: The Basis of Presocial Behavior from a Lewinian Perspective," *Journal of Social Issues* 28 (1972), 191–218.

31. B. Zeigarnik, "Ueber das Behalten von erledigten und unerledigten Handlungen," *Psychol. Forsch.* 9 (1927), 1–85. The complete translation—"The Retention of Completed and Uncompleted Activities"—is available from University Microfilms. A fourteen-page abstraction may be found in Willis E. Ellis (Ed.), *A Source Book of Gestalt Psychology* (London: Routledge and Kegan Paul, Ltd.). This summary is also Bobbs-Merrill reprint P-375.

32. Koffka, *Principles of Gestalt Psychology,* 340.

33. Janet, *Psychological Healing,* 661.

34. A R. Pachauri, "A Study of Gestalt Problems in Completed and Interrupted Tasks," *British Journal of Psychology* 25 (1935), 365–381, 447–457.

35. Alfred Jay Marrow, "Goal Tensions and Recall," *Journal of General Psychology,* 19(1938), 3–64.

36. *Ibid.,* 37–45.

37. Annie Van Bergen, *Task Interruption* (Holland: North-Holland Publishing Company, 1968).

38. Zeigarnik, "Ueber das Behalten," 18 (19 of translation).

39. J. Brown, "Ueber die dynamischen Eigenschaften der Realitäts—und Irrealitätsschicten," *Psychol. Forsch.* 18(1933), 2–26. The translation "On the Dynamic Properties of the Levels of Reality and Unreality" is available from University Microfilms.

40. Zeigarnik, "Ueber das Behalten," 81 (94 of the translation).

41. S. Rosenzweig, "An Experimental Study of 'Repression' with Special Reference to Need-persistive and Ego-defensive Reactions to Frustration," *Journal of Experimental Psychology* 32(1943), 64–74.

42. Alfred F. Glixman, "Recall of Completed and Uncompleted Activities Under Varying Degrees of Stress," *Journal of Experimental Psychology* 39(1949), 281–296.

43. Robert Sears, Chapter in C. P. Stone, *Annual Review of Psychology,* Vol. I (Stanford: Annual Reviews, 1950).

44. Thelma G. Alper, "Memory for Completed and Incompleted Tasks as a Function of Personality: An Analysis of Group Data," *Journal of Abnormal Social Psychology* 41 (1946), 403–420.

45.   Thelma G. Alper, "Task-orientation and Ego-orientation as Factors in Reminiscence," *American Journal of Psychology* 59(1946), 236–248.

46.   Alper, "Memory," 1946; and "The Interrupted Task Method in Studies of Selection Recall: A Re-evaluation of Some Recent Experiments," *Psychological Review* 59(1952), 71–88.

47.   Helen Block Lewis, "An Experimental Study of the Role of the Ego in Work: I. The Role of the Ego in Cooperative Work," *Journal of Experimental Psychology* 34(1944), 113–126.

48.   Solomon E. Asch, *Social Psychology* (Englewood Cliffs, New Jersey: Prentice-Hall, 1952), 312.

49.   *Ibid.*, Chapters 10 and 11.

50.   Murray Horwitz, "The Recall of Interrupted Group Tasks: An Experiment of Individual Motivational Involvement in Relation to Group Goals," *Human Relations* 7 (1954), 3–38.

51.   Morton Deutsch, "A Theory of Cooperation and Competition," and "An Experimental Study of the Effects of Cooperation and Competition Upon Group Process," *Human Relations* 2 (1949), 129–152, 199–232.

52.   Cf. William Kessen, "An American Glimpse of the Children of China: Report of a Visit," *Social Science Research Council Items,* 28(1974 September), 41–44.

53.   Helen Block Lewis and Muriel Franklin, "An Experimental Study of the Role of the Ego in Work: II. The Significance of Task-Orientation in Work," *Journal of Experimental Psychology* 34(1944), 195–215.

54.   Personal communication from Mary Henle.

Chapter V

MENTAL SATIATION*

Anitra Karsten

I. INTRODUCTION TO THE PROBLEM

When one observes a child in a free situation, unfettered by external tasks, one sees a succession of different activities, each one growing out of the preceding activity. Sometimes the activities change rapidly, sometimes slowly. For a while the child plays with a ball, then with a hoop or a doll, then begins

*Translated by Ms. Marsha Horwitz. The original article, "Psychische Sättigung," was published in *Psychologische Forschung,* Vol. 10 (1928), 142–254. Permission to publish this translation was generously granted by Springer-Verlag.

a game of hide and seek with other children. The transition from one activity to another is strongly influenced by the actions of the other children, by the events, and generally by the type of valences which the child encounters. However, even when the child is left to himself, he does not remain for very long at one activity; rather, after a certain time, he tends to go on to other activities.

Physical fatigue can play an important role here—for example, when the child has run around for a long time and wants to rest. Frequently, however, the transition from one game to another is not the product of muscular fatigue. The child has simply had enough of one action, and wants to do something different. Such tiring of an activity is particularly striking in those cases in which the child repeats an action again and again, or demands its performance repeatedly until suddenly the demand for it abruptly turns into aversion.

Miss Goldberg, a doctoral candidate, has been observing such processes with children for a long time, both in free observation and in experimental arrangements. One example she mentions is that of a three-year-old boy who enthusiastically opened and closed a door eighty-two times, and then, during the next two repetitions, revealed a sudden subsiding of enjoyment in this popular activity—after which he could not even be talked into continuing with the play.

Such cases of mental satiation due to the repeated performance of certain actions are also known among adults. In vocational psychology we encounter the problem of work monotony, and it is known that whether a specific action becomes monotonous does not only depend on the character of the action, but also on the relationship between the particular action and the particular individual.

Mental satiation processes also play a large role outside of actual vocational work. They can affect the most diverse actions, commonplace ones such as playing piano, listening to lectures, reading books, and also situations such as socializing with a particular person. Matters of mental satiation are, for example, often a problem in marriage.

The most general condition which we will designate with the term *mental satiation* is the condition in which a particular action or situation initially possesses a positive valence for the person (the action being performed with pleasure, the situation being sought out) and then, with repeated execution, or long duration, the positive valence disappears and is replaced by a neutral condition or a weak negative valence. If in spite of this, one continues to perform the particular action, oversatiation ensues. There is a very close parallel here with processes which show a direct connection to certain needs. For example, actions which are longed for during the hunger state of the need can, in the course of satiation and oversatiation, be rejected to the point of nausea.

An experimental study of mental satiation must first determine the different satiation phenomena and the stages and phases which are observable in the total satiation process. An experimental investigation which is primarily geared to description (Part I of this work) may provide the basis for the discussion of causal dynamic problems. For example, one may consider questions about the relationship between the satiation process and the particular structure of the action, including the action's initial pleasantness or unpleasantness. And one may also examine the general question of the conditions which result in the satiation process or in the specific phenomena of satiation. (Part II of this work deals with some of these questions).

From the experience of satiation in everyday life, one acquires some points which must be considered:

1. The transition from the unsatiated to the satiated condition can occur quite suddenly or very gradually. One must not only consider the moment of satiation, but also the complete process of satiation, including its preliminary and subsequent stages.

2. Satiation can affect a region of actions or situations of a very diverse magnitude. One can be tired of playing a certain étude, of playing études in general, or of playing the piano at all. Indeed, one may have had enough of music, so that one does not want to hear an opera or concert. Questions arise such as whether or not belonging to a specific region is something characteristic of satiation, and if so, how the regions can be delineated, and what determines how large or small a region will become satiated.

The experience of daily life shows that each satiation can be of a different endurance. In some cases, after even a few hours or days the satiation can give way to a new hungering condition for the particular action. In other cases, oversatiation seems to bring a very long term, even a permanent, rejection.

3. Finally, in the experimental investigation of the satiation process, as well as in other psychological investigations, one must keep in mind that actions which are the same externally can have a very different meaning psychologically. Work in vocational psychology shows that the same action can assume a monotonous or a nonmonotonous character according to the prevailing vocational desire of the particular person (1). Therefore, in each individual case, one must pay attention to the specific relation the subject has to the concrete action. Thus, one cannot evaluate an action as simply defined by performance alone; rather, one must consider the significance which the action has for a particular subject in the totality of a particular situation and as a concrete process of events.

4. In order not to extend our problem too far, as much as possible we have attempted to exclude from our investigation the question of fatigue.

The connection between fatigue and mental satiation is, in itself, quite amenable to experimental investigation. In fact, we arranged some preliminary tests. However, it soon became evident that a very complicated and extensive complex of questions exists here, especially since the concept of fatigue has by no means been clarified by physiology (2). In any event, fatigue and mental satiation are not identical. This is obvious from the fact that a condition of oversatiation can continue even after such long pauses—days or weeks—that fatigue can no longer be considered as the cause. Furthermore, there are cases in which satiation is achieved with more difficulty in a state of fatigue than in a state of alertness; for example, when one is somewhat lax and generally indifferent. In other cases, irritability, which increases with fatigue, may lead to a rapid satiation.

In many cases, as we shall see, a clear difference is felt between muscular fatigue and mental satiation—for example, when, in spite of every desire to work, muscular fatigue hampers continuation. On the other hand, fatigue must often be interpreted as a mere symptom of mental satiation.

In experimental investigations of fatigue, reference is sometimes made to a certain mental discomfort which can appear as a complicating factor in fatigue processes. In fact, fatigue experiments (the tests with ergographs, as well as the Kraepelin tests with continuous calculation) can to a certain extent be interpreted as satiation experiments. It may be difficult, especially when one considers the results of our own work, to distinguish between what is due to fatigue and what is due to satiation in the fatigue investigations that have been performed.

Without overlooking the need for a more extensive explanation of these matters, we have interpreted the concept of *fatigue* as essentially *muscular fatigue,* and have attempted to eliminate the problem of muscular fatigue in so far as it was possible.

5. A further limitation on our work stems from the necessity of beginning our experimental investigation of such a large problem area with a definite, specific case. We did not proceed from the sensory blunting of impressions, nor from the state of having enough of certain situations (such as the continuous company of a particular person, or long work on a difficult mathematical problem) but, rather, from the satiation of certain repeatable actions, which themselves only lasted a short time. We must rely on future investigations to show the extent to which our results have more general significance.

In extensive preliminary experiments, we strove to become oriented to the satiation process as manifested in quite diverse actions, pleasant and unpleasant, manual and intellectual, playful and serious. A number of these actions are mentioned in Section II; however, space limitations prohibit an extensive description of satiation in each of these different activities. For quantitative questions, we have limited ourselves to the description of satiation in only two activities—sketching or drawing figures, and reading poetry.

II. THE EXPERIMENTAL METHOD

The Situation

The problem of satiation essentially concerns a question of the inclination of the subject to perform certain actions or to remain in specific situations. It is primarily a question of the movement of inclination or disinclination, and only secondarily a question of shifts in the ability to perform.

Because of this, we did not usually create a strictly defined work situation: for example, we did not prescribe at the outset a definite number of repetitions. Rather, breaking off depended on the inner desires of the subject, and thus was determined to a great extent by his will. The tests could have been arranged so that task-free situations were created—ones in which specific actions would only have been suggested by means of the situation. The work would then only be indirectly influenced by the experimenter in so far as he selected the situation, the milieu in which the test took place. It is possible to investigate satiation processes through such means (3). However, we wished to use the spontaneous breaking off by the subject as our main criterion of satiation. The moment of this breaking off does not only depend on the degree of satiation, but also, naturally, on the strength of the forces which urge the subject to continue. Therefore, we could only use the moment of breaking off as a criterion of satiation, to the extent that the forces to continue were at least approximately equivalent in the various cases. In very free situations, it is very difficult to make any precise determination of this factor.

Therefore, we finally used *semi-free situations* in which the subject is given a task, but allowed to break it off whenever he wishes. For example, we gave the following instruction: "Do the work as long as you enjoy it. When you no longer want to do it, you may stop."

Such an instruction, no matter how it is formulated, is never understood in the same way by the various subjects. Therefore, great weight was not placed upon the literal instructions. Rather, we wanted subjects, who began with different opinions, to receive on the basis of a conversation with the experimenter a rather uniform picture of what the experimenter expected of them, and what was left up to their own preference.

In fact, the subjects did not tend to follow their first desire to break off, either because of the total situation (which fundamentally pressed for work), or because of their ambition, or because of certain views the subjects held about the will of the experimenter. On the other hand, occasionally there occurred chance impulses to stop that were unrelated to the situation.

For quantitative comparison, it would seem theoretically relevant to designate as a *satiation point,* that moment, or that phase, in which the action or situation is just relinquishing its pleasant or neutral character and is assuming a negative valence. If this satiation point is to lead to an actual breaking off by the subject, the total situation would have to be as free of other forces as possible: in any event, there should no longer be any factors pressing for continuation. However, in a situation relatively free of forces apart from the satiation process, every small chance force will be felt relatively strongly. Thus, in reality, chance, and, therefore, invisible factors would play an unduly large role. Apart from the technical difficulties of producing force free situations, this theoretical consideration led us to not choose the neutral satiation point, but rather a somewhat later stage, the phase of light oversatiation. The degree of oversatiation at which the subject breaks off the action, depends on the strength of the pressure in the direction of continuing the work—a strength which is exerted on the subject by the whole situation, including the behavior of the experimenter.

We proceeded so that the experimenter left the breaking off expressly to the subject himself, but adjusted his behavior so that a certain weak pressure remained on the subject not to break off too quickly. This pressure could naturally be formed with various degrees of strength, and was chosen in its strongest form in a series of preliminary tests during which we aimed for oversatiation (see the later example of Subject D). In the main experiment, on which the quantitative results are primarily based, the pressure on the subject was significantly less. To achieve exactly the right amount of pressure, the behavior towards each individual subject had to be somewhat different, depending on the attitude the subject naturally had. Sometimes, care had to be taken that he did not excessively force himself to continue in spite of satiation. At other times, an overly-relaxed cessation had to be corrected by a gentle pressure to continue. The influence of the experimenter essentially took the form of questions, such as: "Don't you like it anymore?" "Are you finished already?" "Perhaps you want to try a little more?" The reaction of an individual subject to these questions clearly revealed the degree to which he rejected the satiated work.

Naturally, the pressure on the subjects to continue, and the degree of satiation were not exactly alike in the various cases. Moreover one might object that this procedure left far too much to the timing of the experimenter. In this regard, we maintain that the task of producing situations which are dynamically similar can best be performed when the experimenter intrudes according to the circumstances, rather than by following strict formulas. Certainly, the experimenter must support his judgment of the inner state of the subject, and not only on the basis of outlining the circumstances, but also on the basis of the subject's reactions to probing remarks made by the experimenter.

This is not to say that no definite objective criterion can be decided upon; the results of our work may open up prospects for this.

Questions of quantitative exactitude are really problems of degree. In accordance with our basic idea that in the investigation of a new area qualitative examination should take precedence over quantitative, we have kept quantitative analysis to a minimum.

The experiments were arranged in two different ways: Sometimes one prescribed task was repeated until satiation (spontaneous breaking-off), while at other times, an activity was only repeated a few times before being changed for another activity. In these later cases, the instructions for the various activities were given before satiation, with order to discontinue when the subject had had enough of the whole series of activities. Either the experimenter gave absolutely definite instructions—forbidding any outside preoccupations (such as playing with objects on the table, singing, or smoking), and forbidding any large alterations in the structure of the task (such as drawing circles instead of strokes, singing instead of reciting poetry)—or the subject was allowed complete freedom in carrying out of task, without being restricted by the experimenter in any way.

Introspection, Spontaneous Reactions, and Observation of Behavior

Since satiation usually entails a relatively long process, often lasting for hours, it has been necessary to include the subject's spontaneous reactions during the experiment, as well as his personal observations as told afterwards.

When a subject's behavior was generally inscrutable, questions about his thoughts had to be asked. However, the silent subject was not compelled to reveal his thoughts, as this might have influenced the satiation process too much. Often, when the subject was hard at work, carefully worded inducements to talk did not disturb the course of the particular activity. This was particularly successful when the experimenter had won the confidence of the subject, and was regarded as an integral part of the total situation rather than as some sort of external enemy.

On the whole, introspection had to be considered within the framework of the subject's general behavior, as reflected in his movements, his friendly or hostile reactions to the measures of the experimenter, and his spontaneous utterances.

The manner of work, its quality and quantity of errors, alterations, tempo, and so forth, must be regarded as parts of the subject's general behavior. When the activity brings about visible results, as in the case of drawing, the general character of the work may lead to some obvious conclusions.

The experiments were carried out during the years 1924–1926 with fifty adults (4). Most of these were students, although three were unemployed. The subjects were, in general, ignorant of the ultimate aim of the experiment.

I should like to thank Professor Kurt Lewin for his unfailing help and advice, Professor Kurt Koffka for useful hints, and Mr. F. Hoppe for his assistance during the experiments.

The Activities

The tasks can be divided into three types of activities:

1. Continuous activities such as drawing, or turning a wheel.

2. Activities which come to an end but must be repeated, such as reading a short poem or drawing an inkspot. When such an activity is repeated very many times it may, in the end, acquire the character of a continuous activity.

3. Activities which go on for a long time but eventually come to an end, such as playing chess. Activities of this kind proved unsuitable for our purposes, as the special nature of the activity came to play too great a role.

Activities frequently mentioned later are described here in detail. Examples of continuous activities:

1. Small vertical or horizontal strokes had to be drawn on sheets of foolscap. Either single strokes had to be drawn continuously, or some sort of rhythm had to be maintained—such as three strokes alternating with five. In many experiments, after one rhythm was satiated, the subject was changed to another rhythm until he was thoroughly fed up with every sort of rhythmic stroke-drawing.

2. The thimble-game. Hollow pegs had to be put into holes. Either they had to be placed one after the other as long as the subject desired to continue, or else the board had to be filled as quickly as possible.

3. A large light wheel had to be turned.

Activities which came to an end include:

4. Reading poems. Short poems were to be read aloud or recited by heart. Poems by Heine, Goethe, Schiller, Morgenstern, and Klopstock were used.

5. Drawing. Drawings were to be copied, prescribed patterns to be continued, objects to be drawn. Free drawing was also a permissible activity, with or without instructions from the experimenter.

6. The godfly game—nagging games that tested the subject's patience. Numbers, letters, or specified shapes were to be formed out of small pieces of variously shaped paper, such as triangles and squares.

7. Stick and ball games. Little interesting sticks and balls had to be made into various shapes.

8. Colored pieces of paper had to be stuck on a sheet of paper to resemble certain figures which were prescribed by the experimenter.

III. EXAMPLES OF THE PROCESS OF SATIATION

Before giving a systematic survey of the phenomena appearing in the satiation process, we will describe several concrete examples of the course of the process. A fairly comprehensive description is necessary in order to obtain a clear picture of satiation. For instance, heavy satiation is relatively disrupted, showing a swift mixing and confusing of various different phenomena. Therefore, too peremptory a schematization would give an overly simple picture of the course of the process, without giving an adequate representation of the opposing forces and their development.

For an example of the satiation process, we have chosen the relatively neutral and boring task of drawing strokes, mainly because of the opportunity it provides to review all the different phases of the process. Later, we shall augment the characteristic peculiarities of this particular satiation process by examples from other activities.

[*I have omitted the first of Karsten's two examples (Subject D) and Figures 1–7 and 21–25. This material supports Karsten's statements, but it does not add other insights. The text may be obtained from University Microfilms and the figures from the original article. Karsten shows that, as Subject D continues to draw strokes on the page, she begins to vary the nature of the strokes. These variations, which represent the beginnings of satiation, often occur spontaneously, without the subject's planning them. As satiation proceeds, the subject's behavior begins to disintegrate and the units of behavior (for example, a line of strokes) lose their coherence. Karsten wonders whether the variation of the activity postpones satiation or is a sign of satiation, and whether the final disintegration of the activity (the subject cannot draw any more strokes) is due to muscular fatigue or mental satiation—Editor.*]

We first had a specific action performed to the point of complete satiation. The examiner then gave the subject a new task which involved a substantially more extensive change than any of the variants which had been used by the subject. However, this new action was not completely different in its nature, but was, on the whole, in the same action region. In our example, the subject was satiated on the activity of hatching in the rhythm 3,5—and then given the new task of hatching in the rhythm 4,4. We selected this second task so that the identical muscles had to be used in the most identical way possible. (In both cases, it was a question of the same muscular actions, that is, drawing short, vertical strokes.) This second task was also to be performed to the point of satiation. It was followed by additional tasks of the same nature: drawing strokes in different rhythms until the subject refused to take on any further hatching tasks.

Even then the question of which region of actions was satiated remained open. How would the subject react towards actions which deviated by one step from the previous actions? Therefore, we gave him new tasks: drawing a continuous figure, "copying objects," and so on.

(Here we are dealing with causal-dynamic questions only in so far as they can be answered on the basis of the qualitative course of action. For the meaning of the quantitative results, see Part 2.)

In the case of subject Tr., the satiation process displays the phenomena observed in the first example. Even their distribution throughout the total course of action corresponds to a great extent to the events in the first example.

Again variations appear very soon (Fig. 8) and at the beginning are frequently spontaneous. At first the subject does the hatching conscientiously. Line 1 began with a group of three, and since the line ends with a group of three, the next line will begin with a group of five. This alteration in the outsets of the lines continues spontaneously. The subject only becomes aware of the pattern in the sixth or seventh line, and since he likes it, he continues it consciously.

In this example, other variations are greatly influenced by the fact that mistakes occur quickly. The subject errs for the first time in line 8, and then errs three times between lines 8 and 15. He says that errors occur primarily when he is thinking of something else. He corrects the errors, but then has a defensive attitude towards them. This strongly affects his over-all behavior in this stage of the process. For example, this was a factor when the subject complained that he always forgot what group to begin the new line with. (In reality, he only made one error of this type, in the twelfth line.) The lines began to tend upward towards the right in a somewhat slanted fashion. The subject even tried once, in the eighth line, to suppress this slant. Then he started a new line (16) with the intention of making the lines completely horizontal, and the strokes "beautiful." (We must leave open the question of the extent to which a tendency for variation is having an effect in addition to the struggle against errors.)

But this struggle against the willfullness of the work was not successful for long. In the seventeenth line, errors again appeared in the groups. The subject wanted to correct them, but for the first time the error had quite a striking and ugly effect.

This greatly annoyed him, and at the same time, the work became increasingly worse until we find connections between the lines and other signs of careless hatching at line 26.

An increase in tempo appeared in this page of the test. As is typical, this increase in tempo at first happened of itself, and was then consciously taken on and continued. At the same time, this occurred in a form which gave the whole task a new meaning: "I want to see how fast I can hatch." This restruc-

Task   Line

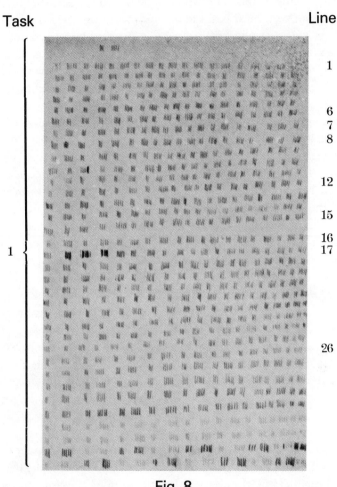

Fig. 8

FIGURE 8. Subject TR. First day. Task: To mark strokes in the rhythm 3/5.

turing of the task into a speed test led to a whole series of new experiences.
The rhythm became more pronounced. An accompanying action appeared, the
subject counted out loud, "1, 2, 3; 1, 2, 3, 4, 5; 1, 2, 3." The set for speed became
so central that the alternate starting of the lines with a group of three and then
of five was given up. It was very striking how with this change of meaning the
work was again performed beautifully, neatly, and precisely (line 26).

Of course, this neat performance did not last very long (only about three
lines); then it again became worse and the strokes of the line became rather
thick "of themselves." After this, the subject intentionally drew the next line
as thinly as possible. Here he was already introducing a conscious variation.
Alterations soon follow one another more quickly than before; the last two
lines of the page have thick group pairs following thin group pairs. At the end
of the page, which took twenty minutes, the subject looked from the sheet to
the experimenter without saying anything. Then the experimenter turned the
paper over. The subject did not follow this suggestion happily, and tried to
transfer the responsibility for stopping or continuing to the experimenter: "If
you want me to work for a specific length of time I'll do it, of course."

Figure 9 gives a picture of the manifold variations which then set in and
which we will not describe in detail. As in Example 1, it was confirmed that
the variety of variations is substantially greater in this later stage of satiation
than in the initial stage. The patterns introduced finally became artificial and
farfetched (e.g., the last third of the page). In fact, the subject was consciously
looking for new patterns. The original rhythm 3,5; 3,5 was really given up
completely. The actual construction of the action is, for example, on line 23:
1, 2; 2, 1, 2; 2, 1, 2 etc.. The task set by the experimenter was only outwardly
fulfilled. Just as in Example 1, the subject actually only obeyed the instructions
pro forma. He had actually already given up the correct fulfillment of the task,
but in such a hidden form that his behavior somehow satisfies the demands.
But he is not yet aware of his giving up; he is not yet in the stage of rebellious
resistance.

It is interesting that often the variations which the subject hit upon proved
to be uncomfortable during performance. On line 18, for example, the subject
suddenly began alternately to draw the strokes in an upward and then in a
downward direction. Likewise, the rhythm of 3 strokes weak, 5 strokes strong
(line 1) proved so uncomfortable that it had to be quickly given up.

However, it is not only discomfort which leads to alterations. This becomes
particularly clear in the phase during which conscious looking for new patterns
begins. The subject felt the tendency "to do something else." "Change in itself
is fun for me." (Moreover, in this first case, even the consideration of how one
can change the pattern was sufficient to cause a spontaneous switching of the
pattern. Later, as we have said, direct seeking of new patterns became a

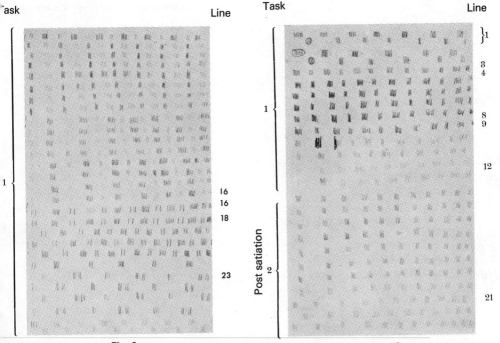

Fig. 9

Fig. 10

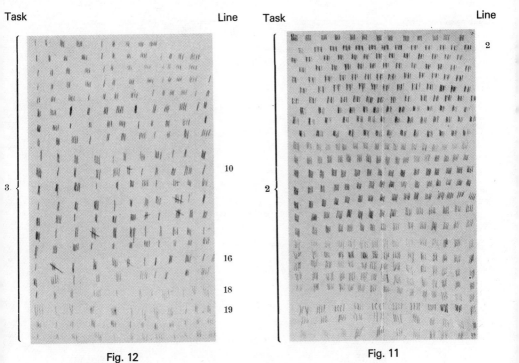

Fig. 12

Fig. 11

FIGURES 9–20. Subject TR. First day. Tasks 1–15: Strokes in different rhythms followed by drawing.

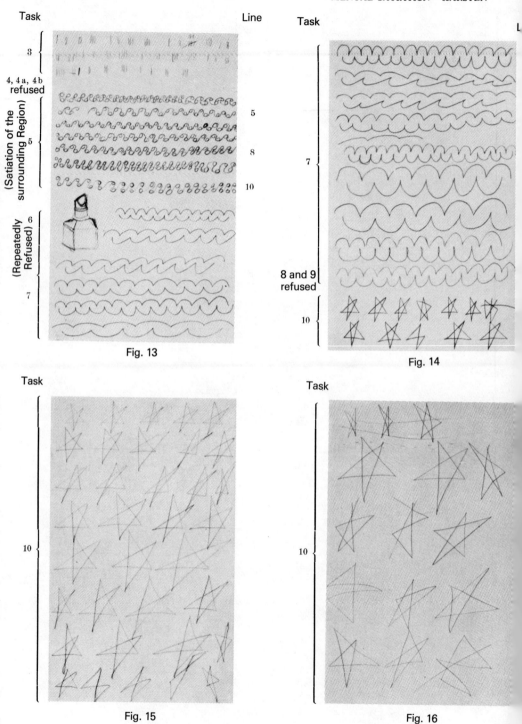

Fig. 13

Fig. 14

Fig. 15

Fig. 16

Task

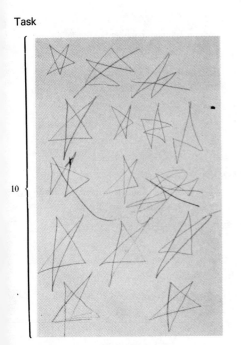

10 {

Fig. 17

Task

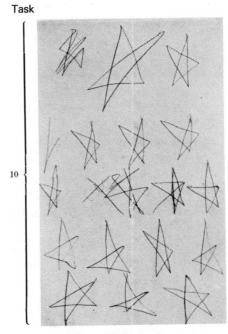

10 {

Fig. 18

Task

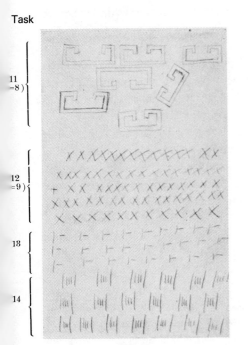

11
=8)

12
=9)

13

14

Fig. 19

Task

15

Fig. 20

necessity.) With the urge for change of any sort, the subject at times fell into patterns which at an earlier stage had proved to be too uncomfortable (*e.g.*, on line 9). Such patterns could now be executed in a surprisingly smooth fashion and without errors (lines 9–16, almost three minutes).

Page 2, moreover, fully shows the influence of unit boundaries on the appearance or lack of variations. The uniform placing of the groups of three and five (to a certain degree beneath one another) was substantially determined by the total configuration of the page. It is very clear how the line proves to be the completely dominant unit. The transition to a new variation does not occur within a line, but almost exclusively at the start of a new one.

The second page took somewhat less time (15 minutes and 15 seconds) than the first page (20 minutes). After the total time of 35 minutes and 15 seconds the subject had had enough, but a slight suggestion by the experimenter was still sufficient to get him to start the third page.

At the close of the second page, the subject had begun a completely new kind of variation, distributing the groups of three and five on two different lines, rather like a checkerboard. He continued in this manner, and at the same time introduced an additional alteration which was outwardly very coarse: he surrounded the group of three with a circle. He was told not to do this. However, by now the subject was no longer simply obeying, and he drew an additional circle, observing: "Why can't I do it anymore? It is more pleasant when I do."

In the third line, the subject again tried to exert great effort to draw "beautifully," but he no longer was able to continue neatly to the end of the line. The strokes again became connected and thick.

Faced with the blatant succumbing of his good intentions to the willfulness of the work the subject became furious: he drew thick strokes, and no longer worried about the experimenter's forbidding him to connect the strokes or about the disintegration of the gestalt (lines 4–8).

Finally, he tried a new way of drawing strokes for the last time (line 9). He made the strokes "very fine" to save his hand which was very "tired." After a small improvement in the work, the subject made many mistakes; sometimes he crossed out the mistakes more or less angrily, and no longer with the intention of correcting them. Only the initial figures of the line remained relatively orderly to the end.

After one hour and ten minutes (line 12) the subject refused, with great determination, to continue hatching in the rhythm 3, 5. (Thus, the last half-page took 35 minutes; the subject worked very slowly here and with many long pauses.)

Post-satiation (Fig. 10, problem 2 to Fig. 13, problem 4C). In accordance with what was said above, the experimenter now presented a new task to which the subject agreed without any great resistance, and which he began after a few introspective statements. The task was to hatch in the rhythm 4, 4. Although when each part is viewed seperately, this action consists of the same parts as the former action, the first eight lines (1 minute and 25 seconds after the beginning of post-satiation) were carried out completely in order, and without any substantial variation. The same strokes, drawn with the same muscles, which so recently had presented a picture of complete disintegration of the gestalt with crookedly and slantedly executed strokes, were now performed neatly and correctly as parts of the new task. The short interval between the preceeding action and the new action cannot be credited with having caused fatigue to subside, because during the slow period of the first action—especially in the last part—intervals of at least the same length occurred without the appearance of such a recovery effect. This shows that the transition to the new task must be considered as the deciding factor. Moreover, not every interval has the psychological character of a pause.

In the course of the second task, the same phases appeared as in the first task and approximately in the same sequence. The only difference was that the individual phases followed one another much more rapidly. On the ninth line (line 21 of the third page), mild variations became noticeable, but very soon (line 2 of page 4, after 1 minute and 55 seconds, Fig. 11) very pronounced types of variations appeared. At the same time, the subject, by the structure of the action, let himself be led into error—several times on line 2, 5 lines were drawn instead of 4—and the experimenter had to call attention to this. After a short period of improvement, a distinct gestalt disintegration of even the individual strokes occurred (at the end of the page). After 20 minutes and 20 seconds (one hour, 35 minutes and 20 seconds since the start of the experiment), the subject refused to continue the action.

Then the experimenter gave the instructions for a third task: hatch in the rhythm 1, 2, 3, 4; 1, 2, 3, 4, which was again accepted without resistance. Although the transition took place this time without pause, the strokes were suddenly drawn in a straight and neat fashion again. (Compare the obvious difference between the last lines in Fig. 11 and the first line in Fig. 12.) To be sure, errors were frequently made from the start. Very quickly the subject no longer concerned himself with correcting the errors, but simply and crudely crossed them out. In line 18 (21 minutes, 20 seconds to 26 minutes, 35 seconds), the subject drew for the first time with his left hand, thereby transferring to another group of muscles, without essentially improving his performance. The following return to the right hand (line 19) revealed no clear recovery. Only the last group on the page (like the last group on the preceding page) was performed neatly. It is noteworthy that the subject paid less attention to the end of the individual lines on this page than he did elsewhere. The action was continued on the ninth page (Fig. 13) for only three lines. Then the subject resorted, as a variant, to a very artificial way of holding the pencil. The subject then broke off, completely exhausted, in the middle of the line. (The third task lasted 30 minutes, 10 seconds.)

The gestalt disintegration of the individual strokes was not as clear this time as it had been previously.

The subject refused to do any other tasks with stroke rhythms (Task 4, 4a, 4b). The entire activity of drawing strokes lasted 105 minutes, 10 seconds.

Satiation of the surrounding region, Fig. 13; task 5, to Fig. 20. After the satiation of the first task, the subject willingly accepted the second task. The repeated performance then led to satiation of this action too, and in a considerably shorter time. In making the transition to the new, third, stroking task the subject was still willing on the whole, but from the start errors appeared frequently. (Of course it is possible that the rhythm 1, 2, 3, 4 was somewhat more difficult than 3, 5 and that this played a role.) After satiation of this task, however, the subject no longer agreed to the introduction of a new variation of the same sort as those between task 1 and 2, 2 and 3. He has had altogether enough of hatching to a certain rhythm.

The question now is whether the satiation was limited solely to the action region of hatching, or if it reached over into other regions. How would the subject react to an even greater degree of variation? The experimenter immediately gave instructions for a new task, which had certain characteristics related to hatching—for example, drawing with the pencil—but which was on the whole completely different. The task was to copy certain continuous patterns.

The experimenter drew the figure each time with words: "Do you want to draw this figure? You can draw as long as you want to."

Fifth task—First figure, figure 13. The subject began the work very happily; in general, he liked to draw very much. (What is described below was also typically evident with subjects who did not like to draw.) Apparently such drawing of designs was neither affected by the preceding satiation process, nor, as far as could be seen from the subject's first reaction, had it been clearly co-satiated. However, very quickly, satiation symptoms also became evident with this figure. The figure was not very difficult in itself, although the first line was drawn incorrectly and only in the second line (fifth on the page) was the correct execution begun. But it began to be scattered in irregular, deviating variations which clearly give the impression of gestalt disintegration (lines 8–10).

Now within the drawing of the figures there began a similar play as occurred within the hatching. Variations and gestalt disintegration were followed by satiation, whereupon the experimenter went over to a new task which the subject took on more or less gladly: at first drawing an ink-well (Fig. 13) and then a double wavy line, in which variations as well as Gestalt disintegration clearly become evident (Fig. 13–14). When the change became too great, under the pressure to do as much as possible as quickly as possible (Fig. 14, line 5), it was forbidden by the experimenter. The subject got hold of himself and performed good work, but he did not stand the pressure to work neatly for long. Even before the end of the page, he suddenly stopped although on the whole he found the figure beautiful to draw. Then the subject had enough of drawing patterns—two similar suggested patterns were rejected—yet he was still prepared to draw pentagrams in a continuous line (task 6).

The first figures were executed very neatly and well, but, very quickly, symptoms of satiation appeared, and, in this case, in a particularly instructive form. Even in the first and second line mistakes were made. In Figures 15 and 16, the performance becomes more and more disordered. At the same time, the tendency observed in the first example to fill in a line, and finally a whole page with as few figures as possible was clearly evident. (Note the step by step progress in this regard.) At this time, the division by lines, very clear at first, was lost. On page 5 and 6 (Figures 17 and 18), it can hardly be noticed.

Besides errors, gestalt disintegration gradually appeared and the execution becomes forced. This must be stressed all the more, because at first drawing figures was regarded by the subject as a direct relief from hatching. It is also noteworthy that the figures were not disagreeable to the subject and that he did not draw them carelessly for this reason. On the contrary, the subject still found them quite pleasant to draw; he struggled in vain against his inability. At the same time, outbursts of anger occurred more and more frequently, together with angry crossing out and simple scribbling. After such emotional outbursts, a certain recovery occurred with extraordinary regularity.

With the satiation of the pentagram figure at the end of Figure 18 (where, by the way, there was again good performance at the end), a reversal in the whole behavior of the subject took place. Through instructions for a new drawing task, the meaning of drawing was shifted in the direction of "What kind of figures will I get?" The subject was anxious for new patterns. After the satiation of the pentagram, the meandering design which he had previously rejected now occurred to him (task II), and he began spontaneously, without instructions, to draw this pattern (Figure 19). Even with this personally chosen pattern, variations and satiation occurred very quickly.

The next tasks—12, 13, 14, and 15—again assigned by the experimenter were carried out very neatly, but, especially since the experimenter forbade pronounced variations, they were only performed for a very short time. The subject had reached the point where he simply stopped doing the task when the experimenter warned him against variations. The last figure (Figure 20) was not even carried out for a complete line. At the top of the page, in the middle of the line, the subject stopped. These figures were boring to him: by now his drawing had suffered so much, that he was not even prepared to draw somewhat more prettily.

Now after two and a half hours, the relatively large region of figure drawing —drawing the figures of the types descussed above—was also satiated.

It is noteworthy that, in a fashion analogous to the typically good concluding performances within each figure, the whole process was characterized by particularly good and neat performances shortly before the end. The subject spontaneously went over to drawing a task which had been rejected before, and even the following figures were carried out extremely neatly, without gestalt disintegration or emotional outbursts, albeit only for a short time.

At this point there was a transfer to a completely heterogenous action, namely to reading poems by Heine and Goethe. We will not go into the details of this activity. Here, too, satiation finally occurred with phenomena which were analogous in particular, as well as in general, to those just discussed.

Our example, in its qualitative course, shows clearly that we are, in fact, dealing with mental satiation. Muscular fatigue may also have played a part to a certain degree, but it cannot be considered here as the decisive factor. The transfer from the right hand to the left brought no substantial alleviation. (Although one could also conceive of a co-fatigue.) Most important, the satiation was no longer present, or in any event no longer present in the same degree, as soon as the subject transferred to a new action, even though it consisted of muscularly identical operations. (We will return to the connection between satiation and fatigue later.)

The satiation phenomena in this second example, show extensive correspondence with those of our first example. Therefore, we will not systematically compare the phenomena of the two examples separately, but rather will include them in a general survey of all the satiation phenomena which occurred in the various activities that we used.

IV. PHENOMENA OCCURRING DURING THE SATIATION EXPERIMENTS

Naturally, not every satiation process contains all the phenomena described here. First, we will discuss the more superficial factors and then gradually go on to those which are dynamically more fundamental.

1. Division of the Action into Subunits

The tasks in our experiments predominantly consisted of continuous actions. Even of the tasks which had ends to begin with—reciting poems, game of gadfly, and so on—some changed into continuous actions through the constant repetitions. Nevertheless, the work tended to show distinct divisions into units and subunits of various magnitude.

Figured unities. In the example given above, hatching, the page tended to play an important part as a unit. Each page presents a rather uniform configuration, although they deviate noticeably from one another. Subjects at times rejected an attractive new variation in design in order not to spoil the uniformity of the page. Often the pages were framed by similar initial and concluding signs. The last, as well as the first, lines or figures on a page were frequently performed especially well.

In the total behavior of the subject, the significance of the page as a unit of work also was frequently expressed. For example, one subject would not relinquish a fountain pen which was almost empty before the page was finished. Only when beginning a new page, did he accept the pencil offered by the experimenter. At points of light satiation, the subjects gladly break off right after completing a page.

The individual lines, too, usually appeared at first as rather distinct subunits during hatching. Before satiation, as in the case of whole pages, the lines were carefully carried out to the edge of the page. Within this smaller subunit, the beginning and end were frequently performed better than the middle. Apart from the times of greatest satiation, attention was paid to at least completing the line before breaking off. Also, at first, variations tended only to appear at the beginning of a new line.

In drawing, as long as it was a question of continuous patterns, the line played a very important part, as, for example with the variations shown in Figures 13 and 14. Page and line were much less important in the case of individual figures. Frequently, new distinct unities were formed from the particular structure of the specific figures (*e.g.* clumps of hexagons). The individual figures were always completed, except at times of greatest satiation. If the performance was so poor and hopeless that it was left unfinished, the subject tried to get rid of it to a certain extent by crossing it out. With the gadfly task, and the thimble, the particular tasks (*e.g.*, a board filled with thimbles) formed the natural subunits of the process.

Connections of Meaning; Action Unities. In reciting poems, the strophes form unities: their unity is apparent in uniform stress, in pauses, new starts, and so on. To a certain extent the lines of the strophes are their subunits. Essentially, however, in the reading of poems, at least at the start of the experiment, the poetry was recited in accordance with its content; the pauses were not made at the end of the lines.

Besides these meaning unities which, in the case of the poems, grow out of the specific nature of the action material, more or less distinct unities of meaning are present within the action process of all activities, and are of great significance for the course of the process. The action can have the meaning:

"Follow those requirements which I have agreed to as a subject." Implied in the term "psychological experiment," for the subject there is often something mysterious, curiosity arousing, and, at the same time, something which concerns his own ego. The action, can suddenly acquire the meaning of a speed test for the subject. The tempo can become faster by itself, and the subject takes on this getting faster, thereby changing the whole meaning of the test suddenly so that he now tries to achieve a high-speed performance. Such meaning contexts can cause distinct structuring with specific subunits in the action process. For example, if the change of the meaning of the work into a speed action means a pronounced break, new subunits frequently occur. Thus, one subject, within a series of thimble tasks, tried to execute a crescendo to the point of fastest performance, then he dropped off in speed, only to attempt a new record by filling out the board with a new start which he hoped would surpass the old one.

Such contexts of meaning often are connected with the genuine needs, actual will goals, and deeper strata of the person, and play a considerable role in all of our work. (We will have many other examples of this to mention.)

The structuring of the action unities becomes still more apparent by the fact that the conclusion of larger units (*e.g.*, the pages in hatching) is underscored by distinct concluding actions. Such concluding actions appear in many different forms. One subject finished the page somewhat spontaneously with his signature. Other subjects used an energetic stroke as a concluding action. Another placed the book energetically on the table with the words "Period, concluded, done!" Another subject, after finishing the thimble game, shoved the board away. There are all sorts of degrees of intensity in such concluding actions, ranging from merely looking up from the work at the experimenter to emotion—angry crossing out of the whole page with hard strokes to even standing up and walking out of the room. Emotional outbursts occurred with particular ease after the conclusion of such large action unities, and then, although they naturally did not merely represent a concluding action, they frequently had something of this concluding character. Furthermore, even the simple concluding actions frequently not only had a concluding character, but also the significance of erecting a dividing wall between the subjects and the finished action which they were about to place aside.

2. Gestalt Disintegration

Figure Disintegration. With increasing satiation, a process becomes evident which can be characterized as a disintegration of the action unities. The larger unities, such as the pages in hatching, begin to become confused, and finally to break up into independent smaller parts, consisting only of individual lines or short groups of lines.

The smaller unities,—for example, the lines—are also affected by this disintegration. If variations only began at the start of new lines, now they are begun in the middle of the line. Even with the individual patterns the disintegration does not stop. Parts of the design which were initially completely dependent can acquire independent life.

For example, a figure that consists of circles connected to each other by curved lines can disintegrate into circles and independently curving lines. The following case shows the fashion in which subunits can become independent main sections, decisive for the action process: After drawing circles, for his next pattern, the subject was to draw triangles made out of ten circles arranged like ten-pins. At the start of the experiment, this design doubtlessly would have been interpreted as a completely new assignment, a different type of action. By the stage of gestalt disintegration, however, the subject rejected the design because it again consisted of nothing but circles.

Thus, the work was not only less orderly, looser, with less definite borders and conclusions, but it really had disintegrated into nothing but independent pieces, these no longer comprised dependent parts of more comprehensive unities, but stood next to each other unconnected, as a mere total of sum (5). It may be that such simplifications to more primitive, less detailed and organized unities, occur as part of the satiation effect, just as they develop during the first performance of a new action under the tendency for the smoothest action process that is possible.

We will illustrate the extent to which this break-up of originally larger unities happens in the case of the thimble game.

In the beginning of this task, filling of the one board with pegs has the significance of an action unity. With increasing satiation, the total action disintegrates into filling out individual rows, or groups of holes such as the upper, middle, or bottom rows of the board. At the same time, the borders between the successive board units become blurred. Frequently, a change occurs from the finite action of "fill each board" to the continuous action, "stick in one thimble after the other." Thus, the disintegration of the original larger unities (the boards), through the blurring of their borders, leads to a course of events which is superfically much more comprehensive—in other words, to a process which could at first seem to be an enlargement of the action unit.

But, as the satiation continues to progress, this continuous action, which at first runs in a relatively uniform flow, tends to disintegrate into nothing but very little actions, each with its own end: stick in one thimble, plus stick in one thimble, plus stick in one thimble, and so on. The action disintegrates into individual parts which no longer even show the character of a continuous action.

The breakup of the action can progress still further: finally the individual motions necessary to "pick up the thimble from the table" and "to insert it in the board" are performed separately. In a similar fashion, hatching can disintegrate into individual actions of: "take up the pencil correctly," and "draw the second stroke." In such a stage of disintegration, nothing at all remains of the original task, whether it be drawing figures, hatching in rhythm, or the thimble game. The significance of the task has been lost. In its place meaningless and difficult muscle movements appear. Especially characteristic of this stage of satiation is the loss of meaning of the task which we will discuss more fully below.

When the task loses meaning (meaning disintegration). As an example, we shall describe the course of events in a task in which meaningful material in the strict sense was involved—specifically, repeated recitation of a poem. The subject said about the first stage of the test that mere reading was impossible for him, that he would try really to "recite." In the process, each new repetition resulted in a different interpretation; different words or lines stood out each time, and new aspects of the meaning of the poem were continually found. At the same time, "reading" completely receded into the background. It was not the recitation, but rather, the content of the poem itself which constantly appeared in a different light. "Making new discoveries" was at the very center of interest of the action. (Here we also have an example of variation in poetry recitation.)

At best, an attempt was made to achieve the most adequate reading possible, a harmony between meaning and emphasis. Sometimes a new interpretative variation of the meaning can result by accident from recitation; thus, the recitation at the start of the experiment is not just reeling off words, but is intimately connected with the meaning of the poem.

The opposite of this meaningful attending to the content consists of a merely superficial reading in which one no longer feels the essence of the poem. At first, the subject resisted such superficial reading whenever the temptation to do so occurred. But in the course of the experiment, the process inevitably began. With time, the repetition of certain individual expressions becomes striking. The subject already knows them; they provide nothing novel, yet continue to recur. These words no longer take part in the meaning changes of the whole, and are soon dragged along like dead weight during each repetition. If, with time, several such words appear, the external superficial verbal quality acquires great emphasis, and mouthing these words destroy the meaning of the recitation. No further progress is made on interpreting the content of the poem. Recitation in itself recedes, and speaking comes more and more into the foreground until the action has become one of mere reading away. These individual repeated words explode the totality of the poem, and its sense becomes powerless against them. Even the other words which at first do not become obvious repetitions in the continually changing larger whole, also develop into unconnected repetitive phrases with a gradual exhaustion of the content.

Now the subject tries to bring about a meaning intentionally. The more effort he exerts, the more the action falls apart. He pays attention to every word, every movement is stressed for itself. In this way, a larger context really becomes quite impossible.

With such disintegration a strong devaluation of the task typically occurs. Not only reciting poetry, but also the other actions such as the thimble game, pattern drawing, and hatching in rhythms are designated as being meaningless, "stupid," or "aimless" in this stage of strong satiation, although word meanings are not involved in these other tasks.

As has already been pointed out, the task as a whole acquires a certain meaning for the subject—for instance, that of a "record performance" or an "experimental action"—which can shift during the course of the process. This attitude of the subjects insures that they hardly ever experience the task set for them as something unreasonable or absolutely meaningless. The thimble game, for example, usually immediately arouses the interest of the subject. Even when the subject feels somewhat repulsed by the task at the start, as is frequently the case with hatching, the task still has a purposeful character and possesses the indefinite meaning of being a test action. The action is begun to comply with the instructions of the experimenter. As a rule, the prevailing meaning of the action is then to see what kind of an action it really is, what comes out of it, what's behind it.

In the course of the satiation process, as the variations on the action are exhausted and complete action disintegration appears, the action loses its meaning as a task. The continued repetition of stroke elements, or of individual arm movements, is felt to be senseless, particularly as the dissolution into action fragments progresses. (This is true even though the performance of such action fragments could have been set up as the testing action by the experimenter from the start. There are important problems here which appear to be worthy of further experimental investigation.)

This experience of loss of meaning is particularly noteworthy, because as satiation increases, objectively meaningless actions, such as explosions of anger, occur more and more frequently and crassly. Thus, from this point of view, the way for emotional outbursts appears to be prepared by the loss of meaning of the task during action disintegration. The subjects themselves did not tend to experience the emotional outbursts as senseless during the outburst, although a certain senselessness can be attached to these outbursts when they are seen in retrospect.

Disintegration of the situation. The gestalt disintegration, reminiscent of a degeneration process, can also include the situation. At the beginning of the process, the total situation, together with the task, tends to form a relatively uniform action field. With strong satiation, the work before the person, and the situation he is in, are experienced as sharply separated. The work, in itself, and the situation, in addition, can then be experienced by the subject as two unpleasant facts.

It should be noted that gestalt disintegration occurs gradually during satiation, and is closely connected to the previously described division into action units and subunits. Large action changes, such as breaking off, at first take place only at the end of more comprehensive unities, such as whole pages; less significant action changes, such as variations, can take place at the end of a subunit, such as a line. With progressing gestalt disintegration, even the larger action changes take place at the conclusion of the smaller segments,—at the end of the line—while the slighter changes,—the variations—take place even within the lines. Finally, even breaking off can occur within a line or within an individual figure. Within both the gestalt structure of the work product, and within the action event, smaller and smaller sections functionally acquire the position of decisive unities.

This gestalt disintegration does not have to occur from above the larger whole. At times a detail suddenly takes on particular stress, and gradually several such superficial details come together until the unity is thrown apart, as in the poetry recitation.

3. Performance Deterioration: Errors, Unlearning, Forgetting

The appearance of errors or of deficient execution in the work is closely related to the gestalt disintegration apparent in satiation. One could consider these phenomena to be simply special cases of the gestalt disintegration. However, we mention them separately because they represent especially obvious, tangible phenomena, and because they have a special character for the subject within the gestalt disintegration.

In these cases it is especially clear how little the continuous performance of an action, as such, is suited to bring about improvement or mastery. The individual action parts by no means associate with each other more firmly and uniformly through repeated performance. Even when fatigue is not decisive, during continued performance the action units finally begin to break apart, errors occur, and performance deteriorates to a point where the subject is unable to continue.

The errors, themselves, can be varied in nature, and depend on the material and the special gestalt of the tasks involved.

During the rhythm hatching, the individual groups may get too many or too few strokes. The subject may give in to the peculiar nature of the rhythm. He lets his hand take care of the hatching, but then, following simple gestalt laws, the rhythm 3, 5; 3, 5, may change into the symmetrical rhythm 4, 4 or into the rhythm 3, 6; 3, 6. At other times, a subunit is erroneously repeated, thus 3, 5, 5; or a subunit is left out: 1, 2, 4, 5 instead of 1, 2, 3, 4, 5. Such performances can be related to the disintegration of the action into small subunits (we shall see another case below). Repetitions, such as drawing circles twice within patterns are not infrequent.

The work may be performed carelessly, messily, and imprecisely. For example, the transition from one stroke to another no longer takes place in the air: rather the subjects carelessly lets it be seen on the paper. This carelessness and indifference is also expressed by the fact that lines which should be angular are rounded off, or arches are drawn too flatly (Figure 14, line 2).

Frequently, the errors have the character of quick finishes. In the case of the pentagram, which is at first performed correctly, the figure is eventually finished with too few corners and lines. (Figure 14, the third figure of the bottom line, and Figure 15, the last line; also Figure 16). In the case of the poems, mistakes (slips of the tongue), stuttering, and stammering occur.

The errors which appear in the course of the satiation action can certainly not be characterized completely as mere errors of oversight; rather, in the later stages of satiation, the satiation is frequently so strong that in spite of the most rapt attention, good will, and effort the subject can no longer correctly perform the task.

Repeated performance can, therefore, lead to a temporary unlearning of the action as it was at first mastered, as, for instance, in the pentagrams of Figures 14–16. Above all, the continuation of continuous patterns simply cannot be achieved in this stage (see Figure 13).

Closely connected with this phenomenon is the condition in which understanding new tasks is made very difficult by high degrees of satiation. If the experimenter gives the subject a new task, the subject must first correctly understand this new task. This is most evident in the case of somewhat difficult, continuous patterns, the correct execution of which substantially depends on understanding the construction of the figure. But even in the case of hatching to rhythms, understanding is necessary.

One subject said: "I must first crystalize the meaning of the assigned rhythm from the words of the experimenter; it must be grasped." The subject must figure out a rhythm, such as 4, 3, 2, 5, in order not to lose it during the performance. (4 plus 3 equals 7, 2 plus 5 equals 7;) it is clear how performance errors can arise as gestalt disintegration progresses.

Even pronounced errors, misunderstandings, become more frequent. The figures to be drawn are not understood (Figure 13), or the subject simply hears incorrectly. For example, in the rhythm hatching, the instruction—carry out the rhythm 8, 6 three times—results in the rhythm, 8, 6, 3.

Finally, we should mention, in this context, a sort of forgetfulness on the part of the subject which appears during phases of high satiation. The subject has known how to make a figure, or has figured out the solution to a certain teaser problem, but when performing during a phase of high satiation, he forgets how to do it. There is a halt; it is as if reason had suddenly stopped functioning.

When the subject has had enough of reciting the assigned poetry and is supposed to switch over to reciting poems from memory, he may suddenly be unable to think of any poem. Such forgetfulness is not an attempt to trick the experimenter, for the subject will take great pains to try to think of a poem. For instance, one subject said, "It is unbelievable. I know so many poems by Goethe, and now I can't think of a single one." At times, the action can acquire new interest for the subject, and then the figure continues, although just a moment before it was not possible to continue.

It seems plausible, inasmuch as a symptom of inner resistance could exist here, to connect such forgetfulness, unlearning, and inability with the cases of forgetting in the situations to which Freud has called attention (6).

In fact, it is possible that an inner resistance does, to a certain extent, play a part in the development of such phenomena. However, we do not believe that it is the sole decisive factor here. Without a doubt, much can be explained directly by the gestalt disintegration. For with increasing satiation there appears a tendency away from the work the creation of a front against the work —not always directly against the work—an attitude which can, in part, be traced back to work deterioration and errors.

The errors frequently appear in batches. After a batch of errors, a certain recovery from the satiation often can be observed. This is similar to the way recovery occurs after emotional outbursts.

As the errors increase, and the quality of the work deteriorates, they lose the nature of exceptions and accidents. They become, so to speak, an ingredient of the work, and begin to ruin the work for the subject. As we have mentioned, errors are usually carefully corrected in the beginning, but, in later stages of satiation, they are simply crossed out (for example Figure 8, lines 8 and 17; Figure 12, lines 10–16; and Figure 13). Even this crossing out becomes more and more sloppy and emotional in the course of satiation.

The mistakes are relatively early instances of outbursts of emotional tension, culmination points. They have the effect of elevating the subject's distaste for the work.

4. Variation

Apart from the disintegration of action unities, another phenomenon which we have mentioned plays an important part in the development of errors: variations which appear as errors from the point of view of performance.

Variation is perhaps the most typical phenomenon of the satiation process. The subject does not hold to the task exactly as he has been given it, or as he first performed it, but rather continually alters the tasks.

Two main types of variations can be distinguished: the change of the external action structure and the change of the significance, or meaning of the action for the subject. Naturally, there are many gradations.

Alteration of the action structure. We can give only a small sampling of the great abundance of variations which have occurred in our tests. The examples all stem from experiments in which we were able to obtain satiation. In the few tests in which we were not able to obtain satiation, few if any variations appeared. We will return to these tests later. The subject Tr shows a rather large number of stroke variations.

If we arrange the stroke variations according to the tasks which the subjects are given, we find that, in hatching, the style of the strokes—their length, breadth, position (vertical, horizontal, oblique, curved)—is altered. The strokes can be brought together in many ways to form larger groups; for example, at times, even two lines were brought together. Sometimes, the groups are broken apart; instead of the assigned rhythm 3, 5, the subject drew 3, 2, 3, or 3, 3, 2; instead of 6, 6, 2, 2, 2, or 3, 3. The most diverse patterns and changes in the strokes' emphasis are brought together. Tempo and rhythm changes are very frequent.

Variations more extensive than those listed above usually appear later. They include the following: instead of strokes, dots are made; circles are drawn around the strokes (Figure 10); in place of strokes, figures are made such as circles, rectangles, crosses, and so on.

Even the manner of hatching is changed. For example, hatching is done from left to right or from top to bottom, alternating with the left and right hand. Tools are used as aids; the pencil is fastened to a paper clip, or taken between the teeth, and hatching is continued in this way.

With drawing, we also find diverse variations. Many of the ones mentioned above are also found in this task. The larger unities which arise in the drawing are always different in nature. The patterns are decorated in various ways. The figures are filled with strokes, thus giving striking expression to the new interpretation of the drawing as a plane figure instead of as an outline. Through hatching, parts of different lines are connected so that completely new plane figures are produced. Between two treble clefs, a note is added. A spiral comes to look like a bird's body.

Some additional variations: If the subject is given the assignment of drawing a flower or an animal, the flower is drawn at various stages of its development —as a bud, as a blossom, or as a withered flower with hanging petals. The animal is drawn in different positions—sitting, sleeping, ready to attack. The task, "Draw eyes" is varied, so that the eyes are drawn with different expressions—friendly, gentle, serious, and angry. When the task "Draw a man" is to be repeated, the subject begins correctly with a man, but later the subject makes a bus near him—the man has become a bus driver.

Variations do not only occur during hatching and drawing, but also in all of the other tasks used in our experiments. For example, in the thimble game and in spinning the top, the tempo was varied: the subject works first with the right hand, then with the left hand; he goes forwards and backwards; he sets the thimble in along the horizontal lines or along the diagonal lines.

In poetry reading the tempo is varied, or the emphasis is changed. The subject can go from a very monotonous recitation to an exaggerated, parodic reading. Sections are no longer said out loud but are whispered or not said at all. Sometimes, only the melody to the assigned Heine poem was sung and the text completely left out. In some cases, the subject recited poems completely different from the ones assigned by the experimenter.

Alteration of the action's meaning without essential change in the action structure. In the case of Subject D, we have already mentioned that hatching did not always mean simply hatching. Often the task is interpreted as an intelligence test, or else is changed during its performance. For example, from "Hatch as long as you like," the subject makes "Hatch as quickly as I can," thus turning the task into a speed test.

If we consider the original attitude of the subjects toward the experiment, we find two types of subjects: (1) Those who relate to the task as they would to a task in everyday life, and for whom a certain task or piece of work of a definite quality is to be done. Subjects who only have a slight familiarity with psychology usually belong to this type. (2) The psychologists are prevalent in the other group. They maintain a passive attitude and let themselves be carried away by every idea that hits them.

The first group usually had established a goal at the very beginning of the task. Subject Ha "is doing work;" Subject D is showing that he can "work for an indefinitely long time." (We will return to this attitude again.) At times, the subjects found the instructions too vague—"Just hatching is to work without any purpose"—and the subjects could not stand this for long. They come to the test to accomplish something. The instructions do not give them anything definite to aim at, for which reason the subjects fall into an indefinite, unpleasant state which exerts a pressure towards solution. The subjects attempt through performance to uncover what is really meant by the instructions. The instructions are felt to be somewhat "dishonest." Since the task, itself, does not permit many opportunities to interpret "what is meant by this," the subjects take on themselves one of a few constantly recurring responsibilities, such as do as much as possible, work as quickly as possible, and so forth.

Rarely, however, do the subjects stay with the same extra goal. As well as the previously described action variations, the significance of the task, its sense, frequently succumbs to change. For example, the subject wants to hatch very beautifully or decoratively. He then wants to see "how much one can hatch," or he continually varies the style of the hatching, because change as such is enjoyable.

A favorite occupation of the subjects is to trick the experimenter by secretly doing something not allowed for instance, varying an action in spite of an order not to do so. One subject, for example, secretly drew a head out of strokes by connecting the strokes to unities such as hair and eyes. He did this in so subtle a manner that the experimenter did not notice it. The subject betrayed himself in this case by a satisfied smile, and when the experimenter finally asked what was going on, the subject admitted that he was drawing a head. The experimenter still could not recognize the head, whereupon the subject made the drawing clearer.

Furthermore, the strokes themselves can lose the character of strokes. The example previously mentioned is a case in point. There, the strokes actually signified eyes, nose, and so on. The subject was, in reality, drawing a head, which was something completely different for him than just hatching. Additional changes in meaning are present when the subject suddenly interprets the strokes as a sea, cattails, or decorative patterns. These variations tend to occur more frequently and become even stronger as satiation increases.

The functional significance of variation. If one seeks to understand the functional significance of variation and the causes of its appearance, the course of the variations within the satiation process provides an essential starting point.

The first variations at the very start of the new task tend to occur of themselves. For example, the subject is working on a hatching task and during this proces the tempo increases, the hatching becomes more comfortable. Or, while drawing a pattern, the lines tend towards certain changes—a rounding off, or accentuation of the corners (7).

Such spontaneous variations in the first stage of the repetitions are usually only noticed by the subject after they appear. Frequently, they are then consciously adopted and often they are then extended into new variants.

The spontaneous variation typical of the initial stage gives the impression that an adjustment of the action structure is involved, so that smooth work is made possible.

The frequency of variations of this sort decrease relatively rapidly. Then, even in the first stages of satiation, the subject starts to look for changes, for diversity. He thinks out variations for himself. We saw in the example of Subject Tr, how this search for new variations became continually more difficult; the obvious variations were exhausted; the variations began to seem sought after (Figures 8, 9, and 10).

With increasing satiation, the variations tend to change more and more frequently, and, at the same time, the extent of the variations becomes greater. The task is now only superfically fulfilled. Finally, even the appearance of the given task is completely deserted.

The subject, of course, tends scarcely to be aware of the extent to which variations are steadily increasing with the increasing satiation. Hand in hand with the magnification of the extent of the variations goes something which one can designate as an extension of the "zone of identity;" that is, the periphery of that which is experienced by the subject to be the same, or at least a similar action, extends farther and farther out. Changes in the action, which the subject rejected in the stage of light satiation as much too noticeable, are frequently performed readily in the later stages without a sense of doing something different or forbidden. As a consequence of this extension of the identity zone, even great variations are not felt to be such.

One could attempt to interpret the transition to even greater variations as due to the objective operation of the extension of the identity zone. However, the extension of the identity zone can only explain why a big variation is viewed as something completely natural and is executed without any qualms. The question remains as to why, after the initial adjustment of the action, the subject resorts to new variations. Indeed, the longer the task is carried out the more variations he turns to. By his total behavior, it becomes clear that as the numbers of repetitions increase the subject is trying to get away from the original action in every way; he is tired of the original work. He would like to leave the field but is under the pressure of the task (8). Now, since the instructions are vague enough to leave the subject room enough to move around in, the subject does not have to simply break off. Instead, he can leave the original action by means of a tactic which does not directly collide with the instructions—that is, the tactic of variation.

One proof of the fact that variations are functionally equivalent to breaking off is the phenomenon that the subject usually breaks off very quickly when he is forbidden any variations. (This proof is technically difficult to achieve because a command from the experimenter can easily cause a new incorporation, "Obey; only do exactly what the experimenter says." The forbidding can only be used as proof when it leads to a situation that is similar to a situation in which the action has exhausted all possible variations.

The subject progresses through variations to new regions. In comparison to the original action the region of actions is magnified. This leaving the field through variations soon leads again to satiation of these neighboring regions. The neighboring region also acquires, in this way, a negative valence. If the subject does not wish to break off, he must progress to new regions and thus resort to greater and greater variations. In the process, of course, he tries to keep within the framework of the instructions as much as possible. But, as we have seen, under the increasing pressure of satiation, the instructions are only followed in a relatively superficial sense; the experimenter is even deceived when possible.

When a sufficiently large variant is no longer possible within the framework established by the instructions, leaving the field ultimately becomes possible only through breaking off, that is, so to speak, through open resistance to the experimenter.

5. The Performance of the Task as a Secondary Action (Nebenhandlung)

Connected with the tendency to leave the field is another typical phenomenon which is especially noticeable in the early stages of satiation: for a time, the test action becomes a secondary action. This happens, when the subject begins another occupation which is outside of the test action and performs the former as the main action. For example, in the hatching tests, whistling and singing may become the main action, while the test task is executed more or less on the side as an accompanying mechanical action, or as a method of keeping time. Sometimes, the subject tried to start a conversation with the experimenter. (Here the behavior of the experimenter made it difficult for the subject to get away from the test situation. The experimenter would not join in any conversation.) At other times, the test action was performed completely mechanically, and the subject was, in reality, occupied with thoughts about something else, allowing his thoughts to run free, paying attention to what was happening in the courtyard, or looking at the sky.

When the test task is performed as a secondary action, the subject is, in reality, occupied with something he enjoys. Through this device, the test task loses its unpleasant nature; it is no longer there any more, or there only very slightly. The subject can detach himself from the test situation. This detachment varies in completeness; for example, the progression from hatching to another type of main action can come to pass through the fact that a certain variation of hatching has animated certain rhythms, which have led to a specific melody, which is now sung. At first, the test task and test situation tend to be relatively animate next to this new action. As the subject involves himself in the new activity, he detaches himself more and more from the test situation. Hatching has become keeping time to the melody. Indeed, the melody is usually not even directed by the beating time, but rather, hatching as a method of keeping time is a secondary ingredient in the total process. The original main task then loses its emotional import. No wish to break off or to continue exists any longer. There is only a running off, which occurs without any longer closely touching the ego. If, in the meantime, the subject pays attention to his work, he only has a pleasant feeling of being undisturbed, of being quietly busy, broken in like a well-worn phonograph record. Even the gestalt disintegration fails to appear when the task is performed as a purely secondary action (a fact which is of great theoretical significance).

Pushing the task away from the vicinity of the central Ego into a peripheral stratum appears to be an extraordinarily effective method of obviating satiation. If the subject succeeds in performing the task completely as a secondary action, and if the test situation is not essential for the new main action, the performance runs very smoothly without satiation phenomena, without errors, and even without variations. (This also supports the observation that the variations are directly connected with the satiation process.) The work looks very even. The only action changes which still appear are occasioned by the short period of adjustment to the task.

Problems with secondary action performance. Treating the assigned task as a purely secondary action which is performed mechanically and in a very peripheral sphere is something that most subjects tend to be unable to maintain for long. More or less quickly, disturbances of the condition appear; these vary considerably in their nature according to the particular structure of the action in question and the test situation. For example, after a time, satiation of the personally chosen main action may occur. (This occurs very quickly if the subject has not completely detached himself from the test situation.) The subject also begins to vary the new action; for example, he changes his tempo in singing, or alternates between singing loudly and softly. If he gives in to looking at the sky, his eyes begin to hurt; if he lets his ideas wander about, he becomes tired of "sitting around."

Frequently, the disturbances are also caused by the fact that performing the assigned test task as a secondary action meets with difficulties. This is true for all precise actions, and in general for all actions which demand complete attention—for example, the more difficult rhythms in which one can easily miscount. If errors occur which are noticed and corrected by the subject, the equilibrium in the performance of the two actions is disturbed. The test task again comes into the foreground; it becomes the main action, and thus the test situation also becomes dominant again.

It tends to become more difficult to perform the task as a secondary action in the later satiation stages than in the initial ones. At the earlier stages of satiation, when the subject has been somewhat drawn into some new main work, the slipping away of attention does not tend to have a strong impact, and in any case is not experienced as something unpleasant. With strong satiation, however, the subject soon becomes alert to the fact that his thoughts are straying from the test task. The subject wants to work, but his thoughts inevitably wander off to other things. The compulsive character of slipping off into other tasks is experienced with pain by the subject; and with increasing satiation, he becomes generally more sensitive to the uncontrollable quality of this process. This is not only noticeable because the subject has a particular work set towards his main task, but also because the subject tends to feel more strongly bound to the work as the difficulties connected with satiation appear. The condition of compulsive slipping away can become so tormenting that the subject breaks off the activity for this reason.

The strength and compulsiveness of the tendency to slip away from the work gradually grows with increasing satiation, and is expressed in the degree of the subject's sensitivity to accidental stimuli and disturbances. At the start of the work, such stimuli from the environment are noticed scarcely or not at all. Even when the experimenter is called out of the room, the subject continues to work without even lifting his head. Gradually, however, aspects of the environment acquire importance for the subject. For example, the subject notices what the experimenter is doing, or hears the noise and conversation in the corridor. He becomes more interested in everything around him than in the work he is doing.

The increased sensitivity to secondary stimuli is also gradually experienced as something unpleasant. In spite of a subject's compulsive interest, he experiences the environmental happenings as disturbances. For example, he can find the way in which his pencil scratches the paper very disturbing. He is, frequently, nervously oversensitive to his own situation. He is not only tired and unhappy, he even starts to notice this distinctly.

Thus, in the change of the actual task into a secondary task, in the slipping off to other main actions, and in the noticing of every unimportant thing, leaving the field plays an important part. However, the subjects are by no means always inclined to follow this tendency easily. Rather, along with the increasingly compulsive tendency to leave the field, a countertendency sets up a strong bond to continue the action. This makes it difficult for the subject to relegate the main task to the role of a secondary action, and causes him to dwell on disturbances as the satiation increases. We shall see that the same phenomenon is decisive in the actual breaking off of the action in the concluding stage of the satiation process.

6. The Direction of Aversion

In the course of the satiation process, a tendency away from the work appears. The initially pleasant or indifferent primary action has acquired a distinctly negative valence. Against what in particular does the aversion of the subject direct itself?

Very frequently, it is the task itself which assumes negative valence. The subject becomes angry, furious, about the work. An emotional reaction of this sort to the work is usually preceeded by a diminishing evaluation of the intrinsic (or objective) value of the work. The hatching gradually becomes "stupid," "idiotic," or "useless." The poem is now judged to be "poor." As mentioned above, the gestalt disintegration, especially the loss of meaning of the task, plays a part in this devaluation.

But there may be other objects of the subject's aversion.

In cases in which the original task is performed as a secondary task, the aversion can be directed against the present main action. For example, poetry recitation may be protected from the threatening danger of gestalt disintegration and devaluation by the fact that speaking has been shoved into the foreground. Then the speaking acquires a negative valence. Speaking becomes strenuous without the content of the speech becoming important; the subject no longer thinks about the fact that he is reading a poem. But if this fact does occur to him, it frequently seems "too stupid for a poem to be misused for the sake of such speech," and the subject then breaks off.

The situation or the experimenter can also be the object of the aversion. Aversion to the situation is particularly clear when disintegration of the total work field leads to the situation becoming detached from the task. Then, the situation can be felt to be an obligation (such as an obligation to work, to sit there), which oppresses and angers the subject. If hatching has been satiated, and the subject is asked to recite poems, he may refuse with the excuse that he cannot recite any poems in "this situation," since "it wouldn't do the poem justice," or "it isn't appropriate." If the subject does make an effort to recite a poem (frequently beginning by singing the melody of the poem without words), the aversion is often turned against the experimenter. For example, one subject commented, "I would enjoy reading the poem, but outside of the experiment, or alone. The experimenter only disturbs me."

In other cases, too, the aversion of the subject can be directed against the experimenter. After all, it is he who is forcing the subject to work. One subject was happy at the thought that in an experiment of his own he could take revenge on the experimenter. "Later, I intend to torment the experimenter vigorously." Another subject said, "It is more pleasant when you keep track of the time; then you also have something boring to do. The joy I feel at your displeasure gives the work more meaning for me." Aversion to the experimenter finally leads to resistance to the experimenter's instructions, and disregard of his orders. The aversion appears to easily turn against the situation or against the experimenter, especially when the subject is inwardly closely bound to the test task for some reason.

Finally, the aversion can be directed against his own person or condition. The subject can become irritated with himself after making errors. He can find himself "very foolish" for reading poetry, because he is sitting around doing something useless. In these cases, the poetry reading touched a personal core which the subjects did not want to reveal, and which they wanted to keep untouched. These subjects liked to read poems, but alone and quietly to themselves.

Thus, the negative valence produced in the satiation process is not necessarily limited to the action itself, but can affect the situation, the experimenter, and the subject's own ego. One might picture a gradual extension of the negative valence (9). However, from the very start the narrower work field is a dependent part of the whole situation, and the latter is affected by the satiation unless specific reasons lead to a strong seclusion of the narrower work field.

The extent of the aftereffects of satiation are determined by the particular direction of the aversion, and the manner and degree of communication between the specific work sphere and other psychical spheres. For example, one subject who liked to read poetry found that poetry reading was ruined for months by the few test hours. For this subject, the test had the characteristics of a very natural vital situation, in which he performed the assigned activity exactly as he would have done at home. Thus, this subject really read the poems just as if he had done so spontaneously.

Since the subject was inwardly close to the action during the test, no wall was erected between the action and his central emotions, as usually happens because of the strange situation or shyness. Precisely because of the close communication between the action and a genuine need, a strong oversatiation occurred in the test, and continued to work even in the natural situation of daily life. This is the opposite condition from that which occurs when the task is finished peripherally as a pure secondary action.

7. Positive Valence for "Opposite" Tasks

If satiation leads a subject to become tired of a certain task or a particular object, other things can simultaneously acquire an increased positive valence. This phenomenon is found in everyday life and was frequently observed in our tests.

A few examples: After repeatedly copying the alphabet, one subject wanted to dance the shimmy. After a complicated and difficult drawing, a second subject asked to draw something "easy, and harmonious." When cutting fabrics for sewing became meaningless for a third subject, she wanted to perform a "sensible cutting task of a very different nature, like give someone a boyish bob." When the reciting of poetry was satiated, other subjects wanted to read softly to themselves; in so doing, sometimes they desired something particular, usually a novel. If a subject was tired of the test situation altogether, he wanted to start conversation.

On the whole, therefore, the positive valence seemed to appear for opposite tasks of some sort.

The more precisely one knows the satiated region, the easier it will be to predict what will take on a positive stimulus for the subject. At first, the scope and nature of the actions which acquire a definite valence through satiation tend to be loosely defined. The more the satiation encompasses a specific region, the less diffuse the positive valence seems to become.

If the first task was pleasant for the subject, he may be able to become interested in another task which was somehow related. For example, drawing a spiral put one subject in a good mood, and awoke in him the desire to wrestle with someone.

8. Actions of Restlessness, Emotional Outbursts

With increasing satiation, a growing disquietitude becomes noticeable in the subject. This can finally transfer into marked emotional outbursts. The subject becomes nervous, jumpy under the pressure of the work; he has a strong sensation of "wanting to run away." The subject feels "nervous fatigue"; he is unsatisfied, impatient, out of sorts; everything seems "awful" to him. The disquietitude also affects the behavior of the subject, his motions. The subject pulls the chair back and forth, constantly changes his position, has twitches in his fingers, leafs through the book of poems, makes faces. The subject tries to pull himself together; but if errors nevertheless occur, or if his speed diminishes, the subject becomes angry, bemoans the fact that he is so dull, that he cannot carry out the work as he would like to. He senses that he is in a conflict which he wants to get rid of as soon as possible. Mistakes are no longer corrected, but are crossed out more or less furiously.

The repeated and increasing errors finally bring the subject to greater and greater emotional outbursts. The anthology is thrown onto the table; the materials for the puzzle-task or the thimbles are thrown into disorder; the pencil is flung away, or the subject hits it so hard on the paper that it tears the paper; angry strokes are drawn this way and that. Finally, the subject would like to destroy everything, especially the product of his work. It may happen that the subject expresses this wish outright and asks the experimenter for permission to do so. Great irrascibility and emotional sensitivity appear.

If the subject is given an activity as a new task which is only vaguely reminiscent of previous tasks, the subject will say that he "already did that" and become insanely angry. Likewise, if the subject fails on a task which he had already mastered, or if he does not immediately understand a new task, an unmotivated violent emotional outburst easily can occur.

Frequently, the emotional outbursts occur in bunches after stretches of especially long or strong control. Outwardly, the emotional outburst is preceded by especially good work; the transition to the emotional outburst occurs relatively suddenly and unexpectedly. Therefore, the total course of events by no means exhibits continuity. In its turn, the emotional outbursts frequently bring about a certain relief or alleviation, and thus better work again.

Of course, if the emotional outburst has been violent, the subject rarely resumes the activity again. But usually a mild suggestion on the part of the experimenter tends to be enough to induce the subject to resume. For the subject is usually terribly ashamed of his lack of control, he wants to make up for it, to be good, and to do whatever the experimenter wants. Naturally, this attitude does not usually last for long, and, finally, the subject breaks off the test for good.

9. Breaking Off

After a more or less lengthy performance, subjects break off spontaneously. (We will deal later with the particular circumstances under which this is not the case.)

Satiation is not the only reason why subjects may discontinue the task. At times, for example, they break off because they simply cannot succeed in drawing a particular figure. As one said, "Ah, I just can't do it! That's all!" If, after many failures, one drawing is finally successful, a subject may break off because he is afraid that the next attempt would not be as successful. While such excuses may also be found with real satiation, there are cases in which the total behavior of the subject, particularly his attitude towards similar new tasks, proves that his stopping has little or nothing to do with satiation.

Since a number of other satiation phenomena are available, we can generally say with assurance if breaking off is basically due to satiation. The test arrangement, in which after the satiation of one action we progress to the satiation of additional actions, provides an opportunity to observe breaking off in various degrees of total satiation.

In early satiation stages, the subject tends to break off at a logical point, at the end of a subunit. Breaking off at that point is "easier than later on," "occurs of itself," and "one does not have to worry about it further." At times, the subject also undertakes to hatch to the end of the page. But during the performance, the subunits become smaller, the subject forgets his purpose, and is eventually satisfied with a smaller amount.

In the later satiation stages—with actions following the first satiation—breaking off becomes more difficult. The subject would like to stop, but finds no motive which he can give the experimenter. Anything he thinks of is not quite sufficient. He is, himself, surprised at the fact that he still continues to work. One subject remarked, "It's just like when one has had enough lemonade and still keeps drinking." Or it's "like when one wants to finish reading one more chapter in the evening even though one cannot keep his eyes open."

In part, this is connected with the fact that, because of gestalt disintegration, the work has no natural subunits with definite concluding points, but flows on continuously. As one subject said, "It could go on forever like this." In this stage, dislike does not simply lead to breaking off; rather, the subject suddenly feels bound to the presence of motives. In fact, the subject typically stops with a jerk, without considering whether the problem is finished. As a conclusion, the action is often done well once more.

The excuses of the subject become more numerous and especially more weighty as satiation increases. He is "tired;" he "really can't work anymore." A hundred things occur to him that he must take care of. He becomes impatient; he hasn't "any more time" and breaks off. (Yet, he can still talk for a long time after the experiment.) He will use the smallest external provocation for motivation, for instance, "The page in the experimenter's notebook is filled." Thus, the subject is under a strong pressure to come up with either genuine or concocted excuses. Frequently, the breaking off occurs during an emotional outburst.

Breaking off becomes more and more difficult for the subject as satiation increases. At first glance, this fact appears completely paradoxical, since satiation presses directly for leaving the field—breaking off—and the forces which press for breaking off naturally become stronger with increasing satiation.

Basically the same paradox is present during the development of the restless actions and emotional outbursts previously described. As we saw, such restless action clearly bears the stamp of a desire to leave the field. One must wonder why the subject does not simply follow this tendency, particularly since he is doubtlessly in a condition in which the task already has a strong negative valence.

It is plausible to assume that the directions of the experimenter keep the subject in the work field against his will. But this is by no means the case. At periods of great satiation, the subject actually wants to stay with the work. He struggles, as we have described above, against the fatigue in his arm, the disintegration of the gestalt, and the loss of meaning of the poems. He struggles against these processes which exist as something objective, which bend his own will and threaten to completely break it.

Even though initially the instructions of the experimenter may have been decisive for the subject, it is the conflict between the tendency to leave the field and to remain at the work, rather than the struggle between the subject and experimenter, which leads to the restless actions and the emotional outbursts. In the course of the work, the quasi-need has entered into communication with genuine needs; the subject has made the work into his own work. The resistance which he finds in carrying out the work, caused by the satiation phenomena, may in turn hold him all the more powerfully in the work field (10).

In this light, the appearance of excuses also acquires a special significance for breaking off. Not only for the experimenter, but also for himself, the subject must have a justification for the fact that he finally breaks off. Otherwise, breaking off would have the character of defeat.

Thus, the satiation process, insofar as it creates difficulties for the subjects, at the same time tends to cause a reactive bond between the subject and the unpleasant work. The subject's growing will to work, and the work's negative valence become juxtaposed. In dynamic terms, a tension field, determined by two opposing forces, is present. The tension of this field grows with increasing satiation.

The increasing tension finds expression in restless actions and emotional outbursts. At the same time, the free movement of the subject, especially the possibility of leaving the field on the basis of a decision, becomes more limited as the strength of the tension field increases. This explains the paradoxical phenomenon that breaking off becomes more difficult as satiation increases.

The correctness of such an interpretation is also supported by the frequent observation that breaking off does not occur in the moment of highest tension, but during a certain relaxation of the tension. For example, the subject is just about to complete a main section of an action, or the solution to a puzzle, and is happy about it. In such moments of relaxation the decision often occurs "just to finish the page," and then to stop.

A certain relaxation might also play a part in the cases in which the subject suddenly breaks off. When the subject has gone so far that he says, "Now I could go on like this for hours if you want me to," he controls the situation; the actual difficulty seems overcome.

If the subject breaks off his activity, he frequently adds something from the feeling of freedom: the last row is drawn especially completely, the subject makes the full dozen of a figure, he fills out the blank spaces on the page with hatching lines, or he recites dramatically.

A second typical situation in which breaking off occurs is after the emotional outburst of anger. It, too, results in a certain relaxation of tension. But here, it seems to be of special importance that the outburst is so distinctly a new situation for the subject; he suddenly finds himself outside of that tension field of work which had held him prisoner for so long.

10. Removal of Satiation by Incorporation (Einbettüng) into a Different Context

During the transfer from the first to the second hatching task, satiation was largely removed although the task (hatching in the rhythm 4,4) consisted of the same action parts as the first task (hatching in the rhythm 3,5). Even the objective phenomena of satiation, for example, gestalt disintegration, disappeared. Fatigue also vanished, even though the same groups of muscles continued to be used in almost the identical way. This condition can be described in the following manner: the satiation of an action ("Draw a stroke") can be removed if one incorporates it into another unity.

To investigate the question of whether incorporation into a figurally different action structure is necessary to remove satiation, or whether a change of meaning is enough, we regularly asked the subject at the close of the second test day to repeat the action which he had just performed to complete satiation. However, we chose a different motivation, so that the identical action took on another meaning for the subject. For example, the last drawing was to be repeated on the back of the page to identify it for the experimenter, or the subject was to show how quickly and in what manner he performed the last task, etc. At the same time, the aid and friendliness of the subject was appealed to, so that he lost the position of "subject."

Through thus incorporating the task into a different context the subject could, without exception, be induced to resume the completely satiated task, and without the task causing him any great difficulty.

Change in meaning and of figural action structure occurred in the following case: A subject had written a b a b a b . . . until he had enough of "writing in general" and actually ran away from the table. The subject was immediately thereafter asked by a person entering the room to write his name and address. Several a's and b's occured in both. The subject at first refused, and asked the other person to do it himself. But when the person stated that he was collecting handwritings of acquaintances, the subject did it willingly.

Even hoarseness and fatigue disappear occasionally with a different incorporation of the action. The subject who was hoarse while reading poems suddenly talks very normally when he wants to say how unpleasant the test is, or when he wants to make any other remark. Or the subject who "can no longer lift her arm from fatigue" when she is supposed to hatch easily strokes her hair when she wants to put it into place.

If the test is finished, frequently the fatigue completely disappears. If the subject had broken off because he physically could not continue working, he now begins spontaneously to correct his work or to fill in the spaces. Playing around afterward with the pencil or the thimbles occurs. At times the subject again recites some verses from the satiated poems. During statements of personal observation, the subject begins, unasked, to illustrate how he worked during the various stages.

Finally, reference must be made to a case that we will discuss later. In this case, the same subject who became satiated after a relatively short time, on another day performed the same task without satiation, and almost without symptoms of fatigue over a very long period of time until the experimenter broke the task off.

Here, we can only establish the fact of immediate resumption after a change in meaning. The important question of how lasting an effect such new incorporations had could not be systematically persued. In any case, however, spontaneous variations through changes of meaning have frequently proved to be quite persistent.

11. Continuous Work Without Satiation

In the case of a few unemployed persons who were compensated for their time, there was not any noticeable tendency for spontaneous breaking off. In fact, the other satiation phenomena, such as restless actions, gestalt disintegration—indeed, even mild variations—were lacking. After two, even after four hours, hatching looked exactly the way it did at the beginning. These subjects were happy to have something to do in order to earn money. The type of work, apart from very dirty or very heavy work, was of no importance to them (11). With the unemployed it is a matter of having a set to work, and the test assignment is a mere occupation without particular character (12). This attitude paralyzes the satiation process in a similar but even more effective way than performing the work as a secondary action.

These experiments show forcefully that repetition as such is not a sufficient cause for satiation. Even Munsterberg (13) has pointed out that very monotonous occupations do not become boring for individuals in spite of their performance for years. Lau has stressed the importance of the dominant goal of one's will (14). The following case shows that it is not a simple matter of personality.

Subject D had been satiated in an earlier hatching test after one hour and twenty minutes. The test involved was the one described above, in which marked variations, distinct emotional outbursts, and finally spontaneous breaking off ensued (Figures 1–7). The same subject, however, during a second hatching test some time later, worked on for two-and-a-half hours straight—until the experimenter broke it off. The subject filled thirty-three pages without any satiation phenomena. Apart from the very slight fluctuations of adjusting to the work at the start, the work proceeded without any noticeable variation.

The subject had wondered if he could possibly hatch "for an infinitely long time,"—indeed, mainly out of theoretical interest. Thus, the meaning of the work had changed, so that hatching was no longer the actual action which the subject was performing. Hatching itself and its character, as in the case of the unemployed, had become unimportant; in reality the subject was in the process of pursuing a problem which interested him.

(The case is similar to writing a letter. Then the letters are mere agents, (15); one is not employed with writing down letters, but rather ideas.)

For superficial reasons the tests were broken off by the experimenter after two-and-a-half to four hours. Thus, it still remains open whether, after longer work, satiation would finally have been reached. However, one must point out that even mild satiation phenomena failed to appear. The particular manner of hatching used by Subject D could not be the main factor, because the tests with the unemployed involved hatching in the rhythm 3, 5; they made very similar strokes as Subject Tr did at the beginning of the task (Figure 8).

We will return later to the reasons for the lack of satiation in these cases.

12. Fatigue and Satiation

We cannot conclude our survey of the phenomena of satiation without summarizing our findings on the significance of fatigue symptoms. While we did not make any systematic tests for fatigue symptoms, it is clearly evident that muscular fatigue and satiation are two different things.

Fatigue can occur before satiation. For example, one subject who was unaccustomed to hatching became tired rather near the start of the test. However, in order to fulfill the purpose of the test, he did not permit himself to be hindered by his fatigue. The next day he complained that his hand hurt. Here was, without doubt, a case of real muscular fatigue.

In the case of an unemployed paper hanger, fatigue symptoms also appeared during hatching. They subsided in the course of the work. At first, he held the pencil awkwardly and could not achieve the proper relationship to the task. Half jokingly he apologized, looking at his hand, saying he was not used to the work. Conversely, the subject can be satiated without being tired, for instance, in the puzzle task.

However, we must point out that in the satiation process, symptoms of fatigue frequently appear. We can distinguish two types of physical fatigue in our tests:

1. Local fatigue occurs. In hatching, drawing, or the thimble game, the subject's fingers or hand hurts. While turning the wheel, the whole arm gets tired. The subject tries to protect himself and hatches very lightly; he tries out

different hand positions to make the work easier; he alternates working with the right hand and the left; he shakes the hand or arm.

2. A general fatigue occurs. Then the subjects speak of a numbness in the head. Or they become dizzy; their heads are swimming or buzzing. Related to these cases is a third symptom: becoming hoarse. While reading poems, for example, the subject begins to speak unnaturally. He becomes hoarse and cannot produce a word. In one case, a subject who in the first testing session after hatching had to read poems to the point of satiation, became very hoarse while hatching in a second test session. There was no explanation; but any poetry recitation became impossible. Thus a phenomena appears here which would be termed hysterical in medicine. (The female subject in question is very tempermental and stubborn, but not hysterical.)

Frequently, it is impossible to see to what degree genuine fatigue is involved, and to what extent the fatigue must be viewed as a mere satiation symptom. Even in the latter case, simulation is not involved. All such fatigue has the distinct character of an objective difficulty that is encountered by the subject, and against which he tends to violently struggle. He is very angry at the fact that he cannot work; he inserts pauses, and exerts an inordinate amount of energy on the technique of performance. By these means, however, the work only becomes more convulsive and poor.

In spite of this external picture there is no mere peripheral muscular fatigue. This is especially evident from the fact that, with sudden removal of the satiation, the fatigue can completely disappear in an instant—especially when new incorporation changes the meaning of the activities.

Nor can one, even generally, state that fatigue accelerates satiation. We have observed many times that being tired can have an effect that is similar to doing the work as a secondary action. Thus, subjects who became tired and sleepy during the work could, for that very reason, more easily continue the work. In fact, in the very condition of freshness and vitality there is the possibility of an intimate communication between the action and the inner-personal strata of the ego, a communication which plays an important part in satiation.

EDITOR'S SUMMARY OF THE QUANTITATIVE RESULTS

[After a brief summary of her qualitative results (in Part I, Section V), Karsten describes an attempt to use quantitative measures of satiation to examine how variation delays satiation. (Part II, Sections I through V). These sections are not as theoretically relevant, and therefore in the rest of this chapter, I shall simply summarize the results. The complete translation may be obtained from University Microfilms. In addition, I shall discuss here the related work of Alex Freund.

To discover how variation affects satiation, Karsten compares two different types of variations for the activities of drawing lines and reciting poetry. In the first type, the subject is completely satiated in one aspect or subregion of the activity—drawing lines in the rhythm 3, 5, reciting one of Heine's poems—and then is offered a variation in some other aspect or subregion of the activity—drawing lines in the rhythm 4, 4, reciting another of Heine's poems. Upon satiation of this second variation, they are then offered a third. This continues until the subject refuses to accept any more variations on drawing lines, or reciting Heine's poetry. Having satiated the basic region of the activity in this way, the subject is now offered activities in the surrounding region of drawing anything, or reciting anything, until satiation occurs here, too, and the subject refuses to continue doing any drawing or any reciting.

In the second type of variation, the subject is not allowed to satiate on any one aspect or subregion of the activity. Rather, the experimenter keeps suggesting variations within the basic region of drawing lines (or reciting Heine's poetry) before the subject satiates on any one aspect or subregion, and until the entire basic region is satiated and the subject refuses to continue. Then, as in the first type of variation, the subject is offered activities in the surrounding regions of drawing anything (or reciting anything).

By recording the time which it took the subject to satiate, and the number of units of work performed before satiation (a somewhat less satisfactory measure), Karsten was able to compare whether satiation of the basic region of an activity took longer with Type 1 or with Type 2 variations. And, of course, she was also able to see whether satiation of the surrounding region occurred more or less rapidly after the different types of satiation. Since subjects differ quite a bit in how rapidly they satiate on such tasks, Karsten planned to use each subject as his own control, counterbalancing the subjects so that five had Type 1 variation on the first day and the other five on the second day. For all subjects, drawing was done in the morning and recitation in the afternoon.

Unfortunately, since almost all of the subjects satiated much more rapidly on the second day of the testing, it was impossible to really use each subject as his own control. On the first day, the five subjects with the first type of variation took an average of 35 minutes to satiate, as compared with an average of 29 minutes with the second type. The range of individual differences (from 7 to 65 minutes) prevents this difference from having any significance. On the second day there appears to be a significant interaction effect. The subjects who experience the first type of variation after the second type take an average of only 8 minutes to satiate, as opposed to 22 minutes for those who experience the second type. However, the result may well be due to the experience of the previous day—those subjects with type two variation having exhausted more possibilities, and so on.

There are no significant differences on how quickly the surrounding region satiates. The range of scores (from 0 to 96 minutes) indicates that individual preferences for drawing are more important than the experimental variation. However, it is interesting that, on the first day, two of the five subjects with Type 2 variation in the basic region showed immediate satiation for the surrounding region, in spite of the fact that no drawing of any sort other than lines had been performed. Karsten speculates that these subjects may have experienced the continuous variations as a sample of the more extensive region, which includes free drawing.

There is an interesting range of individual differences in the subjects as they progress towards satiation with Type 1 variations. Some subjects spend a considerable amount of time on a few (from 3 to 7) variations of rhythm, and then show satiation for the entire region; while others flit rapidly from one to another variation (from 21 to 28 times) before they show satiation for the entire region. The latter subjects satiate more quickly over the entire region; their average is 17 minutes, compared to 49 minutes for the other subjects. Also, in general, the more variations used, the shorter the time to satiate each variation.

Karsten's theoretical interpretation of these relationships is to postulate that some subjects have more permeable boundary walls, walls that leak. The more permeable, the longer the individual subregions take to fill, but the more the surrounding region is satiated in the process. As evidence for this interpretation, she points out that within each subject, the satiation time for each subregion decreases as the subject progresses from one variation to the next. On the other hand, one would expect that if permeability were a general characteristic, subjects with high permeability (slow satiation of a few subregions) would also leak into the surrounding region of all drawing, and hence show more rapid satiation of this region. This is not noticably true.

On the basis of her results, Karsten concludes that variation neither stops satiation, nor reflects a recovery from the satiation process. Rather, variation simply postpones satiation by enlarging the region of activities that are satiated.

For my own part, while I find it interesting that neither type of variation is superior to the other in delaying satiation, I am not sure any theoretical conclusions can be drawn. My reason for saying this is that there are many ways in which subjects vary the activity of drawing lines other than by varying rhythm. The bulk of variations must include activities such as slanting the lines, varying their length, spreading them out, making patterns out of them, and so forth. The experimental manipulation of varying the rhythm seems relatively weak in comparison. Furthermore, if a subject expects to be interrupted by an imposed variation of rhythm, he may well begin to curtail the spontaneous variation of other factors. The result might be less, or the same amount, of variation than exists in Type I variation. Therefore, I cannot reach any conclusions as to what the experiment shows.

Freund's Experiment

The fact that satiation occurs much more rapidly when the self (or central region of the person) is involved was the starting point for an investigation by Alex Freund (16), another student of Lewin's at Berlin. Freund reasoned that the experience of tension must indicate self-involvement. On the basis of reports of increased tension during the period just before menstruation, he concluded that at the beginning of the menstrual period, activities which would ordinarily be surface activities would move closer to the self and be more central. (His reasoning is not spelled out in any more detail.) Following Karsten's thinking, such activities should satiate more quickly. Accordingly, he administered a series of seven activities, most of which involved drawing patterns such as a honeycomb pattern, to women on the first day of menstruation and in the middle of their cycle. Each time, he instructed his subjects to stop working on an activity as soon as they were "fed up with it." To balance out any effects of repeated testing, he tested one group of subjects for the first time during menstruation, then again in the middle of the cycle, and finally again during menstruation; while another group of subjects were tested for the first time in the middle of their cycle, then again during menstruation, and a last time again in midcycle. Twelve subjects with normal and regular menstrual cycles who were, however, hospitalized with gynecological problems, were used in the study.

Freund found that all twelve women satiated more rapidly during the first day of menstruation then in the middle of their cycle. Satiation times were from 9 per cent to 50 per cent faster, with an average satiation 32 per cent earlier than in midcycle. Accuracy was unimpaired, and work speed was slightly higher in ten of the twelve cases.

To investigate the effect of menstrual tenseness on the ability to perform activities, as opposed to satiation (the disinclination to continue with an activity), two other activities were included in each testing series. One of these was an accuracy test which involved counting a number of closely spaced lines; the other, a speed test, involved stringing as many pearls as possible in a five-minute period. With these two activities, unlike the other seven, the subjects were asked to do their best. Since the results clearly show no decrement in either accuracy or speed, Freund concludes that menstruation affects inclination but not ability.

While Freund's experiment is straightforward and precise, there are, of course, a number of factors which make one cautious in completely accepting the theoretical rationale for the results. First, since both the experimenter and the subjects knew when menstruation was occurring, there is the possibility that the subjects were unconsciously influenced to give the predicted results. Second, the subjects may simply have felt they had more right to stop when they were menstruating. A more convincing technique would be to test a much larger sample of women two times, fourteen days apart, and then select only those cases which later proved to have one of the test days fall a day or two before menstruation began—Editor.]

VI. ON THE CAUSES OF SATIATION

The explanation of variation as an escape from the field leaves open a question which is fundamental to the nature of the satiation process: why does an action which begins as pleasant, or relatively neutral, gradually become unpleasant and unbearable when it is repeated? A few tentative considerations concerning this central question will now be presented.

It is conceivable that an action would become easier and more pleasant because of the practice of repetition. When, instead, the work becomes more unpleasant, one may theorize that the performance of an action leads to a kind of self-blocking which impedes the repeated performance of the action. Such a thesis would make the fact of repetition as such responsible for the growing unpleasantness.

For a long time, repetition has been considered to be the cause of learning, mastery, or association. And since this concept has proved to be untenable, one might immediately doubt that satiation is due to repetition as such. And in fact, our tests show that there are cases where, in spite of the most extensive repetition, satiation fails to appear. Indeed, whenever there is an absence of satiation we find a pure repetition of the same identical action. In contrast, satiation regularly goes hand-in-hand with strong variation, a continuous change of actions. Thus, one cannot view repetition in itself as critical. Rather, one has to look for specific concrete structure peculiarities, either in the action and situation, or in the corresponding mental system.

Exhaustion of Need Tensions
We may assume that the performance of work by the subject flows from certain quasi-needs or genuine needs. Perhaps, if this energy source is exhausted with the first performance of the task, any further repetitions are felt to be unpleasant because there is no available tensed mental system.

To support this thesis, one could point to the fact that satiation is removed when one brings the action into communication with another genuine or quasi-need—as when the action is incorporated in a different context.

TABLE 1
Comparative Satiation Times on Agreeable, Disagreeable, and Neutral Tasks.

Each task column is sub-divided into S. (subject), T. (time, Sec. or Min./Sec.), and Ave. (average). Values are read as best as possible from the rotated table.

	Hatching (S. / T. Sec. / Ave. Sec.)	Drawing (S. / T. Min.Sec. / Ave. Min.Sec.)	Writing (S. / T. Min.Sec. / Ave. Min.Sec.)	Punching holes (S. / T. / Ave. Min.Sec.)	Turning a wheel (S. / T. / Ave.S. Min.Sec.)	Stick-and-ball game (T. / Ave. Min.Sec.)	Sticking on paper (S. / T. / Ave. Min.Sec.)	Thimbles (S. / T. / Ave. Min.Sec.)	Rolling balls (S. / T. / Ave. Min.Sec.)	Number of cases	Ave. on the task (Min./Sec.)
Very agreeable	Z. 9; A. 27 — 18; 38	D. 45 / 30 / 35 / 20 / 1 / 42; Ave. 39								10	1 15
Agreeable	Z. 10; A. 65 — 38	L. 43 / 1 40 / 31; A. 22 / 54 / 2 30; D. 1 50 / 2 35 / 45; Ave. 1 19		Z. 6 5; T. 6 5; Ave. 6 5		L. 4 15; T. 4 15; Ave. 4 15			L. 19; T. 19; Ave. 19	14	6 15
Neutral	V. 50; 50	D. 3 20; 3 20	L. 17 30; D. 49 20 — 24 7; 30 19		Z. 8 6; T. 8 6; Ave.S. 8 6 J.	J. 18 5; T. 18 5; Ave. 18 5			L. 45; T. 45; Ave. 45	8	23 15
Disagreeable	Z. 30; 30	L. 1 40 / J. 10 / V. 20; Z. 15 / L. 38 / A. 38; 37	L. 5 15 / 9 40; Z. 6 15 / 1 30 / 7; 5 56	L. 1 15; T. 1 15; Ave. 1 15	J. 0 8; T. 0 8	J. 6 55; T. 6 55; Ave. 6 55	L. 1 15; T. 1 15; Ave. 1 15	J. 3 15; T. 3 15; Ave. 3 15	L. 2 50; 2 50	16	2 50
Very Disagreeable	Z. 15 — 3; 9	J. 6 / 8 / V. 2; L. 22 / 38; 15		J. 1 20 / 53 / L. 15; 49	J. 0			J. 50; 50		12	26

That there is a relationship between satiation and central strata is shown by the results with Subject D and with the unemployed subjects. In these cases, there was no satiation because the subject inwardly stood above the work, or because the action was performed as paid employment and the nature of the work was of no importance. Therefore, if satiation is to develop as a result of repetition, there must be communication between the action and the central intrapersonal mental strata.

Evidence for this is also given by the suspending of satiation whenever the action is performed as a secondary action.

Finally, the necessity of communication with central strata is shown by yet another fact which we must now mention: One can ask whether pleasant, indifferent, or unpleasant actions are satiated more quickly. It would seem obvious that actions that are unpleasant in themselves would satiate most rapidly, and that pleasant actions would change more slowly into unpleasant ones. A comparison of 61 cases of different actions from different test arrangements shows that such an assumption is erroneous.

The same action can manifest different degrees of pleasantness and unpleasantness with different subjects, and with the same subject on different days. In setting up Table 1, we used only those cases in which we had trustworthy statements about the pleasantness or unpleasantness of the action at the start of the work.

The results in Table 1 show that it is the indifferent actions which are satiated most slowly, rather than the most pleasant ones. The pleasant actions, like the unpleasant, are satiated more quickly than the indifferent ones. With striking regularity the satiation velocity increases with the degree of the pleasantness and unpleasantness.

Since not every action falls into every category (very pleasant to very unpleasant), and since the average satiation times for the different types of action are quite strongly differentiated, arriving at a mathematical average (last column) is not completely correct. However, the rule is strikingly well confirmed for each of the individual action types.

Thus, there is a rather close relationship between satiation and contact with intra-personal strata. However, the conditions are not such that the satiation is postponed through contact with central strata, as one would expect if the availability of energy sources for action was crucial for work without satiation. Rather, conversely, satiation occurs more quickly when there is contact with central strata.

The Satiation Process as a Movement of the Will-Goal

The structure of the satiation process indicates that it is not equivalent to the satisfaction that appears upon reaching the goal of some well-delineated task, such as the solution of a math problem. In dynamic terms, it is not a matter of how a tension system operates to the point of release, as in the problem of finished and unfinished action; rather, it is a matter of whether after the release of such a system, the subject is in a position to continuously produce new tension systems for the same action.

At the same time one has to view the supply of energy within our tests as practically inexhaustible (although we do not have to presuppose Adler's theory of unlimited psychical energies).

Therefore, although satisfaction and dissatisfaction, success and failure, play a part, the concept of a satiation process seems to designate a sequence of events which is essentially characterized by a modification of the goals of the will. The total constellation of events results in certain inclinations and disinclinations with regard to the tasks which must be repeated, and it is this movement of the will goal (17) that appears in our tests as the satiation process.

Such an interpretation is in accord with the fact that the unpleasantness of an action does not simply continuously increase during the satiation process. Rather, even with unpleasant actions, the tendency to perform an action frequently increases at first, and later shows clear fluctuations.

Accordingly, one must ask how the inclination and disinclination to perform similar tasks is shifted by repetition:

The activity ceases to offer anything new. The following is a rather obvious explanation for the change of the positive character of the action during continued repetition: the action maintains a positive character as long as it offers something new. If during repetition the subject learns the action so well that he completely masters it, it becomes uninteresting and finally positively boring.

In fact, much seems to support such an interpretation in the satiation process. Even the main phenomenon, variation, could be easily derived from a tendency for something new and more interesting.

Nevertheless, this in itself does not seem to fully explain the phenomenon of satiation. The most contradictory fact is that relatively indifferent activities do not lead to a rapid satiation, but to a slow one, and that the steering of the activity into the periphery, that is to say the indifferent, is a basic aid against satiation. While in certain cases of satiation the subject tends to employ some interesting variation, the subject's general attitude is not necessarily a desire to be continuously occupied with something interesting. In the later stages of satiation, the subject does not refuse to carry out the activity because it is uninteresting, but rather because, with all the good will and exertion in the world, he simply cannot do it any more.

The disintegration of the gestalt. In the course of satiation, an accelerating state of disintegration could be observed both in the demeanour of the subject and in the results of his work. We could point to this state of disintegration as the cause of the growing dislike of the subject for his work, and in fact it has a bad effect on his work. But then we must ask ourselves, what is the cause of the disintegration of the gestalt? It is not clear why gestalt disintegration occurs during the continuous repetition of an activity. One could attribute the disintegration and the dislike to satiation, or even vice versa.

Marking time (on a treadmill). Let us peruse the structural peculiarities of the course of events in the experiment. Repeated activity is a type of activity which is the exact opposite of final activity. The latter, for example, the completion of a chair, or the painting of a picture, go through changing phases to a final objective. However, even when the subdivisions of a repeated activity are in themselves final activities (this is true of repeatedly reading poems, and to some extent of drawing strokes), repetition leads the whole activity to automatically acquire the character of a continuous, endless activity. The mere fact of an end is not critical. The task "Draw 3000 strokes" is not an end action, because the goal is so far removed that the structure of the actual execution is untouched by this ultimate end to the work.

This characteristic alone does not, however, account for the increasing unpleasantness. There are endless activities which produce absolutely no signs of satiation in some people. Stonebreaking or any other occupation which bears the characteristic of endlessness can be carried on for years and years without satiation.

Endless activities like those which were used in our experiments belong to a special type. Endless activity can be carried out continuously in the same way as a final activity. Generally, such activity proceeds forward, with some momentary difficulties and detours, and even with the feeling of making no progress; but it never quite reaches the state of continuously marking time. However, in our experiments (and the same is probably true of all everyday situations in which satiation phenomenon appear), there is no progress at all. Bricklaying does not necessarily make a house. After reading a poem for the tenth time, one is no further forward than after the ninth reading. Likewise, the fortieth repetition of stroke-drawing is the same as the thirty-ninth. It is of little significance that the page is being filled up. The endless activity in our experiments sooner or later becomes only a marking of time.

Nevertheless, the continual dwelling on the same place cannot be regarded as a sufficient explanation for the gradually increasing unpleasantness. Why does not the subject spend more time on a pleasant than an indifferent activity? The subject is not actually standing still, he is continually active, and accomplishing a certain amount of work. He is applying concentration and some effort to the task in hand, without its ever becoming exactly an *oeuvre*. This feeling of meaninglessness, experienced in the later stages of satiation, expresses itself in disintegration and the making of errors.

The theory that satiation is caused by a continuous subjective input of energy without apparent effect or real progress explains the exceptions in our experiments. Thus, Subject D in the second experiment wants to find out if satiation always sets in; therefore, the continuance of the experiment represents real progress for him. And the unemployed, to whom it only matters that the activity is not too unpleasant, are pleased to remain on the job in order to make money. (The fact, for example, that a clerk is quickly tired of filing letters in contrast to an inexperienced worker (17) would be explained by the fact that the clerk knows she is not doing something that will further her career.) When an activity is carried out as a sideline, there are scarcely any cases of satiation, because subjective input of energy is generally absent, as well as the unpleasantness caused by nonaccomplishment.

Finally, we can explain the fact that there is no real unpleasantness during the variations of the first phase of the satiation process. The first repetition of the individual activities do not bear any characteristics of marking time, despite the fact that objectively there is no greater feeling of accomplishment than with later repetitions. The subject learns something new, and he thinks about how he will carry out the task, so that the work seems neither stupid nor pointless.

On the other hand, the idea of progress in these activities lasts only so long as the task really offers something new to the subject. Thereafter, the subject begins consciously to do variations. This later results in a strong revulsion against the satiated variations.

The contrast between progressive work, and the feeling of discrepancy that arises from a large input of energy that only results in an apparent marking of time, may explain why the activity becomes unpleasant during repetition, even though there is no physical tiredness or other factors to be taken into consideration.

This discrepancy becomes particularly striking when a new activity must be started and an old one destroyed. In that part of the experiment where small sticks and balls were joined together in various patterns, the fact that the pattern had always to be taken apart again was particularly unpleasant for the subject. This destruction of his own work quickly led the subject to refuse to do any more. Stonebreaking in prisons belongs to this category. It is similar when the experimenter ignores the work of the subject, or fails to treat his work with proper regard. (For instance, the experimentor lets completed work drop from the table to the floor, and restrains the subject from picking it up, saying "Leave it there, I don't need it.")

Stable fields of consciousness. Certain other circumstances play a role in the satiation of the situation. Situations which demand intense concentration, yet possess no inherent positive or negative valences, require one to maintain an artificial field of consciousness with a definite structure that permits no interruptions from without. Such situations, including beginners learning typewriting or vocabulary, nearly always become unbearable in the long run. This can apparently be explained as follows: the outward, and in particular the inner situation, of any one person only remains constant for a short time, because the tensions in the remaining mental regions must sooner or later make themselves felt. If a field of concentration is to be maintained undisturbed within the same structure, continuous re-intensifications of effort are required to do this, and the whole thing eventually becomes impossible.

Furthermore, it is obviously difficult to maintain for long a situation in which acute tension prevails. Experiments made with children watching films have shown that their attention is not held by a gradual building-up of tension, and that their behavior in such circumstances regularly shows an inner or outward going out of the field.

Is there a unified theory of satiation? When seeking any uniform theory of satiation, one must remember the extraordinarily broad range of questions with which we have to deal. The variation tendency during repetition is to be found in the satisfaction of vital needs, notably in sexual matters, as well as in every day work, in problems of endurance in sport, and even in fashion.

This theory may play a role in such occurrences as the alternation between work and play, and changes in visual perception. According to unpublished tests by Köhler, the regular change in the interpretation of figure and ground in looking at so-called reversible figures seems to be produced by a kind of local satiation. Finally, satiation can occur either in specified work, or in the company of certain people or in a particular situation.

For a clear conception of the satiation process, it is of essential importance to know if all these variation tendencies are based on the same laws and dynamic factors, or whether it is only a question of outward similarities. This can only be answered by further experiments and analysis. These must also show why people are not satiated by their day-to-day work.

Further experimental research on mental satiation that is important in education necessitates a precise investigation of the significance of success and failure for the satiation process.

1. Lau, *Beiträge zur Psychologie der Jugend* (Langensalza, 1921). Vernon refers to the difficulty of testing the problems of monotony in factory work by using certain laboratory tests, *e.g.*, with ergographs. *Cf.* E. Myers, "The Study of Fatigue" *The Journal of Pers. Res. 3*, 9(1925).

2. Arnold Durig, *Die Theorie der Ermüdung*, cites the definition of Herrmann: "Fatigue is the condition into which the muscle falls through strenuous or enduring activity. Since this condition doubtlessly represents only a certain increase in those changes which occur with every contraction, albeit only in an insignificant amount, it is advisable and basically common usage to designate as fatigue the relatively continuously progressing change in the muscle caused by muscle activity." *Körper und Arbeit, Handbuch der Arbeitsphysiologie*, ed. Edgar Atzler (Leipzig: Thieme, 1929), 201. Also, Thorndike, "Mental Fatigue," *Journal of Educ. Psych.* 2. Mental fatigue also includes mental satiation in Thorndike and others. Also, *Psychologie d. Erziehung* (Psychology of Education), tr. Bobertag (Jena, 1922), 260.

3. The experiments of F. Fränkel are cited by Lewin in "Filmaufnahmen über Trieb-und Affektäusserungen psychopathischer Kinder" (Films of expressions of drive and emotion of psychopathic children), *Zeitschrift für Kinderforschung*. 32, 414-447.

4. W. Blumenfeld, reported about his own work at the 10th German Symposium for Experimental Psychology in 1927. Although it starts with another problem, that of practice, it seems to have yielded very similar results. Since our work was already concluded, unfortunately we cannot go into the substance of his oral report, but we would like to refer to it.

5. Moreover, the gestalt disintegration frequently shows similarities with that gestalt disintegration which is noticeable in the copying of patterns by the feeble-minded. See Rupp, "Über optische Analyse," *Psychol. Forsch.* 4, 262.

6. *Zur Psychopathologie des Alltagslebens* (Vienna, 1920), 174.

7. Werner, "Studien über Strukturgesetze," *Zeitschrift fur Psychologie* 94, 248ff.

8. Lewin, "Kindlicher Ausdruck," *Zeitschr. f. Päd. Psych.* 28(1927), 518.

9. Schwarz, "Über Rückfälligkeit bei Umgewöhnung." *Psychol. Forsch.*, 9, 135, 158.

10. N. Ach, *Über den Willensakt und das Temperament* (Leipzig, 1910).

11. Lau, *Psychologie der Jugend.*

12. Zeigarnik, "Das Bahaltenerledigter und unerledigter Huandlungen," *Psych. Forsch*, 9(1927) 54.

13. Münsterberg, *Psychologie und Wirtschaftsleben* (Leipzig, 1912), 117.

14. Lau, *Psychologie der Jugend.*

15. Heider, *Ding und Medium*, Supplement 7 of the Symposium, 1927.

16. A. Freund, "Die psychische Sättigung in Menstruum und Intermenstruum," *Psychol. Forsch.*, 13 (1930), 198–217. A translation, "Psychical Satiation in and between Menstrual Periods," is available from University Microfilms.

17. Lau, "Willensziele und Willenszielbewegungen," *Psychotechn. Zeitschr. 1*, (5) (1926), 148.

Chapter VI

THE TRANSFORMATION OF ACTIVITIES

In advancing the idea of intention-systems, I noted that when a person becomes involved in an activity, he transforms the activity so that it may develop a character that was not anticipated by the experimenter. In this chapter, we shall see that as long as involvement continues, an activity will constantly be transformed and developed into somewhat different activities. This seems to be a general principle governing all of our activity, from the writing of a word or the listening to a sound to, on a larger perspective, the development of a scientific investigation or the pursuit of a career. Not only is this process of transformation intimately intertwined with the process of satiation, I believe that it is involved whenever substitute satisfaction occurs, and whenever motives are transformed. In fact, it is only when these transformations fail to occur that we invoke concepts such as "rigidity" and "fixation."

In this chapter we shall see that it may be possible to develop a taxonomy of activity that is based on different types of development, and an algebra of how activities transform—the rules for when they change and when two different activities may be considered identical.

THE SATIATION AND PROGRESSION OF ACTIVITY

The Necessity of Variation

Let us review the highlights of Karsten's data from our own perspective.

Reading over the rich array of phenomena which Karsten presents, we are again struck by the vitality of the relationship between the person and the activity in which he is engaged. This relationship is an affective one; that is, the self is involved. The person enters into a project, gets rid of a bad performance, concludes actions by erecting a dividing wall between himself and the work, and in many small ways demonstrates that he and the material are parts of one gestalt.

As this gestalt begins to satiate, variations occur, at first spontaneously, later as a result of the person intentionally exploring different ways of performing and different possible meanings. It is an essential aspect of a variation that the person experiences himself as performing the same activity, and at first, varia-

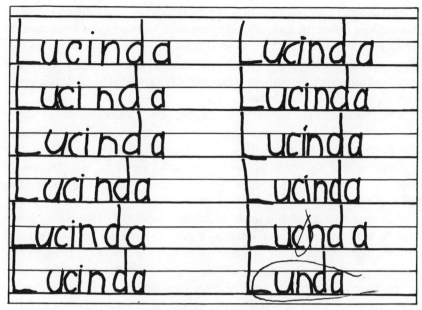

FRONT SIDE OF PAGE

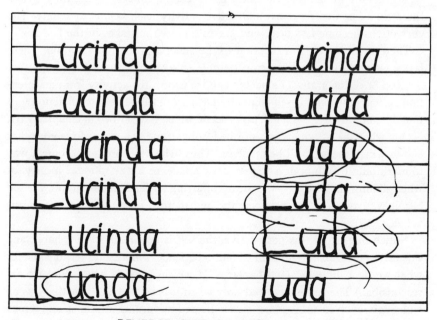

REVERSE SIDE OF PAGE

FIGURE I. Satiation in the First Grade

tions that occur are quite close to the original version of the activity. However, it is not long before the zone of identity expands, and variations begin to occur which initially would have been rejected as a different activity, rather than seen as a variation of the same activity. In this way, the activity's identity is preserved, although the activity is considerably expanded for instance, seeing how quickly one can hatch lines.

When variations can no longer occur, the person enters the final stage of satiation and the gestalt between person and activity begins to disintegrate, so that the task becomes meaningless and errors occur. It is of crucial theoretical importance that this disintegration cannot be prevented if variations or changes in the activity are stopped. An activity which is continued must either develop or disintegrate.

Failure to understand this process leads to a good deal of the misery generated by some of our school systems. Figure 1 shows a first-grade exercise brought home by the writer's six-year-old. The teacher, attempting to give children practice in writing their names, has provided the child with a model to repetitively copy. Notice how the copy—which begins quite well and is not supposed to be varied—gradually disintegrates. At the start of a new unit (the reverse of the page), the copy again begins well but then disintegrates even more rapidly until, finally, the name is no longer recognizable. The teacher—who probably thinks that the child has "become careless"—dutifully circles the errors; but this repetitive corrective activity itself begins to satiate. The corrections become less neat, and she misses two mistakes in the last row.

There is, however, an exception to the general process of satiation. There is one way in which a person can continue an activity without having it either develop or disintegrate. The person can transform the activity from an intention system in which his self is involved as part of the gestalt, to an action unit that does not involve the self. This process, which is described in Chapter VIII, occurs when the activity is transformed from an end to a means for some other end in which the self will be involved. Thus, when the strokes become a way to mark out a rhythm, or a way to draw a face, or a way to make money; or when signing one's name is the means of giving a friend an autograph, the self becomes involved in the new activity, and there is no satiation of the means activity.

Notice that, from this perspective, the self is not involved in a habit, and this fact is undoubtedly related to our experience of not being responsible for what we do habitually. (In chapter VIII we shall see in what sense we are responsible.) The self is involved only when it is related to the activity as an end. Such involvement is sometimes indicated by various emotions, and it may be recalled that Karsten found that activities which were inherently pleasant or unpleasant satiated more rapidly than activities towards which the subject was indifferent. Hence, a person can prevent an activity from satiating by withdrawing self-involvement and making the activity mindless, a mere habit, or a means to some other end. We may, therefore, summarize Karsten's findings by stating that activities which are repeated must either expand or satiate as long as the self is involved in the activity.

Or we may state that, under the conditions of Karsten's experiment, a person may participate in an activity in two ways—with or without self-involvement. In the latter case, the activity will be mindless or habitual or merely a means to some other end. In the former case, the activity must continue to develop.

One of the central tenets of gestalt theory is that all systems move towards equilibrium and stability. While the final state of a system need not be lacking in tension (often a system may be in considerable tension, but in equilibrium with surrounding states that are also in tension), and while the very movement towards equilibrium may establish a subprocess that temporarily moves away from equilibrium as a detour to final stability, the basic dynamics of gestalt systems always work towards a state of equilibrium.

I can agree that in the establishment of a gestalt, the best possible organization is achieved, and that this system always moves towards a balanced state. Many of our activities reflect such a progression—from means to an end, from a strange organization to a stable assimilation, and so on. But how are we to account for the fact that some activities must develop if they are not to disintegrate? It seems to me that this press for the establishment of new goals, new gestalts, cannot be understood in terms of a movement towards equilibrium. Rather, it indicates the existence of another fundamental trend in nature —a trend away from the stability and towards new organizations.

I do not mean this as an argument for vitalism, for this trend may also be present in nonliving organizations, and the trend towards equilibrium is just as present in life (1). Rather, it seems to me that the move towards the increasing development of organization may actually be implicit in the principle of Prägnanz, if we think of that principle as being the maximization of good form in the sense of a constant tendency to transform chaos into cosmos. Nor is such an interpretation completely antithetical to gestalt psychology; for, as Koffka has observed:

> . . . to say that a process, or the product of a process, is a gestalt means that it cannot be explained by mere chaos, the mere blind combination of essentially unconnected causes; but that its essence is the reason for its existence . . . (2).

The investigation of satiation may be viewed from the perspective of Frankl's observations that persons must have meaning in their lives (3). For a person to repeat an activity, either the activity must gain its meaning through serving some end, or the person must vary the activity—create a new goal— in order to preserve the activity's meaningfulness. When this can no longer be done, the gestalt disintegrates and the activity becomes meaningless.

The Theory of Satiation

It will be recalled that Karsten's final theoretical formulation states that satiation occurs whenever there is a "continuous subjective input of energy without apparent effect or real progress." The specification "continuous subjective input of energy" was included in order to distinguish cases of satiation from those where satiation did not occur in spite of the objective input of energy, as in the case of the paid workers who failed to satiate. However, it is not clear why in these cases there was no subjective input of energy. I believe that a more precise formulation for the facts can be articulated by using the concept of involvement. We may state that:

1. There is no satiation, in spite of pure repetition, when the subject is not at all *involved* in the activity. Thus, to the extent that the activity is simply a means for another end (for example, a way of making money), or to the extent that the subject is indifferent to the nature of the activity—that is, it is neither inherently pleasurable nor unpleasurable—or to the extent that the activity is secondary to some other activity of interest (for example, carried out as a rhythmic accompaniment to a melodic line), the activity is not subject to satiation. If the activity is distant from the subject, if the subject is isolated from the activity, if there is no involvement between person and activity, no intention system, then satiation cannot occur.

2. Conversely, precisely when a subject is most involved with the activity in its own right, when the activity is an end in itself rather than a means, then the relationship with the activity is most subject to the satiation process. That is, there is a need for variation, and if this is not realized, gestalt disintegration will ensue.

We will, therefore, amend the statement on the essence of satiation to read: *satiation occurs when there is involvement in an activity without apparent effect or real progress.*

We must now inquire further into the exact meaning of the apparent effect or real progress of an activity, for it appears that the meaning of "progress" may depend on the type of activity we are dealing with.

It is clear that in Karsten's type of experiment, the subject is in a different relationship to the activity than he is with the finite tasks that Ovsiankina and Zeigarnik used. In their work, the subject is engaged in an activity which is dominated by an attempt to reach a goal. Thus, there is some distance between the subject and some end which he desires, and progress of the activity means progress towards this end. The person may succeed or fail in reaching this external goal, and, as we shall see in Chapter XIII, this has implications for the person's ability, whether or not the subject's self-esteem is involved. In Karsten's experiments, the subject is already in the region of the goal. There is no distance, no real difficulty in achieving a goal, and hence the subject cannot try to reach it. Therefore, too, there can be no implication about the subject's ability; he merely has to act to achieve the desired effect. The activities are more like the continuous activities used by Ovsiankina and Zeigarnik, where there is constant repetition which is not directed towards a goal.

There are a number of types of such activities. First, of course, there are consumatory acts, such as eating food as opposed to obtaining it. Henle (4), observing that most psychologists focus on goal-directed activity and stop their analyses when the person or animal is in the goal region, has called for more investigation into what happens when the goal is reached. In this regard, Sheffield (5) has presented some evidence that suggests that reinforcement is based more on consumatory activity than on goal attainment. Since Karsten uses the term *satiation*, it is tempting to think of her as investigating consumatory behavior. Indeed, Lewin states, ". . . an activity can be viewed as a consumption which changes the underlying need and, therefore, the positive valence of an activity into a negative one. As a result of this consumption the valence of 'similar activities' also becomes negative . . ." (6). Unfortunately, such an analysis blurs any distinction between goal-directed and consummatory activities. In fact, we believe that there is a distinct class of activities that are consumatory in nature. Engaging in such activities provides direct pleasure, and satisfies underlying needs. However, such activities do not show the type of satiation that Karsten describes. They are performed with relatively little variation, and continue until pleasure diminishes, without any development of the activity. For such consumatory activity, progress of the activity appears to mean progress in assimilation. Such activities do not have to involve physical needs, such as hunger. For example, when a composer finally completes a piece, he may play it repeatedly, simply enjoying the sound of it as he assimilates the new organization of notes. Such consumption continues without variation until the enjoyment slackens—presumably as the arrangement is somehow digested. In Chapter XII, we shall see that the emotion of pleasure functions to permit the consumption or assimilation to occur without the person's immediately moving to another activity, as he so often does.

Second, there is the sort of mindless activity that is required for many jobs, and that we sometimes engage in to avoid anxiety, to release tension, or when there is simply nothing better to do. Thus, Lewin (7) draws a distinction between means-end activity, and cases where "the activity is its own end"—referring to events such as a child swinging a fishing pole, pushing a truck back and forth, or "walking aimlessly about." It is interesting to note that we have no data on what proportion of our time is actually spent in such mindless activity, and Ryan (8) argues convincingly that it should be investigated in its own right. Since many industrial and military activities involve work of this sort—continuous work that must not be varied—satiation is an inevitable problem. Maier (9) discusses this and various remedies, such as job rotation, the division of such activity into arbitrary units so that one experiences some sense of progress, and the use of rhythm. And Ryan cites a study by Baldamus (10) which specifically investigated repetitive industrial work. Baldamus asserts that such continuous tasks have a pull or "traction" which keeps the person engaged with the activity. He states, "Traction is, in a sense, the opposite of distraction. It is a feeling of being pulled along by the inertia inherent in a particular activity. The experience is pleasant, because it is associated with a feeling of reduced effort" (11). In spite of the importance of this sort of activity, it is relatively noninvolving; progress is rather irrelevant as long as there is progress in serving some larger end; and its rate of satiation is low. Clearly, Karsten is not working with such behavior.

Finally, there is a class of activities that include activities such as exploratory activities (for instance, a child's repeated opening and closing of a door), play activities, and many creative endeavors. While such activities do not really have a goal in the sense in which tasks do, they do have a direction that is revealed as the activity proceeds. In fact, it is the progression of these activities that distinguishes them from consumatory and mindless activities. Although the person is not trying to reach a goal, and is not moving towards a goal, he is allowing the activity to happen, and it is going somewhere, unfolding along definite lines. We might say that the person is be-ing rather than try-ing, and this distinction is probably related to Maslow's distinction between "being" and "doing" cognition (12). Unfortunately, we do not have a word like "task" to characterize activities which have a direction but not a goal, but I shall use the term *ings* (as in explor*ing*, play*ing*, creat*ing*) to denote such open-ended activities.

One *ing* that is of particular importance in education has been termed "messing about." Hawkins (13) defines such activity as the free and unguided exploratory work that a child engages in when he first encounters new material —letters, chemicals, pendulums, and so on. The messing about with the material allows the child to gradually assimilate the material's basic characteristics so that an apperceptive background is developed. Until this occurs, the analytical work of tasks such as learning to read or formulating scientific laws cannot really occur. Holt (14) points out that such messing about is important whenever a person is confronted with material that is not yet organized into familiar patterns. He gives as examples his own attempts to understand a loom, a Scandinavian language, and a rugby match. In attempting to solve a problem with such material, analytical reasoning is powerless because the variables are not clear; and if the person is not going to be overwhelmed with anxiety, he must simply begin to play until he achieves some familiarity with what is going on.

Now the meaning of apparent effect or real progress will depend on the type of activity. If we are dealing with a finite task, then progress means progress towards the goal of the task. If we are dealing with consumatory activity, progress means the gradual assimilation of some material. But if we are dealing with an *ing,* progress means a progression (expansion) of the activity in its own right.

Correspondingly, these different types of progress are stopped in different ways. In the case of finite tasks, the person may be halted by a barrier that he is unable to surmount and that frustrates his progress. In this case, as the person moves against the barrier, tension is generated within the gestalt. When this tension (or pressure) becomes great enough, no further differentiations may be made. This appears to be the type of satiation which Koffka has in mind when he compares its dynamics to trying to continually pump air into a tire as the pressure builds up (15). In fact, in Dembo's experiment (Chapter X) we shall see that this sort of tension may reduce differentiation and produce a general regression. It seems probable that such buildups of tension occur in cases where the person is maintaining a stable field of concentration in order to master vocabulary, a musical passage, etc. The fact that a period of time away from the task will allow one to perform the task more adequately ("reminiscence"), and the frequent superiority of spaced as opposed to massed practice, attest to this sort of an effect.

In the case of consumatory activity, progress is stopped by the assimilation of whatever material is being consumed. The activity is no longer pleasurable, and there is no motivation for it to continue. Nevertheless, it should be noted that this type of satiation still depends on self-involvement. Persons who are overweight because of continual eating activity may be failing to satiate because they are uninvolved with eating *per se.*

Finally, in the case of *ings,* there may be nowhere else for the activity to go. That is, progression may cease because the person is unable to create any further variations, form any other units or organizations. This appears to be the type of satiation with which Karsten is dealing. When it occurs, if the person attempts to perform the activity without disengaging himself, there will be signs of gestalt disintegration.

Thus, while satiation occurs whenever a person is involved in an activity that is not progressing, the reasons for the lack of progression vary as much as the reasons for regression. However, in all cases, the person can no longer organize a gestalt which includes himself and the activity.

Here, we are primarily concerned with Karsten's research, with its emphasis on the progression of activity in the sense of the activity's going somewhere as the subject forms a series of intention systems that broaden the scope of the activity. However, when we examine Hoppe's study (Chapters XII and XIII), we shall learn that this is not only true in the case of *ings*. Rather, we shall see that when a person is successful in reaching the goal of a task, the satisfaction of the intention system leads to the formation of yet another intention system that extends the activity.

The Progression of Activity

While Karsten's study focuses on satiation, we have seen that her experiment may be viewed as a study of the progression of activity. Indeed, by slightly modifying her technique, one could establish ideal conditions for the study of the natural progression of activities.

Note that Karsten's technique simply consists of giving the subject a simple task, one that the subject is able to perform, under conditions where there is no question of experimenter evaluation, and asking the subject to continue the task until the subject wants to stop. For the purposes of obtaining satiation, Karsten prevented a full range of variations from occurring and applied some pressure to get the subject to continue until they "really" wanted to stop; however, we think it is clear that any variation could be permitted, and the subject's wishes could be completely respected. Under these conditions, and with a suitable assortment of tasks, one could explore the nature of the natural development of activities and of task involvement. It is interesting to note that Cohn (16) has suggested a somewhat similar technique as a therapeutic measure. In her procedure, the person sets aside ten minutes by himself in which he commits himself to the idea that he must do what he wants to do (not simply what he feels like doing or what he thinks he ought to do). We hope that there will be studies which utilize these techniques in the future.

For the present, there are some important facts that may be derived from Karsten's observations if we view her study as an investigation of task involvement, rather than of satiation. Let us, therefore, review her data from this different perspective. The progression of the relationship between person and activity seems to be as follows. The person begins the activity with some positive interest. Gradually, however, this interest recedes, and some related activity seems more interesting. For example, a subject who is drawing lines feels it would be nice to slant them differently. Karsten observes that it is not that the activity becomes negative so much as it simply loses its attraction, and another idea occurs which appears attractive. Of course, this process is not necessarily conscious. So the activity expands and progresses as a result of the tempting positive valences which spring up nearby. Seen in a positive light, these variations are a sign that the activity is developing. The trailing trough of this wave of development is the area which is now left behind and is neutral or satiated.

For example, a person who begins by drawing lines in a 3, 5 rhythm begins to slant his lines to the left rather than the right. Then, it occurs to him that the contrasting rows of lines could be made into a pattern. Having finished the pattern, he begins to make the lines as freely and as quickly as possible. Each variation expands the original activity. While making a pattern is not the same activity as drawing lines in a 3, 5 rhythm, it includes the earlier activity and hence is an extension of it. While this expansion does not relieve the satiation which is behind it, the extension keeps the activity progressing.

When the activity can no longer go anywhere, either because it is fully developed or because of restrictions on what is permitted, the activity is satiated and the person normally stops. What constitutes full development will depend on the nature of the person, his needs and talents, and the external supports he has. The accounts of prodigies and persons with genius suggests that when they are engaged in their favorite activity they do not satiate; rather, the activity and their involvement in it keeps developing. Most persons, however, soon run out of ideas (or lack the ability to execute new ones), and then lose interest. At this point external supports are crucial. If the atmosphere is nonevaluative, and if another person can provide a suggestion or technique which will enable the activity to progress, then development rather than satiation will occur. (In open education this procedure is known as extending the activity.)

Holt's observations of children often show how activities may naturally be extended in a free atmosphere (17). For example, a seven-year-old boy saw an article on underwater swimming and became involved in the scuba equipment, the colorful fish, and the idea of an underwater world. His mother found him another article about divers exploring the vases and weapons of a ship sunk thousands of years ago in the Mediterranean. The boy became fascinated by the idea of these beautiful objects lying unknown for so long. An adult friend found him books about the pre-Homeric civilizations that had produced the objects. These books referred to Homer and the Trojan war, and led him to read a juvenile version of the *Iliad*. This led him to read of the seven cities of Troy, and he became interested in uncovering ancient cities and archaeological expeditions. Thus, the activity of scuba diving extended easily to Schliemann's archaeological diggings.

In the above example, it should be noted that as the activity was extended, completely new intention systems were developed. Thus, Asch notes:

> New and important needs can grow out of a free exploration of the surroundings
> and a tendency to constructiveness. They are often not in the service of other
> interests, although they can be brought into important relations with them. To
> maintain otherwise, to refer new developments always to earlier conditions, is
> to obscure what is most significant in the historical process (18).

Asch points out that persons have an objective interest in both the objects
and persons in their surroundings, and that human activities grow out of
insights into the relationships between these objects and our needs. Hence, our
interest extends beyond the initial goal of our activity, to the activity itself and
the objects it involves, until we often find ourselves becoming involved in new
activities and objects that were originally simply means. This is, of course, the
inverse of the process we described earlier whereby a person disengages himself
from a repetitive activity by transforming it into a mere means for some other
end.

Often, the extension of an activity is only possible when new materials or
ideas are available. And Jokl (19) has noted that sometimes new training
techniques will extend the range of an activity so that the whole progress of
a sport or an art is advanced by making activities less susceptible to satiation.
(Chopin's *Études* are an example.) Far too frequently, development is hindered by external restrictions about what is permissible, and, as in Karsten's
experiment, persons are restricted by what ought to be and what is "sinful."

When an activity becomes satiated the person's attention is no longer preoccupied, and other interests, which may have been quite dormant, are liable to
revive. We wonder what governs these revivals—which interests will emerge
—and whether Karsten is correct when she suggests that they will, in some
sense, be opposites of the activity that has been satiated.

While the natural response to satiation is to stop the activity, the person's
ambitions or external pressure may force him to continue. At this point gestalt
disintegration begins to occur and the resulting errors remind the person that
the activity has a will of its own which cannot be ignored. The *ing* has become
an impossible task. Faced with these errors, the person becomes frustrated or
discouraged, as well as satiated, and develops the aversions, devaluations, and
emotional outbursts which Karsten describes. While he may attempt to leave
the field by altering the meaning of the task, he cannot really break off until
the tension is reduced in some way.

It is interesting to note that similar progressions occur with *ings* such as
listening. Thus, if one concentrates on a simple noise, such as a ticking sound,
variations begin to occur which, in the absence of other stimuli, can become
full hallucinations. While Karsten's experiments all involved the satiation of
motoric activities, it is quite possible that similar processes are involved in the

satiation which occurs in perceptual activity, such as figure reversals. For example, in Hans Wallach's studies of visual reorganizations, the continued seeing of one stimulus pattern provokes perceptual reorganizations which might be considered as variations of the activity (20). He had his subject view a pattern of diagonal lines which moved downward relative to the background, but which could be perceived as moving either downward or to the side. Although the downward motion was predominant, eventually a reversal would occur and the movement would appear to go to the side. If the subjects gazed for long at a pattern which could only be seen as moving downward, they were satiated and predisposed to see the ambiguous diagonal lines as moving to the side. The effect of seeing the lines move to the side could be inhibited by having the right half of each line colored red. In this case, to see the lines as moving sideways, one might have to see them as changing color from black to red. However, the satiation becomes so strong that the subject's experience is reorganized by the creation of a completely new gestalt. The subject suddenly sees the lines as moving sideways under a transparent red surface.

While perception is often counterposed to motoric behavior, the sensory-tonic theory of perception stresses their interrelatedness, and Chein's psychology emphasizes the common status of perceptual and motoric behavior as motivated activity (21). Certainly, perception is an activity, and the phenomenon of habituation—the fact that repeated applications of a stimulus results in decreased responsiveness—may simply be a form of satiation. If this line of thinking is correct, then I would expect that the variable of involvement would prove as important in the satiation and development of perceptual activity as it is in the case of Karsten's activities. Thus, if a subject's involvement in looking at a figure were increased by subtly increasing the emotional impact of the figure, or decreased by preoccupying the subject, the rate of perceptual satiation (or development) should be correspondingly affected.

Finally, it should be noted that the analysis of the development and satiation of involvement in an activity needs to be extended to the important area of the development and satiation of involvements with other persons.

Before we leave the area of satiation, we wish to suggest that one other possible avenue for satiation research lies in the peculiar intensity which perceptual meanings may attain during satiation. In Schwarz's study, (Chapter VIII), the reader will discover a brief account of the satiation which occurs when a subject fixes his attention on an action unit that is normally a habitual means to an end. The sudden self-involvement causes the former action unit to splinter, suddenly become prominent, and enter the ego-vicinity of the subject, loaded with distinguishing marks they previously lacked. Thus, the subject suddenly notices that part of the apparatus has a scratch, that the apparatus is stained brown and the grain is visible, and so on.

The apparent intensity of these perceptions with their quality of unique specialness or meaningfulness reminds us of the effects of LSD, intensive meditation, and Werner's discussions of "primitivization" (22). The dependence of this phenomenon on gestalt disintegration suggests that satiation procedures might be a direct and inexpensive way of investigating such phenomena in the laboratory.

SUBSTITUTE SATISFACTION

In discussing the progression of an activity that is satiating, we noted that true variations of an activity are always variations of the same activity. What began as the activity of hatching lines in groups of four may change to hatching lines in groups of four that all slant to the right, then change to slanting all the lines to the left, and then change to making rows of lines that alternately slant to the right and to the left. While in one sense the goal of the subject has changed completely, in another sense he is still hatching lines in groups of four. The activity has expanded and yet retained its identity; otherwise the person would have to get involved in a completely different activity.

While in Karsten's experiments we begin by knowing the identity of an assigned activity, teachers in open education who wish to extend an activity have the problem of discovering the identity of an activity that spontaneously occurs. For example, in one case, a group of children began pushing cars about the classroom as rapidly as they could. Since the teacher diagnosed the activity as "racing," she attempted to extend the activity by getting them involved in stories about races of various sorts. She was completely unsuccessful in this endeavor, and returning to observe the initial activity, finally identified it as an activity of "speeding." With this correct conception, she was successful in extending the activity to become an investigation of how fast different things can go.

The extension of activity that is involved in the progression of satiation may be closely related to the extension of an activity that is involved in substitute satisfaction. Let us see how this is so.

It may be recalled that the subjects in Ovsiankina's experiments engaged in at least two different types of alternatives to full resumption of the activity in which they had been interrupted. One of these consisted of partial resumption, such as thinking about the solution to a puzzle or putting some pieces of a mosaic in place. The other involved a diffusion of the original goal, such as resuming work on a mosaic but using pieces somewhat haphazardly without really trying to accurately copy the model; or turning to the objects used in the interrupted activity but playing with them or using them for some other purpose. Later, we shall see that Dembo found that when her subjects were frustrated in their attempts to reach a goal, they sometimes completed an analogous task. For example, subjects who were unable to throw a ring over a distant bottle placed it over a nearby hook.

Such behavior raises a number of interesting questions. Do such alternatives serve as a satisfactory substitute for the initial activity in that they release the tension system (fulfilling the intention) behind the initial activity? How are such substitute activities related to the phenomenon of symptom substitution and motive transformation which Freud described? What are the dynamics underlying substitution, and to what extent can substitution occur on different levels of reality and in different areas of motivation? A number of Lewin's students were challenged by these problems and I shall summarize their attempts to attain a solution. (The complete translations may be obtained from University Microfilms.) However, I must warn the reader that these experiments, while often ingenious and always instructive, only begin to suggest answers to some of the above questions.

The Studies of Lissner and Mahler

In Lissner's experiments(23), after the subject was involved in a task he was interrupted and given a second task which was similar in some way to the first. The subject was permitted to complete this second task, and while he introspected and the experimenter busied herself with taking notes, there was an opportunity for him to spontaneously return to the first task if he so desired. In this way, it was possible to see if the second task had been an adequate substitute for the interrupted task, satisfying the tension system which had been created, and decreasing the probability of a resumption of the first task. (Lissner first shows, replicating Ovsiankina, that there is about an 85 per cent chance of resumption if no substitute task is provided.) Lissner's findings may best be illustrated by a number of examples:

1. If the interrupted task was a jigsaw puzzle, a different jigsaw puzzle proved to be an adequate substitute; but a puzzle which involved making a square out of a number of geometric parts was not a substitute—that is, after putting the square together, the subject still resumed work on the jigsaw. A jigsaw puzzle of equal difficulty is a better substitute than one of lesser difficulty, but the latter is better than a difficult square puzzle.

2. If the interrupted task was molding an animal out of plasticene, covering the metal form of an animal with plasticene did not decrease resumption. Even cutting an animal out of paper was not a substitute, although it was as difficult as molding it.

3. If the interrupted task was to fold a boat out of paper, folding an airplane out of paper was a good substitute. However, in working with plasticene, subjects who became involved in molding a particular animal (for example, a

tiger), rather than in making just any animal, were not satisfied by molding a different animal.

From the above results we would have to say that one activity may substitute for another if its *process* has the same name—molding, folding, cutting—but not if its *product* has the same name—a boat, an animal. I assume that this means that the subjects were involved in the process, rather than in the superficial product. That is, the subject's goal, or the activity in which he was engaged, literally involved process more than product. Thus, a goal was to make something by folding paper rather than to somehow or other make a boat.

It is evident that one must be careful if one wishes to specify the psychological activity in which a person is engaged. In Lissner's experiments, a subject who was objectively making a boat by folding paper was psychologically closer to making something out of paper than to making a boat. One can, of course, think of activities where the product is more important than the process. For example, a person's objective activity might be sawing wood to make a boat —that is, something that will float on the water and carry things—but psychologically he is making a boat, as shown by the fact that riveting aluminum was a substitute whereas sawing cordwood was not. I shall call this a product activity in contrast to the process activities used in Lissner's experiments.

If we interpret Lissner's findings in this way, the activities which were adequate substitutes were close to being another means of reaching the subject's personal goal. It should be noted, however, that if the subjects had simply been asked what they were doing, they probably would have responded by saying something like making a boat, assuming the questioner could see the paper, and may well have been unaware that the basic activity in which they were involved was closer to making something by folding paper.

By chance, a somewhat different type of substitution occurred in one experiment. The interrupted task was making a mosaic copy of the figure of a man, and the second task was drawing the same figure, which included lines corresponding to each of the different mosaic blocks. Thirteen of the twenty subjects simply drew the requested figure, and since drawing is a different process from the making of a mosaic, eleven of these subjects resumed the mosaic as soon as they had the opportunity. However, seven of the subjects connected the drawing with the making of the mosaic. That is, in drawing the mosaic they took into account the exact number and color combination of the available mosaic blocks. Only three of these subjects later resumed work on the mosaic. Note that it does not appear that the subject gave up the process of making a mosaic man for the goal of drawing a man, but that they literally made the mosaic on paper instead of with stones. As in the previous cases, the substitution helped the subject achieve something close to his initial goal. Nevertheless, this is certainly a different type of substitution than is involved in changing jigsaw puzzles or making airplanes rather than boats.

An investigation of this second type of substitution, substitution which involves a change in process and not just in product, was performed by Mahler (24). Unfortunately, her procedure establishes a connection between the substituted activity and the interrupted activity, so we do not learn anything further about the important act of connecting. But her findings do help clarify the nature of the character of an activity.

In order to insure a connection between the potential substitute task and the original task, Mahler, unlike Lissner, invited the subject to complete the interrupted task by means of the substitute activity. Thus, the two tasks were not presented as independent from one another. After completion of the substitute activity, she permitted the subject to return to the interrupted task if he so desired. The substitute activity was always some form of the original activity (for example, sketching out a mosaic) and Mahler attempted to vary the reality of the substitute by having the subject act, talk, or simply think through the activity.

In the course of the investigation it became obvious that the subject's own goal (how he construed the task) was an important factor in determining substitutability. Two tasks which superficially looked similar could be quite different activities. For example, in one task the subjects were to write a different number on each page, and in another task to write a different number in each square of a checkerboard-like pattern. While superficially similar, most subjects construed the first task as numbering the pages, and the second task as counting the squares. Hence, when the tasks were interrupted and the task of saying the numbers was substituted, the latter proved to be a good substitute for writing on the squares, but *not* for writing on the pages.

On the basis of a number of such results, Mahler determined that there were two different characteristics to activities: "problem solving," where the goal involves finding a solution to a problem; and "realization," where the goal involves realizing (making real) a product (often this takes the form of producing a visible product). Some activities, such as counting, primarily have a problem-solving character, whereas others, such as numbering, primarily have a realization character. However, many activities are constituted by beginning with a problem (how to arrange a mosaic), but ending with a realization (putting the pieces in form). And an activity can change its character. For example, coloring a picture may begin with a simple realization character, but then the subject may suddenly want to make a harmonious color pattern and thus cause the activity to take on a problem-solving character. The distinction between problem and realization character would, of course, apply to product as well as process activities.

In determining the efficacy of an activity as a substitute, it becomes crucial to know the point at which the original activity is interrupted. This is because its character may change, thus affecting whether or not the second activity can help the subject achieve his goal. For example, the activity of making a mosaic begins with the problem of how to arrange the blocks, and ends with the physical realization of this arrangement. (That both parts of the activity are crucial is shown by the fact that if a subject is interrupted after he solves the arrangement problem but before realization, he spontaneously returns to the task.) Suppose the subject is interrupted and given the substitute task of drawing the pattern (a partial realization of the mosaic). If the interruption comes before the solution of the problem of how to utilize the stones, the drawing has no substitute value. If, however, the interruption is after the problem has been solved, the drawing has a definite substitute value (only 17 per cent resume the mosaic whereas 100 per cent resume without the substitution). In short, the character of the activity of drawing could substitute for the realization character, but not for the problem-solving character of the activity of making a mosaic.

It is important to note that talking about how to finish the mosaic had no substitute value, whereas the drawing did. Talking could not realize (bring into reality) the mosaic. On the other hand, when a task had primarily a problem-solving character, such as an arithmetical task, saying the answer was an adequate substitute for writing it.

It might be thought that since the problem posed by an arithmetical task could be solved by thinking, interrupting the writing of answers and asking a subject to simply think through the answers would be an adequate substitute. However, this did not prove to be the case. Even when the subject can privately check his answers, he does not feel the task is completed until he communicates the answer to the experimenter. Mahler points out that the communication of the answer is required to make it a social fact; to make the answer real, it must be recognized as a fact by the experimenter. Thus, tasks such as figuring which seem to have only a problem-solving character, also have a realization component. However, in these cases, the realization (translation into reality) is established by the creation of a social fact, rather than by some visible product such as a finished mosaic.

To summarize: activities have two different components, problem-solving and realization. A new activity can substitute for a prior one only if it fulfills both components, or if it occurs after the other component has been completed. If the realization component is creating a social fact, this may be accomplished by talking rather than acting. But if the realization involves a visible product (such as a mosaic), only another visible product can act as a substitute.

Note that in spite of the advance in specifying an activity's character, we are still dealing with substitute activities which are only successful when they help the subject fulfill a goal or activity which is quite similar to his initial goal. In those cases where subjects return to complete part of an unfinished task, or where they simply play with the materials, it is possible that the activities were not really true substitutions, but rather reflect aborted intention systems in which the subject was never really involved in the first place. That is, the involvement in the original activity may have been rather sparse, with the original commitment limited to doing only a part of the task, or to simply using the materials that were available. In such a case, the subject's subsequent behavior would reflect a complete return to the original low degree of involvement.

Theoretical Considerations

In considering how substitution occurs, Lissner reasons that the substitute activity must somehow provide a release for the original tension system. This obviously cannot occur if the second task's tension system remains independent from that of the first task. It can only occur if the two tasks become parts of one larger tension system. Then they would be connected, and the release of tension in the second task's system would afford release or partial release to the first task's system.

Under what conditions could two tension systems become part of a larger whole? In Lewin's conceptualization there are two sets of factors which would be of influence: (1) The "qualities" of the two systems (the thickness of the boundary walls, the fluidity of the medium, the relative strengths of the different tensions). We shall consider some of these factors in the next section and others in Chapter XI. (2) The "relative position" of the two systems (their proximity to one another, their potential means-ends connections, and so forth).

The reader should recall that in our own conceptualization, tension systems are not pressurized cells, but rather intention systems—gestalts that are moving towards closure. From this view, the combining of two intention systems is a constitutive act rather than the result of pressures bursting through boundary walls. The objective factors which Lewin discusses may all be translated into subjective terms which, I believe, makes the process of substitution much clearer.

The proximity of two different tension systems is not simply governed by similarity, but by whether the systems belong to the same region. As we shall see in Chapter IX, there are different regions in our psychic organization. For example, the region connected with a person's professional life may be relatively isolated from the regions of his personal life. If this is the case, then dissimilar activities in the professional region (dining with a colleague and adding some figures) may be closer to one another than to similar activities in the personal region (eating with a spouse and balancing a check book). Hence, the proximity of a second activity to the interrupted activity may depend on whether the second activity is in the same region—that is, perceived to be part of the same task. From our own phenomenological perspective, the subject may even include two quite dissimilar activities in the same region by some embracing act such as thinking of both activities as "experimental tasks."

While it is not exactly clear how to apply this line of thinking to the results summarized above (neither Lewin nor Lissner give concrete examples), I believe one might proceed as follows. Suppose a subject is folding a paper boat, is interrupted, and is given the task of folding a paper plane. He is likely then to connect the two activities and form a larger whole—the activity of folding papers into objects. He is likely to do this because the two activities are similar and in the same region of performing experimental tasks. Hence, just as two similar objects may be seen as a unit, the two activities may become parts of a larger unit. In a somewhat similar fashion, if a subject perceives that drawing the pieces of a mosaic may be a means to the end of realizing the mosaic, he connects the activity of placing solid pieces with the activity of drawing. Thus, doing a mosaic by placing solid pieces becomes transformed into doing a mosaic by drawing the pieces. It may be added that the formation of the larger unit may be almost automatic, or it may require an act of insight.

This way of conceiving of substitution receives support from an experiment of Henle's (25) in which she applied gestalt principles to the organization of the behavioral field. She reasoned that the similarity between two tasks is always relative to their background. Hence, a subject should only form a unit between two tasks, and thus show substitution if the two tasks were more similar to each other than the background formed by the other tasks which were being performed. Accordingly, Henle gave her subjects a series of five mazes to perform. In the first condition, all five mazes were similar; in the second condition, the first three mazes were similar but the fourth and fifth maze were different (though similar to each other). In both conditions the subjects were prevented from finishing the fourth maze, but allowed to finish the fifth maze. Then the experimenter observed whether or not they went back to do the fourth maze. The results show that the fifth maze only had substitute value in the second condition. We may, therefore, infer that the subjects grouped the fourth and fifth mazes together as similar only when these two mazes stood out against a background of dissimilar tasks. Hence, a gestalt principle is indeed affecting what must be an active organization of the behavioral field.

If we are correct, then it is incorrect to think that one activity literally substitutes for another one. Rather, the subject connects the two activities, so that each is transformed into a part of a new and expanded activity—an enlarged intention system—that may be satisfied. A subject who was making a paper boat and is asked to make a paper airplane is suddenly engaged in the new activity of making things out of paper. Thus, even with these simple substitutions, there has been a transformation of goals or activities.

One wonders if this dynamic can also account for the transformation of motives involved in reaction formation and sublimation. For example, if a child were engaged in the activity of making a mess, but enlarged this to the activity of being involved with a mess, then cleaning up a mess might become a satisfactory substitute. Similarly, making sexual love might be enlarged to loving and, hence, satisfied by taking care of. Such an explanation would stress the role that crucial decisions may play in the development of a person, in the manner explicated by Charlotte Buhler (26). In this connection, it is interesting to note how few studies we have on the phenomenology of motive transformation in everyday life.

We have been discussing substitution as a function of the dynamic of connecting two different intention systems. In addition to this dynamic, an activity might be a satisfactory substitute if it were completely unrelated in form, but met most of the underlying needs initially met by the original activity. In this case, one means would simply replace another means to an end, and the two means would not necessarily have to be connected. The second activity would simply connect directly to the underlying needs.

Of course, this type of substitution could occur only if the original activity had not become fixated,—that is, developed into an autonomous need in its own right. In fact, such fixation sometimes occurred. For example, it often occurred when subjects began molding an animal out of plasticene. If they became involved in making a cat, the activity of making a dog could not substitute, presumably because making an animal was not satisfactory. Indeed a dynamic definition of fixation (or an "autonomous motive system") might be that the activity cannot be enlarged, and hence other activities cannot be made a part of a new whole.

THE CONCEPT OF RIGIDITY

Lewin believed that one quality of a system that would effect how easily it would combine with other systems was its rigidity, a quality that he related to the thickness of the walls of the tension systems. The concept initially grew out of a study by Koepke, who worked with Lewin at Berlin.

Koepke's Study

Working with feebleminded children, Koepke (27) discovered that their tendency to resume interrupted tasks was even greater than that of normal children (as long as the task was in sight). However, in contrast with normal children, Koepke was unable to obtain substitution effects. His initial task consisted of making the figure of a car out of formed pieces of paper. When the task was interrupted and the children were given the task of making a car out of sticks and rings, most normal children did not wish to go back to finish the original car, whereas most of the feebleminded resumed the task.

Koepke attempted to obtain substitution in the feebleminded with a whole series of ingenious methods. He used green paper pieces instead of red pieces to make a car. No substitution. He asked his subjects to copy an animal, and interrupted them with the task, "Now draw the same animal again." Still no substitution. He then attempted to make the substitute act more important. Thus, he asked the children to make a basket out of sticks, and interrupted them with the task of making the basket and filling it with apples (made out of plasticene). There was still no substitution—although this time the resumption of the original task was somewhat delayed. Finally, he tried a series of tasks—making five bridges out of wooden cubes and rectangles. In one condition the five bridges had no meaningful relation with each other, while in a second condition they were connected to each other and led to buildings. In both conditions the second bridge was interrupted by the experimenter who gave the child the third one to complete. In neither case was there any substitute value—though many of the children completed all five bridges before they returned to the second one.

Koepke concludes that for his feebleminded children (aged eight and nine, classified as moronic rather than imbecilic—thus not greatly impaired) substitution cannot occur because their tension systems are more rigid. Thus, the systems cannot communicate to form a whole—a new system—and each system remains isolated with the subject fixated on the original task.

On the basis of this, and other studies, Lewin formulated the idea that the boundaries of intention systems (the walls of the regions) could be conceived as being of varying thickness. The thicker or more rigid the wall, the less the region was capable of joining with another region to form a larger system.

Lewin primarily uses rigidity as a construct, rather than to refer to a type of behavior. Thus, Kounin (who did his dissertation with Lewin at Iowa) states, "Rigidity is that property of a functional boundary which prevents communication between neighboring regions" (28). The more rigid a boundary, the less possibility of tension spreading from one cell to another (the greater the degree of tension difference that can be maintained), and the less chance of cells joining with each other (the greater the functional segregation of the regions).

It should be observed that while rigidity of behavior could be due to the rigidity of boundaries, it might also be due to a lack of differentiation, or to the person being in an insecure situation.

Kounin's Study

From the idea of rigidity as a property of boundaries, Kounin derived a number of predictions (29). One of the most straightforward of these is that the more rigid the boundary, the less effect a change in one region would have on a neighboring region. Hence, he deduces that if a subject is satiated on one activity, the effect on the satiation rate of another similar activity (a proximal region)—its co-satiation—should lessen with increasing boundary rigidity. To test this Kounin makes two assumptions: that rigidity (as a boundary property) increases with feeblemindedness, and that the degree of differentiation within a person is reflected by his mental age (as given by the Binet test). He then compares three groups of subjects with the same mental age (from six to eight): normal children from six to eight years old; young feebleminded subjects, from ten to seventeen years old; and older feebleminded subjects from twenty-nine to fifty-four years old.

The subjects are shown how to draw simple animals by using a large oval and smaller ovals and lines, until they feel confident in making cats, bugs, turtles and rabbits. Each subject is then asked to draw cats until he becomes satiated with minimal pressure. He is then asked to draw bugs until this satiates; then he passes on to turtles, and finally to rabbits. What Kounin shows is that the older feebleminded subjects have the least amount of co-satiation. That is, satiating on cats doesn't affect their rate of satiation on bugs, and so on. This effect is obtained in spite of their taking a somewhat longer absolute time to satiate on the first activity. The normal children show the greatest co-satiation. Kounin also reports that the older feebleminded subjects become suddenly satiated in contrast to a more gradual process in the normal group.

Using the same group of subjects Kounin also establishes that the feebleminded subjects have a more difficult time in shifting sets (sorting cards on the basis of color rather than form, or vice versa) and an easier time in reversing habits (using the apparatus described in Chapter VIII, Kounin shows that the feebleminded are subject to less relapse pressure.) While these findings may also be deduced from the assumption of greater rigidity, we believe that the derivations are more tenuous and that other explanations are equally plausible.

Critique of the Concept

In the course of their investigation into the rigidity of problem-solving behavior in normal persons, the Luchins (30) have attempted to relate rigid behavior to Lewin's construct of rigidity. In the Luchins' "water jar problems," a subject is given a series of problems that can be solved in a given way. After he has developed a set for this type of solution, he is presented with some apparently similar problems. The first two of these can be solved in a different and simpler way, while the third requires that the different solution be utilized. Depending on conditions, such as the amount of stress, the degree of commitment to the first solution, and whether or not the crucial problems are isolated from the first problems, a considerable proportion of subjects will not only maintain their set and miss the objectively easier solution, but will even fail to solve the third critical problem. The Luchins' report an attempt to relate such rigid behavior to the individual differences in degree of rigidity obtained by measuring the extent of co-satiation (31). (The less the co-satiation, the thicker the boundary walls, the more rigidity.) However, no relationship was found between the two measures of rigidity.

Parenthetically, it is interesting to note that there are limits to the efficiency of satiation as an aid to perceptual reorganization. The Luchins report one study in which subjects were given one solution until they were thoroughly satiated (32). When, after from 11 to 203 problems, the subject refused to do any more, he was given the crucial problems. Since only one of thirty subjects used the easier method on the first two problems, and twelve failed to solve the third problem, we may conclude that satiation was of no benefit. Indeed, in this sort of problem, repetition appears to have the major effect of strengthening the set.

Lewin's concept of rigidity has been criticized by the Luchins, who give an excellent review of the theories of rigidity by Lewin, Werner, and Goldstein, contrasting and relating their respective positions (33). They note that the latter two theorists, unlike Lewin, take rigidity to refer to a type of behavior. They also account for rigid behavior in different ways: Werner using the constructs of undifferentiation and disintegration, and Goldstein the impairment of the abstract attitude. The Luchins suggest that Lewin's construct of rigidity is itself a rather rigid construct. They state, "Nowhere, it seems to us, does Lewin come more dangerously close to the concept of an 'essence' of the person which is independent of field conditions . . . than he does in his construct of rigidity as it is formulated in his theory of feeble-mindedness" (34).

We certainly agree with this statement (and we might add that cell walls have to be strong in order to maintain tension in the face of other pressures), but then how can we account for the data on substitution and satiation? The

Luchins point out that there is a hidden assumption in the Lewinian account. This assumption is that the activities are similar (that the regions are proximal). This seems so evident to us that we are apt to forget that in the experience of a feebleminded subject the activities are probably not experienced as similar. But then the regions are not proximal, and we may account for the lack of the communication required by substitution and co-satiation in terms of position and without any reference to rigid boundaries.

The Luchins' explanation assumes that the feebleminded experience an activity much more concretely than the average person does. Thus, each activity is quite special and unlike other activities. In this regard we may note that Maier (35) cites an instance of a feebleminded boy who continually washed large quantities of dishes without satiating. According to Maier, each dish was individually recognized, greeted with pleasure, and placed in special places in the cupboard, the favorites in the most desirable places. Such behavior seems related to the rather special quality of experience that may be induced by certain drugs, or that we may recall from our childhood. As we mentioned earlier, this quality may be obtained when we direct our attention to a satiated activity that is used as a means.

Of course, we still might want to co-ordinate this way of experiencing things as special, or being fixated with the strength of an intention system. However, such a system might be proximal to a system that appeared quite dissimilar to us. Further, if we view these experiences as special rather than rigid, we are more apt to think in terms of related field conditions instead of fixed personal attributes.

Perhaps it is in this regard that we should mention Forer's study on the Decroly method of teaching reading (36). The Decroly method involves teaching children to read by teaching them short complete sentences, rather than words or letters, as units of meaning. While the bulk of Forer's study is a demonstration that the superior recognition of larger whole is due to the increased meaningfulness of the material, and cannot be attributed to such factors as visual patterns, a section of the investigation deals with the effect of having children act in response to the visual presentation. (A part of the Decroly method involves having the child act out sentences such as, "Open the window.") When she was using single words as stimuli, Forer showed the children a card with the name of an object upon it and had the children place the card on an appropriate object in the room. The children were enthusiastic about this activity, and indeed behaved as though they were completing an uncompleted task or gestalt. To place a sign saying "shoe" on a shoe evidently gave the activity closure. As Werner and Kaplan (37) have observed, in the early stages of language acquisition the name of an object belongs with the object as part of it. On the other hand, when adults were asked to perform equivalent actions—they were given names in arabic script—they disliked putting the cards on objects—it was a distraction. Again, rather than accounting for the strength of the children's action gestalts in terms of rigidity of cell walls, it seems more profitable to think in terms of the special properties of concrete events and the quality of related intention systems.

In summary, we should note that there is no question that there are times when activities do not undergo the transformations that are involved in satiation and substitution. At these times we may speak of the person as being fixated. Rather than attempting to explain these occurrences in terms of rigidity (thick cell walls), we prefer to think in terms of the activities being special to the person. We hope that this specialness will eventually be explained in terms of field conditions—for instance, how the activity is embedded in other activities.

FOOTNOTES

1. Ehrenfel argued that there were two opposing principles in the universe—a vitalistic tendency towards order and a tendency towards disorder that stimulated the principle of order to react with new forms. However, the Berlin gestalt school opposed any dualism between life and death, or inorganic, processes. Cf. Fritz Heider's interesting account "Gestalt Theory: Early History and Reminiscences," *J. Hist. Beh. Sci.* 6(1970), 131–139.

2. Kurt Koffka, *Principles of Gestalt Psychology* (New York: Harcourt, Brace and World, 1963; original, 1935), 683.

3. Viktor E. Frankl, *Man's Search for Meaning* (New York: Washington Square Press, 1959).

4. Mary Henle, "On Activity in the Goal Region," *Psychological Review* 63 (1956), 299–302.

5. Fred D. Sheffield, J. J. Wulff, and R. Backer, "Reward Value of Copulation Without Sex Drive Reduction," *Journal of Comparative Physiological Psychology,* 44 (1951), 3–8.

6. Kurt Lewin, "Behavior and Development as a Function of the Total Situation," in Kurt Lewin, *Field Theory in Social Science* (New York: Harper and Row, 1951), 284.

7. Roger Barker, Tamara Dembo, and Kurt Lewin, "Frustration and Regression: An Experiment with Young Children," *University of Iowa Studies of Child Welfare,* 18 (1941) No. 1, 62.

8. Thomas Arthur Ryan, *Intentional Behavior* (New York: Ronald Press, 1970).

9. Norman R.F. Maier, *Psychology in Industry,* 3rd ed. (Boston: Houghton Mifflin, 1965).

10. W. Baldamus, "Incentives and Work Analysis," *University of Birmingham Studies in Economics and Society,* Monogram A1(1951).

11. Ibid., 42. Cited in Ryan, *Intentional Behavior,* 103.

12. Abraham H. Maslow, *Toward a Psychology of Being,* 2nd ed. (New York: D. Van Nostrand, 1968).

13. David Hawkins, "Messing About in Science," *Science and Children* (February, 1965).

14. John Holt, *How Children Learn* (New York: Dell, 1970), 142–156.

15. Koffka, *Principles of Gestalt Psychology,* 411.

16. Ruth Cohn, "I Must Do What I Want To," *Voices* 4(1968), 29–33.

17. Holt, *How Children Learn,* 135.

18. Solomon E. Asch, *Social Psychology* (Englewood Cliffs, NJ: Prentice-Hall, 1952), 345. For his account of the development of new motives, see 336–348.

19. Ernest Jokl, "The Acquisition of Skills," in Erwin W. Strauss and Richard M. Griffth (Eds.), *Phenomenology of Will and Action,* Second Lexington Confer-

ence on Pure and Applied Phenomenology (Pittsburgh: Duquesne University Press, 1967).

20. Hans Wallach, "Ueber Visuell Wahrgenommene Bewegungsrichtung," *Psychol. Forsch.*, 20 (1935), 325–380. A brief abstract may be found in David Krech et al., *Elements of Psychology*, 2nd ed., (New York: Knopf, 1969), 169 and 173.

21. Heinz Werner and Seymour Wapner, "Toward a General Theory of Perception," *Psychol. Rev.* 59 (1952), 324–328, and Isidor Chein, *The Science of Behavior and the Image of Man* (New York: Basic Books, 1972).

22. E. H. Shattock, *An Experiment in Mindfulness* (New York: Samuel Weiser, Inc., 1958), and Heinz Werner, *Comparative Psychology of Mental Development*, revised ed. (New York: International University Press, 1957).

23. Kate Lissner, "Die Entspannung von Beduerfnissen durch Ersatzhandlungen," *Psychol. Forsch.*, 18(1935), 218–250. The translation: "The Satisfaction of Needs by Means of Substitute Actions" may be obtained from University Microfilms.

24. Vera Mahler, "Ersatzhandlungen Verschiedenen Realitätsgrades," *Psychol. Forsch.*, 18(1933), pp. 26–89. The translation, "Substitute-Actions on Various Levels of Reality," may be obtained from University Microfilms.

25. Mary Henle, "An Experimental Investigation of Dynamic and Structural Determinants of Substitution," *Contributions to Psychological Theory* 2(1942), No. 3.

26. Charlotte Buhler, "The Goal Structure of Human Life," *Journal of Humanistic Psychology*, 1(1961), 8–19.

27. Paul Koepke, "Substitute Satisfaction in Normal and in Feebleminded Children," an unpublished manuscript of 19 pages, may be obtained from University Microfilms. Lewin's summary and discussion of the data is in Chapter 7 of Kurt Lewin, *A Dynamic Theory of Personality* (New York: McGraw-Hill, 1935).

28. J. S. Kounin, "Experimental Studies of Rigidity," *Character and Personality*, 9(1941), 251–282,

29. Ibid, 254.

30. Abraham S. Luchins and Edith Hirsch Luchins, *Rigidity of Behavior* (Eugene, Oregon: University of Oregon Press, 1959).

31. Ibid., 222–223.

32. Ibid., 224–226.

33. Ibid., Chapter 2.

34. Ibid., 63.

35. Maier, *Psychology in Industry*, 535.

36. Sarah Forer, "Eine Untersuchung zur Lese-Lern-Methode Decroly," *Zeitschr. fuer Kinderforsch.* 42(1933), 11–44. A translation, "An Investigation of the Decroly Method of Learning and Reading," may be obtained from University Microfilms.

37. Heinz Werner and Bernard Kaplan, *Symbol Formation* (New York: Wiley, 1963).

Chapter VII

THE STRUCTURE OF ACTIVITY

WE have been considering the dynamics of action, that intentions energize our behavior. But there is also a structure to our activity; it is organized and sometimes follows rigid forms. Intentions, valences, and forces are important concepts, but so are associations, fixations, and personality structures. In Chapter II, we saw how Lewin demonstrated that behavior would not occur without the dynamics of intention, but Lewin did not deny that associations were also necessary to behavior. Without an intention to read, a printed word cannot lead to reading, but the best of intentions to read cannot lead to reading without the necessary associative structures. Thus, Lewin saw the performance of a habit as dependent on an intention energizing an associative connection between stimulus and response.

However, when we closely examined an intention we found that this dynamic actually has a complex structure. Rather than simply being a source of energy that could be conceptualized as a region under pressure, we found an involved structure with interdependent parts—the "intention system" described in Chapter IV. Likewise, in the next few chapters we shall discover that an examination of the apparently simple structural concept of an association reveals a complex set of dynamics. We shall have to replace the idea of an association as a simple connection, an S-R bond, with the conception of an association as a complex organization with its own internal dynamics. In fact, as we proceed, the distinction between dynamic and structural concepts will be replaced by a view of all behavior as a dynamic structure of activity whose units are always intention-systems rather than mechanical connections. In the next chapter, we shall examine the study by Georg Schwarz that makes this conceptualization possible. It may be best introduced from the perspective of Koffka's theory of association (1).

In his analysis of associative learning, Koffka argues that an association does not occur either as the result of a mechanical connection or an intentional force. Rather, he asserts that associations are the products of organizations of experience—gestalt forms. Whenever a part of one of these gestalts is provoked, forces arise that tend to evoke the whole. Hence, when a stimulus communicates with a part of such an organization, we are apt to have associative responses that complete the organizational gestalt.

Note that in such a view, the energy for the association resides in the gestalt organization and need not rely on the person's intention. For example, if one person intones, "To be or . . .," another person may unintentionally think, " . . . not to be," thus spontaneously completing the whole. However, for a stimulus to provoke an association, it must first communicate with a part of the whole that has been previously organized. Rather than accepting Lewin's view that the energy for an association must come from an intention, Koffka suggests that intentions affect associations by influencing the communication between the stimulus and the organization. That is, if a person is confronted with the stimulus "black," an intention to give opposites will establish a communication between the stimulus and the "black" that is part of the organization "black-white." Whereas an intention to give "sayings" may establish a communication between the stimulus and the "black" of "black and blue."

While I accept Koffka's assertion that associations are the result of organizational dynamics, the way in which he phrases his argument suggests that a stimulus exists independently until it communicates with part of an organization. However, from the perspective of either field theory or phenomenology, a stimulus does not exist for the subject until it is responded to. Hence, I would carry Koffka's argument a step further and suggest that the stimulus itself is already a part of an organization and influenced by organizational dynamics. When I present a subject with the stimulus *blue,* he may organize the stimulus in different ways. If I ask him to "look at the word," he is apt to organize the stimulus as a word-to-be-read. If I now ask him to report the color of ink in which the word is printed, the organization (word-to-be-read) will interfere with the intention of reporting the different color in which it is printed. If, on the other hand, I ask the subject to "count the letters," the subject does not organize the stimulus into a word. For the subject there is no word-to-be-read present, and hence no interference with the task of counting the letters. Thus, intention (set, or will) affects how the stimulus itself is organized and hence how the subject responds. In fact, later we shall see that *will* may be regarded as the organization of behavior.

Let us review these theoretical developments:

1. Ach demonstrates that the force of a subject's intention can be experimentally pitted against the force of habit. However, this latter force is conceived to be due to a mechanical connection established by the repetition of a stimulus and the subject's response.

2. Lewin shows that this "force of habit" really stems from the person's intentions. However, habit is still conceived to be a mechanical connection that is energized by the intention.

3. Koffka argues that a habit should not be conceived of as a mechanical

connection, but rather as a dynamic organization. When one of the parts of this organization is evoked, a force is exerted to re-establish the whole. The evocation of this part will occur when a subject's intention establishes a communication between the stimulus and some part of the organization.

4. I agree that habits should be conceived of as dynamic organizations. However, I assert that stimuli do not exist as stimuli independently from a person's activity. Any stimulus acquires its meaning from being part of an organized activity (an intention system). Once perceived, the stimulus leads to a response which promotes the intention. The meaning of this response is, of course, related to the meaning of the stimulus. As in Koffka's conceptualization, this process is governed by the dynamics of closure.

All these facets of the problem of association are illustrated in the study by Schwarz that we are about to examine. This important study has been completely overlooked. In part this is probably due to its length and complexity, but in part I believe it has been neglected because it really does not fit anybody's theoretical predilections.

Schwarz works with "relapse errors" (negative transfer)—the forces that make one reach for the pencil where it used to be. Building on Lewin's work, he shows that the course of energy for the old habit does not come from a stimulus, but from an intention—the very intention that is not being actualized.

However, in line with Koffka's thinking, he shows that the constraining connections which lead to the relapse are not an interfering habit in the sense of a connection, but a gestalt—an "action unity."

The traditional connection (S-R) is usually formed by contiguity and strengthened by repetition; the action unity is formed and gains its strength by the various gestalt factors which promote a solid unit. Schwarz's specification of these factors for action units is an original contribution of the highest order. Further, by using different experimental arrangements, he is able to create different types of action units, and thus manipulate the amount of relapse error independently of the number of repetitions.

Finally, by examining the experience of his subjects and subtle nuances of their behavior, Schwarz discovers phenomena that would be overlooked by an investigator who was simply concerned with the quantitative aspects of overt performance. The latter would merely note that negative transfer (relapses) occurs when the habit strength of a new response approaches the habit strength of the old response. Schwarz, however, succeeds in distinguishing between two qualitatively different types of negative transfer. One of these is experienced as a force of habit, the other as a confusion about what to do. These different types of relapses are explained in terms of differences in the structure of the action units that develop. And these structures are shown to be affected by the subject's intentions.

The reader must be warned that this is a difficult study to grasp in its entirety, because of the large number of details which are involved in its over-all execution. However, if he patiently examines each of these trees, and keeps his bearings, he will finally be rewarded with an elegant forest of new ideas.

FOOTNOTES

1.   Kurt Koffka, *Principles of Gestalt Psychology* (New York: Harcourt, Brace and World, 1935), 556–590, 607–614.

Chapter VIII

ON RELAPSES IN RELEARNING*

Georg Schwarz

[*I have combined the first of Schwarz's articles with the second, originally published ten years later. Both articles are based on the same data, and deductions from Part II are relevant to the full understanding of Part I.*

Originally, Part I contained the data on relearning, backlearning, and confusion errors, and a brief discussion of the role of action unities in relapse pressure. Part II focused on the development of action unities and the experiments on relearning suggested by their analysis. I have changed the order, so as to present

*Translated by Ms. Marsha Horwitz. The original article, "Über Rückfälligkeit bei Umgewöhnung," was published in *Psychologische Forschung,* Part I, 2(1923), 86–158, and Part II, 18 (1933), 143–190. Permission to publish this translation was generously granted by Springer-Verlag.

the data on relearning, the full discussion on the development of action unities, the experiments on relearning suggested by the analysis, and, finally, the data on backlearning and confusion errors. In order to conserve space, I have omitted material whenever this would not detract from the main thrust of Schwarz's thesis. Both the original articles may be obtained from University Microfilms— Editor.]

I INTRODUCTION

According to association theory, learning and learning errors are attributed to the fact that associations arise between two psychic events *a* and *b*, which have repeatedly occurred directly after one another. An association, acting as the motor of a psychic event, causes *b* to tend to occur after the appearance of *a*. This is said to become evident when one tries to associate *a* with a new experience *c*. The formation of a new association, according to this theory, is inhibited by the already existing association.

Associations are also said to be the cause of the relapses which are evident when instead of reacting to *a* with *c*, the subject again reproduces *b*.

Lewin (1) proved, however, that the coupling which is produced when two actions repeatedly follow one another is by no means the motor of a psychic event. He showed that relapses do not take place under certain conditions in spite of many repetitions and strong associations, while they do occur under other conditions even with little repetition and weak association.

Thus, the problem of learning and relapses is in need of new investigation. [*I have omitted a page which describes different types of relapses, and moved two paragraphs to the procedure section—Editor.*]

Munsterberg (2) believed that relearning tests could not be undertaken in the laboratory since the deviation of the subject from the purpose of the experiment (relearning) is not possible. Thus he placed the test in everyday life, and carried out a series of observations on himself in the course of several months:

1. In addition to his usual ink bottle on the left side of his writing case, M places a second bottle on the right edge of the case which is to be used exclusively from then on; the left one is emptied. M thus establishes relapses.

2. M transfers the place of his pocket watch from the left vest pocket to the right pocket of his trousers, and establishes that he still continues to reach automatically into the vest pocket.

3. M locks the door which leads from his work room directly to the hall, which he has been using up to now, and he takes a detour through the anteroom. Here, too, relapses are observed.

Munsterberg's results will later be compared with our own. Munsterberg undertakes his interpretations on the basis of mechanistic psychophysics.*

These studies place stress on quantitative performance results, and as a rule do not at all go into the qualitative character of the actions. At present, however, since the purely associative explanation has become untenable, the very questions concerning the nature of habituation, the structure of the incorrect actions, and of relearning are again under discussion. Therefore, for us a qualitative analysis is primarily necessary.

II METHOD

Life offers us a great number of examples of performance habits (*cf.* Munsterberg's experiments). When we attempt to rearrange such a performance habit in the laboratory we succeed readily. Thus we can lift a door handle which we have thus far pressed, without any difficulties. On the other hand, difficulties may suddenly become evident, as in the following case. After changing the mechanism of the door handle, one sits down to his usual work, and after a time wants to open the door, perhaps to receive a visitor. Frequently, one will still press the handle again, lost in thought from carelessness or from habit (3).

These and numerous similar observations cause one to conclude that the comprehensive action context plays an essential role.

Preliminary experiments with a three-part action (similar to the one used later as a "middle action") had not yet yielded any habit errors. In order to obtain sufficiently pronounced errors, we had to incorporate the habit action into a larger frame of actions in which it plays a relatively unimportant role.

Apparatus

Thus an apparatus was constructed (Figure 1) which is used as follows: a ball having a diameter of 1 cm. (a marble) is tossed into one of three funnels F_1, F_2, or F_3 and runs over the duct D into the box B. There it remains until the subject has pressed the lever L which projects horizontally from the box; then the ball runs over duct E out of the box and is to be caught by the subject. The lever returns automatically to the horizontal position.

These three manipulations of the apparatus—tossing the ball, pressing the lever, and catching the ball—which must all be carried out with the right hand, are incorporated into a more comprehensive action, a frame action. This frame action consists of an initial action, the selection and removal of the ball from a bowl (BB) standing at the left of the apparatus, and an end action, placing the ball on a design (PD) which forms a name. The weight of the whole action

Review of earlier studies omitted—Editor.

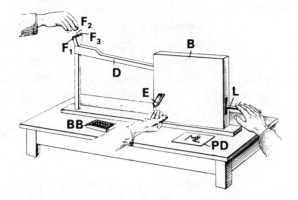

FIGURE I. The Apparatus Used for the Tests.

In the bowl BB on the table are various colored balls (marbles). The subject takes one of these balls with his right hand, and tosses it into one of the three holes (F_1, F_2, F_3) of the funnel, so that it rolls down the duct D which ends in the box B. Due to a device within the box and not visible to the subject, the ball remains lying in the box until the lever L is pressed. When this is done, the ball immediately rolls out over the short exit duct E, where the subject must catch it with his right hand after quickly releasing the lever. Then the ball is placed on the placement design PD. The lever returns automatically to its original position. It is possible to rearrange the inside of the apparatus so that the ball rolls out of the box when the lever is lifted instead of pressed.

lies on this final action. After the final action, the subject moves on to the selection of the following ball.

Therefore, the whole action is a goal action leading to a specific end, in contrast to a continuous action, which may continue any length of time. Within this goal action, three main parts and a total of about five subparts can be distinguished according to task:

1) Initial action: *a)* choosing the ball in the bowl; 2) Middle action: *b)* tossing the ball into the funnel, *c)* pressing the lever, *d)* catching the ball; 3) Final action: *e)* placing the ball on the design.

The middle action is physically represented as a path which leads from a starting point to a certain goal. The individual parts of this path action have no material relationship to the goal of the total action; they can be changed without in any way affecting the action's goal.

After learning this total action, a change in the apparatus can be made out of the subject's view, so that the lever must now be lifted instead of raised if the ball is to appear at the exit duct.

Since with further performance of the test the final action is gradually performed more fluently its dominating position is weakened. Its stress tends to become equal to the relative lack of stress of the middle action, and it is necessary to introduce factors which will counteract this process. The stress of the frame action can be restored by an increase in its difficulty, which can have an effect on both the beginning and final phases. For instance, various types of curves, intertwining letters, and fantastic figures can be placed, partially from memory, after the plans have been shown once.* Or, red, green and yellow balls can be used with increasing difficulty, by requiring the subject to avoid using the same colors next to one another, or by requiring a specific color sequence, for instance, red-green-yellow, or yellow-red-green-yellow-green.

Procedure

The experiments were carried out from December, 1923 to August, 1924 in the rooms and with the materials of the Psychological Institute of the University of Berlin, and with the support of the Cooperative Aid Society (Notgemeinschaft) of German Science. The work was inspired by Dr. Lewin, who also aided the course of the tests with his advice. May I here express my gratitude for the friendly help of those just named. The author is also indebted to those who helpfully conducted some tests, and also to the 53 subjects who made themselves available for a total of 95 tests.

To limit the length of this presentation, the results of only one subject will be described for each specific test arrangement, although we almost always had a series of other confirming results at our disposal.

Instructions. The action of the apparatus is demonstrated to the subject. Verbal instructions are only given with respect to the frame action.

Preliminary Practice. The subject carries out the whole action several times to become familiar with the operation of the apparatus, especially the use of the lever. Generally 2–5 tosses with balls suffice here. To be sure, some subjects need up to 30 tosses. In the following descriptions of the tests, generally the tosses necessary for preliminary practice are not presented separately. They appear in the calculations among the tosses of learning.

Learning. The total action is practiced with the subject until a firm habit is produced in the performance of the middle action. This is generally the case after about 90 tosses. The frame action is prevented from becoming automatic by regularly giving new instructions of increasing difficulty after every 30 tosses.

Toss 1—30: A name is to be laid out; no instructions on color choice. Toss 31—60: A new name is to be laid out; the same colors may not be used directly after one another. Toss 61—90: A third name is to be laid out; a definite three-part color order is prescribed.

Relearning. The apparatus is changed in such a way that the lever which

_____
* Figure omitted—Editor.

thus far has been pressed, is now lifted. Relearning is generally completed after about 45 tosses. Initial and final actions are made more difficult: a sine curve, a lower-case Greek or Latin letter must be laid out in a new color sequence.

Back-learning. After renewed alterations of the apparatus by the experimenter, the lever must now be pressed again. Generally back-learning has been completed after about 15 tosses. Initial and final actions are made still more difficult: complicated intertwining letters, or fantastic figures which have been shown once must be laid out in a new color sequence by memory.

Renewed Learning. The lever is again lifted. At the same time, new and more complicated instructions are given for the initial and final actions.* Although this is at first uncomfortable for the subject, all partial actions must be carried out with the right hand. We did not investigate whether habituation also arises when the actions are carried out partially with the right hand and partially with the left.

Personal Observations

The experimenter was able to establish with certainty errors in the tasks, such as incorrect lever use or false starts in that direction, by observing the subject. Insight into the psychological conditions for the subjects' behavior could only be obtained by using the subjects' personal observations (4). The subject was able to make his statements during the action, or else he could from time to time pause in his action and during this pause render his personal observations on his experiences during the last toss period.

By pauses for statements, the course of relearning and back-learning was hindered, and relapses were strengthened. At the same time, important observations could be made. For this reason, testing with pauses for statements was preferred.

Since during the stage of learning, as well as relearning and the following stages, the inner development progressed more rapidly at first, and the experiences were richer, and since we were interested in the most accurate investigation of every phase of the development, more pauses for statements were included at the beginning.

The subject was generally asked: During the stage of learning, after toss 5, 10, 20, 30, 45, 60 and 90. During the stages of relearning, back-learning, and renewed learning, after toss 3, 6, 10, 15, 20, 30, and 45. Five tosses generally take 40 seconds.

---

the results from back-learning and renewed learning have been shifted to a later section—Editor.

III RELEARNING: SUBJECT A, RELAPSE PRESSURE

Learning in test A stretched over three test days.

Learning. The lever is pressed. On test day 1, 110 tosses; on test day 2, 110 tosses; on test day 3, 57 tosses. Not until the third test day is the lever use changed, immediately after the 57th toss.

Relearning. The lever is lifted. 56 tosses. New instructions for the frame action are given with toss 1 and 26. Pauses for statements after toss 5, 10, 16, 21, 25, 31, 36, 40, 45, 50, 56.

Course of Learning

At this point we shall give only a short description of the learning process. At first a chain of relatively independent, hardly connected, partial actions is carried out (selection of the ball, tossing into the funnel; pressing the lever; catching the ball; placing the ball on the design), a series of (relatively) isolated unities. In accordance with the test transcript, which is described in more detail later, we shall speak here of a "sum action" *(a + b + c + d + e).*

Gradually, the stress of the individual partial actions shifts; the individual contours become hazy, and new ones appear; a process, complicated at times, having repeated re-centerings takes place.

The action finally occurs as a unified action, as an action unity (5) *(abcde)* the parts of which can only be separated to some extent as being successive; however, even this division does not correspond to a parallel psychic one. With future repetitions the action unity becomes rigid.

Course of Relearning

The purpose of the arrangement proves to have been achieved. Immediately after changing the instructions on lever use, a strong relapse tendency to press occurs which is only overcome gradually. We divide the course of this relearning into sections, using psychological criteria. The course in detail is evident from the subject's personal observations:

Section I (Toss 1—5). The subject makes an incorrect start in his hand movement for lever use. Short of the lever, he corrects himself (Toss 1—3) or else he forgets the correction and uses the lever incorrectly (Toss 4 and 5).

The subject says about Toss 1—3: "Every time I wanted to press down the lever; but at the last moment it occurred to me that I had to lift it. It was the moment that the ball bounced in the apparatus, perhaps a little earlier. . . ."

About Toss 4: "When I had tossed the ball I wanted to sit somewhat more comfortably and in the process I hit my right foot against the table leg. As a result, the balls I had already laid out rolled from the sheet, and at the same time I pressed down the lever. Since I was distracted by the rolling balls, I only pressed it down part way and therefore I immediately pressed down again and more firmly. But since the ball did not come out of the apparatus I became confused and it occurred to me that I had used the lever incorrectly."

In Toss 5 the subject again made incorrect use of the lever.

Section 2 (Toss 6—16). The subject keeps the performance of lever use in mind and immediately begins the hand movement for lever use correctly. He explains Toss 11—16: "Lever use is still not completely a matter of course for me. I always thought: Lift it up! I think I no longer have a tendency to press the lever down."

Section 3 (Toss 17—25). The subject only makes a false start in his hand movement for the lever use in the first tosses of each cycle, after the pauses for introspective statements, but then corrects them (toss 17, 22, 23). The correction takes place at an earlier and earlier stage, and with less and less intensity.

Toss 17—21: "The first time (toss 17) I wanted to press down the lever. But then, want is not the right expression; it was really weak; at the last moment I did it correctly without any particular intensity. The second time (toss 18) I clearly thought about lifting it up. From then on I used the lever automatically, and almost as a matter of course."

Toss 22—25: "The first time (toss 22) I wanted to press the lever down, but I noticed it and, in fact, this time I noticed it a little earlier than otherwise. The second time (toss 23) I thought of it even earlier, perhaps when my hand passed over the center of the apparatus. The third and fourth time (toss 24 and 25) I used the lever rather automatically."

Section 4 (Toss 26—56). The subject begins the hand movement toward lever use correctly right at the funnel. At the first toss of each cycle he is often aware for a moment of the manner in which the lever use had previously been carried out; the awareness of the action required resists this (toss 26, 41, 46, 51).

Toss 26—31: The first time while tossing the ball I had a vague idea of an action in which I must not press the lever down. From the second toss on (toss 27 ff), lifting the lever was a matter of course for me."

Toss 32—36: "I no longer feel any desire to press the lever down, and I do not pay any particular attention to the lever."

Toss 37—40: "The whole action is a matter of course for me."

Toss 41—45: "The first time (toss 41) I had a weak sense or an idea of pressing the lever down. But this was immediately rejected with anger that such a thing could still occur."

Toss 46—50: "At the first toss (toss 46) I remembered the previous times when I was always tempted to act incorrectly the first time . . . a struggle was not necessary."

Toss 51—56: The first time (toss 51) I felt something that had to do with pressing down; I cannot even call it an idea. While lifting the lever my had describes a kind of loop. The second time (toss 52), I had this loop clearly in my mind."

Degrees of Relapse Tendency

By drawing upon the various symptoms of difficulty, the following eight degrees of relapse tendency can be distinguished and arranged systematically. These are used in Figure 2 as the basis for a curved representation of relearning. The strongest degree of relapse tendency is designated as step 8.

8. The hand movement is begun incorrectly; the lever is incorrectly used (Toss 4 and 5).

7. The hand movement is begun incorrectly, but is corrected shortly before or at the moment of contact with the lever (toss 1—3, 17).

6. The hand movement is begun incorrectly but corrected earlier, on the way from the funnel to the lever (toss 18, 22, 23).

5. The hand movement is begun correctly. The subject is aware for a moment of the action performed earlier; the awareness of the required action resists this (toss 26, 41).

4. Same as 5, but awareness is more fleeting (toss 46).

3. Same, but awareness has almost totally disappeared (toss 51).

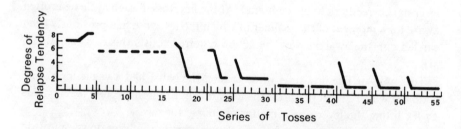

FIGURE 2. Course of Relearning in Subject A.

On the ordinate are the degrees of relapse tendency described in the text; on the abscissa, the series of tosses is indicated. The pauses for statement are rendered by vertical lines between the numbers of the tosses. The curve is broken at these places; continuing it would falsify the picture.

Tosses 6–16, where the subject performs the action correctly by employing a conscious pressure for mastery, cannot validly be included among any of the eight steps. Viewed from the perspective of achievement they do not belong to steps 6–8 (errors on false steps). On the other hand, very different psychic conditions are involved in steps 1–5. Therefore, the results of these tosses are shown with dotted lines—rendering the improvement of outer achievement by lowering the curve to an intermediary step.

2. Lever use occurs "as though of itself"; first step of the mechanization of the required action (toss 19–21, 24–25, 27–31).

1. The same, but still more clearly pronounced; second step of mechanization (toss 32–36, 37–40, 42–45, 47–50, 52–56).

Dynamic Factors

Let us consider the curve with regard to its dynamic factors, *i.e.*, not the events as such, but the forces which are present in the psychic field during the various phases of the course of events.

At the beginning of relearning the subject formed the intention of carrying out the actions, so that the balls are chosen in a different color sequence, the lever is lifted, and a new name is written out. But this intention is without success with regard to lever use. At the very beginning, false actions occur regularly; even when the lever itself is correctly handled, the start of the hand movement begins falsely (toss 1–5).

The subject's corrective measures are not directed toward strenghtening his intention to use the lever correctly; rather he endeavors to keep in mind the directions on lever use (6). He thinks about it always (toss 11; probably including all of the tosses between 6 and 16). The effect of this awareness does not only mean an intensification of attention; it also means a re-centering of the whole action, so that the center, the main stress of the action, which hitherto lay on the final action, now shifts to the lever use. This re-centering invokes a relative independence of the lever use; the subject carries out the lever use as it were as a seperate action beside the whole action, and thus he is able to master it better. The relatively good achievement in this phase therefore indicates, psychodynamically, something essentially different from the later phases of relearning. The good outer effect does not mean that there are no forces in the direction of habit errors, but only that they are being overcompensated elsewhere.

The not completely successful intention at the start of relearning was more general, and dealt with the whole of the action, leaving the structure of the action unchanged. The subsequent successful intention, however, is an intention which restructures the action and which lends the lever use a higher stress rank.

When the lever use has been stressed several times and carried out as it were as an independent action, the relapse tendency (toss 17) is considerably weakened. Now, under the pressure of the tendency for the flowing course of the total event and the stress of the final action, the destruction of the relative independence of the lever use begins again; the frame action again becomes dominant.

After the subject has kept the lever action in mind from Toss 6-16, and has correctly begun the hand movement, he believes he has overcome the relapse tendency, and after a pause for statements, he again performs the lever use without special stress on toss 17. Study of the curve shows us, however, that a relapse tendency continues to exist, although at a diminished strength. While the relapse tendency becomes weaker during the time of a toss period, it always gains strength with each pause, that is, with the first toss of the next cycle.

If the relapse tendency diminishes from toss 17 on, this is expressed by the fact that it appears more weakly with the first pause of every succeeding cycle (with the exception of toss 23) than with the first toss of the preceding cycle. From toss 26 on, the relapse tendency no longer has any influence on the effective action of the subject, but is only documented in the "idea". Here, constantly weaker after-images appear: the subject is briefly aware of the previous action as "idea", "weak feeling" (toss 26 and 41), "memory" (toss 46), "not even an idea" (toss 51).

Let us once more list the factors which promote the relapse tendency: 1) pauses for statements; 2) increasing the difficulty of the initial and final actions. This can be accomplished by instructions or it can occur through difficulties arising from the task. The lever use loses stress; and 3) through disturbances which lead the weight of the events to lie completely outside of the action (cf toss 5 and 4).

Corrective Actions

When subject A does not use the lever incorrectly more often than in toss 4 and 5, this is due, besides the restructuring intention, to the appearance of involuntary corrective actions. Thus, for example, Subject A, in tosses 1–3, wants to press the lever, but he notices his error, and, short of the lever, he quickly brings his hand around to lift it: "In the last moment it occurred to me that I had to lift it." Such "ideas" of an imperative nature appear again in toss 17, 18, 22, and 23. The ideas fail to occur when a disturbance takes place (toss 4 and 5).

As soon as the relapse tendency weakens and occurs only as an idea, the corrective action also vanishes into ideas, a fleeting awareness of the corrective action counteracts the fleeting, after-imagelike awareness of the relapse (toss 26 and 41). When a very weak relapse tendency occurs, no corrective process counteracts it any longer (toss 46 and 51).

The place of the corrective action within the whole action is not stabile. In toss 1–3, the corrective action occurs directly at the lever after it has already been touched (If this last minute is missed, incorrect lever use must occur, as it does in toss 4 and 5.) In toss 17 the corrective action again takes place at the lever, which is, however, no longer touched; in toss 22 it occurs somewhat before the lever, and in toss 23 midway between funnel and lever.

The place of the corrective action thus travels in sections to the funnel, and thereby it becomes transferred back in time within the whole action; indeed, this occurs parallel with the weakening of the relapse tendency, as a glance at the curves indicates, and also parallel with the weakening of the corrective action (7).

When the place of the corrective action has reached the funnel, it does not travel on to the initial action. Rather, the corrective action, which has already vanished into ideas, takes place before tossing or during tossing the ball into the funnel (toss 26 and 41).

IV RELEARNING: SUBJECT B, CHANGES IN STRESS

Since in the case of Subject A the tendency to press the lever could have been intensified by the common pressing down on the door latch, with Subject B *lifting* the lever was learned on two testing days. In all other respects the arrangement was formed according to the plan given in the introduction:

Learning. On the first testing day, 140 tosses; on the second testing day 56 tosses; on the second testing day there followed the relearning in which the lever is pressed—96 tosses.

Relearning. A relapse tendency of the same total strength as in the case of Subject A, is displayed, despite the altered test arrangement. Although it runs differently in its details, the same psychic conditions and dynamic factors are detectable.*

Changes in Stress

Particularly noteworthy is the repeated change of stress between the frame action and lever use which causes some errors (see Table 1). After the subject experienced the intensity of the relapse tendency in toss 4, he keeps in mind the lever use in toss 5 - 8, and thus causes the re-centering of the total action in favor of the lever use, as well as rendering the lever use independent. In doing so, he carries out the frame action with less stress; and in toss 8 he selects the wrong color. Consequently, in toss 9 he again stresses color selection, but is then about to incorrectly carry out the now less-stressed lever use, and only corrects his hand movement at the lever.

The stressed and therefore controlled action, the main action, is thus correctly carried out while the action which is performed without stress, the secondary action, can be done erroneously, or in other words, the relapse tendency is effective when the lever use is performed as a secondary action, but ineffective when it is performed as the main action.

*Figure similar to Figure 2 omitted—Editor.

TABLE 1

The Change in Stress between Lever Use and Frame Action with Subject B, and its Significance for Errors

Toss	Lever Use	Frame Action (Initial and Final Action)
4	unstressed (error)	stressed
5–7	stressed	unstressed
8	stressed	unstressed (error)
9	unstressed (error corrected later)	stressed
10–12	stressed	unstressed
13–18	stressed	unstressed
24–26	stressed	unstressed (error)
27–31	stressed	unstressed (error)
32	unstressed (error)	stressed

This is confirmed by the further course of relearning. After the false beginning in toss 9, the subject performs lever use as the main action in toss 10–12; from toss 13–18 he aims at especially controlling the start of the hand movement to the lever use at the funnel; for, in so far as no other corrections occur, it is decided at this point whether the lever will be correctly or incorrectly used. Beyond this, however, the subject again places an incorrect color sequence twice (from toss 24–26 and toss 27–31). Now he feels sure that he no longer senses a relapse tendency. But when he now stresses the frame action again, he immediately makes incorrect use of the lever in toss 32. Therefore, he once again performs the lever use an an independent action from toss 33–38. With toss 43 he feels the relapse tendency for the last time. From then on he can perform the whole action without having to give special attention to the lever use.

Corrective actions occur at the lever in toss 3 and 9, but only in the subject's mind in toss 43. When there is no correction in toss 4, this can be explained by the fact that, as the subject asserts, he is acting completely absentmindedly. Further tests with Subjects C and K provide similar results.

Criteria for the Strength of the Relapse Tendency

The necessity to compare quantitatively the strength of the relapse tendency in various test arrangements forces us to seek criteria for such a comparison. The following come into question:

1. The number of incorrect uses of the lever. However, even in the presence

of a rather strong intensity of the relapse tendency, incorrect uses can fail to appear if corrective actions occur.

2. The number of hand movements which were started incorrectly. Here one must consider, however, that even when a relapse tendency is present, the hand movement can be started correctly due to a particular intention or a controlled execution as an independent action, as for example in the case of Subject B, toss 13–18.

3. The spread of the relapse tendency—that is, the number of tosses from toss 1 on, over which the relapse tendency stretches. We will consider the last toss with relapse tendency as that one in which the subject still carries out a corrective action mentally (as B in toss 43), or in which the subject still performs the lever use or the start of it because of a particular intention, and thus does it as an independent action. Thus considered, the longest lasting relapse tendency occurs in the case of Subject B where it lasts from toss 1–43. In order to be able to compare relapse tendencies, a relapse tendency having the duration of 45 tosses (to simplify calculation, 43 was not selected) is given the number 100 per cent.

For subsequent compilations it has proved expedient to represent the strength of the relapse tendency by the three criteria just discussed (Table 2).

TABLE 2
The Strength of the Relapse Tendency in Tests A and B

Test	Incorrect Uses (F)	Falsely started hand movements (f)	Spread of the Relapse Tendency	
			over the tosses	in % of our normal case (45 tosses)
A	2	7	1–23	51
B	2	2	1–45	93

V TESTING CONDITIONS UNDER WHICH THERE IS NO RELAPSE TENDENCY*

Tests Without Pauses

If the relapse tendency occurs more strongly after pauses for statements than before, such a regular re-intensifying of the relapse tendency cannot take place

Material is combined here from two different sections in the original article—Editor.

when the subject makes his statements on the side without stopping the action to do so. This thought was confirmed by Test A.A., among others. After the Subject A.A. had lifted the lever 88 times, he had to press it during the stage of relearning. According to his statements, he "immediately adjusted to pressing"; he undertook a certain recentering of the action unity, and rendered the lever use independent. Never did an incorrect use of the lever or a false start for lever use occur. The subject had no opportunity whatsoever to experience the intensity of the relapse tendency, as had subject A and B. Approximately from toss II on the dominance of the lever use receded again.

When the pauses for statements are discontinued, a pressure for control is sufficient at the start of relearning to quickly cause the relapse tendency to stop. The fact that relearning is made difficult by including short pauses for statements has also been confirmed with two other subjects. This is surprising, since, as we know from the experiments on the establishment of associations, the first learning of nonsense syllables is promoted by pauses. We shall return to this fact later.

Intervals Between Tests

There are two different test arrangements which bear on the question of the significance of an interval of one or more days for the relapse tendency.

1. With Subject F, learning was undertaken on the first test day, but relearning was not undertaken until the following (second) test day. The precise test arrangement was as follows: *First Test Day:* Learning (105 tosses). Pressing the lever; *Second Test Day:* Relearning (32 tosses). Lifting the lever.

The relatively strong relapse tendency which is common in relearning did not occur at all in this test.

2. Backlearning was not undertaken until a subsequent testing day with Subject A. The test already described involving this subject was continued on a fourth test day after 30 days. In this test, too, no relapse tendency occurred.*

We must therefore state that when tests are continued on subsequent testing days, the old action unity from which relapses usually emanate is still present, but that when it is performed in our tests no particular psychic forces appear which are noticeable as a relapse pressure.

Table omitted which shows that the relapse tendency does not reappear with repeated relearning and backlearning; also a discussion, which concludes that the failure of a relapse tendency to appear cannot be due to forgetting the mastery of the learned action or to a disintegration of its unity— Editor.

VI FAMILIARIZATION

[*In this section, which I have abridged, Schwarz discusses the possibility that relapse errors might really be learning errors which are simply due to the fact that the subjects have to learn a new action—the motions involved in raising the lever instead of pressing it. In refuting this possibility, he makes an interesting distinction and an analysis of the required movements which are presented below. Schwarz draws a distinction between "familiarization" (the achievement of facility in an action) and the "learning of a habit." The former involves the training of a substantial ability by practice and drill until mastery is acquired and the action is performed with stability and smooth timing; for example, a subject is finding a balance between the tempo of his movements and the tempo of the apparatus, such as the speed with which the ball rolls down the duct. He then shows that the additional familiarization that occurs when a subject must lift instead of press is independent from the relapse pressure—Editor.*]

In the case of Subject A, learning the lift movement occurs in the following way. In the stage of learning when the lever was to be pressed, the subject had kept his palms down while throwing the ball and while pressing the lever. During the introduction to the catching movement he then turned his hands 180°, as is natural, and thus had his palms up while catching.

The conditions are different, however, during relearning, when the lever is to be lifted. When the subject has tossed the ball (palm down again), he must turn his hand 180° on the way from the funnel to the lever in order to then be able to use the lever in such a way that he shoves the hand, palm up, under it and thus lifts it up. After the lifting of the lever, he now need only shift his hand sideways without turning to catch the ball with his palm up.

One wonders whether the essential difficulty of relearning consists in the fact the subject finds the addition of turning in the hand movement from the funnel to the lever difficult as a task in itself. In this regard, let us study the development in Subject A. Of course, he carries out the first lift movements somewhat gingerly and sometimes clumsily; the turn is added somewhat jerkily and abruptly. However, during this period of familiarization tosses occur in which a pronounced relapse appears, and the turn, which is in itself tolerably mastered, is totally forgotten or performed later as a corrective action, either directly at the lever or a short time before. Even the experimenter can distinguish rather clearly between clumsiness in the performance, and the very different relapse; and this distinction is completely apparent in the subject's personal observations.

In the further course of Test A, the differences also become evident. Clumsiness in performance, substantial nonability, can be overcome by practice alone; but relapse must be overcome by something which the subject frequently experiences as a kind of counterpressure. While the progress of drill is not disturbed by pauses for statements, relearning is disturbed considerably.

From Toss 32 on, actual relapse no longer occur. Now it becomes evident that the subject must perform an increase in work with the turning movement between the funnel and lever, and must therefore hurry. With Toss 36, this tempo difficulty was also overcome. The action is performed more smoothly and more fluently, the turn is carried out smoothly on the same course from the funnel to the lever. Finally (with Toss 56), the subject states that a new movement, a "looping motion" has been formed.

In contrast to Subject A, Subject B has to drop the turn, with the transfer from lifting to the pressing movement. He feels a certain constraint while pressing the lever. He does not know what to do with his fingers, especially his thumbs during the action; lifting, he says, had been more satisfying. This constraint, experienced when the subject is pressing, returns at times in later tests combined with a certain feeling of dislike, but without in any way being connected with relapse. The case is similar with other subjects (W,F) where the situation is similar.

VII FIELD FORCES

[To explain the occurrence and the overcoming of the relapse tendency, Schwarz works with two major concepts: *field forces,* and the structure of *action unities.* In the original articles, the sections dealing with these concepts came after additional data which dealt with backlearning and confusion errors. Since the concepts of field force and action unity are primarily applied to the relearning data, I have moved the data on backlearning and confusion errors to the end of the chapter—Editor.]

Field forces appear to be of great importance for the occurrence of errors, and also for their prevention—although they cannot be observed in all cases. The objects of our environment are not by any means neutral to us in our capacity as acting beings, but rather they challenge us to particular actions. These challenges can exhibit various strengths (from the irresistible attraction to the cautious suggestion); furthermore, they can be positive (attractive) or negative (repulsive) in nature. In all these cases, we can speak of the valence of an object.

In succeeding test series, the presence of valences will be compellingly evident from the statements of the subject. But even in the previous tests, the imperative thoughts, for example, and the corrective actions related to them seem, in part, to be due to a warning character ("Don't press!") which is peculiar first to the lever and later to the funnel.

To illustrate the phenomenal effectiveness of the warning character, we present a statement by Subject D from a later test. This statement describes the imperative effect of the whole lever area: "I almost would have pressed the lever. The area above the lever stopped me when I wanted to put my hand down. A signal effect of this area set in. When I had moved about halfway to the lever, it increased. Then there was a kind of throwing about, a transition into another movement; one turns around into another action, without one noticing much on the surface, half actively, half automatically." The lever seems to assume a warning character through the intention for the new variant which is effective against the relapse tendency, even in the first tosses.

The warning character of the lever becomes even stronger through incorrect use. Such an error weighs heavily psychically, because not only does the subject believe he has shown a weak side to the experimenter, but the whole action also stops: the subject is holding his hand at the exit duct to catch the ball, but it doesn't appear. Thus the subject has to use the lever again, and as a rule, forgets in the process the place where the ball is to be put which he had already spotted before, and now must look for again. He has also forgotten the color sequence, which he is usually always aware of, and has to reconstruct this again by studying the balls already placed.

These relatively serious results of incorrect lever use affect the subject in such a way that he becomes angry and usually ashamed, too. The significance of the lever becomes greater psychically and its warning character stronger. At the same time, the decisive factor is not the number of repetitions, but rather the intensification of the tension situation.

For the lever to become effective, it is not necessary that the subject touch it or look at it (in the further course of the test the subject no longer "sees" the lever at all). It is sufficient that the subject has the lever present in his mind. This condition is not fulfilled when the subject is completely absentminded, and is not at all aware of the total situation including the lever (toss 4 of relearning in the case of Subject B), or when, due to disturbances, there is great stress outside of the test arrangement (toss 4 of relearning in the case of Subject A). Then the corrective actions do not occur.

The movement of the corrective actions to the funnel is evidence for the fact that, in the course of the test, the field of the effectiveness of the warning character spreads out more and more in space, during which time the imperative idea becomes fainter and fainter the further away from the lever it occurs.

Subject W told the following as an example of an analogous warning character and its movement: The subject enters an unfamiliar country house. One door is so low that he must bend over to walk through it. Soon the subject bumps his head on the door beam. The second time he thinks of it just as he is right before the door, and almost bumps his head again. The third time he thinks of it sooner. Finally, he is completely familiar with the fact that he has to bend to go through the door; relearning has been completed.

Even during backlearning (Subject C), the subject's behavior is perhaps influenced by field forces. Whereas during relearning the subjects exert the counterpressure against the relapse pressure during the whole course, Subject C does this only after tossing the ball into the funnel from toss 1–4 of backlearning. Asked at a later time, the subject states that he did indeed form an intention, but that the hand movement toward lever use took place in part involuntarily.

Drawing upon the statements of this subject and our other experiences, perhaps the development occurs as follows: during relearning, after the subject has seen through the performance structure of the required action, he tries to control the start of the hand movement toward lever use at the funnel (as also Subject B, Toss 13–18 of relearning). Therefore the funnel has acquired meaning as the place where the hand movement lever use is to be started, and started correctly. The funnel has, therefore, assumed a valence and a warning character. The subject probably strengthens this by the fact that before toss 1–4 of backlearning, the subject intends, albeit not with great decisiveness, "Pay attention at the funnel!" From Toss 5–8 the subject only generally adjusted to control, without special reference to the funnel.

It is striking in this development that the lever does not again assume a valence in the sense of the required action (a valence which then again intensifies the relapse pressure when the lever use is changed), with the progression of relearning as it had during learning; but that the funnel now becomes the outstanding spot. This is in agreement with our other results: Only those places which are psychically relatively important can assume the importance of a valence to an action. During the stage of relearning, however, the functional center of gravity of the lever use shifted more and more to the funnel; this latter object received the meaning that the lever use must be started here and started correctly. As paradoxical as this may sound, the lever itself psychically lost meaning for lever use, even though its technical and physical meaning remained the same.

VIII ACTION UNITIES DURING RELEARNING

When the subject learns to use the lever in a different way, one wonders whether a new action unity is produced, and if so, whether the old action unity is destroyed or if it continues to exist side by side with the new one.

The action which was carried out at the beginning of the tests was a chain of relatively independent partial actions which were only loosely connected. It was a sum of relatively isolated units, an aggregate action: a + b + c + d + e.

Then the contours blurred; recenterings took place, and finally the action occurred as a gradually solidifying action unity: abcde.

As an external criterion for the action unity, there is the externally fluent course of the action in contrast to the previously uneven and somewhat choppy course. There is no contradiction to this in the fact that the initial and final actions *(a* and *e)*, which have been subjected to regular change, assume a stress; while the ever-constant middle action *(bcd)* becomes more strongly self-enclosed and is performed without stress. In this way the action unity receives a definite structuring and accentuation:

A bcd E

Those letters printed together indicate a high degree of consolidation, whereas those capitalized are relatively stressed.

If one seeks an analogy in sense psychology, one can perhaps consider a series of chords which are first presented as isolated chords. A presentation of these chords in immediate succession, so that the whole forms a unified musical phrase, would correspond to the final action unity. In our case, the initial and final chords would be stressed, and the three middle chords especially closely connected.

Examples of analogous structuring in the optic and accoustical fields can easily be found for all the other action unities and variations which occur in this work. But one must not overlook the fact that in our discussions of the existence and variation of action unities, we are not speaking about the structuring in which the action event appears to other people, or to the subject himself, as a perceived object, but about how the action event itself is structured according to its dynamic factors.

If this action unity were destroyed with the start of relearning, the fluent course of the action event should cease and the action should be again performed as a sum-action. But it is evident from the personal observations of the subject, and this is confirmed by the observations of the experimenter, that while the action acquires a "jagged" quality between the funnel and the lever, in all other respects it continues to be carried out fluently. While, due to the new lever use, the subject adds the turn between the funnel and lever somewhat clumsily or omits it, he otherwise continues to apply his previous learning.

One can, therefore, only speak of a destruction of the action unity between funnel and lever; in other respects, the unity continues to exist. With the progression of the learning process the partial disturbance is overcome, and the whole action is again carried out smoothly and fluently.

The restored action unity is not the same as the original, but it is strongly related to it. The subject is conscious of continuing to perform the "first" action simply with a certain change. Thus Subject D states, "I am using the old complex of parts from the lever to the exit duct, even the transition from the lower part of the duct to the lever has remained. I am using what I learned. It is not the substitution of one complex by another. Rather, only a nuance of the action has been changed, a qualitative change—as though I had to press harder."

Subject D.D states, "The process has a new way, a different note, but without being different."

These statements indicate that the subject continues to carry out the first action unity, which simply experiences a reforming with respect to one part of the action. This reforming does not merely indicate that one part of the action is carried out differently with respect to performance. When the subject performs the action during the stage of learning and presses (or lifts) the lever, he doesn't know that he could also carry out a certain part of the action in a different way.

But when the subject lifts (or presses) the lever in the stage of relearning, he finds himself in a totally different psychic posture. He has become aware of the fact that the lever can fulfill its function by being lifted or pressed, depending on the interference of the experimenter. What had previously been a single given action now appears to be one of two possible actions. The subject sees before him a unity of a more complicated type of structuring, a unity which is carried out in one variation or another. The action performed first now, in retrospect, acquires an index c_1:

$$A \; bc_1d \; E$$

which previously would have had no justification; it acquires, in retrospect, a pendant meaning. The action which is to be performed now is:

$$A \; bc_2d \; E$$

But the subject cannot simply carry out this new, required action. He sees, to his surprise and anger, that he is subject to a pressure in favor of the old action, a relapse pressure:

$$\rightarrow A \; bc_1d \; E$$

and must produce a counterpressure to keep c_1 at a distance:

$$ab \; \underset{\downarrow c_1 \downarrow}{\overset{c_2}{\rule{0pt}{0pt}}} \; de$$

whereby he recenters the action unity so that ab on the one side, and de on the other side, come together more strongly and the lever action c is rendered relatively independent. Finally, the relapse pressure is overcome, relearning is completed, and the reformed action unity is carried out in a structuring analogous to the one of the old action unity.

$$A \; bc_2 d \; E$$

Whereas at the beginning of relearning the lever use took place incorrectly "as though of itself," now, according to the statements of the subject, it occurs correctly "as of itself." In other words whereas at first the subject was under pressure in favor of the old action, now he is under a pressure in favor of the action demanded by the instructions.

$$\rightarrow A \; bc_2 d \; e$$

The reforming of the action unity during relearning, the weakening of the relapse pressure, and the strengthening of the instruction pressure do not occur continuously but are disturbed again and again by pauses for statements.

IX ATTEMPT AT A THEORETICAL EXPLANATION OF THE RELAPSE PRESSURE

To succeed in proving that the presence of an action unit with a particular structure is a psychic condition for the appearance of relapse, we must explain that under these conditions: 1) A relapse pressure is present; 2) This relapse pressure appears more strongly after short pauses which serve for personal observations than before; and 3) After longer pauses (one day or more) it is no longer present.

One might consider an analogy with the interruption of actions. If an action is interrupted before it is finished, there exists a tension pressing for conclusion of the action. In our case, however, no action is interrupted. Even when the concept of the total action is not limited to a single toss, but is spread out to the group of tosses necessary for laying out a name, an interruption of these total action does not, as a rule, occur. Numerous tests show that relapse pressure is also present with customary strength when one frame action is concluded with learning, and a new frame action is begun with relearning.

Nor can one say that after performing the tossing action ninety times the pressure exists to continue performing it. The subject does not feel any such pressure whatsoever. This is apparent with Subject F, for example, when the test was broken off after the stage of learning.

Rather, a pressure for performance of the old action is evident when the new action is begun. Only then are the forces which press for relapse acute, only then does the subject feel an explicit compulsion. Accordingly, the energy from which the relapse pressure occurs seems to flow from the intention for the new action. Nowhere does another source of energy exist.

At first these results seem paradoxical. For according to this, the intention, which in itself is directed at the new action, is supposed to form the energy source for two contradictory actions. But since no other energy source is present in this performance habit, the conclusion is inescapable.

If one attempts to obtain a more precise idea of how it can happen that two contradictory actions can be fed by the same source of energy, one will have to keep in mind that the relapse tendency does not occur if one carries out a very different action, rather than an action which is closely related in its structure. The fact is that very special conditions must be present with reference to the action structure. These special conditions are taken into account in our tests, by the fact that we change one part of an unstressed middle action which is incorporated in a stressed frame action. Thus, the relapse tendency only appears when the intention is directed at a total action which only differs from the old action in its details. In both cases we are faced with actions which are psychically very closely related when one considers the total character of both actions.

Moreover, in our case at least, there is a direct agreement in the first phase of both contradictory actions. Therefore, the quasi-need set by the intention comprises, at least in part, the very same psychic system as the earlier actions. Once such psychic systems have developed, if the momentary quasi-need is satisfied, they might remain for some time, even in an untensed condition, as a kind of empty form. Due to the action unity created by the first action, and the corresponding unity of its tension system, the tension condition equivalent to the quasi-need must expand over the whole system. Thus it happens that with the intention to perform the total action, new energy is brought to the old partial action at the same time as it is brought to the partial action which is actually intended. This energy becomes manifest in a tendency toward the old action, that is, in a relapse pressure.

When the area to which these actions belong is not yet very differentiated psychically, then if the action is performed simply on the side, a relapse danger could even appear in the following way: with the general application of the subject to this action area, the energy flows to the system which is completely formed and still standing in the foreground from the immediate past.

The quasi-need set by the intention will at first be more of an advantage to the old action, and thus to the relapse pressure. This is because it is a solidly formed system which is in close communication with the initial part of the action. On the other hand, such a system is not yet available for the new partial action, but must still be gradually formed. Thus, relapse errors ensue insofar as special measures do not sever the communication of the partial action in question from the total action (which is now again placed under tension by the intention).

Such a severing of communication is by no means readily possible. For the partial phase of the event the subject must, therefore, neutralize the cause of the motorics by special control measures, and must instead carry out the endangered partial action as an independent action. In this case, the course of the event appears to be one single action when judged by performance, but psychologically two actions really exist. These correspond to two relatively separate systems, so that one phase of the old action is suppressed while the other action takes place.

These results confirm Lewin's statements that certain action unities form the prerequisite for the appearance of habit errors, but that the unity structure itself is not the source of energy of these habit errors.

The fact that the relapse pressure is relatively large again after short pauses for statements, that it is larger than at the close of the preceding group of tosses, may be evidence that the new partial system which has just formed is not yet completely firm in its structure and its communication with the total system. In fact, this renewed reappearance of the relapse pressure does not occur when pauses are not inserted until after the stable development and fixing of the new system.

When, as in our tests (8), the relapse tendency is not noticeable if one day is inserted between learning and relearning, one might attempt to explain this by the fact that in the course of this time the first system produced has disintegrated due to normal life processes. This is contradicted, however, by the fact that the subject still can do the old action on the second day, and that therefore the total structure formed through learning is still present, and can again be produced by the simple act of intention.

There might be a very important theoretical meaning to this fact. The ability to perform certain action unities which one was not at first able to do corresponds to the formation of certain dispositional structures, or, in our terms, certain inner systems. These systems can still be present at a later point in time: one can still do the action. Of course, ability can be destroyed by other types of influences.

From this question of the survival or nonsurvival of a system, one must separate the question of whether such a system is in a tension state at a given movement. Systems which were originally in a tension state can also continue to exist in an untensed state. (Thus, we arrive at a very similar distinction as the one established by Zeigarnik on completely different foundations. In her work the difference between the systems found in the tension stage and the untensed stage is shown by effects on memory.)

It might be possible that relapses in relearning do not occur after a one day interval because the similarity of the two actions in question—in the sense of their belonging to the same undifferentiated area—is no longer great enough for the easy occurrence of sliding over from one action to another. Only further investigations would be able to give us information about these questions.

The concepts which we use here to explain relapse pressure—particularly the concept of the systems corresponding to quasi-needs in tensed and relaxed condition, the idea of their communication with other systems due to immediate functional proximity or partial identity, and the concept of loosening and forming communications—doubtlessly have certain formal similarities with the concepts of channeling and inhibition *(Hemmung),* the formation of simple and complex associations in the sense of association theory. On the other hand, there are profound differences. Particularly, the fact that the repeated execution of two actions and the associations so formed are not considered to be the cause of habit errors. Rather, the tension evident in the relapse pressure is due to the quasi-need produced by the new intention. Also, the repeated, successive performing of the actions is by no means sufficient cause for the fact that the tension produced by the new intention is also evident in the performance of the old action. On the contrary, certain unified action structures must have formed, indeed, unified systems of a very definite structure. These facts completely go beyond the boundaries of what is contained in the way of conceptual facts in the old concepts of association and channeling, and they compel us to a more far-reaching conceptualization.

One wonders whether the break in communications between the part to be changed and the whole action must necessarily be a relatively long-lasting process, or whether an action type can be formed from the outset so that the switch can be undertaken more easily. We shall later see that this is quite possible.

X THE NATURE OF ACTION UNITIES*

Criteria for an Action Unity

Using the following criteria, one can determine which action unities are present in an individual case.

Personal observation. In sensory psychology, such as in psychological optics, the respective unities are as a rule given directly in the perception itself as phenomenal units of the object.

In determining the action unity, one turns first to the personal observation of the subject. But this manner of determination is frequently substantially more difficult in this case, because while actions can be made the object of personal observation, they by no means have the natural position which an object of observation has in perceptual psychology. The subject is active, but

*[*This section is taken from Part II of Schwartz's work. I have omitted the introduction, and some paragraphs that seemed peripheral to the major line of development, and have included only one example of a process wherever a number of examples were given—Editor.*]

does not experience his own actions as objects. And even when the subject is prepared for personal observation, the type of unity form of the action is an object which is relatively hard to grasp, because it is seldom a part of the actual accomplishment of the action. The majority of subjects do not go beyond very obvious observations, perceiving only with difficulty the development of their own action, especially since this development occurs gradually and not in jumps. Only the records of subjects with very good observation—we had only about 12 such subjects among 53—offer sufficient material.

That a repetition of observation substantially changes the unity synthesis is a process with which we are familiar from the unities of perceptual psychology.

Behavior. Besides personal observation, certain clues are given by the externally observable behavior of the subjects—whether the action is smooth or jerky, whether the subject pauses, and so on. To be sure, these could also mislead us.

Dynamic criteria. Besides the direct criteria of unity, there are indirect ones, such as the various effects and susceptibilities which distinguish a sum of actions from an action unity. These dynamic criteria for unity are doubtlessly the most important. They will acquire more significance as the dynamic definition of unities (as functionally self-contained systems in Köhler's sense) becomes authoritative instead of a phenomenal definition. Once we prove that certain dynamic factors are dependent on the unity synthesis of an activity, as in the case of relapse, these dynamic facts can in turn be used as criteria for an action unity in any concrete case. First, to be sure, the criteria of personal observation and behavior must be referred to.

Action Unities During Learning

In order to have a precise understanding of the action unities which come into question in our tests, it is necessary to pursue the transofrmation of action unities from the beginning.

After the first 2 or 3 tosses in which the subject becomes roughly familiar with the apparatus so that surprise experiences become more seldom, the following action unities tend to be present for all subjects: the selection of the ball (a), throwing (b), use of the lever (c), catching (d), and placement of the ball (e).

With further tosses, an extensive change in action unities becomes apparent in the course of practice. To illustrate such a course we will first present a concrete example with good personal observation. Subject R executed 79 tosses, lifting the lever:

Personal observation of a subject. Section 1, tosses 1–27. The subject has been instructed to place the the balls together to form a name.

Toss 3–7: "During toss 3 it was still difficult to be almost simultaneously at the funnel, lever, and exit duct. Gradually a rhythm forms among these three actions. Placement of the balls is an appendage. Selection is unnoticed and completely forgotten."

Toss 8–13: "The rolling of the ball on the duct is boring; it should go more quickly. It is a waiting period; I wait for the ball to roll into the box and I find this unpleasant."

Toss 14–20: "When the ball is at the bottom of the duct it makes a different sound, and then I know that I must grasp the lever. . . . Selection and tossing of the ball is one action. Waiting for the sound is a gap in the action. The sound is the signal for lifting the lever. Lifting the lever and catching the ball are closely connected, but they are not one action. At the beginning, when I was not aware of the sound, the pause before lifting the lever did not tear the action apart."

Toss 21–27: "The rhythm is there again. I am very relaxed now; the tension has disappeared. I still hear the changed sound at the end of the duct, but it no longer plays any part, because I am lifting the lever by feeling, according to a sense of time."

Section 2, Toss 28–52: The subject is forming a second name. The same colors may not be placed next to one another.

Toss 28–32: "The effort necessary for choosing the balls disturbs me very much. I have to look at the sketch again and again to see whether the color is right."

Toss 33–44: "Selection of the balls is easier now."

Toss 41–52: "Before, placement of the balls was an appendage and the working of the apparatus was essential. Now it is reversed: selection and placement of the balls are the chief actions."

Section 3, toss 53–79: The subject is forming a third name, this time with the color order red, green, yellow.

Toss 53–57: "Selection and placement make up the main action; working the apparatus is the means to the end. I would not like to call it a secondary action, because the action involving the apparatus is actually much more complicated. Tossing the ball, lifting the lever, and catching the ball are practically one action. I cannot distinguish the individual parts; it is as if I were doing it unconsciously. Only rarely do I feel the pause before use of the lever."

Toss 71–79: "Selection is now rather easy. It is very difficult to name the main thing, everything is now balanced. It is one action; there is no longer any appendage."

Survey of the course of the unity's transformations. In rough terms, the course of the unity transformations is the following:

During tosses 1–13 the action is carried out relatively as a sum of actions. It is focused on the working of the apparatus; the frame action (i.e. choice of the balls and filling the pattern) completely in the background. Soon unifications occur. From tosses 14–20 two subunits—*a b*—and, more loosely, *c,d,e* arise. They are at first separated by a pause, but are finally borne together by an overlapping rhythm (tosses 21–27).

With altered instructions for the frame action (toss 28 ff.) new accents are given, and thus combinations which have already arisen are destroyed and new ones begun. Now a completely changed synthesis exists. The frame action *(a and e)* is the main action; manipulations of the apparatus are carried out as secondary actions, come closer to one another (tosses 28–52), and soon form a unity which is carried out mechanically (toss 53 ff). Even when frame action and middle action finally melt together to form one unity, the middle action forms a particularly firm bond within it (toss 58 ff) (9).

In order to arrive at a more general point of view, we shall schematically present the types of unities which arose in the various phases of the unification process. It is evident that any attempt to adequately represent the various action unities is forced to differentiate not only genuine action unities from summative concurrence, but also combinations of varying degree. This is analogous to the differences between strong and weak gestalts. (10).

We differentiate four closeness grades for the combination of parts in the whole, for which we use the following signs, starting with the strongest closeness grade:

1. ⬜ 2. ⬒ 3. ⬚ 4. no border

Basic Synthesis Forms

There seem to be certain general synthesis forms, corresponding, for example, to the symmetrical structure of optical figures.

1. The relatively undivided action unity, for example, the simple lifting of the lever which appears phenomenally as unified action:

2. The action unity, which consists of two or more relatively independent subwholes, in which the subwholes are separated by a caesura (break, division) (Figure 3).

FIGURE 3. Action Unity with Independent Subwholes.

In Toss 14 to 20 of our sample, there is an example of such a synthesis form which is somewhat more complicated (Figure 4). The first subwhole which represents a solid unity, but is less stressed, is formed by selection and tossing. The action pause while the ball rolls on the duct works as a caesura. The second subwhole consists of the use of the lever and catching. These are stressed and intimately connected, but are not firmly melted together. Placement is an appendage. The pause is more a part of the first subwhole.

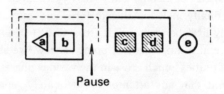

Pause

FIGURE 4. Complex Action Unity with Independent Subwholes

3. Main block with up-beat and end (Figure 5). In this case, it is characteristic for the stress to be in the middle actions which are felt to be related. The initial action is an unimportant up-beat, the final action is an appendage. Such a type is clearly pronounced in tosses 3–13.

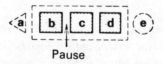

Pause

FIGURE 5. Main Block Action Unity

4. Cloak action" with embedded (unstressed) middle action (Figure 6). This is a reversal of main block action. The parts of the cloak (initial and final action) do not meet in time or space (see toss 28 ff. especially 58–79 of our sample).

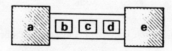

FIGURE 6. Cloak Action Unity

5. Spiral form (Figure 7). The last part of the total action leads into the first part of the following action, or draws it immediately after itself. Thus the action has no actual conclusion and new beginning, but continues to run, as it were, in a circle; or, more accurately, an always continuing spiral.

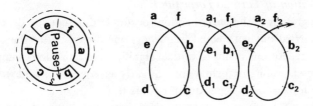

FIGURE 7. Spiral Form

In our test arrangement, the combining of the old end-action and a new initial action occurred in the following way. The subject makes the decision on the color of the ball to be chosen. The lifting of this color from the cup of balls, which is the factual beginning of the new action, is psychically the result of the preceding decision. The actual selection is placed back in time within the total action.

Some subjects resist the advancement of the decision, and psychically as well as physically begin the action at the ball cup. But they often forget the last placed color, and must look back at the design.

While it is clearer to symbolize the spiral form of the action as a circle, this is not exact. Exactly speaking, the new a, b, c, which follow the old e are not psychically the old a,b,c again, but a_1, b_1, c_1, and so on, and would therefore have to be represented by a spiral. This spiral would have as many coils as there are tosses which combine to form the unity.

Now let us survey the course of our sample from Subject R with regard to the typical basic synthesis forms. From the original un-unified sum action, a main block action emerges, along with the significance of manipulating the apparatus. But this is of short duration, for the main block is exploded (toss 14 ff.) by the pause caused by the ball rolling down the duct. This gains significance in the subject's experience, and the unity composed of two sub-wholes arises. When, with the 28th toss, selection and placement take on critical significance because of special instructions on the use of the balls, a new synthesis form begins, the cloak action, which is finally clearly pronounced with the 53rd toss. When the action is again carried out easily, the frame action begins to lose meaning. Selection and tossing of the ball sink to preparation, placement deteriorates to become only a final note, and use of the lever and catching remain as the only high points—but still without much significance.

The action again approaches a main block form, only to revert to the cloak form whenever specialized instructions are given concerning the frame action. As the action event becomes still more monotonous, the spiral form is found in advanced test stages.

The Integration of Parts to Form the Whole

The integration of the partial actions occurs at different speeds, even when they are carried out with equal frequency, one directly after the other. The number of repetitions is not of critical significance. Thus, for example, selection and tossing unite to form a unity as early as toss 14–20, while tossing and use of the lever remain separated for some time.

Also, the mechanization of parts which have already combined to form a unity need not occur at the same time. Thus the middle action of toss 53–57 is carried out mechanically, while the frame action still requires the control of the subject. Already existing unities can disintegrate and new ones arise. Thus the unity produced by selection and tossing disintegrates with toss 28, and later tossing enters a new unity with the other manipulations of the apparatus.

We were able to determine the factors which are significant for integration and separation of partial actions. In general, similarities and conformities among the action parts encourage their unification while oppositions and differences hamper it.

1. *The general motor character.* There is a hampering effect on unification when the partial actions are unevenly and sharply set off from one another, as when a "point" follows a "round" motion. On the other hand, it is beneficial when one action follows another without a change and difference being felt at the same time. The movement of the hand from the lever to the exit duct, for example, can be an unforced continuation and conclusion of the hand movement which began at the funnel and continued over the lever.

2. *Tempo.* An even tempo in the execution of the partial actions promotes unification, uneven tempo holds it up. Thus, in our sample case, selection and tossing do not combine as long as selection is done at a relaxed tempo and tossing is carried out rapidly (toss 1–13). Not until toss 14, when there is a tempo adjustment, does unification occur.

3. *Stress grade.* Evenly unstressed execution of the partial actions favors unification. We cannot decide from our examples whether evenly stressed execution of the parts also encourages unification.

Unevenly stressed part actions which are pronounced in their character do not unite. Thus selection and tossing do not merge from toss 1–13; frame and middle action do not merge until toss 53–57. Only after stress differences have disappeared or weakened does unification take place—toss 14 ff., or toss 58 ff.

Already existing unities are destroyed by strong stress differences which suddenly appear. Thus the unity consisting of selection and tossing disintegrates with toss 28, where selection takes on a strong tone. This example of a gestalt disintegration is typical.

4. *Goal.* Subordination of the parts to the same goal favors unification; varying goal determination disturbs it. For example, the merging of the manipulations of the apparatus is encouraged when the subject experiences them as a means to the goal of placement of the figure.

Later we shall see how connection of several tosses is promoted by their subordination to the common goal of laying out a rather complicated figure. On the other hand, unification of catching and placement is disturbed by the fact that the subject views catching as a means and placement as the goal.

5. *Meaning.* If the total action is meaningful, this seems to favor integration; meaninglessness, on the other hand, has a laming effect on unification. We will later meet with a pointed example of this when the total action becomes meaningless as a result of the weakening of the frame action.

6. *Rhythm.* Execution of the partial actions in a rhythm favors unification (see Toss 21–27 of our test sample).

7. *Linkage (Interlinkage).* Unification is favored if the action parts are linked with one another; that is, one part must follow another in a specific way or become engaged with it. Thus the unification of the manipulations on the apparatus are promoted by the fact that the use of the lever has to occur at a specific time after tossing, and catching has to occur at a specific time after lever use; whereas, on the other hand, tossing can follow selection after a relatively arbitrary time interval.

8. *Pauses.* Pauses inhibit unification to the extent that they are psychically experienced as pauses, and they are particularly strong in their effect when they are accompanied by feelings of dislike. Tosses 14–20 of our sample offer an example of the separating effect of the pause.

9. *Effects of the whole as a functional unity.* Which factors prevail with regard to integration or separation of the parts does not only depend on the nature of the individual neighboring parts, but also on the nature of all the other parts and of the whole in general. Whether, for example, parts c and d are motorically similar or dissimilar can only be decided when one knows the motor nature of parts a, b, and e and can judge whether the similarity between c and d is more compelling than that between b and c, as well as between d and e.

The situation is the same when we speak of agreement in stress degree, tempo, and so forth. Our statements on affinities and opposites have only relative meaning.

The pause which becomes apparent from toss 8 on does not only separate parts b and c in the 14th toss, but also promotes the merging of a and b. In this case, too, the total action assumes a completely new synthesis form in this way. To be sure, it is a contributing factor that b experiences a decrease in its importance for other reasons, and that its unification with a is thus favored.

From the same initial synthesis form of the total action, to the same end synthesis form, various courses are possible according to which factors determine the integration or separation of the parts. Frequently, lever use and catching first enter into a bond which forms the nucleus of a main block form, while tossing is still separated by a pause. However, in other cases the main block includes pause and tossing from the beginning.

Mechanization as an After-effect of Unification

In many cases the subject describes the firmly unified action, particularly the middle action, as "mechanical", "automatic," or "unconscious." This mechanization of the action can be more closely evaluated in the following way:

The nonmechanized action offers difficulties and demands a higher degree of command. The subject is thus relatively active and is conscious of doing something relatively important. In contrast, the mechanized action runs, as it were, by itself on a well-traveled path similar to a mechanism that is wound up; the subject simply initiates it. Newly appearing difficulties which force renewed control temporarily remove mechanization, either completely or in part.

2. The nonmechanized action has a greater proximity to the ego; it lies within the subject's zone of the present. The mechanized action has undergone a withdrawal from the central ego, an independence; it is something peripheral, which no longer belongs, as it were, to the person.

In this sense the mechanized action is described as follows by Subject HH: "Somewhat reminiscent of falling asleep. One works intensively, thinks somewhat, and yet it is covered with a veil." Later: "The action is completely blurred: the procedure has become automatic and indefinite. The action is present but completely unclear, far away, as sometimes a memory is far away in time." And by Subject F. "The whole thing is something outside myself." When he later has the action present, he says: "I am completely awake."

3. The nonmechanized action is described as broader, slower, the mechanized action as more narrow, shorter, faster. This is related to the fact that in division and stress, the nonmechanized action is more varied while the mechanized action is more uniform.

This is evident from statement made by Subject HH on the mechanized action: "The whole action is much more blurred. At the beginning it was more divided; now everything seems to proceed faster. It also becomes smaller in space; shrunk together; my movements have become smaller." Later, "The action is still more uniform and more connected. The action's expanse is much smaller than at the start. At first there were large movements; I had to go back and forth to the right and left with my body; now everything is within reach of my hands."

The process of becoming narrower does not progress simply with repetition of the action. If individual action parts acquire greater stress, the action can again become broader.

The Creation of Stress and its Significance for Synthesis

The stress of partial actions has already been mentioned as one of the factors which influence the integration and division of the unities. A more intensive investigation of its significance is also of practical value, as we wish to use stress later as a means of changing the structure of the complete unity.

Factors decisive for Stress. Below we classify the factors which are decisive in influencing stress within our test arrangement and probably more generally.

1. *Inability.* Actions which the subject must first learn technically, or must practice are more stressed than actions which are already technically mastered. Thus, in the first tosses, lever use and catching are stressed; while the technically simpler actions of selection and placement of the ball are carried out unstressed.

2. *Technical difficulty.* Actions which are technically difficult (even after a certain preceding practice stage), and which require attention are more stressed than technically uncomplicated actions. Thus, lever use and catching are stressed as long as the subject attains coordination by paying attention to signals—the sound of the ball in the apparatus—while the simpler act of tossing is unstressed.

3. *Compulsion to make a decision.* Actions which require a decision or resolution are more stressed than actions whose execution is completely clear. Thus, in the later test stages, selection is frequently stressed when the instructions leave the choice of ball color free and the subject has to decide on the color. Nothing depends on this choice of color; there is no possibility of error.

This stress is independent of where the act of selection actually takes place, and instead it is situated where the decision is actually made. Thus, the stress is transferred from the ball box to the pattern if the subject makes up his mind at the pattern about the color to be chosen.

4. *Gravity of the errors.* Actions in which the subject is afraid of committing decisive errors are more stressed than actions in which errors are insignificant. Thus lever use takes on great stress in relearning as soon as the subject recognizes his tendency for mistakes which hold up the whole action event.

5. *Significance of the unity as a functional unit.* The significance of the factors influencing the stress of a particular part is also determined by

the way in which they are effective within the total action. In many cases the stress of one part is phenomenally weakened in the presence of stronger stress of other parts, and phenomenally strengthened in the presence of weaker stress of other parts. For example, lever use and catching immediately lose their stress, without any objective change in the manipulations of the apparatus, when the frame action takes on a stronger stress.

· *The significance of stress for the total synthesis of the action.* A typical example of the significance of stress for our experiments is the complete change of the main block form into the cloak form and back as the result of stress shift. The main block form which exists in the presence of unstressed frame action:

a bcD e

is replaced by the cloak form when the frame action is made more difficult and thus is more strongly stressed:

A bcd E

This cloak form again reverts back to a (weakened) main block form with gradual recession of significance of the frame action.

a bcD e

A further example: An action which is divided into two sub wholes can only maintain this synthesis as long as each of the subwholes has a specific weight. If the stress of one of these subwholes is substantially intensified or weakened, then this or the other subwhole will become an up-beat or an appendage, and the action form will have changed.

More Comprehensive Unity Formation and Disintegration

Unity formation. As has already become evident from the description of the spiral form as one basic synthesis form, the unification process is not concluded by the unification of the actions belonging to one toss. Rather, several tosses can experience connection between them. In this process, the linkage of a selection with the preceding placement, and the uniform goal served by a number of tosses can work as unity forming factors.

At first the subject carries out each toss separately as an isolated action. Then a whole series of tosses is carried out to fulfill a larger assignment, for instance, laying out a name. There is a transitional stage in the merging of a unity of tosses which serve to lay out a name. It consists in the fact that the (three-part) color sequence appears as a unity forming factor. For example, the subject places a green ball, and, in the manner described above, he sees from the design that red and then yellow are now to follow. After these three tosses a certain conclusion is reached; a caesura occurs after which a new comprehensive action begins.

At a further stage, the 20–30 tosses necessary for laying out a figure are placed in one uniform action, as long as mistakes and misplacements do not cause fractures and waverings in the stability.

Even in the comprehensive action unity, the frame actions or the final action alone can be especially stressed. Here too, stress shifts can occur in that the frame actions gradually lose their stress, and catching may temporarily become more distant.

Unity disintegration. Further observations cause one to suppose that in the comprehensive action unity a certain disintegration is underway. We are stating this supposition cautiously, since decisive evidence is lacking. Nevertheless, for dynamic criteria for a loosening of the action unity, one might consider the following data: the comprehensive action unity is easier to interrupt by the experimenter than the firmly bound, mechanized unity which only comprises one toss; also, the tendency of the subject to resume the action is weaker. Furthermore, there are phenomenal criteria to justify our supposition, and the observations of others. (13).

As described earlier, a unified, mechanically executed action was experienced as unconscious, outside the subject's actuality zone, spacially narrow, short in time. Now a period ensues in which this condition begins to reverse itself to a certain degree. The action phenomenally splinters; the individual parts again become more prominent, and again enter the ego-vicinity of the subject. They now are loaded with distinguishing marks which they previously lacked. For example, it is now a part of tossing that the front funnel has a scratch; and it is noticed in lever use and catching that the apparatus is stained brown and that the grain is visible. Also the subject notices things which have nothing to do with the action, for example, the street noise from outside, the fact that there is a map of Berlin on the wall, that the water pipe is dripping.

Let us ask ourselves which factors could cause a loosening of the action unity. Karsten's experiments on psychic satiation have shown that continued repetition does not have the effect of stabilizing the unification of the action. In our tests, too, repetition driven beyond a certain limit seems to promote the appearance of unity-destroying factors:

1)As a result of the numerous repetitions, the subject is able to do everything.

2)The continued repetition appears senseless to the subject. The action no longer offers him difficulties nor stimulation.

3)The composite nature *(Teilhaltigkeit)* of the comprehensive unity perhaps works as a unity-destroying factor. It is characteristic that the unity does not loosen at the points of unification which have only existed for a short time, namely, between placement and new toss, but it loosens as a whole.

Integration and disintegration of action unities under the influence of stress changes. It was possible to ascertain the following:

1) Originally independent action unities of the same stress degree integrate easier to form a dynamic unit than those of different stress degrees; 2) Originally independent action unities of low stress degree unite more easily than strongly stressed action unities; and 3) Action unities which are divided within themselves (with differing stresses) show a lower tendency to gestalt disintegration than do relatively undivided or monotonously divided action unities.

1 and 3 appear to contradict each other. But with closer study their mutuality is easily seen; they can be interpreted as special cases of the following more general statement: Restructurings in the organization (whether it be integration or disintegration) occur more easily when neighboring action unities have an even degree of stress, and with more difficulty when the stress is uneven.

This statement, which we derive from purely empirical findings, becomes clearer through a consideration which is based on the concept of the boundary. The restructuring of action unities involves a change in the relative strength of the boundary between the parts. This boundary will, from the start, have a strength which depends on the tensions of the action unity in question.

If neighboring systems have tensions of varying strength, it is necessary that the boundary which separates them have a dynamic stability such that it resists the pressure of the stronger tension upon the weaker. Otherwise, the systems could not maintain their structure without compromise. In such a case, any factors which have an effect on the restructuring of both systems must be relatively strong.

If neighboring systems are equally strongly tensed, on the other hand, the dynamic stability of the boundary between them is of less importance. Even weak walls are capable of preserving the existing structure as long as it is a question of resisting the pressure which emanates from the structures themselves. Factors which have an effect on the restructuring of these systems only need to be relatively weak.

Effects of the Tension of Intention

If the subject forms the intention of carrying out a toss, or placing a name or a figure, the intention is the content of a quasi-need; and a pressure, a state of tension, arises which presses for the execution of the intention.

Acceleration. With continued execution of the action, this pressure can have the effect of causing faster and faster performance of the action. Thus, Subject HH says, "I would like to go faster and faster. I couldn't bear to go more slowly." Subject B-3: "I have the tendency to bring the ball as quickly as possible through the apparatus, and once I took 2 balls at once. The traveling of the balls is too slow for me; I sit before the machine and can't do anything about it."

Completion. The tension which presses for the execution of the intention also has the effect that the subject does not like to be interrupted in the action. (12).

Subject Q, for example, who is told to stop in toss 18 after throwing the ball into the funnel, still pulls the handle (he has to use a handle instead of a lever), and catches the ball. When asked, he stated, "I did indeed hear the instructions but I did not interpret them to mean that I was to stop at that very moment." Even after the subject has been informed that he is to stop immediately when he is given the instruction "Stop!" he still pulls the handle and catches the ball. He explains, "It was more of a battle between the word I heard and the action."

Thus the subject finds it clearly difficult to follow well-understood instructions. This case is typical. In many cases the subject also places the ball in the pattern.

In the case of a unity comprising several tosses, the quasi-need no longer deals with the placement of the ball just taken, but on the structure of the entire figure. Thus, the subject is now also sensitive to interruptions at the conclusion of a toss. It is perhaps due to the action unity's lower stability that the struggle is no longer as animated, and that the resumption tendency is no longer as strong.

Resumption of the interrupted action. When the subject follows the instructions to stop, he has not forgotten that the ball is still in the box, and he immediately carries out the remaining action after the close of the pause, which is used for extensive statements of personal observation. Without being commanded to do so, he catches and lays down the ball. The subject apparently has the tendency to resume and conclude the interrupted action. Thus Subject N. says, "It is a whole, and one piece is still missing."

Ovsiankina's results show that the tension system is sufficient to produce a tendency for resumption of the action, even when no motor unity is present. One wonders whether the tension is weaker in more aggregate actions than it is in unities, and whether, accordingly, the interruption comes more easily. Our observations support this. The looser unity comprised of several tosses is easier to interrupt than the more stable unity comprised of only five partial actions, and the resumption tendency is also weaker.

XI THE SIGNIFICANCE OF THE BASIC SYNTHESIS FORM FOR RELAPSE*

Now we would like to raise two questions:

1. When actions which are subject to relearning have identical elements, does

* *This section is from Part II of the original work—Editor.*

the relapse tendency vary if the basis synthesis forms of the actions are different?

2. Is relapse influenced when the basis synthesis form is changed simultaneously with the relearning?

While investigating these questions, we also obtained results on the significance of the degree of linkage for relapse.

The Relapse Tendency with Various Basic Synthesis Forms

In the basic experiments described earlier, the action had a cloak form at the end of the relearning stage:

$$A \ bcd \ E$$

Now the question arises as to how the action can be given a different synthesis form without changing the elements of the action. Let us go back to our earlier statements on the significance of stress for the synthesis form. If these are correct, then the stress of the frame action stems from the possibility of making serious errors.

Accordingly, if we do not permit such dangers of error to arise, the special stress of the frame action would not occur, and the middle action would have to be relatively strongly stressed because of the functional influences of the unity. Thus the action would have the main block form instead of the cloak form:

$$a \ bcD \ e$$

Therefore, such an experiment would also be a test of the correctness of our earlier investigations on the significance of stress.

In practice we can make the frame action drastically more simple by never giving the subject definite instructions on selection, and by having the subject simply put the balls into a container as a final action. Experiment W_1 was carried out with a frame of action weakened in this manner; it had the following arrangement:

I. Learning (90 tosses): the lever is pressed.

II. Relearning (40 tosses): the lever is lifted.

III. Back-learning (10 tosses): the lever is pressed.

In this experiment the immediate objective of the arrangement proved successful. It became evident that the action had the main block form toward the end of the learning stage, and also retained this form. Thus, a basic synthesis form different from that during the basic experiments had been obtained, and our thoughts on the significance of stress had been confirmed.

Concerning the question of the relapse tendency's dependence on the synthesis form, it became clear that *no relapse at all* occurs for the main block form.

The transition to changed lever use takes place without any aftereffect stemming from the action previously executed (see Table 3).

Experiment E E, was performed with a frame action which was only partially weakened. The initial action was carried out, as in the basic experiments, with increases in the difficulty; yet, as in experiment W_1, the final action consisted of merely putting away the balls. Thus, in the stages of learning and of relearning, the total action had the following synthesis form which was between a cloak form and a main block form:

A BCD e

TABLE 3
The Significance of the Basic Synthesis Form for Relapse

| Experiment | Stage 1 | Stage II (Relearning) | | | | | | |
| | | | strength of the relapse tendency | | | strength of the danger of confusion* | | |
	action unity	action unity	incorrect uses	hand movements begun falsely	spread over the losses	incorrect uses	reconsideration	spread over the losses
C_1	A [bcd] E (cloak form, solid)	A [bc$_2$d] E (cloak form, solid)	3	3	1–25 (56%)	—	—	—
W_1	a [bCD] e (main block form, loose)	a [bC$_2$D] c (main block form, loose)	—	—	—	—	—	—
EE_1	A [bCD] e (loose)	A [bC$_2$D] e (loose)	—	—	—	—	—	—
SS_1	A [bcd] E (cloak form, solid)	a [bC$_2$D] e (main block form, loose)	1	1	5–8 (>9%)	0	1	1
Q_2	A [bcd] E (cloak form, solid)	a [bC$_2$D] e (main block form, loose)	0	2	4–12 (20%)	0	1	1
RR_1	a [bCD] e (main block form, loose)	A [bc$_2$d] E (cloak form, solid)	0	1	1 (2%)	0	5	1–3 and 16–20

Confusion errors will be discussed in the next section—Editor,

Here too there was no evidence of relapse during relearning.

In actions which have the same content in all other respects, the relapse tendency is dependent on the synthesis form. While relapse occurs in the cloak form, it is absent in the main block or similar forms.

To what facts can the lack of relapse in the main block form be due?

Following the earlier results, it probably seems decisive at first glance that in the main block form the lever use can always be carried out with control, and as the principle action in the learning as well as the relearning stage. The subject always has this part of the action under his control, and relapses are not at all possible. Therefore, the situation is different than in the cloak form, where the execution of the frame action as the principle action does not also permit the execution of lever use as the principle action within the same unity.

In our experience, however, the controlled execution of the lever use in the stage of relearning contributes to successfully suppressing a relapse tendency. Here, one wonders why a relapse tendency is not at all present.

Let us study in Table 3 the synthesis form in the learning stages of experiments C_1, EE_1, SS_1, and Q_2. The experiments in which a relapse tendency occurs, whether it be strong or weak, namely C_1, SS, and Q_2, have a cloak form toward the end of the learning stage, whereas the experiments without relapse have a main block form (or, in the case of EE_1, an approximate main block form). This is evidence for the fact that it is not the synthesis form in the relearning stage, but the synthesis form in the learning stage which is decisive for the appearance of the relapse.

A perusal of the experiment transcript shows that it is not the synthesis form in itself which is decisive for the presence or absence of the relapse tendency, but rather the varying degree of linkage in the two synthesis forms. In the case of the action learned in the cloak form, the individual actions are very firmly unified; a strong unity exists. In the case of the action learned in the main block form, the individual actions remain far more independent and never merge firmly together; not even the manipulations on the apparatus merge among themselves. The action remains a relatively loose, splintered, and labile succession—an aggregate action or at best a weak unity. (This is true in spite of the same number of repetitions—a new proof that the latter plays no decisive role.)

The strong difference in degree of linkage can be explained by the varying effectiveness of an essential unity factor in the two synthesis forms, namely, by the varying degree to which the two action forms are filled with meaning.

In the cloak action, the manipulations on the apparatus have the pronounced character of an auxiliary middle action; the main goal action is the frame action. The whole receives its meaning through the fact that this frame action serves to construct a figure or a name.

In contrast, this meaning is missing in the case of the main block action. Just as putting the balls into a container is meaningless if this container is emptied after 30 tosses, and the balls are again dropped into the ball cup so that the cycle can begin again, the manipulations of the apparatus (which are carried out 90 times in succession) are meaningless. The subject does not know for what purpose he is actually performing the action; he remains dissatisfied and bored and dissipates his energies in variable observations on unimportant things like the length of the duct, the size and tempo of the balls, and the sounds in the box.

Perhaps an additional factor is that the stressed performance of the manipulations on the apparatus assures this part a certain independence, and is less favorable for its unification than its evenly unstressed performance in the cloak form.

The contrast between the stability and meaningfulness of the cloak action, and the meaningless, loose succession of the main block action is apparent in the following juxtaposition of typical statements.

Cloak form, Subject R:

Toss 41–52: "Before, placement of the balls was an appendage and the working of the apparatus was essential. Now it is reversed: selection and placement are the chief actions."

Toss 53–57: "Tossing the ball, lifting the lever, and catching the ball are practically one action. I cannot distinguish the individual parts; it is as if I were doing it unconsciously."

Toss 71–79: "It is one action; there is no longer any appendage."

Main Block Form, Subject W:

Toss 31–60: "I no longer have to grope for the funnel, but freely toss in the balls; I have a definite sense of space. All at once I found the duct very long. I pressed more and more so that it might go more quickly. Therefore the crucial point was the *rolling* of the ball until it hit the box."

Toss 61–75: "A kind of rhythm is forming. I am becoming somewhat more relaxed by the rhythm. Before I had it I tried to get something out of this business; now I am content. I no longer have the feeling that the ball is traveling so terribly slowly. I have my greatest enjoyment in the sounds of impact the ball makes inside the box. They are clear, musical sounds, the rest is noise."

Toss 76–90: "The balls seemed somewhat small to me. The rhythm was no longer as pronounced. Again, it was going somewhat too slowly. The two main sounds are even more pronounced."

The varying intensity of the relapse tendency can be explained by the varying degrees of linkage of the two synthesis forms. If a strong relapse tendency appears in a strong unity, no such tendency appears at all in what is almost an aggregate action

Relearning with Simultaneous Change of the Synthesis Form.

The question arises as to whether there is an influence on relapse when the synthesis form of the action is changed simultaneously with the change of lever use.

The action is learned in the cloak form in the usual way with initial and final actions having a strong stress:

$$A \text{ bcd } E$$

With the start of relearning, no further instructions are given concerning the initial action, and the final action consists of simply putting the balls away. Thus initial and final action are completely unstressed; with this radical change in stress the action would have to switch to a main block form:

$$a \text{ } bcD \text{ e}$$

Experiment SS_1 was carried out in this way.

I. *Learning* (80 tosses): the lever is lifted. Stressed frame action.

II. *Relearning* (47 tosses): The lever is pressed. Unstressed frame action.

III. Back-learning (19 tosses): The lever is lifted. Unstressed frame action.

The change of the cloak form into a main block form at the start of the relearning stage was successful. *The change was experienced very strongly* (13). After receiving the instructions, the subject believed that, apart from lever use, he was facing the same action with a simplified frame action. However, when he began the action, he immediately had the completely unexpected impression of carrying out an action which was changed qualitatively. He faltered, felt a restraint, and thought over what was required. With Toss 1 there was a danger of confusion at the lever; the subject was unsure. "I simply didn't know what I was supposed to do. I pulled myself together and remembered the instructions." With Toss 2 the confusion had already been overcome.

A relapse tendency only appeared for the duration of four tosses. At that, it was very weak, and it did not by any means reach the extent and intensity of the pronounced relapse tendencies observed in the basic experiments (Table 3 makes possible a quantitative comparison). The relapse tendency began only after the subject had become a bit more familiar with the action, and it was no longer performed with such care and control. During Toss 5, the subject makes an incorrect hand movement toward lever use, but then corrects it on the edge of the box. During Toss 7, after a pause for statement, he uses the lever incorrectly.

During repetition with a second subject, the experiment ran in the same way.

There are two possible explanations available for the weakness of the relapse tendency. 1) The performance of the action in the main block form during the relearning stage. This involves controlled performance of the lever use as the main action while the frame action is weakened, and thus relapse is effectively repressed: and 2) The change of the synthesis form simultaneous with the change of the lever use. By this change the new action unity is made relatively unlike the old one, and (despite the identical contents) it is experienced by the subject as strange (alien) (14).

Experimental Manipulation of Synthesis Form

We may obtain a test of the correctness of our interpretation if the action is learned in main block form (permiting only a loose combining of the parts), and then organized into a cloak form at the start of relearning by placing stress on the frame action. Now, in addition to changing the lever use, the subject has to exercise control in performing the frame action (which is now offering difficulties). As far as this factor alone is concerned, far more favorable conditions are present for a strong relapse tendency than in the basic experiments. However, from the experiments just discussed, we know that two factors work against the appearance of a strong relapse tendency—specifically, the loose integration of the parts in the learning stage, and the dissimilarity of the actions in the learning and relearning stages. Accordingly we cannot count on a strong relapse tendency.

Experiment RR_1 confirms these considerations. Only one isolated relapse appeared. Specifically the subject started his hand movement for lever use incorrectly, but then carried out corrective action due to an imperative idea. Once again a strong experience of strangeness had a controlling influence on the subject. From Toss 16 to 20 he doubted if he was acting correctly.

We attain further confirmation of our previous results when we compare, in Table 3, Experiment RR_1, just described, with Experiments SS_1 and Q_2. Although in Experiment RR_1 the lever use in the relearning stage is carried out without control and as a secondary action, the relapse tendency is still weaker than in the two other experiments in which the lever use is performed with stress and as the main action. This causes one to again conclude that the strength of the relapse tendency is not dependent on the controlledness of the action to be relearned, but on the synthesis of the action in the learning stage. Specifically, the firmer integration of the action unity in the cloak form promotes strength of the relapse tendency, while looser integration in the main block form promotes its weakness.

EDITOR'S SUMMARY OF FURTHER SECTIONS

[Schwarz's material is so rich and complex that I have elected to summarize a number of further sections that are important, yet that might be indigestible in an unabridged form.* These are as follows:

1. A section in which Schwarz demonstrates that his results do not apply just

* The complete text may be obtained from University Microfilms—Editor.

to changes in use of the lever. Schwarz describes three experiments. In the first, instead of changing the lever action, he varies which funnel the ball is tossed into. In the second, instead of changing the lever action, he changes catching the ball to picking the ball up after it has fallen into a box. In both these experiments, he shows that there is a relapse tendency; that this is due to the firm incorporation of the parts involved in the action unity; and that relearning involves reconstructing the action unity and destroying the command character of the signals. Finally, Schwarz simultaneously changes all three parts of the middle action. This makes the middle action so unlike the previously learned unity that it functions as a completely new action, and no relapse tendency appears.

2. A section on backlearning. Schwarz shows that when the subject back-learns—is forced to return to his initial way of working the lever—he again encounters relapse pressure. However, with each relearning, this pressure diminishes. Since the strength of the relapse tendency is related to the specific structure of the action unity, Schwarz argues that the structure must have changed. Whereas at first the action unit was:

$$A \text{ bcd } E$$

the subject has now discovered that there are two variants, so that the unit becomes:

$$A \text{ b}(c_1)(c_2)\text{d } E$$

The increased differentiation of the unity—a double-tracked action unit—provides the subject with better control.

3. A section on the prevention of relapse pressure: Schwarz provides evidence for his reasoning by showing that relapse tendency is completely prevented if subjects begin with the knowledge that the lever works both ways. Even if the subject only occasionally experiences the other use of the lever, a double-tracked action unit is formed, and no relapse pressure is experienced.

4. A Section on "Confusion Errors". This section introduces a completely new phenomenon. As the subjects develop double tracked action units, they begin to make a different type of error. While there is no relapse pressure, there are sudden confusions about what to do. Schwarz carefully spells out the dynamic differences between relapse and confusion errors, and points out that if an investigator simply analyzed the subject's overt performance, he might never become aware of the different structures that are involved. He shows that, unlike relapse pressure, confusion danger becomes more severe with each switch in lever use. However, it also disappears more rapidly. Schwarz accounts for these details in terms of the field characteristics acquired by funnel of the apparatus. He points out that the funnel assumes its command character

(valence) more rapidly with each switch. Since the funnel's command becomes specific ("Lift" or "Press") rather than the general "Watch out for the lever" warning used to guard against relapse, the funnel's valence works *against* the new response until its command is changed by a new intention from the subject.

Schwarz presents experimental material on the appearance of confusion errors, their development in relation to valences, and the dependence of confusion error on the presence of double-tracked action units. However, Schwarz also shows that sometimes subjects report confusion when basic synthesis forms are changed (see experiments $3S_1$, $Q_{.2}$, and RR_1 reported in Table 3). He does not discuss whether or not this latter type of confusion error is dynamically similar to the type that arises during backlearning. Finally, he gives the comprehensive summary presented in the next section—Editor.]

XII CRITICAL DIFFERENCES BETWEEN RELAPSE TENDENCY AND CONFUSION DANGER

The distinction between relapse tendency and confusion danger is of fundamental significance for future investigations. For this reason the most important differences are contrasted here.

Relapse Tendency	*Confusion Danger*

1. First Appearance

The relapse tendency first appears during the first relearning (on the first testing day). It begins very strongly and leads, as a rule, to errors immediately during the first tosses.	The confusion danger does not appear until after repeated re- and back-learning (on a later testing day), and then at the earliest after the first lever use on this testing day. It begins weakly at first and is expressed in the uncertainty of the subject.

2. Appearance in Later Stages

The relapse tendency can appear again in immediately following stages, but it is far more weak.	The confusion danger can appear repeatedly in immediately-following stages. If its surmounting is to be attributed to a warning, or command character of the funnel, it begins earlier in the subsequent stages, and is probably stronger and disappears more rapidly.

3. Nature, Forces

Relapse Tendency

The subject feels that there is the presence of a compulsion to perform the previously performed type of action. If he succumbs to this compulsion, he still knows which action had been practiced before, and which is now required.

Confusion Danger

The subject feels uncertainty and indecision about which of the two middle actions he is supposed to employ. There is no presence of a compulsion to employ one of the two actions.

4. Struggle

The subject compensates the relapse pressure by a counter pressure (as a rule, stronger control or stress). The action unity is restructured. The lever use is stressed and performed relatively independently.

The subject overcomes uncertainty by reflection and by bringing to mind the instructions.

5. Aids in the Struggle

Hand movements which have already been started incorrectly are frequently corrected by corrective actions due to imperative ideas. These begin as early as the first toss and move from the lever to the funnel in the course of the test, whereby the ideas become less and less sharp. At the funnel they disappear into the imagination.

After some time an inhibition of the action event emanates from the funnel (warning character of the funnel). Later the funnel assumes the function as a guidepost (specific command character of the funnel). With repeated occurrence the confusion danger recedes again very rapidly without the funnel's assuming imperative functions.

6 Characteristic Terminology of the Subject

Among other things the subject uses such expressions as "Stress upwards," "Tendency to lift," "It occurred to me," "Thought about it always."

The subject speaks of "uncertainty," "doubt," "reflection," "hindering tendency," "clarity," "orienting idea."

Although we may not be certain whether relapse tendency or confusion danger is present when we rely on the subject's statements about a particular toss, continued statements and the total picture of the course of action leave no doubt as to which is occurring.

1. Lewin, *Psychol. Forsch* 1 (1922), 191 ff; and 2 (1922) 65 ff.

2. H. Münsterberg, *Beiträge zur exp. Psychol.*, Part I.

3. Lewin, *Psychol. Forsch.* 2 (1922), 104.

4. Ach, *Über die Willenstätigkeit und das Denken,* (Göttingen, 1905), 8 *ff.;* also Ach, *Willensakt und Temperament,* Leipzig, 1910; Koffka, *Zur Analyse der Vorstellungen der Vorstellungen und ihrer Gesetze,* (Leipzig, 1912); Lewin, *Psychol. Forschg.* 1(1922), 193; and Lindworsky, *Der Wille,* (Leipzig, 1923) 6 *ff.*

5. On the term *action unity* see Köhler, "Gestaltprobleme und Anfänge einer Gestalt-theorie," *Jahresbericht über d. ges. Physiol.* (1922) 519; and Lewin, *Vorsatz, Wille und Bedürfnis,* 12 ff.

6. Compare the identical observation made on another occasion by Lindworsky, *op. cit,* 93.

7. The fact that the corrective actions are shifted ahead chronologically within the total action is reminiscent of the fact that, in composite actions in general, acceleration of performance rests to a great extent upon a process which Lewin (*Psychol. Forschg.* 2 (1922), 129), calls a chronological placing ahead *(Früherlegen)* of the activity stimulus." In his experiments with nonsense syllables, realization of the task and the act of attentive concentration is soon pushed from the main period into the preliminary period of the action. Thus, the motor tasks demanded by the subject at that point finally take place directly after the presentation of the external stimulus. In learning to use a typewriter, a similar process takes place.

8. In Münsterberg's tests in which the habit has been produced in the course of months, the first system, and then even the second system, is apparently so stabile that it even survives for a rather long time in a condition devoid of tension.

9. See also the statements on the effect of practice in Lewin, *Psychol. Forsch* 2 (1922), 125.

10. Köhler, *Psychische Gestalten.*

11. Blumenfeld, *Psychotechnische Z.* 3 (1928), 30 and *Bericht über den 10. Kongress für experimentelle Psychologie,* 97.

12. Ovsiankina's results agree with this. See also Lewin, *op. cit,* 49.

13. As we saw on another occasion, the use of a new apparatus, the change of all three parts of the middle action, or the addition of optic signs are not experienced as strange to this degree.

14. Van der Veldt finds that the relapse tendency becomes weaker the more the action in State II becomes unlike the action in Stage I. "L'apprentissage du Mouvement el L'automatisme," (Etudes de Psychologie Publ. sons la Direction de Michotte) (Löwen u. Paris, 1928).

Chapter IX

THE ORGANIZATION OF BEHAVIOR

IN this chapter we shall consider a number of different levels of organization. First, we will interpret Schwarz's findings on the formation of action units, and examine how such "molecular" intention systems are organized. Then, we shall look at a study by Birenbaum on the forgetting of intentions, a study that suggests that intentions themselves may be organized into larger structures— embedded as parts of more extensive intentions. We will also see that intentions may be organized around aspects of the person's situation, and hence affected by situational factors. Finally, at an even higher level of organization, we shall have a brief look at how the entire personality may be viewed as an organization of intention systems.

THE INTENDING AND ORGANIZING OF ACTION UNITS

In order to fully understand Schwarz's results and integrate them with our theoretical position, we will review the dynamics and organization of action units as an intentional process.

The Dynamics of Action Units

We may interpret Schwarz's results as follows: in the course of carrying out a project of action (such as spelling a name with marbles from the apparatus), the subject forms as action unit. This is a true gestalt, whose parts are the dropping of the marble in the funnel, the pushing of the lever, and the catching of the marble. This organization of action which might be called "get-the-marble" is intended by the subject in the same sense that a perceptual organization is actively constituted. The instigation for this organization is that the parts are all means to an end.

Once this action unit has been formed, it ordinarily serves a very laudable function. Rather than intending each step of the procedure, the subject can simply intend the unit—for by intending the whole, all the parts are necessarily present.

However, if one of the parts is changed, the subject is in difficulty. For if he is concentrated on the project of spelling a name, he will intend the means-unit "get-the-marble," thereby intending the action unit which now has an incorrect part. This will occur unless the subject chooses to focus on the means of getting the marble, and hence breaks up the former action unit. In this case, the subject will have no difficulty in performing the correct action—note that there is no mystical force stemming from some objective stimulus. However, the subject will not be unable to use his attention elsewhere, for example, in intending the name he wishes to spell.

We have noted that Lewin and Koffka had two somewhat different ways of accounting for the force of habit. Lewin, conceiving of habits as mere connections, demonstrates that the force of a habit is really due to an intention which energizes the connection. Koffka, conceiving of habits as dynamic organizations, argues that the force of a habit is the force to re-establish the whole that occurs when a part of the organization is evoked.

From Schwarz's study it may be seen that Lewin is correct in insisting that the energy for the unwanted action comes from the subject's own intention. He is correct in the sense that the subject must intend "get-the-marble," or the unwanted action will not occur. On the other hand, we believe that Koffka is also correct when he asserts that this intention must "communicate" with part of a gestalt—the action unit—and that this part must then invoke (energize) the whole unit, including the unwanted action. Thus, there will be no relapse pressure unless the subject's intention communicates with an action unit that has its own internal energy.

Schwarz hints at the independent energy of the action unit when he speculates that the tension to complete a task is partially dependent on the strength of the action unity. Thus, he wonders if tension is weaker in aggregate actions than in unities, and he points out that looser unities seem to be more easily integrated than more stable unities. Speaking of the tendency to complete the task, one of his subjects remarks, "It is a whole, and one piece is still missing." This suggests that the tension is coming from the action unit rather than from some other tension system within the subject. By this I do not mean to suggest that the energy for the formation or invocation of the action unit is coming from the action unit itself, or from some external stimulus; Lewin's experiments show this cannot be maintained. But the energy for the carrying out the action may be coming from the organization within the action unit. This is, of course, close to Koffka's position that the part must invoke the whole.

Since Koffka imagines habits as existing in time, he hesitates to have the organization be the sole source of energy, because the energy would be depleted after one use (1). However, since we believe that the unit is continually re-established by the intention of the subject, we have no problem of energy depletion. According to our theory, the subject's intention (to get the marble) creates the action unit (drop-push-catch). We do not envisage this gestalt existing somewhere as an empty form until it is energized by a tension system which communicates with a part of the whole. Rather, the subject organizes the action unit as a whole—intends it—as a means to the project of action he has willed. Once formed, this whole (the action unit) necessarily implies each of its parts, including a part which is now inappropriate.

It must be stressed that action units differ from habits in two ways. First, they are not caused by the presence of an objective stimulus, even when the latter coincides with a drive state. Rather, they are always organized by the subject who intends them for some project of action. Second, they are not formed on the basis of repeated associations between a stimulus and a response. Rather, they are formed on the basis of the various organizational principles that Schwarz explicates—equal stress, a common means to an end, and so on.

Since Schwarz's work, there appears to have been very few applications of the idea of action units. The only experimental work with which I am familiar involves a study by Adams and McCulloch, in which rats ran down a T-maze to obtain food (2). The food was always placed at the end of the same arm of the T, until the rats were thoroughly trained as to which way to turn. Then the food was switched to the other arm of the T, so that if the rat had previously had to turn right, he now had to learn to turn left. Adams and McCulloch manipulated one very simple variable—the length of the runway to the choice point. The runway was only two and a half feet long for some animals, but twenty-five feet long for others. They reasoned that if the runway was short, the animal would really be engaged in only one action unit—"turning right" or "turning left"; whereas if the runway were long, the animal would form two action units—"go down the runway" and "turn right" (or left). That this understanding of the situation was accurate is supported by the fact that those rats in the short runway immediately oriented themselves towards the turn (for example, by twisting the head), while this was not true in the long runway.

Adams and McCulloch predicted that it would be much easier to simply learn the reversal of a single action unit than to have to learn the reversal of one of two action-units. (It seems to us, however, that this would only be true if both units were part of one gestalt.) As predicted, they found that, upon reversal, the rats with the short runway made substantially fewer errors—only half as many as the rats with the long runway.

It would seem as though the idea of action unit has many implications for studies of both human and animal learning and performance. We hope that some of these will be translated into additional experimental research.

Organizing a New Action Unit

While the subject can perform the correct action as long as he keeps specifically intending it, he needs his attention for other tasks. Hence, once he is confronted with the fact that the formerly helpful action unit "get-the-marble" is now a hindrance, he begins to organize a new action unit. As Schwarz points out, the structure of this new unit must be fundamentally different because the subject now knows that the lever may be set to be either pushed or lifted. Hence, he makes a differentiation and forms a double-tracked action unit. But how is he to form this new unit?

It is evident that the subject intends a new action unit. And we may presume that the subject puts the pieces together in his mind. Although Schwarz does not give any details on this process, Koffka has pointed out how subjects learn nonsense syllables by organizing them into a whole with rhythmic parts (3). But what is remarkable is, that once these pieces are together the subject does not have to keep his full attention on them, but can go back to attending to the name that he is spelling. Indeed, he must do this if the pieces are to be "glued" together, for it is their common character as a means to an end that makes them cohere.

Nevertheless, the subject must maintain some kind of specific intention, for when he is distracted by the introspective pauses which Schwarz inserts, he begins to use the old action again. It is as though the pieces are glued together but still must be clamped for them not to fall apart. This "clamp"—the intention for the formation of the new action unit—must have become a part of the larger action of using the marble to spell a name, but not yet a well-enough established part to take the jar that occurs when the subject shifts to the different activity of reporting his introspections. Hence, the intention is not remembered when the subject returns to the activity of using the marble. Shortly, we shall see that this interpretation fits with Birenbaum's findings on the forgetting of intentions.

If, however, there is no separate intention for the new action unit, how can we account for the presence of the valence that appears when the subject begins to manipulate the lever in the wrong way? We believe that this valence is actually the result of a different intention on the part of the subject. This other intention, quite separate from that which forms the new action unit, is to not make a mistake. This is why the valence only appears when the subject begins to make a mistake because of using the old action unit. This intention is triggered by the incipient mistake, and, as Schwarz points out, occurs more quickly each time and is intensified by the emotional upset of an actual mistake.

The compulsive nature of the relapse pressure and the involuntary imperative "no" of the countervalence remind us of the ego-alien id and a sort of superego counterforce. Since the relapse pressure stems from the subject's intentions, such an analogy suggests that it might be worthwhile to explore the possibility that some id impulses may really stem from the ego's intentions, and do not exist in a completely isolated state.

When the subject has finally succeeded in establishing a solid new action unity, he can relax his control. The new unit easily occurs and no relapse pressure is experienced. If, however, the subject is asked to return to the original action unit, he may experience a different sort of problem—a confusion tendency. In the middle of performing the action, the subject may forget whether to push or lift the lever. Studies by other investigators have shown that shifting the response back and forth is not necessary to produce this effect. A break in the action unit, or some other disturbance, will suffice to produce a confusion error when both action units are equally strong (when the habit strengths are equal). Schwarz's point is that these errors are dynamically quite different, and are overcome by different solutions. In the case of confusion errors, the subject does not have to exert a counterforce against a relapse pressure and form a new intention, he simply needs to decide what to do in the face of his confusion. Once he does decide, assisting valences immediately issue specific commands about what to do, and hence insure the performance of the correct action.

THE ORGANIZATION OF INTENTIONS—BIRENBAUM'S STUDY

Although we have been speaking of the organization of an action unit, a unit made up of what used to be three separate activities, it must be realized that such a unit is the exact equivalent of a unitary intention system made up of what used to be three separate intentions. Just as the intention system "drop the marble" corresponds to the activity of dropping the marble, so the intention system "obtain the marble" corresponds to the activity of dropping the marble, pushing the lever, and catching the marble. The person need no longer make three separate intentions, he has developed an organization of intentions such that he is able to make only one. This suggests that there may be whole systems of intention systems, in which one intention system contains a number of others as parts. Another of Lewin's students, Gita Birenbaum, became involved in working with these systems of intentions in attempting to account for some of her findings. Birenbaum's study is actually concerned with the forgetting of intentions; considerations of space have necessitated its separate publication as one of the monographs of *Psychological Issues* (4). Here we shall give a summary of her results from our own perspective, concentrating on the implications which her study has for the organization of intentions.

The Forgetting of Intentions

In order to study the forgetting of intentions, Birenbaum gave her subjects a series of problems. Each problem (such as "Write the names of famous writers whose last name begins with a *G"*) was given, one at a time, after the subject had completed the previous problem. With each problem the subject was given a sheet of paper, and, "in order to keep track of the papers," the subject was asked, "as a favor to the experimenter," to sign her or his name to the paper before handing it back to the experimenter. The subjects of course agreed to this request, and the experiment began. While the subjects were focused on completing the problems which had been given to them, Birenbaum was interested in whether they would remember to sign each paper or would forget their intentions. To influence this process, she manipulated, or observed, a number of interesting variables.

Birenbaum began her experiments by giving her subjects a series of from ten to twelve problems. In one series, the problems were all of the same type (for instance, different puzzles all involving making a required number of squares out of a fixed number of match sticks; or writing the names of cities which start with *N*, with *G*). In another series, the problems were of all different types. She demonstrates that in both series of problems almost all of her subjects almost always remembered to sign their name to all of the ten to twelve papers. In Lewinian terms, the intention to sign was usually successful in establishing a tension system which consistently operated to influence the subject's behavior.

Such success suggests that the tension system was connected to deeper needs in the subjects, and to their relationship with the experimenter. In this regard, Birenbaum suggests that the acceptance of the experimenter's request, the motivation of the intention to sign, usually is related to the willingness to be a subject, and to a concern for the experiment and experimenter. That is, there is an involvement with the success of the experimenter which leads to a desire to protect the papers from being mixed up.

In a few cases, subjects always remembered the intention to sign but because of personal needs that had nothing to do with the experiment. For example, one subject had the need to show a constant ironic attitude, and signed himself in a way that formed a swear word which he never forgot to display. Another had a personal need for orderliness that completely dominated his behavior and resulted in consistent signatures.

In the case of a few subjects, there was no carrying out of the intention. These subjects became so wrapped up in the personal meaning of solving the problems that the intention to sign the papers never made contact with need systems concerning the success of the experiment. For example, a very ambitious subject, intent on doing the problems better than a friend, never remembered to sign his name in spite of continued reminders from the experimenter. When, however, he was told, "But (your friend) remembered to sign his name," he stated, "Oh, I hadn't realized the signature was important" and thenceforth signed all of the time. In another case, the subject appears to have made a connection between signing and a need to help the experimenter, but the problems took on a meaning which involved deeper needs. He was a chess player who perceived the match puzzles to require the same sort of ability as chess. Priding himself on his ability, he was dismayed to find that he had a very difficult time solving the match puzzle. This so occupied his attention that he continually failed to perform the signature in spite of verbally chastizing himself whenever he was reminded.

In her analysis, Birenbaum discards all those subjects whose over-all personal needs prevented the more typical sort of involvement with the intention to sign. (While it is not clear exactly how many subjects were discarded, it is less than 10 per cent.) It should be noted that the method of experimental phenomenology *requires* such a procedure. If the investigator were making a statement about the impact which certain physical conditions had on her subjects, or if she were interested in the practical problem of delineating the conditions under which intentions are remembered or forgotten, it would be unconscionable to discard some of the subjects. However, the investigation is aimed at discovering the behavior that results from certain specified psychological conditions. Hence, it is essential to eliminate those subjects who, for whatever reason, are in a different set of psychological conditions.

Birenbaum also notes the role played by motivations (tension systems) directed against completing the intention of signing the paper. One of the problems, drawing a symmetrical pentagon, was particularly difficult for the subjects to complete in a satisfying way. Under conditions which promoted forgetting (which we shall elaborate below), this problem was much less likely to be signed than others. The subjects were, apparently, reluctant to sign their names to a shoddy piece of work.

The existence of such countermotives is, of course, the substance of Freud's passages on the forgetting of intention (5). Noting that intentions are usually easily carried out without the person having to worry about forgetting them, he gives a number of examples where a countermotive works against the intention's performance. Thus, Freud notes, with shame, that when he occasionally forgot his house calls, it was always at the homes of his nonpaying clients. Freud was, of course, particularly interested in the fact that the countermotives were usually subconscious—there being some reason why the person could not take the responsibility of owning their existence.

Such countermotives may also be revealed in a person's failing to remember whether or not he has carried out an intention. Thus, Rapaport observes that this forgetting may signal the presence of subconscious motivation (6). Often, Birenbaum's subjects were not sure if they had remembered to sign the paper and checked to make sure; but unfortunately Birenbaum does not investigate the subconscious motivations of her individual subjects, and so we cannot be sure of the extent to which countermotives played a role in the various cases of forgetting to sign the papers or forgetting whether or not a signature was made.

On the other hand, her study reveals quite a different factor which is probably of even greater importance as a condition for the failure to perform intentions. She shows that in addition to the various needs which determine the acceptance of, or resistance to, the intention, there are organizational—structural—factors which affect the relationship between the various intentions. (7). Before we consider what these are, let us return to Birenbaum's data.

Having shown that subjects ordinarily remember to sign the papers whether the problems were of a similar or of a diverse nature, Birenbaum introduced a new variable: after five similar problems (match stick puzzles), she introduced a pause of from five to ten minutes in duration. The pause was either filled with a little trick problem, or with a diverting conversation. After the pause, the subject was given another five match stick puzzles. Whereas before the pause the signature was always performed, on the sixth problem, directly following the pause, eight of the ten subjects either forgot the signature completely or gave an uncharacteristically late performance. However, on the next —the seventh problem—only one subject is late, and by the eighth problem, all ten subjects are again signing the papers with regularity.

How can we account for the momentary forgetting of the intention? Birenbaum points out that the intention is not "forgotten" in the sense that the subject no longer can remember what it was he intended to do. Indeed the tension system established by the intention must still be available, because it leads to the production of a signature on the very next problem. It must, however, have failed to become tensed or in some other way been unable to influence the subject's behavior.

Structural Relations Between Intentions

Birembaum argues as follows: with the average subject, two different tension systems are established at the beginning of the experiment. The major system is concerned with performing the problems. The minor tension system is concerned with signing each sheet of paper. To account for her results, Birenbaum reasons that the two tension systems must begin to merge together to form a larger unit. By the sixth problem this more inclusive tension system is concerned with solving puzzles having to do with match sticks and signing the pieces of paper they are on. The signature tension system has thus been incorporated into a more comprehensive unit. The intention to sign is now a part of an intention to do problems, sign them, and give them to the experimenter.

Now during the pause, the person moves into quite a different region; he is no longer a subject in an experiment, but, rather, a fellow person. When he is suddenly given another problem to perform, he must make a transition back into being a subject. Birenbaum argues that in order to do this, to get involved again, he has to again intend to do problems (to create a new tension system). This he does, but since the new tension system in quite separate from the older system, which had developed to incorporate the signature intention within it, the signature intention is left behind. Hence, it is not present (tensed), and therefore does not influence the person's behavior.

It is important to note that the pause does not create a disturbance because of the mere passage of time, but because the person moves into a different region where different motive systems are active. Thus, subjects may return to the experiment after a "pause" of several days or a month, and immediately sign the papers without being told to do so because they return to the experiment as a subject—have already entered that region. In a somewhat similar vein, the mere repetition of the signature is, in itself, neither a factor for or against the completion of the intention. What is important is whether or not the person intends to sign—whether in our terms the signature's intention system is active.

While the connection with the old intention system has been broken by the pause—since the sixth problem is similar to the problems which preceded the pause—it begins to be joined with the old problem intention system. When the seventh problem is also another match stick puzzle, it becomes fully unified with the original inclusive gestalt. Since the signature system is a dependent part of this inclusive system, the person intends to sign (the system is tensed), and on the seventh and succeeding problems the signature is performed.

In summary, Birenbaum proposes that the signature intention system gets incorporated into a more comprehensive unit. When there is a psychological interlude in the experiment, the subject has to develop a new intention to solve the problem he is given, and hence there is a break between the old global unit and the new intention. When the new intention is incorporated into the old global unit, the signature intention again occurs (the tension system is tensed) and the intention returns.

To bolster this explanation, Birenbaum performs a different experiment. After giving her subjects five match stick puzzles, instead of using a pause she causes a break, by making the sixth problem a different type of problem (naming cities starting with *G*, forming different words from the letters of a given word, and so on). Again, the hitherto regular performance of the signature drops to only a 27 per cent performance, However, this time most subjects do not begin to sign again when the next, seventh, problem is presented. The average performance on the subsequent problems (seven to twelve) rises to only 34 per cent. (This is in spite of the above-mentioned fact that when the subjects are given diverse problems to begin with, they have 100 per cent performance.) We can only conclude that the signature intention has, indeed, been somehow incorporated into an intention system that deals with match stick problems, and hence is unable to influence behavior as long as that intention system is isolated from the governing intention system.

Occasionally, as further problems (all of different types) are presented, a subject may begin to form a connection between the new problem system and the old match problem system—incorporating them both in to a more inclusive "being a subject doing problems" system. If and when this connection is made, the intention to sign will become active again, and the person will resume signing his papers.

It is important to note that Birenbaum, like other Lewin students, can account for individual differences in terms of her general explanatory system. Since the performance of an intention is attributed to the connection, and forgetting to the isolation, of inner intention systems, subjects who form a connected system should perform better than those with a less connected structure. Birenbaum observes that subjects who are less involved with the problems in their own right, and are merely being obedient subjects, will be more likely at the beginning to simply form a "being a subject doing problems" system. Therefore, these subjects will experience no break, and never fail to perform the signature. On the other hand, subjects who are quite involved in the individual problems, emotionally excitable, feeling each event intensely, will be less capable of forming a more inclusive problem sphere; and hence they will never recover the intention to sign. Finally, subjects who are involved, but are more controlled, will temporarily lose the intention but will force themselves to find the more comprehensive unit. Eventually, they will again begin to perform the signature—once they have managed to transform the meaning of the problems so that the test acquires a uniform sense. Birenbaum's data show that the less excitable subjects perform the intention 89 per cent of the time, while the more emotional subjects only perform at a 43 per cent level.

In addition to handling individual differences, Birenbaum's explanation, in terms of the structure of the relevant intention systems, explains the influence of a number of other interesting variables. Some of these work by causing a break between an individual problem and the comprehensive intention system (which contains the signature intention); others exert their influence by promoting or hindering the original development of the more comprehensive system.

In general, any factor that isolates a given problem from the comprehensive intention system (which includes the signature intention) will prevent the performance of the intention. Thus, Birenbaum gives a number of examples when an emotional success or failure experience with a problem causes the problem to become noteworthy for its success or failure characteristics, rather than for its problematic character. This sets the problems off, and hence leads to a failure to sign the paper. If the experience is a deep one, it may even color the meaning of successive problems, separating them from the more mundane, comprehensive intention system and thus causing the forgetting of an intention. The isolating factor need not necessarily be emotional. A problem that is qualitatively different from the others in any way will be somewhat isolated. Thus, one of Birenbaum's problems was to write a stanza from one's favorite poem. This problem was of such a different character that subjects were much more likely to forget to sign the paper.

In general, any factor which hinders the development of a comprehensive intention system (that includes the signature intention) will work against signature performance. This is so because in the absence of a comprehensive system, the person's behavior will be dominated by the individual problems.

A comprehensive intention system may be hindered by creating an emotionally labile condition. Using eight calm subjects with high intention performance, Birenbaum created a competitive situation with a stooge and introduced experiences of success and failure. She was successful in emotionally arousing four of the subjects, and the performance of all of these four subjects dropped from an average of 86 to 64 per cent. (Note that the method of experimental phenomenology requires us to be concerned about the performance of all four of the subjects who became aroused. Each one must show a deficit in signature performance, or there must be some explanation as to why a deficit did not occur. On the other hand, the method is not concerned with the performance of the four subjects who did not happen to become aroused. Since the manipulation was not successful in affecting them, their behavior should simply continue as before.)

Likewise, pauses between problems increased the isolation of different problems, and, hindering the development of a more unified intention system, decreased the chance of signature performance.

On the other hand, development of a comprehensive intention system may be aided by placing a person under enough steady pressure to increase the stability of the situation. Birenbaum choose seven subjects with high emotionality, and hence a low probability of signature performance (46 per cent in the prior experiment). She gave a second series of test problems to these subjects with the added instruction, "Please work as quickly as possible." The subjects became more tense and businesslike, showing little of their former emotional enthusiasm; the signature performance rose to 90 per cent.

It might be expected that very ambitious subjects might see all the problems as chances to succeed, and that this would create a greater unity between the different problems and hence promote a comprehensive intention system. In fact, this great unity and stability are often present. However, the signature intention is never incorporated in this larger unity, which therefore becomes a comprehensive intention system without a signature intention, and hence leads to no signatures. In accounting for the failure of this incorporation, Birenbaum refers to Schwarz's finding that action unities do not develop when there are large stress differences. She suggests that the large stress on the success of the problems prevents this system from merging with the slightly stressed signature intention system. If this explanation is true, then intention systems can only merge when the stresses in the systems are not too different. In Lewin's terms, this makes perfect theoretical sense, since it is necessary to weaken the boundaries between the different systems in order to effect merger, and this would be difficult to do if the tensions were too different. An alternative explanation may simply be that there is no intrinsic relation between an intention to succeed and an intention to do the problems. Hence, the intentions are less apt to be joined together, in the way an intention to help the experimenter would be joined with an intention to sign the problems.

Summarizing the conditions which govern the inclusion of the signature intention, Birenbaum notes (8):

> The incorporation of the intention system into a uniform sphere comprising the main problems can be promoted by a similarity of the problems, a uniform course, an avoidance of too great stress differences between the special intentions and main problems, and finally by a tight but steady total tension situation. The dropping out of the intention system which leads to forgetting is promoted by a qualitative break in the test course (created by a pause or by a transition to problems of a different nature), by emotional fluctuations of the test course, and by fluctuations produced by increasing the tension situation.

THE INFLUENCE OF THE SITUATION

In emphasizing the importance of how the person organizes his action units, his intentions, and his entire system of motives, we do not want to overlook the importance of the situation in determining whether or not an intention will occur. We have already noted that substitute satisfaction—or any sort of development in the organization of an intention—cannot occur if the intention is fixated on some object. While Birenbaum accounts for the forgetting of intentions in terms of how the person has organized his intentions, she is also alert to the influence of field factors generated by the situation in which the person must perform his intention.

The Effect of Field Forces

With respect to field forces, Birenbaum notes that the execution of a behavior—such as carrying out the intention to sign each paper—partially depends on the peculiarities of the immediate surroundings. Thus, there must be an occasion for signing, and there must be an absence of diversions. She states that, "The psychic fields in which the subject moves during the test are generally dominated by the goals of solving the problems which are given to him. . . . Only for relatively short periods of time is the situation free from these towering field forces—only in the intervals betwen problems". It is only at these moments, when the field is relatively free of tension, that the signature intention system (set up by the intention to sign one's name) can bring its influence to bear and give direction to events. Thus, the signature is usually made in the period between problems—either just before beginning a problem or immediately after finishing it. If this period is excluded, the signature intention will fail. For example, with one subject who usually signed the paper before working on a problem, Birenbaum eliminated the period between problems by introducing a new problem before the subject had finished working on the previous problem. The subject became involved with the new problem and forgot to sign the paper. Interestingly, this subject signed subsequent problems *after* finishing the problems.

On the other hand, a situation can develop in which the field of forces is unusually conducive to signing. If, for example, the situation becomes akward because of failures, the subject may escape the field by remembering to sign the paper. The subject may actually gain a substitute satisfaction in remembering to sign. Or, if the subject ponders over a problem, a void may exist, and this will permit the tension system for the signature to begin to function.

Another situational influence stems from the specific problems which are given to the subjects. We have already noted how a problem which is too different from the others, or which causes an emotional experience, will be isolated from the intention system. A problem may also provide a substitution for the signature tension system. One of Birenbaum's problems was to write down one's monogram. Subjects who viewed this problem as an artistic task usually remembered to sign their names. But subjects who saw the problem as simply writing down their initials almost always failed to sign the paper—the initials evidently acting as a substitute for the signature.

A different field influence occurs because of the development of a certain amount of fixation. The intention to sign has created a tension system which is directed at signing paper at a particular time. The paper happens to consist of small white sheets, and to some extent the tension system becomes fixated on this particular type of paper. As an experiment, after a number of problems, Birenbaum gave the subjects a larger piece of colored paper on which to do one of the problems—to trace a figure. She reports that the subjects acted as though the paper were a foreign body, showing a reluctance to sign their names or even give it to the experimenter. The over-all number of subjects performing the signature dropped from 80 per cent to 34 per cent (or in one controlled arrangement from 43 per cent to 22 per cent).

Birenbaum also tried an experiment in which she attempted to create a time fixation by specifically instructing some subjects to sign before actually beginning the problems. When the subjects came to the sixth problem, which was suddenly different from the first five, they showed more resistance to being disrupted—the percentage signing dropping to only 66 per cent rather than the 32 per cent of nonfixated subjects. It if interesting to note that in spite of the fixation to sign before the problem, half of the subjects who remembered the signature were shaken enough so that their signature occurred after finishing the problem. This type of disruption is quite common. Birenbaum notes that when subjects were suddenly given a pause, a different sort of problem, or experienced an emotion, even those who remembered to sign lost their consistency—the signature being signed at a different time or on a different part of the paper.

It should be noted how all of the above observations and experiments reflect the method of experimental phenomenology. The investigator takes advantage of every opportunity to vary conditions and note the effect on subjects' experience and behavior. She is not concerned with the fact that there is sometimes only one subject in a condition. She is continually concerned with attempting to ferret out the essential dynamics of the situation. In many ways, in this experiment in particular, the method reminds me of the technique used by ethologists, such as Tinbergen, in their exploration of the conditions governing instinctual behavior in animals.

Forgetting Intentions as a Function of Situational Structure

The close relationship between the carrying out of an intention and various field forces raises the possibility of explaining Birenbaum's main results in terms of the structure of the situation, rather than in terms of the structure of the intention systems that are involved. I wonder, for example, whether failures to sign the paper could not be explained in terms of the failure of occurrences to which the signature had been fixated.

Let us see how this might be so. Consider the situation of a subject who is told that he will be given problems and asked to sign the papers he turns in. He need not form any over-all intention regarding the problems, because *the experimenter* will give each problem to him. He need only respond by creating an intention to solve each of the proffered problems.

It is clear that these individual problems do, in fact, lose their separate character and merge together to form a unit. This is shown by at least three facts: (a) a set developed, so that when the subject was given a different sort of problem he experienced it as "different"; (b) the subject began to develop a level of aspiration; (c) the meaning of a new problem began to alter the meaning of prior problems—the subject might think of a type of solution and then wonder if it could have been applied earlier. However, this does not necessarily mean that there is a common intention system to solve these problems, nor that the intention to sign becomes an integral part of any intention system having to do with the solution of problems. It seems possible that the signature system actually remained relatively isolated from the intention system or systems which dealt with the problems. This separate signature system might only use the problems as occasions to which it should respond.

On the other hand, the subject cannot count on the experimenter to repeatedly ask him to sign the papers. Rather, the subject must take the responsibility of remembering to sign each paper when he is finished. This responsibility does call for an over-all intention—the formation of an intention system to be alert to those occasions when one should sign the paper.

It should be observed that such an intention system has a point of qualitative difference from the ones which form around solving an individual problem. It is what Chein calls a perpetuated motive—constantly alert for occasions which may call it into activity. The subject must actively find some way of reminding himself to sign—of fixing on the occasions for signing—of imposing a structure on reality.

Some subjects, particularly those subjects who merely wish to do what the experimenter wants, may fix the intention to sign to the global occasion of being a subject. Others, however, may attach their intention to sign to the problems which are being presented. When these problems are all of one type, the intention may become fixated on that one type of problem, which has thus become the occasion for the signature intention. When the subject is presented with a problem which does not have this meaning—whether because the problem is of a different sort, or follows a pause, or arouses an emotion—he fails to recognize the occasion that requires his signature.

Notice that this explanation differs from Birenbaum's in that it focuses on the occasion for the intention, rather than on the place of the intention in the structure of other action systems.

This is not to deny that intentions may be related to broader action systems, that the degree of separation between the intention and other systems of action may vary considerably, and that this is an important variable in the activation of an intention. Birenbaum points out that there can be a complete isolation between one intention system and another, as when one answers an irrelevant phone call that breaks into a conversation; an inevitable dependency between the systems, as when one must pause to thread a needle in order to sew; a necessarily close connection between the systems, as when an experimenter starts a stop watch whenever he gives a timed problem to a subject; or a relatively separate existence of the two systems, as when a subject signs a paper to help the experimenter keep papers together. And it seems evident that the greater the degree of separation between an intention and a larger action system, the greater the probability of the intention failing to influence behavior. It was for this reason that Birenbaum chose to investigate the forgetting of the rather unconnected intention of signing papers. (Previous experimentation showed that the performance of completely isolated intentions was mainly governed by chance occurrences.) Nevertheless, this seems to be a necessary rather than a sufficient condition, and the data of Birenbaum's particular experiments seem to us to be more consistently explained by the nature of the structure of the action systems.

In either case, perhaps the most important result of Birenbaum's investigation is to establish that the forgetting of intentions is not always motivated. Clearly, the failure to perform an intention may be caused by a change in the meaning of a stimulus which would have ordinarily been the occasion for the intention's performance, or by an absence of linkage between the intention's tension system and some activity that is dominating the subject's behavior. While Birenbaum's study investigates the forgetting of an unimportant and minor intention system, her analysis applies equally well to such important perpetuated motives as fastening seat belts and using birth control procedures.

PERSONALITY STRUCTURE AS A SYSTEM OF MOTIVES

Having seen that intentions may become parts of a larger system of intention, we may wonder about the general structure of intentions in the person. May we think of the personality as a well-organized system of intentions? What sort of an organization would we see if we stepped back from a person to gain an over-all view of the structure of his intentions? While we cannot go into the many possible ways of viewing this complex question, which bears on the whole issue of how personality is organized, we do wish to mention Lewin's stand on these questions, and the related position taken more recently by Isidor Chein.

Lewin's View of Personality Organization

Lewin (9) asserted that tension systems (or activities) are embedded in, or belong to, broader systems (structures, spheres, complexes, regions). He argued that in order to understand any given piece of behavior, one must examine the larger system of which it is a part. Each of these larger systems is in itself a dynamic unity, with quite definite boundaries that separate it from other systems. Thus, the total psychic system has a number of relatively isolated regions. While systems in themselves can be strongly unified, and while some systems have a certain amount of communication with some others, according to Lewin the system as a whole is a very weak gestalt.

For Lewin, the ego or self is one region—one complex of systems—within this whole. While it maintains a unique position, and is perhaps more unified than other systems, not all systems belong to one's self, and some systems might have very weak communications with the self region.

While events occurring within one system can influence one another, they are unable to influence occurrences in a different system. Indeed, Lewin asserted that were it not for this relative isolation of systems, and the concurrent possibility of having one system dominate action at any given moment of time, ordered action would be impossible. If a subject was given a number of tasks which were interrupted, and the various individual tension systems were not isolated, the person would be overwhelmed with a diffuse general tension.

As an illustration of the necessity of separation, Lewin (10) mentions the behavior of a person taking moving pictures with the old type of handcranked camera. The beginner is likely to stop turning the crank evenly when something unexpected happens in the picture, whereas the expert has separated the movement of his arm from other impressions so that the cranking is uninfluenced by external events. Thus, his arm movements are a relatively independent action unit—though, of course, they are a part of the larger unit of taking pictures.

Lewin suggests that the dynamics of each system is governed by a tendency to equilibrium within each system and within the whole. (Part actions might, of course, go in the direction of a disequilibrium, as in detour behavior.) He also points out that systems in equilibrium may be, and usually are, still filled with tension. For a system to be in equilibrium, yet tensed, it is only necessary for the system's boundaries to be firm enough to prevent a diffusion of energy to equilibrium at some lower level of tension. Systems may, then, remain in a state of tension for long periods of time, and in the adult there are a number of such systems, each providing a reservoir of energy for action. Of course, in our own view these systems are intention systems, and are as much governed by a dynamic towards creation of organization as by a dynamic of equilibrium; but we can agree with Lewin as to the importance of the structure of the whole of these systems, and their constant governance of behavior.

With such a diffuse view of the psychic system, Lewin did not attempt to portray much of a structure for the person region of the lifespace. His major structural dimension is a *central-peripheral* one, where a central system is defined as communicating with (influencing and being influenced by) many other systems (11). Thus, a central intention system (*e.g.,* to become famous) might influence and be influenced by numerous other intention systems (such as making money, running for public office, and supporting popular causes). When we discuss Lewin's views on development, we shall see that an organization that has central regions is considered to be more developed than one that does not.

The other structural dimension that is sometimes used by Lewin is an *inner-outer* dimension, where outer systems are on the boundary of the systems as a whole (perceptual and motoric systems), and inner systems are separated from the environment by surrounding outer layers. (Note that this dimension is independent of the central-peripheral dimension; since an outer region could conceivably be central and an inner region could be peripheral if it were isolated from most other systems.) The only real use Lewin makes of this dimension is in his article on the differences between German and American character structure (12). Simply viewing personality as a layering of concentric regions, Lewin explains a number of cultural differences by postulating that Germans place the barrier between public and private regions of the personality further out from the center than do Americans. Thus, Americans reveal many aspects of their lives that Germans keep private. On the other hand, Lewin asserts that, once it occurs, the barrier is actually stronger in Americans. The German does admit a few others past his barrier and shares the innermost regions of his person with these close friends, whereas the American tends to have many acquaintances with whom he shares much, but not all.

Taking these two dimensions (central-peripheral and inner-outer) and adding a time dimension (enduring-temporary-monetary), Sanford (13) has suggested a 2x2x3 table for the description of personality structure. Such a scheme can locate many motivational dispositions. For example, a minor intention system that has been insulated by repression but remains susceptible to exactly the right stimulus fits in the peripheral-inner-enduring cell, while the adolescent's intention system for independence fits in the central-inner-temporary cell. Sanford goes on to point out that such a scheme for personality structure should not be confused with a scheme for personality dynamics. In the latter case, he postulates that the major dimension is conscious (ego-integrated) motives—unconscious (defensive) motives. His major point is that this dimension is independent of the two structural dimensions. Unconscious defensive motives are not necessarily "deep" in the sense of being either "central" or "inner"; but rather, they are distinguished by their isolation and their intention to prevent communication between parts of the system.

In his notes on Lewin's theoretical article about intentions, David Rapaport (14) repeatedly emphasizes how Lewin's thinking implies a whole hierarchy of motivations. Intentions are seen as isolated molecular motive systems which establish quite limited ends (to solve a certain puzzle), but ordinarily leave open just how this is to be done (the means that will be used). These motives are embedded in broader motives which Lewin calls "general goals of will" (to accomplish one's occupation, to get a degree, to help a friend). The energy for the intention is derived from the broader motives, the intention being a means to satisfy these broader ends. Lewin also saw fundamental needs such as hunger, and styles of life such as one's manner of dressing, eating, and going to sleep as broad motivational systems which governed many different specific behaviors.

Rapaport points out that Lewin is dealing with what psychoanalysis would term "ego" motives, and that in classical analytic theory these were derived from more fundamental and primitive drives, although current theory would emphasize the relative autonomy of ego motivation. He raises the interesting question of the general relationship between different layers of motivation within the hierarchy of motives. How, for example, do primitive sexual and aggressive drives influence the general goals of will and the specific intentions with which Lewin is dealing? While Lewin would emphasize that a given intention (to read a certain book) might be derived from a more general intention (becoming a doctor), the classical analyst might derive the goal of becoming a doctor from a combination of a desire to help (representing a sublimated sexual wish) and a derived aggressive urge (of mastering and hurting people). Rapaport points out that even the highly derived intention of engaging in a specific task—say of building a tower of blocks—is influenced by the person's interest in (motivation for) the specific activity (building), the specific structure (a tower), and the specific nature of the material (shiny smooth blocks). He asks, to what extent different layers of motivation are derived from each other, and to what extent the different layers are currently influenced by deeper layers as opposed to being autonomous from them.

Rapaport speculates that the various layers of motivation are ordinarily fairly autonomous from one another, but that in certain situations, motives from the more primitive layers break through their boundaries to effect behavior primarily governed by surface intentions. He indicates that it still is unclear as to whether all motives are derived from instinctual drives—and then in the process of satisfying these drives they acquire a quasi-autonomous energy of their own—or whether ego motives have a separate existence to begin with.

Chein's View of Personality Organization

In the course of his portrayal of a deterministic behaviorism that is compatible with the fact of human freedom, Chein (15) has advanced a systematic view of motivational hierarchies that integrates Lewin's thinking with the structural aspects of Freud's system. The key to Chein's system is his definition of behavior as any activity which is both directed towards an object, and included in some other behavior. (For example, reading this sentence is an activity that is a behavior, since it is directed at the sentence and included in the behavior of reading this book.) From this viewpoint, all behavior is motivated by more inclusive behaviors, and a *motive* is simply a behavior that includes other behaviors (reading this book is a motive for reading this sentence).

Chein's motives are activities that function in a way that is similar to Lewin's tension systems (or our intention systems), and he proceeds to formulate an organization of these motives that has the advantage of incorporating the Freudian structures of ego, id, and superego as systems of motives.

Chein points out that most motives are both derived from, and imbricated (intertwined) with, other motives. For example, a subject's motive to solve a problem which is given to him by an experimenter may be derived from motives to help science and please the experimenter; and this motive may, in turn, intermingle with a motive to prove one's abilities, thus producing a motive to select the most difficult problem which the subject thinks he can solve. Many motives are also perpetuated, in that they are constantly tensed —searching for a means of expression. The need to prove one's abilities is often just such a motive. Networks or systems of these derived, imbricated, perpetuated motives gradually develop, and, since motives are behaviors and behaviors are directed at objects, these systems focus around a wide variety of objects (including, of course, persons).

One of the major systems of these motives focuses on the person's self— defined as a generalization of Köhler's, *viz.*, as the point in space-time which is between the in-front and the behind, and between the past and the future; and further conceptualized into a multifaceted self-image. This system of motives, including such perpetuated motives as self-preservation, self-enhancement, and self-actualization, is the dynamic whole which may be termed the *ego*.

If this system of motives is well imbricated, the ego will have considerable unity (the resiliency that is one aspect of ego strength). If it lacks this intertwining, it will be subject to lines of cleavage and potential splits. If the person has developed a perpetuated motive to be concerned with the future implications of his behavior and the consideration of future contingencies, and if this motive is imbricated into the ego system, then the person will have high "ego control."

Another major system of motives does not belong at all to the ego system. It is the system of motives originally held by the person's parent, and now incorporated into the person by means of his commitment to the authority of that parent. In Chapter IV we saw that the subject in an experiment accepts the authority of the experimenter, and hence is motivated to perform actions that he would not perform out of his own needs. Such motives have a "have-to" rather than a "want-to" quality. When the commitment to the authority of the other is internalized, these motives have an irrational "should" quality. This system—the superego—is experienced as a set of external irrational imperatives.

A third major aggregate of motives, the id, is not a system in the sense of the two systems described above. It is largely made up of isolated motives— bits of unfinished business—which have never been incorporated into the ego structure, and hence are experienced as ego-alien impulses.

Since all motives are behaviors, and behavior always involves the body (for example, seeing an object involves the optic system), the various systems of motives are tied together by the fact that they share a common body (with the self as the perceived subject of behavior), and a common fate. This over-all system—a rather weak gestalt—is the person himself, who is inextricably tied to his environment by virtue of the fact that many behaviors in the system are directed at environmental objects.

It is worthwhile noting that both Lewin's concept of a tension system and Chein's concept of a motive are similar in many respects to the concept of *plan* advanced by Miller, Galanter, and Pribram (16). A plan, like a tension system or motive, is a unit of analysis that emphasizes an active organism that knows what it wants, and goes out to get it in a way that takes the environment and the effects of action into consideration. Hence, it implies the utilization of feedback. Further, plans, like tension systems or motives, may be nested, organized into hierarchies, so that plans include subplans and may be incorporated into larger plans.

However, there are some important differences in how these three concepts have been presented. Miller, Galanter, and Pribram note that whereas tension system is a dynamic concept that motivates activity, their own conceptualization of plan is not dynamic. Rather, they prefer to view activity as inherent in life itself, and plans as simply a way of organizing this activity. Seen in this way, they view the plans of a human being as formally similar to the plan inherent in a computer program.

Their conception of plan has been discussed by Chein (17), who accepts their definition of plan as "any hierarchical process in the organism that can control the order in which a sequence of operations is performed." However, his acceptance is contingent upon Miller, Galanter, and Pribram assigning the controlling function to the hierarchical process as such, when *hierarchical* is taken to refer to the simultaneous organization of behavior from an all-inclusive molar unit down to molecular subunits. Such a definition is compatible with Chein's definition of motive. As Chein points out, such a usage is inconsistent with an application to computer programs—where the activity of the computer is completely determined by a succession of events in the machine and events in the environment. (That is, the computer does not engage in planned behavior, it merely follows the plan of the programmer.) Chein also shows that true plans, like his motives cannot really be located in the organism. Rather, they must be conceived as between the self and the environment.

The concept of intention system that was advanced in Chapter IV is partly based on Chein's concept of motive, and is in agreement with many aspects of his portrayal of the personality as system of activities. As is the case with a motive, an intention system is an activity that relates the self to a specific object, often motivating other activities (intention systems) in the process of fulfilling its end. Further, as is the case with motives, intention systems may be perpetuated and are often derived.

There may be, however, one important difference. In my own view, intention systems are not necessarily included in other intention systems so that their derivation is determined by the aims of prior systems. Rather, they incorporate the ends of other systems as motives for the formation of new, autonomous systems. (Indeed, I believe this is the only way in which Chein's imbricated motives could arise.)

When we considered the natural progression and extensions of activity (in Chapter VI) we saw that new intention systems could develop quite independently from the activities that initially introduced the person to interesting new objects in his environment. Therefore, rather than seeing the person as completely determined by his prior commitments and their effects on the environment and person, I see the person as continually redeveloping his commitments as he progresses through space and time. Thus, while agreeing with Chein that freedom means self-determination, I see this freedom as contingent on a continually autonomous reorganization of intention systems—reorganization that takes into account commitments, but is not determined by them. While I believe this is consistent with Chein's general portrayal of personhood, it may necessitate a revision in his definition of behavior as always contained in other behaviors.

The systems advanced by both Lewin and Chein are essentially connative psychologies that emphasize the importance of the person as an actor and the system of activities which he develops. Yet, as Lewin himself observed (18):

> To regard a course of events as a sequence of units of actions is not the only way to divide it. Emotional behavior and moods such as crying, being depressed, feeling happy, or restless can also be conceived of as natural psychological units within the course of events. . . . Obviously these units would not necessarily coincide with the units of action.

In spite of the integrative efforts of Rapaport and Chein, it still seems to me that there is a rather sharp division between theorists like Freud and Rapaport, who begin with instinctual drives and emphasize affective relationships, and those, like Lewin and Chein, who begin with acts that develop into an ego and other systems of motives. Nevertheless, while a complete integration of connative and affective analyses has yet to be achieved, I assume that any successful attempt will build on the above conceptualizations.

Lewin's Theory of Development

When Lewin points out that personality may be considered to be an organization of tension systems, he calls for the study of the development of these systems—the ontogenesis of inclinations, needs, and interests, and where they narrow and where they broaden. He suggests that, like the development of an egg, there is a rhythm to the growth of interests, and that the autonomous steps of growth may show a maturation around points of crises. Unfortunately, there has been little systematic investigation into the gradual development of interests (intention systems) over the life of different persons, or even within the day of a child. In Chapter VI, we noted how all activities in which the person is involved follow a progression in which they expand and in which sometimes radical substitutions occur. Yet we have little empirical data on these progressions in everyday life. Therefore, Lewin's developmental theory is merely an overview of the gross structural changes that are apparent when we consider the over-all development of persons.

Although Lewin is more of an organismic rather than a developmental theorist (19), his approach to developmental issues is similar in many ways to that of Werner (20). Lewin's conceptualization lacks the tremendous scope of Werner's systematic theory, but his focus on human development contains some important suggestions that should be integrated with future developmental theories.

In looking at the gradual development of the human, Lewin sees five separate avenues of developments (21).

First, an increase in the variety of behavior. The adult engages in more types of activity, has a greater number of words, emotions, smiles, and needs. Lewin treats this increase in variety as a simple function of the increased number of subregions in the personal region of the lifespace. He distinguishes between "specification" (or "individuation") as a decrease in homogenity, and "differentiation" as permitting parts to function independently. Thus, differentiation of the motor region enables movement to be more precise and independent from emotional effects.

Second, an extension of the person's activities and interests. While at first glance this factor may appear similar to an increased variety of behavior, what

Lewin has in mind is the increasing scope of the lifespace as a whole. Hence, this factor is somewhat independent, and is most clearly revealed in the development of the time perspective of the lifespace. With development, the person becomes more aware of himself in historical time and more concerned with the future as well as the present.

Third, an increase in the degree of realism. Here, Lewin does not mean a decrease in imagination—which he viewed as essential for good planning and theorizing—but a greater differentiation between what should be attributed to the self and what to the environment. Hence, with development, reality and fantasy (and what is, and what is not dependent on changing moods and needs) are more clearly distinguished. Lewin also saw this factor in terms of the difference between sanity and insanity. In his schematic diagrams it is represented by the distance between the levels of reality and unreality, and by the strength of the boundary separating the personal and the environmental parts of the lifespace. We shall consider these factors in more detail in the next two chapters.

While from a Wernerian perspective the three above factors may be understood in terms of increased differentiation, the next two factors are related to increased integration. Thus, Lewin's fourth factor is the increased organization of behavior. It is interesting to note that he chose the word organization, rather than integration because he did not want the concept to have the implication of being the reverse of differentiation. He points to three separate features of this increased organization:

1) There is an increase in the number of parts (subunits) contained within one unit of action. Thus, both the coordination of subunits in a behavior, and the complexity of the means to an end increase with development, as they are unified by governing purposes or ideas.

2) The organization itself becomes more complex as subgoals or units become parts of larger subgoals or units, so that a hierarchy of units develops.

3) There is an increased ability to deal with complex overlaps between behaviors. Thus, there is an increasing ability to play while one is also conversing, to deal with two levels of meaning at the same time as in lying or joking, to carry through on an activity that is frequently interrupted.

Fifth, Lewin speaks of a factor of interdependence or unity. This factor is actually an aspect or outgrowth of organization. Lewin believed that differentiation increased the number of boundaries, and hence decreased unity, unless organization restored this unit at a higher level. He distinguished between an integrated organization with a unity formed by the interdependence of parts, and the sort of undeveloped unity that consists of dependent parts. The former organization permitted central control over all parts of the structure, while in the latter organization tension simply spread from one region to the rest via the proximity of the regions.

It should be noted that while Lewin conceived of both differentiation and organization as steadily increasing with development, he believed over-all unity often declined in the course of development until the organization of new differentiations resulted in a higher order interdependence.

Lewin was somewhat hindered in his ability to deal systematically with development and unity because of the rather mechanical constructs which he used. Nevertheless, it is remarkable to see how much he was able to accomplish with these constructs. Increasing differentiation is treated as an increased number of cells (subregions) within the person and/or an increase in the strength of cell walls (the stronger the wall the more independence, since tension cannot spread as readily). Unity decreases with differentiation unless organization affects how the cells are grouped. Certain organizations promote unity by facilitating communication between cells. Thus, if cells are strung out along a line, the unity is much greater than if they are grouped about a central cell or cluster. The degree of unity can be quantified by counting the number of cells one must pass through in order to get to any other cell. While central cells influence many other cells, it is conceivable that a central cell may also be part of an outer layer than influences the environment. In general, however, development is seen as leading to an increasing distance between central areas of the self and the environment. This is coordinated to the increased control the person has with less influence of moods on perception and action, and less impact of environmental events on one's self.

Freud, with his interest in emotional dynamics, defined *regression* in terms of a person returning to earlier objects which had been invested with libidinal energy, or reverting to the entire sexual organization at an earlier stage of development. He saw the conditions of such a regression as being frustration of the libido at the current level of development, and an earlier fixation point at a prior developmental stage. On the other hand, Lewin, interested in the person's functional activity, defined regression as a primitivization of behavior. That is, an activity is regressed if it is less differentiated or organized, or shows less scope, or less sense of reality. Although Lewin distinguished between a situational regression and one that was more established, he was primarily interested in the here-and-now conditions that lead to regressed behaviors.

Defined in this way, a distraction is apt to produce regression. Thus, as we mentioned in Chapter IV, the well-known frustration-regression experiment appears to have produced more primitive play activity because the children were preoccupied with the toys that they had been playing with—that is, still involved in the prior activity. Likewise, we saw that Ovsiankina's study of schizophrenics suggests that the regressed behavior of at least some schizophrenics is due to a central preoccupation that prevents them from becoming involved in many current activities.

On the other hand, Karsten's study demonstrates that satiation of an activity produces disintegration (disorganization), and hence regression in Lewin's sense of the term. And, as we shall see in the next chapter, frustration may produce regression. Unlike any of the above conditions of regression, frustration is seen as producing regression by increasing the tension within the lifespace so that cell divisions cannot be maintained and de-differentiation occurs.

It is interesting to speculate on other possible conditions of regression (or development) in Lewin's sense. For example, it seems clear that the dynamics of a T-group (22) provide conditions that provoke a loosening of previous organization, with temporary loss of unity. This, in turn, permits the incorporation of new material in an eventual unity which has more scope. It has been suggested that important personal growth often occurs as a result of this dynamic pattern of thawing, followed by reorganization and refreezing. While quite different in scope, there is a conceptual parallel in Laing's (24) suggestions for handling schizophrenia by creating a secure environment in which disorganization and eventual reorganization can occur.

In general, the relationship between emotion and regression-development is quite unclear. It seems evident that, under some circumstances, emotional concerns appear to greatly decrease time perspective and cause general regression. On the other hand, under other circumstances, an emotion such as sympathy or love seems to greatly enlarge the scope of one's lifespace. This area of research is largely untouched and would seem to be a promising region for exploration. We shall examine a few of the conceptual issues when we consider the nature of emotion, in Chapter XI.

In terms of strengthening an organismic approach to development, our own perspective suggests that it is time to abandon an account in terms of cells— their number, strength of wall, and proximity—and, instead, consider an approach based on types of relationships with the environment. For example, Angyal (25) has suggested two relational trends that have developmental significance. These are a trend towards increasing autonomy (the development of the person as a whole that controls the environment), and a trend towards increasing homonomy (the development of the person as a part of a larger meaningful whole). These trends are not antithetical to each other, but probably are in a dialectic. Yet a third trend involves the need for a person to have a coherent whole to his life as he looks back upon it and towards the future.

We have been interested in observing different courses of development in different persons. For example, some persons appear to show an early development of autonomy at the expense of being out of contact with others; their subsequent development seems to involve the lifting of the boundaries which initially protected their autonomy. Another type of person develops an early sensitivity to others and a high degree of homonomy, but only gradually develops a sense of himself as autonomous. In regard to these problems, it would appear that Rank's (26) conceptualization of the difficulty of achieving separateness without losing contact with the mother (or group or culture) is relevant to the achievement of both autonomy and homonomy. And the reader interested in the polarity between individuation and belonging should also consult the work of Schactel (27) and that of D. H. Lawrence (28), whose interesting ideas have been largely neglected because of the highly colorful but unscientific language in which they are expressed.

Angyal also makes an important structural point when he stresses the split that may occur between the ego and the rest of the person whenever the ego's tendency for hegonomy goes unchecked. This point is related to May's (29) distinction between "intention" and "intentionality," and to the difference Farber (30) draws between "willful" and "willing." In each case, the writer develops the idea that part of a person—the conscious self—attempts to control the person's behavior to the detriment of the person as a whole. Truly responsible behavior occurs only when the person's intention systems accept all aspects of the self.

We have already mentioned how regression may have to occur in order for higher orders of organization to develop, and there is at least some recognition of the importance of this process. However, developmental theorists have not yet addressed themselves to certain types of advanced organization which can not easily be described in terms of a hierarchical integration of differentiated parts. For instance, highly developed mystical states appear to evidence a unity without a subject-object split, and it has been very difficult to describe them in terms that distinguish them from primitive states. However, it seems to me that Herrigel's (31) masterful portrayal of the organization of consciousness attained by Zen masters opens this area to intellectual inquiry. While I cannot digress into a discussion of his description of egolessness and the perception of all things as having equal value, I wish to quote one passage from his work because of its obvious relationship to Schwarz's description of the development of action unities. Herrigel, who is describing his learning of the Zen art of archery, states (32):

> The Master now went on to relate the breathing, which had not of course been practiced for its own sake, to archery. The unified process of drawing and shooting was divided into sections: grasping the bow, nocking the arrow, raising the bow, drawing and remaining at the point of highest tension, loosing the shot. Each of them began with breathing in, was sustained by firm holding of the

down-pressed breath, and ended with breathing out. The result was that the breathing fell into place spontaneously and not only accentuated the individual positions and hand-movements, but wove them together in a rhythmical sequence depending, for each of us, on the state of his breathing-capacity. In spite of its being divided into parts the entire process seemed like a living thing wholly contained in itself, and not even remotely comparable to a gymnastic exercise, to which bits can be added or taken away without its meaning and character being thereby destroyed.

As Herrigel finally masters the technique and loses himself in the breathing, he notes that he begins to feel that rather than breathing he is "being breathed." As his training progresses, distinction after distinction breaks down until, finally, he experiences a complete unity with no distinction between his hitting the target or the target hitting him. Indeed, the ego disappears to the extent that an impersonal "it" brings his shot and the target together. It should be noted that the unity that becomes organized here is not really a habit, because the person is in full control of what he is doing or, rather, not doing —since the whole exercise involves a ceasing to try. Such an activity may be related to the "ings" discussed in Chapter VI. Perhaps if the development of an individual were considered from the perspective of his being a part of the unity of all things, it would be possible to understand such egoless organizations.

FOOTNOTES

1. Kurt Koffka, *Principles of Gestalt Psychology* (New York: Harcourt, Brace and World, Inc., 1935), 573.

2. Donald K. Adams and T. L. McCulloch, "On the Structure of Acts," *Journal of General Psychology*, 10 (1934), 450–455.

3. Koffka, *Principles of Gestalt Psychology*, 564–566.

4. Gita Birenbaum, "Das Vergessen einer Vornahme, " *Psychol. Forsch.*, 13 (1930), 218–285. The translation, "Forgetting an Intention," may be obtained from Xerot: University Microfilms.

5. Sigmund Freud, *The Psychopathology of Everyday Life* (New York: W. W. Norton, 1960), 151–161.

6. David Rapaport, *Organization and Pathology of Thought* (New York: Columbia University Press, 1951), footnote 9. Also see footnotes 30–33 and 35–45, pp. 106–113, that discuss this experiment from the psychoanalytic point of view.

7. For an interesting contrast between forgetting as an affect of reorganization, and "forgetting" because of repression, see Herbert J. Schlesinger, "The Place of Forgetting in Memory Functioning," *Journal of American Psychoanalytic Association*, 18 (1970), 358–371.

8. Birenbaum, "Das Vergessen einer Vornahme," 278.

9. Kurt Lewin, "On the Structure of the Mind," in *A Dynamic Theory of Personality* (New York: McGraw-Hill, 1935). This is a translation of the second part of "Vorsatz, Wille und Beduerfnis . . ." The first part is translated in Rapaport (ed.), *Organization and Pathology of Thought*, Chapter 4.

10. Kurt Lewin, "Intention, Will and Need," in David Rapaport (Ed.), *Organization and Pathology of Thought*, Chapter 5, 142.

11. Kurt Lewin, *Field Theory in Social Science* (New York: Harper, 1951), 122–124.

12. Kurt Lewin, "Social-Psychological Differences Between the United States and Germany," in *Resolving Social Conflicts* (New York: Harper, 1948).

13. Nevitt Sanford, "Surface and Depth in the Individual Personality," *Psychological Review*, 63 (1956), 349–359.

14. Rapaport, *Organization and Pathology of Thought*, chapter 5. Cf. footnotes 23, 26, 30, 32, 35, 36, 39, 40, 43, 49, 52, 56, 57, 61, 67, 69, 78, 100, 115, 121, 127, 137, 140. Rapaport's footnotes are a source of immense value to anyone interested in integrating field theory with psychoanalytic theory.

15. Isidor Chein, *The Science of Behavior and the Image of Man* (New York: Basic Books, 1972).

16. George A. Miller, Eugene Galanter, and Karl H. Pribram, *Plans and the Structure of Behavior* (Holt, Rinehart and Winston, 1960).

17. Chein, *The Science of Behavior and the Image of Man*, 27–28.

18. Roger Barker, Tamara Dembo, and Kurt Lewin, "Frustration and Regression: An Experiment with Young Children," *University of Iowa Studies, Child Welfare*, 18 (1941), No. 1, 62–63.

19. Bernard Kaplan, "Rationality and Irrationality in Development: I. Strife of Systems," Lecture I, Heinz Werner Lecture Series, Clark University, October 9, 1974.

20. Heinz Werner, *The Comparative Psychology of Mental Development*, revised edition (New York: International University Press, 1957).

21. Kurt Lewin, "Regression, Retrogression, and Development" in *Field Theory in the Social Science* (New York: Harper and Row, 1951). This is a reprint of chapter One of reference 18. An appendix of this reference, "Analysis of the Concepts Whole, Differentiation, and Unity," is also reprinted as the appendix of *Field Theory in Social Science*.

22. Leland P. Bradford, Jack R. Gibb, and Kenneth D. Benne, *T-group Theory and Laboratory Method* (New York: Wiley, 1964).

23. Edgar H. Schein, "The Mechanisms of Change," in Warren G. Bennis, Kenneth D. Benne, and Robert Chin (Eds.), *The Planning of Change*, 2nd edition, (New York: Holt, Rinehart and Winston, 1969).

24. R. D. Laing, *The Politics of Experience* (New York: Pantheon Books, 1967).

25. Andras Angyal, *Neurosis and Treatment: A Holistic Theory* (New York: J. Wiley, 1965).

26. Otto Rank, *With Therapy and Truth and Reality* (New York: Knopf, 1945).

27. Ernest G. Schactal, *Metamorphosis* (New York: Basic Books, 1959).

28. D. H. Lawrence, *Psychoanalysis and the Unconscious* (New York: Viking Press, 1960; original edition, 1921).

29. Rollo May, *Love and Will* (New York: W. W. Norton, 1969).

30. Leslie H. Farber, *The Ways of the Will* (New York: Harper and Row, 1966).

31. Eugene Herrigel, *Zen in the Art of Archery* (New York: Panthem Books, 1955).

32. Ibid., 39.

PART TWO:

THE STRUCTURE OF SITUATIONS AND DYNAMICS OF FEELING

INVOLVEMENT IN SITUATIONS

Until Dembo's study, Lewin's psychology is primarily concerned with the person's involvement in an activity. Of course, the interruption or satiation or reversal of an activity always took place in the context of a laboratory situation, but it was the activity that was in the foreground of the inquiry. Beginning with Dembo's study, the focus of investigation becomes the situation in which the person is involved, and the particular activity in which he is engaged moves more into the background.

The Dynamics of Impossible Situations

Although Dembo's study is titled "The Dynamics of Anger" and begins and ends with a focus on the emotion of anger and a search for its essential conditions, the study is primarily concerned with the effects of frustration, and might better be titled "The Dynamics of Frustration."

In frustration-aggression theory (1), whenever the organism comes up against a barrier between itself and its goal, frustration occurs and an aggressive drive begins to accumulate. One of the many important contributions of Dembo's study is to suggest that this is simply not true. She shows that in a situation where the organism is faced with a single barrier, the frustration is easily met by simply leaving the situation. There is no reason for tension to build up, and no function for aggression. Dembo points out that in order for frustration to lead to anger (or regression, apathy, or any important effect), the organism must be trapped in the frustration situation by an outer barrier. Thus, the necessary condition for frustration to lead to aggression includes an outer as well as an inner barrier. It is a sad commentary on the relative lack of scientific community in psychology that this insight, published in 1933, has not been represented in any of the hundreds of publications dealing with frustration-aggression theory.

Having found one of the necessary conditions of anger, Dembo becomes interested in exploring the characteristics of this condition—frustration with an outer barrier—and rather neglects the explication of the sufficient conditions for anger and the essence of anger as an emotion. Instead, the study becomes a study of the condition of frustration, or, more precisely, a study of the dynamics of what might be called "impossible situations." Because of this, the study's results most easily generalize to areas of real life where a person is trapped in an impossible situation. Thus, the reader will see similarities between Dembo's descriptions and John Holt's observations of failing children in a typical classroom situation (2), or Bateson's account of the double-bind situation (3), or a counselor's description of an impossible marriage.

In an impossible situation—which may be characterized by a person's being trapped between two sets of barriers—tension begins to mount, and the person becomes emotional. As this tension increases, boundaries dissolve and the field is broken down so that it is less differentiated and integrated. It becomes primitivized. We shall see that this simplification of the field into a relatively undifferentiated state leads to various types of irrational behavior.

It should be noted that the condition of primitivization is quite different from the condition of preoccupation which was created by Barker, Dembo, and Lewin in their experiment on frustration and regression (4). In that experiment, it may be recalled that the children were frustrated by a barrier which prevented them from playing with the attractive toys. However, there is no evidence that tension built up to create a primitivized lifespace. Rather, the children simply appear to have been preoccupied with the attractive toys. Of course, this resulted in regressed behavior, but the experience of the child and the corresponding structure of the child's lifespace were completely different from the experience and lifespace structure that we shall see in Dembo's experiment.

In Dembo's experiment, and to some extent in Karsten's, the increasing tension creates a primitivization of the field, a slowly growing structural change which is masked at first, but occasionally crops out in irrational behavior. In the following chapter the reader will see how Dembo uses a field approach and phenomenology to attempt to describe the dynamics of such situations.

FOOTNOTES

1. John Dollard, Leonard W. Doob, Neil E. Miller, O. Hobart Mowrer, and Robert R. Sears, *Frustration and Aggression* (New Haven: York University Press, 1939).

2. John Holt, *How Children Fail* (New York: Dell, 1964).

3. Gregory Bateson, Don D. Jackson, Jay Haley, and John Weakland, "Toward a Theory of Schizophrenia," in Warren G. Bennis *et al.* (eds.), *Interpersonal Dynamics* (1st ed.) (Homewood, Illinois: Dorsey, 1964).

4. Roger Barker, Tamara Dembo, and Kurt Lewin, "Frustration and Regression: An Experiment with Young Children," *University of Iowa Studies in Child Welfare* 18 (1941), No. 1.

Chapter X

THE DYNAMICS OF ANGER*

Tamara Dembo

*Translated by Dr. Hedda Korsch. The original article, "Der Ärger als dynamisches Problem,"
was published in *Psychologische Forschung,* Vol. 15(1931), 1–144. Permission to publish this translation was generously granted by Springer-Verlag.

[*I have omitted a seven-page historical and methodological introduction. Dembo notes the paucity of experimental work on emotions and argues that basic laws cannot be discovered by investigating either statistical generalities or symptoms of emotions such as heartrate, or galvanic skin response. She argues in favor of investigating the dynamics of the development of an emotion, focusing on concrete details of the individual case, and carefully noting the relationship among the occurrence of emotion, the total situation, and the course of events surrounding the person who has the emotion. Methodologically, Dembo notes that since accounts of emotions tend to lack developmental details, it was neces-sary for her to rely on the systematic observation of the behavior and spontaneous utterances of her subjects. In order to arrive at the basic dynamics underlying the concrete details of emotional behavior, the smallest details, as well as the larger units of behavior were systematically observed.*

The omitted section, together with other omissions and the study's appendix may be obtained from University Microfilms—Editor.]

I. EXAMPLES OF ANGER IN EVERYDAY LIFE, AND FIRST THEORETICAL CONSIDERATIONS

In what situations can anger be experimentally induced in a subject?

If you ask somebody, "Please, tell me, have you been angry lately? Do you know why? What did you do then?" the answers you will receive will approxi-mate the following:

1. "I was angry yesterday when I was in a hurry to get home, and the number X bus did not stop for me. To spite it, I took the following bus, which was number Y. Normally I don't do that, because Y takes a roundabout way, and it's better to wait a few minutes for the next X bus. But I was mad."

2. "Recently I was angry when I wanted to prove something about which

I was right to an acquaintance. I could not convince him in spite of my efforts. In the end, I began to abuse him."

3. "Recently, I mislaid my keys again. I looked everywhere, rummaged repeatedly in all drawers, but they had completely disappeared."

4. "If you're interrupted in your work time and time again, it is natural to become annoyed, and to yell at anybody who causes the next interruption."

5. "I became quite angry when I went to a concert with an expensive ticket, but because I wanted to save the taxi fare, I got there late."

6. "Poor quality ink, an unsharpened pencil, a spring that keeps snapping off the apparatus—those things get me hopping mad!"

7. "If you give up something in favor of another person, only to find out that he didn't need it at all—that can make you lose your temper."

Looking for a characteristic common to all the cases quoted here, it appears that each time a person tried to reach a goal but, in spite of all efforts, failed to reach it.

If one examines this hypothesis seriously, it turns out not to be universally valid. We gave a crossword puzzle to a crossword puzzle addict, so that we could be sure of his genuine interest and of his seriously attempting to find the solution. The subject was quite involved and tried intensely, but could not find a certain word; nonetheless, he expressed only occasional annoyance. There was no sign of serious anger or of emotional upset. There was definitely a failure to reach the desired goal, yet a marked by angry affect did not materialize. That "I want to, but I cannot" is not a sufficient preliminary condition for the genesis of anger can be seen in examples from everyday life:

When a mother wants to leave the house in a hurry, but is delayed by her baby, she often does not get angry. A person does not get furious each time a bus passes him by. Interruptions of important work do not always produce anger.

Why, then, does failure to reach a desired goal cause anger in one case, but not in another? It might be assumed that the absence of anger in the instances mentioned above could be explained by a comparative lack of intensity in the desire to reach the goal. It would be plausible to think that annoyance increases in proportion to the intensity of desire.

A general statement cannot be made on the basis of this assumption, either. It will frequently be noted that a sudden obstacle arising in the way of a vitally important goal does not lead to an affective outburst, while a trivial disturbance of an unimportant action can cause violent anger. A typical example: persons who show considerable self-control in important matters can lose their temper to a surprising degree when a waiter serves them a cup of coffee that is not quite as it should be. In such cases, it cannot always be argued that the coffee did have importance for the person.

Further on, we shall see that manifestations of affect occur especially easily over unessential matters. We will find the same circumstances at work that are responsible for important tasks remaining undone, while unimportant occupations take up our time. Trifles, mere nothings, things that are really meaningless keep us occupied; partly because the less important things are also the less oppressive ones, and therefore the more pleasurable. Furthermore, having once entered the field of unimportant matters, the meaningless objects assume a dominant role. Behavior is now determined by the forces of the field, and as soon as actions follow its structure, affects can be produced within its limits as well.

The assertion, "The more important the desired object is, the more anger is created by obstacles" is not true, at least not in this form.

At this point, we shall interrupt our theoretical considerations, to resume them after the discussion of our experiments.

In the years 1925–1928, 64 experiments were carried out with 27 subjects. The individual experiments lasted 1-2 hours. In 7 cases, the experiments were continued on the following day. In 3 cases, there were third and fourth sessions. The subjects did not know the problem underlying the experiment. When they felt anger during the experiment, they occasionally stated that the experiment made them angry, but only rarely did it occur to them that anger, as such, was being investigated.

II. EXPERIMENTAL ARRANGEMENTS AND THE TYPICAL COURSE OF EVENTS

For the experiments, we limited ourselves to two setups: "Ring throwing" and the "flower experiment." In the course of our investigation, it will be explained why we selected just these two arrangements. To understand the quality of some of the communications that occurred, it is essential to know that the experimenter was a woman. In our detailed descriptions, we state the sex of the subjects.*

Experimental Setup I (ring throwing)

The subject enters the room without knowing anything about the purpose of the experiment. The experimenter directs the attention of the subject to the wine bottles (1,2) standing on the table (T) by the window (W). Figure 1. The experimenter says: "You have to hit these bottles from this distance." The experimenter points to a chalkmark (C_1) on floor, at about 3.5 meters away from the table. "You have to throw these rings"—the experimenter hands the subject 10 wooden rings, of about .15 centimeters in diameter—"over the

---

*It is also important for the American reader to realize that the cool, rather formal, tone of the instructions is normative in the German culture and would be heard as appropriate rather than harsh by the subjects—Editor

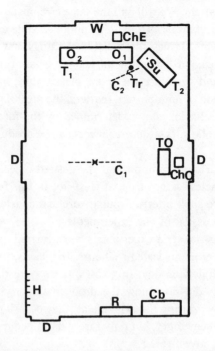

FIGURE 1. Experimental Set-up No. I ("Ring-throwing").

T_1 = table, on which	C_2 = chalk-mark drawn	ChO = chair of observer
O_1, O_2 = 2 bottles, targets	later	TO = table of o
for ring-throwing	T_2 = table, on which	W = window
C_1 = chalk-mark on floor,	Su = substitute bottle	Cb = cupboard
from which S has to	Tr = tripod	R = radiator
throw rings	ChE = chair of experi-	H = hooks for coat
	menter	D = door

bottlenecks. You are to practice until you are able to place ten rings in succession."

The distance is such that it is practically impossible to hit the bottlenecks ten consecutive times; the subject is faced with an insoluble problem. (This fact allows an unlimited extension of the experiment. If the solution were difficult but possible, a sudden solution would mean an undesirable disruption of the affective process.) It is, however, not immediately evident that the task is insoluble. So the subject begins to practice.

Meanwhile, the experimenter has taken her seat on the chair (Ch E) behind the table, and begins to take notes. An observer (O) has been in the room from the start of the experiment. He is sitting to one side on a chair (Ch O) at a table (TO); generally his presence is of no vital significance for the social structure.

Usually, the throwing of the first ten rings is not at all successful; none of the rings hits the mark. During the throwing, the experimenter collects the rings on the table which have missed. When the tenth and last ring has been cast, she picks up the rings that have dropped to the floor.

Outline of a typical course of events in first setup. Only close examination of particular cases permits full insight into affective processes; that is why the course of events has to be described in great detail. Since, however, an unprepared reader would probably be lost in the maze of different phenomena, it seems useful to give an outline of a typical experiment at the start. Thus, we shall describe the general character of the course of events, sketching a picture of the experiment as a whole.

The subject accepts the experimenter's instructions to throw the rings. He throws the first ten rings; sometimes even the first failures lead to an angry exclamation: "Darn it, that's hard!" In general, however, the first ten throws are considered trials,—throws that, because of the absence of an established level of aspiration, do not lead to a definite experience of success or failure. The subject is involved with the difficulties of the task, trying various methods in order to succeed. The rattle of falling rings, or a ring that misses by an especially wide margin, begins to have a disturbing effect. The throws do not improve; the subject becomes restless, runs around, rattles the rings in his hand. In a rising fury, he wants to get on quickly. He changes the target-bottles or feels compelled to stop for a moment. Before coming to rest, the rings roll a while on table or floor, and sometimes spin around; this disturbs the subject's next throw. He says: "I can't go on before the ring lies still."

Once in a while there are two consecutive hits. These are generally bright moments that evoke a joyful "Ah-hah!" The subject beams, if only for a short time.

When the number of hits remains the same, and the subject scores at the most one or two hits our of ten, the result is he finally feels keenly aware of the unsurmountable limitations of his capabilities. (The reason for this is the subject's heightened level of aspiration; *cf.* Hoppe.) He begins to get angry. He feels he is on a treadmill. The arrangement is called "mean," "most annoying," "irritating," "maddening." If the subject still controls himself, he will predict "I suppose there will be a stage when people will throw the rings out of the windows," or make some other such remark.

Experimental Setup II (Flower Experiment)

The bottle experiment is interrupted after each set of ten throws, while the rings are being collected. The interval is a break created by outside conditions. It disrupts the development of an affective process. In order to eliminate this intermission, which does not derive from the events themselves, but rather from the comparatively peripheral peculiarities of the task, another experiment was devised. We called it, for short, the "flower experiment."

The subject enters the room and sees on the floor a square (Sq) of wooden laths (W). Figure 2. The length of each side is 2.5 meters. The back wall of

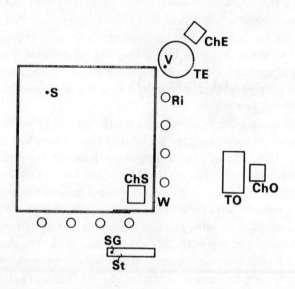

FIGURE 2. Experimental Arrangement II ("Flower Experiment").

S = subject
W = wooden laths forming the square in which S is standing
St = stand, on it
G = goal (a flower)

S_G = Substitute goal, flower on second stand, nearer the square
V = vase with flowers on
T_E = table of experimenter
ChE = chair of experimenter

TO = table of observer
ChO = chair of observer
ChS = chair available to S
Ri = wooden rings disposed of floor, outside square

the square is composed of two partly overlapping, laths, 2 meters and 75 cm in length. Four wooden rings of 15 centimeter diameter are placed at equal distances outside along two sides of the square. In one corner of the square is a chair (ChS). A saw horse 110 centimeters high is placed outside the square at a distance of about 120 centimeters. On it is a flower, the goal, (G.) Sometimes a second stand with a similar flower is placed behind the square, nearer than the first.

The experimenter addresses the subject: "Enter that square, and from there grasp that flower." (The experimenter points out the goal). "Your feet have to stay inside the square, and you must grasp the flower with your hand. The stand, the square, or the flower on the stand must not be moved." The distance from the flower is too great to be bridged by simply bending forward.

The subject enters the square and tries to find the solution. The experimenter goes to her seat (ChE) by the round table (TE) on which flowers and writing materials are placed. She begins to take notes. As in ring throwing, an observer has taken his seat (ChO) before the arrival of the subject; he does not attract attention.

There are two possible solutions to the problem: 1) The subject places the chair that is inside the square, outside, between the stand and the square. He supports himself by placing one hand on this chair while grasping the flower with the other hand; 2) The subject kneels. In this way, he can keep his feet inside the square, and can reach the flower with his hand.

Sooner or later, nearly all subjects find one of the solutions. When a subject has found the first solution, the experimenter asks him to find a second one. That, too, is found in most cases. Then the experimenter asks the subject for a third solution, which is, in fact, nonexistent. Not knowing this, the subject eagerly tries to find the third solution; he suggests variations on the first two solutions, or else advances solutions that do not conform with the prescribed conditions. The experimenter rejects all suggestions as mere variations, or as solutions contrary to instructions and thus prohibited. At the same time, she insists on the existence of a third independent solution, an insistence which spurs the subject on to further efforts. Sometimes, the subject proves by logical deduction that there cannot be a third solution. In most cases, however, the simple statement, "There is a third solution," made by the experimenter is sufficient to stimulate the subject to new attempts. The experiment can thus be extended indefinitely.

Outline of a typical course of events in Setup II. We start once more by outlining a typical sequence of events. The subject enters the square and tries to find a solution. He studies the distance, and by bending forward makes sure that the stand is too far away for him to reach the flower on top of it. He turns around, looking for possible tools; he examines the walls, and asks whether the chair may be used. The experimenter's tactics are to leave the subject to his own devices, to give evasive answers, and to leave him in doubt. On purpose, she speaks inconclusively and vaguely. Sometimes, she will say, "Sorry, I can't tell you."

The subject tries solutions both with the help of tools and without. As tools, he uses the chair, which in fact will yield one solution; but he also tries other objects that cannot be useful in the given situation. He considers at length, for example, the ways in which the wooden rings lying around the square could be used to get hold of the flower. (Later on it will be fully explained why the experimenter put placed the rings as she did.)

The subject takes the rings in his hand and looks at them thoughtfully. Then he tries a different approach: "May I place the chair outside the square?" This idea points the way to the first solution.

The subject is happy, but the experimenter spoils his joy by saying, "There is still another solution." The subject is taken aback and rehearses the instructions to make sure that he has understood them correctly. The experimenter confirms his understandings. The subject looks around again and says, "The rings will do me no good. What kind of rings are they? Are they wood? The subject asks himself these questions, or puts them to experimenter; then he turns eagerly to the task. Soon after, the subject finds the second solution. Now the experimenter calls for a third solution. The subject tries again. He moves closer to the flower, picks up the chair again, trying to rest his knee on it rather than his hand. That does not get him anywhere. The subject lets go of the chair and his attention wanders from the task; he scrutinizes the laths, no longer regarding them as an inviolable borderline, but as ordinary wooden laths that may have spots or may lie unevenly. After a short while, he returns to the task. He repeats his former methods, again in vain. He says things such as, "If I lean forward while you are holding my coat, it could be done." "If I place your table in front of the flower." "Maybe I should take off my shoes." "Should I suspend myself somewhere?" Thus, the subject strains and labors. From time to time he interrupts his efforts, stating that a third solution is impossible. When the experimenter simply replies, "It *is* possible", the subject's efforts are renewed.

At times, the subject turns away from the task, thinking of something that has nothing to do with the experiment. He thinks of his plans for tomorrow, or of something that happened to him on a recent trip. Then the unsolved task recalls him: he makes pointless efforts, has ever-reoccurring thoughts, considers the reiterated statement by the experimenter that there is a third solution, when anyone can see that there cannot be one. "Maybe," the subject thinks, "the experimenter is right after all." In between, the subject notices that the experimenter takes down his every movement.

With increasing intensity, the subject wants to "get the experiment over with, one way or the other, to have done with it." He becomes more and more negative towards the task: "It is nonsense!" "There cannot be a solution!" He ridicules the experimenter's assertion, begins to pace back and forth, considers once more for a moment, then stamps his foot at the next failure. "Enough of that!" "Let's drop it!" "How clumsy can you be?" "What asinine humbug!" "Let the experimenter think what she likes!" The subject then sits down, no longer willing to bother with the task. He remains sitting for a while, in protest. The experimenter keeps writing, face expressionless. At last the subject gives up the protest demonstration; after all, he *must* end it some time. He stands up, but instead of breaking off the experiment, he works at the solution once more.

When events take this course, rising affectivity emerges, which may lead to violent outbursts. The subject scolds, threatens; leaves the square, and thus violates the instructions; grasps the flower, and may even tear it to pieces. If the experiment is limited to a brief time span—about half an hour—it leads as a rule only to superficial affective utterances, such as angry gestures or arguments. This happens, that is, if the experiment is not the second or third in the series, and if no prior affective tension existed.

If, however, the experiment is extended over several hours, or if it is repeated for a second or third time on subsequent days (without, of course, offering a solution to the subject), extraordinarily crass affects will be produced that actually reach the deep strata of the person's emotions. The subject may stamp his feet and scream. It has happened that a subject grabbed the experimenter's hand, when he was disturbed by her while throwing rings, and held it by force. Another subject ran out of the room crying. A third subject, better acquainted with the experimenter, pulled the experimenter's hair. Many subjects refused to go on with the experiment according to instructions.

Some subjects were seriously offended with the experimenter as a consequence of the experiment, although they had known all along that it was nothing but an experiment. They could only be placated by special conciliatory actions. How profound the effect can be may be gauged by the fact that the subjects, in reporting their self-observations immediately after the experiment, were often unable to rise above the events. Sometimes they made false statements, for example, that they had not been angry at all. On the following day, however, they did, as a rule, rectify their depositions.

In the attempt to understand the dynamic structure of affective processes, the investigator must concentrate not only on the climatic outbursts, as has been mentioned before, but must also thoroughly scrutinize the weaker manifestations. Attention must be given to a whole series of events whose affective character is not immediately apparent. Frequently, certain wishes, predictions, or thoughts betray affective tension that is strong and profound, but outwardly still under control.

Finally, we must consider certain actions that at first sight look purposeful and goal-directed, but which, when analyzed more closely, show an affective component. We call them affect-colored actions. One such is, for example, the subject taking up the rings and throwing them angrily at the flower in an attempt to push it to the floor where it could be reached. (Seemingly, this is an attempt at solution, but basically it is affective action.) As we shall see, the borderline between calm behavior and emotional occurrences is fluid.

Cases occur in which no affect is generated—sometimes there are complete experiments which produce no expression of affect, or individual phases and sections which lack affect. The outer conditions were the same as in the cases in which affect was generated. The study of the prerequisites and the laws of affective events also demands the clarification of such an absence of affect.

III. TOPOLOGY OF THE SITUATION AND ITS FIELD-FORCES

The description of a course of events in terms of structures, its totalities and subtotalities, or in terms of rhythms of development, leads to the question of whether any regularity can be found in the chronological sequence of events. The study of a number of records gradually brings the conviction that there is no regularity in the sense that a certain event, *a,* is always followed by another event, *b.* In one case, a forceful affective outburst is preceded by a weak demonstration of affect, in another case by behavior which is seemingly quite detached. Substitute actions are sometimes followed by a frantic effort at solution, while at other times they are followed by a turning away from the task. An attack upon the experimenter appears sometimes after an intermission but at other times after a failure.

The more thorough the analysis, the greater the impression of irregularity. This has contributed to the assumption that affective events are not subject to laws. Actually, the chronological interpretation of the thesis "if *a,* then *b*" is quite misleading, a slip in the quasi-historical direction. The historical course of affective events is essentially cumulative, in Driesch's sense of the word. That is to say, it is a mutual sequence and penetration of objectively non-commensurable events, rather than a genuine totality. The development is not uniform in the sense that one sort of occurrence—for instance, the striving towards a goal, or the rising of anger towards an explosive climax—develops without interference from other events. In our affect experiments, it was especially striking how developing events were temporarily interrupted or replaced by events of a different character. Often, later phases once again took up earlier developments that had been interrupted. However, the structure of the sequence of events as such did not determine conclusively whether an intensification, a continuance, or a tapering off was likely.

Insight into the lawfulness of affect can only be gained by giving up the attempt to use Aristotelian concepts to discover statistical regularities within the course of events itself. Rather, the progress of events depends on the changes in the total situation created by each successive event, and on the consequences of such changes. Events can be understood and conceptually deduced only by means of the dynamic properties of the inner situation of a person, on the one hand, and of the forces of the environment surrounding the events on the other. We will first examine the psychical environment, its topology, its field forces, and its tensions.

In presenting psychological topology, we use the concepts of general mathematical topology, like "connected," "separated," "boundary." Thus, "distances" do not have metrical significance. We also make use of the mathematical concepts of "direction" and "between."

Our basic dynamic concepts are directly related to these mathematical concepts, but in a way they go beyond them, as, for instance, when we distinguish a mere boundary from a real psychological barrier, which indicates an obstacle of definite firmness. It will appear later that the psychical barrier must not be identified with either an actual physical barrier or with an actual social barrier.

We start with a description of the topology and dynamics of the basic situation which generates anger; then we proceed to the specific investigation of the affect. (In the following representation of the situation, we will at first limit ourselves to the most elementary occurrences. Later we will go on to deal with more complex and exact facts.)

We shall begin with the theoretical factors in the total situation. Then, we shall present the real occurrences that derive from these factors, and thus document the existence of the factors.

The goal. The situation of the subject within the experiment is restricted in comparison with his preceding activities and his normal life.

As to its content, the basic situation can be characterized as follows: The subject is faced with a task that he undertakes willingly, he attempts to reach a goal. In other words, a force vector is working on the subject in the direction of a positive valence. This is represented in Figure 3.

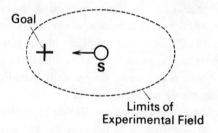

FIGURE 3. Representation of the Goal.

Concerning this vector, we have to consider two questions: 1) What are the conditions of its appearance? 2.) What are the real occurrences—thoughts, questions, or actions—by which it manifests itself?

Causes of the emergence of the vector may be a) the request of the experimenter; b) the attraction of the task itself; c) the difficulty of the task, which challenges the subject's ambition.

a) Having committed himself to be the subject of an experiment, the subject feels obliged to do what the experimenter demands. Even when at times it seem pointless to him to go on looking for a solution, the request of the experimenter, or even the mere thought of the experimenter pushes him to go on trying, "since I am the subject in this experiment"; b) The task, in itself, is interesting to the subject. Either he enjoys finding a way out of a seemingly hopeless situation, or discovering whether and when it is possible to throw rings on bottles from a distance. Sometimes it intrigues the subject to just let the rings fly, or (in the flower experiment) to figure out such an amusing task; c) The subject feels personally involved with the task he has undertaken. It is important to him to know whether or not he will succeed in being skillful and clever, as well as how quickly he can solve the task, compared to others.

There are few cases in which only one cause motivates the subject. Moreover, the subject's motivation changes during the course of the experiment. If, for example, the task in itself becomes meaningless or boring, it may be that a sense of duty (obedience to the experimenter) takes over, or the sudden question, "Were the others able to do it?" In different experiments, changes of this sort occur with different frequency, but they occur in all experiments. Sometimes there is a gradual transition, but usually a sudden emergence of new driving forces is clearly observable.

Nonetheless, we are justified in saying that during a certain experiment a particular driving force has been predominant, even though other motives may have played passing parts for shorter periods. Occurrences that are produced by the vector directed towards the goal are mainly: a) theoretical and manual attempts at solution; and b) questions concerning the usefulness of further effort, which the subject puts to himself sotto voice; "Can anybody solve it?" "Should one try harder?" Such utterances are characteristic of the phases of the genesis or original formation of the goal-vector. If the subjects believe from the outset that the task is insoluble, they usually remain unaffected.

Questions concerning the usefulness of further effort, however, are not only actions directed toward the goal, but are also an expression of having reached a "barrier of difficulty," which we shall now discuss in more detail.

The difficulty of the task (inner barrier). The subject, impelled by the vector, cannot move directly towards the goal. He is separated from the goal by an obstacle: the difficulty inherent in the task. The same instruction that produces the vector in the direction of the goal also keeps the subject away from the goal object. It bars access to it by prohibiting the direct approach (walking up to and grasping the flower, or depositing the rings on the bottles). The condition "Keep your feet inside the square," or "Get the rings on the bottle from this specific distance" stands between the subject and goal like a barrier. This is represented in Figure 4.

Occurrences which are determined by the barrier while the vector is in operation are: 1) being stopped by the barrier; and 2) being repelled in consequence of failure, so there is a wish to get away from the barrier.

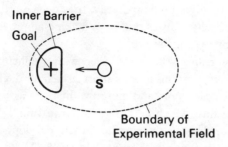

Inner Barrier
Goal
S
Boundary of
Experimental Field

FIGURE 4. Representation of the Barrier.

A distinct experience of the barrier happens to the subject only at a moment of failure. The road he started on turns out to be impassable. The specific conditions of the instruction appear as an obstacle. Repeated inability to progress finally leads to doubts about the possibility of a solution, or to the conviction that it is impossible.

Often the inner barrier, transcending the character of mere difficulty, acquires a *negative valence* (Figure 5). The subject wishes to get away from the

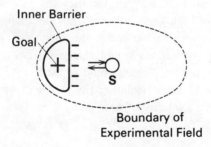

Inner Barrier
Goal
S
Boundary of
Experimental Field

FIGURE 5. Representation of Barrier with Negative Valence.

barrier. He begins to shy away from it, and consequently from his occupation with the task. He would like to avoid running up against the barrier, to give up further efforts, to escape if possible.

Taking into account only the goal-directed occurrences and those determined by the barrier, we have the following picture of the total course of this phase of the experiment. The subject looks for the solution; he tries one approach—it does not work; he tries another—with no success either. "Did the others solve the problem faster?" he asks, and keeps on trying. Again, he runs into the impossibility of carrying out his plan, or into its incompatibility with instructions. He gives up temporarily, tries once more, collides with the barrier again, and finally realizes that he is making no progress at all, that he is encountering nothing but failure.

The subject now realizes that he is faced with a difficulty that cannot be overcome step by step, that this is not a short stretch of rough road over which he has to travel. Instead, more and more the difficulty assumes the character of a real barrier against which he hurls himself in vain.

The complete topology of the situation, then, develops in this case, as in many others, through action within the field itself. (The gradual evolving of the barrier is not peculiar to psychological barriers; it works the same way with physical barriers.)

We might ask why the subject, following the goal vector, does not simply break through the barrier, and move closer while throwing the rings, or step outside the square in the flower experiment? In other words, what constitutes the solidity of the barrier?

Observation shows that the barrier is connected with the goal in a special way. In fact, the goal is not "to reach the flower," but "to reach the flower without moving one's feet outside the square."

Occasionally, one can speak of two existing goals: one is the flower or the bottle itself, the other one is reaching the flower according to the instructions. The two goals contradict one another, but they also substitute for each other. The subjects speak of both goals, although not simultaneously.

The connection between barrier and goal is such that, ignoring the difficulties inherent in the instructions would also mean destroying the goal; the remaining goal, grasping the flower, would be far less valuable. Breaking the barrier by force would mean violating the goal and lowering the level of aspiration. The barrier's solidity is based on its special conditional connection with the task.

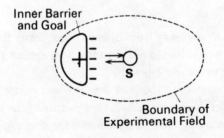

FIGURE 6. The Connection of Barrier with Goal.

The fact that goal and barrier are connected not only topologically, but in a qualitative and contextual manner, requires a correction of our representations. We express this symbolically by joining the barrier to the goal sign, as in Figure 6.

In conclusion, we want to point out that, psychologically, the barrier need not produce only difficulties or counterforces. It can also change the strength of the original goal vector. This becomes most clearly apparent in cases where the barrier strengthens rather than weakens the goal vector: meeting the difficulty can arouse the ambition of a subject, and can make an intrinsically indifferent goal attractive.

Going out of the field, the outer barrier, and tension phenomena When the subject notices that he still remains in his initial situation and is making no progress at all, the direction of his actions may change completely. The negative valence becomes dominant. The repelling forces of the barrier increase to the point that they temporarily become stronger than the attraction of the goal. The subject tries to get away from the barrier, and in that way from the goal. He wants to leave the region where the goal vector operates; he wants to break off the experiment.

In trying that, however, he meets resistance in the form of the outer barrier. The subject has not been expressly forbidden to break off the experiment, but such an action would evidently go against the intention of the task which the subject has voluntarily undertaken. The subject feels committed to this implicit instruction, this unspoken prohibition. In the flower experiment, as with the ring-throwing, he finds himself trapped in a situation that he cannot just simply leave.

As a rule, the outer barrier is experienced by the subject after he becomes aware of the barrier; the outer barrier is not felt clearly until the subject tries to get away. It turns out that the boundary is more than a mere dividing line between the two qualitatively different regions, "experimental situation" and

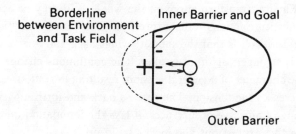

FIGURE 7. Representation of the Outer Barrier.

"life situation," which can be crossed with comparative ease at any time. Instead, it shows a real solidity, having turned into a barrier that severely limits the mobility of the subject (Figure 7). We shall discuss this problem in more detail later on.

The subject, then, is incapable of breaking through the outer barrier. Surrounded by barriers on all sides, he must stay inside the experimental field. Once inside it, he must act in accordance with the field forces operating in the field. Consequently, he works at the task again. The efforts towards the goal, the collisions with the outer barrier, and the return to the experimental field constitute a cycle of events. The subject finds himself in a situation of increasing conflict; contradictory and mounting forces are working on him. He is in a state of mounting tension. This is shown in Figure 8, where the shading indicates mounting tension.

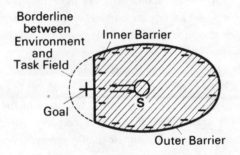

FIGURE 8. Representation of Tension in the Situation.

The situation of conflict can cause the subject to attempt the creation of a new psychic field without physically leaving the goal field. He may, for example, concentrate on reading a book, or try to go out of the field in other ways.

The state of tension, moreover, can have the result that the subject remains occupied with the task, but leaves the real task situation, slipping instead into unreality. Finally, transformations of the whole field may be accomplished. There are substitute actions verbal expressions of affect, and emotional actions.

The over-all result is that the subject swings back and forth. At times this oscillation is stronger, at times weaker. The continuous change of direction acquires the character of a general tension, resulting in restlessness, which, in its turn, increases the tension. The restless back-and-forth movement marks the beginning of affective occurrences; it lays the foundation upon which the various affective expressions and events build up.

Topology of the total situation. As it is important to correctly understand the way in which the total situation builds up, it seems advisable to check the adequacy of our representation of the field. This will be done in connection with just one special aspect, namely, the inner and outer barriers.

In fact, the representation chosen in Figure 8 is not the only possible method of illustration. The separation of the subject from the goal, on the one hand, and from the region outside the experiment, on the other, perhaps might be more suitably rendered by Figure 9:

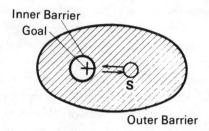

FIGURE 9. An Alternative Representation of the Situation.

Such questions of topological representation are not to be taken lightly. As mentioned above, the adequate representation of a concrete situation is a decisive prerequisite for understanding the event, and for finding out the laws by which it is governed. The topology of the psychic field determines which processes are possible in a given case. Differences in representing the basic topological outlines of a field must have far-reaching consequences for the explanation of the individual events.

Both Figures 8 and 9 are topologically identical in many respects. Both representations have in common the fact that the subject is completely separated from the goal, as well as from the region outside the experimental field. There is further agreement in that, from the subject's point of view, the direction towards the goal, the inner barrier, is not the same as the direction towards the outer barrier. In these respects both representations correspond to the psychic facts.

The topological difference lies mainly in the fact that in the case of Figure 9, the inner and the outer barrier are not connected. In Figure 8, however, there is a connection between the barriers; that is to say, seen from the subject's viewpoint, the barrier has the psychological significance of getting out. Reaching the goal also places the subject outside the experimental situation. In the representation of Figure 9, this fact is not adequately illustrated.

Certain subjective experiences of the subject also point to a representation like Figure 8, in which there is a transition from the inner barrier to the outer.

If, for instance, the subject has an intensive experience of "it can't be done," he feels himself hedged in by a homogeneous wall. The inner and the outer barriers merge to such a degree that it is often hard even for the experimenter to determine whether the subject has encountered one barrier or the other.

The location of the inner barrier as part of the outer manifests itself clearly when the subjects attempt shortcircuit breakthroughs in the direction of the goal. These subjects feel vividly that a breakthrough to the goal would also get them out into the open, away from the unpleasant experimental situation.

The topology of certain advanced phases would be better rendered by Figure 9. Such is the case when the subject at a certain moment wishes intensely to leave the field, and consequently experiences the direction away from the field in clear opposition to the direction toward the goal. The outer barrier is then felt as a closed and independent barrier unconnected with the inner barrier.

It must be kept in mind that, in the course of an experiment, a situation normally undergoes basic transformations of its topology. The barriers not only evolve gradually, but frequently they change with regard to their solidity and their type of mutual interconnection. (It has to be understood that absolute exactness is not essential for the representation of the fields. Initially, there can only be a topologically adequate representation of the situation. Even topologically, differing representations can agree sufficiently to make a first approach to reality.)

We mentioned above that reaching the goal means at the same time that the subject gets out into the open. That might prompt the question whether the dotted arc that is seen in Figures 3–8 should not be omitted. The dotted arc forms part of the boundary that divides the whole experimental field from the environment. The rest of the line developed into the outer barrier during the course of the experiment. Does that mean that the task goal is no longer separated from the surrounding environment? It does not. Even in the later phases of the experiment, the subject does not perceive the task goal as a region of the field of everyday living; it remains definitely part of the experimental situation. After the solution is found, however, the dividing line between the experiment and daily life is no longer a barrier, but only a boundary that can be crossed rather easily.

Summing up: The subject is surrounded by a rather solid barrier, consisting of the outer and the inner barriers. The outer barrier also marks part of the outer limits of the experimental field, including the task goal. The boundary line between the task goal and the field of everyday living does not have the character of a solid barrier.

Events and vectors. In the preceding paragraphs, the claim that there are vectors operating in the direction of certain positive valences is based on the actual occurrence of actions in that direction. It might be questioned whether such inference is justified—and in explaining our procedure, a brief discussion of that question may be appropriate.

There are two ways to ascertain the existence of vectors:

1. A static method, which proves the existence of a vector by creating an equally strong vector in the opposite direction; this should result in an equilibrium of the forces.

2. Inferring the existence of certain vectors from actual occurrences or changes in the course of events.

The start of an event which is in the direction of the task goal does not permit an unequivocal conclusion that a positive valence is operating in the direction of the vector. In itself, it is possible that the vector could be a resultant of other vectors, and that, accordingly, the determining valences must be sought in other directions. Action in the direction of the goal might, for example, be the result of an attempt to escape the outer barrier.

Decisions about whether an event is moving in the direction of a resultant vector or in the direction of a definite positive valence—that is to say, decisions about the existence and the position of the determining positive valences—cannot always be made on the basis of momentary occurrences. As a rule, though, the answer can be found in the way in which events develop over a period of time. In our experiments, this could be done most of the time with sufficient exactness and assurance.

IV. TASK DIRECTED EVENTS (1): REALISTIC SOLUTIONS

We have discussed the general experimental situation and described the genesis of goal-directed actions, the build up of barriers, going out of the field, substitute actions, and affect. In the following sections, all of these phenomena will be traced in detail. We will start with a description of the events stemming from the impact of the forces that push towards the solution of the task.

We do not limit ourselves to the initial situation characterized in Figure 3, where the vector towards the goal completely dominates the field. Instead, we shall deal also with all the events moving in the direction of the goal which can be observed in subsequent situations after the inner and outer barriers have fully developed.

[*I have omitted a section in which Dembo discusses the wide range of events that occur, the different ways in which these might be classified, and the usefulness of different classification schemas in avoiding a onesided or premature interpretation. This material may be obtained from University Microfilms. Dembo points out that sometimes conspicuous phenotypical differences, such as the difference between planning and acting, can be relatively unimportant to understanding the dynamics of a particular case; and therefore a classification*] *based on dynamic considerations is warranted. Such a classification would have to include the intensity of the subject's involvement in the task, his level of aspiration, and the degree of reality of his efforts. I have moved the discussion of the level of aspiration to include it here, rather than later, as Dembo originally had it—Editor.]*

Intensity of Involvement

Inquiring into the dynamic properties of an occurrence against the background of the topology of the total field, one has to find out the direction, and, following that, the intensity of the event.

It is important for the total course of the experiment whether the subject works intensely at the task, investing his whole personality in it, or whether he is uninvolved in the task, and only following the instructions in a pro forma, detached manner.

General remarks about measuring strength of involvement. Extreme differences in the intensity of involvement can be observed without difficulty. Subtle distinctions, however, cannot be discerned so easily, and there are considerable difficulties in establishing conceptual definitions of the gradings in question.

Efforts at solution consist of different kinds of processes. It is impossible to assign well-defined degrees of intensity to processes which are generically distinct.

1. It could be assumed prima facie that an action represents a more intense effort than mere planning. Such is not always the case. Moving the chair in the flower experiment or even throwing the rings can, in individual cases, take place without real effort, and can be less intense than thinking out in concrete detail ways of solving the problem.

2. It could be supposed that the first attempt at a certain approach should be valued higher than a mere repetition of the same approach. This is not always correct; frequently it is only the repetition of a previously attempted approach that develops into a serious effort.

3. Even the comparison of wishing with mental or external action cannot be handled by assigning a lesser degree of intensity to mere wishing. The comparatively inactive state of wishing can, on occasion, indicate a rather high degree of involvement. Moreover, it must be taken into account that the intensities of wishing and of action are not commensurable. A person can wish for something intensely, yet, with a certain psychic constellation, never reach the stage of really trying. The dividing line between wanting a goal and taking action in its direction is very important. This become apparent: 1.) if a *need* is felt, but no corresponding action is taken (intensity of need, but no intensity of action); 2. if there is resistance to the action, but not to the need; and 3. if action is enforced, (but no need is felt.

However, at the moment, it is not our job to reach a decision about the strength of the needs that dominate the behavior of the subject. We are concerned instead with the force of the actual efforts, with the intensity of involvement. (It is self-evident that the question of whether or not a goal is reached by a certain action cannot serve as a criterion for the intensity of involvement.)

In determining the degree of intensity, another difficulty is encountered: an expressive gesture, an action, a question by the subject may correspond to his inner state, but may also correspond to his tendency to conceal his real inner attitude. One can, for instance, look fixedly at an object with thoughts else-where, not thinking at all of the object in sight. One pretends to try; one may, for example, repeat certain attempts at solution such as walking toward the flower, or looking around as if for suitable tools.

It is the immediate experience of the experimental situation, in which the individual event is not encountered in an abstract but in a living context, that allows the observer to evaluate the differences in the intensity of effort. This is the case even in many of the overt cases.

In the following discussion, we shall use for illustration only the cases with no discrepancy between outward behavior and inner state of mind. We distin-guish three groups: strong, moderate, and slight involvement.

Strong involvement. It is characteristic of strong involvement that the sub-ject strives for the goal with all his might. It means serious work, a full belief in the possibility of solution, a real search for a passable road.

Examples: One subject bends his body towards the flower, trying to grasp it with outstretched arm. He does not succeed. Frequently, in really intense efforts, the failure is easily tolerated. The subject tries again, harder. He stretches so far forward that he loses his balance and has to step outside the square. He returns to his old place immediately and resumes his efforts. Then he considers where he could support himself so as to bridge the distance between the square and the flower stand. The chair catches his eye; he places it between the square and the stand.

Another subject starts out by taking a ring in his hand, trying to pull the stand in his direction by means of the ring. The experimenter points out that, according to the instructions, the flower has to be grasped by hand. The subject remains standing, ring in hand, and asks; "Do I need some support for the solution?" The experimenter replies, "I cannot precisely tell you." Thereupon, the subject seriously ponders the question of how to reach a distant object with or without support.

The modes of behavior described above reoccurred in many variations with all the subjects. As far as actions are concerned, subjects bend forward; stand on tiptoe in order to reach farther; let themselves drop towards the stand; try to support themselves in various ways; kneel; sit down or lie on the chair between square and flower, keeping their feet inside the square; try to pull up the stand; measure the distance with their eyes; look around in the hope of finding some kind of tool. The subjects also bombard the experimenter with questions: "Must I first leave the square to solve this?" "With the rings or the chair?" "May I use a stick?" "May I remove objects from the walls?" "Is it permitted to use the laths, the sticks on the floor?"

Such questions may also form a transition to less intense attempts at solving the problem. What is true for a given case has to be determined in each particular instance.

Observations regarding the timing of the emergence of intense efforts show that as a rule, the start of the experiment produces a series of intense efforts. Later, these efforts occur in spurts, intemingled with less intense attempts or other occurrences. Sometimes, however, intense efforts appear as isolated, momentary events. There are also cases in which intense efforts do not occur at the start of the experiment, but develop gradually. This happens, for example, when the subject does not believe at the start of the experiment in the possibility of reaching the goal.

One type of intense effort consists in making a premature attempt at a solution. A solution is not thought through to the end, but is initiated before the subject knows what steps to follow. A chair is picked up and is placed closer to the goal, inside the square, because the subject has a hunch that "somehow the chair will lead to the solution." The subject puts questions to the experimenter: "May I jump?" "May I stand on the rings?"

Premature preparations and questions appear because the tendency towards the goal is so strong that finally something has to be done in its direction. Unable to keep still any longer, the subject starts action prematurely. (The same phenomenon can be observed in sports, for instance, in racing.) Ill-considered solutions can also be based on other circumstances. They can indicate weakness of effort, when they simulate effort.

Sometimes ill-considered solutions are the result of a certain economy of effort. The subject offers the sketch of a solution, intending to embark on more thorough thinking only after the experimenter confirms that he has been trying in the right direction.

Moderate involvement. Less intense efforts at solution often take the form of recapitulation, elimination of false solutions, preparations, or questions to the experimenter that have been answered previously by the instructions.

The subject say, "I can solve the problem by the old method" (recapitulation). "The chair will not do it." "The distance is too great for bending forward" (elimination of false solutions). "Stay inside and grasp it" (recapitulation of instructions). "With my hand only? No throwing, no pushing!" "The condition of the experiment is, keep my feet inside the square" (recapitulation of instructions). "I'll first have to think about it" (preparation).

Moderately energetic attempts at solutions occur usually when the subject continues trying even though he is tired or exhausted, or when he undertakes the task unwillingly for the second or third time, after a previous solution.

Most conspicuous among the moderate attempts at solution are recapitulations of old solutions. This is extremely frequent. It seems to be based essentially on the following factors:

Moderate involvement corresponds to a state in which the subject works at the task much more intentionally than he does when deeply involved. The explanation for this paradoxical fact is that, as a rule, intense involvement implies being completely gripped by the task, creating powerful tension in the foundations of the psychic system. This produces occurrences related to actions that stem from basic drives. Such actions do not necessitate a special effort of will, a forcing of oneself to work on the task. Weaker tensions, however, are generally expressed by intentional voluntary actions. By a consciously willed action one can start out on a given road, but it is less easy to find a new, creative way. Thus, lesser involvement, in spite of willed efforts, often leads to a mere recapitulation of former, accomplished solutions, and not to those processes of development and transformation that characterize involuntary efforts.

Some of the recapitulations seem to originate in the following manner: a subject decides to resume the unpleasant task but, at the same time, basically rejects it. He feel detached from the task, and the recapitulation of the old method provides a means, used also in everyday life, of regaining inner contact with the task. Thus, recapitulation can be a prelude to genuine involvement.

Finally, it should be pointed out that recapitulations also occur after extreme confusion or drastic failures. Here, too, they are usually conscious attempts at getting back into the proper task situation. (Occasionally, intense efforts can also lead to recapitulation. In that case, they disturb productive thinking. The best way to get rid of such disturbances is for the subject not to resist them but to allow the recapitulations to cross his mind at will. The phenomenon of the resurgence of old solutions is connected with the general phenomenon of goal-directedness in such situations.)

Slight involvement. A very slight degree of involvement manifests itself in the remark by one subject: "I have not forgotten the flower, but it does not disturb me." The subject's weak efforts keep him in contact with the task; he does not abandon it, but he assumes an almost passive attitude, scarcely trying for a solution. Slight involvement is frequently characterized by a merely formal connection with the task, not by genuine action.

Changes in intensity of involvement. No generally valid statements can be made concerning the chronology and sequence of the different degrees of intensity. Intensity can gradually decrease, but it can also jump upward; it can remain on the same level for extended periods, or it can change repeatedly. It depends on, among other things, the success or failure of the subject's actions, that is to say, on his painful contacts with the inner or outer barriers. It also depends on the experimenter's interference, encouraging or otherwise. If it suddenly occurs to the subject that his performance might be compared to the performance of other subjects, the intensity of his efforts may increase by leaps and bounds. If the subject's thoughts have strayed from the task for a while, the return to the task will frequently be weak; sometimes, however, his conscience will spur him on to more intensive efforts.

We have not been able to observe a typical increase of effort intensity along with an increase in affectivity. On the other hand, in our experiments, a considerable degree of involvement forms the necessary precondition for the emergence of affect.

Level of Aspiration

During the discussion of various degrees of intensity, the goal was assumed to be given and constant. In fact, there may be various goal transformations. In some of these, the connection between the old and the new goal lies in the fact that the new goal is a natural preliminary step towards reaching the original goal. For example:

At the start of the experiment the subject undertakes the task of throwing ten rings on the bottles. He undertakes the task without knowledge of its difficulties or of his own abilities in that direction. At first he tries to get the rings on the bottles without attaching definite expectations to his performance. He only wishes, somehow, to do as well as possible.

His first failures show the subject that the task is not easy. He realizes that much practice will be needed. He indicates this to the experimenter by remarking casually during the 2nd series of 10 throws, "I'll have to order dinner to be brought here," and by asking at the end of the series, "Has anybody ever accomplished the task from this distance?" The experimenter answers, "Yes." The subject responds, "I don't believe it."

During the third series, one throw succeeds. The subject remarks with satisfaction: "Well, at least one." Evidently, the subject considers he has succeeded because one out of ten throws was a hit, although the task is to throw ten rings on the bottle, and consequently he has failed. After the first trials, the goal of ten hits has turned into a distant goal in the future. The goal to be tackled immediately, which therefore has become decisive for success or failure (the new *real* goal), is now to score at least one hit. At the same time, the real goal has acquired the character of one step on the road to the future, ideal goal, which at the moment has no reality. (Frequently, the conscious goal is more vague: as many rings as possible. At the moment of performance, however, the experiences of success and failure demonstrate what was the genuine real goal.)

The degree of expectation, the level of aspiration, as indicated by the real goal, has grown out of the given situation, and shifts as the situation changes. If, for example, the goal of one hit has been realized, the subject feels he has taken a step forward and aspires to more.

In our example, the first hit was followed by several series without any hits. The subject was thrown back to his beginning level.

When after an unsuccessful series of seven the subject scores a hit again, he experiences it as success, and says, "In time you get practice." He does not evaluate the hit as chance victory, but as an expression of his abilities. This is followed by a shifting of the level of aspiration to "more than one hit." When, during the next series, another hit is booked, it is no longer valued as a success. The subject then says: "Funny, I can't get beyond one hit." Evidently, the real goal of the subject has changed. His level of aspiration now is more than one hit.

When in one of the following series of ten the subject scores two hits, he says triumphantly: "My goodness! I'm surprised at myself, got two rings on! Fabulous!" During the next-following series, the subject has only one hit which he ignores, at least outwardly.

In order to stimulate the subject in the direction of the full goal, the experimenter allows him to step closer to the bottles. But even then the final goal does not become dominant; instead, the subject starts on fresh trials to find out how much can be attained in the present situation. Since the number of hits in this series is four, the level of aspiration for the next series becomes more than four.

In the next series, the subject scores five hits. He asks the experimenter, "Was it four or five?" When he receives the answer, "Five," the subject, gratified, says, "Aha!"

The further course of this experiment gives a characteristic picture of the shiftings in the level of aspiration, since in this case the amount of achievement at any given moment is such that the height of the level of aspiration finds precise expression. (Such a course of events is understandably rare.)*

* *Because Hoppe's experiments* (Chapter XII) *are a quantitative elaboration of this phenomena, first described by Dembo, the remainder of this example has been omitted—Editor.*

V. TASK DIRECTED EVENTS (II): UNREALISTIC AND SUBSTITUTIONS SOLUTIONS

While goal transformations are involved in changes of the level of aspiration, the events are determined simply by the original goal, and move directly towards it. The real goals successively approach the original, ideal goal in a step-by-step fashion. They are genuine part-goals which represent an approach to the original goal, which is clearly preserved in the process. Quite a different set of goal transformations are involved in events which are not simply in the direction of the original goals. These are unrealistic and substitute solutions.

Unreal Solutions

Many attempted solutions made by the subjects either go contrary to instructions, or they ignore the facts, especially the facts of the physical environment. One subject, for example, envisioned himself floating above the stand. He said later, "I shall fill the room with water and swim to the flower." Several subjects expressed the desire to hypnotize the flower.

When such a solution occurs to the subject, he does not usually see it as a joke, but rather, fleetingly, as a kind of solution; often it even satisfies him for the moment. This very satisfaction indicates that the old situation no longer prevails. The precise definition of the goal, the real qualities of the barrier and of the actual environment, are no longer in existence. Essential details of the situation, the goal, the barrier, and the admissible means of action become blurred. The whole situation grows vague, schematic, general, and independent of the concrete difficulties. Without realizing it, the subject replaces the task "To reach *this* flower from *this* distance under *these* conditions" by the more generalized task "To reach a distant object," "Bridge a distance," or "Create connections." The original task is thus reduced to a generalized schema, a schema which sometimes includes remnants of the old situation, such as the instruction that it is a flower that must be reached.

The transition towards a schema can also occur as a "reasonable" consideration of possible solutions without being fantastic or imaginary (1). However, the cases that we are discussing here transcend this framework more or less strikingly. For example, the subject may see his arm, separated from his body, moving towards the flower in a hallucinatory way. This and other imaginary solutions, when they appear cumulatively and especially when the subject advances them seriously, are essentially different in character from real solutions. The subject has left the factual area for a sphere of unreality. He moves in a field in which the rules of reality are no longer, or no longer completely valid; here, he can act wishfully.

One subject proposed: "I'll stop the clock; then I shall be inside the square and with the flower at the same time." Many subjects coax the flower by words and gestures. Slipping into unreality does not always have to take the form of mere fantasies; it may appear in the form of suggestions that at first seem more realistic. One subject, for example, announced, "I will place the rings on the floor between the square and the stand and will walk to the flower using them as steppingstones." This plan, it is true, is much more concrete than the schemes mentioned above, but being obviously contrary to instructions, it is quite impracticable from the start.

For a long time, psychology has made use of concepts such as "unreality." Dynamic differences between reality and unreality, however, have not been conceptually clarified in psychological theory. Without entering into a detailed discussion, we want to point out that questions of unreality are in many ways related to the problems of fantasy, of dreams and insanity, of lying, play, symbolism, as well as to the problems of religion and supersition, and of confrontations between truth and imagination. It is to be emphasized that not only must reality and unreality be distinguished, but a whole continuum of degrees of reality as well. Not only imaginings possess a certain degree of reality, but also speech, actions, and thoughts do. The degree of reality is not only a property of the individual, psychological event but also of the situation; the environment of a person (at least of an adult) shows a stratification according to degrees of reality. The subject can move on a plane endowed with a higher or a lesser degree of reality.

A transition into unreality cannot be represented on the same plane as is shown in Figure 8; it requires leaving the level of reality. In topological representation, the differentiation of the degrees of reality necessitates a special dimension of the psychological environment. The total psychological situation has to be presented in at least three dimensions. In the following, we shall not deal with the different degrees of unreality; we shall generally speak only of reality and unreality.

In our case, the level of unreality, in its topology and its field forces, is a kind of rough mirror which reflects conditions on the level of reality (Figure 10). As the degree of unreality increases, however, the inner and outer barriers lose their firmness. The subject has more freedom of movement on the level of unreality. At the same time, the goal becomes blurred, less well defined.

The Genesis of Unreal Solutions

The transition to a new and unreal situation can be described only in general terms. It may be a gradual transition. The subject "frees himself" from the old solutions; he discards his previous concepts about the situation; he looks around for new means and ways. All this loosens up the old situation and transforms it. In order to find a solution, the subject must think—that is, he

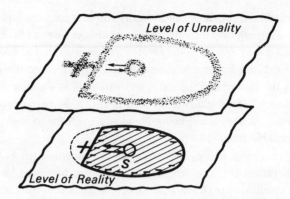

FIGURE 10. Representation of Different Levels of Reality.

must operate with thoughts. In a way, this already means a move in the direction of unreality. It can easily lead to the subject's evading a collision with reality altogether. Not infrequently, the transition is initiated or encouraged when the subject goes beyond the particular considerations, and instead consciously thinks through the general possibilities of the solution in conceptual terms. Oversatiation, with the same attempts at solution and repeated mistakes, also creates a tendency towards the transformation of the task and a slipping into unreality. These are the factors that, starting from realistic efforts, lead to unreal solutions.

Apart from this, an inner state of tension may also cause the transition into unreality. This happens, above all, when the desire to find a solution becomes so elemental that the subject is completely dominated by it. Then, the subject no longer simply has the desire, but comes under its power and is entirely obsessed by it. In such a case, the subject is easily driven into unreality, into the sphere where no real barriers exist, and where success can be achieved by wishing.

The commanding wish that assails a person and carries him away according to its own laws occurs in everyday life mostly in connection with strong, affective goal-directedness (for instance, love). If such passionate desires meet obstacles, it often leads to romancing, that is, to a prolonged occupation with the desired goal in which the connection with the reality level is almost completely severed. The decisive factor is again not the intensity of desire, but the relation between the desire and the person, that is to say, whether the person has the desire or whether the desire has overcome the person.

The same factors that cause a shift towards unreality also motivate the person to remain in unreality. Staying there is more pleasant than operating on the level of reality, which is rich in failure and not very agreeable. In unreality, the subject has greater mobility. Difficulties have disappeared, in part or altogether. Chances of success are greater. Here one can romance; one can dream happy dreams.

Why then does the subject not linger indefinitely in happy unreality? Why does he return to reality to labor again at a level full of failures?

Solving the task in unreality, the subject may well have a momentary feeling of having reached the goal of his endeavors. But it is just such a reaching of the goal that will awaken the subject to the fact that the essential functional consequences which would have followed the reaching of the real goal, and which heretofore have played an important role for him, have failed to materialize. The experimenter does not acknowledge the solution; the unrealistic solution does not open a way out of the whole experimental situation, as would have been the case with a real solution. In other words: the unreal solution does not eliminate the real existence of the inner and outer barriers which limit the subject's freedom of motion.

Substitute Solutions

Unrealistic solutions no longer correspond to the original goal. The same is true of a second group of events, which, however, manifest different characteristics: substitute solutions.

Examples. In the ring-throwing experiment, as mentioned earlier, there are not only the two goal bottles upon which the subject is to throw the rings, but there is also another bottle left "by chance" on the side table by the experimenter. When the subject throws the rings from the shortest distance, it is more accessible to him than are the two goal bottles. Although the subject is instructed to throw the rings over one of the bottles designed as goals, and although there are no misunderstandings about the instructions, the subject at times throws a ring on the more easily accessible bottle on the side table (substitute goal object). It sometimes also happens that the subject throws the rings over a near by tripod instead of over the designated bottles.

In the flower experiment, the subject does not reach for the goal flower as instructed, but instead takes a flower "left lying from the preceding experiment" on a second stand near the experimenter (substitute goal object). Sometimes, he seizes a flower that stands in a vase on the experimenter's table.

The subject does not throw the rings, but he grabs a long stick and *slides* the rings over the bottle neck with its help, although this is forbidden (substitute procedure).

In the flower experiment, the subject sometimes leaves the square of laths in spite of the prohibition, and goes to fetch the flower that he could not reach if he followed instructions (substitute procedure).

There are many variants of substitution. In the examples cited here, the substitution sometimes changes the goal object, in which case either a superficially similar object, bottle, or flower, or an apparently different one, tripod, becomes the goal. In other cases, the substitution takes the form of a change in the procedure. In all cases, the task is essentially transformed.

As a rule, it can be said that substitution is not a conscious process of the sort: "Instead of that flower, I will take another, more easily reached." In most cases, the substitution is not planned in advance. Usually, the subject realizes the substitution only after completing it.

A more thorough investigation into the psychological definition of substitution reveals extraordinary problems. The following two difficulties of demarcation exist:

1. A whole group of actions that include certain transformations of the task can also be interpreted as different routes or detours to the original goal. If, in spite of the prohibition, the subject were to pull the flower from the stand towards himself with the help of a stick, this action would imply substitution; the evading of the real task would be definitely contrary to the intent of the instructions. But when the subject places a chair between the square and the stand, that is to say, when he uses an admissible instrument, there can be no question of substitution in spite of the fact that at the moment when this solution is found the meaning of the task has also undergone a transformation in the eyes of the subject.

There are many transitions between those transformations of the task's intent that are a prerequisite for any real solution, and those transformations that must unquestionably be regarded as substitutes.

2. The second, more significant difficulty, may be illustrated by means of an example: If the subject throws the ring on the bottle nearby, it is without doubt a substitute action; the substitution is equally obvious if the ring is thrown on the nearby tripod. If, however, the subject throws the ring on some spot before him, then the throw can be interpreted not only as a substitute action, but also as playfulness, or as an affective discharge, or as practicing. No less problematic is the use of the concept of substitution when the subject plays with the rings without throwing them.

Conceptually, the difficulty is the following: how far can a transformation deviate from the original goal, and what sort of transformation can it be, without necessitating the statement that it no longer constitutes an event directed towards the original goal, but is an independent, substitute event?

In spite of the difficulties, there remain a large number of events which can without hesitation, be characterized as substitution. The following considerations about the genesis and the dynamic properties of substitution processes are primarily based on these events. In this discussion, we will deal only with a limited number of questions, since an elaborate theory of substitution would transcend the framework of this study.

Genesis of Substitute Solutions

Looking for the origins of substitution, one comes across a multitude of different conditions. Sometimes, the striving towards the goal is of extraordinary intensity. The substitute action seems to stem from a determination to reach the goal at any price. Not infrequently, substitution occurs at a moment when the subject is quarreling with the experimenter; this gives it the character of a fighting action. Occasionally, the substitute action emerges suddenly and abruptly, and apparently surprises the subject as much as the experimenter. Sometimes, substitution means settling for less. In other cases it indicates an evasion of certain demands made by the experimenter. Sometimes the object that resembles the goal seems to have an especially strong attraction for the subject.

Dynamically, all the cases above involve an event which is fundamentally determined by the tendency towards the original task goal; and we are going to use the term *substitute* only when this dynamic fact is present.

The Identity Theory. Although the concept of substitution plays a prominent role in Freud's psychopathological theories, and although it is used to explain many events, there is no precise theory which deals with the problem of why substitution occurs under a given circumstance.

Generally, it seems to be considered sufficient to establish the similarity involved in cases of substitution. This becomes evident particularly when substitution problems are linked with problems of symbols and taboo. Similarity is regarded as a kind of partial identity. If the substitute and original goal are fundamentally identical, there seems to be no need to look for a special cause to explain the emergence of substitution. We shall refer to this theory as the theory of substitute identity.

The logical structure of the concept of similarity implies that it is possible to establish similarities between any events whatsoever. This fact makes the use of the substitution concept particularly dangerous—as became evident enough in the psychopathological theories.

The phenomenon of identity or similarity between the substitute goal and the original one is as striking as it is precarious for any theory. Let us examine the validity of this theory, which regards similarity as the cause of substitution, in those cases which seem to be particularly favorable to the theory, that is, where considerable similarity exists. Consider the following: while throwing rings, the subject switches from bottle 1 to bottle 2, which stands in a symmetrical relation with the first at the same distance from subject. In the flower experiment, where the subject has tried at the start to reach the flower with his right hand, he now extends the left. In the ring-throwing example, the identity of both goals is especially clear since the instruction is, "Throw the rings on one of the two bottles (1 and 2)." Thus, formally the goal is one originally given by the experimenter. However, the second bottle is not the first. We are dealing with a typical replacement of one goal by another. The theory of identity would say: The transition to the second bottle occurs because it resembles the first.

It is precisely these cases in which there can be the least doubt of identity that best serve to demonstrate how inadequate identity is as an explanation for the emergence of substitution.

In the case of the bottles, if both are in fact identical for the subject, there is no reason why the subject should switch from the first bottle to the second, rather than stay with the first. In no way does he mistake the first bottle for the second. The entire behavior and the statements of the subject make it abundantly clear that the subject undertakes a transition to something new and different when he switches bottles, the more so when he realizes the substitutive character of the event. Occasionally, the subject feels embarrassed when he switches from one bottle to another one that evidently does not offer a better chance. Likewise, the replacement of the right hand by the left in the flower experiment occurs under conditions which leave no doubt in the subject's mind that he has not improved, but worsened his chances.

The act is not a confusion, but a change. The transition to the second identical bottle is essentially based on the non-identity of the bottles. The subject wants to remove himself from the task of throwing rings on the first bottle. He wants to leave the original goal. The cause of the substitution in the ring experiment is the tendency away from the goal object to which he is still tied at the moment. It is only under the pressure of getting away from the first goal that the similarity of the bottles gains significance for the substitution. The fact that a second, nearly identical goal, is ready at hand opens an easy and noncommittal path to doing something new for the subject.

Other cases show with equal clarity that identity is not the decisive cause of substitute actions. The substitute bottle provided on purpose by the experiment, or the flower deposited nearby, are often not considered as goals by the subject; while other objects, like the tripod, the blocks, or the coat hooks objects with much less resemblance to the bottle, are used as substitute goals.

This is equally true if, rather than the phenomenal, the functional identity is considered. In ring throwing, for example, one would expect substitution with objects particularly suited to have rings of the given size thrown on them. Frequently, the subject chooses a substitute that surprises the experimenter, ignoring objects that, owing to their greater similarity, seem much more suitable.

We can, then, make the general statement: neither a phenomenal nor a functional identity of the goal object as such leads to substitution. Actually, the substitute bottles and the substitute flowers have been present since the start of the experiment. However, substitution appears only in certain phases within its course. Well-defined, special conditions are needed if identity is to bring about substitution.

The identity of the goal objects alone is not decisive. A whole series of other factors must be considered, to wit: the position of the goal within the field, its distance from the subject, the intensity of desire for the goal, the affective situation, and the momentary attitude of the subject towards the experimenter. It is the total dynamic constellation of the field and of the person that determine all events, including the historical course of the experiment—although the effect of the latter is often hard to analyze in detail. Above all, the individual subject's thought processes play an essential role; they give to the separate objects in the environment their special significance, which differs from case to case and is often subject to considerable change.

Sources of substitute actions. What are the determining conditions that create a tendency towards substitution? In some cases, this seems an easy question to answer. If a subject switches from the first bottle to a second, practically equivalent one, the tendency away from the first goal was his chief motivation. It is the tendency to go out of the field that evidently determines the subject's behavior. (It must be specially emphasized that the tendency to go out of the field in all these cases is not due to the attraction exerted by the environment, but is primarily a tendency to get away from the goal.) The tendency to go out of the field is made even clearer by the subject himself in the following example of the use of a substitute instrument: The subject refuses to pick up the rings after throwing because he is in a revolt against the experimenter. The experimenter repeatedly tells him to do it. The subject seizes the tripod, and triumphantly picks up the rings with this incongruous instrument, feeling that he has evaded the command. Here, too, the substitute action is dominated by the outspoken tendency away from the original task. Similarly, the tendency to leave the field is dominant in the subject who throws the rings on the coathooks at the other end of the room while running away from the experimenter.

In all these cases, the situation is dominated by a vector that, due to the negative valence exerted by the difficulty barrier, pushes away from the original goal towards something else. Going out of the field takes the form of substitute action.

Aside from the substitutions that are dominated by the tendency to go out of the field, there are a number of cases in which the situation is evidently different. In these, an unusually strong tendency towards the goal seems to be responsible for the substitute action. We shall discuss these cases at length because they will also throw new light on the cases mentioned before.

We start with the subject who suddenly notices with surprise that a second flower is lying on a stand near the rear of the square. He asks, "I guess that is not the right one?" and receives a negative reply. Although the subject is now aware of the fact that the other flower is not part of the experiment, this flower keeps obtruding itself on him. Once more, the subject feels compelled to say, "So this is not the one!" After a while the other flower disturbs him again, disturbs or attracts. Anyway, the flower on the stand does not leave the subject in peace. He remarks on it; sometimes he asserts emphatically, "I'm not going to touch that one!" Yet, not much later, he seizes the flower whose attraction he has fought consciously for so long. Drawn by the object's fascination, he acts almost compulsively. The process of attraction is not always so prolonged. Frequently, the substitute action occurs immediately at the moment when the attraction is first felt.

If the subject is asked immediately after a substitute event to describe the occurrence precisely, he does not find anything to say except, "Suddenly I saw a flower there, and I had to take it."

Similarly, it comes as a surprise to the experimenter, and to the subject himself, if in the ring-throwing he sometimes casually drops a ring over a nearby bottle, only to resume the throwing at the goal bottles directly afterward.

The genesis of this variety of substitution becomes intelligible only when two phenomena that go beyond substitution are considered: 1) the directedness of objects; 2) the subject's freeing himself from his rigid adherence to the instruction.

Directedness. The subject tries to find a solution to the task. This search transforms his perception of the field in a definite way. Before the instruction is given, the objects in the room represent certain valences unconnected with the task goal. The rings lying beside the laths may evoke the desire to roll them, a chair may look inviting to sit on, the flowers standing on the table look as if they have pleasant fragrance, and so forth.

When the subject begins to search for a solution to the task, most of the objects in the field of perception acquire a more or less marked relation to the solution (2).

The over-all situation becomes tense, and the tension towards the goal seems to carry along everything inside the field. The subject sees the objects in terms of the direction of the goal; that is, he views them as possible obstacles, disturbances, usable instruments, as something other subjects might have used as a goal, and so on.

By the same token, the events during the experiment are usually seen in relation to the goal. The subject sees, for instance, a small feather floating towards the flower, and he says, "Can this give me a clue?" The constant relating of all objects and events to the task goal goes on to the extent that even unsuitable objects are used as instruments, or irrelevant actions are made in the direction of the goal. Sometimes, in our experiments, the range of connected events was so unlimited that the more absurd transformations took on an almost paranoid character. (The referral to specific superstitious connections also suggests itself.)

The greater the tension, the more compulsively the objects seem to offer themselves as tools. In the long run, the subject can hardly defend himself against these often senseless offerings.

Some examples to illustrate these statements: Eight wooden rings are lying on the floor. The rings, "evidently" put there on purpose, are time and again related to the solution by the subject. Although the subject must realize that the rings are useless, since the flower has to be grasped by hand and the stand must not be moved, he cannot resist their attraction. In his search, he keeps thinking of a solution with the help of the rings. There was hardly a subject who did not yield to their attraction and pick up the rings that "have something to do with the solution."

Since a real solution of the task by means of the intruding objects is impossible, as the subject eventually realizes, these objects not only acquire significance in the direction of the solution, but they are also resented as "nuisances." They bother the subject, preventing him from a forthright, objective search for the solution. On the one hand, the subject hopes to make use of the rings; on the other, he would like to eliminate them in one way or the other. Being in doubt about the possibility of using the rings, the subject picks them up, for example, and then puts them down on the floor emphatically. With particular insistence the chair standing inside the square of laths will offer itself as a tool after the first two solutions. In order to stop its importunity, the subjects occasionally sat down on it. (This reveals at the same time a form of substitution. If the subject cannot utilize the chair as a tool, he uses it at least to sit on.)

Another example: For a long time, one subject believed the fact that the rear side of the square consisted not of one, but of two laths was relevant to the task. He was greatly disturbed by this thought and felt extraordinary relief when it occured to him that "the rear wall of the square is simply put together by two laths because one would not be long enough."

Thus, with sufficient tension on the part of the subject, the objects and events of the situation acquire the attributes of being useful resources or of being disturbances, beyond the dictates of commonsense.

We also want to make the point that the substitute actions that are oriented in the direction of a goal which is different from the original one are based on the general directedness of the field of action (unless the substitution stems from the tendency to go out of the field). Objects that are out of the question as tools for reaching the original goal, but which show a certain resemblance to the main goal, acquire a goal character, owing to the goal-directedness of the total field. According to this thesis, the substitute goal does not have to be a substitution for the original goal in the literal sense of the word. The fact is rather, that a very strong general directedness can lead not only to the inclusion of nonsensical means and ways, but also to the acquisition of a positive valence by a goal which does not correspond with the intent of the original task. This goal can either be in addition to the original goal or a replacement for it.

Where certain objects or events are transformed into tools, ways, means of approach, and so on, to the original goal, we shall speak of the *special directedness* of a field. The term, *general directedness,* on the other hand, includes the fact that substitute goals can also acquire a positive valence apart from the original goal.

Later on, in discussing the relation of the subject to the experimenter, we shall encounter the phenomenon of induced positive valences which are based on the fact that the forces of the experimenter dominate the experimental field. Conditions of general directedness can be interpreted in a similar way: the positive valence of the task goal creates a field of forces that, when sufficiently strong, dominates the total field and has different effects on the various elements of the field. It not only induces positive valences in tools in the sense of special directedness, but it can also lend to certain elements acquiring an actual goal character in the sense of general directedness. When the vector towards the goal, extending tension over the total field, bestows positive valence on other objects as well, a situation is created in which both the original goal and the substitute goal have a positive valence.

Although the strength of the positive valence in the substitute goal is generally inferior to the strength in the original goal—except for the moment of substitute action itself—substitute goals are nearly always considerably easier to reach than the main goal. Their positive valence is only induced, but they are not removed from the subject by so strong a barrier of difficulties. Under these circumstances, the question is not so much why substitute actions occur, but rather why they do not occur regularly with all subjects.

Indeed, a substitute goal as such develops extremely frequently; for example, whenever the subject conceives the idea of grasping the second flower. If, nonetheless the substitute action is not always carried out, the reason lies partly in certain inhibitions: the substitute goal seems somehow "wrong," "forbidden," or "of inferior quality."

Loosening of Ties. There is a second prerequisite for the emergence of substitution: the subject must have broken loose from his firm tie to the instructions, to the original task goal.

In our discussion of unrealistic solutions we gave examples to show how a subject, after trying in vain to solve the problem, lapses into the fantastic. These cases also demonstrate that the task loses, at least temporarily, the precise form given it by the instruction. Such loosening not only blurs the boundaries between permissible and prohibited resources, but, after continued unsuccessful efforts, it also affects the whole situation in a more or less marked way. (Karsten has discussed cases where psychic satiation led to the deterioration not only of actions, but also of the total situation. In our experiments, intensive but ineffective efforts produce a structural loosening, similar in many respects.) Finally the loosening encompasses the task goal as well. This provides the prerequisite for a situation in which the attraction of a substitute goal, based on the general directedness of all objects towards the goal, does not meet with sufficient resistance.

The loosening process is promoted by the fact that even legitimate efforts towards the goal necessarily include factors that involve loosening. In spite of our analysis of similar processes connected with the problem of unrealistic solutions, it seems useful to sketch once more the development of such general loosening up: The subject has found the solution to the problem. If he is to find the second solution, he has to think freely and without constraint. He must try to reinterpret in his mind both the instructions and the total situation. In order to find a new method, a person has to consider without prejudice even forbidden ways. Only in that manner is it possible to think out the limitations, and thereby find the gap in the forbidden region.

We shall try to demonstrate that there is no fundamental difference between the use of fantastic or forbidden ways of solution, on the one hand, and the transition to substitute goals on the other.

Basically, the use of a forbidden tools or approach, for example, leaving the square—also implies changing the task. The goal is no longer "To seize the flower without leaving the square," but it is "To seize the flower that lies on a stand near enough to reach." This problem is entirely different in quality. With respect to the lessening of difficulties, there is, in principle, no difference between the transition to a shorter distance in ring throwing and the choosing of another, nearby target bottle.

Nonetheless, the use of resources contrary to instructions is less easily interpreted as substitution. The change in the original task is not as evident. The transformation of the goal through an altered method of solution does not have to be less significant, but it is less overt and actually occurs with less difficulty than an overt substitution of the goal. The reason for this seems to

be that, within the framework of a goal-directed action, the means of procedure, the tools and manners of approach, appear to be less fixed than the goal
object. They seem changeable, and therefore more open to loosening up than
does the goal, which from the beginning has been an unequivocally defined,
definite object.

The total course of events that ends in substitution often exhibits special
qualities characteristic of substitution processes. As borne out by daily experience, relaxation at any one point of a situation can easily lead to relaxation
at other points.

The subject finds himself in a situation where it is difficult to keep the wall
between himself and the forbidden region intact. Self-control is especially hard,
because the goal could be reached easily by forbidden means. If the loosening
process has started, this means the subject has taken the first tentative step in
the forbidden direction—he has thought of a possible substitute solution, or
asked the experimenter whether a certain act may not be permissible after all.
This event has already brought him nearer to the prohibited area. The first
tentative steps into the forbidden region bestow a much higher degree of reality
on the prohibited zone than before, and at the same time they weaken the
boundary between it and the subject. At the time, the subject, shocked at
himself, may return to the legitimate region. After a while, however, he will
be considerably more receptive to the allure of forbidden things. Finally, the
subject may end up under the spell of valences that dominate the forbidden
region. These valences now determine his behavior even though, in the beginning, he may have thought that he was only entering the forbidden region
tentatively and not really in earnest.

Such progressive developments can be observed in everyday life in connection with addictions, or in cases where the relinquishing of one conventional
tie, to the surprise of the person himself, leads to the radical relinquishing of
all conventional ties. Not infrequently such developments play an essential role
in the genesis of substitute actions.

The Combination of Escape and Goal-Directed Actions in Substitution. In
tracing the sources of substitute action, we found that, dynamically, substitute
action can in part by explained as a going out of the field, as an escape away
from the original goal. Next, we discussed a second group of substitute actions
which stem in the final analysis from a vector in the direction towards the
original goal.

It is essential for the understanding of substitute actions to realize that
actually these two groups are not separate, but that every substitution is always
at the same time both an action towards the goal and an escape from the goal.

We have already pointed out that a substitution which must be interpreted
as an escape, for example, the switch to the second, symmetrical bottle, is

carried out under the disguise of a seemingly goal-directed action. The subject does not go out of the field by leaving the room or turning to different activities; but during his flight to the substitute goal, in a certain sense he stays with the original task. At this point, it must be emphasized that this staying is not only a phenomenon; both an escape and a new approach to the task-goal are dynamically in existence.

Corresponding statements can be made for the second group of substitute actions in which the tendency towards the goal is primarily conspicuous. When the subject, under an overwhelming pressure in the direction of the goal, succumbs to the attraction of a forbidden tool, or reacts to a substitute goal like the second flower, neither of those actions points exclusively in the direction of the original goal: the new goals lie in a different direction from the real goal. In these cases, too, the substitute action constitutes at the same time a deviation away from the real goal.

In conclusion, we can state that substitution is always the effect of a conflict between the tendency towards the goal and the tendency away from the goal: both of these dynamic components find expression in the substitute action itself. The amount of influence exerted by one component or the other differs widely in different cases. In some cases, escape, in others, action towards the goal, is decisive for the experience of the subject and for the dynamics of the event. That is why the distinction between the two groups of substitute actions —substitution as escape and substitution as attraction towards the goal— retains a measure of significance.

Substitution and Level of Aspiration. Since shifts in the level of aspiration also involve transformations of goals, the question arises as to whether the setting of a level of aspiration is actually a substitute action. The question seems especially pertinent because normally a substitute goal is much more easily attainable than the original goal, so that the subject often feels afterward that he has slipped downward to an inferior goal. Shifts in the level of aspiration also often involve having the real goal made an easier task than the ideal goal. Furthermore, as with substitution, the change in the level of aspiration preserves a sufficient identity with the original goal. Formally, therefore, we would be justified in claiming the existence of substitution in all cases of changed levels of aspiration, when, as in our example, the real goal does not yet coincide with the ideal goal.

It is, of course, possible to broaden the concept of substitution enough to include shiftings in the level of aspiration. Yet, we do not consider such a broadened definition useful for our purpose, because dynamically the conditions in the cases of substitution which we have discussed are rather different. In shifting in the level of aspiration, while the real goal changes, the main goal is preserved. The real goals successively approach the original goal in an attempt to reach it step by step. They are genuine part-goals. In substitution, however, dominance is acquired by a goal that does not represent a real approach to the original goal.

Substitution can be claimed only when the subject stops permanently at a lower level of aspiration—when the real goal no longer represents a step towards the ideal goal, but has instead become an independent goal in itself.

In such cases, we will speak of *resignation substitutes,* in contrast to the cases in which the substitute goal is a step on the way to the original goal. If the substitute goal is situated in a different direction, we shall speak of *genuine substitution.* (Occasionally there are cases of genuine substitution in which the subject acts as if, somehow, the substitution were, after all, a step in the direction of the original goal, and pretends to use the substitute goal for practice. For example, in the flower experiment, a subject compares the distance from the goal stand to that from the substitute stand. Seeing that reaching the flower on the substitute stand presents no difficulties, he says: "I shall first try to take this flower, and then the other one." That looks like practicing, but is nothing of the kind.)

Insofar as the level of aspiration enters into genuine substitution at all, it acts as an obstacle. By its very nature, the dynamics determining the level of aspiration push towards the highest possible goal. Thus, they form an obstacle to substitution, both of the resigned and of the genuine variety.

The Dynamics of Genuine Substitution

It is now clear that genuine substitution does not serve as a step on the road to the original goal. Still, it must be kept in mind that the vector towards the substitute goal comes into being because of the dominance of the vector towards the original goal over the total situation.

As we have pointed out earlier, with genuine substitution a tendency both away from the goal and a vector towards the goal are always in simultaneous operation. This creates a duality: on the one hand, dependence on the original goal, on the other, independence from it. This becomes clearer from a somewhat different angle if one considers the effect which the substitute action has on the state of tension in the psychic system that forms the base of the goal-directed action. How does substitute action affect the satisfaction that usually forms the concomitant of reaching the original goal?

Let us contemplate a typical course of events. In the flower experiment, the generated tension has led to a spread of general directedness towards the goal, encompassing all objects in the environment in the fashion described earlier. This directedness is considerably intensified by the spatial restriction inherent in the experiment, the subject's seclusion and confinement. (Not infrequently, the subjects complain about being imprisoned.) Under these conditions, the few objects that are close to the subject, who is virtually inside a prison, acquire an even stronger positively compulsive relationship to the experiment. Consequently, the subject considers the significance of the second flower; he inquires about it, and, as has been already mentioned, receives a noncommittal answer. Thus, the second stand presents a disturbing unsolved enigma. Finally the subject acts just to put an end to the uneasy interval; with a sudden, decisive movement he grasps the flower on the near by stand.

Often, the experiment will then pursue its course as follows: the experimenter does not budge. Very quickly the subject realizes that, in spite of his temperamental action, nothing has changed in the experimental situation. He understands that it was a useless reaching for a useless object, that is to say, an object that is of no use as a tool for obtaining the original goal. Sometimes he would like to retract his action; occasionally, he even puts the flower back on the stand.

The subject, then, is not at all satisfied with reaching the substitute goal; as a rule, he is dissatisfied. (Though substitute actions do not result in anger.) Attainment of the substitute goal never brings the relief and relaxation of tension that normally characterize reaching a goal. Even momentary satisfaction is not always apparent, even in cases where the substitution evidently marked the termination of a prolonged conflict.

Satisfaction with genuine substitution is observable in cases where the substitute action is an act of rebellion against the experimenter, or represents a kind of coy teasing of the experimenter. In any case, the subject's behavior makes it eminently clear that with respect to the main goal, the substitute action does not bring a relaxation of tension in its wake.

This fact, too, indicates a considerable dynamic distinction between the system of tensions that generates the substitute action and the system geared to the main goal. It is true that, in the last resort, the tension towards the substitute goal was also generated by pressure towards the original goal. However, in the very cases which end in substitutions, the tension towards the substitute goal seems to have become comparatively independent.

In conclusion, it should be stressed once again that in genuine substitution the events are akin to unrealistic attempts at solution. They possess the character of direct wish fulfillment inherent in actions outside the sphere of reality. Conversely, fantasy solutions always to a degree present the characteristics of substitution. Both processes have in common the fact that they are generated by pressure towards the real goal, while the action does not really move in that direction.

VI. BARRIERS AND THEIR EFFECT ON THE GOAL VECTOR

Collision with the Inner Barrier

As we have seen, the inner barrier develops in the attempt to reach the goal.

Working towards the goal, after some time the subject notices he is not getting anywhere. He has the experience of walking a treadmill and says so. He asks himself whether the difficulty barrier can be overcome or whether the task is insoluble.

If the barrier is felt as a surmountable difficulty, contact with it assumes the character of a fight with the barrier, or of running alongside it in search of an opening. Both are identical with attempts at solution.

If a stage is reached when the subject experiences the barrier as insurmountable, this leads to occurrences which we will discuss in some detail. These are the situations in which the difficulties acquire most distinctly the character of a barrier.

At times, soon after the beginning of the experiment the remark, "There is no solution" is made in an unmistakably definite tone. Yet immediately afterward, without expecting a reaction from the experimenter, the subject resumes his efforts at the task. Such a remark about the task's impossibility can be an exaggerated expression of a sudden collision with the inner barrier, which, however, has only a momentary impact and remains without deeper effect on the total course of events.

The lingering by the barrier may also last longer. The subject may embark on systematic considerations, or may stop because of doubt about the possibility of a solution.

Usually a full conviction of the task's impossibility does not last long. It quickly gives way to doubt again. Rarely does a subject become convinced with finality of the impossibility of a solution. Yet, for a while, he may come back time and again to the assertion, "There is no solution."

If the subject regards the task as insoluble for a period of time, it can mean for him one of two things: either he believes that the task is objectively insoluble, or he considers it beyond his own personal abilities. (It is an interesting problem under what circumstances the subject takes upon himself the blame for failure, and under what conditions he holds the objective situation responsible.)

Consequences of collision with the inner barrier. The situation of the subject, when he stands in doubt in front of the barrier, must be called labile. Such a labile state of doubt becomes, in the long run, intolerable. And, indeed, it does not last long. Often, a mild stimulation by the experimenter,—sometimes the simple statement, "There is a solution"—is sufficient to prod the subject into returning to his task.

Actions that occur after collision with the barrier are: *a)* an attempt to go out of the field completely; or *b)* giving up the belief in the impossibility of the task and making fresh efforts at solution.

The attempt to go out of the field can be observed above all when the collision with the barrier has "hurt" the subject. We will later analyze this action, which in our experiments usually ended with a return to the field of the task.

As for the return to efforts at solution: Logically the conviction that the barrier is insurmountable should cause the subject to permanently give up his endeavors. In reality, all the subject returned to the task again and again, as a rule almost immediately after proclaiming its impossibility. The reasons for these surprising returns vary. They depend on the motivations that formed the basis of the subject's efforts.

If the subject is guided by ambition, he usually experiences the distress of getting stuck as a deficiency in his own capabilities, just as he would ascribe a success to his own powers. In either case, ambition spurs the subject on. Ambitious persons in collision with the barrier are only tied more closely to the task. This is why ambitious persons try each time to solve the task with renewed vigor.

However, the same ambitious subjects develop phases of determined attempts at escape, because of their embarrassment with the total situation. Cases occur in which ambitious subjects want to give up the search for a solution after the first failure. They would rather suffer a minor defeat than a major one.

In the rare cases in which an ambitious subject considers the barrier an objective impossibility, the experimenter can easily change that interpretation and shift the blame onto the subject's inadequacy. The simple statement, "There is a solution," made by the experimenter is sufficient. The subject then returns immediately to the task.

If the subject is motivated in his efforts by interest in the task, it is more likely that he will realize the objective impossibility, since from the start he is less inclined to personal interpretations. This makes it easier for him to break away from the task. A subject with a detached point of view often looks upon his own inability as an objective fact. He does not feel hurt or irritated. To a certain degree, he sees himself as an instrument for reaching the goal, as part of the situation. He acknowledges the inadequacy of his performance as an objective reason for ending the task situation.

The logical consequence for a subject who realizes the impossibility of the task would be a tendency to go out of the field. Nonetheless, the simple statement, "There is a solution," made by the experimenter, is enough to keep even these subjects inside the experimental field. Since the subject does not feel personally offended, the total situation is without much tension; new, if half-hearted, efforts are then made.

Some pages back we mentioned that it is not always interest or ambition that makes the subject strive toward the goal; it can also be a willingness to oblige the experimenter. If this is the case, the subject tries to be a good subject, and failure is of minor significance. Solving the task, or not solving it, is not as important as the effort in itself. The subject's aim is to "carry out the experimenter's wishes obediently." Thus, just acting in the direction of those wishes gives the subject a measure of satisfaction. Even when he realizes the objective or subjective impossibility of the task, the tendency to leave is not very strong. Seeing that his efforts are important to the experimenter, at least that is what the experimenter lets him believe, the subject goes on trying. In such cases, the efforts are not especially intense, but they are persistent.

On the whole, we can observe in our experiments that if the subject is ambitious, collision with the impossibility barrier will lead to a strengthening of the hold of the experiment on the subject. In the presence of impersonal, objective interest, neither persisting nor wishing to escape is strikingly conspicuous. If the effort stems from the desire to oblige, the subject will stay with the task even if he is not really involved in it.

Repeated collision with the difficulty barrier may finally lead to a kind of exhaustion of all motivation. For a while, the ambitious subject does not show any ambition. The interested one loses his interest. The obliging subject tires of his compliance. After some time, however, new efforts will be made, either based on the same motive as before or on another one.

Change of motivation is not always caused by collision with the barrier. It may, for example, be caused by a remark of the experimenter's that triggers certain trains of thought. The experimenter may say, "Several other subjects have not solved the task in that time, either." It depends on the subject's source of energy whether he will stress the fact that other subjects did not solve the task either, in which case he feels reassured, or whether he focuses on "several" and "in that time," in which case he feels anxious.

Firmness of the Outer Barrier

After frequently renewed futile attempts, every serious endeavor towards the goal may finally cease. Then the subject begins to work at the task with minimal intensity in a merely formal way, or he leaves the field for a while. Yet, he does not succeed in leaving the field permanently, for in that attempt he runs up against the outer barrier.

In the following section we shall discuss the many forms and ways of movement in the direction of the outer barrier. Here, we will only examine why the subject hardly ever breaks through the outer barrier, but reverts to the task field after colliding with it. What is the reason for the extraordinary firmness of the outer barrier, a firmness which keeps the subject within the task field in spite of his manifest tendency to go out of the field? The obvious explanation is to hold the experimenter's prohibition responsible for the firmness. But, as a rule, no special prohibition is needed. The subject remains in the task field of his own accord, or after trying to leave, he returns to the task voluntarily.

Of a number of factors responsible for this remarkable behavior, we shall name only the following:

1. The subject has declared his willingness to participate in the experiment. His willingness is usually connected with basic regions of his life. There may be the "professional obligation" of a psychology student, or perhaps the subject has undertaken the experiment as a service to serious research. Although the task in front of the subject is only an experimental task, he experiences leaving this task as a neglect of duty. The duty jeopardized by breaking through the outer barrier is no mere experimental matter, but concerns the subject's whole way of life. It is this fact that constitutes one of the essential causes of the dynamic solidity of the outer barrier.

2. At first, failure of the subject in front of the task is just an experimental failure. Its degree of importance, compared to serious failures in ordinary life, is not very high. (Actually, as long as the subject stays completely inside the task field, the task is important to him. Its comparatively low degree of importance becomes apparent to the subject only when he is on the brink of going out of the field.)

If the pain of failure should make the subject go out of the field, it would mean that he took the experimental mortification so seriously that he had to flee in earnest. The subject would not like to take this painful situation seriously; even less would he like to show his distress to the experimenter. So he remains in the task field as long as he can stand the mortification.

Breaking through the barrier, which promises to free the subject from the embarrassment of hopeless endeavor, would at the same time create increased embarrassment: tearing down the outer barrier destroys the boundaries between the experiment and ordinary life. The subject would leave the experimental situation, but at the cost of establishing a connection between his painful incompetence and his general lifespace.

The subject, consequently, refrains from breaking through the barrier even without an explicit prohibition by the experimenter. In most cases, the subject waits until the experimenter breaks off the experiment of her own accord.

Hope

Trying to accomplish his task, the subject has continually run into the difficulty barrier before the goal, the inner barrier, and has finally given up his belief in the solubility of the task, or at least his belief in his own ability to solve it. The inner barrier has acquired the character of being insurmountable. Now, the forces of repulsion gain dominance. They produce an attempt to go out of the field.

However, the outer barrier also proves too strong. For better or for worse the subject returns to the task field. Whereupon, not infrequently, work at the task assumes a different character. The attack against the inner barrier is now not so much an effort to solve the problem as an urge to get out of the field, no matter by what means. The solution of the task means an opened way to freedom; if the problem is solved, the experiment will be terminated, and the subject rescued from his distressing situation.

The more painful the total situation, the more clearly the subject will realize that the inner barrier forms only part of a barrier that surrounds him on all sides. The subject, after colliding with the outer barrier, returns with comparative ease to action in the direction of the task. The unification of the inner and outer barriers is probably responsible for this phenomenon to a large degree.

In its role as an outer barrier, the barrier in the direction of the goal even seems to have certain advantages for the subject. He cannot hope to overcome the rest of the outer barrier, especially if it is connected with his sense of duty, by active endeavor. In that respect he can only give in, or risk a violent breakthrough with all its unpleasant consequences. (The breakthrough almost unavoidably carries the embarrassing failure over into life.) In the direction of the goal, however, the subject can at least try to find a painless way out of the distressing situation by means of active endeavor; he can do something; he can give scope to his restlessness.

Even such active initiative in the direction of the inner barrier is undertaken on the basis of a minimal hope that the problem can be solved. The existence of hope is in no way a purely intellectual matter. Even when the subject has already logically proved to the experimenter that the task is insoluble, nonetheless, in a surprisingly short time, he will revive hope that some way out will be found. Like a drowning man catching at a straw, the subject clings to every possibility, be it ever so vague. The stronger the urge of the subject to reach the goal, the less is the real foundation needed for the emergence of hope, in comparison to a sober evaluation of the given circumstances. The basis needed for hope diminishes as the rate of tension felt by the subject increases. (We find these facts confirmed in daily life: years may pass after a mother has heard of her son's inexplicable disappearance—and *still* she hopes for his return.)

Vacillation (pendulum swing). The oscillation between attempts at solution and attempts to go out of the field is one of the most striking phenomena in all our experiments. It usually starts at an early stage and continues more or less conspicuously through the entire length of each experiment.

The oscillation is a consequence of the fact that the field is dominated by almost equally strong vectors, which are pointed in opposite directions. It reveals clearly that the situation is one of conflict (3).

The antagonistic field forces intensify the existing tension and may lead to outbursts of affect. Before that occurs, however, the conflict situation will manifest itself in the behavior of the subject who follows, in turn, now one and now the other of the two opposite vectors. This back-and-forth pendulum motion is most marked when the behavior in the conflict situation lacks self-control.

VII. GOING OUT OF THE FIELD

Being out of the field without breaking through the outer barrier

We have elaborated upon the fact that the attempt to leave the painful field through the outer barrier is nearly always abortive. This seems to be contradicted by certain occurrences. Often the subject manages to free himself, at least temporarily, from the task and from the painful situation inside the task field—that is, he changes over to another field for a while by occupying himself with other things.

In ring throwing, for example, the subject listens to the various sounds made by the rings when knocked against something. Or, in the flower experiment, he pulls a sheet of stationery from his briefcase and starts to write a private letter. He asks whether the illustrated magazine on the table is the current issue and checks on it when the experimenter gives an evasive answer. The subject considers how to meet a friend after the end of the experiment, and so on and so forth.

The length of time during which the subject slips away from the task varies, but it cannot be doubted that, for a while, he has managed to really remove himself from the task field.

How can the subject leave the task field without breaking through the surrounding barrier? It is characteristic of all the cases of leaving the field scrutinized here that the subject does not leave the experimental field bodily. In the flower experiment, for instance, he remains in the square of laths, even though his thoughts are far away.

It would be misleading to identify the cases discussed here with the transitions to pure thought-operations or fantastic imaginations characteristic of unreal solutions. It is true that going out of the field often takes the form of thinking. This does not constitute a direct or indirect effort at solution; rather, it is a genuine occupation with something different. Above all, going out of the field not only takes the form of mental, but also of physical action—letter writing or reading. Both inner mental and outer physical being out of the field can thus be accomplished without the subject crossing the outer barrier.

In the topology of the situation in question, this could be done only if the subject seeks out or happens upon a region inside the experimental field which qualitatively does not belong to the task field. We shall call such a region, a special region inside the field. It is shown in Figure II.

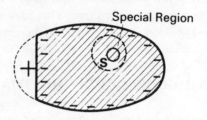

FIGURE II. Representation of Special Regions.

Is such an interpretation really correct? Does not the occupation with other things imply that the subject is, for the moment, situated outside the outer barrier? A more thorough analysis of our experiments confirms that the subject has left the task field, but is still situated inside the outer barrier.

Transition to being out of the field occurs without any experience of collision with the outer barrier. This is most easily understandable when being out of the field is a thing of the mind. As we have seen, there are no definite barriers in the unreal zone; the subject can slip easily into unrelated thoughts. In the zone of unreality, he then is outside the unreal outer barrier (See Figure 12).

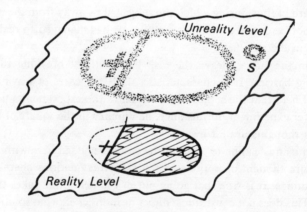

FIGURE 12. Escaping the Field on the Level of Unreality.

At the same time, on the reality level, he remains inside the outer barrier. This finds manifest expression in his bodily fixation in the experimental field.

The physical forms of being out of the field are possible because the experimenter is bound to leave a certain margin of mobility for the subject inside the experimental field. The subject can use this margin to mark off the region inside the task field which does not belong to the task. By means of certain prohibitions, the experimenter can narrow down the margin of freedom to a degree, but he cannot eliminate it altogether. We carried out a number of experiments, trying to restrict free mobility. We forbade the subject to rise from his chair, to do anything but work on the task, and so forth. A complete elimination of the margin of mobility was not practicable, because even intensive occupation of the subject cannot prevent a certain margin of freedom for eyes and hands. Transition to a special region inside the reality level of the task field can occur without the subject having to break through a barrier. The boundary between task field and special field is easily passed by the subject; as a rule it is not even marked clearly.

The subject's state during his being out of the field also shows that in a certain sense he is still situated inside the outer barrier. Even when the subject has turned to another occupation, or is dreaming passively, a constraint, a restriction of his mobility, is manifest. The constraint is spatial: the subject cannot go wherever he wants (as he would, once outside the barrier). It is also temporal: the subject feels obliged not to let his thoughts wander for too long, and after a while he regularly returns to the proper task field. Constraint is also experienced subjectively: although the subject may read the illustrated magazine, he is at the same time aware of the fact that he really is in an experiment and can expect an instruction by the experimenter any moment. Even while being out of the field, the subject often feels restricted.

Ways of Going Out Of The Field

If we try to survey the ways of going out of the field, without making a distinction between actions which are in the direction of the outer barrier and actions which are a slipping into a special field inside the task field, we can distinguish momentary, temporary, and permanent being out of the field. Furthermore, there are cases of abortive going out of the field, which can be defined as attempts to leave it.

Attempts to go out of the field. One subject suggests to the experimenter, "Let's break it up, let's stop it!" He describes his motivation: "When it's no fun, when you don't feel like it, you know you're through." A second subject asks, "How long are you going to carry on? I beg to observe that I'm hungry. You let me go the last time then." A third subject says, "I should not like to bore you, nor myself either!"

In all these cases, the subjects suggest more or less explicitly that the experiment should be broken off. They do not act on their own; they only "make a suggestion." The subjects nonetheless acknowledge their position as subjects. They do not completely conform, however; they look for a way out. Here we have an unequivocal attempt to leave the experimental field, which means action in the direction of the outer barrier.

Much less frequently our experiments produced attempts at transition into a special region within the task field. The subject asks, for example, "May I read the paper?" In contrast to attempts in the direction of the outer barrier, these actions do not take the form of suggestions, but rather of questions. The subject wants to test what is permissible. He would like to know whether an activity, such as newspaper reading, certainly on the fringe of legitimate action, is located inside or outside the region of free choice allotted to him. (See Figures 13a and b.) If the experimenter's answer shows that the activity in question is still located on this side of, and not beyond, the barrier, the subject can use it as a special region. This is proof that the outer barrier is not completely fixed.

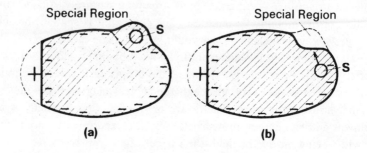

FIGURE 13. Special Regions Internal (a) and External (b) to Barrier.

Momentary being out of the field. Between two efforts at the task, it suddenly occurs to a subject that he did not call Mr. X to whom he wants to speak over the telephone; another subject remembers she has forgotten to get something on a shopping list. Another subject is sitting on the chair working at the task; he is staring at the floor and notices a spot that distracts him for a moment. In these cases, the subject turns away from the task just for a moment and then returns to work on it immediately.

Temporary being out of the field. In the flower experiment, a subject may study the rings which he has picked up first because he wanted to use them as tools for solving the task. He observes their smoothness and roundness. He turns them around in his hands, plays with them, makes them spin on the floor like a top. Or a subject forgets the existence of the task for a while, thinking instead about some personal concern of his own. Another subject carefully examines the objects lying on a nearby chair. He picks up a copy of *Life* to read for a while. A different subject starts a conversations with the experimenter; he asks whether the experimenter was at a certain lecture.

Temporary being out of the field takes the form here of active engagement in alien matters. It can also happen that the subject will be temporarily out of the field, not doing anything. The subjects describe this state as "drowsing." It means a lessening of endeavor to the point of complete passivity. For a time, the subject becomes "tired," "sleepy," "indifferent."

Permanent being out of the field. A permanent being out of the field, a final breaking off without return to the experiment, happened only once. The subject had paved his way to freedom in advance by setting a definite deadline, at which time he would break off the experiment—"I'm leaving at 1:15!" He later postponed that deadline a few times. (We shall speak later of cases of affective breakthroughs that are actions of protest against the experimenter, yet actually do not terminate the experiment.)

Neither mental going out of the field, nor transition to a special region inside the task field will enable the subject to leave the field permanently.

Genesis of the Various Kinds of Being Out Of The Field

Up to now, we have classified the kinds of going out of the field according to the exterior criteria of the duration and success of the action. Yet their significance goes deeper.

From the start, it is noticeable that the futile attempts to go out of the field are nearly always directed towards the outer barrier. Momentary and temporary going out of the field, however, moved regularly in the direction of a special region within the task field. Transition into the special region is usually not preceded by any attempt.

The difference in the events which occur in going out of the field in the direction of the outer barrier compared with the special region is based on the dynamic difference between the boundaries. As mentioned before, the task field is separated from the free environment by a barrier. The special region, however, is as a rule not separated from the task field by such a barrier. The road into it is open, as in the case of ring spinning, so that usually the subject is not even aware of the boundary zone. This explains the absence of special, subjectively experienced attempts in the direction of the special region: a vector in that direction immediately leads to actual transition.

The boundary of the environment is a genuine barrier. That is why real attempts are made in that direction. They are characterized by serious endeavors to surmount a difficulty barrier. They constitute a search for a way out, comparable to the efforts at task solving, at surmounting the inner barrier.

The degree of tension in the situation plays an essential part in the genesis of the going out of the field in either direction. Yet, since the special region in the task field is not isolated by a definite barrier, a subject lapses in its direction frequently without even subjectively realizing the painfulness of the task field.

One dynamic effect of the lack of a barrier between the task field and the special region is that, in the long run, the tension in the task field extends to the special region. Actually the subjects do not find peace in the special region. When a subject catches himself outside the proper task field, he often returns to the task remorsefully, as it were.

We have distinguished two kinds of being in the special region: momentary and temporary. But here, too, not only temporal but also qualitative differences are to be found.

By momentary being out of the field, we mean the cases in which absence from the task is so brief or insignificant that the total course of the experiment is hardly disrupted. It is dynamically characteristic of this kind of being out of the field that the subject cannot help its occurring. As a rule, it happens suddenly and unexpectedly.

The occurrence of momentary being out of the field is favored by the fact that during the experiment the subject is in a state of general readiness for new ideas, and of restlessness. This state is good soil for the growth of tension systems which existed already, prior to the experiment, in the form of unfinished actions (4) and intentions (5). It also helps small, unimportant positive valences to attract attention and provide distractions.

Temporary being out of the field can develop from the momentary situation. However, it frequently does not start with sudden ideas, but rather with a gradual slipping away from work at the task. It should be noted that sometimes temporary being out of the field occurs officially. Such a temporary being out of the field, suggested by the subject, is called a *recess*. The subject wants to relax a little. On grounds of fatigue, satiation, or the pretext of mustering new forces, he asks for an interruption. The subject experiences this request as completely fair; he does not think that he is asking for anything forbidden. If the subject were to ask not for a temporary break, but rather for a final termination, such a request would profoundly change the character of the event.

Limits of the Subject's Mobility

We have, so far, discussed the topology of the situation; the subject's actions in the direction of the task goal; the actions produced indirectly by the vector towards the task goal (fantastic and unrealistic solutions); the actions in the direction of the outer barrier; and being out of the field in a special region inside the task field. If we survey the various possibilities regarding the location of the subject, and the direction of his activity, the result is as follows:

Location. The subject may be: in the real task field; in a special field within the task field; in the region of unreality either inside the unreal task field or outside of it. Theoretically, a fourth location, outside the real task field, could be postulated. For the reasons given above it is a rare occurence experimentally. However, many subjects mentioned it in their self-observations directly following the experiment.

Direction of activity. There are different directions of action for each location. If the subject is situated in the real task field, his actions can be directed towards the task goal (efforts at solution); or his activity can lead away from the task either in the direction of the outer barrier (suggestions to break off the experiment), or in the direction of a special region inside the task field (requests for permission to enter such region); or he can move away from the reality to the unreality level.

Dynamically, these actions can be triggered by the positive valence of the goal, or by a negative valence in the opposite direction. (Action in the direction of the task goal).

If the subject is situated in the special region within the task field, he can engage in activities inside that special region, or try to return into the task field.

If the subject is situated on the unreality level, his activity can either take a direction toward the (unreal) task goal (fantasy solutions); or take a direction towards the (unreal) outer barrier (temporary going out of the field); or he can try to return onto the reality level. In these cases as well, the determinant may be a positive or a negative vector.

The three locations and the various actions originating from each of them delineate the circumference of the area of free mobility available to the subjects in our experimental arrangements.

The subject is not immediately aware of the boundaries of this area, and the limitations imposed by the boundaries on the direction of his actions. What was said earlier about the gradual development of the barrier between the subject and the task goal holds true as well for the extension of the region of free movement and its limitations.

When the subject enters the experiment, his situation is still quite open; he does not yet know its boundaries, its difficulties and its pitfalls; moreover, he does not yet feel surrounded by a barrier. The inner and outer barriers develop later in due course. But even then, the subject experiences his mobility as unlimited, at least in one direction: the direction of unreality.

In addition, even the outer barrier is not completely fixed and firm from the outset; rather, it is changeable to a certain degree. On occasion, even a single playful spinning of the rings seems to the subject to be a forbidden activity, outside the barrier. On other occasions, even prolonged fooling around with the rings does not give the subject a feeling of having come in contact with the barrier of the forbidden area.

Sometimes, the subject carries on a lengthy conversation with the experimenter without feeling that he has left the region of the task field. At other times, he will not ask a second question because the first one gives him a feeling of collision with the forbidding barrier. Thus, even on the reality level, the margin of permissible action varies in scope from one subject to the other; and for the same subject, it varies at different moments in time.

On the whole, the course of the experiments tends to demonstrate that the subject, on the one hand, constantly hits upon new, thus far unrealized, possibilities of motion. On the other hand, it becomes more and more evident that none of the actions opens a way to freedom.

In trying to escape to the unreality level or into a special field, the subject meets with similar experiences. He has given free rein to his mind, has thought about things that are totally unconnected with the task, in fact, he has gone out of the field for a period of time. Sooner or later, however, he will realize that such being out of the field is fundamentally unreal; his body remains tied to the experimental field.

He fares no better when some involuntary and compulsive substitute action gives him a feeling of freedom for a moment, only to push him back immediately into a greater resentment of his futile action and his imprisonment in the task field.

Time and again, different actions seem to open up new regions of mobility for the subject. Each time, they end up in the experience that that mobility, too, is limited, and that the field of mobility is not an open but a closed one.

The freedom gained by the subject because the outer barrier is transposable, allowing him to move into the special region or into unreality, has the drawback that it can provide only very shortterm relief. Going out of the field during the experiment never leads the subject to freedom; instead, it makes him feel more forcibly the limitations upon his freedom, and throws him back into the task field each time.

The solidity of the impassable barrier heightens the tension. With renewed energy, the subject turns to the only place in the barrier that seems surmountable—the inner barrier—so that he may attain freedom by solving the problem. Excited and emotionally charged, the subject tries again for a solution, and then goes out of the field again. The first instance of being out of the field frees the subject from his situation of failure only temporarily. After a certain time, the barrier is as solidly impassable as ever, and the ensuing failure of goal-directed action is even more painful in its effect. The tension keeps mounting due to many factors: the failures of efforts at the task; the solidity of the barrier during attempts to cross it; the unreality of escape while being out of the field; the transition from unlimited freedom to limited freedom. Barriers wherever the subject turns. Every action in the field leads to them. "You want to jump out of your skin!" Such is the strange interaction between tension and imprisonment, between insecurity and uncertainty in the situation, the restless sequence of violent actions in ambiguous but basically identical opposite directions. All these lead up to the genuine affect of anger, and may already be part and parcel of it.

VIII. SUBJECT AND EXPERIMENTER

The Relationship Between Experimenter and Subject

As mentioned before, the experimenter's presence strongly influences the course of the experiment. Her importance varies for different subjects, and changes during the course of an experiment. The experimenter's significance for the subject may be of different kinds: 1. She may be the driving force motivating the efforts at solution; the task is undertaken "to oblige her." 2. She is in the position of a fellow person who is better at the task than the subject. 3. She sets the task goal, but also bars the access to it; she is, therefore, an inner barrier. 4. She is also a barrier that surrounds the field, preventing escape. 5. She is a possible tool. 6. She is a person outside the task field who can be used to get out of the field. 7. She is an annoying stumbling-block, a changeable and provoking creature who actively interferes with the course of the experiment and who turns out to be an enemy.

The experiment proper is preceded by a situation that is essentially characterized by a social relationship between the subject and the experimenter. If, for example, the subject is a student who has volunteered in answer to the experimenter's direct invitation, then both subject and experimenter are joined in a collegial atmosphere of semiscientific, semisocial mutual obligation. The over-all character of the starting situation differs with different subjects. Students specializing in psychology, for example, who have already been experimenters themselves, experience a sense of cooperation with the experimenter more strongly than others. With other subjects, curiosity often plays an important motivating role.

In any case, the situation at the start of the experiment, before the introduction of the experimental task, must be characterized as a social interrelation of two persons without any explicit subordination of one to the other. This is represented in Figure 14.

Once the instructions are given, the situation changes. The objective task takes predominance. The topology and the field forces develop, as described

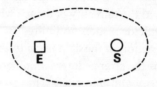

FIGURE 14. Initial Relationship of Experimenter and Subject.

in the preceding sections. The experimenter disappears temporarily behind the objective situation, and for a time she may, psychologically speaking, be practically nonexistent.

That disappearance, however, is neither final nor lasting. Soon the experimenter will reappear for shorter or longer periods, although in a different psychological role.

While the subject is working on a solution in the flower experiment, the presence of a better informed person, as the experimenter is *ipso facto* supposed to be, can gain essential significance. The relation with the experimenter can then assume the form of a social relationship to a fellowman, and can lead to the subject's asking for help.

The presence of a better informed person gains particular significance as soon as the subject begins to doubt the possibility of a solution. The task situation in the later stages is maintained mainly by the experimenter's insistence that there is a solution. In the affective states discussed earlier, when hope is very important, this flat statement by the experimenter plays a decisive part. For the subject, the experimenter's thesis becomes a fact, because the experimenter is in a position where she should know. (If the subject answers the experimenter by saying: "That's a lie!" the accusation is more an expression of anger against the experimenter than an assertion of real disbelief.)

The superior knowledge of the experimenter has, moreover, been proved to the subject by the fact that he eventually found the first two solutions, which at first he did not believe in either. Further proof lies in the calm, unobtrusive, almost casual assurance with which the experimenter confirms the possibility of a third solution, whenever asked.

Characteristically, it also matters to subjects whether the experimenter knows best because of her information about the task, or because of her superior abilities. The subjects test the cleverness and the skills of the experimenter. In ring throwing, for example, many subjects suggest to the experimenter that she should first demonstrate what she can do. In the flower experiment, they ask whether the experimenter devised the experimental arrangement herself, or whether it was the director of the study, the professor himself, who did it. One subject submitted a complicated puzzle to the experimenter, just to test how smart she was.

As a rule, the subject expects the experimenter to be superior to himself. The eminent position of the experimenter in the experimental situation, the fact that she conducts it, seems to endow her not only with more social power, but also with more abilities and omniscience than the subject. Comparable situational conditions often make a child believe, for example, that his father can do anything; similarly, in political life people will credit members of the government with great abilities.

The fact that the experimenter is smarter than the subject causes the subject to endeavor to reach the level on which the experimenter is situated; this puts the subject in a position which can be described as one of inferiority. Such a situation is not always unpleasant. However, in our experiments, the superior partner is just sitting there, observing the efforts of the subject without lifting a finger. She remains a spectator when she could be a help, and this can create a conflict between the subject and the experimenter. The experimenter is felt to be an observing nuisance, and the subject will reproach her. "You are just nodding your head, pleased to get results"—that is, you are profiting egotistically from other people's distress.

Apart from the general personal relationship, the existence of more or less clearly marked relations between the special topology of the task situation and the experimenter gradually becomes apparent. To begin with, it becomes clear that the type and solidity of the inner barrier depend fundamentally on the experimenter. The subject asks the experimenter about the exact conditions of the task. For the subject, the experimenter's replies have significance which is more than an objective explanation; very soon the replies acquire the character of permission or refusal. Whether the subject can pursue the course towards the goal that she suggested does not only depend on the nature of the task, but also on the experimenter's acquiescence. The experimenter's severe strictness is accentuated by her repeated rejection of the subject's suggestions for a solution.

The annoyance of the rejection is increased because it always takes the same form. The experimenter says, "That is only a variation of your previous solution"; or merely, "Forbidden"—which is even more annoying. This "Forbidden" squashes the subject's proposals, and moreover it accentuates the dependance of the inner barrier on the experimenter.

Similarly, the type and the solidity of the outer barrier are closely connected with the experimenter. In trying definitely to go out of the field, the subject resents the experimenter as an obstacle. Hence he asks frequently; "How long do you want to go on with this experiment?" The subject's experience of collision with the outer barrier is often that it would be in the experimenter's power to remove this solid obstacle. In such cases, the subject appeals directly to the experimenter. "Break it off!"; or he tries in a devious way to get the experimenter to agree with this.

When the subject temporarily retires into a special region inside the task field, the experimenter also plays an important role. We have seen that transition into a special region, for instance, playful handling of the rings, is open to the subject and is frequently achieved unnoticed by the subject. Return to the task field, however, is often influenced by the experimenter's presence. The experimenter may ask the occupied subject, "Well, what about the solution?" Or the subject himself becomes aware of the silently watching experimenter, and he returns penitently.

The experimenter may act still another part in the task field: she may be an objective tool, a helpful instrument for reaching the task goal. In the flower experiment, the subject may say, "Give me your hand, I shall lean on you," or he asks her, "Maybe the solution is that you must hand me the flower?" Here, the directedness of the objects towards the goal also includes the experimenter.

Similarly, the experimenter can become a helpful instrument for the subject in his attempts to go out of the field. With the tendency to go out of the field, the corresponding directedness of all objects can make the subject conscious of the experimenter's position outside the task field. The subject may, for instance, start a conversation with the experimenter, talking about the theater, the weather, or some other extraneous topic. In this way, he can make use of the experimenter in order to leave the task field for a while.

Finally, the experimenter can assume the position of an anger-provoking element, an enemy. This development will be understood when we proceed to describe the transformation of the total situation as it evolves from the relationship discussed above between the subject and the experimenter.

Genesis and Topology of the Situation of Struggle

The experiment proper was preceded by a situation dominated by the social relationship between the subject and experimenter, as shown in Figure 14. This was replaced by an objectively oriented task situation, which in turn gradually developed into a situation with outer and inner barriers and with certain vectors—in short, with a definite topology on both the reality and the unreality levels, as (represented in Figure 10.).

During the evolution of this topology, there are, however, moments when the subject-experimenter relation as a social relation returns to the foreground. (In some sets of experiments, this transformation appears as a gradual development, in others as an irregular changeover.) This reason for this transformation is the more and more clearly emerging fact that not only one particular property of the objective task situation but, in the last analysis, *all* the properties depend on the experimenter's will. The task that dominates the situation has been set for the subject by the experimenter. It is rather surprising that the immediate connection between the task and the experimenter's will never causes the subject to experience the task as an arbitrary, personal device of the experimenter's; instead, he accepts the task as an established objective situation. He begins to feel his dependence on the experimenter's will only when he runs into difficulties, on collision with the solid barrier. The collision, due to the close links between the task goal and the barrier, also brings home the subordination of the goal to the experimenter's will. What is true of the inner barrier soon becomes equally apparent in the case of the outer barrier. It becomes more and more evident that even the special region inside the task field, and the unreality level to which the subject escapes when temporarily going out of the field are not safe from the intrusion of the experimenter; the experimenter can easily recall the subject to the task field at any moment.

All actions, in whatever direction, bring the subject in contact with the experimenter. The subject need not be explicitly conscious of the connection between the goal, the inner and outer barriers, and the experimenter; he just feels himself to be more and more in the experimenter's power field.

Actually, the given situation that underlies the field forces which act on the subject within the experimenter does not consist of natural valences and barriers that would function in the same way outside the experimental situation. The valences of the experiment are derived or induced (6). They are based on

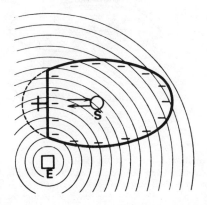

FIGURE 15. Representation of the Power Field of the Experimenter.

the fact that the experimenter, as a consequence of her powerful position, has created a well-defined, special field. Dynamically speaking, a field of forces originating with the experimenter has given certain valences to certain objects in the psychological environment of the subject—the flower or the bottle—and has induced a prohibitive character in certain actions. Fundamentally, the whole topology of the situation turns out to be essentially determined by its location inside the power sphere of the experimenter. This is shown in Figure 15.

It is not possible to discuss at length here why we represent the existence of a power sphere as a psychological field or forces rather than ascribing a special valence to the experimenter. It is sufficient for our purpose to use for an illustration a homogenous field of forces spread uniformly in all directions, although, in fact, there is no such homogenous spreading.

When the subject experiences that the objective task field is subordinate to the experimenter's will, it can have important consequences for the actions of the subject. Apart from the possibility of overcoming the difficulties in an objective way, the subject then glimpses a second way out: destroy the field of forces responsible for the firmness of the barrier. For this second way, it is essential to break the experimenter's power over the situation. This means that, for the subject, the experimenter acquires the position of an enemy; the situation turns into a situation of struggle. It does not matter much by what means the struggle is carried on. What is essential for the subject is to handle the

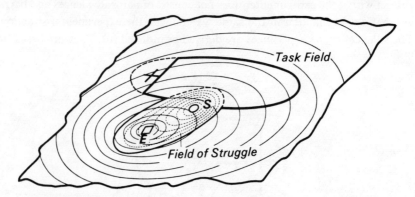

FIGURE 16. Representation of the Situation of Struggle.
    The outer barrier encloses the task-field as well as the field of struggle (catch and throw). In this respect, the field of struggle is equivalent to a 'special region inside the task-field' (figure 13a). Should the subject succeed in gaining the upper hand permanently, the whole task-field with its vectors and barriers would be destroyed in as much as they depend on the experimenter's power-field.

situation in such a way that it will not be dominated by the experimenter's field of forces, but by his own (7).

The result then, is a situation where subject and experimenter face each other as antagonists. The experimenter and the subject each dominate a social field of forces—shown in Figure 16. The original connection of this situation of struggle with the specific task can be almost completely lost in the process.

When the topology is transformed into that of a battlefield, sometimes it changes the whole basic structure of the situation. In other cases, it means only a temporary modification; or else the task situation may be overlaid by the situation of struggle.

The Struggle

Events occuring during the situation of struggle can differ greatly in kind. Their chronology, their sequence, and duration also vary considerably with different subjects.

The forms of the events in our experiments and their manner of development show clearly that struggle is an act of human interaction (8). It belongs to those situations that must be characterized as ones of social interaction. In our experiments, the struggle frequently emanates from specifically social actions of the subject. In a certain way, the emergence of a situation of struggle means resumption of the social situation as it was at the start of the experiment. The dynamic dependence of the task on the experimenter frequently leads first to a discussion, which may be initiated by the subject's asking a natural question about the exact conditions of the task. This creates a relationship between the experimenter and subject in which they face each other as equals. The result may be a free dialogue in which the topic of the experimental task may be abandoned.

It is true that such a conversation in which the subject really feels free is a rare occurrence. As a rule, if the subject starts to discuss something that is alien to the task, this is only a form of struggling with the experimenter, and is at the same time, a way to go out of the field.

Onset of Struggle. As a rule, genuine aggressive actions do not appear without preliminaries. When the subject feels his difficulties as coming intrinsically from the experimenter, the situation may be one of antagonism; however, the outbreak of hostility is sparked by a particular event.

With affective outbreaks, a special supplemental event is needed to change a situation of latent animosity into one of overt fighting. In our experiments, the supplemental events usually appear in the form of provocations by the experimenter.

Since our experiments are aimed at creating the affect of anger, the experimenter is apt to resort to provocations. The form of such provocations varies greatly, and is determined by the sensitive, vulnerable spots that the experimenter can find in the subject. In the ring experiment the provocation is carried out openly. After a while, the experimenter begins to interfere. She will intercept the rings thrown by the subject in midair, either by hand or by means of a stick; or she may rock the bottle back and forth, or put her hands on the bottle to prevent the rings from landing. The experimenter acts in this way when a sort of stagnation threatens, or when the task is already almost solved, or when the subject begins to show signs of anger. Such provocations nearly always result in fighting reactions on the part of the subject.

As a matter of fact, the experimenter can behave in such a way that a conversion of the objective situation into a personal struggle will be avoided. If she says, for example, without irony, "I am sorry, but I am not allowed to give you more detailed instructions," this will accentuate the impersonal, objective element in the situation. In that case, the subject will turn his attention to the task. By and large, such objectivization definitely counteracts the emotion of anger.

The few subjects who assume a hostile attitude towards the experimenter from the beginning will usually initiate a fight by reproaching the experimenter, even without provocation. The reproach may be half-joking, as with the subject who said, "You're jinxing the rings!" Subjects in a situation of struggle resent the experimenter's actions, even if she is only quietly sitting and reading, and consider them as mean, hostile activities. Then, such occurrences can have the effect of supplementary events.

The first provocation by the experimenter comes as a surprise to the subject. It may spark a brief outburst of rage, have the effect of a blow between the eyes. After that, the situation will change; the subject takes up the fight and carries it on with gusto, often giving the fight a decidedly playful tone. In ring throwing, for instance, the subject may try to seize a moment when the experimenter is not looking, suddenly throw at the other bottle, or only pretend to throw in order to fool the experimenter, and so forth. When the experimenter has intercepted the rings several times, the subject says, "All right, let's play," and starts throwing the rings purposely onto the experimenter's stick.

The conversion of the objective task situation into one of social fighting is usually received with pleasure by the subject, and not without reason. It releases the subject from his subordinate position as a subject. He gets out of the task field, is freed from his difficulties. At last, he enters a field in which he immediately occupies a more favorable position and has a better chance of success than in the task field. Thus, he engages in the struggle with fresh vigour, all the more so since this struggle often has a not-too-serious, playful aspect.

Different Kinds of Struggling. The struggle with the experimenter can be

carried on overtly or covertly. The subject may directly refuse to obey instructions. He does not go on throwing rings, and otherwise disobeys explicit
directives by the experimenter. A physical struggle may occur, such as the
subject's seizing the experimenter's hand when it interferes with the throwing.
The subject hurls abuse at the experimenter or threatens revenge: "Just come
to X department, and we'll needle you with electricity."

It suddenly occurred to one subject that he could turn the tables; instead
of trying, he could do nothing and keep the experimenter waiting. In another
case, when the experimenter intercepted the rings, the subject threw them to
her on purpose, teasing her. "All right, all right! I'll be glad to throw them
to you directly!" The subject ridicules the experimenter. He thumbs his nose
at her, or he picks up a substitute flower and fastens it with a sneer in the
experimenter's buttonhole. The struggle seems especially mean when it assumes the form of amiability. One subject observed that the experimenter was
cold. He asked her politely, "May I bring your coat?" In the prevailing
situation of struggle it was not exactly pleasant to the experimenter to see her
weak point discovered and her weakness catered to so courteously. It gave an
effect of pure irony.

Another form of struggling is defiance. In the flower experiment, for instance, the subject picked up the rings that were arranged outside the square
and put them away because they disturbed him. The experimenter restored the
disturbance; she deposited flowers in place of the rings. The subject collects
these, too. The experimenter goes on to deposit more flowers, later also other
objects, in the same places; the subject goes on picking them up. The subject
uses this activity, which theoretically could go on forever, in order to move
outside the task field and to gain the upper hand over the experimenter. Each
new removal has the character of a new fighting action: "Who will hold out
longer?"

Fight Actions and transformations of the field of struggle. In many cases, the
transition from work at the task to struggling against the experimenter has the
effect of expanding the experimental field. Suddenly it appears that, apart from
the task region and the previously explored special region, there are after all
more regions available within the experimental field—the picking up game,
throw and catch, and so on. A new region, such as throw and catch, has certain
objective properties; the objective properties of the new field are important as
a basis and as instruments for the struggle.

The subject's transition into the new field is the best way for him to pull out
of the experimenter's power field, and to build up on his own a field of struggle
which the experimenter cannot avoid. The experimenter is compelled to react
to the subject's challenge in such a way as to retain the upper hand. The means
she uses for this purpose are essentially the same as the subject's. Such a battle

can considerably exacerbate the anger situation. As a rule, the experimenter must try to prevent the fighting game in the new field from going on too long, for that would mean that the subject has succeeded in going out of the task field. She tries to force the subject back into the task field, preferably after suffering defeat. To be forced back, in itself, means a defeat. Inside the task field, the subject is subordinate again to the experimenter. For these reasons, the fight itself frequently has the character of a struggle for position.

If a fighting game seems to go on for too long, with the subject refusing to obey the experimenter's summons to the task, the experimenter will simply remind him, "You are a subject, after all." As a rule, such a reminder is effective.

It sometimes happens that the subject calls the experimenter back to her place. In ring throwing, for example, the subject may request the experimenter to pick up the rings that have dropped to the floor, for that is her assignment. Or, in a commanding way the subject says to the experimenter, who is already picking up the rings unasked, "Pick them up, pick them up! You even have to hand them to me!" The subject savors his momentary superiority.

If the situation of struggle becomes sufficiently accentuated, actions of the subject within the original task field can lead to a fight by objective means of the sort described. Just as action in the direction of the task goal may sometimes be nothing but flight out of the field, so an additional effort to find the solution may take on the character of an aggressive action against the experimenter. Finding the solution would mean a victory over the experimenter, and a destruction of the field dominated by the experimenter's forces.

As a rule, the struggle proceeds so that both the subject and the experimenter make use of the objective properties of the battle zone—for example, the rules of a fair catch-and-throw—for their own purposes.

The struggle is not always carried on in this objective form. It can also consist of flat disobedience on the part of the subject and flat commands on the part of the experimenter. (In the army, when any request for objective explanations is ruled out on principle, the term used is "direct order.") This form of fighting is dangerous for the experimenter because a direct order can easily provoke a sharp refusal to obey, a refusal against which the experimenter is essentially powerless. The subject, too, dislikes resorting to direct disobedience, because such a reaction nearly always has an affective character. To react emotionally, however, is in itself a kind of defeat. Disobedience occurs most frequently in connection with returning to the task field, yet in an acute fighting mood other commands may be rejected as well.

The situation of struggle, and the genesis of affect. The fact that the task situation may be converted into a field of social struggle between the subject and the experimenter is of essential significance for the generation of affect.

The stimulation of affective occurrences by the power struggle is based on several factors, some of which follow. We observed above how the counteraction of vectors induces an oscillation back and forth, and how this oscillation demonstrates to the subject the available margin of free mobility, while finally making him more conscious of his limitation, the restriction in his freedom. The subject realizes that in the end all his various single actions amount to the same thing. At first the possibility of a transition from the task field into new special regions of the field of struggle brings new leeway; however, this proves to be useless in the end, as long as the experimenter retains the upper hand. Thus, a new element of unrest enters the total situation, and new hopes are shattered. Task situation and the situation of struggle are fused, and prove to be, in the last resort, identical.

In discussing the importance of the struggle between the subject and the experimenter, it must not be forgotten that in the total course of the experimenter the struggles have only the character of episodes. On the whole, the situation of the subject is characterized by the task field whose development has been elaborated in the preceding chapters. The topology of that task field with its specific boundaries, conflicts, and tensions remains predominant. In general, the function of the fighting action is only that of an additional pressure which helps to bring the latent affect out into the open.

IX. EXPRESSIONS OF AFFECT

In the situation as analyzed above, the subject cannot manage to go out of the field. Collision with the barriers increases his insecurity or hopelessness. Finally, events occur which in everyday life are usually described as outbreaks of anger.

We will first present some examples of the expressions of affect in the narrow sense of the word; we will go on to group the different anger phenomena, and will finally discuss questions of intensity of affect. In order to facilitate later groupings, we have added to the examples a nomenclature of the events.*

Examples**

The following examples have been arranged in order of the progressive degree of affective intensity. It should be remembered that the respective affectsform only phases of the total course of events, and that those phases do not always occur at the end of the experiment.

*These descriptions are given in parentheses after each example—Editor.
** *In order to conserve space, I have included only three of the seven original examples. The other four examples, together with a listing of the various manifestations of affect, may be obtained from University Microfilms—Editor.*

Affective intensity often is manifested by gesture as well as speed and pitch of speech, that is, by facts that cannot be reproduced here, even though the nomenclature in the parentheses could only be unequivocally justified with their help.

Example I

Flower experiment; the subject is a male student. Subject: "You know, I would have given up already if I did not know that logical thinking alone is not enough in magic tricks. They are sometimes possible, even if logically they seem impossible." After a short interval, the subject suddenly says with energy: "You finish it! I can't find it." (Affective refusal in affective tones. At the same time challenging of experimenter.) Subject gesticulates angrily. Experimenter: "You will still find it." Subject does not answer, plays with rings, rattles them nervously. (Restlessness in mood and motions.) Paces back and forth restlessly, stops in front of flower, keeps rattling rings. Subject: "There just is no other solution." Goes on rattling nervously, (restlessness in mood and motions), then says, "I must sit down." (Affective exhaustion)

Example IV

Flower experiment: subject is a male student. Subject: "You are just sitting there, nodding your head, pleased as Punch to get results." (The subject points out that the experimenter's correct behavior, her response to the subject, is a lie, really serving quite a different purpose. This reproach is based on affect; in other experiments, the subject would accept such behavior on the experimenter's part without objection.) Subject picks up a cleft stick that is lying on a nearby chair. He says, "That would do fine as a pincer to pinch the flower. I'm really getting wild!" (This example might seem to be less affectively charged than the preceding ones. One could almost believe that the pincer suggestion was an attempt at solution. The concluding words, however, reveal its affective content, visible earlier in posture and tone of voice. In reality, the desire to catch the flower with a pincer expresses a destructive tendency, a wish to harm the irritating object.)

Example VI

Flower experiment; the subject is a female student. This experiment ended with the subject's rushing out, although before that occurrence she did not make an especially emotional impression. According to her own statement, she had been in an irritable mood even before the experiment. The experiment was the last straw.

The whole experiment did not last longer than about thirty minutes. The first ten minutes were taken up by efforts to find the third solution. (The subject had found the two possible solutions during a previous session). To start with, the subject is calm, only her voice sounds irritable. Also irritable is a remark concerning the rings that must not be used to seize the flower: "Then I'll just push the things aside," accompanied by a push with her foot against the laths.

The subject sits down, saying; "Now I'll sit down comfortably, just to laugh at you. I'll not take the least trouble. (Consciously exaggerated pose of being at ease.) Why does the experiment take so long?" Experimenter: "Experiments last so long because persons sit down, taking their time." Subject: "Are you going to conduct more experiments?" Experimenter: "I don't know." The experimenter leaves the room, the observer remains alone with the subject. Subject: "What are you writing down?" Observer: "Everything." After an interval, observer says, pointing to the task: "There is a solution." Subject: "Out of the question. (Energetic refusal.) I'm not that dumb." (Affective choice of words.) For two minutes the subject sits still, her expression serious, her eyes downcast. (Inhibition. Normally, the subject is a very lively person.) Observer: "Are you working on the solution?" Subject: "Not really, I consider it impossible. And when I consider something impossible, there is an end to it. Why are you stressing the possibility?" Observer: "Because there really is one." Subject: "Then it is a trick—either the flower has to be moved, or the stand. And if it is not found, what are you going to say?" Observer shrugs his shoulders. Subject: "You can keep me sitting here for as long as you like, I'll never get it." Subject sits still, as if in thought, sighs (sighing), sighs again after a little while. Experimenter returns to the room: "Well?" Subject: "Do, change to something else as soon as possible, I'm through with this." Experimenter: "What are you doing?" Subject: "Sitting and lazing. (Exaggerated calm on emotional basis.) There is still some suspense because you are telling me that it is possible. By myself, I'd do something else." After a brief interval, the subject begins to speak spontaneously: "What a serious face, I'm spoiling your mood. (Projects on the other person the unpleasantness she herself is feeling.) I shall sit here until one o'clock—I could do all kinds of things—no earthly reason why I should—do you expect me to describe something? I have experienced quite a lot, also thought of reading: reading the paper. Can't remember what." Experimenter remains unconcerned. Subject: "That expression of yours is quite intolerable. (An unessential circumstance is represented as the main reason for anger.) You could do something at least. I thought I was going to do nice things here, throw hoops, and so on. Now I am sitting here with nothing to do." (Complaints.) Short interval. The subject begins to push the laths on the floor around with her feet. She pushes one lath aside with her foot, making it look like unintentional by play.

Gradually, this comparatively quiet fooling around changes into excitement; (Excited fooling) the laths are scattered around (Affective action. Destruction of set up.) Experimenter laughs. Subject feels this laugh as clearly derisive. It acts as additional pressure (later we shall discuss the importance of additional pressure), and she flares up agitatedly: "I don't feel like laughing! It's no laughing matter to me!" (Loss of self-control. Outbreak. Stressing of painfulness. Seriousness of condition. Defensive attitude.) Subject jumps up, says quickly: "I'm leaving now," runs out of the room. (Flight.) Experimenter follows her and finds her crying by the window in the adjoining room. (Weeping.)

Experimenter tries to calm the subject. She points out that it is only an experiment, not serious. "But it is serious", replies the subject, "very serious indeed. No matter, whether it was an experiment or not. It was distressing."

After calming down, the subject reports: "You came in with such an expression on your face! Awful! I was nailed to the spot. At first I wanted to throw the stick, smash the vase, the inkwell, everything, so that it all would crash to the floor and go to pieces. But I felt nailed down to the spot. Inside that space—the square of laths—there was nothing I could do; it obstructed everything. Useless talk. Self-conscious conversation, too artificial. I got the idea, away from here! It gained momentum. Scattered the laths. Out!—if I could have done something drastic, I could have acted it out. But throwing the laths only intensified the previous excitation. The situation was completely real."

Manifestations of Anger

A survey of the manifestations of anger in the examples mentioned above shows an extremely variegated picture* It demonstrates immediately that the breakdown of affective experiences and emotions into their elements of sensation, emotion, and volition is completely inessential for the problem of dynamics. Anger can be documented in the most variegated and heterogeneous forms of overt behavior. Correspondingly, there is great variety in the subjective, experiential phenomena of anger. The course of the experiments furnishes sufficient proof that all the cases provoked genuine anger; the subjects acknowledge this fact in their depositions.

The grouping of the diverse manifestations of anger is not easy. The reasons for this lies partly in the variety of phenomena. Sitting quietly in a chair, for example, may be an expression of anger just as well as wildly running around; laughter may express anger as well as tears, courtesy as well as rudeness, obedience as well as defiance. The final conclusion seems to be that nearly any form of human behavior can take on the significance of an outburst of anger in a given situation. If the total context is disregarded, the manifestation of anger by affective courtesy, for instance, differs only in hardly perceptible ways

* *There are over forty categories in Dembo's list—Editor.*

from genuine courtesy. An additional difficulty lies in the fact that the connection of the external manifestation of affect with the inner affective state of the person is far from simple or unequivocal. The very fact that expressions of anger may be either open or covert or perverted in various ways makes them equivocal. Nor does the intensity of emotional expression parallel the force of the inner emotional situation. It is well known that a person can boil inside without evincing any gross apparent manifestation. These facts necessitate a differentiation between the external manifestations of affective behavior and the underlying affective state. Changes occur not only in the topology of the situation, which is transformed by the affective event, but also comprise such inner changes as the heightening of the subject's sensitivity and irritability, or changes in his attitude towards things or demands.

However, the forms of affect manifestation are certainly not unimportant. They, too, are determined, and, in the case of open affective manifestations, they directly reflect the inner emotional state to a great degree. In the grouping that follows we have taken the overt cases as the starting point to guide us. We have grouped the covert forms with the corresponding overt ones. Mixed forms in which several affective directions converge, such as affective joking, are not dealt with as a separate group.

The number of possible systems for grouping is, of course, large. We have chosen the one below because of its direct connection with the essential dynamic factors. In every grouping of this kind, the transitions are fluid. Since psychic phenomena can be interpreted in different ways and are layered in different strata, the classification of specific cases is always difficult.

We have selected as the main groups for the classification of anger manifestations: a) pure expression of affect; b) affective actions; and c) affective coloring of other events.

Pure expressions of affect. In this group of manifestations, affect is disclosed unequivocally. Here belong, for example, angry gestures, screaming, abuse, stamping of feet, weeping, restless running around, and so forth. These pure expressions of affect, considered as typical expressions of anger in daily life, form, as we know, only one of many groups of affective processes.

Pure expressions of affect, just as other processes mentioned above, can occur as momentary events or as lasting ones. As a matter of fact, a pure expression of affect rarely extends over a very long period of time, at least if we disregard extremely strong affects of anger, which did not occur in our experiments. In sustained protracted outbreaks of anger, pure affect is typically intermingled with other forms.

Pure expressions of affect occur, on the one hand, when the affect is very intense; in extreme rage, for instance, a person may writhe and squeal. On the other hand, pure expressions of affect are also typical of very weak affects. In that case, there will be a momentary explosion, and while the form of expression—abusive phrases—is exaggerated, the intention is not very serious. With moderate affective feelings, pure expressions of affect are rare.

It is difficult to establish a conceptual demarcation and definition of pure expressions of affect in contrast to other forms of affective manifestation. It will be noted that the subjects' actions discussed in the preceding sections, such as efforts to reach a goal, and events around barriers, were all related to the environment. Those events were directly determined by the direction of certain elements of the psychological environment towards a goal, a certain barrier. That applies to physical actions as well as to actions of word or thought. In comparison, the pure expressions of affect seem to be expressions of an inner excitement without relation to a definite goal. It would be erroneous to characterize the differentiation by seeing the source of action as in the person in the one case, while attributing the goal-directed action exclusively to environmental circumstances in the other. In reality, the inner state of the person is equally decisive as a source of goal-directed actions (9).

A more thorough investigation shows that this characterization is not quite correct. It is true that pure expressions of affect are an expression, an emergence of an internal state, independent from the environment. Yet even the stamping of feet, and certainly the insults, contain a component directed against the experimenter, or against the experimental setup, or against the unpleasant situation. Even screaming is not only a form of self-expression, but also an expression of relevant content. The very quality that distinguishes the expression of anger as anger, that discriminates it from restlessness or other excitations, is often connected with the relation of anger to the environment. However, the pure expressions of anger are relatively independent of the special topology of a given situation; stamping of feet has nothing to do with the object of anger, and abusive gestures and phrases used by the subjects were rather stereotyped. The individual subjects employ the same derogatory expressions that they are accustomed to use in everyday life—Damn! Phooey! That's mean! Disgusting! Complete nonsense!

We do not intend to trace these gestures and other expressions of anger that are not dependent on any special topology back to an inheritance from formerly purposeful actions, as Darwinists might be inclined to do. We attribute them to the typical internal affinities of different anger-provoking situations, and to the extension of affective anger-provoking tension to all of the objects within the environment. We shall discuss this relationship later.

Affective action. Apart from pure expressions of affect, there are actions that are doubtlessly related to the special objects and to the special topology of the situation, but which at the same time create the impression of affective manifestations.

In ring throwing, for example, the subject throws the ring at the experimenter. Contrary to instructions, the subject makes a grab at the flower. He threatens to tear the flower apart or actually does so. He threatens to break the bottle and is pleased to see it wobbling when hit. He handles the rings so carelessly that one of them breaks in two. He rushes off into the adjoining room.

The manner of these actions is frequently crude, harsh, impulsive, or unconsidered. It shows great phenomenal similarity to pure expressions of affect and to affectively colored actions.

The affectivity of such behavior does not end with its manner; it also extends to the goal, to the contents of the action. The action is aimed at destruction and demolition, at smashing up everything.

Seen from outside, the direction of affective actions frequently coincides with the direction of non-affective actions (10). If, for example, the subject hurls a ring at the experimenter or pushes a lath aside, the action could easily be interpreted either as an action towards the goal barrier, or as a hostile action directed against the experimenter's dominance. Affective action, however, differs from sensible actions insofar as it loses its character of being a means towards an end.

Action against the barrier, for example, is carried out even if it destroys the original goal, thus making it impossible to find a solution. Overcoming the barrier has become a goal in itself. Intermediary goals have lost their function as subsidiary steps towards a mere comprehensive goal (11). Thus, actions assume the typical qualities of meaninglessness and the impulsivity characteristic of affective behavior. It is destruction, the urge to get it over with at any price.

Still, the direction of the affective action, like non-affective action, is determined by the essential properties of the special topology in the situation. Therefore, the only directions in question are towards the inner barrier and the goal; towards the outer barrier; against the experimenter; and against any irritating object in the environment.

A particularly important group consists of those affective actions against the outer or inner barrier, which we characterize as "break-throughs." Ignoring all inhibitions imposed by the instructions or by decorum, the subject is driven impulsively towards the goal. He leaves the square to seize the flower; he walks up to the bottle to slam the ring on it; he runs out of the room. Like all other actions, the breakthrough through the inner barrier can take the form of thought or speech as well as of physical action. Usually, the action stops in the realm of wishes and words, but actual physical breakthroughs do occur on occasion. Such an actual physical break-through is like a sudden short-circuit (12). It is only after such an action that the subject realizes that it did not achieve a real solution to the task, and was only an uninhibited attack against the disturbing barrier, or against the experimenter's prohibitions.

Affective actions, and the breakthrough in particular, are events of puzzling equivocality. They are based on a change of subordinate goals into dependent goals, that is to say, on a disintegration of the situation. At the same time they are indications of an especially strong and rigid fixation on the task goal. The task goal is being affectively simplified, leaving nothing but the external, primitive goal content: the bare grasping of the flower, however achieved, or the bare external fact of the rings resting around the bottle. The overly strong fixation of the subject on the goal, combined with the primitivization of the goals, finds expression in action at any price, in the breakthrough. In addition, affective breakthrough shows a momentary affective loss of inhibitions. The loss of inhibitions becomes apparent either when the subject consciously violates specific instructions, or when the barriers fall by themselves. Speaking of unreal solutions, we have demonstrated how the subject (in the course of his reasonable thought operations) slips into the level of unreality, and how the specific conditions of his instructions (together with other real barriers) gradually crumble by themselves so that the subject reaches dreamlike wish fulfillment. The affective breakthrough is directly connected with these processes: obstructive reality gets ignored, at first in dreams and then, with rising affectivity, also in speech and action. Thus the affective breakthrough in the direction of the real goal, though more primitivized, shows a close affinity to substitute action.

In the same way, the breakthrough through the outer barrier, the affective going out of the field, is partly based on the fact that the barriers fall by themselves. Some subjects cannot help it: time and again things occur to them that interrupt their work at the solution, and against their will push them temporarily out of the field. The subjects complain that they cannot do anything about it. However, the affective breakthrough can also occur as an intentional action, especially as an act of defiance against the experimenter or as an affective escape. Such acts of defiance are fighting actions against the experimenter, which, like the breakthrough through the inner barrier, have raised negativism against instructions to the realm of the absolute and the meaningless.

It should be noted that in our experiments the breakthrough beyond the outer barrier, that is to say flight, indicates an extraordinary degree of affectivity, and only happens when the subject does not care any more. The situation has become so painful, affecting the subject so profoundly, that the frontiers between the experiment and real life have been wiped out during the moment of escape.

Affective coloring. Apart from pure expressions of affect and affective actions, there exists another manifestation of affect: affective coloring.

If the subject says to the experimenter "Break it off now!" the tone of command may reveal a certain affectivity. If the subject betrays irritation when asking, "Must I go on trying?" the affective coloring is unmistakable. In a similar vein, the subject's suggestion to pinch the flower with pincers must be characterized as affective coloring.

In general, events with affective coloring do not present the lack of inhibition and meaning that characterizes affective actions, yet they reveal restless and destructive features, if in a covert way. The affective coloring is often more or less absorbed by the non-affective events to which it is attached, and is therefore often hard to detect. In general, we are inclined to regard affective coloring as a symptom of stronger affectivity than many dramatically pure expressions of affect, for it is always meant seriously, without exaggeration.

Affective coloring can show in verbal expressions as well as in the character of actions. Also, the general state of the person can be colored affectively.

The general situation is affectively colored when a subject is easily offended, grim, sarcastic, fatigued in his whole presence and behavior. We speak of these states as affective moods.

Intensity of Affect

Criteria of affectivity. It cannot be doubted that affects have different degrees of intensity, varying considerably in individual cases. It is, however, extremely difficult to evolve definite criteria for the intensity of affect. The reason for this lies partly in the fact that the intensity of expression is by no means a reliable indicator of the intensity of the affective state from which it flows. (Compare the discrepancy between the intensities of state and expression in goal-directed events). Discrepancy between inner emotional state and motoric action can be caused by the subject using self-control to stem the outbreak of affect into movement. But, even without such self-control, the presence of the experimenter, for instance, or other circumstances in the psychic environment may by themselves inhibit or transform motoric expressions.

There are also cases in which, for reasons of situation or character, motoric expressions are exaggerated (though such cases did not play any important part in our experiments). They are often found with psychopathic children (13).

Apart from cases in which the discrepancy between intensity of expression and intensity of the affective state is based on inhibition (or exaggeration) of motoric action, there are cases in which an intense affective state does not demand an intense affective expression. Some highly affective moods, such as hurt feelings or a general affective mood deterioration, apparently do not produce as immediate a tendency towards motoric expression as that which characterizes most other affective occurrences.

Intensity of emotional state, then, will have to be distinguished from intensity of expression. Yet, even considered separately, it is difficult to establish general psychological criteria for each.

The difficulty in determining the intensity of affective expressions is due to their being so heterogeneous. How can the intensity of a verbal articulation of desire be compared with the intensity of a gesture, an affective action, an affective thought, or a pure expression of affect? Or, even within the realm of affective action, how can flight, for example, be compared with throwing things at the experimenter?

It is not necessary to go into these questions at this point because the intensity of the manifestation is without basic significance for dynamic problems. It is more essential to discover the affectivity of the inner state. Yet, it seems nearly impossible to find a frame of reference within which to distinguish the different degrees of affect.

Nonetheless, at times the differences in intensity are so palpable that gross differences can be determined with sufficient accuracy. An affective momentary occurrence, like the use of invective at the start of the experiment, undoubtedly corresponds to a far less affective state than an affective breakthrough, like flight from the room. Here, in spite of the heterogenous manifestations, a comparison of intensity is feasible.

In this comparison, as in many other cases, the effect of the affective event can serve as a criterion. By *effect* we mean the degree of transformation of the total inner and outer situation produced by the affective event. An example: the invective used in the beginning of the experiment is phrased extravagantly, it is not meant very seriously, and it leaves the topology of the situation almost untouched, while affective flight radically changes the environment and with it the whole situation.

One of the essential criteria for affective change in the inner situation is the subject's heightened irritability. One of the most important properties of affective events, one that determines the force of its effect, is its degree of reality.

Degrees of intensity and increase in intensity. A survey of the force of impact of the various manifestations of affect in our experiments permits the following generalized statements:

Earlier, we pointed out that it is not possible to coordinate the major manifestations of affect, pure expressions of affect, affective actions, and affective coloring with well-defined degrees of intensity. Pure expressions of affect occur not only in cases exhibiting the highest affectivity, but also frequently in those with a low level of affectivity. In the latter case, they are typical momentary events. Their independence from the special topology of the situation indicates that the manifestation of affect is still nothing but an isolated island in an otherwise unchanged flow of events. Furthermore, pure expressions of affect generally take the form of speech or gesture, and being slightly exaggerated, by and large they have a comparatively low degree of reality.

Affective action and affective coloring correspond, as a rule, to a much higher degree of affectivity. Their very nature implies a material relation to the special properties of the situation. It is evident that a real breakthrough, such as the short-circuited grabbing of the goal or sudden flight from the room, will radically change the topology of the situation. Even just smashing the bottles or breaking a ring will radically alter the situation, if perhaps only in one (not very important) spot. The total course of events shows, for example, that cracking bottles or hurling a ring at the experimenter are expressions of minor affectivity, compared with breaking through the inner or outer barrier. Herein lies proof of the validity of using strength of impact as a criterion for the intensity of affect: the destruction of a bottle or throwing a ring at the experimenter produces a lesser and more transitory change of situation than does a final breakthrough.

Next to the contents of an affective action, its degree of reality is decisive for its force of impact. There are, as mentioned above, all sorts of possible transitions between a physical action, a threat or a request to the experimenter, a general expression of desire, and a mere thought. A threat, in itself, can be meant more or less seriously; it can take the form of an actual announcement of an affective action in the immediate future, or of a moderate hint that another subject in the same situation might easily commit a certain affective act. Similar shadings exist with wishes and thoughts. Affective actions of minimal reality level are no more affective than the pure expressions of affect at the start of the experiment.

The criterion of force of impact, then, explains why the breakthrough represents one of the most forceful affective actions that can occur. However, it does not immediately clarify why pure expressions of affect, for example, a fit of rage, are typical manifestations of both low and extremely high degrees of affectivity, since pure expressions of affect are characterized by nondependence on the special topology of the situation.

When based on low affectivity, the independence of pure expressions of affect from the special topology of the situation is understandable because, at that point, the expression of affect still is nothing but a superficial momentary event. In violent outbreaks of affect, conversely, the same manifestation signals the fact that the barriers and inhibitions that determined the special topology of the situation and the inner state of the person have been, or are in the process of being demolished. Affectivity as such, chaotic fluctuation in the course of events, action and counteraction of the field forces, will flood the total situation, submerging all details of its special structure. Then the pure expression of affect is no longer a momentary occurrence; instead, it characterizes a phase, and what was not fully serious before has now become an earnest matter.

As mentioned before, all sorts of affect—except for the most violent states of affectivity—do not appear as a prolonged, coherent sequence of events. Instead, they occur sporadically during the experiment, at shorter or longer intervals. Yet these sporadic manifestations of affect are by no means unrelated. One manifestation of affect may seemingly be without effect and obliterated by subsequent events; yet, later manifestations usually relate back to the previous ones, building up on the base they supply.

Such subterranean connections are characteristic of affective actions. Frequently, there is an escalation of affectivity, with a rising level of reality in the affective action and a gradual increase of interference with the existing topology. Typical, above all, is the transition from thoughts to words, and from words to actions (14).

As an example: a subject reasonably exploring possibilities in the flower experiment suddenly gets the fleeting idea that "the simplest way would be to just walk over and take the flower." Later on, he suddenly says, "I'm going over to take the flower!" changing wishful thought into a half-threat. Nonetheless, he continues trying to find the solution, until finally the breakthrough to the goal, the grasping of the flower, occurs as an impulsive action.

Not infrequently, a gradual increase of the reality level, interrupted by intermittent non-affective phases, can also be observed in cases of affective coloring.

At first, there may be efforts to reach the goal in the direction of genuine action. In the flower experiment, for example, the subject considers the possibility of using the rings as tools. He picks them up, wishing vaguely to utilize them somehow in the direction of the goal. Thoughtfully, he turns them this way and that. After a while, when his thoughts return to the rings, he moves them more violently, and already it is obvious that the rings will come to grief.

Continuity of this sort, typical of the recurrence of affectivily-colored processes, and above all of affective actions, appears rarely in pure expressions of affect. The reason for this is probably that, unlike affective actions, pure expressions of affect are rarely fundamentally imbedded in the meaningful context of the total course of events; instead, they are rather isolated phenomena.

X. PRECONDITIONS AND DYNAMIC SIGNIFICANCE OF AFFECTIVE OUTBURSTS

Basic Affectivity and Additional Pressure

The topology and the constellation of forces in the situation, the constant collision with barriers, the swings towards the goal and away from it, the limited freedom of motion—these and similar factors combine to create an inner and outer state which we call *basic affectivity*. Yet, genuine outbreaks of anger rarely occur unless some anger-provoking particular event, beyond the general basic affectivity, creates an additional pressure, acting as the straw that breaks the camel's back (15). Such additional pressures derive from events that stand out as comparatively isolated individual occurrences against the background of the steady course of events.

Events creating additional pressure can be very different in kind. The kinds typical of our experiments, are the "almost-event" and provocation by the experimenter.

Almost-event. In ring throwing, hits and misses are not the only things to be evaluated as successes or failures. There is also one psychologically distinctive group of throws where the rings almost settle correctly around the bottle: the rings already touch the bottle or even encircle the bottleneck, but then they slip aside after all. Such near-successes, almost reaching the goal, can be taken in different ways by the subject. The subject may be pleased that he came so close to complete success. Frequently, however, the effect is just the opposite: the subject is much more annoyed by a throw of this sort than by an ordinary miss.

The paradoxical fact that a complete failure produces less frustration than a near-success derives from the following circumstances: When the first part of the throw-curve already clearly indicates failure, the subject only wants to go on quickly to the next throw. The throw does not stand out against the continuous activity of ring throwing. (The statements of the subjects show that the speed of the rings' flight allows time for such observations. Even the brief occurrences between the ring's flying and its sliding down to the table are consciously experienced in detail.) If, however, the start of the throw heralds a hit, the subject gets completely absorbed in the momentary happening. His attention is glued to the ring, expectation mounts to a climax, focussing on just one point. His concentration can be compared to that of a runner, who, close to the goal, makes a last desperate effort. If the correct landing of a single ring is already familiar to the subject, an analogous almost-situation can develop with respect to a larger unit such as the series of ten throws.

If the promising throw ends in success, a strong outbreak of joy may follow. Conversely, failure in this case is experienced with extraordinary intensity. After raised hopes, the subject sees himself suddenly thrown back to a lower level of aspiration. In everyday life, too, almost-situations of this sort, when events have focussed on one definite moment for instance, a bus missed by a split second—are particularly painful.

Provocation by the experimenter. In the discussion of the relations between the experimenter and the subject, we pointed out that as a rule a subject enters into fighting actions only as a consequence of special additional pressure, usually provided through provocation by the experimenter. The provocation may result in an affective outbreak as well as in a fighting action.

The process is important enough to be considered in detail with the aid of an example. An already tense situation makes the experimenter laugh. The subject says, "I don't feel like laughing at all. I could not laugh now!" He jumps up. "I'm leaving now!" and runs out of the room. The experimenter's provocation was unintentional, but it provided enough additional pressure to trigger off a serious affective action, a breakthrough through the outer barrier.

The inordinately strong effect of the experimenter's laugh in this case is explicable by the convergence of a series of factors: 1) The subject believes that the experimenter is laughing at his distress. He feels that the experimenter is seeing through him, in spite of his self-control; 2) His feelings are hurt because he is being laughed at while performing a good but difficult deed; 3) As a definitely social action of the experimenter's, the laughter hits into a deep stratum of the subject's social identity, and brutally touches a most sensitive spot; 4) The laugh shows up in high relief the contrast between the dominant position of the experimenter and the helpless position of the subject; 5) The experimenter's laugh, by proclaiming the existence of the subject's strenuously controlled affectivity, makes that existence undeniable to the subject as well. (We cannot enter more deeply into the general problems of the equivocality and many facets of many psychic events, especially ones of an affective nature.) In opposition to the experimenter's unseemly behavior, the subject says, "I do not feel like laughing at all," thus accenting the existence of his affect all the more. He can no longer control himself, and runs out of the room.

Effect of additional pressure. The example clearly demonstrates why the special occurrence precipitated the outbreak of affect. The subject had strenuously controlled his affectivity, that is, had tried to prevent the high state of inner tension from carrying over into his motor activities and erupting into the open. He tried in every way to keep a hold on himself and to cover up his excitement. Suddenly the subject felt himself stripped of his disguise. The experimenter's laughter showed that his self-control could not prevent others from seeing right through his behavior into his state of mind; the limits that he had kept up so carefully were not real solid barriers. The experimenter's laugh, hurting him in the innermost core of his being, shattered the boundary between the environment and the inner regions of his soul. It signified a sudden expansion of the experimenter's field of forces into regions that up until then were inaccessible to him.

It was the additional pressure that pierced the wall between the inner regions of the soul and the environment, and consequently between the inner state of mind and motor activity. For motoric activity, just like the systems of perception, functions as a boundary layer between the intrapsychic systems and the environment (16). The first effect of the process is to topple the protective barriers sufficiently between inner affectivity and motoric action to reveal naked affectivity. The subject openly acknowledges his anger. The inner state of excitement thus gains power over the motoric layer dividing it from the environment. At first, it finds expression in words in actions, or in a low reality-level, rather than in affective actions. The content of the words, too, is still well under control—just a statement "I don't feel like laughing at all," even though the tone reveals excitement. One senses that certain barriers still prevent the outbreak of affectivity.

The mere statement, however, establishes the acknowledgment of inner affectivity to the outer world. The open acknowledgment invests it with enough reality to break down the barriers between the inner regions of the soul and the environment. Affective action without inhibitions, a breakthrough through the outer barrier, follows; at first in the form of mere verbal expression, and then, immediately after, as physical action.

Here, as in many other cases, the impact of additional pressure creates a sudden additional heightening of tension that burdens the inner emotional systems beyond capacity; the tension acts as the last straw. Moreover, it impairs the functional firmness of all boundaries within the system. As a rule, the environmental occurrence will knock down the boundary wall between the intrapsychic systems and the environment. After that, the way is open for the breakthrough of general affectivity into motoric action. It is not a particular property of the example just given, but rather a frequent occurrence. Different circumstances become entangled in such a way that the breakthrough, originally sparked by a minor incident, quickly gains momentum and assumes gross forms of expression.

In theory, the collapse of boundary walls could be caused solely by a gradual increase of tension beyond a certain limit. Actually, such cases may occur. It could also happen that the additional event weakens the firmness of the system's boundaries without actually increasing the general state of tension. In reality both circumstances frequently may coincide.

An essential characteristic of additional pressure is the suddenness of the event. This adds to its special impact. The suddenness is an essential precondition for weakening the regulatory functions, for example, self-control, and not giving them time to handle the interference. This factor may play an important part in the impact of almost-events. Thus, the regulatory functions are not able to prevent a breakthrough of affectivity into motoric action. The strength of basic affectivity, the character of the person, and the special structure of the individual case will determine how forceful an additional event must be in order to make the affective outbreak inevitable.

Additional pressure and the situation of struggle. As mentioned above, the consequences of provocation by the experimenter may be either a fighting action or an affective outbreak. In our experiments, fighting actions and affective outbreaks are therefore equivalent in this respect.

Both processes have another element in common. The resorting of the subjects to fighting actions is nearly always an expression of affectivity (except when sparring is entirely playful). It means leaving the field of objective engagement.

Furthermore, fighting actions, and even the existence of a fighting situation, tend to increase affectivity. Struggle, like conversation, is a specifically social situation between the experimenter and the subject. The emergence of a situation of struggle will immediately involve the subject's social identity, which is particularly vulnerable. In the situation of struggle the experimenter and the subject meet as equals. At the same time, the subject is doubly sensitive to his personal dependence on the experimenter's will. Consequently, the events lose most of their experimental character and change into a real-life situation. The field of struggle extends to the experimental task, events become increasingly serious. An atmosphere is created in which affective excitement can reach considerable depth. In our experiments (with one exception) the genesis and development of situations of struggle played an essential role in generating strong affects.

The situation of struggle also produces a closer connection with the deeper layers of the soul, and this may have an effect on the affective outbreak by loosening the firmness of boundary walls in the intrapsychic systems. It may be recalled that the barriers of the objective task situation become temporarily immaterial when the task situation is converted into a situation of struggle. The outer barrier opens up, only to make the restrictions of liberty all the more irksome afterwards.

The search for additional pressure. If the basic affectivity is very strong, or if the boundary firmness between inner systems and motoric action is low, the outbreak of affect hardly needs additional events to break down the walls. Yet even in these cases, as a rule, some individual event sparks the outbreak. It may be of a trifling nature and create the impression that the subject is actually trying to find an opportunity to break out. As it was with goal-directedness, so it can be with anger: given sufficient intensity the entire situation can be engulfed, so that finally everything is experienced as the additional pressure which provokes anger. In the flower experiment, for instance, the subject wishing to get away from the flower is especially annoyed that it is beautiful, "that it is such a gorgeous specimen!" The subject misunderstands everything and resentfully sees only the wrong side. Almost paranoically, he relates quite harmless incidents—the experimenter nodding to his statements to herself, for instance—and feels annoyed. A ring slipping through his fingers is enough to make him explode in a furious, "Ridiculous!"

The Nature of Outbursts of Anger

The development of the general situation and the manifold events that arise from it have now been discussed in detail, as have also the special occurrences that precipitate affective processes. It remains to investigate the significance of outbursts of anger from the dynamic point of view.

As a criterion for the intensity of various manifestations of affect we have used their force of impact. We determined this by measuring the changes in the intrapsychic systems and in the environment. The next problem is: what is the nature of these changes?

The outburst of anger is an expression of changes in the situation, which the outburst itself carries farther and may bring to completion. Essentially, the changes consist in a more or less sudden loosening or breaking down of functional barriers in the total field, that is to say of barriers in the environment, of interior boundary walls in intrapsychic systems, and of the functional boundary between the inner systems and the environment. The breakdowns produce an equalization of the different tension levels between the intrapsychic systems and the psychological environment. Besides, it is possible that an excessive degree of tension becomes insupportable, forcing the person to break through the field's boundaries and to enter calmer fields of forces.

In the following discussion, we are going to dwell only briefly on the problems of energy in these events. We will inquire more closely into the breaking through of the various limits and boundary walls.

Firmness of boundaries in minor manifestations of affect. As we have seen, the typical manifestation of minor affect is an isolated momentary event, usually a pure expression of affect without a deep connection with the course of events. At this state of slight basic affectivity, when comparatively small causes produce uninhibited expressions of affect, it merely shows the general *openness* of the subject. The subject has not yet withdrawn into himself, not encapsulated himself against the environment. For example, he is completely accessible to the experimenter's instructions and is genuinely involved with the particular problems and difficulties in the environment.

The core of the person's individuality has hardly been touched as yet. Only the peripheral layers of the soul's inner region have been reached by the experiment. These peripheral layers have comparatively easy access to the motoric region, which is situated between the environment and the inner systems. This is diagrammed in Figure 17. Thus, superficial affectivity can easily be produced, only to be discharged with equal ease in superficial manifestations of affect.

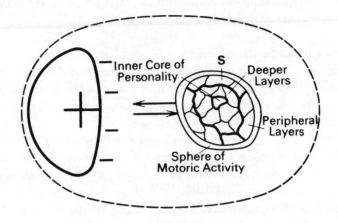

FIGURE 17. Condition of the Subject in Superficial Affect.

It is characteristic of subjects who never develop strong affects in the course of the experiment that they remain willing to comply with all the experimenter's directions. Their peripheral layers remain open to the environment, while the more central layers remain untouched or are kept as uninvolved as possible. This type of subject is highly self-controlled.

Firmness of Boundaries and state of tension. When various conflicts and recurrent failures increase the tension in the situation, the subject tries to protect himself against the danger of deeper involvement by encapsulation or

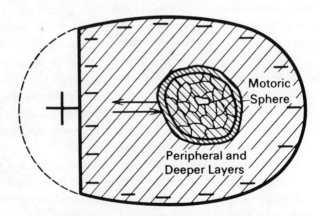

FIGURE 18. Condition of Subject Attempting to Control Affect.

by self-control. The mounting inner tensions can no longer express themselves directly. Instead, the intermediary layer between the inner systems and the environment—the region of motoric action and discharge—is being blocked; see Figure 18. While the question of exactly how this block is created must remain open for the moment, it is clear that this blocking then favors the development of unbalanced tensions within the intrapsychic systems, which in turn increase the urge to abandon all restraint. At the same time, the subject tries to follow all the roads that might lead him out of the unpleasant situation.

Rising affectivity develops when subsequent changes bring about increasing pressure on the boundary walls of the intrapsychic systems, on the barriers in the environment, and on the borderline between the two regions. Finally, the affective outburst destroys all boundaries. The rising pressure on the functional walls and barriers is an immediate consequence of the growing state of tension inside the individual regions, for higher tension within a system always means increased pressure against its outside walls.

At the same time, pressure against the boundaries is created by the subject's active attacks against the barriers. It is characteristic of the tendencies directed against the solidity of functional walls and barriers that they flow from factors in the situation which are in part without, or even contrary to, the subject's intention, and which are in part actively brought about by the subject. It is an important attribute of strong outbursts of anger that the person resists the destruction of limits while at the same time he wishes for it.

The process of loosening up and breaking through the various boundaries will now be traced in detail.

The Loosening and Breaking of Boundaries—Primitivization

Loosening up and destruction of barriers in the environment. The barriers determining the topology of the task field only develop gradually (see Section III), and gradually they acquire the firmness characteristic of the later stages. A certain firmness of barriers is a prerequisite for the development of tension. (Tension in the intrapsychic systems is likewise contingent on sufficient firmness of boundary walls within the systems.) If the tension goes on increasing, the limits of the field are strained; and if our basic concepts are correct, this strain will show in the direction of each barrier that surrounds the field of tension. Such processes can actually be observed.

Boundary line between reality and unreality. The first boundaries to be blurred are those between reality and unreality. In our experiments, tension originates on the reality level. Yet it is not surprising that evasions in the direction of unreality can easily lead to fantastic solutions or substitute actions (see Section V). While on the reality level, the subject is encircled by the inner and outer barriers, and the transition from reality to unreality is normally fluid. No solid barrier intervenes in that direction. Nonetheless, there is a tendency to keep one's feet on the ground, that is, to stick to the reality level, at least as far as action is concerned. (The reasons for this will not be analyzed here.)

The effacement of the dynamic separation between the zones of reality and unreality manifests itself, above all, in the more than normal homogenization of the two regions. Hallucinatory experiences emerge. And, under the stress of affect, a curse—that is, a magic tool which normally has a decidedly unrealistic character for the adult European—may acquire a touch of reality. Also, as mentioned in Section VI, hopes can be based on extremely slight real foundations when affectivity is strong.

As a rule, transition to the unreality level happens inadvertently, but active measures in that direction are not uncommon either. A considerable number of subjects tried to hypnotize the flowers by their glance, or to coax it, "Dear flower, come to me!"

Inner and outer barriers. Evasion into unreality is no real road to freedom. The only way left is destruction of the inner or outer barrier on the reality level. There, firm barriers are found in contrast to the boundaries of unreality. The subject realizes that the barriers cannot be surmounted in the normal way. The result, as discussed earlier, is violent attack, and in the end affective breakthrough.

These events consist largely of active actions, yet displacement of barriers can also occur on their own. There are expansions and restrictions of the field of motion which hardly change the rigid limitations of the field, but do make them vaguer and less tangible. This strange loosening up is complemented by the changing significance of the field, which may be experienced as either a task field or as a field of struggle. This adds up to more and more insecurity. A general deterioration becomes imminent, which not only encompass the barriers proper, but step by step will affect all substantial boundaries of given objects and events within the total field.

Natural boundaries, conventional ties. To a certain degree, every stressful tension tends to blur and to dissolve the natural boundaries and differentiations of objects and events in the environment. The goal-directed vector dominates the whole situation. A general directedness of all objects towards the goal is the result. This directedness is apparent in the way that objects will reasonably change their significance, turning them into tools and other resources. If it is strong enough, it will lead to the acceptance of substitute objects as goal objects and consequently to substitute actions.

With strong anger affectivity, this general directedness of objects will also demonstrate the ambivalence characteristic for situations of conflict. The tendency to become a goal or a tool can spread to the degree that finally every object will lose its natural significance, offering itself instead to the subject. Being unusable, however, the offered object has a disturbing effect, and instead of furthering action, it creates new impediments. In the same way, the character of barrier can more or less engulf all objects and produce a homogenization destructive to their natural, objective function.

The destruction of objective structural ties manifests itself most openly in substitute actions, or in irrational acts like scolding or breaking inanimate objects, like the rings. It also engulfs the conventional social rules of behavior. Conventional limitations of expression and of struggle with the experimenter are abandoned.

Finally, the struggle between experimenter and subject encompasses all objects. This, too, indicates the disappearance of natural limits. As the experience of barriers and disturbances widens, the subject sees himself as fighting his whole environment, which turns into a single undifferentiated, hostile field of tension.

Indetermination, sense, and nonsense. Apart from the homogenization of contents, which unifies the total field (showing everything under a single aspect), the individual objects and events also take on a strange ambivalence; they even seem to contradict each other.

The mere fact that subjective factors (which depend on the inner state of the subject) assume so much weight in determining the significance of objects is sufficient to undermine the inner stability of the field, which normally derives from its immediate connection with the objectively given circumstances. The situation of inner conflict is reflected in the inner contradictions of objects or events. Action in the direction of the task goal also simultaneously acquires the character of flight. The rings in the flower experiment become a tool to which the subject pins his hopes, and at the same time a toy that helps him to go out of the field. When the experimenter tells the subject to pick up the rings from the floor in the bottle experiment and the subject does so by means of a tripod rather than by hand, this action represents both obedience and defiance, both picking up and not picking up. The second flower, the substitute flower, is at the same time attractive and disturbing: it is identical with the goal, but it is not the goal. Each substitute goal and each substitute action, (throwing the rings over clothes pegs) reveals this inner contradiction. Lastly, the experimenter herself is a helper to whom one can turn, but also an enemy who creates all difficulties.

Thus, all objects and events have a dual contradictory significance: They are at the same time both themselves and their opposites. The field thereby loses its inner structure. Not only are the main directions lost because the inner and outer barriers have become indistinguishable, but even the details within the field lose all definite directedness. A multitude of heterogeneous possibilities and hopes take over. New possibilities continue to seem to open, but none of them will stand up. The subject considers a variety of different details that in the end turn out to be but variants of the same idea. The end result is an unintelligible unstructured unit, homogeneous and hopeless.

Correspondingly, the dynamic vectors show a simultaneous action and counteraction of field-forces of approximately equal strength. Initially, the vector towards the goal was met by a vector in the opposite direction, produced by the inner barrier's gradually developing negative valence (Figure 5). Similar conflicting vectors were created by action in the direction of the environment (Figure 8). The subject's further experiences, when he tries to escape into a special region, or go into unreality, or make use of some device or instrument, expose him more and more to contradictory impulses generated by approximately equivalent field forces. Every possible action, every single object makes his experience more acute. Where earlier a single definite direction was dynamically prevalent at any given moment, now there is conflict—that is, a relative equilibrium of opposite forces, a situation of tension, as shown in Figure 19.

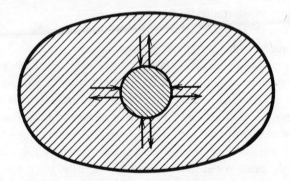

FIGURE 19. Primitive Unification Due to Extreme Affect.

The state of strong outbursts of affect is specifically characterized by this homogeneity of the total field. This is, however, not based on total harmonious structuration, but on the deterioration of all definite organized structure. Homogeneity is created by the dissolution of all ties. Finally there is a whole, characterized only by its completely closed boundaries and the intolerable incompatibility of all forces at every point of the field. It is a most powerful dynamic unit, made up of contradictions and absurdities.

Disintegration into separate elements. Disintegration should be understood in connection with the following circumstance: The struggle against the barriers, especially against the inner barrier, starts as a reasonable means toward an end. The task goal is to be reached, therefore the difficulty barrier has to be overcome. Later, when the attacks against the barrier become affective, the struggle can become an end in itself. The unreasonable and nonsensical quality characteristic of affective events is, in part, due to the fact that the derivative goal (overcoming a barrier) has significance only as a subordinate moment in a larger context, but acquires independence in the course of events. It is then pursued at any price, regardless of the context.

The breaking down of meaningful comprehensive units occurs chiefly, though not exclusively, with affective and fighting actions. It is an essential expression of the affective deterioration of all field structures and boundaries. In its turn, it increases the general dissolution implying an extreme primitive equalization.

Loosening up and destruction of boundaries between intrapsychic systems. A process of equalization by the destruction of inner boundaries, similar to the one described for the psychological environment, also takes place in the intrapsychic systems. Of course, in our experiments, the latter process is revealed much less markedly than the former. Our main source of information is from the depositions following the experiment.

What is most visible is the strong inner tension. Signs of restlessness, as well as the content of thoughts, hopes, and wishes, indicate that tension reaches the deeper layers of the personality as affectivity rises, until finally the superficial matter of the experiment turns into something far more serious.

Expanding tension weakens the usual functional isolation of the central nuclear layers of the person. However, not every contact with the deeper layers brings about the kind of equalization that is characteristic of the affect of anger. It is not a simple weakening of functional boundary walls. This would leave the total structure intact; rather, it is a general blurring, a confusion that makes surface and depth indistinguishable.

The subject loses his control of inner regions which he normally keeps well protected and firmly in hand; he may start talking about personal matters. Here, too, the over-all conflict is apparent. Afterward, the subject regrets his frankness.*

Most interesting are the subject's statements about the thoughts in his mind during the experiment. They are important because they are accessible only through the subject's report. At first, the subject talks excitedly in rather incoherent sentences, at times hard to follow: "Idiotic nonsense! If I cannot leave before there are ten rings on the bottle, I'll be throwing for all eternity!" The subject starts the proper report of the experiment only at the specific

* *The following example of this phenomenon is taken from the appendix of the original work—Editor.*

request by the experimenter. He relates in detail what he thought and what he did. "You want to know exactly what I was thinking—well, in that case! I thought of three things that had become pointlessly unpleasant. A certain feeling (gesture of displeasure and embarrassment). The whole activity of the Institute is after all silly, a pointless game. No suspense, no anticipation. Some time ago, that was different. Like the ring throwing. Everything seems stupid and futile. One good thing, though: at the moment when you begin to see clearly, it is all over." The subject's speech is still hard to follow. Apparently the subject wishes to say that the ring throwing and his whole course of studies follow the same pattern: early expectations that are disappointed. At the same time, this is an outburst and a statement about a very vital question. During and after our experiments, we frequently got surprisingly comprehensive statements of this sort from very personal, seemingly unrelated regions. The same subject brings up yet another personal, very serious matter. His way of reporting, however, is getting calmer and more organized.

"The second matter was connected with a person from whom I had expected great things—well, it's all past now. Thoughts of it crossed my mind during the experiment. There had been a reason to break it off, but I can't recall what it was. What I had hoped for was gone beyond return. The feeling was stronger than the reason for it. Thirdly, I thought of something more connected with the experiment. I had an invitation to a friend's birthday party for this afternoon, but I was busy with X, so I declined. When I heard later that I would be free this afternoon, I decided to go anyway. Then you called (the subject was on another floor of the same building), and I agreed to come for the experiment. I had been wishing for a long time to be your subject. Now, sitting down on the couch, I was annoyed with myself for having stayed here."

In conclusion, the subject speaks once more about the painfulness of the experiment. "By the way, even now the whole thing is disgusting." The experimenter (comfortingly): "It is because you are tired." The subject: "Oh no! Sometimes you feel like talking about yourself, but not just when you are a subject." The subject's belated regret at his having spoken too frankly shows how deeply he was affected by the matters reported.

The surfacing of deep personal layers, combined with a total state of high tension and an inner slackening of limits, may be responsible for the primitivization discussed above. The externalization of goals apparent in breakthroughs and substitutions, the magical, animistic, and hallucinatory quality of events, and the exaggerated hopes and the like, are all proof of the fact that the proper limits between certain intrapsychic regions and layers have disappeared, and that it is not only in the environment in which levels of reality are no longer clearly separated.

The loosening up and destruction of the boundary layer between the environ-

ment and the intrapsychic systems. Exaggerated verbal expressions, gestures, and actions demonstrate not only the loosening up of intrapsychic regions and of the environment, but also the loosening up of the layer that separates both and connects the psychologic environment and the intrapsychic regions. We have already characterized the genuine outburst as a smashing of the boundary-stratum, as a discharge of inner tension by means of motoric action. Now it becomes clear that when the obstacle of this particular limitation is removed, so that the subject loses control over his actions and speech, it is only a special moment in the general slackening and destruction of all walls and barriers within the total field including the environment and intrapsychic systems.

A certain loosening up of the motoric boundary layer will often manifest itself early in the experiment as visible restlessness. The weakening of boundaries between inner and outer events that exist in nonaffective states of mind becomes apparent when objects and events in the environment are no longer perceived according to their own, objective nature, but become abnormally dependent on the personal state of the subject, even to the point of falsification. Thus, when an affective outburst permits violent expression of wishful actions that normally are carefully suppressed, this is only the climax of a gradual process. Poignantly and in high relief, it reveals a development which, while it was less visible or intentionally covered up, was always dynamically decisive for basic affectivity and its mounting intensity.

Primitive Unification of the Total Field in Affect, in Fatigue, and with Children

As we have observed, manifestations of the affect of anger are extremely diversified, changing, and heterogeneous. There are goal-directed actions such as movements towards the goal proper or towards substitute goals, or fighting actions against the experimenter, or different kinds of going out of the field. In addition, there are direct expressions of anger such as abuse, yelling, attempts to break objects, and breakthroughs to the goal. These events occurred both on the reality and on the unreality level, in the form of words, fantastic ideas, and exaggerated hopes. Even the appearance of the environment, its total character as well as the experience of individual objects and events, may undergo deep seated transformations.

Now it becomes apparent that all these seemingly heterogeneous events can be derived from a few, comparatively homogeneous, fundamental dynamic factors. The topology of the situation creates a conflict between the action and counteraction of field forces in various directions. The situation becomes increasingly hopeless. The ensuing strong tensions lead to a loosening up and destruction of all boundaries in the total field.

As we have seen, the various affective events can all be derived from this loosening of boundaries within the total field. The boundaries within the total field include the barriers in the environment, the boundary walls of the intrapsychic systems, and the motoric boundary layer between the environment and the intrapsychic systems.

If the affectivity is more than superficial, the subject will make efforts at self-control or encapsulation of affect. He does this in order to counterbalance the threatening collapse.

If the subject fails to rise above the situation, and if neither the subject nor the experimenter can effect a favorable change in the situation, a true violent outburst will follow. Such an affective outburst necessarily implies a breakthrough of inner tension into motoric action and the demolition of certain barriers, boundaries, or ties in the environment.

A person's state immediately preceding and during the affective outburst is characterized by a special directness and the absence of all considerations. This is dynamically explicable by the heightened tensions, and by the loosening up or destruction of the limits that determine the fine structure of the total field.

In our experiments, neither the tensions nor the deterioration reached their greatest possible extent. Still, the situation was sufficiently drastic to illuminate the occurrence in its various ramifications.

The loosening up of limits discussed here is not identical with the inner loosening up which occurs for example, when fatigue causes fluidity of the psychic substance (17). (A kind of affective fatigue also occurs in our experiments. It is, however, shortlived and occurs after an affective outburst.) In both kinds of loosening up, the walls and barriers inside the total field are weakened. The affect of anger, however, is distinguished from fatigue phenomena by the existence of a particularly firm barrier which surrounds the field of mobility for the subject on all sides. Loosening of the fine structure is in part simultaneous with, and in part caused by, the development and the stiffening of the outer barrier. With fatigue, the loosening of inner boundaries goes hand-in-hand with an increasing fluidity and a weakening of the total tension; with anger, the state of tension is heightened, an eventuality which would be impossible without the outer barrier. The loosening of fine structure in affect means, at the same time, an increase in the dynamic unification of the total field, a change in the direction towards an undifferentiated but strong gestalt.

The unification, based on excessive tension and the loosening up of fine structures inside the field, precedes the outburst of affect. It produces a primitivization of the total field, a simplification of its structure. An outer barrier, firm though strained to the utmost, now encircles a tense inner field. Within this field only the motoric boundary layer between the environment and the intrapsychic system remains distinguishable; See Figure 19.

The unification into a primitive whole imbued with utmost tension creates the strength and the weakness, the power and the absurdity of affect. The destruction of the fine structures and the unification of the total field produced the unconditional, powerful, and all-encompassing character of affective events. The deterioration of the walls between the outer and the inner regions, between surface and depth, create—in spite of all tendencies towards self-control—a strong entanglement, an unusual merging of active volition and compulsion, of wishes and actions.

Our concepts of the dynamic foundations of affect receive confirmation when they are compared with the primitivity of children—which is akin to the temporary primitivization which occurs with adult affect. Compared to the adult, children represent a much more unified dynamic whole. There is less differentiation between surface and depth; the boundary layer between the environment and the intrapsychic systems is dynamically weak (18). The state of adult affect, therefore, is comparable to a state of childishness in some ways. Actually, we have observed many modes of behavior that are usually considered characteristic of children: little differentiation between reality and unreality, easy encroachment of excitation of one psychic region upon another, slight fixation on the firm, objective properties of objects, magic and animistic modes of behavior, greater directness, fewer inhibitions, and so on. Children are easily incited to affectivity. This demonstrates that their total personality structure is permanently inclined to enter the state that generates affectivity.

Still, it would be a mistake simply to identify the dynamic state of the total field during the adult affect of anger as the dynamic state of a child. It is true that in both cases the solidity of the walls between the intrapsychic systems and the boundary layer, and between the intrapsychic system and the environment is considerably reduced, with corresponding consequences. Yet, an essential difference exists: the child's psychic systems are originally undifferentiated and characterized by a general plasticity of the psychic substance, while adult affectivity removes the existing differentiation as well as loosening or breaking existing walls and barriers. The difference appears most clearly in the processes of self-control. The eruptive nature and violence of a genuine outburst of anger are evidence that the affective whole does not represent a harmonious co-ordination of a closely connected but in itself well-organized system, but is instead based on the breakup of fine structures.

An investigation of the aftereffects of affect is beyond the scope of this study. It would have to deal with the dynamics of the return to calmness and equilibrium. According to Freud's thesis, an affective outburst should bring about a discharge of tension. This might also be expected in our own representation of its dynamic development. In some cases, especially those climaxed by crying or by violent, irrational fits of rage, a certain release of tension indeed seemed to follow. In other cases, the affective outburst did not seem to have a noticeably relaxing effect. Our observations did not yield a uniform picture. We were reminded of the problems connected with substitute satisfaction. Here, as there, the subject allowed himself to be carried away by his anger, moving in a certain sense from the reality level into unreality, so that he then has to find his way back. Undoubtedly an outburst of anger involves a considerable expenditure of energy; but the dynamic relationship between the discharge of energy and the relaxation of tension is by no means unequivocal. A thorough study of the total field which exists before and after the outbreak of anger would be needed to establish such a connection in each individual case.

XI. THE SPECIAL TOPOLOGY OF THE EXPERIMENTS AND CASES OF ANGER IN EVERYDAY LIFE

Our findings concerning anger are based on situations determined by a special topology and a special constellation of field forces. The question suggests itself of whether the findings are valid only for this special topology, which includes the development of an outer and an inner barrier, or whether they are of more general significance.

We are inclined to ascribe general significance to the processes derived from the tension and the destruction of the fine structures and of the boundary lines within the total field. However, the type and location of field forces, as well as the special topology of the initial situation, may show considerable deviations in other cases.

All the same, it is noteworthy that even rather specialized properties of our experimental topology could be observed in instances of spontaneous anger, and with much more frequency than might be expected. Some examples follow.

Example 1. We start with an example which at first seems completely unrelated to our experimental situation. A woman wanting to attend a party in a new dress notices spots on her dress. Unable to remove the spots, she gets angry.

What is the topology of this situation? A strong positive valence is in evidence, as well as a tension created by her putting on the new dress and heading for the party. Suddenly a barrier, the spot, arises between the person and her goal. It creates a situation closely corresponding to the initial situation in our experiments; this is diagrammed in Figure 20a.

This situation would not be sufficient to generate a major affect of anger. If the spot were easy to remove, there would be no anger at all. Sometimes, though, the mere fact of having been soiled can provoke a reaction of anger. The fact of having been soiled is irreversible.

Another factor is of decisive significance for the outburst of anger. At least for the moment, the situation seems hopeless. If the barrier cannot be removed quickly, in this case, it cannot be removed at all. It would be too late. Moreover, as a rule, the total situation makes it difficult to beg off at the last moment —she feels social obligations, has made arrangements, and so on. Thus, the woman is not only separated from her immediate goal by a barrier, but she is also encircled by an outer barrier, as shown in Figure 20b.

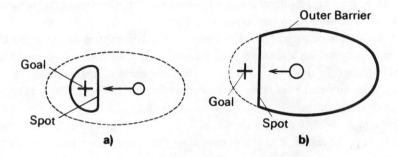

FIGURE 20.

a. A Condition of Frustration.   b. The Condition of Being Trapped in Frustration.

In order to meet our experimental conditions for generating the affect of anger, there must also be penetration to the person's inner core. If the woman concerned does not care much about clothes, or if she is not interested in the party, no serious affect of anger will be forthcoming. The anger affect may also relate directly to the ruined dress. Then the hopelessness may be connected with fear of irreparable damage.

Anger will be especially strong if the person is in a hurry, because then a strong basic affectivity and a certain inner loosening up are both present. (It seems highly immaterial for the emergence of anger whether the basic affectivity is produced by the anger situation or by something else, such as a desire to hurry.) In this situation, the affect of anger is inadequately strong. It may be precipitated by some trifling thing, such as not immediately finding a piece of apparel. The explanation lies in the presence of the almost factor which, operating as additional pressure in the case of our experiments, played so important a part in generating the genuine outburst of anger. Thus, the building up of the situation, its field forces, and the topology of barriers show a surprising similarity to the situation in our experiments.

Example 2. Anger upon missing a bus by a hair's breadth involves similar factors. There, too, general tension and the almost are present. There, too, the affect of anger will gain major intensity only when the fact of missing the bus makes it likely that one will be late for the goal; this gives the situation a kind of hopelessness.

If the case becomes so hopeless that the whole trip must be given up, the anger may be relatively shortlived, because a completely new position has been reached necessitating a restructuring of the total situation. The greatest extent of annoyance is reached when the situation is almost hopeless. Then, there is an oscillation between hope and despair, between the desire to get there and giving it up. This results in pendulum swings in the meaning of the situation such as we observed in our experiments.

Finally, it is essential for the outburst of affect in missing the bus that the person, once having almost reached his goal, is thrown back to a position far away from it. In this case, as in many other instances of anger, being thrown back from the goal may be more important for the outburst of anger than it is in our experiments.

Example 3. A frequent source of anger is being repeatedly disturbed while at work. Here, too, the person is working towards a goal. Typically, in this situation, the worker is at the same time thrown off his position. Each new disturbance mandates a transition from the work field into another field; the outer barrier of the work field must be crossed. Time and again, the person actively has to build up a new work field; as a rule, fearing fresh disturbances, he will try to encapsulate the new field as much as possible.

The topology of the field, shown in Figure 21, is characterized by inner and outer barriers, which corresponds to the structure of our experimental samples. Affectivity created by disturbance will develop in proportion to the importance of the work and to the general degree of tension in the situation. Almost-factors also play an important part, as well as the experience of being thrown back to the repeated necessity of repeatedly restructuring the tension

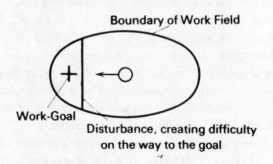

FIGURE 21. The Situation of Being Repeatedly Disturbed.

forces of the work field. The temporary breakdowns of the outer barrier will keep destroying the fine structure of the field.

Example 4. Anger occurs when time and again keys are mislaid, or tools, such as a pen, do not function. In these cases, the special properties of the momentary situation—a goal with an inner and/or outer barrier—frequently correspond with Example 1. However, the following factor is added: repetition of the same difficulty gradually assumes the character of something inescapable and hopeless. The recurrence of the difficulty creates a sense of helplessness; there seems to be no way out of one's own impotence. The person keeps slipping back to former situations, and in this way the structure of the field gains a weight and firmness beyond what it would have if the particular case were not seen by the person as an example. The process is the same as in our experiments where the repetition or duration of the experiment were of essential significance.

Example 5. Conditions are somewhat more complicated if a person is late for a play because he could not make up his mind to use an expensive means of transportation. The situation of failure is obvious. Its topology, however, appears different from the other examples in that the inner barrier is apparently missing. This applies to the cases when anger does not set in, at least not strongly, before the latecomer has arrived at the play.

In these cases, as in many others, the outburst of anger occurs post factum, when it is too late. The essential feature is that shortly before the present situation an inner barrier from the goal to get there on time did in fact exist. It was already thinkable that the chosen way of approach was the wrong one. But only after the fact can the person gain certain knowledge that his incorrect behavior has rendered the inner barrier in front of the goal (timely arrival) impassable and thus made the situation hopeless. The true structure of the situation is felt only when the situation is no longer present, but is already past. It is true that usually also the present situation is impaired by the belated arrival.

It is especially galling for a person to have seen the correct way without using it. The barrier has become impassable through his own fault. This turns the direction of the anger against the person himself, and occasionally against others who, supposedly or factually, are equally to blame.

As pointed out earlier, the value of our particular experiments for the clarification of the dynamics of anger cannot be judged by the statistical frequency with which the phenomena occur in everyday life. Efforts to use homogeneous concepts in order to represent all cases of similar historical manifestations will be misleading rather than helpful in clarifying dynamic processes. Nonetheless, it is evidently of interest to demonstrate, as our examples have done, that the topology of our experiments characterizes a large number of anger incidents that grow out of the chance episodes of living.

[*Space limitations prevent the inclusion of Dembo's appendix, which contains descriptions of the behavior of two different subjects. It may be obtained from University Microfilms. In addition to many examples of the phenomena which are discussed, these other observations may possibly be important:*

Affect appears to emerge when the situation becomes an impossible one. It then declines and the subject again becomes immersed in the task. The task again proves difficult and substitution phenomena, attempts to escape the field, and so on, all fail to bring relief. The situation seems impossible again and affect rises again; it then declines and the pattern is repeated. Each time things get a bit more uncontrolled.

At times, apathy, or purposeless rigidity occurs rather than anger. Occasionally, pain occurs.

The relationship between experimenter and subject occasionally reminds one of that of a Freudian therapist and patient. By remaining aloof and insisting there is a solution, the experimenter places the subject in a completely impossible solution that could be solved only by a radical shift in the power relationships involved. The subject would have to take the responsibility of ending the experiment.

The subject is completely dominated by the authority of the experimenter. No matter how impossible the situation appears, and no matter how hard the subject trys to convince himself or the experimenter that there is no solution (or at least that he cannot find it), the subject seems incapable of taking the responsibility of breaking off the experiment of his own accord. At best he continues to ask for permission to leave. Even then, the subject may be afraid of being assigned the problem to do at home—Editor.]

1. Selz, *Über die Gesetze des geordneten Denkverlaufs* (The Laws of Orderly Thinking), 1913.

2. Köhler, W., *Intelligenzprüfungen an Menschenaffen* (Intelligence Tests with Anthropoid Apes) (Berlin, 1921), 26.

3. A conflict is defined as a situation governed by the clash of field forces of approximately equal strength that operate in opposite directions. Lewin, *Die Entwicklung der experimentellen Willenpsychologie und die Psychotherapie* (The Development of Experimental Psychology of the Will and Psychotherapy) (Leipzig, 1929), 14.

4. Zeigarnik, B., "Das Behalten erledigter und unerledigter Handlungen," *Psychol. Forsch.* 9.

5. Birenbaum, G., "Der Vergessen von Vornahman," *Psychol. Forsch.* 13.

6. Lewin, K., "Environmental Forces in Child Behavior and Development," in Murchison, *A Handbook of Child Psychology* (Worcester, 1931), 115.

7. Similar situations evolve frequently with promises of reward or threats of punishment. Cf. Lewin, K., "Environmental Forces in Child Behavior and Development," in Murchison, *A Handbook of Child Psychology* (Worcester, 1931), 33 ff.

8. Clausewitz: *Hinterlassene Werke: Über Krieg und Kriegsführung* (Posthumous Writings on War and Strategy) (Berlin, 1832–37).

9. Lewin, K., "Zwei Grundtypen von Lebensprozessen" (Two Basic Types of Life-processes), *Z. Psychol.* 113, 209 ff.

10. Köhler, W., *Intelligenzprufüngen an Menschenaffen* (Intelligence Tests with Anthropoid Apes), Berlin, 1921. Similar affective behavior is also observed in anthropoid apes.

11. Compare the concept of disintegration in Karsten's work on Psychic Satiation.

12. Homburger, *Psychopathologie des Kinderalters* (Psychopathology in Childhood) (Berlin, 1926), 335. Also Karsten, A., "Psychychische Sattigung," *Psych. Forsch.* 10, 172 ff.

13. Homburger, *ibid*, 361 ff; and Lewin, K, *Trieb-und Affekt-ausserungen psychopathischer Kinder (Expressions of Drives and Affects in Psychopathologic Children), Z. Kinderforshung* 32 (1926), 432.

14. See Karsten, A., "Psychische Sattigung," *Psych. Forsch.* 10, 156, on sins of the mind preceding short circuited action.

15. The concept of basic affectivity does not imply the thesis of continually produced affective energy. Cf. Apfelbaum, *Affektdynamik*, (Leipzig, 1927), 23.

16.   Lewin, K., "Environmental Forces in Child Behavior and Development," in Murchison, *A Handbook of Child Psychology* (Worcester, 1931), 120 ff.

17.   Zeigarnik, B., "Das Behalten erledigter und unerledigter Handlungen," *Psychol Forsch.* 9, 65 ff.

18.   Lewin, K., "Environmental Forces in Child Behavior and Development," in Murchison, *A Handbook of Child Psychology* (Worcester, 1931), 121.

Chapter XI.

THE STRUCTURE OF SITUATIONS, EMOTION, AND UNREALITY

THIS chapter begins with a consideration of various types of situations and the method involved in their description. Then, we shall turn to the "impossible situation" described by Dembo and consider some of the issues that are raised by her description of the dynamics of frustration, and the implications these have for a general theory of the emotions. The difference between emotions and emotionality will lead us to a discussion of the nature of unreality, and I shall attempt to demonstrate that there are actually two different types of unreality. Finally, we will conclude by discussing a few of the problems involved in the acceptance of various realities. Dembo's study also raises issues about the nature of will and freedom, but we shall delay our discussion of these topics until Chapter XIII.

THE DESCRIPTION OF SITUATIONS—TOPOLOGICAL PSYCHOLOGY

While Dembo's study confines itself to a description of only one type of situation—the situation of frustration with an outer barrier—that I have named the "impossible situation," the depth of her inquiry provides such a wide range of concepts that we are able to use them in describing several other types of situations as well. This is fortunate, because once we become familiar with the concept of a situation, we discover that there are many different types, that many have important structures that had been completely overlooked, and that all behavior may be analyzed in terms of the structure of the situation in which it occurs. Thus, in the next chapter, when we examine Hoppe's study of the level of aspiration, we shall essentially be examining what might be called the "test situation"—a situation in which one can either succeed or fail with consequent effects on the ego; in a moment we will consider the situations of reward and punishment; we may consider the behavior of children in the frustration-regression experiment to be the effect of their being in the situation of being preoccupied; and, in general, we may imagine a whole typology of the situations in which we find ourselves in our everyday lives.

The description of behavior in terms of situation and the search for a systematic language with which to describe situations is an essential feature of Lewin's psychology. The elaboration of this endeavor receives it fullest statement in Lewin's *Topological Psychology* (1), and the interested reader should go to this book to gain a full appreciation of Lewin's enterprise. In this section, I shall simply give a sketch of this approach. Let us begin by considering some other analyses of situations that were made with the concepts used in the Dembo study. Then we shall examine some of the conceptual developments in the description of situations that occurred after Dembo's study.

The Situation of Reward and Punishment

The usefulness of the topological description of situations is neatly shown in Lewin's analysis of the differences between the situation of reward and punishment (2). First, Lewin considers the general problems involved when an adult wants to get a child to do something that the child doesn't want to do. He notes that one of the most efficient methods the adult can use is to embed the activity in a context which makes it more meaningful to the child. Thus, learning to read letters may become intrinsically interesting if one embeds the letters in whole sentences which the child must act out (as in Forer's study of the Decroly reading method) (3). Lewin points out that this use of the concept of the whole governing the meaning of the parts is a much more effective approach than trying to increase the attractiveness of letters by adding positive stimuli, such as putting pretty pictures on a page of the reader. In turn, the whole activity of reading is made more meaningful if it is a part of preparing for another activity, such as a birthday party.

There are times, however, when rather than attempting to change the intrinsic valence of the activity, an authority will choose to use reward or punishment as an external motivation to perform the activity. At first glance, the situation of reward and that of punishment may seem quite similar—in both cases an external motivation is being applied to secure conformance. However, if punishment is chosen, the negative valence of the punishment will tend to force the child to leave the field. Therefore, in order to keep the child in the situation where the punishment will force him to perform the unwanted activity, an external barrier will have to be utilized. Unfortunately, as we have seen from Dembo's study, such a situation will lead to an increase in tension. As a result of this tension, the child may react with emotional outbursts, with flights into unreality, with a struggle of wills with the authority, or with an "encysting" reaction as the child withdraws into himself.

On the other hand, while the use of a reward may require a barrier to prevent the child from taking the reward without performing the activity, since the forces are in the direction of the goal, there is no need for an outer barrier, and hence there will be less tension and fewer negative consequences.

The presentation of the essence of these situations of reward and punishment by means of topological diagrams provides the reader with an immediate intuitive grasp of the fundamental differences between the two situations.

The Relationship Between Barriers and Forces

Subsequent to Dembo's study, Fajans (4), one of Lewin's students at Berlin, studied the relationship between distance and force. Working with infants and children, she hung a desired object (such as a piece of brightly wrapped chocolate) in such a way that it was out of reach of the child's grasp. She then observed the child's behavior, noting how many seconds the child spent actually trying to reach the object, indirectly trying to reach it (pleading with the experimenter), passively standing around, or leaving the field by going off and playing with something else. By varying the amount of distance between the goal object and the child's grasp, she could then determine the effect which distance had on the attractive power of the goal.

Her observations show that when the desired object is close, both infants and children keep actively trying to reach the goal; whereas when the object is distant they passively stare at it, turn toward and away from it, and finally leave the field. In Chapter XIII, we shall discuss other aspects of this experiment, such as the impact of success and failure on the child's behavior. Here we simply note two important points. First, even when there are no longer attempts to actively reach the goal objects, the infants—and, to a lesser extent, even the children—still orient more toward the goal when it is close than when it is distant. Hence, we may conclude that the force exerted by a valenced object is greater when the distance is less. Second, the infants are obviously more tense when the object is close. Since this tension must be the result of a conflict of forces, there must be some negative force opposing the positive force toward the goal. This negative force can only come from the infant's being unable to reach the goal. Thus, we may conclude that a barrier is able to acquire a negative valence, and that the negative force from this valence must, like positive forces, increase as distance decreases. Note that such a negative force is a driving force that is quite different from the restraining force that is a necessary property of any barrier.

While barriers themselves may acquire negative valence, a series of experiments by Herbert Wright (5) demonstrate that barriers may also increase (or maintain) the positive valence of the goal that is behind them. His first study examines the choice behavior of waitresses selecting desserts from a cafeteria counter. On any given day the desserts were all of one sort (for example, apple pie), but were placed on the counter in two rows—one 2 inches, the other 14 inches from the edge of the counter. Wright observed that when the waitresses selected dessert for their customers, they picked a dessert from the near row 97 per cent of the time. However, when they chose a dessert for themselves, they picked a dessert from the far row 60 per cent of the time. That is, the effect of slightly obstructing the desserts apparently increased their attractive valence. He also found that the extent of this effect was proportional to the initial valence of the dessert. That is, the more attractive the dessert of the day, the more likely the choice of an obstructed dessert.

Continuing his study in the laboratory with preschool children, Wright shows that the children indicate that toys which are in a cage appear more attractive than toys outside the cage, and that they prefer to be given (for keeps) a ball that is far away, or a lollipop that is out of reach, than a ball that is closer or a lollipop that is within reach.

In discussing his results, Wright points out that they may be accounted for in two different ways: (1) the presence of a barrier may increase the valence of the obstructed goal; or (2) the barrier may maintain a valence that would disappear if the person were in the goal region. Without a barrier, the person would be in the goal region, and hence the valence might decrease because of a decrease in tension or because of the person's new perspective.

Wright's results raise a question as to whether the magnitude of a force always increases as distance to the goal decreases. The answer seems to depend on the meaning of distance. In Fajans' experiment with decreased distance, the goal appears closer in the sense that its attainment seems more possible, and force increases. In Wright's studies, the goal is at hand, so that there is no question as to the possibility of obtaining it. In fact, it may be incorrect to speak of a "barrier" being present. The "further" goal is distant, in that it is in a region other than the one occupied by the person. Whenever Wright attempted to increase valence by using a barrier that necessitated more effort or affected the possibility of attaining the goal, he was unable to obtain an effect. For example, in one of his experiments, he had children come into a room where two pieces of candy were suspended by strings. One could be immediately reached, while the other required the child to step up on a chair to reach it. This maneuver was evidently perceived as a real barrier, and the children all chose the more accessible candy. Clearly the relationship between barrier and distance requires further study.

It is interesting to note how Wright's procedure clearly distinguishes activity as a means and as an end. When the person chooses a means, as in selecting a dessert for a customer, he always picks the easiest object; it is only when the object is an end, one's own dessert, that it is chosen when it is further away. In fact, I suspect that the phenomena may always hold for ends, and that when other conditions are equal, a choice of the closer of two objects is an indication that it is a means. For example, a waitress who chooses the closer of two pieces of pie for herself may simply be choosing a means toward the end of finishing her meal, rather than seeing the particular pie as having any value in its own right.

Lewin himself was, of course, committed to the conceptual analysis of concepts such as barrier, valence, and goal. His most comprehensive attempt to define such concepts in a systematic way focuses on the concept of force as the key to the fundamental problems of psychological dynamics (6). And while his attempt was not fully successful, the very difficulties which become apparent from his analysis (for example, in defining psychological distance) provide a starting point for future analyses.

Conflict Situations. Lewin discussed a number of conflict situations. The most interesting of these is the situation in which there is an approach-avoidance conflict (7). We have seen that the force of attraction or repulsion increases as the distance to the valenced object(s) decreases. Lewin reasons that the continued existence of the situation of approach-avoidance conflict necessarily implies that as the ambivalent object is approached, the strength of the negative force must begin later, but increase more rapidly than the positive force otherwise the person would simply either go towards or away from the object. We have already seen from Dembo's study that conflicting forces create tension. Now, as may be seen from Figure 1, if we assume that the person approaches until the two forces are equated, then if the negative force is increased the amount of tension will actually *decrease,* and vice versa. Likewise, a good deal of tension or a strong withdrawal is an indication of a powerful attractive force, for otherwise the person would not come so close

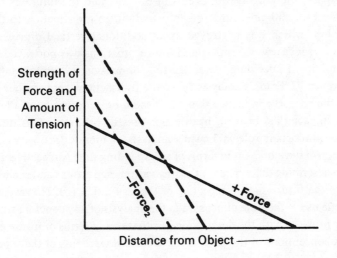

to a strong negative force. Note how the behavior of the person logically follows from the structure of the situation. The deceptively simple analysis reveals an inherent structure that could be (and is) often overlooked. Shortly, we shall see how the structures can account for some of the phenomena related to attitude change.

When Lewin turned to the analysis of larger social situations, he again made use of the concept of tension. In the situation where one group is trying to change the norms or procedures of society at large, they are essentially trying to change customs that are held in place by a whole set of forces. An analysis of the situation will reveal that some of these forces are preventing changes in the customs while other forces are actually working for changes. That is, the customs are really held in a "quasi-stable" equilibrium by a set of opposing forces (8). The group working to change the customs may do so either by attempting to increase the forces for change or by decreasing the forces against change. However, there is a critical difference between these strategies. If the former is adopted, there will necessarily be an increase in the tension of the situation, with the resulting consequences, while if the latter strategy is successful, the change will occur with a decrease in tension.

Additional Concepts

While many of the concepts used in a field approach are developed in Dembo's attempt to describe the situation of frustration—life-space, boundaries, barriers, forces, tensions, subregions, and level of unreality—there are some additional concepts that were employed as other situations were analyzed.

Perhaps the most fundamental of these additions is the *time dimension* of the life-space, the portrayal of events in the past and the future as they are experienced in, and affect, the present situation. In a distinction to the level of unreality, which was portrayed as an additional vertical dimension, the person's present view of his part and future situations was portrayed along a horizontal line. In deciding to add the time dimension, Lewin was influenced by Lawrence K. Frank's analysis (9) of the transactions between our present view of the past, the influence this past has on our conception of the future, and the impact this, in turn, has on our present behavior. This dimension played an important role in Lewin's analysis of morale (10), as well as his description of development in terms of an expanding time perspective. It is also useful in describing differences in the way various age groups and social classes structure the future time perspective of their situation (11). However, Lewin made little use of the time dimension in the analysis of any concrete situations. A major problem with the description of situations in terms of future expectations, or conceptions of the past, is the sheer awkwardness of the topological representations. As a result, I believe that only the present dimension receives really adequate coverage.

Another important conceptual addition is the idea of *overlapping situations* (12). The idea here is that one is often in more than one situation at the same time, although one of them may be much more in the foreground of experience. One of Lewin's examples is of a woman who, on the one hand, is in the situation of working in a factory, while on the other, she is also in the situation of her home where there is a sick child (13). Each of the overlapping situations may be regarded as having a certain "potency" that affects how pronounced it is, and hence its ability to affect current behavior.

As we saw in Chapter IV, it is possible to describe a child in the frustration-regression experiment as being both in the former situation of playing with enchanting toys *and* in the current situation of being behind a barrier playing with less desirable toys. To the extent that he is involved in the former situation —that is, the more potent that Garden of Eden is—the more preoccupied he is, and the less he can be involved in his play in the current situation. Therefore, the play becomes less constructive than it was before the child was introduced to the enchanting toys. In Chapter XIII we shall see that it is also possible to regard a *decision* as a choice between overlapping situations. That is, a decision determines which of two or more situations a person will be in, and hence what he will be affected by.

Finally, Lewin greatly elaborated the concept of *regions* within the environmental part of the life-space, and added the idea of paths connecting different regions (14). Both of these concepts are developed in several ways. Lewin makes good use of the idea of region in describing the different possibilities which a situation offers to a person. When the environment is subdivided into regions, the person is in one of these regions and outside of others—which may be next to the person's region ("connected" to it) or separated from it by other regions ("distant"). The concept of region may be coordinated with a spatial position (a room), a social position (the upper-middle class), an activity (playing basketball), a group (a family), or anything else that permits a person to be in or out of it. The region in which a person stands is important, because his perception of his situation depends on what region he is in; and when a person moves from one region to another, his perceptions undergo radical changes. On the one hand, his neighborhood is changed, since his is now surrounded by different regions, and hence subject to different forces and opportunities. On the other hand, the character of the new region is different. Because of these perceptual shifts, it is always important to know whether a person stands inside or outside of the region of others with whom he is interacting. If the person is in a different region, his perceptions of the "same" thing will be quite different. Because of the importance of the person's perception of his situation, Lewin observes that to understand a person's behavior, the first question one should ask is what region the person is in.

Attitude Change

It has been repeatedly demonstrated that when a person is induced to perform an action that he would not otherwise perform, his attitudes often change in a direction that is more consonant with the initially alien act. This attitudinal change is most apt to occur when the person is ostensibly offered a choice about whether or not to perform the act, at the same time that situational forces incline him to accept the induction. Kelman (15) has outlined a number of different dynamics that may be involved in the attitude change under such circumstances.

First, the induced action may provide an occasion for the person to re-examine his attitudes about the other. Having a choice leads the person to find attitudinal support for the action he is about to take, and hence leads him to persuade himself. Likewise, the action may provide an occasion for the person to have unanticipated new experiences with the object. If the person has been given a choice, and is not antagonistic toward these new experiences, he may well change his attitudes to fit the new information.

Second, once the person has taken the action, his life-space becomes altered, and the new psychological intention brings new forces into play. The person finds himself in a new region, where the balance of approach and avoidance forces may be different. This is particularly pertinent in cases where the approach gradient is steeper than the avoidance gradient, or where the resistance to the action is due to the price one has to pay to come into a closer association with the object. In either of these cases, once the action is taken, the person finds himself in a region where the approach gradient is stronger, and he is now bound to the object that he previously avoided. Kelman's article gives several interesting examples of these sorts of circumstances and the general principles that may govern their occurrence.

Third, once the action has been taken, new elements and new forces enter into the life-space. On the one hand, taking one step may commit the person to additional steps—he may have formed a unit between himself and the action; on the other hand, since he has undertaken the action, his subsequent definitions of objects are affected by the fact that he acted in a certain way (for instance, the other is a friend because a friendly act was directed toward him), and by the fact that self-evaluation may be involved (one is stupid if he directs a friendly act toward an enemy). The potency of these new forces will, of course, depend on the degree of personal involvement in the action.

The reader should note that the above dynamics are all ways of accounting for attitude change without resorting to either a general theory of cognitive dissonance or a general theory of self-attribution, and that it might be interesting to experimentally vary the degree of reality of the induced action.

Structure and Atmosphere of the Environment. Lewin spoke of the movement of the person from one environmental region to another as a "locomotion." When a region acquires a valence it creates a force on the person towards such a locomotion. This movement might require the person to go through certain intermediary regions (a "path") in order to reach his goal. For example, in order to reach the region of "practicing medicine," a person must pass through the region of "entering medical school," which in turn requires the person to pass through the region of taking chemistry courses and so on. The person might also find himself in a different region, or find a change in path, because of a restructuring of the life-space. For example, the person might discover a paramedical program, a new region which, if passed through, might lead him in the region of practicing medicine.

One important characteristic of situations is the *space of free movement*— the extent to which a person can locomote from one region to another and how easy or difficult this movement is. Ordinarily, various paths lead from one region to another, but sometimes barriers completely prevent access to a region and the person may be deprived of important goals. Such barriers may not even be evident to a person who is outside of the situation. For example, many persons are unaware of how a flight of steps is a barrier to a person in a wheelchair, or how the lack of familiarity with application procedures is a barrier to a person in the lower class. The construction of a ramp, or the presence of a helpful neighborhood worker may greatly increase the space of free movement in these situations. It should also be noted that an unstructured region is equivalent to a barrier, because the person does not know how to get through such a region.

In Lewin's later work with groups, the experienced environment was treated in terms of the situation's atmosphere. Thus, we may speak of a situation having a "repressive" or a "playful" or a "cooperative" atmosphere. Ronald Lippitt, one of Lewin's students at Iowa, began the studies of group atmosphere by experimentally creating "democratic" and "authoritarian" atmospheres, and contrasting the behavioral effects that these atmospheres produced (16).

Working with groups of children (ages ten and eleven), Lippitt created different atmospheres by having the adult leaders behave in different ways. The authoritarian leader induced group goals by the strength of his own power field. While he acted in a matter of fact rather than hostile manner, he ignored the goals of individuals that did not coincide with his own. Further, he kept the future as his own possession, inducing immediate actions without really sharing his vision of where these actions would lead. The democratic leader induced actions by helping members move towards their own goals. He gave them a future time perspective, and by pointing out a variety of means that could lead to each goal, gave each individual member a range of choices that could be self determined.

As a result of the different behavior of the leaders, the atmosphere in the authoritarian group was a restrictive one that reduced the space of free movement, and reduced each group member to an impersonal group unit that was directed towards leader-induced goals. In the democratic group, there was a free atmosphere, and as members gained knowledge about how to work with various art materials, there was an increase in this space of free movement. Each group member was an individual subpart with a unique position and particular personal goals and friendships that were respected.

These different atmospheres led the persons in each group to react in certain ways. Under the restrictive atmosphere, children began to constantly search for the leader's approval (the only way they could gain uniqueness), and tension began to develop that was expressed in several instances of scapegoating and a wild sort of explosiveness. In the free atmosphere, children were much more independent of the leader, showed more cooperative behavior, and calmly merged their individual efforts towards a group goal. In brief, I would say that the children in the free atmosphere showed more task involvement, and hence more capacity to cooperate, while the children in the restricted atmosphere showed more ego involvement. This effect may be related to Asch's theory that ego centeredness results from the thwarting of needs to be part of a group (see the discussion in Chapter IV).

Subsequent studies by Lippitt and White (17) demonstrated that the tension generated by a restrictive atmosphere might lead to either aggressive scapegoating or pervasive apathy, depending on other conditions in the group. They also showed that a third type of atmosphere could be created by a laissez-faire leader who failed to provide any real leadership for the group. Under these conditions the members of a group could not mobilize their individual interests into a group goal, and consequently suffered low morale and could not accomplish any group work.

Of course, I have given only a brief sketch of the above studies, omitting many rich details, simply attempting to orient the reader about their place in Lewin's over-all conceptualization. It may be seen that any given situation has a particular atmosphere—an over-all field influence—that will exercise effects on the behavior that occurs in that situation. Thus, there will be a particular atmosphere in any psychology department that will effect the creative work and the personal relationships in that department.

The Method of Description

Since the central characteristic of a region is neither its size nor its shape, but simply whether a person is inside or outside of it, Lewin initially used topological mathematics as a systematic language with which to describe the regions of the life-space. However, in order to be able to describe paths, which also have direction and length, he later introduced a "hodological" description of the space (18).

In my own opinion, the heart of Lewin's approach lies in the description of situations, rather than in the use of topology or egg-shaped diagrams. This is not to say that topological diagrams may not be helpful in describing a situation. They may encourage systematic thinking, and the necessity of choosing how to portray the situation may force the investigator to decide what the situation is really like. Thus, Dembo must choose whether or not to represent the goal and the barrier as connected, as in her Figure 6, and must choose whether or not the inner and outer barriers are connected, as in her Figures 8 and 9. However, if the investigator feels that he *has* to use topological diagrams, they may be much more of a hindrance than a help. In fact, they may get in the way of an accurate description of the situation.

Lewin's basic dictum is to be faithful to the situation. One must begin with the phenomenon. Then after looking, if one uses some sort of systematic conceptualization, it will be helpful—because one will be forced to look even more closely in order to make conceptual choices.

A second important methodological point is Lewin's insistence that one should not build up a picture of the situation by adding up disconnected descriptive elements. Rather, he advocates an over-all sketch of the situation which captures its fundamental structure. Then one can gradually specify details and differentiate elements. Thus, he argued for a method of gradual approximation from the whole to the parts.

Finally, a related point: the field approach tries to be sensitive to the larger situation in which a given situation is embedded. There are many fundamental situations, such as oppression, that are part of the human condition and cry out for description. In order to meet the challenge of accurately describing these situations, the investigator must have the courage to look at them and the freedom to describe them with new forms of systematic conceptualization.

THE NATURE OF EMOTION

The frustrating situation that Dembo describes, the impossible situation, produces a state of emotionality that leads to increasing primitivity, and finally to irrational behavior. This finding raises the more general issues of what emotions are, under what situations they occur, and how they are related to rational and irrational behavior. First, let us recall the major points which Dembo makes in regard to the specific case of frustration; then we shall inquire into the general nature of emotion.

Dembo notes that when a person is in an impossible situation—unable to reach his goal and unable to leave the struggle—the conflicting forces generated by the person attempting to go through the barriers that surround him produce a state of tension in the field (the life-space). Just as the molecules of a heated gas bump against the sides of their container and increase the pressure within the container, the person bumps against the barriers that surround him and increases the tension within the life-space. This conceptual description of the underlying life-space is coordinated to the basic affectivity of the surface description of the person—his impatient movements and feelings of frustration.

On the conditional genetic level, as the tension increases, boundaries in the life-space begin to dissolve and the space becomes more primitive and undifferentiated. This conceptualization is coordinated to specific experiences and behaviors, such as seeing the flowers that can be reached as similar to the goal flowers that cannot be reached. In this regard, I believe that one of Dembo's most important insights lies in the idea that the strength of an emotion may best be gauged in terms of how much it changes the person's life-space.

Finally, under the stress of an "almost event," or the provocation of the experimenter, the tension dissolves the boundary separating the person from the environment. There is a loss of self-control, and an affective outburst, and the person finds himself engaging in some irrational behavior: shouting angrily at the experimenter, or reaching for the wrong flowers.

Now Dembo's conceptualization is specifically applied to the conditions of frustration and the emotionality and irrational behavior which it may produce. But the very terms used—emotionality, anger, and so on—suggest that the description may be applicable to emotional behavior in general. To see how this may be possible, we turn to Sartre's theory of the emotions.

Sartre's Analysis and the Self-Boundary

Dembo's description of frustration has many features which are confirmed by Sartre's examination of emotion in general (19). As in Dembo's analysis, Sartre views emotion as a more primitive state in which the person is no longer so separated from objects in his world. He points out, for example, that if one sees a horrible face at the window, an essential aspect of feeling horror is preserving the face as present. The face is not experienced as "out there," separated from the self by the walls of the house; it is experienced as *here*. Thus, in emotion, the objective world falls away, and, in Sartre's terms, the self falls into another mode of being in the world.

For Sartre, too, the fall is a magical act which is undertaken when nothing else is possible and which might be said to be on the level of unreality, or to unite the two levels. Just as Dembo's subject reaches for the flower that is at hand, magically grasping the real goal, Sartre's subject faints in a magical avoidance of danger. For both Dembo and Sartre, emotion transforms the world.

Yet there are places in Sartre's analysis where he seems to consider these magical acts to be functional, rather than a mere expression of tension. Thus, he analyzes the joy of meeting a lover or an old friend in terms of the emotion's being a sort of magical incantation that permits an immediate union with the other. This union, which one would have to say is on a present level of unreality, gives the person a brief respite from the psychological work that must be performed to realize this union in the future, to bring it into being by talking and listening and doing things together on the level of reality. While this emotional magic does express tension, it seems a good deal more beneficial than fainting in the face of danger, or exploding with anger. I stress this point because I believe that emotions are basically functional, and only become emotionality under certain field conditions.

If the distance between the self and the objective world is indeed lessened whenever we experience emotion, then we may certainly represent this fact by speaking of a loosening of the boundary between the intrapsychic system, or self, and the environmental part of the life-space, the not-self.

It is worthwhile to note the peculiar character of this boundary. Elsewhere, Lewin makes a number of points about its nature (20):

The person may be more or less differentiated from the rest of his reality. A child only gradually distinguishes himself as a separate entity, and until a boundary develops there *is* no separate self and no concept of some things as belonging to the self.

Even when the self is relatively separated from the environment, it may be unified with certain other persons or objects. Thus, the mother, or a favorite toy, may be a part of the child, or a lover be a part of the self. In such cases, the presence and absence of the other may have dramatic effects on security, and the other may be a point of special sensitivity to the invasion of environmental forces. Whether or not an object belongs to the self depends on current tension systems. Thus, an incompleted product is more apt to still belong to the self, and hence the person is more susceptible to its being attacked or destroyed than he is after its completion, when it is more separate from the self.

The firmness of the boundary determines the extent to which environmental features and tensions influence one's intrapsychic state. Thus, if a family is moving, or a mother is tense, a child (whose boundary is not as firm as an adult's) will himself become tense. Likewise, the extent to which external impressions touch the nucleus of the self and affect it (and one's moods)—the sensitivity of the person—depends on the solidity of the boundary.

Conversely, the thinner or more permeable the self-boundary, the less a person controls, so that needs and tensions may break through to influence overt behavior. Furthermore, intrapsychic needs and tensions will influence one's perceived environment to a greater extent. Thus, animistic thinking and physiognomic perception will occur. And, since the perceived environment will be more connected with, and influenced by, the self's needs and wishes when the self-boundary is not firm, there will be less separation between the plane of reality and the plane of unreality. Thus, the person may enter the region of unreality. In this region, as defined by Dembo, the person can do what he pleases and wishes can come true. In Freudian terms, the person's thinking becomes dominated by the pleasure principle rather than the reality principle, and primary-process thought starts occurring. This regression (really a type of primitivization) is not, of course, wholly dysfunctional. In the service of the ego it is a temporary surrender which may lead to creative solutions. However, such unrealistic thinking may also escape from the person's control and begin to dominate. Dembo notes a number of instances where the field is experienced as ego-alien and forces behavior the subject does not want to happen. Thus, a subject who is playing with a fantasy may suddenly come under its power and be dominated by an unrealistic idea. Similarly, a subject may come under the spell of valences, as when he keeps compulsively thinking about how to use the clearly useless wooden rings that lie nearby. A somewhat different set of ego-alien forces may be involved when subjects go out of the field and on to the level of unreality, or into an overlapping situation against their will, as when persons who are trying to concentrate on a problem find themselves distracted by a multitude of other thoughts. In this case, the effects of satiation permit competing intention systems to assert themselves. Finally, affective breakthroughs and attacks against the experimenter were often, at least partly, unintended by the subject, who sometimes would much rather have maintained control.

Koffka's Theory

On the basis of the studies by Dembo and Karsten, Koffka attempted to conceptualize emotions as *intra*-ego forces (21). In doing this he appears to have been attempting to reconcile two different sets of facts. First, it seems clear that the primitivization which Dembo describes as characteristic of emotionality is due to tensions within the self. This is also true of some satiation phenomena which result from intra-ego tensions, and which Koffka, accordingly, conceives to be emotional phenomena.

Second, a person may experience fear only after he has run away from danger; and it is possible that a person might run away without experiencing any fear at all. Koffka can handle these facts by having the behavior of running away guided by field forces between the person and the environment, and coordinating the experience of emotion to separate tensions within the ego. (These tensions might be established after running as an adjustment to the field forces, or they might not occur at all if the danger was easily avoided.)

Thus, Koffka's analysis asserts that a behavior such as a flight from danger is initially controlled by stresses *between* the dangerous object and the self. These stresses may then causes stresses within the self, such as the emotion of fear. This emotion is then treated as equivalent to a tension system within the self—that is, a need to flee from the danger. This intra-ego tension may then persist after the actual danger is over, so that the person experiences fear after he has stopped running. Thus, the original stress stems from field relations, but this, in turn, stresses the ego, and these stresses may then begin to control the behavior of the person.

From my own viewpoint, Koffka's analysis overlooks one essential point: the flight from danger presupposes that the object is experienced as a dangerous object that must be fled from. That is, the object is experienced physiognomically. In fact, Koffka makes this very point elsewhere. Speaking of physiognomic characters, he states (22):

> ... they arise in objects when these objects are in dynamic relations with the Ego, when, otherwise expressed, a state of tension exists between them and the Ego. It is important to keep in mind that the kind of tension will vary for the different physiognomic characters. Not only will it be different in sign—positive or negative—and in degree, but also in quality. The kind of tension will determine our responses: attack, flight, approach, success, disregard, compassion, and so forth.

Now, Koffka himself points out that physiognomic characters such as "the horrible, the majestic, the enchanting," must arise in an organization which includes the ego. Further, this ego must not be separated from the environment —in the way that civilization encourages—but is rather unified with the field (though obviously not merged, or there would be no ego there as a separate part). But this appears to be the very unification that Dembo and Sartre are referring to when they speak of the boundary dissolution between self and environment that occurs in emotions.

In fact, from our perspective, when Koffka describes physiognomic character, he is doing a beautiful job of describing emotions. In his account of such physiognomic objects as the "horrible" and the "enchanting," and his account of our response to such objects with activities such as flight, and compassion, he seems to be describing essential emotional structures. Indeed, I have advanced a theory of the emotions which specifies the structure of each of the various emotions in terms of a systematic pattern of such relationships between the self and the environment (23). Why, then, does Koffka turn around and consider emotions to be stresses within the ego?

I believe that this is because Koffka, like many other theorists, is conceiving of emotions as dysfunctional. His account of physiognomic character is basically a positive, sympathetic, functional account. If there is danger, one had better flee it; if there is need, one had better have compassion. Whereas his account of emotion is a rather negative account—experiencing fear after the flight, tension, outburst, neurosis, and so on.

In general, there seems to be a marked distinctiveness of emotions, which is shown in the terms used by most theorists. Thus, we "fall" into emotion, the experience is more "primitive," and emotions are related to the release of "tension." One could imagine that the disappearance of a boundary between self and not-self might be described as "transcendent," to result in increased "unity," or to be related to compassion or serenity. Indeed, we find these very terms used by a few theorists, such as Hillman (24). Either we are dealing here with two different sorts of theorists, some of an Appollonian and some of a Dionysian bent, or there are two quite different sets of phenomena which appear similar when we attempt to formally conceptualize them. I suspect that both of these factors are at work in the confusion about emotional experience. Thus, the "return" to unity may actually be a higher-order organization that only occurs through an apparent disorganization.

In any case, I believe that Koffka places emotion within the ego because he is really talking about emotionality or disorganization. He fails to recognize that he described emotion in its functional aspect when he discussed physiognomic character.

Emotions as Organized Patterns of Relationships

My own position is that emotions are organized patterns of relationships between the self and the environment. These patterns are basically functional and are closely related to the situation in which the person finds himself. They occur when the boundary between self and environment weakens, and they function to promote greater autonomy and homonomy for the person. On the other hand, I would agree that emotionality is a disorganization that results from increased tensions within the field. I see such emotionality as a degraded form of emotion that occurs when emotion has been encapsulated, and which subsequently produces a dissolution of the boundary between reality and unreality. (Often this emotionality is induced by attempts of the self to maintain its hegonomy over field organization.)

Let us see how this view of emotion applies to Dembo's study. First, it should be observed that the dynamics of increased tension, primitivization, and boundary dissolution which she describes account only for the increase in general emotionality and its eventual outburst in irrational behavior. However, as Dembo indicates, a description of these dynamics are not sufficient to predict exactly what sort of irrational behavior will occur. That is, we do not know under what conditions there will be an outburst of anger rather than a magical substitution or a flight into unreality.

Next, I believe that it is important to distinguish between two qualitatively different types of anger. An earlier introspective study by Richardson makes a distinction between anger preceded by irritation, and anger preceded by humiliation (25). Richardson notes that the former may be discharged by a nondirected aggressive outburst, and that the irritated person actually hopes that no harm is caused by his outburst. The latter, on the other hand, is only resolved if the humiliated person specifically reduces the ego of the person who caused the humiliation to occur. In such cases, outbursts have no cathartic effect.

Now, in Dembo's study we really have two different situations somewhat analogous to irritation and humiliation. The first of these we have discussed in some detail as the impossible situation. In Dembo's experiment, we essentially have a satiation situation, similar to Karsten's experiment, but more irritating because the subject is not permitted to stop. As in Karsten's experiment, primitivization develops beneath the surface of fairly smooth behavior. But Dembo does not permit her subjects to stop, and the tension mounts until it finally explodes in a burst of irritation. While some event always triggers this explosion (though the trigger is sometimes sought), and this almost event or provocation may be accidentally provided by something which the experimenter does, there is nothing personal in the explosion. It is not really caused by the experimenter nor directed at her. In a later experiment of Dembo's, reported by Koffka (26), subjects were placed in an impossible situation without the experimenter's being present; these subjects exhibited a freely expressed irritated anger that was not directed against the experimenter, and which left them without any feelings of upset about their experience.

On the other hand, it seems clear that the subjects in Dembo's original experiment were placed in a somewhat different situation; their frustration was not of an impersonal nature, but was maintained by the will of the experimenter. This situation involved a struggle of wills, and as Koffka notes, the ego of the subject was put under pressure by "its subordination under the will and whim of the experimenter" (27).

Here it seems that the anger is of quite a different quality. The subject is not simply irritated; his will is being challenged by the will of the experimenter, and his anger resists this challenge. The subject is also in a bind, because the angrier he gets, the more obvious it is that he has been gotten to, and hence the more inferior he has become. Here, then, we have an anger which is not simply an impersonal explosion, releasing an intrapsychic tension, but rather an interpersonal assertion of the subject's personal will against the will of the experimenter.

My own investigations into the phenomenology of anger have revealed that this type of anger only arises when there is a challenge to the person's will—to what he asserts (28). Further, this challenge is to what the person asserts ought to exist, rather than to simply something he wants to exist.

Returning to our initial problem of how to specify the conditions under which different sorts of affective outbursts will occur, I postulate that, given a state of basic affectivity, the emotion of anger will occur only when the subject perceives that there is a challenge to what he asserts ought to exist. Thus, at the moment of anger I believe the subjects must have felt that the experimenter *ought* not to subject them to an impossible situation, or that it was *wrong* for her to be so rude. Rather than being merely an aimless expression of tension, or a blind intent to destroy so that one can break free, I believe that the emotion of anger is a specific emotional pattern that is directed against the will of another who is creating an intolerable reality. As such, it is fundamentally an assertion of the subject's own will as to what reality ought to be like.

Note that, while the presence of the emotion indicates an underlying tension in the field and a weakening of the boundary between the self and the other, the particular emotion arises as an organized pattern in a situation with a definite structure—there has been a challenge to what the subject asserts ought to exist. Further, the emotion is basically functional in that it psychologically removes this challenge and re-establishes the reality that the person asserts ought to exist, thus preserving his autonomy and values.

THE NATURE OF UNREALITY

In the situation created by Dembo, the outburst of anger does not succeed in permanently reorganizing the social situation. This is because the experimenter resists the reality asserted by the subject's anger and insists on her own definition of the situation. The experimenter's will is too strong for the subject to prevail, and all his actions and emotions are futile. (We shall examine why this is so when we consider the nature of will in Chapter XIII.) Hence, the subject's emotion appears irrational. However, for the subject's basic emotionality to lead to truly irrational behavior, it seems to me that he must begin to confuse the level of unreality with the level of reality. To see how this may occur, and to examine the nature of irrationality and the structure of unreality in more detail, let us return to the dynamics of the impossible situation.

It should be observed that all the time that the increasing tension is leading to a primitivization of the field, the person is trying to escape from the field. In addition to attempting to break through the barriers, Dembo notes two other responses which are topologically distinguishable. These are: (a) the retreat into unreality; and (b) the creation of special subregions that are within the field of reality by fluid boundaries, where the person can move freely and wishes can come true unhindered by the obstacles of the real world. Dembo conceives of the subject entering this realm when he slips off into a daydream. On the other hand, the special subregions of the field are akin to private kingdoms within the real world. Within these narrow limits, the subject's own will can determine his behavior, free from the imposing tension of the field. For example, the subject may decide to ignore the experimenter and read a magazine. We believe that the distinction between these two different methods of escape is potentially of great importance. However, when it is examined closely, the distinction raises a host of questions about the nature of unreality and the difference between "willed" and "unwilled" behavior.

Lewin himself always coordinated reality with the firmness, and unreality with the fluidity, of the material of tension systems. Thus, he essentially defined reality in terms of its resistant properties—what is real is what may offer resistance to the will, whereas wishes can freely shape the unreal. However, Dembo's distinction between a level of unreality and a private subregion on the level of reality suggests that there are different ways to escape from reality, and perhaps different sorts of unrealness.

We wish to know whether the distinction can help us understand a whole series of different sorts of unreal behavior. Can it help us with the differences between primary and secondary process, between dreaming, schizophrenia, and hysteria, between fantasy and play? Can it help us with the many uses of reality within the series of experiments that we have considered? For we have meet the concept of reality or realness on several occasions. Ovsiankina mentions that for some of her subjects the interrupted task remained "the real task," and the subjects never became fully involved in the task which was used to interrupt them. Brown varied whether intelligence test items were real items or just filler items. Finally, Mahler attempted to vary the reality of substitute tasks by having subjects actually perform, talk about, or simply think of doing the activity. And it will be recalled that she discovered that there was a component of many tasks was a realization component, which involved some aspect of task being brought into reality. When Dembo speaks of a plane of reality as opposed to a plane of unreality, we wish to know whether her concept of reality is the same or different from all these other uses of the term.

To answer these questions we must make a detour and examine whether or not an activity that is on the level of unreality can substitute for an activity on the level of reality.

It may be recalled that a number of studies showed that it was sometimes possible to substitute one activity for another, so that the intention to perform the first activity was released by the performance of the substitute. Thus far, we have largely considered substitute actions which occurred on the level of reality where the material of the tension systems is solid, rather than fluid. Since Dembo's subjects, trapped in an impossible situation, sometimes spontaneously imagined fantasy solutions as a substitute for reaching the real goal, the possibility arises that substitute actions on the plane of unreality may be able to release intention systems on the plane of reality.

Mahler's Study

To investigate this process, Mahler (29) placed subjects in a situation where they had an impossible problem to solve: she asked them to bring a balloon which was three meters away over to themselves without leaving their position. A number of interesting looking tools were lying about the room, but in fact could not be used to reach the balloon. In these circumstances, about one-third of the subjects spontaneously began thinking of solutions with a magical or unreal character. For example, they wished for a vacuum cleaner to suck the balloon to them; or imagined the ability to create an earthquake; or started to talk to the balloon and reassure it so that it would come. These unreal solutions were not satisfying, and the subjects always returned to the plane of reality with an unchanged intention system. In fact, if the experimenter asked for a magical solution, many subjects rejected the idea out of hand. Subjects who did comply still returned unsatisfied to the real task.

In order to encourage the possibility of spontaneous fantasy solutions, Mahler interrupted some subjects in the middle of their efforts to reach the balloon and gave them the substitute task of making up a fairy tale. It is fascinating to note that nine of fifteen subjects spontaneously told a story which involved reaching the balloon or some obvious equivalent like the moon. Of these nine stories, seven ended successfully and two unsuccessfully. However, this spontaneous substitute action did not release the original intention system; eight of the nine subjects again resumed the task of trying to get the balloon. Of the six subjects who failed to mention the balloon, five also resumed the task.

Mahler next attempted to loosen the situation so that the subject could more easily make a transition into unreality. She structured the entire experiment in a playful vein, beginning with a supposedly true ghost story about the room in which the experiment was held. Then the subject was asked to get a piece of paper, and found written on it, "Whoever finds me is to go to the table at the window." There followed a series of written requests for various actions, one of which involved reading a fairy tale in which magic was involved. Finally, the subject found the critical task of reaching the balloon (which was three meters away). After trying unsuccessfully for about six minutes, the subject found a "magic" stick with which he could make the balloon come to him. After some "magic thinking," the experimenter gave him the balloon and the subject found another piece of paper, ordering him "to write down the names of ten fairy tales." The experimenter then busied herself in making notes, thus giving the subject an opportunity to resume the task of reaching the balloon, or to show a partial resumption by thinking about or talking about it. Under these conditions, the unreal magic solution has some substitute value, and the percentage of resumption drops from 92 to 57. Furthermore, the subjects who did resume the task appear to be those who had difficulty in entering the unreal situation from the beginning.

Thus, activities and solutions that are on the level of unreality appear to have substitution value, but only when the subject is on the plane of unreality to begin with.

Substitution in the Frustration-Regression Study

When children were separated from the toys with which they had been involved, their play sometimes appeared to have the meaning of substitute activity. Barker, Dembo, and Lewin classified this play as either "real" or "unreal" substitution (30). In the former category were episodes where children played with the available toys as a substitute for, or a means to, the unaccessible toys. For example, one child used an available fishing pole to "fish" through the barrier, pretending to catch the obstructed toys. In the latter category were episodes in which a child simply talked about the unaccessible toys, without the talking being an attempt to influence the experimenter. For example, the child might say, "It looks like Christmas night," or "My house is that color."

Later, when the investigators made a count of all emotional expressions, they found that in periods of time when real substitution was occurring, the subjects were calm and happy. In periods of time when unreal substitution occurred, the children did not express the unhappiness and restlessness that were characteristic of periods of extreme frustration. However, neither did they express any happiness. The experimenters state, "These findings suggest that unreal substitutes reduce the pain and tension of frustration, but do not supply the satisfactions of reality . . ." (31).

Sliosberg's Study

Further information on the dynamics of unreality is given by the experiments of Sliosberg, who studies the substitution of various objects in children's activities (32). In general, her procedure was to involve a child in playing with one object and then suggest that he put it aside and play with some substitute object.

In serious nonplay situations, Sliosberg shows that children (from three to six years of age) are well aware of the difference between real and pretend objects. If, for example, a child is promised a piece of candy, but given a piece of cardboard which the experimenter calls candy, 32 per cent of the children refuse it altogether, 20 per cent treat it as cardboard but do something with it, 22 per cent begin to play with it as a toy, 8 per cent calls it "play candy," and others treat the cardboard as candy but with gestures that indicate they see through the game (for instance, smilingly saying how good it tastes). Sliosberg points out that on the level of reality the cardboard remains outside the region of eating, while on the level of unreality it is within the region of eating. She shows that the transition to the level of unreality is much more apt to occur when the situation is loose and the child is not yet eating real chocolate, than when the situation is fixed by the real prior activity of eating. The most fixed situation, with the least possibility of a transition to play, is when the goal is close but not yet attained.

Experimenting with different objects, Sliosberg shows that a pair of scissors is not as bound to the activity of cutting as a pair of play scissors. And 40 per cent of the younger children "scribble" with a cardboard "pencil," although the situation is a real rather than play, situation. However, such behavior is dependent on needs being low. When needs increase, the situation becomes firm. For example, if there is a competition for cutout figures, no child will accept play scissors.

Now, if the situation is loosened by working with a child who is playing, the same objects that would be rejected in a real situation are quite acceptable. If the experimenter offers the child some "chocolate" (cardboard), it is usually accepted and treated as (play) chocolate. In fact, within the play situation the older children accept many substitutes (a stick for a doll) that the younger children refuse. The older are more able to influence the meanings of objects, whereas the younger are more bound to reality so that the toys must be more real; a stick doll is less satisfactory than a real doll, for example, since without a mouth it cannot eat. In all cases, objects which were not part of the play were still treated as real, and attempts at substitution were rejected.

Sliosberg shows that even in a play situation some objects have more fixed meanings than others. If, for example, a child is building something with blocks, he will accept plasticine or stones as a substitute. But he will refuse to accept wooden animals. The animals are somehow not proper building materials. An object such as a toy animal has a meaning which conflicts with certain other meanings with almost a "moral" force.

Sliosberg called the property of an object that causes it to be viewed in only one way its "fixity." She shows that an object's fixity is less as a child gets older and begins to separate himself more from objects. However, fixity increases whenever the object is a dependent part of a broader situation.

Towards the end of her study, Sliosberg makes the important assertion that play does not really occur on the level of unreality. True, the fluidity of the meanings of objects and their properties, and the dependence of meaning upon the will of the person are properties of both play and the level of unreality. However, Sliosberg argues that objects are treated logically in play, whereas in dreams or psychosis, prelogical or primary process thought abounds. For example, pieces of wood that in play are "milk bottles" are treated as though they might break, and the child doesn't really try to feed the doll chocolate. Therefore, play is more accurately described as occurring in a special region within the level of reality.

Two Types of Unreality

Sliosberg's argument that play occurs in a special region on the level of reality seems intuitively correct. However, I have difficulty in accepting her argument that play should be so regarded because objects are treated logically. For in that case fantasy, which often treats objects or persons logically, would also have to be considered a special region on the level of reality, whereas it is one of Dembo's prime examples of activity on the level of unreality. I believe that the issue of whether or not thinking is logical should be coordinated with the integrity of the boundary between reality and unreality, and kept separate from whether or not the person is on the plane of reality. Thus, I would treat primary-process thinking, dreaming, and irrational behavior as evidence of boundary dissolution between the level of unreality and the level of reality. But a person might be daydreaming on the level of unreality, and yet keep in contact with reality by maintaining the boundary between his behavior and the plane of reality.

It seems to me that the reason that play is on the level of reality appears to have more to do with the fact that the meanings involved in play are public rather than private meanings. Hence, the difference between what is real and what is play might better be related to the difference between perception and imagination. In play, the meanings which I give objects, acts, or events are meant to be shared meanings. Anyone who watches children at play may see innumerable negotiations over what something is or is not going to mean. Not only the child but the other must be careful with the play "milk bottle." On the other hand, in fantasy, dreams, and schizophrenia, there is no thought that another person with a separate perspective could view the event.

In play, objects may be imagined to have a meaning that they do not ordinarily possess, but this play meaning must be logically related to the object and publicly acceptable. This may be easily demonstrated by attempting to get a child to accept an unordinary play object. For example, in playing "farm" with my four-year-old, I noticed that a small cup could conceivably be imagined as a hen. I proposed that the cup was a hen and began to have it walk around and "cluck," but this was met by the objection, "That's not a hen, it doesn't have a mouth." I took a crayon and drew a mouth on the front of the cup, but there was another objection—"It doesn't have any eyes." I remedied that and asked if it were now a hen. However, there was one more objection, "It's not a hen, it doesn't have a tail." I took a small feather and fastened it to the handle of the cup (which had been a good enough tail for me), and held the object up for inspection. After a second of skeptical scrutiny, Lucinda's face cleared, and reaching for what was now a hen, she began to walk and cluck it about our farm.

In contrast to play, in fantasy we are on the plane of unreality because there is no other perspective than our own. In play, as when the subject in Dembo's experiment decides that it is time to read the paper, the person knows that he is imposing his perspective on the world. Now of course, in a sense this does make things less real, for it neglects other perspectives; play is not real. But this is quite a different path away from reality. In play, unlike fantasy, we make our impositions on a real world.

When a person is on the level of unreality, the boundary between the levels of reality and unreality may remain intact, as in fantasy, or it may vanish, as in dreams, schizophrenia, and the unreal substitute actions which Dembo describes. Likewise, when a person has created a special region within reality, the boundary between the levels of reality and unreality may or may not be intact. The boundary is intact in the case of play; but I believe it vanishes in cases of hysteria, and when we indulge in what Sartre calls "bad faith" (33).

If my analysis is correct, there are at least two different ways to escape reality or be out of touch with it. We may enter a level of unreality where an essential aspect of our experience is that our work has no other possible perspectives; or we may create a subregion within reality in which we impose the meanings we desire on a world that we know may have different meanings from those we give it (we know that the objects of our world can be seen from other possible perspectives). In the latter case, we may say that our behavior has a low degree of reality because its validity is limited to a subregion which does not take into account the perspectives of the generalized other. We are living behind a boundary that is erected by our will, and imposed between us and other perspectives and meanings. (It should be remembered that this boundary may or may not be under our conscious control.)

While Dembo's analysis lays more stress on the retreat to a level of unreality, it is clear that when persons are in an impossible situation they often attempt to escape the reality of the unpleasant alternatives by escaping to a special region of reality where events have a more comfortable meaning. Sometimes other persons will join them in this play region and pretend that it is reality; indeed, when faced with unacceptable alternatives, an entire group may retreat into its own isolated version of reality. Elsewhere, I have shown how this may occur at the highest governmental levels (34); and Janis has documented a number of cases where a number of decision makers may concur in an unrealistic course of action (35).

In the case of either the level of unreality or a special subregion in which the person's behavior has a low degree of reality, a person may decide to enter the level or region, or he may find himself in it. That is, in Lewin's terms, the entrance may be either "controlled" or "field dependent." Note that the latter case is not necessarily unwilled, because an intention may have established the field of forces to which the person responded. However, if the person is in a special subregion within reality, he has a mastery of the region. There is an assertion of will that determines what objects and events within the region will mean. On the other hand, if a person is on the level of unreality, I believe that there is a letting go, a surrender of will, so that meanings may be found rather than given.

It may also be seen that, in a sense, there are two different meanings to *real*. When Dembo speaks of unreality, she is referring to activities that are on the plane of reality—where reality is hard rather than fluid, and wishes and fantasies cannot change its shape. However, when Brown speaks of real test problems in contrast to filler items (Chapter IV), he is referring to activities that are not isolated within a special (play) region of reality, items whose success or failure will have a meaning in the public domain.

It should be noted that the concept of a subregion within reality implies that the person experiences a broader reality with different meanings outside of the subregion. However, in hysteria or bad faith—where the distinction between the level of reality and unreality has been lost—the person will be unaware of this broader reality, and will impose his private meanings without being aware that he is playing and that his meanings are not publicly valid.

THE ACCEPTANCE OF REALITIES

The distinctions made above raise the general question of just how events are admitted, or denied access, to our reality. While this topic clearly requires a book in its own right, I want to at least make a brief sketch of a few of the interesting problems and promising approaches in this area.

Different Realities

Ordinarily, we assume that there is only one reality. However, in actuality, the reality that exists for a person who is inside a situation is quite different from that of the outsider who is objectively viewing the situation. Thus, in her work in rehabilitation psychology, Dembo (36) has pointed out that the reality for a person who has lost a limb or a loved one is quite different from the reality of the professional or friend who may want to help the person inside the situation. In fact, the meaning of a helping act may be quite different depending on whether one is helping or being helped. Likewise, Leviton's work shows that the meaning of hope depends on whether one is a client or a professional (37). To most clients, hope means present comfort and an incentive to work because of the expectation of future improvement, while a realistic approach may mean depression and withdrawal. On the other hand, to many professionals, realism means acceptance without false hopes. Thus, most clients prefer a hopeful rather than a realistic outlook, while most professionals prefer realism. As Leviton observes, "Clients stated that if they don't have hope for improvement they can't see the sense of working hard at therapies, but few of them felt, as several professionals did, that if improvement is expected patients will wait passively for it and not work hard" (38). Obviously, effective communication between persons who are in different positions—professionals and clients, teachers and students—depends on the recognition of these different realities.

Although in practice it is difficult for us to be aware of the different realities inherent in different positions, in theory it seems easy to account for these differences in terms of there being different perspectives on one reality. However, we have no adequate way to represent the interesting situation that occurs when a person experiences another whose reality is completely different from his own. This may occur when a person meets someone from a different culture or class, when he meets a person who is in a world of his own, or when he simply becomes intimately acquainted with another person. It is interesting to note that the shock of this different reality is sometimes met by seeing the other as playing (that is, being in a subregion of his own reality), or by maintaining other types of distance between oneself and the other (39). While we cannot deal with this issue here, it should be noted that Lewin briefly discusses the problem when he attempts to deal with disagreements between husband and wife in terms of overlapping life-spaces (40). The issue is also a concern of Schutz's when he discusses the problem of conceptualizing the reality of Don Quixote (41), and is a central theme of Castaneda's dealing's with Don Juan (42).

The Reality of Unreal Acts

It would be interesting to state the conditions under which a person's own unreal acts may become real. To understand this problem, we must return to the issues raised by substitute activities. While an intention that has not been fulfilled (an unreleased tension system) is often expressed in fantasy activity or in play, and while this substitute activity occurs more easily in the fluid region of unreality, or the self-willed region of play, both Sliosberg's and Mahler's experiments suggest that substitutions which occur in fluid or play regions cannot satisfy intention systems that develop in the more solid region of reality. The activity of imagining a magical solution that gets a balloon is not the same as the activity of really reaching it, and cannot substitute for it. Hence, unreal substitutions have a basically nonfunctional aspect. Because of this, Lewin himself was puzzled as to why attempts at substitution occur so frequently in fluid regions.

In everyday life, it is also true that many substitute actions which occur in fantasy, on the plane of unreality, do not satisfy the original tension system. The process of symptom formation, and the evidence that the removal of one symptom may simply result in a new symptom are prime examples. However, there is also evidence that suggests that symbolic acts may sometimes provide a complete release for the underlying tension. From my own experience I know that a person who is angry at another may draw a nasty picture, or pretend to hit the other, and find that this substitute expression completely reduces the anger. Therefore, we must conclude that the experiments that we have described above simply did not create the right conditions for such successful substitution to occur.

It seems to me that symbolic actions attain substitution value only when they get away from the person's control. The action of either playing or fantasizing begins as an act of will, as the person establishes the play region or the level of unreality in which meanings depend on what he desires. However, the meanings of the events within this region or level are apt to attain an independence of their own. If and when this happens, the symbolic events become real. That is, an action that was initiated with a low degree of reality —either in fantasy or in play—breaks away from the person's self-control and takes on a meaning (which may have been previously prohibited) that gives the action a high degree of reality. When this occurs, the person's life-space becomes restructured and the original intention system can be fulfilled. Similar conditions may often be present when symbols are created in a successful work of art.

In this connection, it should be noted that intention systems can be released in at least two different ways. Ordinarily, we think of release occurring by an intention being fulfilled. But is also possible for the situation to change so that the intention is no longer needed. If a friend unexpectedly comes for a visit we no longer need to write him; if an insult that we are about to avenge turns out to have been an innocent remark, there is no further need for our anger. Substitute actions on the symbolic level may often achieve the release of intention in this latter way. That is, they may operate by providing an entirely new meaning for the situation in which the person finds himself.

To summarize: the substitution of one activity for another may occur in at least two different ways. In Chapter VI, we saw that it may occur on the plane of reality if the original activity is transformed into a more general activity, so that the substitute activity can satisfactorily release a more general intention system. On the plane of unreality, substitute activities often occur when the person has no available means of satisfying his needs and goes into a fantasy world of his own. However, such substitution is not satisfying unless the boundary between unreality and reality loosens and permits a reorganization of the life-space. This may occur when a fantasy escapes from the person's control and influences the meaning of the real situation. If a reorganization on the level of reality does not occur, the substitute gratification is lost when the person returns to reality.

FOOTNOTES

1. Kurt Lewin, *Principles of Topological Psychology* (New York: McGraw-Hill, 1936).

2. Kurt Lewin, "The Psychological Situations of Reward and Punishment," in *A Dynamic Theory of Personality* (New York: McGraw-Hill, 1935).

3. Sarah Forer, "Eine Untersuchung zur Lese-Lern-Methode Decroly," *Zeit fuer Kinderforschung* 42(1933), 11–44. A translation, "An Investigation of the Decroly Method of Learning and Reading," is available from Xerox: University Microfilms.

4. Sara Fajans, "Die Bedeutung der Entfernung fuer die Starke eines Aufforderungscharakters beim Saugling und Kleinkind," *Psychol. Forsch.* 17(1933), 215–267. The translation, "The Significance of Distance for the Strength of a Valence in Infants and Young Children," may be obtained from Xerox: University Microfilms.

5. Herbert F. Wright, "The Effect of Barriers Upon Strength of Motivation," in Roger G. Barker, Jacob S. Kounin, Herbert F. Wright (Eds.), *Child Behavior and Development* (New York: McGraw-Hill, 1943).

6. Kurt Lewin, "The Conceptual Representation and Measurement of Psychological Forces," *Contributions to Psychological Theory* 1(1938), No. 4.

7. Kurt Lewin, loc. cit., and "Behavior and Development as a Function of the Total Situation," in *Field Theory in Social Sciences* (New York: Harper and Row, 1951).

8. Kurt Lewin, "Frontiers in Group Dynamics," in *Field Theory in the Social Sciences* (New York: Harper and Row, 1951).

9. Lawrence K. Frank, "Time Perspectives," *Journal of Social Philosophies* 4(1939), 293–312.

10. Kurt Lewin, "Time Perspective and Morale," in Goodwin Watson (Ed.), *Civilian Morale* (Boston: Houghton Mifflin, 1942).

11. For a review of this literature, see Robert Kastenbaum, "The Dimensions of Future Time Perspective, an Experimental Analysis," *Journal of General Psychology* 65(1961), 203–218.

12. Lewin, *Principles of Topological Psychology*, 137–139.

13. Ibid., 22.

14. Ibid., 88 ff.

15. Herbert C. Kelman, "The Induction of Action and Attitude Change," *Proc. XIV. Internat. Cong. Applied Psychol.* (Copenhagen, 1961).

16. Ronald Lippitt, "An Experimental Study of the Effect of Democratic and Authoritarian Group Atmospheres," *University of Iowa Studies in Child Welfare* 16(1940), No. 3, 43–195.

17. Ralph White and Ronald Lippitt, *Autocracy and Democracy* (New York: Harper, 1960).

18. Kurt Lewin, "The Conceptual Representation and Measurement of Psychological Forces."

19. Jean Paul Sartre, *The Emotions: Outline of a Theory* (New York: Philosophical Library, 1948).

20. Kurt Lewin, "Environmental Forces," in *A Dynamic Theory of Personality* (New York: McGraw-Hill, 1935).

21. Kurt Koffka, *Principles of Gestalt Psychology* (New York: Harcourt, Brace and World, 1935), 405–416.

22. Ibid., 362.

23. Joseph de Rivera, "A Structural Theory of the Emotions," *Psychological Issues* (in press).

24. James Hillman, *Emotion* (Evanston, Illinois: Northwestern University Press, 1961).

25. Roy F. Richardson, *The Psychology and Pedagogy of Anger* (Baltimore: Warwick and York, 1918).

26. Koffka, *Principles of Gestalt Psychology,* 673.

27. Ibid., 674.

28. de Rivera, loc. cit.

29. Vera Mahler, "Ersatzhandlungen verschiedenen Realitätsgrades," *Psychol. Forsch.* 18(1933), 26–89. A translation, "Substitute Actions on Various Levels of Reality," is available from Xerox: University Microfilms.

30. Roger Barker, Tamara Dembo, and Kurt Lewin, "Frustration and Regression: An Experiment with Young Children," *University of Iowa Studies in Child Welfare* 18(1941), No. 1, 163–164.

31. Ibid., 200.

32. Sara Sliosberg, "Zur Dynamik des Ersatzes in Spiel-und Ernestsituationen," *Psychol. Forsch.* 19(1934), 122–181. A translation, "A Contribution to the Dynamics of Substitution in Series and in Play Situations," is available from Xerox: University Microfilms.

33. Jeal Paul Sartre, *Being and Nothingness* (New York: Washington Square Press, 1971, original, 1953).

34. Joseph de Rivera, *The Psychological Dimension of Foreign Policy* (Columbus, Ohio: Charles E. Merrill, 1968), 78–82.

35. Irving Janis, *Victims of groupthink: A Psychological Study of Foreign Policy Decisions* (Boston: Houghton Mifflin, 1972).

36. Tamara Dembo, "Sensitivity of One Person to Another," *Rehabilitation Literature* 25(1964), 231–235.

37. Gloria Leviton, "Professional and Client Viewpoints on Rehabilitation Issues," *Rehabilitation Psychology* 20(1973), No. 1.

38. Ibid., 43.

39. For different types of psychological distance, see Thomas Kreilkamp, "The Dimensions of Psychological Distance," unpublished dosctoral dissertation (New York University, 1968). For the distance created by deception, see Joe K. Adams, "Deception and Intrigue in So-called 'Mental Illness'," *Journal of Humanistic Psychology* 4(1964), 27–38.

40. Kurt Lewin, *Resolving Social Conflicts* (New York: Harper, 1948), Chapter 4.

41. Alfred Schutz, "Don Quixote and the Problem of Reality," in *Collected Papers*, Vol. II (The Hague: Martiners Nijhoff, 1964).

42. Carlos Castaneda, *Journey to Xitlan* (New York: Simon and Schuster, 1972).

Chapter XII

SUCCESS AND FAILURE*

Ferdinand Hoppe

It is not necessary to give a detailed argument in order to show that the question of origin and effect of success and failure is of thoroughgoing importance for psychology. The concepts of success and failure play an important part in Adler's theory reference of encouragement and discouragement. They are also very important in animal psychology and in our conceptions of psychological development. The principle of selection, on the basis of which the child or animal learns to behave correctly and adequately over and above mere instinctive actions, is ascribed to success and failure, or rather to the experiences of pleasure and displeasure connected therewith.

Karl Buhler (1) for instance, explains "The human trainer works with reward and punishment, whereby he is only imitating what nature does; for under natural conditions the animal learns through success and failure. Consider, for instance, the hen at the garden fence. The first time she will run back and forth along the obstacle in a restless and confused manner, until accidentally she finds a hole which is suitable to slip through. The second, third, fifth, time the change in the hen's behavior is hardly noticeable, but if the process occurs several dozen times, she will gradually reach the goal more and more

*Translated by Dr. Sibylle Escalona. The original article, "Erfolg und Misserfolg," was published in *Psychologische Forschung*, Vol. 14(1930), 1–62. Permission to publish this translation was generously granted by Springer-Verlag.

quickly, and finally she avoids all unnecessary ways by going to the goal directly. The *pleasure of success* has given this particular behavior an advantage, the displeasure of failure has repressed the other; there is now a clear, and sufficiently rigid *association between definite sensual impressions and the movement-complex of the successful behavior.*"

The question with which the following experimental investigation is concerned, was not, at first, too narrowly defined. We wished to gain a general impression of the formation and the psychological effect of success and failure experiences.

Chapter I and the corresponding experimental setup I leads to the basic problems of success and failure.

We found it necessary to emphasize, in this study, the qualitative aspect of the processes in question rather than the quantitative ones. We do not mean to say, however, that we wish to discuss only phenomenological questions. Functional-dynamical problems stand in the center of our considerations. Before starting a quantitative investigation, however, it has to be determined what kinds of dynamic problems are of importance, and which concepts are to be used for their adequate representation. For such purposes, a thorough investigation of a few cases usually proves more useful than a broad, statistical approach. As far as the quantitative results are concerned, therefore, the individual experiments bear more the character of a first orientation, in a field still new to experimental research.

I. SATIATION, SATISFACTION, AND RESUMPTION

The point of departure for these experiments were problems which had come up in Karsten's study in psychological satiation (2) and which are connected with a selective effect of success and failure by means of associations of pleasure and displeasure.

The developmental-psychological thesis of the selection of actions through the repetition of an association of pleasure with successful actions and displeasure with unsuccessful actions meets with a difficulty, insofar as we know that even a successful action, when it is repeated several times, does not always lead to a fixation of pleasure, but under certain psychological conditions, may lead to extreme displeasure. Instead of a satisfaction, and an inclination to repeat the action, there occurs then psychological satiation, that is, a disinclination to repeat the action. In order to approach the question of the selective effect of success and failure, we must first attempt to clarify the dynamic difference between satiation and satisfaction.

One might be inclined, at first, to regard satiation as well as satisfaction as equivalents for the release of tension systems. But the investigation of A.

Karsten showed that the two are not the same. An activity may have given satisfaction, but one need not be tired of it; there may even be a tendency to repeat it. It is quite possible, however, to be extremely satiated with an activity without feeling any satisfaction about it at all. And furthermore, there are cases in which an activity yielded satisfaction and nevertheless satiation occurred.

Satiation and satisfaction are, therefore, not identical. By way of preliminary clarification of the difference, Karsten points out that the questions of the presence or absence of satiation, and of the presence or absence of satisfaction, really belong to different realms of investigation. We want to give a short explanation of the difference.

If somebody intends to carry out an action with a definitely planned goal, for instance to write a letter or to read a certain article in a newspaper, the carrying out of this intention will, usually, satisfy the quasi-need which corresponds to this intention, and the corresponding system will be released of tension (3).

After the execution of such an action, one will usually turn to new goals, begin other tasks for which a quasi-need had been present beforehand, or carry out a new, not previously intended action. It may also be the case, however, that after the action one does not turn towards entirely new goals, but to those which are similar or identical with the first one. After having read one article, one may like to read another article, after having played one piece on the piano one may wish to play another one. Sometimes, however, for instance after many repetitions of one and the same action, there exists a disinclination to carry out the same, or similar actions. One turns to a different kind of action. The question as to which actions or which goals attract a person after completion of an action, we shall call a question of *goal formation*. We speak of goal formation during the transition to a repetition of an action, as well as during the transition to a new action (a change of goal).

How this goal formation takes place in a concrete case depends upon a number of different factors in the psychological outer fields *(des In- und Umfeldes)* of the particular person. It is of special importance whether other objects or events which have a strong negative or positive valence are, at the moment, near by.

Psychological *satiation* is defined by a definite direction of goal formation after the execution of an action. Satiation means that, on the basis of the previous repetitions, there is no inclination to turn towards similar actions; in other words, there exists a marked tendency towards a change of goal.

In *satisfaction,* however, we are dealing with the equivalent of the release of the tension system corresponding to the need underlying the previous action, and not, at least not directly, with the direction of future behavior.

According to the conception of satiation and satisfaction outlined here, we will have, after completion of an action, in both cases a release of the tension of the original system underlying the action. Without the existence of a corresponding need, the inclination or disinclination to repeat an action would be caused merely by the experiences of pleasure or displeasure fixated to it through the association of the experiences of pleasure or displeasure with the action.

In the following, we shall use the term *fixation* only in this special sense. We do not mean the determination of the valences of action corresponding to a need, but the fact that an action may have a positive or negative character from previous experiences without the existence of an acute tension system.

The assumption that, disregarding other valences in the field and other needs, in the case of satisfaction there is a tendency towards a repetition of the action, but in the case of satiation a disinclination to any repetition of the action, corresponds to the usual conception of the selective effect of pleasurable and displeasurable experiences on future repetitions.

Experimental setup I. We constructed a series of experiments which were to test spontaneous resumption of actions after satiation and after satisfaction.

Each experimental day every subject had to carry out one action until satisfaction was achieved, and another action until satiation was achieved. After the experiment, the subject was left alone in the room for a certain length of time, during which time the experimenter secretly observed the subjects' attitude towards the actions,—that is, whether he resumed them or turned away from them.

We assumed that a subject is satisfied after a good success. In the task, "To place on hooks sixteen rings, which pass by on a moving belt," (Giesecher *Zwangslaufapparat*) (4), the subject should be satisfied by a success when he was able to place all sixteen rings on the hook. In fact, the behavior of the subject conveyed this impression. He was glad that he had been able to do it, and expressed his satisfaction by praising himself and communicating the good result to the experimenter. After such an experience of success the task was said to be completed, and the subject was left alone. Another task was: "To copy, with a straight wire, the model of a wire doll as exactly as possible." This task was considered completed by the experimenter when the subject said that he had finished and spontaneously put the task down.

With other subjects, the same tasks were repeated until the subject was satiated by the action, stopped working on it spontaneously; even slight pressure from the experimenter could not move him to begin anew.

Experimental technique. The room in which the experiment was conducted was separated into an anteroom and the real experimental room by means of a cardboard. The subject at first entered the anteroom, which was again separated into two parts by means of a curtain, and through a second door entered the real experimental room.

The experimenter concluded the experiment with the words: "We will stop now, the experiment is finished. I would only like you to tell me your introspections, now. Will you please excuse me for a moment, I just want to take these pliers to Mr. X; he is waiting for them."

The experimenter then left the room and went to his place of observation, not without having noisily opened and closed the door which led to the outside.

In the wire bending experiment, the experimenter operated an electrical bell contact which was fastened to his chair, and hurried outside as if he had been called through the bell signal.

During the whole experiment, a small motor, which was invisible to the subject, was kept running in order to cover up possible noises. The experimenter observed the subject through a small hole in the cardboard wall. The absence of the experimenter usually lasted from three to six minutes. After this time, the experimenter again opened the outer door, and entered with excuses for having kept the subject waiting so long. Now the subject reported on his introspections.

The results show that all ten subjects resumed the task after satisfaction. After satiation, there occured no resumption in seven cases, while three subjects spontaneously resumed the action.

These results seem to confirm the above assumptions about the nature of satisfaction and satiation. The cause for the regular resumption of the action after satisfaction would be then that the action is repeated because the subject is satisfied, because pleasure has been fixated to the action.

Resumption and Repetition

However, a detailed analysis of the behavior of the subjects and of the spontaneous remarks during the experiments and the introspections shows that usually the action is not repeated because the particular subject likes it so much that he wants to do the same thing over again. On the contrary, the repeated action is based on entirely new goals, which are different from the original goal.

One subject, for instance, wanted to see whether the ability once shown will remain, and therefore began to bend a new wire doll. Another subject, using his wristwatch, tested the speed of the moving belt and tried the action anew with the goal to see "whether it can be done simpler and faster." A third subject tried in the resumption, to always put two rings on the hook at once. Another subject began, in the resumption, the bending of the wire figure from the other end than usual. This resumption occurred, incidentally, even though the experimenter had by mistake removed the pliers with which the bending was ordinarily done.

Therefore, in the spontaneous resumption after satisfaction, we are dealing not with a simple repetition, but with the presence of new goals. However, these goals are not altogether foreign to the situation; the new goals are tied up with the original ones, but go much farther (5).

The new goal goes farther than the original ones even in the rare cases where the spontaneous resumption looks outwardly like a mere repetition. In those cases, the subject was usually not quite satisfied with his achievement and carried out again only those parts of the task which he had found particularly difficult before. This kind of resumption occurred most often in the bending of wire task. The bending of the round parts was difficult for many subjects because they were not used to working with the pliers. Characteristically enough, the resumption of this task consisted often in the subject merely correcting the faulty parts of the original product, or training himself in bending the wire round.

Therefore, the spontaneous resumption after satisfaction does not mean a true repetition, but psychologically the beginning of a new task with another goal.

This fact is of essential importance for the theory of these processes. For it is now not possible to explain resumption after satisfaction either by the earlier tensions, or from the connection of the earlier action with a pleasure quality:

1. If one assumes that, in spite of the satisfaction, there remains a residual tension from the original quasi-need, one would have to expect that this tension demands an identical repetition. In all cases where the new action is directed towards a new goal, different from the original one, this assumption is inadequate.

2. Similarly, the assumption of an associative fixation of pleasure with the original action cannot be true, because again the resumption should take the form of an identical repetition, and this does not occur.

The fact that resumption after satisfaction does not consist of a mere repetition shows that, dynamically, the conditions are rather more complicated. The particular kind of change of goal which occurs here, in which new goals are aspired to that have some relation to the original goal, makes it necessary to consider not only single goals and single actions, but to look as well for goal associations and more embracing wholes of action.

A consideration of the three exceptional cases of spontaneous resumption after satiation takes us in the same direction. A more detailed analysis shows that here, also, the conditions are rather complicated. It seems at first paradoxical that a person should spontaneously resume a task which he had spontaneously interrupted before, and which he did not resume even after mild persuasion by the experimenter. This is particularly strange since the pause between the two events was insignificant.

The remarks of the subjects show that in the cases which led to a resumption, the spontaneous interruption of the previous process cannot be viewed as satiation in Karsten's sense of the word. There was, in these cases, an action as a whole which had a certain goal structure, and the course of the action was greatly influenced by experiences of success and failure.

The actions which were continuously repeated in Karsten's satiation experiments were small, relatively isolated wholes. The carrying out of single actions (for instance, reading a poem aloud, drawing short lines in a definite rhythm, and similar tasks) did not offer the subjects any particular difficulties. The actions were usually not of a kind which would lead us to expect a spontaneous resumption. Repetition of a task after execution is brought about only by the instruction, so that a new but identical goal is continuously being formed. There is, therefore, genuine repetition present.

Nevertheless, a certain change is also noticeable here, because a series of such repetitions of a single action soon lends the process as a whole the character of a continuous action. The single action has then, to a certain degree, the character of a dependent part, and the different positions of these identical parts in the course of the action as a whole (for instance, small lines at the beginning or the end of a page) means a change. Essentially, however, the process as a whole is to be characterized as a series of identical actions.

In our experiments, however, the relation between the single action and the process of repetition as a whole is essentially different. In Karsten's tasks it was usually not a question of whether the subjects were able to meet the demands of the tasks. Experiences of success or failure therefore never occurred, or only at the beginning of the experiment. (Only in the later stages of satiation does the decreased efficiency again lead to success and failure experiences. For the basic structure of the processes investigated by Karsten, however, this factor is not very important.) In our experiments, however, we have demands which the subject can meet only partially and with difficulty. The repetitions, therefore, bear the character of an attempt to approach a definite goal step by step. We are right from the first not dealing with true repetitions. The subjects do not just continuously mark time; and such a marking of time is, as Karsten emphasizes, a main condition for the occurrence of satiation.

This interlocked goal structure is particularly marked in the moving belt task in which the subject is asked to hang up as many rings as possible. In such a task in which the subject tries to improve his record (a "record" task), he feels after each repetition that he has progressed, stayed where he was, or regressed. It is obvious that here experiences of success and failure are of great importance for the tendency to continue or interrupt the task. In fact, as we shall see later on, the cause for spontaneous interruption in our satiation experiments is not true satiation, but rather a series of failures.

Also, the (exceptional) resumption after satiation is, in our experiments, connected with experiences of success and failure, just as is the resumption after satisfaction. Here, too, the conditions are by no means such as would be expected according to the thesis of the fixation of pleasure and displeasure. It is not because the subject was satisfied with his achievement (fixation of pleasure), but precisely because he was dissatisfied that he resumed the action in these cases.

The following can be stated about the effect of success and failure on resumption: dynamically, we are dealing not with questions of the fixation of pleasure or displeasure with regard to definite actions which are to be repeated, but with questions which concern the position of an individual action in a more embracing organization of actions, and with the relation of a partial goal to a more embracing goal as well as with the special properties of such comprehensive goal structure.

II. THE LEVEL OF ASPIRATION

Before we will be able to clarify the effects of success and failure we will, therefore, have to investigate the general dynamics of such associations of actions, and the origin and development of experiences of success and failure (6).

How does it come about that a person experiences success or failure? What must the subject achieve in order to believe that he has completed an action successfully or unsuccessfully?

If we analyze the behavior of the subjects in our experiments in this respect, we find that sometimes rather different achievements are experienced as successes or failures by the various subjects. Also, for the same person, the experiences of success or failure are not tied up with a definite, fixed achievement. The value of the same achievement is judged differently in the various stages of the whole experiment. If, for instance, the subject manages, the first time, to place eight rings on the moving belt, he considers this a success. He judges the same achievement as failure, however, when the real goal of the task—to place all sixteen rings on the moving belt—has once been reached. A seemingly simple, but fundamental fact is that the occurrence of the experience of success or failure is not tied up with any definite achievements, and the particular effect of an action is not necessarily a psychological datum. It becomes a success or a failure by its relation to an aspired goal, an ideal or other norm which functions as a momentary measure of the effect of an action in its significance as an achievement. Probably, the effect of an action has the character of achievement only through the presence of such a goal.

In the cases investigated, the subjects always approached the task with certain aspirations and expectations which might change in the course of the action. The totality of these expectations or aspirations for the future achievement of a person, a totality which shifts after each achievement, and which is sometimes vague and sometimes precise, we shall call the *level of aspiration* of the person. According to the circumstances, the level of aspiration may move anywhere between the goal, "to get a maximum of achievement out of the action," and the "renunciation of any achievement."

One example: in the Placement of rings, a subject has, right from the beginning of the action, the feeling of facing a task which is too difficult for him. "I will never be able to do all of this." He is satisfied at first by the partial goal to place as many rings as possible. The height of the level of aspiration would not be determined at this time by a definite number of rings, but would be relatively vague because the subject has, as yet, no conception of his ability in this action. The subject works, at first, without a definite goal. The first time he places four rings on the moving belt. This achievement does not have the character of an express success or failure because the subject had not expected any definite level of achievement. It is different, however, when he approaches the action for the second time. He has now a definite conception of the difficulties of the task, and since right from the beginning his goal was to place as many rings as possible, he will no longer be satisfied with placing three rings: four rings is the minimum of what he now wants to achieve, for he now knows that he is able to place four rings. If, in the third repetition, he manages only three rings, this means a failure and he is annoyed and angry.

If, in the further course of events, the achievement rises to six rings, this is felt by the subject as a success. In the further course of events, he is able to place eight and later ten rings. Both times success is noted. But now the number of rings decreases again to six. Six rings, which had been judged a success just a minute ago, is now felt to be a disagreeable failure. The level of aspiration is no longer, as formerly, four rings, but has risen to more than six rings.

Finally, the subjects dares to demand from himself the placement of all sixteen rings; he shifts his level of aspiration to the maximal height, and no smaller achievement is judged a success any more. Frequently, even the placement of all sixteen rings at one time does not suffice for the success, but the subject has the goal to place all sixteen rings every time. If the subject finds that he can realize this maximal achievement with a certain speed, he again raises the level of aspiration, and spontaneously asks for a greater speed of the moving belt.

It also occurs that the level of aspiration is shifted in such a way that the subject leaves the original task situation and adjusts his aspirations to a goal which is only loosely connected with the real goal of the original task, but which lies on the way towards it. In the top game, in which a top is to be led over a curved track, one subject, for instance, attempted at first "to start it right." Successes and failures were then not judged according to whether the person managed to lead the top over the track, but according to whether he was successful in starting the top correctly.

Whether achievement is experienced as success or failure depends not alone upon the objective quality of the achievement, but also upon whether the level of aspiration appears to be reached or not to be reached. The same achievement is, according to the height of the momentary level of aspiration, once experienced as success and another time as failure. If there is no level of aspiration, the achievement corresponds neither to a true experience of success, nor of failure.

The level of aspiration, the height of which cannot be stated for every moment, can be determined mainly by the help of the following means: 1) The direct indications of the subjects concerning their levels of aspiration; 2) The occurrence of experiences of success or failure from which the position of the level of aspiration can be inferred indirectly with some precision.

To the direct indications of the subjects about their level of aspiration belong all remarks about their goals and expectations; for instance, "That is much too difficult for me, I will try this figure first." "Now I want to shoot from a great distance." "I will have to hit 100 at least once."

From an experience of success we can conclude that the level of aspiration was lower or just as high as the achievement in question; from an experience of failure that the level of aspiration was higher. Experiences of success and failure usually alternate, so that the real height of the level of aspiration can be determined from above and from below through averaging.

Finally, certain conclusions about the level of aspiration can be drawn from the way in which the person enters into the task, and from his attitude to the task. It is quite possible to distinguish whether a subject participates eagerly and wants to solve the task under any circumstances, or whether he just pretends to occupy himself with the task. One can state, therefore, to what extent a certain level of aspiration determines the behavior of a subject.

If one uses these various methods side by side, the particular level of aspiration can be determined fairly accurately.

III. SHIFTING THE LEVEL OF ASPIRATION

Experimental Setup II

For the following experiments on the investigation of the level of aspiration and its shifting, we purposely chose actions of rather different types. Our intention was to discover possible dependencies of the level of aspiration upon the structure of the action. Besides record tasks, such as target shooting, we gave tasks which had, right from the beginning, a definitely outlined goal, such as thought problems, and also tasks which did not have a fixed goal but nevertheless did not have the character of record tasks.

We wished to arrange setup II in every detail so that the possible shiftings of the level of aspiration were easily and accurately observable. As far as possible, we avoided exerting any pressure upon the subjects, in order not to set too rigid goals for the subjects from the outside.

The instruction was approximately: I will now give you various tasks which you are supposed to solve. The experiment does not require you to solve these tasks. The only important thing is that you react to them freely and naturally. If you do not feel like continuing one task, and would like to have another one, just tell me so.

Furthermore, the materials for all tasks lay on the table, so that the subjects did not find any difficulty in going from one task to the other. We kept to one task situation, but through a minimum of requirements, we left as much room as possible for the free inclinations of the subjects. The subjects were also allowed to whistle, smoke, and walk around during the experiment.

We thereby achieved a state in which the subject did not feel dominated and controlled by the experimenter. During the experiment, they conversed with the experimenter about the difficulties of the task, about their wishes in regard to success, and about their chances. Occasionally, the subjects reproached the experimenter for giving them such a "stupid" task, and sometimes they asked him for help in the execution of the task. The experimenter was in no way an authoritative person. Through this kind of a situation it was possible to gain immediate insight into the momentary level of the aspiration of the subjects. The partially spontaneous remarks of the subjects during the experiment were supplemented by detailed introspective reports at the end of the whole experiment.

Nine different tasks were used in this experimental set-up:

1. The *problem knot:* A body composed of many small wooden parts is to be taken apart and put together again.*

2. *Nuisance:* A game to test patience in which blocks, arranged on a board,

* *Illustration omitted—Editor.*

have to be laid into figures upon the model of various patterns.

3. *Solitaire:* A board game in which stones, arranged in a certain way on the board, have to be taken away in such an order that finally only one block remains in the center. There is only one solution, which it is difficult to find without help.*

4. *Top game:* A small top has to be led over an S-curved track of cardboard.

5. *Modeling:* The subject models any figure he wishes out of plasticine.

6. *Task with matches:* Ten matches which lie side by side on the table are to be arranged in five pairs by causing each match to jump over two other ones before it is put next to another match. Here also there exists only one solution which is difficult to find.

7. *Thought problem:* Three persons A, B, C, sit together. Each of them has a blackened face without knowing it. Each is laughing about the two others because they are black. Finally A knows, and only on the basis of a thought process, that he himself has a blackened face. Question: How does A know that he is black? The solution to this task is very difficult and was found only by one subject who knew the task beforehand. It is: A thinks how B may explain to himself why C is laughing. B thinks, of course, that C is laughing about A, because B does not know that he is black himself. Therefore, A's face must be black.

8. *Shooting through a hole:* The subject shoots with a rubber gun at a hole 15 centimeters wide and 3 meters distant.

9. *Target shooting:* With the same rubber gun.

The fact that these actions are of very different types makes it possible to observe how the level of aspiration and its shiftings depend upon the structure of the particular task. The target shooting is an example of a record task; the thought problem, the solitaire game, and the task with matches are tasks with a fixed and definite goal; modelling, shooting through a hole, and the top game are tasks in which the goal is not fixed, but which do not have the character of record tasks.

The experiments were distributed over two days. Usually, we gave the actions one, two, three, and eight on the first day, and the other actions on the second. This order was not kept constant very strictly because the experiment took into account the wishes of the subjects to a very high degree. The materials of the finished tasks were not taken from the table, so that the subject always had the possibility of resuming the completed task.

The experiments were carried out with thirty-six actions (four subjects, nine actions each). Since a series of shiftings of the level of aspiration occurred in each of the thirty-six actions, the total number of separate facts available for tabulation is rather high (almost 100).

Approach to the Task, Trials, and the Beginning Level of Aspiration

Most of the tasks were unknown to the subjects, so that they had no definite idea about the relation between the difficulty of the task and their ability. They had, therefore, no fixed beginning level of aspiration. They began by testing the possibilities of success. The positive or negative ending of this trial did not usually lead to experiences of success or failure, but merely meant for the subject a statement of fact—"it is possible or impossible." (A certain shading of success or failure is sometimes present, since the tryout does not always occur without definite expectations.)

During the trial, the subjects usually gain a certain over-all view not only of the difficulties of the task, but also of the path towards the goal—whether one has to work steadily and cautiously; whether one energetic action may lead to the goal; whether training is necessary. Frequently the subjects think it impossible, at first, to completely reach the goal set by the task. They establish for themselves a preliminary intermediate goal, which they believe themselves better able to reach.

The problem knot, for instance, was very difficult for all the subjects. It was necessary to gain by means of a carefully planned procedure a clear insight into the way in which the different wooden parts are interlocked. This was best done by taking the knot apart step by step, that is, by always putting together again the pieces which one had just take apart. Only one subject used this method; all the others took it apart in a more or less planless way. In such difficult tasks, the subject doubts from the beginning his ability to solve the task; nevertheless, he begins working, and with a goal which he believes he might be able to reach, namely to "put the thing together somehow."

The adjustment to a level of aspiration as low as possible at the beginning of the task was also to be observed in the placement of rings, in the previous setup. The subjects almost invariably asked at the beginning for a lessening of the speed of the moving belt, or they systematically skipped one hook.

The fact of the trial, and of the adjustment to a level of aspiration as low as possible shows that the subject, in approaching the task, wishes to take the smallest possible risk of failure, to avoid failure altogether, or to secure a success by setting the goal very low.

Shiftings of the Level of Aspiration as Effects of Success and Failure*

In order to express the lawfulness of the shiftings of the level of aspiration in numbers, we give, in Table I, all observable experiences of success or failure and their effect upon the level of aspiration.

---

* I have omitted a page of text and eleven figures which illustrate the effect of success and failure on shifts in the goals of individual subjects working on individual tasks. These may be obtained from University Microfilms—Editor.

TABLE 1
Shifts in the Level of Aspiration (LA) After Success and After Failure

Shifting of the L A	Raising	Lowering	Staying the same	Realization of previous successes	Discon-tinuation
After Success	52 (32%)	0	5 (3%)	0	18 (11%)
After Failure	0	45 (27%)	19 (12%)	2 (1%)	24 (15%)

The listing of 165 shiftings of the level of aspiration from the different experiments shows that the level of aspiration was raised after success in 52 of the cases, but never after failure; while it was lowered after failure in 45 of the cases, but never after success. The level of aspiration remains the same after success in five cases, and after failure in 19 of the cases.

We shall deal later with the forty-five residual cases which consist, partially, in a going out of the field (spontaneous discontinuation of the action and beginning something entirely different), and partially in a later realization of an earlier achievement which had not previously been experienced as a success, but which is now realized as such. The last named cases are connected with spontaneous discontinuation, and must, therefore, be regarded as special cases under this category.

The same relation, in regard to the distribution of the cases, results if only the cases of experimental setup II are listed, and also if one considers each subject separately. It is true that some characteristic changes in the numerical relations appear, but they do not influence the main result in the least.

The Effect of Success

The typical effect of success is, as was mentioned before, a raising of the level of aspiration. This becomes apparent mainly, among other things, by the fact that the subject wants to begin the same task again, but with a higher goal. The subject wants, for instance, to carry out a second, more difficult nuisance task.

The raising of the level of aspiration usually lies within the limits set by the instruction. Sometimes, however, a subject leaves behind the goal which the instructions provided, and sets himself a more difficult task. For instance, in the shooting at a hole task the subject will, after he hits the hole, spontaneously increase the distance, or try to shoot with the left hand, and so on.

In a series of successes, the subject raises his level of aspiration until he is certain that he has gotten everything possible out of the task. This may occur when the nature of the task does not allow for further raising of the goal, or because recurring failures show that the subject has reached the limit of his ability.

The Effect of Failure

After failures, we usually find a lowering of the level of aspiration. In the nuisance task, for instance, a subject will limit himself to laying "only this one triangle" while his original goal was to lay "as many figures as possible." (Quite analoguous phenomena are often found with children.) After further failures the subject wanted only to "put the blocks back in the box," and when he did not even succeed in this, he asked the experimenter for help, or "packed the blocks using the pattern."

Such a lowering of the level of aspiration in steps was generally easily recognized by the way in which the subjects reacted to offers of help made by the experimenter. In the problem knot, each subject at first refused very shortly all attempts of the experimenter to assist. They meant to do it all alone. After some unsuccessful trials, however, they accept help from the experimenter, or even ask for it.

The direct asking for help is often preceeded by an uncertain inquiry about whether the work so far was correct. The confidence in the subject's own abilities is already much disturbed, and when the experimenter confirms his failure, he lowers his level of aspiration even further and asks for information about how to go on, or at least how to begin.

After some more unsuccessful trials, the subjects finally attempt to put the parts together "somehow." There is now no hope of reaching a satisfactory solution. The partly nonsensical putting together of the parts does not give the impression of a serious attempt to find the solution; it is, rather, an occupation which has little connection with the original task (7).

In other cases, after failures the subject sets himself a very easy task. If success does not occur even then, the subject not infrequently becomes furious and throws the materials on the table; or he satisfies himself with a minimal level of aspiration—that is, he asks the experimenter to tell him the solution.

If we insist that the subject continue the action in spite of constant failures, the growing disinclination increases until it leads to genuine outbreaks of rage.

These observations, as well as an occasional hiding or putting aside of the materials used in the task, ("in order not to see them any more") show the strength of the disinclination which is caused, or at least strengthened, by the fact that the failures force the subject, as in the satiation processes, to continuously mark time. A similar case was present where one subject, who after two hours of unsuccessful efforts had almost succeeded in putting the problem knot together, found that the one part which he needed to complete the task had been put in at a wrong place earlier. He then threw away the whole thing with the remark, "I would rather have the unpleasant feeling of having it unfinished than do the whole thing over again."

If finally, after continuous failures, the subject drops the action, he sometimes points out his earlier successes: "At least I have achieved this and that." It is not necessary that these achievements were experiences of success while they were carried out; according to the new low level of aspiration, these achievements are now valued as successes. In such cases, we speak of a later raising of earlier achievements to successes.

Partial and Accidental Successes and Failures

According to Table I, the level of aspiration is shifted after success or failure in the majority of the cases (97 of 165), but in 68 cases it remains at the same height; or the subject discontinues altogether. In a consideration of these figures, it must be kept in mind that not all successes and failures are of equally moment.

It is possible to distinguish several degrees of importance. For successes, one might speak of: (1) a complete success; (2) a partial success; and (3) a single success (or single partial success) after a series of failures. For failures, one might speak of: (1) a complete failure; and (2) of a single failure after a series of successes. (We are counting the partial failures as partial successes.)

TABLE 2

Shifts in the Level of Aspiration Distributed According to Full and Partial Success and Failure

	Level of Aspiration			Discontin-uation	Discontin-uation and realization of previous successes
	Raising	Same	Lowering		
Full success	44	3	—	10	—
Partial success	7	2	—	—	—
Single success after failures	1	—	—	8	—
Series of failures	—	8	45	23	2
Single failures	—	11	—	1	—

Table II shows the 165 statements about shiftings of the level of aspiration distributed over these different types of success and failure. We can differentiate our previous total result by saying: A raising of the level of aspiration occurs usually after a full success, and a lowering of the level of aspiration occurs almost exclusively after a series of failures. The shifting of the level of aspiration usually takes place, therefore, not after the first success or failure, but after a good or poor achievement has been repeated two or three times.

We have to distinguish various cases, in such repetitions of actions, which look alike externally, but which mean different things psychologically. In the nuisance task for instance, a subject wants to pack the blocks, which he had packed just before, once again with the remark, "I want to see whether I can really do it." Only when he succeeded a second time did he begin to also lay in other figures. In this case, we are dealing with a true repetition of the action; the level of aspiration remains the same. The subject is not sure after the first success whether his level of performance has really reached his level of aspiration. He wants to ascertain whether he can take the single success seriously, whether it was not an accidental success, and whether he has the right to give himself credit for the result. Only the repetition provides the possibility of realizing the success as a fact, and therefore effects a raising of the level of aspiration.

The action of one subject, who repeated the part of the problem knot which he had already solved correctly in order to "comprehend the thing clearly once more" before he continued to put the parts together, served the same purpose. The following remark of another subject points in the same direction. He said about the placement of rings: "If one succeeds once, one does not immediately think, 'Now it will work,' but, 'Perhaps this one was accidental'."

The cases in which the subject counts the first positive effect actually as a success are to be viewed somewhat differently. Here, the subject now wants to achieve the same success several times in immediate succession. This occurs frequently in the shooting and the top game, where the goal of the action is not to get it right once, but to master the action. It is necessary for this, however, that one hit several times. In these tasks the transition from the being able to do it once, to mastering it is the most relevant way to raise the level of aspiration. In these repetitions of actions with the same goal, it only seems as if the level of aspiration were the same; in reality it is mostly a raising of the level of aspiration.

Single failures have usually no influence upon the movements of the level of aspiration (see Table II), because within a series of successes they are not regarded as significant; the subject considers them to be accidental, or at least he wants to give the experimenter the impression that they were. In many cases, he does not feel them as failures at all.

Most often, the subject indicates at once a reason for this one failure, which, in a way, excuses him. Of the shooting, for instance, it will be said that "the gun went off too soon," or that the shot scattered. Of the top game, a subject will say that "he did not start it right," or that "the top is not quite all right." In the placement of rings, it will be stated that a crooked hook or ring is to blame for the failure. It is thus explicable that a single failure led in no case to a lowering of the level of aspiration, since it does not show up an insufficiency in the subject's own abilities, but only in one of the materials used. (The tendency to shift the blame for a failure away from oneself and upon a thing can be found also in failures which are not accidental, and indicates a relation between the level of aspiration and the self-confidence of the subject.)

That the subjects disregard single failures among successes—that is, that they have the tendency to hold on to the total success as much as possible— is related to the behavior of single subjects in the raising of the level of aspiration after successes. They begin, right from the start, with a very low level of aspiration, as a kind of a safeguard against possible failures; only slowly and cautiously, always distrustful of their own achievement, do they raise their level of aspiration.

Spontaneous Discontinuation

After a series of failures, but also after a single success within a series of failures, the action can be spontaneously discontinued.

The interruption after a series of failures is readily understood. The disinclination grows with each failure, and is finally more effective than the quasi-need to complete the action. It is less obvious why the subjects spontaneously discontinue after a success. Table II shows that such a discontinuation occurs almost always after single successes (8 of 9 cases). In order to orientate ourselves about the process of discontinuation, we first gathered as many cases of this sort as possible and examined in each the course of events.

One subject had modeled a figure and was very much satisfied with his performance. (Modeling was a successful task with all subjects because the subjects were free to choose the figure which they wanted to make; all subjects chose figures which they knew how to do.) He nevertheless did not stop to improve his work, and showed no inclination to discontinue spontaneously. Even when there was nothing to be improved any more he did not stop abruptly. The subject looked at the product and praised it, and tried in every way to tarry with it as long as possible. Only a question of the experimenter about whether he would like to do something else caused him to turn towards a new action.

The discontinuation of the task is different in the shooting. Frequently, subjects discontinue because the task does not provide an opportunity to raise the level of aspiration any higher. In shooting at a hole, for instance, many stop with the words: "I know that now. Now I would only want to shoot at the target, otherwise the thing does not offer anything new." Since target shooting is not permitted, the continuation of the same action has no more meaning for the subject, and would be a mere marking time.

The following is a different case: One subject had shot 29 times with a great many successes, and he kept making the conditions more and more difficult. He finally found that he failed more and more frequently. He decided to stop, but wished under no circumstances to end up with a failure. So the last shot was always followed by another one, until he finally achieved a good success; he then discontinued the task.

The failures here forced the subject to lower his level of aspiration once more at the end, from "always hitting the center" to "hitting the center at least once more." These failures at the end are, however, not felt very strongly, in view of the many previous successes. They are usually explained by the fact that the eyes or the hands of the subject are tired.

The number of shots given before the spontaneous discontinuation varies for the individual subjects between two and thirty.

Especially interesting is the following case in which the subject said after the first two shots, which hit well, "That is enough, I can shoot." Either this achievement really seemed to the subject the optimal possible achievement, so that a raising of the level of aspiration was out of the question, or the subject was afraid to meet with failures in the continuation of the action.

The most frequent type of spontaneous discontinuation is probably the following: A subject has, in consequence of constant failure, lowered his level of aspiration step by step; finally there occurs a success, perhaps an accidental success. In this case, the subject does not raise his level of aspiration again, but discontinues at once.

In the top game, for instance, one subject tried for quite a long time to make the top spin over the track, but did not even succeed in starting it correctly. Finally he succeeded once; the top even went over part of the track. The subject immediately discontinued with the words, "I know now what the main point is."

Also, in other tasks like the thought problem, the game of solitaire, and the task with matches, many subjects were satisfied with knowing the principle of the solution after they had not been able to find the solution itself.

The high number of cases in which a single success after a series of failures led to discontinuing the action, is probably caused by the fact that the many previous failures had shown the subjects that a complete success was impossible for them to achieve.

If there is no success whatever, the subject finally discontinues even with the lowest level of aspiration. He often asks the experimenter to at least show him the solution. After such a defeat, he often spontaneously reaches for those actions in which he had been more successful before; he consoles himself with his previous successes. If a subject says he want "to try it again later on," it also often means such a consolation. Even this means retaining a last, though very low, level of aspiration.

While we shall discuss individual differences later, we may summarize our feelings about discontinuation as follows: Discontinuation occurs after successes if a raising of the level of aspiration seems impossible, either because the limits of personal ability, or the nature of the task, or the instruction prevent raising the level. After failures, discontinuation does not occur until the last possibility of achieving a success has been used. A single success or partial success, after many failures does not lead to a raising of the level of aspiration, but to discontinuation, if the previous failures have demonstrated the impossibility of a complete success. Even after failures, there remains the tendency to find some kind of satisfaction—whether it be through the expectations of a later successful trial of the same task, or through a consolation with one's successes in other fields.

IV. IDEAL GOAL AND REAL GOAL

The Goal Structure and the Level of Difficulty of the Task

In the following theoretical consideration, we shall make use of a number of concepts which are not always easy to apply in all concrete cases. Nevertheless, the distinctions involved are hardly avoidable if one does not want to limit oneself to a few special cases.

Although the level of aspiration and the goal of a task are intimately connected, they are not simply identical.

In our experiments, and in many cases in everyday life, the goal of an action is, at first, given from the outside. The task may appear in the form of an instruction, of an order or wish from a strange person, or as directly demanded by the thing itself, by the nature of the situation. The goal of an action—and we wish to stress this point in particular—may have a certain significance and objectively be a part of the task, even if the subject has not completely made the task his own, in the sense that the goal of the task corresponds to a level of aspiration.

This becomes most clear in the cases where no real level of aspiration is formed, even though there exists a goal of an action. When a subject, for instance, first tries out the task, the goal of the action is definitely given (for instance, putting together the problem knot), but the subject has, at first, no definite aspirations as to his level of performance, and no true experiences of success or failure result.

Also, in the more instinctive actions of the small child, probably often there exists a goal but no real level of aspiration.

The case is similar where the subject's attitude toward the task is purely objective; the task exists for the subject as such to a certain degree, but there is no level of aspiration in regard to his own performance.

Also, in cases where a level of aspiration exists, the goal, which the subject experiences as belonging to the task, is to be distinguished from the momentary level of aspiration, which changes with success and failure.

The individual tasks differ greatly in regard to the level of difficulty of the assigned goal. We shall speak here about differences in the level of difficulty of the tasks. We are referring thereby to differences in the difficulty of the goal which are caused by the instructions, by general external conditions, or by the nature of the task itself.

Furthermore, a task does not always have a definitely fixed level of difficulty. It usually allows for a certain natural latitude of gradations of difficulty.

The height of the goal which corresponds to the perfect solution of the task, we designate as the *natural maximum* of the task. The height of the goal which has to be reached if the task is not to lose its character as a task, we designate as the *natural minimum* of the task.

According to this point of view, we may group the tasks given in our experiments as follows:

I. Those for which the natural maximum of the goal of action is almost at the same time the natural minimum; for each lowering of the goal means (nearly) giving up the task. In the solution of these tasks there are only the two possibilities: all or none. The problem knot, thought problem, task with matches, and similar ones belong to this group. The solution of these tasks is, so to speak, one event, after which it would be meaningless to attack the task again.

2. Those tasks which possess a certain, but not very considerable, latitude in gradations of difficulty. The natural maximum and natural minimum do not coincide, but the distance between the two is not very great.

Examples of this are the nuisance and the top game, as well as some other tasks in which the main point is a series of successful performances, rather than a single solution. In the nuisance and the top game, the natural maximum would lie in the mastering of the task, that is, when the subject is able to lay several figures or to lead the top several times over the track. The natural minimum for the nuisance game would be to lay at least one figure, and for the top game, to lead it over the track at least once.

Also, these tasks may, occasionally, take on the character of all-or-none tasks, namely, when a single performance is so difficult for a subject that the single performance becomes the main task—In the nuisance game, for instance, when a single figure is very difficult to lay.

3. Those tasks for which there is a great distance between the natural maximum and the natural minimum. In between, the task allows for many gradations.

In the shooting, for instance, the natural maximum of the task lies, approximately, at being able to hit the center of the target with certainty from a great distance; the natural minimum would be to hit the center at least once under easy conditions, or to hit the target at least once. Between these two goal positions, there lie a number of possible gradations. The distance from the target may be varied; or the number of times which one wants to hit in one series; and finally also the technique of shooting—shooting freely or with a rest, with both hands or just with one. The number of such steps may, of course, be limited by the experimental instructions.

The latitude for shifting the level of aspiration is particularily broad in the modeling. The subject may choose an easy or more difficult object, and he may want to make just a rough likeness or a figure as true to nature as possible.

4. Those types of tasks which do not have a natural maximum or minimum. In the record tasks, for instance, the latitudes for shifting the level of aspiration may be so unlimited, especially upward, that we can no longer speak of a natural maximum.

The distance between the natural maximum and minimum, as well as the kind of gradations possible, are usually experienced by the subjects as something objectively given, as a goal structure which belongs to the task as such (in the momentary situation.)

The Structure of the Task and Shifting of the Level of Aspiration

We wish to trace, briefly, the influence of different goal structures upon the effect of success and failure. The subject's behavior is not altogether determined by the goal structure. His level of aspiration may, as we have seen, go below the natural minimum of a task (for instance, when the subject asks the experimenter to tell him the solution.) Nevertheless, the objective goal structure is doubtless of importance for the behavior of the subjects, and it is conceivable, for instance, that the distance between the natural maximum and minimum is one of the factors which determine whether the level of aspiration is shifted after a success or failure, whether it remains the same, or whether the subject discontinues spontaneously.

In Table III, we give the sums of actual shifting (relative to the total number of experiences of success and failure observed), grouped according to the different types of tasks.

In the group of tasks in which the natural maximum and minimum lie close

TABLE 3
Effect of Task Structure on Shifts in the Level of Aspiration after Success or Failure

	Elbowroom between natural maximum minimum is Small				Elbowroom between natural maximum minimum is Large				
	Solitaire	Thought Problem	Matches	Problem-knot	Hole Shooting	Target Shooting	Nuisance	Top	Modeling
After success LA raised*	–	–	–	–	7	3	6	3	2
After failure LA lowered	2	2	2	12	–	2	7	5	–
After success LA stays same	–	–	–	1	2	–	1	1	–
After success Discontinuation	–	1	–	1	1	2	2	1	3
After failure LA stays same	1	2	–	1	4	–	2	1	–
After failure Discontinuation	3	1	2	2	–	1	1	3	–
After failure Realization of earlier successes	–	–	–	2	–	–	–	–	–

*LA = Level of Aspiration

together (or coincide), a shifting of the level of aspiration occurs less frequently (45 per cent) than in the group of tasks with a large latitude between the maximum and minimum height of the goal (62 per cent).

That no instance occurs of raising the level of aspiration after success in the first group may be explained by the difficulty of these tasks, which made real success impossible. Partial solutions were, in these tasks, not experienced as true successes. In the few cases where the subject really had the success of finding the solution, discontinuation occurred, probably because the task did not allow for a further setting up of goals.

In the all-or-none tasks, there occured quite a number of shiftings of the level of aspiration after failures, even though the lowering of the level of aspiration leads below the natural minimum goal, and is therefore identical with giving up on the task. This is probably to be explained by the fact that inability to solve these tasks is usually experienced as an intellectual failure by the subjects. This usually puts the subject under strong pressure from the general situation, and such a strong pressure may change the effect of the natural goal structure very considerably.

The Ideal Goal and the Changes in The Degree of Its Reality

The momentary level of aspiration of the subject usually corresponds to one of the goals which are made possible by the goal structure of the task. A series of factors indicate, however, that the behavior of the subjects is determined not only by the momentary goal—which is determined by the momentary level of aspiration—but also by a farther-reaching, more comprehensive goal. This goal goes farther than the changing, momentary goal, and is psychologically more or less real according to the difficulty of the individual task.

One subject described this fact as follows: "There exists a whole hierarchy of goals. The top one of these is to carry out the task in the given time; but this is out of the question, even though it is somehow present."

The comprehensive goal, which is not acutely present at the moment, but which stands behind each single action and determines the subject's behavior as a whole, we shall call the *ideal goal.* It is to be contrasted with the *real goal,* which corresponds to the level of aspiration for a momentary achievement.

One subject, for instance, said in the nuisance task: "I must try first whether I can pack the blocks back into the box." In this case, packing is the real goal, while mastering the nuisance task is the ideal goal behind the individual action.

The ideal goal has usually the position of the extreme value, which corresponds most often to the natural maximum of the task.

In record tasks which, as we have seen, possess no natural maximum, the height of the ideal goal is frequently determined by a desire to beat the performance of the previous subject. The subjects ask how well the other subjects did in the same action. Sometimes, especially after failures, the subject is satisfied with an ideal goal of doing "at least as well as the others did."

The distance between the real and ideal goal may be of varying size, and may change during the course of the action. When, for instance, the subject raises his level of aspiration after success, the ideal goal usually remains the same. It is most often the highest achievement of which the subject thinks himself capable. Experiences of success or failure do, however, change the degree of reality of the ideal goal, in the sense that the ideal goal becomes generally more real the more the actual achievement approaches it. It loses reality the greater the distance between ability and desire, that is, between the real goal and ideal goal.

When, for instance, a subject approaches the top game with the words: "This action is much too difficult for me, and I will never be able to do it," the degree of reality of the ideal goal, to master the task according to the instructions by the experimenter, is very small. If the subject then has some partial success he gets much more courageous. He does not think the ideal goal so impossible to reach. It remains on the same level, but gains in reality.

In another experiment, the task was to set up a perpendicular pole with the aid of a clamp and three short sticks in a time interval given by the experimenter. In spite of eager attempts, the subject was not able to put the pole upright. The goal in approaching this task was to manage the thing in the given time. Failures in the attempt to fix the clamp effected an immediate lowering of this goal (retreat). The real goal was then to erect the pyramid, it does not matter in how much time. But when the subject believed, even for a moment, that he had reached his goal, the speed of the work gained in importance again. In the next moment, it lost again because the subject found that he had not been able to do it in the given time. This behavior shows clearly how the ideal goal, to carry out the task in a given time, became psychologically more real as soon as a success occured or the subject expected a success to occur; while it lost in reality as soon as the hope for success was seen to be a delusion. Also, in this case, the height of the ideal goal remained unchanged.

The ideal goal may lose all reality, and thereby become ineffective for the further course of events in the action, if, in consequence of a series of failures, the subject lowers his level of aspiration so that the distance between ideal and real goal becomes too great. This may, among other things, lead the subject to discontinue the action, instead of raising his level of aspiration after a success following a series of failures.

This was the case in the incident mentioned before where the subject, after many failures in the nuisance task, finally wanted "at least to pack them." When this, too, offered him difficulties, the packing became, for him, the main goal. He quite forgot that the real task was not packing the blocks, but laying of figures. When he had finally finished packing the blocks, he stopped contentedly.

However, the momentary real goal may rise to the height of the ideal goal; the ideal goal may become the real goal if previous successes make it appear possible to reach the ideal goal. The ideal goal may, after it has been reached, even become the point of departure for additional raising of the goal.

In the nuisance task, one subject began, after a series of smooth successes, to develop one figure out of the other. He thereby increased the difficulties of the task over and above the demands made by the experimenter. After the first ideal goal had been reached, he set up a second one which was, in this case, something like "to find new possibilities for the solution."

It also means an exceeding of the original ideal goal if a subject, in shooting at a hole and aware of having solved the task, begins to change the distance. Here, too, the subject wants to get as much as possible out of the task, even to the point of exceeding the original instruction.

We summarize briefly once more: Whether a person experiences his achievement as success or failure depends upon the level of aspiration, the total of all subjective goals and expectations. This has to be distinguished from the concept of the level of difficulty of the task, which is determined by the nature of the task, and which the subject experiences as something given from the outside. The level of difficulty of the task is characterized by the degree of difficulty of the task, its goal structure, and especially by the latitude between the natural maximum and minimum of the task.

Aside from the real goal, which corresponds to the momentary level of aspiration of the subject, there usually exists a comprehensive ideal goal. While the real goal is usually raised or lowered after successes or failures, the ideal goal does not (at first) usually change after success or failure. The degree of reality of the ideal goal, however, does change with the distance between the real and ideal goal.

The height and the shiftings of the level of aspiration are primarily determined by the following factors:

1. The establishment of the level of aspiration at the beginning of a task (beginning level of aspiration) depends upon the outer level of the task, which is given with the instruction and the nature of the task. It also depends upon inner factors, such as the ideas of the subject about his abilities in relation to the difficulty of the task, his ambition, and his caution.

2. The shiftings of the level of aspiration depend upon the relation between the actual level of performance and the height of the momentary level of aspiration.

If the performance reaches or exceeds the level of aspiration, it is—if the achievement is valued as genuine and not as accidental—experienced as a success. Otherwise, it is experienced as a failure. After success, the level of aspiration is raised, or (particularly if a single success occurs after a series of failures) the action is discontinued. After failures, the level of aspiration is lowered, or the action discontinued. In no case is the level of aspiration lowered after success or raised after failure. (The cases in which the level of aspiration remained unchanged are here disregarded, because the successes or failures in question were not taken seriously by the subjects.)

The Dynamics of the Laws of Shifting

If one attempts to theoretically deduce the laws governing the shifting of the level of aspiration, one meets, at first, with considerable difficulties.

We began with the assumption that after the satisfactory completion of an action, as well as after satiation, there no longer exists a system in a state of tension in that direction, and that a possible resumption or nonresumption would have to be explained by the fixation of a positive or negative valence to the action.

It would be possible to explain, through the fixation of a valence, why an action is continued after success and discontinued after failure. However, this explanation would not explain the main phenomenon that the subject does not simply repeat the action after success, but instead raises his level of aspiration. Furthermore, the not infrequent cases in which the subjects discontinued the action as a consequence of a success also would remain unexplained. (It is obvious here, as mentioned before, that the fact of success rather than satiation leads to the discontinuation.)

The impossibility of explaining these observations becomes a paradox when the following is taken into consideration: If behavior were exclusively determined by the tendency to secure pleasure in as intense and as certain a way as possible, that is, to secure as many and as strong experiences of success as possible, the subject could not do worse than to raise his level of aspiration after success.

This is so since, as we have seen, the presupposition for the experience of success is that the level of performance exceeds the level of aspiration. In order to secure as many experiences of success as possible, the subject should then tend to keep his level of aspiration always below his level of performance. After failure, the level of aspiration should not be lowered gradually and slowly, but the subject should immediately go down to such a low level of aspiration that further failures are avoided.

The shiftings of the level of aspiration become understandable only if we take into consideration not only the single partial actions, but also the over-all dynamic relations. The considerations about the real and ideal goal show that the individual action does not correspond to an isolated quasi-need, but that the momentary real goal often belongs to a hierarchy of goals. Even though the psychological effect of a single action (for instance, the single shot in the target shooting) depends upon the momentary level of aspiration, this is a relatively separated tension system. The simultaneous presence of the ideal goal indicates the existence of a more inclusive tension system which is characterized by the ideal goal, and in which the real goal is only a dependent element, only a provisional goal.

The raising of the level of aspiration after success may, to a certain extent, be explained by this comprehensive goal of the will. Also, in our tasks, a single action which is a full success means only progressing towards a goal which is set very much further away. Relative to it, the single action has the position of a preparatory action. It is like the first phase in the carrying out of an action to complete the action as a whole.

However, the discontinuation after successes, as well as the behavior after failure, is still unexplained. Also, the question remains open as to why, under certain circumstances, success leads to a raising of the level of aspiration above the originally given task or above the original ideal goal.

The shiftings of the level of aspiration become completely understandable only if one goes back to the more inclusive goals of the person, goals which far exceed the single tasks. They concern the self-worth of the subject. In contrast to the level of aspiration which pertains to specific actions, we shall call this more inclusive factor the *ego level* of the subject.

V. THE LEVEL OF ASPIRATION AND SELF-WORTH (EGO LEVEL)

The Ego Level

A series of facts make it clear that the shifting of the level of aspiration depends not only upon the special properties of the single task, but also upon the attitude and the character of the subject.

The level of aspiration to which the subject adjusts himself at the beginning of the action *(beginning level of aspiration)* is frequently different for the different subjects in the same task.

In the nuisance task, for instance, one subject tries at first the easiest task, packing the blocks; another tries a somewhat more difficult figure; and the goal of a third subject includes, right from the start, the solving of several tasks.

It seems that the tendency to choose a level of aspiration which is high or low at the beginning is characteristic of the subject.

The beginning level of all tasks was lowest in Subject 14. This cautiousness is not caused by continuous failures—his achievements correspond to the average—but must be regarded as a property of the character of this person.

The relation between the height of the beginning level of aspiration and the personal characteristics of the subjects is likewise clear in the case of Subject 19. Even though he had experienced failures almost entirely, and therefore had to lower his level of aspiration by a great amount every time, he always began each new task with the highest goal.

Individual peculiarities which go beyond the single task are also evident in the way in which, after failures, the aspiration level may sink gradually or else abruptly and in great steps. The same holds true for raising of the level of aspiration after success. Subject 14, for instance, raised his level of aspiration only by very small steps.

The total behavior of the subjects shows that success and failure have an immediate relation to the central "I" of the subject. Successes heighten (raise) self-confidence, especially the inner attitude of the subject towards the experimenter.

Successes tend to make the subject happy, and frequently lead to spontaneous exclamations: "Look how clever I am! I have done this beautifully!"

One subject, who particularly emphasized his success to the experimenter, felt, later on, "quite swell headed." Other colloquial expressions for persons who make much of themselves—as, for instance, "He has a big head," or "he acts big"—also express the greater circumference of the person in relation to the environment.

Not only success and failure as such, but especially the feeling of the *belongingness* of this feat to the person, the regarding of the performance as an expression of his own value, is dynamically of importance. This shows itself, among other things, in the fact that the subjects very frequently attempted to push the responsibility for the failure away from themselves. Usually, the subjects blamed, in these cases, the materials.

In the top game, it is the bad top, and in the shooting, the gun which "starts too soon." In the bending of wire, the wire was too thin, and in the placement of rings, the hooks were "crooked"; in one of the experiments, where a pyramid had to be erected from four wooden sticks and a fastener, "the fastener did not grasp right." Characteristically enough, the subjects began to speak of the shortcomings of the materials only when they experienced failures.

In such cases, the maliciousness of the object frees the subject from the responsibility for the failure. One tries to withdraw from the fact of the failure as much as possible by looking for the cause of the failure not in one's self, but in the neutral sphere of objects.

Another method for pushing away the responsibility onto the objective sphere is sometimes present when the subjects state that the task is "too difficult" (for them to do). Frequently, this does not mean, "*My* abilities are poor," but, "You ask for the impossible; I am, therefore, for objective reasons common to human nature, unable to fulfill the task." Thus, the responsibility is shifted from the self to something neutral, namely to human nature as a given biological factor; and the real experience of failure is, accordingly, lacking.

Frequently, such a pushing away of the responsibility occurs with a bad conscience. One subject even indicated that he himself does not believe it to be so, and that it was only an excuse.

The tendency to get rid of the responsibility for one's failure is so strong that the subjects frequently try actually to deceive the experimenter. In order to make it appear as if they had really solved the nuisance task, some subjects tried to take away from the table one of the blocks in such a way that the experimenter would not notice it. Especially when it was difficult to find out the truth of the matter, the subjects were inclined to lead the experimenter astray. In the task with matches, they frequently jumped just over one match, instead of over two as was required by the instructions, and then maintained stubbornly that they had reached the solution in the correct way. Only when the experimenter asked them to give the solution a second time did the subjects admit the deceit.

These attempts to deceive indicate that the relation between the I and the outer field, and especially the attitude to the social field, is of essential importance for the shifting of the level of aspiration.

Success and failure are evaluated in the first place in regard to the importance of the self as a social being.

The social factor becomes apparent, also, in the fact that subjects who, as a consequence of failures, gave up an action in the presence of the experimenter and did not wish to begin anew, attempted the task once more when they were left alone. The subject was afraid of a failure in the presence of the experimenter, but he was not at all, or hardly at all, afraid when he was alone. The social factor of the presence of the experimenter essentially sharpens the experience of failure.

The same relation between success and failure and social importance causes the anger of the subjects during failures to be directed immediately against the experimenter as the representative of social pressure. The whole behavior of the subjects sometimes takes on a tone of hostility to the experimenter (but not, however, in an entirely serious way). Especially do the subjects tend to shift the blame for the failure onto the experimenter who gives such "stupid tasks."

There exists, therefore, a dynamic relation between the level of aspiration for each single task, and a more embracing ego level which rests on one's self as a social being. The strength of this connection becomes perhaps most clearly evident in the fact mentioned earlier that experiences of success or failure are lacking as soon as the result of an action is not regarded as an achievement of the self—for instance, when the responsibility is shifted to the working materials, or in the trials at the beginning where the result of an action is experienced as being conditioned by the materials.

Concerning the Dynamics of the Ego Level

The shiftings of the level of aspiration, unexplained until now, as well as the different forms of behavior after success or failure become comprehensible if one takes into consideration the interaction between success, failure, and the ego level, and if one assumes that there exists a general tendency to keep the ego level as high as possible.

The existence of this tendency can be proved by a series of facts:

The tendency to keep the ego as high as possible is directly expressed in the tendency just described to shift the responsibility for failure from one's self to an objective sphere, or even to conceal failure through attempted deceit. (Such a failure to consider the achievement as belonging to the person occurs also after success when the success is felt to be accidental, or when the task as a whole is considered too easy. It is, however, much rarer after successes than after failures.)

Another means is to devalue the task, to depreciate it, and to consider it as something indifferent. In the task with matches, one subject says: "That is probably some nonsense which you made up yourself." He approaches the task seemingly without interest. When he could not find the solution after some trials, he gave up and refused to be shown the correct solution by the experimenter. He wished to stick to the assumption that the task was unsolvable. "No, I'd rather not, it would embarrass me." It happens sometimes that the subject, after a series of failures, does not work at the task ostentatiously and playfully.

Behavior of this sort leaves no doubt about the fact that there actually exists, in our experiments, a strong tendency to protect one's self from failures, or to keep the ego level high in spite of failures.

What the basic cause of this tendency is, and upon what conditions its strength depends, cannot be discussed in detail here. We do not believe that we are dealing with an instinct which does not have to be explained any further (for instance, a drive towards higher goals, or towards power). It seems, on the contrary, that this tendency is bound up with the position of the person as a whole in the social field.

The Conflicts in Establishing the Level of Aspiration

The tendency towards maintaining a general Ego level as high as possible is also one of the decisive dynamic bases which underlie the laws of the shifting of the level of aspiration. It means a continuous pressure to shift the level of aspiration upward.

In the first place, this pressure explains why the subjects occasionally set themselves a goal which exceeds the natural maximum of the task, a behavior which cannot be explained by a fixation of pleasure to the action, or by an after effect of the original quasi-need.

Also, the way in which the level of aspiration is shifted within the natural latitude of the task depends upon the relation between the level of aspiration and the Ego level. The tendency to keep the Ego level high expresses itself here in two ways: in the tendency to avoid failure, and in the tendency to achieve success with a level of aspiration as high as possible. The two effects of the same dynamic basic tendency usually resulted in behavior in opposite directions.

On the one hand, the fear of failure causes the subject to set the beginning level of aspirations as low as possible, to try the task out first (without becoming too engaged in it in an involved personal manner), to raise the level of aspiration after success only in small steps, and to lower it as much as possible after failure. On the other hand, the subject is driven towards the opposite behavior by the desire to realize success with the highest possible level of aspiration. He wishes to raise the level of aspiration in big steps after success and to lower it only a little after failures; he wishes to choose at the beginning of a task a high goal in spite of the danger of failure, since it shows self-confidence to risk everything bravely at the beginning.

The two tendencies, which originate from the same source, typically lead to a conflict situation. This conflict is the basic situation from which the single shifts of the level of aspiration, their kind and direction, arise.

The effect of this conflict is further complicated by the fact that there exists not only the question of leaving the level of aspiration on the same level, or of raising or lowering it by small or large steps, but also the question whether one should continue one's efforts for the solution of a task (on any level of aspiration), or whether one should discontinue.

A conflict situation usually exists, also, for spontaneous discontinuation of an action, after success as well as after failure.

In the interruption of actions after success, two situations are possible: The subject, after a series of failures, has finally had a success; with this, he wishes to secure for himself a "good exit," even if the corresponding level of aspiration is quite low. Or the subject progressed from success to success, and discontinues the action because no higher success can be expected from it. In both instances, the interruption means the renunciation of the hope of achieving success on a higher level of aspiration than the one achieved, and the conflict situation is apparent from the behavior of the subjects. The subject does not stop as if the action had reached its natural end, but each time it is a real decision which ends the conflict situation.

Example of a good exit: One subject actually said, "I wouldn't like to stop after a failure. All is well that ends well."

Example of discontinuation after a series of successes: One subject hit 100 twice in succession in the shooting task. He said, "Now I had better stop. Otherwise, it will get worse again."

The two first shots of Subject 21 hit the center. He stopped with the words, "Wonderful, I shoot very well, I wouldn't have thought that." In answer to questions, he declared that he thinks a failure after such an achievement absolutely impossible. "Why should I go on shooting?" This only shows that he does not really believe in his ability in shooting. The behavior expresses the same tendency, to assume importance through a self-confident way of acting, as was expressed in the tendency mentioned above of the subjects to set the beginning level of aspiration high, in spite of the rules of caution.

A similar conflict situation also frequently exists in discontinuation after failure. On the one hand, the desire to achieve at least one success drives the subject to attempt the task again and again, on a gradually lowered level of aspiration. On the other hand, it seems to the subject that he commits himself less when he discontinues after a failure to reach a high goal than when he fails, even though he has lowered his level of aspiration greatly.

On the whole, we find a tendency (to a different extent in the individual subjects) to satisfy oneself with a small success, rather than to discontinue after a failure without lowering the level of aspiration but keeping the Ego level high. We sometimes got the impression of a strong overestimation of the value of the success, when the subject tried in every possible way to succeed, even if with a very low level of aspiration. He asks, for instance, the experimenter to tell him the solution and thus gains, at least, the knowledge of the solution. If a successful ending cannot be achieved, in spite of the lowering of the level of aspiration, the subjects sometimes try, as was mentioned before, to realize now as success an earlier achievement which had not then been considered a success, or even to simulate success. The subject maintains, for instance, that he grasped the principle of the task, even when this is not at all the case. If even such an inferior success cannot be reached, the subject consoles himself with the hope of a possible later resumption. In this way he, at least, lowers the degree of reality of the failure.

Individual Differences

Even though the general laws of the shifting of the level of aspiration, and the basic dynamic factors concerned, are the same for all subjects, considerable individual differences are present. They consist primarily in the way in which the subject deals with the conflict situation described. There are, of course, certain variations from task to task, but aside from this special behavior, characteristics of the particular subject are clearly recognizable.

The individual differences concern the relative height of the level of aspiration; the strength of the tendency to raise the level of aspiration to the highest possible point; the tendency to raise the level of aspiration after success; to lower it after failure; the tendency to make large or small steps in one or the other direction; the strength of the tendency to discontinue after failure rather than gradually to lower the level of aspiration; and, finally, the degree to which the subject has the tendency to console himself or to obliterate the unpleasant reality in some other way. We are, therefore, dealing with differences in ambition, in cautiousness, in self-confidence, in the fear of inferiority, in the degree of self-assurance, and in the courage to face reality.

We compared, for each subject, the percentage of the frequency with which he raised, lowered, or maintained his level of aspiration.* A consideration of these averages shows a few interesting points [clues]. A characterization of each individual's behavior becomes even clearer when the curves of the actual course of events are considered, since with these one can trace the position of the single shiftings of the level of aspiration within the events comprising the whole task.

Subject 16. Subject 16 presents the picture of a person who has a good sense of reality, who meets the conflict between cautiousness and ambition in a calm manner, and who keeps to a middle line. A statistical analysis shows a regular distribution. Usually, there is a raising of the level of aspiration after success, and a lowering after failure. The level of aspiration remains the same after failure more frequently than after success. This, however, is probably caused not by a special persistency in defense of the level of aspiration, but rather by the fact that the subject shows, on the whole, good achievement. Thus, most failures have the character of single failures.

The percentage of the frequency with which the subject went out of the field is relatively high. Also, the curves show that even though the tendency to carry success as far as possible is relatively strong after failure, the subject tends to discontinue. He thereby recognizes the failure as a reality, rather than allowing his level of aspiration to be lowered more and more (see, in contrast, Subject 19).

Subject 21. Subject 21 is closest to Subject 16. He also has a rather strong ambition and considerable self-confidence. Just as with Subject 16, the beginning level of aspiration is generally high. Most characteristic of Subject 21, perhaps, is the tendency to discontinue an action abruptly, after success as well as after failure. If, on the basis of his abilities he has the experience of failure right at the beginning, which occurs quite often as a consequence of his high level of aspiration, he almost always discontinues. The level of aspiration is,

*I have omitted these four figures. They may be obtained from University Microfilms—Editor.

therefore, seldom raised or even kept the same (especially in target shooting and shooting at a hole).

The tendency to go out of the field after failures, rather than to lower his level of aspiration gradually, is even more obvious in Subject 21 than in Subject 16. (See the frequent attempts to go out of the field in the nuisance task.) In the top game, however, Subject 21 continuously lowered his level of aspiration after failure. We have to keep in mind here that this subject, more than others, tends to devalue actions in which he is unsuccessful, and to carry them out in a playful manner. Such a devaluation of the activity is almost equivalent to an actual discontinuation, and contrasts with the escapist tendency to devaluate failure later.

Subject 19. Subject 19 also begins all tasks with a very high level of aspiration. This is the more remarkable because this subject fails almost entirely. One would expect that he would, after having failed in one task, choose the beginning level of aspiration for the next task somewhat more cautiously.

In the statistical grouping, the high percentage of the frequency of lowering of the level of aspiration after failure attracts our attention. This is connected not only with the high absolute frequency of failures of this subject, but also especially with the fact that failures, at a high level of aspiration, do not lead to discontinuation (as in Subject 21), but to a lowering of the subject's level of aspiration. The curves of the course of the whole experiment show that this subject always lowered his level of aspiration very slowly and gradually. Furthermore, he allows his level of aspiration to be lowered until it lies below the natural minimum of the task. This subject is the only one who, while discontinuing a task, often consoled himself with the expectation of a possible resumption of it.

The gradual lowering of the level of aspiration might show that the subject had backbone or that he lacked it. (Otherwise, this subject would prefer to discontinue completely, like Subject 21, instead of lowering his level of aspiration so far.) The truth is that both factors are present and do not contradict each other. We are dealing here with a certain persistency in sticking to a thing, in holding on to something, which frequently accompanies a lack of courage in facing reality. (To a much stronger degree, this phenomenon can be observed in hysteria (8).)

In Subject 19, insufficient courage to face reality was also observable in his reactions to unpleasant facts. Even the fact that he does not discontinue, in spite of continuous failures, means in this case an unwillingness to realize failure. The fact that the subject begins the next task once again with a high level of aspiration is only a gesture which shows that he does not sufficiently take into account his abilities. It is as if the subject wanted to make up for the failures by at least setting his level of aspiration high, that is, by demanding much of himself. (This tendency is related to the subject's tendency to console himself, and is not done just for the benefit of the experimenter.)

The feeling of inadequacy, which underlies the overestimation of the value of mere intention in contrast to reality, also expresses itself in this subject in very marked emotional outbreaks after failure (9). They are exaggeratedly violent and seem, for this very reason, somehow "false," almost as if he wished to emphasize his level of aspiration to the experimenter, and thereby the "unusualness" of the failure.

On the whole, it is characteristic for this subject that the conflict, which is necessarily present, is felt particularly strongly on account of the especially great fear of inferiority on the one hand, and the exaggeration of the level of aspiration on the other. The situation was not solved through the decision to discontinue, which was demanded by the situation, but became a permanent condition. (This subject was actually affected by the failures for weeks after the experiment.) The indecisiveness is perhaps causatively connected with the lack of courage to face reality.

Subject 14. The subject just described might also be regarded as an example of a case where the danger of failure was very much heightened by an ambitious assumption of a level of aspiration which exceeds abilities, thereby leading that much more certainly to failure. In Subject 14, however, the fear of failure leads him to choose a beginning level of aspiration which is as low as possible. In almost all actions it lies lower than that chosen by other subjects, even though Subject 14's average performance corresponds quite well to that of the other subjects.

The cautious behavior of this subject also shows itself in the fact that he raises his level of aspiration after success only by small steps, and that he always lowers it after failure. (The statistical grouping shows him to be the only subject whose level of aspiration never remained the same after a failure.)

It is surprising to see how much the behavior of the subjects, in discontinuation, in the shifting of the level of aspiration, and generally in their way of dealing with the conflict arising in the experiments, corresponds with their behavior in everyday life. We have known these subjects for several years and can assert that the characteristic differences which were noticeable in the experiment can be observed in their behavior in life situations which extend over months or years. We suspect, therefore, that such experiments are quite suitable as a basis for the investigation of individual behavior differences in situations of success and failure, for the study of attitudes towards "inferiority" (Adler), and for the investigation of the whole complex of important questions connected therewith.

The individual differences, like the preceding phenomena, indicate that the laws governing the shifting of the level of aspiration are generally based on a conflict situation, which in turn goes back to the tendency to keep the ego level as high as possible. (A teleological consideration, which we do not think correct, might lead us to formulate the facts as follows. The shiftings of the level of aspiration has the function of protecting the subject, as far as possible, from an injury to his self-confidence.)

EDITOR'S ABRIDGMENT AND COMMENT

[The rest of this article contains two more sections, with twelve figures, and a summary section—about 30 per cent of the total. This material, which is not as theoretically relevant, may be obtained *in toto* from University Microfilms. It may be summarized as follows.

After the observations reported above, Hoppe attempted to experimentally produce changes in level of aspiration. His initial attempt was a failure, which nevertheless helped the development of his conceptualization. Giving the subject a task, Hoppe varied the time in which the task was supposed to be done. In an attempt to produce strong feelings of success and failure, he gave times which were far too long or far too short for the particular task. He found, however, that this made the task too easy or too hard, and the subject failed to experience either success or failure. The subject did not feel responsible, and either did not get involved, or created a substitute goal which was not as involving. Fulfillment was experienced as success, and nonfulfillment as failure only when the time limit was close to the subject's actual abilities. Noting exactly where these limits of ability lay, Hoppe found that the region of difficulty in which experiences of success could occur was almost the same region in which experiences of failure could occur. As Hoppe states, "Experiences of success occur only where experiences of failure can also be expected with a reasonable degree of probability, and the other way around, experiences of failure occur only in a zone where success is possible" (10).

Recognizing this limit on his technique, Hoppe began to use a "deception watch" which he could ostensibly set for one time while it was actually set for a different time. In this way he could set the timer to ring just before or just after his subject finished a task with a time limit. He was thus able to experimentally produce success or failure. He discovered that his deception was apt to be discovered when time was considerably speeded up to produce failure. However, when success was at stake, subjects could double or even triple the time period (from one to two or three minutes) without experiencing the deception. Hoppe also learned one other important fact. If the subject was involved in setting the goal—for instance, if he suggested the time limit—then even if the time was far too long or too short, there was still an experience of success or failure.

Satisfaction, Goal Formation, and Learning

In a way, the early quantification of analysis in terms of level of aspiration detracted from an elaboration of the qualitative significance of goal setting. It should not be forgotten that Hoppe was initially dealing with the problem of why his subjects repeated a successful action. He found that the repetition was by no means an automatic repeating of an action that had been associated with pleasure, but instead involved the creation of a new goal. The new goal motivated action toward it, and hence psychologically there was no repetition at all.

With the emphasis on the new goal as indicating a level of aspiration, Hoppe never does return to his initial problem, and simply assumes that his subjects resumed action because they were not yet satisfied. But the initial problem is too good to remain so slighted. We must ask whether or not an analysis in terms of goal formation would also help us to understand the hen who gradually goes more quickly to the hole in the fence.

It is clear that a good deal of trial and error learning can be accounted for in terms of changes in goal formation. In a sense, Tolman's analysis of changes in means-end relationships is precisely such an account (11). For example, suppose that a hen's behavior is initially governed by the goal of getting beyond a fence. Then this activity could be described as "finding a way through the fence." Once the hen has found a hole in the fence, she may adopt the new goal of going to the particular place where she has found the hole. Once this is so, she is engaged in the somewhat different activity of "going to the hole." Thus, more quickly repeating the behavior of going to the hole need not be conceived of as an association that has been based on the pleasure of success, but rather may be seen as a different behavior based on a new goal.

Rather than fixing a behavior pattern, the role of satisfaction in such an account of learning would be to free the animal or person from the prior goal so that the new goal could be established. Thus, in our example, it is dissatisfaction that would keep the hen trying to find a way through the fence, while satisfaction would permit the goal to change to "going to the hole."

Thus, paradoxically, it is dissatisfaction which keeps the animal or person performing the same activity (trying to find a way through the fence), even though frustration may lead to different ways to do this. And it is satisfaction which, by removing the goal, creates a situation which will either lead to a new goal, or to satiation and a cessation (or disintegration) of the activity. It is important to note that in such an analysis the role of pleasure (as opposed to satisfaction) is to permit repetition of the activity—which then becomes a consummatory rather than a means-end action.

Of course, in humans it is important to realize that learning something may itself be a task, and that the intention to learn is equivalent to being engaged in the activity of learning something, or repeating something (12). This task, like any other unfinished task, tends toward completion, so that there is a tension to finish the learning. The intention system that is formed (the activity of learning) may be regarded as providing a structure such that correct or successful responses are included or incorporated in whatever system is being learned (13).—Editor.]

FOOTNOTES

1. Karl Buhler, *Die geistige Entwicklung des Kindes* (Jena, 1922). See also Koffka, *Die Grundlagren der psychischen Entwicklung* (Osterwieck, 1925).

2. A. Karsten, "Psychische Sattigung," *Psych. Forsch.* 10, 142.

3. Lewin, "Vorsatz, Wille und Bedurfnis," *Psych. Forsch.* 7 (1926). The processes of such a release of tension have been investigated in the studies by B. Zeigarnik, "Über das Behalten erledigter und enevledigter Handlungen," *Psych. Forsch.* 9, and M. Ovsiankina, "Die Wiederaufnähme unterbrochener Handlungen," *Psych. Forsch.* 11.

4. Giese, *Handbuch psychotechnischer Eignungsprufungen* (Halle, 1925), 288.

5. Ovsiankina ("Die Wideraufnähme unterbrochener Handlungen," *Psych. Forsch.* 11, 338) also found that a tendency towards resumption was sometimes noticeable when there were still "new possibilities open." Otherwise completed actions were not spontaneously resumed.

6. Some of the properties of the level of aspiration and its shifting, which we discuss, are mentioned in T. Dembo's study, "Der Aerger als dynamisches Problem," *Psych. Forsch.* 15(1931).

7. Compare with the similar handling of objects in the anthropoid apes. W. Köhler, *Intelligenzprufungen an Anthropoiden* (Berlin, 1927).

8. See, for instance, Kretschmer, *Medizinische Psychologie* (Leipzig, 1926), 215 and 219.

9. Kurt Lewin, "Trieb-und Affectausserungen Psychopathischer Kinder," *Z. Kinderforschg.* (Berlin, 1926).

10. Ferdinand Hoppe, "Erfolg and Misserfolg," *Psychol. Forsch.* 14(1930), 1–62. The translation of all sections of the original article omitted from this chapter may be obtained from Xerox: University Micrifilms, "Success and Failure." The quotation cited is from page 101 of the translation.

11. Edward C. Tolman, *Purposive Behavior in Animals and Man* (New York: Appleton-Century-Crofts, 1967).

12. Compare Thomas Arthur Ryan, *Intentional Behavior* (New York: Ronald Press, 1970), 178–187.

13. Ibid., 180. Ryan cites the work of J. Nuttin, *Reward and Punishment in Human Learning* (New York: Academic Press, 1968).

Chapter XIII

CHOICES AND THEIR DETERMINATION

THE studies of Hoppe and Dembo demonstrate how situational factors such as success, failure, and frustration can affect a person's activity. But it is also true that a person's active choice may affect the situation he is in. In this chapter, after noting further evidence as to the impact of success and failure on activity, we shall examine the nature of personal choice and how it affects one's situation. First, we shall consider the role of choice in goal-formation and its influence on the will to try; then the choices involved when one's worth is at stake in interpersonal relations; and finally, returning to Dembo's study, the choice about what to believe and the issue of whose will shall govern a person's reality. We shall see that the interplay between situational forces and active choices raises a number of interesting questions about the nature of will, reality, and freedom.

THE EFFECTS OF SUCCESS AND FAILURE

Hoppe's results suggest that success in an activity leads a person to raise his level of aspiration while failure (or anticipated failure) leads to a lowering of goals or to discontinuing the activity. Such results raise many related questions such as whether success in one activity may affect one's goal in another activity, and whether success and failure have more general effects on behavior.

Jucknat's Experiments

While Hoppe's last technique allowed the experimental creation of success and failure, the subject's level of aspiration could only be inferred from the subjects' remarks, or their subsequent experience of success and failure. Another of Lewin's students, Jucknat (1), decided to use the experimentally more rigorous procedure of controlling success and failure, and establishing their effect on an independent measure of level of aspiration that could be obtained before any performance. Accordingly, she designed a series of ten increasingly complex paper-and-pencil mazes. After performing a sample maze, the subject could choose which maze to perform, thereby establishing his level of aspiration before he engaged in the task. After succeeding or failing on the chosen maze, he could select another maze, or discontinue the experiment. Jucknat rigged her mazes so that one series was a set of ten solvable mazes, whereas the mazes in the other series were all unsolvable. She could thus be assured of a success or failure experience, and see the effects on the subject's level of aspiration as indicated by the next maze he chose in the series (or by his withdrawal). Half of the subjects were first exposed to the success series and then given the failure series; half experienced the reverse order. It should be noted that most subjects were between ten and fourteen years of age.

Confirming Hoppe's results, Jucknat found that the level of aspiration is raised after success, and the frequency and extent of the shift depends on the strength of the success, as measured by the time and effort required to solve the maze. However, it is interesting to observe that only 42 per cent of the subjects who experienced success continued to the most difficult maze. Many subjects discontinued the experiment when they began to meet with difficulty, thus avoiding a risk of failure.

Subjects who experienced failure tended to drop their level of aspiration, but only until they became convinced that they could not seem to master the mazes. They then discontinued the experiment rather than dropping to far simpler mazes.

Jucknat observed that after experiencing success, a subject became confident and decisive, evidencing a knowledge of what he did and didn't want. His work sped up and the manner became more fluid, showing a general loosening up, a freedom, and a joyful quality. After failure, a subject became more serious and intense, and showed difficulty in making decisions (as revealed by longer decision times to choose the next maze or discontinue). However, in general there were more individual differences, a greater number of characterological factors, that were revealed by the failure experience.

In this connection, we wish to mention Cartwright's investigation into the effect which failure has upon the attractiveness of an activity (2). His subjects were given a number of tasks and told that the purpose of the investigation was to see if people tended to do better on the tasks that they wanted to perform. Under these conditions, if a person was told he had taken a longer time to finish than any other subject, he tended to see the task and similar tasks as less attractive than he had previously. This was particularly true when subsequent failure was anticipated. In fact, Cartwright notes, "There is some indication . . . that anticipation of failure more unequivocally reduces attractiveness than the actual experience of failure" (3).

While the above findings were the average effect, in a substantial number of cases, failure produced an increase in attractiveness. Probably this was due to the subject's experiencing the experimenter's remarks as an obstacle or a challenge rather than a failure; and Cartwright notes the necessity for a theory of failure that has more sharply defined conceptual properties. Of course, if we take overt failure as a starting point, there are numerous factors to be considered. These are different ego defenses which may be utilized (4), and Aronson has shown that unsuccessful effort may create dissonance that is reduced by increasing the attractiveness of the disappointing outcome (5).

Returning to Jucknat's investigation, we must note that her technique permitted the examination of the important question of whether or not success or failure in one activity would transfer to affect the subject's level of aspiration on other activities.

Considering first the limiting case of an identical activity, we may ask what happened when subjects who had experienced success or failure in the first series of mazes were given a second series of mazes. The results show that after success in the first series, 60 per cent of the subjects choose a more difficult maze to begin the second series than they had chosen to begin the first series, thus demonstrating a raised level of aspiration.

Although the new mazes were approached cautiously (nobody chose mazes as difficult as those they solved towards the end of the first series), the subjects were confident and made their decisions quickly and with few fluctuations. After failure on the first series of mazes, 67 per cent of the subjects showed a lower level of aspiration on the second series than they had initially demonstrated on the first series. Still, they tended to choose a maze that was somewhat more difficult than ones of a similar type at which they had been unsuccessful.

Those subjects who experienced failure on the first series of mazes showed more activity in the success series of mazes than the subjects who had begun with the success series. They more frequently raised their level of aspiration, thereby completing more mazes. However, they did not raise their aspirations in such large jumps, and eventually they wound up with a lower final level of aspiration than the first group of subjects. In general, the new-found success brought relief and interest in the task, but the subjects never showed the free and easy approach of those who had experienced success without the prior trauma of failure. The latter subjects, confronted for the first time with failure, behaved exactly as the earlier subjects had behaved. They were literally somewhat paralyzed by the sudden failure.

Like Hoppe's finding that subjects could more easily distort time when it served the interests of their self-esteem, Jucknat found an interesting phenomenon with similar implications. Among the subjects who had first experienced the failure series, a fairly common defense had been to begin to think that the mazes were in fact unsolvable. With the experience of success, all the subjects changed to believe that the earlier mazes were solvable. However, whereas before many subjects had demanded to be shown how to solve the failed mazes, now all forgot to remind the experimenter of his promise to show them the solution at the end of the experiment.

In order to better investigate the extent of transfer from one activity to another, Jucknat modified her technique. She created a number of series of tasks which were graded in difficult along a ten-point scale (mazes, arithmetical problems, block designs, and so on), and which could serve either to induce success or failure, or to be a standard series against which level of aspiration could be determined. Her technique was to show the subject a standard series and have him make a choice as to which problem he would do (thus establishing the level of aspiration), but then, on a pretext, she would give him some other task or series of tasks which would induce success or failure. Then going back to the standard series, she again had the subject choose which level of difficulty he would like to try. In this way, she could determine the effect which success or failure in one type of activity had on a before-after measure of level of aspiration in a different type of activity. While subjects tended to simply repeat their first choice on the standard series (they, of course, had some tension to complete the particular task they had chosen), Jucknat found that if the standard series was not numbered (or distinguished in some other way) the lapse of a week's time permitted fluctuation in the choice and thus allowed changes in the level of aspiration to be measured.

Using tasks that were somewhat similar, but where it was not clear whether or not the same abilities would be needed, such as different types of seeking games (mazes and "find the cats"), or different sorts of mathematical problems, Jucknat established that success in one activity did raise the level of aspiration for another somewhat similar activity (about one step measured a week later). Failure, on the other hand, did not significantly lower the level of aspirations.

When the tasks were completely different, such as mazes and mathematical problems, there were no transfer effects.

In order to obtain transfer over different tasks, Jucknat tried building up the success or failure experience, and generalizing it by giving the subjects a number of different activities. For example, after determining the subject's level of aspiration by having him choose a maze from a standard series of ten, she would give the subject success experiences on a riddle and a series of block patterns, and a series of figuring problems. Then, a week later, the subject would again pick a maze from the standard series. Under these conditions there was a strong transfer effect, the level of aspiration going up after success and down after failure. In evaluating the generality of this transfer effect it should be noted that the presence of a series of task in the success and failure experience seemed to be a necessary factor in the transfer to the standard series. Also, of course, the subject was, in both cases, in the same general (experimental) situation.

Theoretically, there are at least three different ways transfer can occur: (1) In performing the first task the subject may learn that he has or lacks certain specific abilities that he believes are needed for the second task. (2) The subject's general feeling of confidence may be altered by the experience of success or failure. (3) The subject's even more general feeling of self-worth may have been altered. In Jucknat's last experiment it would seem that perhaps general confidence in the experimental situation had been affected. In the case of Hoppe's one subject who experienced the aftereffects of failure for several weeks, it would seem that self-worth may have been affected (6).

Fajans' Study

While both Hoppe and Jucknat noted various general effects which success and failure had on the performance of their subjects, their primary interest was in the specific effect on the subject's level of aspiration. Another student of Lewin, Fajans (7), working with infants and children, focused on more general performance effects. She hung a desired object on a string in such a way that it was just out of reach of the child's grasp and then carefully observed the child's behavior. Her first publication (8), which we considered in Chapter XI, shows that the force exerted on the child decreases as the distance to the object increases, and that the barrier to achieving the goal can acquire a negative valence that leads the child to leave the field.

In the success condition of the experiment, after four minutes of the rather frustrating situation the string was surreptitiously lowered so that the child could just grasp the object, thereby achieving a hard-earned success. (If he stopped trying, the experimenter suggested that he try again.) After a five-minute break, during which the child played with various toys, another object was hung from the string, again just barely out of reach. After four minutes, the child's striving was again successful. Finally, after another break, the procedure was repeated for a third time. In the failure condition of the experiment, the string was never lowered, and thus the child experienced three consecutive failures.

It is not surprising, of course, that in the success series the time spent trying to reach the goal increases from the first to the third period, while in the series of failures the time decreases. What was somewhat surprising was the dramaticness of the effect. Active children were made even more lively and active by success, while children who had been backward, embarrassed, and extremely passive began showing active, confident behavior. On the other hand, failure transformed both active and passive children into children who showed a lack of confidence and certainty. Children who had been active left the field (in some cases leaving the room), while children who had been passive were trapped and embarrassed, and began daydreaming or stood passively sucking their thumbs.

Of course, after the experiment was over, Fajan consoled the children who had been in the failure series and let them reach the candy. Seeing how much this restored them, she ran another series of experiments in which she utilized the five-minute break periods to console and encourage the children who had experienced failure. She found that in about three-fourths of her cases, the children responded with free and more active behavior, maintaining the time they spent in actively trying to reach the goal. In the other quarter of her cases, her attempts at consolation were taken as a sort of one-upping behavior, and were automatically rejected. She discovered that even after success experiences, encouragement strengthened the success experience, especially in passive children.

Fajan reports other interesting individual differences among her subjects, but these results are secondary to her major finding of the tremendous impact of success or failure on children in this particular situation. It is important to note that these effects, which were also obtained with infants, appear to simply depend on whether or not the child reaches his goal. That is, although children attempt to protect themselves from visible failure with its attendant shame or embarrassment, the child does not have to be praised or shamed or ego-involved in any special way in order for simple success or failure to dramatically influence his basic confidence and the level at which he actively tries to reach goals.

On the other hand, I feel it is important to remember that the basic self-worth of the children, their general experience of wellbeing, may have been largely dependent on how they perceived themselves to be treated by the experimenter. That is, in a situation which is governed by how the experimenter arranges the goal, the meaning of success or failure may have largely been "The experimenter treats me well," or "The experimenter treats me badly." Like Little Jack Horner, success may have meant "I am well treated, what a good boy am I." In any case, it is clear that success and failure may have enormous effects on the will to try.

THE WILL TO TRY

We cannot attempt here to completely summarize the vast literature on the level of aspiration subsequent to the studies described above (9). On the one hand, there have been numerous investigations into some of the personality differences which Hoppe described. Ambition has been measured by McClelland's development of measures of need achievement (10). Fear of failure has been measured by Mandler (11) and other investigations of test anxiety. And considerations of both the need to achieve and the fear of failure have led to Atkinson's demonstrations that persons with a high need to achieve set moderate levels of aspiration which avoid both extreme risk of failure and too easy successes (12). The one variable which has been neglected is courage. Adams (13) has pointed out that there have been an unfortunate dearth of studies dealing with the courage to face reality, or any other type of courageous behavior. The one exception with which we are familiar is Jahoda's discussion of independent behavior in the face of conformity pressures (14).

On the other hand, there have been studies on the impact which social norms have had on the individual's aspiration. And there have been a number of attempts to use the idea of level of aspiration in the analysis of social movements. Here the central argument has been that an oppressed people will be apathetic until slight improvements occur which establish some hope for successful change. The resulting rise in level of aspiration then provides the motivation for a social movement towards improved conditions.

A third line of development has stemmed from the further analysis of the test situation, and the basic conflict which a person faces as he decides to what extent he should raise or lower his level of aspiration. Since this is of particular theoretical relevance, we will attempt to sketch an outline of some of the developments in this area.

Deciding the Level of Aspiration

As Hoppe pointed out, a person in a test situation must decide what level of aspiration to commit himself to—what to really *try* for—and in this decision he is caught between his desire to achieve success and his desire to avoid failure. Elaborating on this, Lewin, Dembo, Festinger, and Sears (15) speculated that the level of aspiration is determined by the subject's attempt to maximize his chance of a positive experience. They reasoned that the subject must subjectively believe that he has a certain chance of success and a certain chance of failure (such subjective probabilities would not necessarily add up to the objective probability of 1.00). Further, the experience of success must have a certain amount of attractive valence, and the experience of failure must have a certain negative valence. Any given level of aspiration might, therefore, be conceived of as having an attractive force that was equal to the subjective probability of success, multiplied by the valence of success at that level, and a negative force equal to the subjective probability of failure multiplied by the valence of failure of that particular level. Lewin and the others argue that the subject will choose the level of aspiration which maximizes the sum [(subjective probability success × valence success) − (subjective probability failure × valence failure)].

This analysis appears reasonable, and indeed is related to the whole general approach to decision making known as "utility models." These models all envision the decision maker as attempting to pick the alternative which will be most useful to him. However, in spite of the analytical usefulness of such models, I have criticized this approach to decision making as applying only to choices about the means to a goal. The goal itself (the end toward which the action is directed) is chosen by a completely different process (16). In fact, it is not really chosen so much as it is created—designed specifically to meet the person's situation in a way that advances the person's interests.

Such goal formation is intimately related to the meaning which the situation has for the individual. That is, there are different possible meanings to the situation which the person confronts, and the goal the person chooses to advance his interests establishes one of these as *the* meaning of the situation. In order to form a goal that will meet all of his interests, a person may prefer to give the situation a meaning that distorts reality, rather than suffer the pain of giving up some of his interests. Such distortions must be distinguished from the courage involved in asserting a personal meaning with the faith and risk, a subject that we shall discuss here later.

Let us apply a goal model to the situation described by Hoppe where the subject is confronted with a task and must decide what goal to set for himself. If the subject's primary interest is in the task, then he will not be primarily concerned with success or failure at all. He will simply establish a goal that will explore the properties of the task and challenge his abilities in the manner described by White (17). His level of aspiration will always be a bit higher than his current ability, because, as we saw in Chapter VI, he cannot simply repeat an activity or he would satiate. Success and failure have an effect on his goals because the person cannot set a goal that is much greater than his ability. In fact, at the actual moment of trying, I believe that a person can try only to the extent that he believes that he can succeed if he tries hard enough. To really try, one must think one can; and failure will always come with a sort of shock, and at least initially, be attributed to chance or insufficient effort, rather than a lack of ability.

The close psychological relationship between trying, and thinking that one can is demonstrated in Fajans' experiments when the distance between the child and the goal object is varied. When the desired object is (objectively) just out of reach, both infants and children actively try to reach the object; whereas when the object is moved so as to be clearly out of reach, they simply passively stare at it, turning toward and away from the goal, and finally leaving the field. If the goal is moved back to its first distance it is, evidently, no longer perceived as obtainable, and there are no longer attempts to reach it.

Now suppose a situation in which the subject is ego-involved. First, let us suppose a subject who is primarily interested in raising his ego level. In such a case, the person will attempt to create a goal that will eventually insure the experience of success. Of course, as Hoppe shows, in order to do this he must risk some chance of failure, and the person cannot possibly insure success or avoid failure. However, what is important to his ego level is whether or not he experiences himself as a success or a failure. This experience will depend on why he believes he has succeeded or failed, and as Wiener has indicated (18), he may attribute the objective success or failure to any of a number of factors. For example, he may attribute a failure to bad luck, or to lack of enough effort, or to the task's being too difficult, rather than to his own lack of ability.

My point is, that exactly what factor success or failure is attributed to depends to a large extent on the goal the person has created. For example, if a person is to experience success and attribute it to his own ability, he must have set himself the goal of succeeding. Otherwise, a success will be attributed to chance or the ease of the task. In turn, the goal a person creates will depend on his beliefs about what he can or can't do. For a person to set himself the goal of success, he must be prepared to try to achieve the goal, and hence must believe that he may be able to achieve it.

We have been speaking of a person who is trying to succeed; however, if a person sets himself the goal of avoiding any real failure, he will not really commit himself to succeeding. His belief that he won't succeed will influence goal setting in such a way that he will either fail to really try, will choose such an easy goal that failure is not possible (and hence neither is subjective success), or will actually try to fail (in order to be in control of the failure).

Of course, given ego involvement, persons high in need achievement will tend to establish the goal of succeeding; and persons low in the need to achieve, or high in the fear of failure, will tend to establish the goal of not really failing. My point is that goal setting is not a resultant of these two forces, nor a computerlike calculation of probabilities, but rather, involves creating a goal that satisfies the person's central interests and affects the meaning of the situation. The level of aspiration is a product of this creation. To fully understand how such goal setting works, we must examine the relationship between success, failure, and self-worth.

The Relationship Among Success, Worth, and Trying

In Hoppe's analysis, both the desire for success and the fear of failure are motivated by the more general goal of maximizing one's self-worth. There are, however, at least two different ways in which success or failure can influence self-worth: either by the direct value of success, or indirectly by its implication for valued qualities. Let us first consider the direct value of success.

Success can mean objective achievement, and as McClelland has pointed out, many persons and cultures value achievement for its own sake (19). In cultures where achievement is valued, child-rearing practices encourage achievement and the child's learning to do things for himself, to be independent and self-sufficient. While McClelland does not develop his analysis in terms of group norms and self-worth, it would seem that in cultures where there is a norm for achievement, individuals are valued in terms of their achievement, and hence their own feelings of self-worth will depend on their achievements. In this view, the development in the individual of a need for achievement is based on the underlying need to be accepted and recognized by the socializing group. When the group's norms are internalized, the person will feel worth while when he is achieving; the raising of one's level of aspiration will be motivated by the need to achieve, and hence to be worthy—to be valued by others.

Although we have been discussing the raising of the level of aspiration by attempting excellence in some activity, it is also possible to *broaden* one's aspiration by being ambitious in many different areas. In stressing a person's need to be recognized by others, William James (20) pointed out that "self-feeling" is bound up with success in the social roles to which a person commits himself. In a complex society such as our own, there are many different successes to which a person may aspire. James notes that a person who is committed to being a boxer must try to win in the ring. His personal level of aspiration will involve beating opponents whom nonboxers would not dream of fighting. On the other hand, a person who is committed to being "cultured" will aspire to have a level of taste in music and art which will be completely foreign to persons committed to other roles. Hence, there are as many different successes as there are roles which we wish to play.

James suggests that one's self-feeling is determined by the ratio between the number of successes and the number of pretensions. Hence, a person might increase his feeling of worth by either achieving successes or giving up pretensions to roles in which he cannot succeed. While James speaks of the relief which follows the abandonment of pretensions and the acceptance of a less glorious but realistic self-image, it would seem that many more persons attempt to increase their self-worth by trying to increase the numerator of James' fraction.

Thus, in general, this need to achieve success and secure recognition motivates the raising of one's aspirations. Although a person may renounce goals because of not wanting to be disappointed by failure, if this were the only motive for setting a low or narrow level of aspiration, we would hardly speak of a fear of failure. To explain this fear, we must turn to the second way in which success or failure can affect self-worth.

This second way is through the implications which success or failure has for ability or other personal qualities which are valued by one's group. Cultures which value achievement are apt to value either abilities, or some other quality over which the individual has little direct control but which can be inferred by his achievements (whether these are the power and superiority stressed by Adler, or the state of grace stressed by Weber). Fear of failure is probably largely a matter of fearing that one lacks these valued qualities, and hence should avoid testing the matter by setting a low level of aspiration (not really "trying"), or by actually trying to fail.

The first of these possibilities is clarified by Heider's analysis of ability (21). He states: If one tries, then if one can, one will succeed.

Earlier, we noted that in order for a person to really try, he must believe at the moment of trying that he can. The function of the emotion of confidence is to establish this belief so that trying can occur. However, after trying he may find that he has or has not succeeded. If he has tried, he will attribute a success to the fact that he can; but if he has failed he may initially attribute his failure to bad luck. If failures continue, and the person does not deny reality, he must eventually conclude that his failure is due to his lack of ability. One function of the emotion of security is to permit the person to relinquish his commitment to his belief in his ability so that he does not continue to distort reality.

Accordingly, if a person tries and has success, he knows that he can (he has the ability); while if he tries and he fails, he will eventually know that he cannot (he lacks the ability). However, if a person does not really try, a failure will not necessarily indicate a lack of ability (that one cannot); and by not trying, a person can protect himself against the fear of failure, which is actually usually a fear of lacking some ability, of being not worth while.

Of course, there is a penalty for this evasion of reality. If one does not really try and yet does succeed, the person will not really be sure whether the success was due to his ability or was simply due to chance. Until he begins to take a risk and really try, he cannot begin to attribute success to his own efforts, and hence to his ability.

The fear of failing and not being worthwhile, of course, is intensified by the presence of an examiner, particularly if one believes the examiner expects one to fail and will look down upon the failure. Thus, Katz (22) has demonstrated that black students perform more poorly on "intelligence" tests when they are conducted by a white examiner than when the same tests are administered by a black examiner. If the same test is called a "coordination" test, the results are reversed.

A variant of the defense of not trying is actually trying to fail. This defense has been elaborated by John Holt (23), who details several cases of children who protect themselves against failure by purposely failing. This seeming paradox is understandable if one remembers that one is really protecting oneself against the loss of self-worth that is often the result of objective failure. By trying to fail, the person maintains control over the meaning of the situation. The objective failure does not mean that one lacks ability because it was due to one's trying to fail.

It should be noted that these defenses against failure are not easily explained by a utility model of decision making. Rather than maximizing utility, the positiveness of success has been completely abandoned and the subjective probability of failure reduced to zero. On the other hand, they may easily be understood in terms of a goal model of decision making. In the terms of this model, the person has formulated a goal which serves his major interest of protecting his self-esteem. He achieves this by not really risking his ability while he pretends to himself that he has it. This is an example of what Sartre terms "bad faith," and relates to a lack of Tillich's "courage to be" (24).

TESTS OF WORTH

Until now we have been speaking of tests of ability. In Hoppe's situation, the subject's self-worth is dependent on the level of his achievement, however, the general lines of our analysis may be applied to a much broader range of situations. Hoppe himself notes that self-worth may be dependent on other things besides achievement. He mentions that value may be placed on being loved, or on friendship, and that in some cultures it is placed on one's birth (or class or caste). It is possible, therefore, that our analysis may be extended into these other areas. Even in these other areas there are certain test situations which the person experiences as establishing the reality of his worth. The suitor at the moment of proposition; the friend who is suddenly dependent on his companion's caring; the aristocrat who may or may not be recognized, may be in the same conflict of hope and fear which Hoppe describes.

One extension of the analysis beyond achievement situations may be realized by replacing the concept of "trying" with the concept of "openness," the concept of "ability" (can) with the concept of "worth," and the concept of "success" with the concept of "being cared for." We may then assert: If one openly expresses a need, and if one is worth while, then one will be cared for.

Now, if a person is fairly secure about his worth he can fairly easily take the risk of openly expressing his needs. He will then expect to receive love, just as a person who tries and is confident in his ability will expect success. If the person does not receive love, he will probably defend against the implication that he is worthless by devaluing the other person and/or severing the relationship, just as a person who is confident in his ability may conclude that a test was bad, or the materials were flawed. Nevertheless, ultimately his worth is dependent on being cared for when he expresses a need.

Similarly, a person who is not sure of his worth, like a person who is unsure of his ability, may be unwilling to risk finding out the reality of his situation. Just as a person may not really try because he is afraid of failing, a person may not really express his needs because he is afraid they will not be met. Of course, by not expressing them, the needs remain unmet; but the person knows that they are unmet for that reason rather than because he is not worth while. He thus avoids the test.

Likewise, just as a person may try to fail in order to maintain control over the failure, so that it does not have the meaning of failure as a lack of ability, a person may express his needs in a way that guarantees they will not be met. He may follow Dan Greenburg's advice to ask for a date for New Year's Eve on December 30th or on June 1st (25).

Older (26) has described still another defensive means of expressing needs. In what he calls "pseudo-testing," rather than openly expressing a need, the person keeps placing subtle demands on those whom he loves. Unfortunately, when these demands are met the person still feels worthless. This is because there is no real evidence of worth, since he controlled the giving by making a demand, rather than by openly expressing a need and taking the risk that the other might not care for him. While such demands usually create an ultimate rejection, the test of worth has been avoided. In ability testing, one must risk failure in order to achieve success; so here, also, there must be a risk in order for there to be a possible success—the free giving that would bring assurance of one's sense of worth.

In extending the analysis of test situations beyond the level of aspiration for task performance and into the area of love and friendship, we do not mean to imply that all activities are always dominated by an emphasis on success or failure, or tests of basic worth.

As we have noted (in Chapter IV), when the ego recedes into the background and our needs involve the needs of the task, or of others, or ideals, or of our own selves, then success and failure are not so dominant. The person is not preoccupied with keeping his ego level as high as possible.

In this regard, we also want to mention Dembo's distinction between "comparason values" and "asset values (27). The former values always depend on a comparison between the person and others. Thus, for me to be valuable means that I have more money, beauty, intelligence, or talent than someone else. The latter values are simple assets which are valuable in themselves. I can buy something I want, attract someone's regard, solve a problem, drive a car, appreciate these values in their own right without doing any comparing. While success and failure affect whatever I do, and may establish or destroy an asset value, they need not raise or lower my ego level unless comparative values are involved.

Furthermore, it should be noted that a sense of worth does not necessarily depend on being valued by significant others. Frank's work (28) suggests that a sense of worth may also be bound up with a person's having some meaning to his life, and this may simply be attained by the person recognizing himself as a part of some greater whole. Hence, persons may also attain a sense of worth by dedication to a cause, or by their relationship with a personal God. In this regard, William James (29) asserted that the primary motive for prayer was the desire to communicate with One who would recognize the rightness of one's position (and, hence, recognize one's worth) when other persons could not. It has also been noted that persons who receive inadequate love when they are children, and hence grow up with a low sense of worth, may sometimes achieve a sense of worth by developing a faith in a God who loves them.

However, it is precisely when we are not sure of our worth that test situations become so anxiety provoking. Hoppe observes, "A common feature of the defenses employed to protect the ego level is the resulting lack of *involvement* with the reality of the task and its implications." We would say that in the case of all the test situations that we have discussed, the lack of courage to become involved and to face reality involves a basic lack of confidence in one's worth. Hence, however it may be developed, a sense of basic worth appears critically related to the courage to be.

WILL AND FREEDOM

At some point in Dembo's experiment, each subject realizes that the impossible situation which he is in is maintained by the will of the experimenter. It is she who has given them the task to begin with, who insists that there is a solution in the face of all evidence and his own reasoning to the contrary, and who will not permit him to acknowledge defeat and leave. The subject attempts to muster his own will, to insist that there is no solution, or that at any rate he personally cannot find it. However, his protests are to no avail. The will of the experimenter prevails in its determination of reality.

The Nature of Will

There are many ways to conceive of "will." Rather than attempting to discuss these various possibilities here, we shall briefly present one point of view that can provide a framework for understanding the contributions of the Lewin group. This point of view draws on different ideas expressed by Ricoeur in his analysis of will (30), Chein's analysis of motive (31), and my own analysis of decision making (32).

As we noted in discussing Ovsiankina's work, we may view a will activity as an intention system—an organization of behavior that tends towards completion—and a gestalt which consists of three interrelated parts: the motivation for the activity, the personal choice to undertake the activity, and the project of action itself. In Lewin's terms, these may be regarded as equivalent to "needs," "goal setting," and "goal striving."

The motives for the intention system may be regarded as other ongoing activities to which the person is committed. While the new activity would not be undertaken if it were not for these motives, the former activities become motives only as a part of the new whole (activity) that has been formed.

The choice of the projected action actually involves its formulation. In order to choose to act, the person must respond to the situation which confronts him and give it a meaning which fits the structure of the situation as well as the demands of his own interests (the prior activities to which he is committed) and emotions. The choice of which of these interests will motivate the project reinforces which interests are his, and hence influences his identity as a person. The decision to undertake the project commits the self, which now becomes responsible for what will transpire. The decision is basically an organizing of behavior. This organization sets the goal for the new activity, which may become a wellspring for further activities in the future. As we have just seen, such goal setting is involved whenever a person establishes a level of aspiration.

The project of action itself (to which the person is committed) may be regarded as the set or intention or tension system which is at the heart of Lewin's analysis. It is the person's goal striving, and organizes his field of forces. It is this part of the gestalt of willed activity, the product of choice, that appears as the force of will, and that is so relevant to an analysis of the struggle of wills.

Own Will and Other Will

We have spoken of will as an organization of behavior which determines the directionality and forces in a person's situation. But we may also ask *whose* organization is going to determine the environmental field. For a person experiences the force of wills other than his own. The child who finds that he *has* to relinquish his plaything to the outstretched hand of the expectant parent, or the politician who finds that he *has* to hold a fund-raising dinner for the president (33), experiences strong forces from the will of an other. Furthermore, this alien will may be internalized. Thus, in Chapter IX, we saw that the imperatives of a person's superego may be understood as stemming from the parent's motives maintained by the person's commitment to the authority of his parents. In all of these cases, we are interested in will as a center of power or influence. This is the sense in which Dembo is using the term when she refers to the struggle between the forces of the experimenter and the subject. Such a usage—will as a source of forces—is useful if we are to discuss whether it is the person's own choices (intentions) or the other's choices (intentions) which are to determine the situation. Lewin spoke of this in terms of how the valences within a field were going to be determined. Were the valences determined by the person's own need? or were the valences induced by the other's needs? In Chapter IV, we saw that this was a critical factor in the determination of whether the person experienced wanting to complete an activity or having to complete it.

This way of looking at will has the advantage of drawing attention to the fact that either the person's or the other's will may organize the environment experienced by the person. Thus, in Dembo's experiment, the person's own mind (will) told him there was no solution to the problem, whereas the other's will insisted there was. When the subject buys the experimenter's idea, and once again begins to try to find a solution, we may say that the field (with its meaning of a problem with a solution) has been determined by the will of the experimenter. In Lewin's terms, the subjects are in the field of force of the experimenter, a field which can induce valences and create barriers, and whose existence, in the case at hand, is dependent on the authority which the subject grants the experimenter (just as a child may grant authority to his parents).

Returning to the other's forces, it should be observed that the commands, assertions, and seductions of another's will all work by inducing valences in the person's life-space. In fact, one might view "self-control" in an analogous way. That is, in the case of self-control, we might regard the person as inducing valences in his own field, organizing the field so that he can walk by a growling dog with a steady and calm air, proceed with a difficult task in the light of possible failure, control his temper in the face of provocation, and so on, not because of his own forces—which would have him run, give up, and explode —but because of his own induction of "other" forces. Furthermore, it is interesting to note that *values* have the same property of inducing valences in the life-space. Lewin observed that values have the same conceptual status as authority—although they are one's own authority rather than the authority of an other. (Perhaps we could conceive of values as ideals which a person creates on the level of unreality—not as mere wishes, or as hopes, but as standards that will exert the force of what ought to be on the events that actually occur.)

In addition to own forces and other forces, Lewin mentions "impersonal" forces—the matter-of-fact demands of an objective situation (34). For example, there is the impersonal demand to stop for a red light or to discuss a problem with a co-worker in a cooperative work group. In Chapter IV, we saw that such forces were related to external need character, and are experienced when a person is task-involved rather than ego-involved. Unlike "other" forces, such impersonal forces are unlikely to arouse antagonism. However, there is always a possible danger involved in using impersonal forces, in that a person may not realize his own responsibility for the establishment of such forces. The fact that the demands of war for anti-personnel weapons and prison cages is experienced as an impersonal force may cancel the individual's own responsibility for accepting these demands.

The existence of impersonal forces raises the question of whether all the forces we experience are related to personal will—intention systems—or whether there are also impersonal sources of force. This question has not really been dealt with in any of the work with which I am familiar. Thus, when Köhler (35) investigates "requiredness"—our experience when one object or event *requires* another, as when a certain suit requires a certain type of tie— he chooses to simply establish the fact that we do experience objective forces that are not experienced as stemming from the self, and may be regarded as "vectors" in the environment (36). In one sense, these forces are completely independent of our personal will. Once a key is established, certain chords are required. In another sense, however, we know that this is a matter of certain standards—cultural norms and tastes—that we have grown up with and have accepted. I believe that these standards, like the values that we establish are maintained by our will, although they are impersonal and bind us and others alike. Hence, while the process is quite different from acts of personal will, the source of these impersonal forces still lies in our personal activity. Shortly, we shall see that such standards are usually related to the "social reality" established by groups.

To return to "other" forces, it should be noted that when we speak of one person's will as affecting another person's organization of reality—when we use the concept of will in an interpersonal way—we are simply extending that usage of will which denotes an intention system. While a simple intention system only organizes the person's own life-space, it is clear that an intention system could be directed at influencing another person's will, organizing *his* life-space. Of course, such an intention system might or might not be successful in that endeavor. When we are only speaking of the degree to which an intention system organizes the person's own life-space, we may speak of *strength of will* as indicating the extent to which the person pursues his goal. When we are speaking of the degree to which an intention system organizes another person's life-space, we may speak of *power*.

Lewin, focusing on situations where there was a conflict of wills, defines the other's power to get the person to perform some act in terms of the ratio: maximum force which the other can induce in the person's field/minimum resistance the person can offer. However, Cartwright (37) has suggested that a more general definition of the other's power can be stated in terms of the other's ability to perform acts which will instigate forces in the person's life-space. He then draws a distinction between power as the ability to instigate forces, and *control*—the ability to have these forces lead to desired behavior.

Since the exercise of power consists in performing acts which will bring the desired forces into play, one of the other's major resources is his skill in formulating these acts. In this regard Cartwright cites Meyer's distinction between a positive and a negative command. The former—"You may play with that truck"—specifies a clear direction of action, whereas the latter—"Don't play with those blocks"—is unclear about a desired direction, and hence yields weaker forces. In a related vein, in Chapter XI, we saw that actions by the person that are induced by the other will lead to greater forces in the person's life-space if the person is given a choice of actions.

Power—the ability to perform acts which will induce forces in a person's life-space—is also critically dependent on the relationship between the other and the person. In his analysis of the basis of attitude change, Kelman (38) distinguishes three types of influence which suggest different basic relationships between the other and the person. In the crudest of these, the other simply has some resources which the person needs, or some punishing capacity that the person fears. The use of such resources may get the person to comply with the other's desires, but the person's behavior is completely dependent on the other's sanctions and has had no effect on the person's beliefs or reality. In our own view, the other has power, but not authority; and really only affects the person's behavior by bribes or threats, rather than the induction of valences which really shape the person's life-space.

A much more pervasive influence occurs when there is an identification between the other and the person. Given such a relationship, or the possibility of one, the other may induce forces that shape the person's beliefs; and these influences will be maintained as long as the identification persists (39). We suppose that when the person recognizes the other's authority, such an identification exists.

Finally, the person may be in a relationship where he internalizes the other's reality so that it becomes his own; this affects his values in a way that is no longer dependent on power or identification. Of course, in Dembo's experiment this type of influence does not occur. We are dealing there with a subject who only temporarily gives the experimenter authority, and allows his reality to be influenced by this relationship of identification.

Will and Reality

From our discussion thus far, it may not be apparent how close a relationship exists between will, on the one hand, and reality, on the other. In a sense, will determines what a person's reality will be, organizing the field of his experience and giving meaning to the situation in which the person finds himself. In the case of a decision, Lewin notes that there is a restructuring of the field so that one of a number of overlapping situations acquires full potency. We might say that this dominant situation now becomes the person's reality. In the case of a simple intention system, for example, the intention to build a house, the person may begin noticing types of houses, and what was some "woods" becomes a possible "house site." In the case of an interpersonal intention, for example, the intention to have one's child pick up his room, the parent may assert that "The room needs picking up," a "reality" that the child may recognize not at all.

Now, since the source of will may be one's own or another's, it is apparent that the very texture of reality may be supported by one's own intention systems or by the intention systems of others. In fact, much of our reality is supported in yet a third way—by the groups to which we belong. Many of the impersonal forces to which we are subjected, and those attitudes that are based on our identification with others, are examples of the importance of groups as sources of will.

Lewin observed that the group is often the ground on which a person stands, and therefore to change the attitudes of an individual, one often must change the beliefs of the group to which he belongs. In his later experiments with attitude change, he showed that new behavior was most likely to be induced when individuals made a decision to act as part of being in a common interest group (40). This same sensitivity to how much of our reality is anchored in group beliefs affected Lewin's instigation of "action-research" (41) to help persons and communities modify their behavior in socially desirable ways. For example, Lewin argued for the importance of a group within a community doing a "self-survey" to determine the extent of the discriminating practices within the community, and also for the involvement of all groups that needed to be affected by social changes.

To some extent, we choose the groups to which we belong. If these are democratic cooperative groups, their reality reflects our own will. Thus, a large part of the reality of an emotionally mature adult who is living in circumstances of economic and political freedom may be self-determined. However, to the extent a person is emotionally, economically, or politically dependent, his reality may be largely determined by the will of others.

The dependency on others which makes reality particularly susceptible to the will of others is maximal during childhood. Lewin notes that in the world of the child the "will of the adult is the strongest and hardest reality," and says that the child's world is largely determined by the social field of forces generated by the authorities in his life (42). We have seen the tremendous impact which adult-controlled success or failure can have on the child's whole demeaner and his will to try. And Wiehe's study (43) shows how strongly the behavior of a child is affected by the mere presence of a strange adult. He demonstrates that when a stranger is at a distance, the child becomes overly boisterous; if the adult moves physically close to the child, the child's behavior becomes inhibited.

It is in this context that Lewin makes one of his most important social commentaries. In a chapter which has been largely overlooked he discusses the different ways in which a child may develop his conceptualization of reality (44). Noting that adults have the propensity to make *their* wishes be the basis for the child's reality, he observes (45):

> The more a pedagogy is based on obedience, the more this outside will becomes the supporting scafford of the child's reality. . . . If, in such a situation, the sphere of power of the adult, his position of authority, should for any reason collapse, the structure of the level of reality on which the life of the child rests psychologically must also collapse. This occurs when the child becomes independent, usually at the latest, with puberty. Such a collapse is usually bad for the child especially because the constraint situation in which he has lived is not only an inimical pressure but at the same time the crutch of his existence.

Lewin points out that there is an alternative way for the child to develop a sense of reality. Adults may arrange for him to be in a situation where he can choose his own activities in accordance with his own needs and experience the "objectively conditioned difficulties" which stand in the way of his attaining his goals. When reality is established in this way, it does not need the supports of external authority.

A second important advantage of this latter pedagogy is that the child does not have to squelch his own imagination. Lewin was conscious of the importance of having a close relationship between fantasy and action, the levels of unreality and reality. He notes that in wishful thinking the level of unreality is unrelated to the future level of reality, while in narrow realism the person is unable to perform imaginative long range planning. Thus, he observes that in either case, "The individual does not believe he has the power to form the world according to his wishes" (46).

Likewise, in his article on morale (47), Lewin points out that the heart of morale lies in having both high ideals and a high degree of realism. He notes that one of the largest challenges facing the adolescent involves his leaving his small primary group to meet a larger reality that will enlarge the scope and the time perspective of his life-space. The trauma of this challenge may lead a person to react by either restricting himself to a very narrow time perspective —having no ideals and trivial personal pursuits—or by abandoning considerations of the actual structure of the present reality, and thereby living only in terms of ideal goals and what ought to be. Thus, Lewin sees the mature person as one "who takes his goal seriously enough to do what is necessary to change the present state of affairs" (48).

Nature of Freedom

The extent of our freedom of behavior is limited by a number of factors that are internal as well as external. Chein (49) has observed that our freedom "from" is limited by internal compulsions and pressure, as well as by pressures from various external sources of power; and that our freedom "to" is limited by our own lack of ability as well as by external barriers. However, the crux of winning ourselves more freedom in all these areas involves being free to will our own reality, to have the power to determine our own experiences.

One of the most interesting aspects of Dembo's study is the fact that no subject determined his own reality, rejected the authority of the experimenter, and quietly left the experiment. In a subsequent study, Frank showed that subjects would engage in obviously impossible tasks as long as the experimenter asked them to perform the task. He concluded that the subject, ". . . makes an implicit contract which strongly inhibits resistance to any activity required by the experimenter" (50). This contract is so strong that Orne (51) related the power of the experimenter to the power involved in hypnotic suggestion, and studies by Milgram (52) and by Zimbardo (53) have dramatically illustrated how difficult it is for subjects to act on the basis of their own reality and values rather than those determined by the experimenter. While these latter studies demonstrate the full range of the experimenter's power, I believe that the conceptual issues involved in the subject's freedom are most clearly revealed in Dembo's experiment.

Here we have subjects who are, themselves, convinced that in reality there is no solution that they can find. Yet the experimenter keeps insisting on another reality. What prevents the subjects from dismissing her authority and exercising their freedom to leave? Of course the subjects did agree to be subjects, and they did give the experimenter authority over their behavior; but they could always take this authority back. They could withdraw their support and leave. Yet they did not. Should we simply say that this was their choice, or can we say that they were not free to choose?

We may approach this question from two perspectives. From the first perspective, we may see that the subjects were not free to choose to leave. For we assert that in order for a person to be free within a situation, he must perceive a choice, must see some viable alternatives. From this perspective, the achievement of freedom may be regarded in the light of creative problem solving. For a person to obtain freedom, he may have to see the situation in a new way. Now, not only do some situations provide less freedom for the person in the sense of having more barriers, less clarity, and less space of free movement, but also, some situations have conditions within them that work against a person seeing them in a new way. Such situations leave the person's freedom dependent on someone who stands outside of the situation and can help. For example, in discussing the problem that a child has in learning to detour away from a goal in order to reach it, Lewin notes (54):

> If the affective connection between the child and the goal is too strong the relative detachment and inward 'retirement' from the valence which is so favorable to the perception of the whole situation and hence to the transformation (restructuring) of the total field, which occurs in the act of insight is much more difficult.

Likewise, in his work on problem solving, Karl Duncker (55) shows that if an object in the environment is "embedded" in the environment by virtue of its functional position, other possible uses for the object are much less apt to be seen. In one of his experimental problems, the solution involves tying two sticks together, and the subject needs a piece of string. If there is a piece of string that is hanging on the wall, the subjects will quickly seize it. However, if there is a calendar that is hanging by a piece of string, many subjects will fail to see the piece of string that is potentially there. This quality, which has been called "functional fixedness," may also be applied to the role of the person in a situation. Thus, we believe that part of the reason Dembo's subjects could not leave is because they were embedded as subjects in the context of an experiment. As a part of this whole, it was difficult for them to see themselves as free agents. For them to leave they would have had to tear apart the experiment in the same way a person had to tear apart the calendar to get the string. To achieve freedom in an impossible situation, a person must separate himself out from the functions that are being required of him by the situation.

A field condition which works against this separation, and against any freeing increase of perspective, is the condition of tension. It may be recalled that Karsten describes how her subjects could not leave an activity that was satiating until tension had been reduced. Karsten describes how separating from the activity is more difficult as satiation progresses. She notes, "The free movement of the subject, especially the possibility of leaving the field on the basis of a 'decision,' becomes more limited as the strength of the tension field increases." The subject can only leave after tension has been decreased by reaching the end of a unit, or after an emotional outburst (which may place the subject in a new situation), or when some event leads the subject to feel that he is in control.

In fact, the very ability to make a clearcut decision and exercise one's own will may depend on having some degree of separation between the self and ongoing activity, so that the person is not embedded in an activity. This factor may explain one rather neglected aspect of Frank's studies on subject's resistance to personal pressure from the experimenter (56).

After preliminary experiments demonstrated that subjects usually do whatever the experimenter requests, Frank created the following situation that was designed to provoke resistance to the experimenter's will. He seated his subjects at a table, made a row of twelve crackers, and announced to his subjects that, "This is an experiment on persuasion. I am going to try to make you eat the twelve crackers in the first row on the tray. Whether you eat them or not is entirely up to you and doesn't affect the experiment one way or the other. But if you resist, I shall try to make you eat them anyway." Whereas control subjects—who had simply been told to eat the crackers—almost always dutifully complied, the above challenge provoked quick resistance from 76 per cent of the subjects, and the remainder of the subjects reported that they immediately made a decision not to resist the experimenter. That is, in either case the subjects quickly made a strong-willed decision about what to do. When they did decide to resist, they used rapid maximal resistance with no subsequent yielding, and they seemed in complete command of the situation with no signs of tension.

A third group of subjects began the experiment as the controls did. That is, they were seated and simply told that the experiment required them to eat the row of crackers in front of them. However, once they engaged in the activity —while they were eating the second cracker—they were given the same challenging instructions that had provoked resistance in most of the experimental group. Yet under these circumstances, only 45 per cent of the subjects resisted; and even in these cases, the average subject showed a vacillating will with fluctuations in resistance, confusion, and emotional tension. Either the subjects were unsure as to what behavior would constitute resistance, or the fact that they were embedded in the activity of eating hindered their ability to make a decision.

As important as involvement, tension, and other field conditions are, they are only one aspect of freedom, and we may view freedom from quite a different perspective. Wertheimer (57), in a poignant chapter about a person's search for the meaning of freedom, concludes that freedom is not only a condition in the social field but also "a gestalt quality of action." That is, an action may be inherently free in the sense of being self-determined.

From this existential perspective, we may assert that the subjects were free to choose, that a person always has the choice to organize the field in alternative ways. We believe that one of these ways will be a valid assertion of what the person really wants to will, an expression of his own self. We believe that this choice occurs when the person realizes (makes real) the basic nature of a situation which he previously was only contemplating. In Dembo's experiment, the subject may imagine that there is no solution; but he fails to transform that imagination into reality. This issue is discussed in more personal metaphors in the writings of Carlos Castaneda (58). It is this choice to constitute reality, to "recognize necessity," to "see truth," that makes a person free. Although the subjects *say* that there is no solution, they do not take the responsibility of *acting* on this truth and leaving the experiment. Note that if the experimenter did show them a solution, they would be very surprised, and they might even say, "How very stupid of me not to see that." But their self-worth would not be at stake—they would not *be* stupid—because they did not risk any aspect of their identity.

What Dembo argues is that the subjects in her experiment could not leave because if they left they would connect the experiment to the rest of their lives —destroy the boundary between the experiment and their life. From our perspective, we would say that the subjects could not take the responsibility for leaving (assume that authority) because the experiment would then no longer be just an experiment, but would become real. If a subject left, he would be asserting, realizing, that there was no solution to the problem. If by any chance there *was* a solution, which the experimenter could then demonstrate, the subjects would not only feel foolish, they would *be* foolish. Given the relatively small discomfort involved in staying in this particular impossible situation, no subject was courageous (or foolish) enough to assume responsibility and take this risk.

I believe that an equivalent choice which requires risk and courage stands between a person and freedom in all impossible situations.

FOOTNOTES

1. Margaret Jucknat, "Leistung, Anspruchsniveau und Selbstebewusstein," *Psychol. Forsch.* 22(1937), 89–179. A translation of a somewhat abridged, 66-page version, "Performance, Level of Aspiration and Self-Esteem," is available from Xerox: University Microfilms. This translation is complete in regards to the empirical results, but omits some theoretical considerations expounded in the original.

2. Dorwin Cartwright, "The Effects of Interruption, Completion, and Failure Upon the Attractiveness of Activities," *Journal of Experimental Psychology* 31(1942), 1–16.

3. Ibid., 13.

4. Saul Rosenzweig, "An Experimental Study of 'Repression' with Special Reference to Need-persistive and Ego-defensive Reactions to Frustration," *Journal of Experimental Psychology* 32(1943), 64–74.

5. Elliot Aronson, "The Effect of Effort on the Attractiveness of Rewarded and Unrewarded Stimuli," *Journal of Abnormal Social Psychology* 63(1961), 375–380.

6. See the data on subject 19 in the previous chapter (section on Individual Differences).

7. Sarah Fajans, "Erfolg, Ausdauer, und Activität beim Saügling und Kleinkind," *Psychol. Forsch.* 17(1933), 268–305. A translation, "Success, Persistence and Activity in the Infant and Small Child," is available from Xerox: University Microfilms.

8. Sara Fajans, "Die Bedeutung der Entfernung fur die Starke eines Aufforderungscharakters beim Saugling und Kleinkind," *Psychol. Forsch.* 17(1933), 215–267. The translation, "The Significance of Distance for the Strength of a Valence in Infants and Young Children," may be obtained from Xerox: University Microfilms.

9. Of special note is a study by one of Lewin's students at Iowa—Sibylle Escalona, "The Effect of Success and Failure Upon the Level of Aspiration and Behavior in Manic-Depressive Psychoses," *University of Iowa Studies in Child Welfare* 16(1940), 197–302.

10. D. C. McClelland, J. W. Atkinson, R. A. Clark, and E. L. Lowell, *The Achievement Motive* (New York: Appleton-Century-Crofts, 1953).

11. G. Mandler and S. B. Sarason, "A Study of Anxiety and Learning," *Journal of Abnormal Social Psychology* 47(1952), 166–173.

12. J. W. Atkinson, "Motivational Determinants of Risk Taking Behavior," *Psychological Review* 64(1957), 359–372.

13. Joe K. Adams, "The Neglected Psychology of Cowardice," *Journal of Humanistic Psychology* 5(1965), 57–69.

14. Marie Jahoda, "Conformity and Independence," *Human Relations* 12(1959), 99–120.

15. Kurt Lewin, Tamara Dembo, Leon Festinger, and Pauline Sears, "Level of Aspiration," in J.M.V. Hurt (Ed.), *Personality and the Behavior Disorders* (New York: Ronald Press, 1944), 333–378.

16. Joseph de Rivera, *The Psychological Dimension of Foreign Policy* (Columbus, Ohio: Charles E. Merrill, 1968), 112–122.

17. Robert W. White, "Competence and the Psychosexual Stages of Development," in Marshall R. Jones (Ed.), *Nebraska Symposium on Motivation* (Lincoln, Nebraska: University of Nebraska Press, 1960).

18. Bernard Weiner, *Achievement Motivation and Attribution Theory* (Morristown, New Jersey: General Learning Press, 1974).

19. David C. McClelland, *The Achieving Society* (Van Nostrand, 1961).

20. William James, *The Principles of Psychology* (Dover, 1950, original 1890) 310–313.

21. Fritz Heider, *The Psychology of Interpersonal Relations* (New York: McGraw-Hill, 1958), Chapter 4.

22. Irwin Katz, Edgar G. Epps, and Leland J. Axelson, "Effect Upon Negro Digit-symbol Performance of Anticipated Comparison with Whites and with Other Negroes," *Journal of Abnormal Social Psychology* 69(1964), 77–83.

23. John Holt, *How Children Fail* (New York: Dell, 1964).

24. Jean Paul Sartre, *Being and Nothingness* (New York: Washington Square Press, 1971, original, 1953), and Paul Tillich, *The Courage to Be* (New Haven: York University Press, 1952).

25. Dan Greenburg and Marcia Jacobs, *How to Make Yourself Miserable* (Random House, 1966).

26. Julles Older, "Pseudo-testing," Unpublished doctoral dissertation, New York University, 1968.

27. Tamara Dembo, Gloria L. Leviton, and Beatrice Wright, "Adjustment to Misfortune: A Problem of Social-psychological Rehabilitation," *Artificial Limbs* 3(1956), 4–62.

28. Viktor E. Frankl, *Man's Search for Meaning* (New York: Washington Square Press, 1963).

29. James, *The Principles of Psychology,* 316.

30. Paul Ricoeur, *Freedom and Nature: The Voluntary and the Involuntary* (Evanston, Illinois: Northwestern University Press, 1966), 227.

31. Isidor Chein, *The Science of Behavior and the Image of Man* (New York: Basic Books, 1972).

32. Joseph de Rivera, *The Psychological Dimension of Foreign Policy,* Chapter 4.

33. John Connally, "Why Kennedy Went to Texas," *Life Magazine* (November 22, 1967), 86A ff.

34. See Kurt Lewin, "Behavior and Development as a Function of the Total Situation," in *Field Theory in the Social Sciences* (New York: Harper and Row, 1951). See p. 260, for an illustration of how interpersonal conflict may be

diminished when personal forces are translated into impersonal ones. See Lewin, *Resolving Social Conflicts* (New York: Harper and Row, 1948) Chapter 8, for a chronic conflict in industry.

35. Wolfgang Köhler, *The Place of Value in the World of Fact* (New York: Meridian Books, 1959), Chapters 2 and 3.

36. Maurice Mandelbaum attempts to establish that these vectors are the basis for our experience of moral demands. Such an experience occurs whenever a person apprehends the "fittingness between a specific envisioned action and the situation in which he finds himself." *The Phenomenology of Moral Experience* (Glencoe, Illinois: Free Press, 1955), 69.

37. Dorwin Cartwright, "A Field Theoretical Conception of Power," in *Studies in Social Power* (Ann Arbor, Michigan: University of Michigan Press, 1959).

38. Herbert Kelman, "Processes of Opinion Change," *Pub. Opin. Quart.* 25(1961), 57–78 (Bobbs-Merrill reprint P-191).

39. It should also be noted that some of the effects of induced actions that we considered in Chapter XI depend on whether the induced action brings the person into a closer relationship with a group with which he identifies.

40. Kurt Lewin, "Group Decision and Social Change," in Harold Proshansky and Bernard Seidenberg (Eds.), *Basic Studies in Social Psychology* (New York: Holt, Rinehart and Winston, 1965). For more recent research on this topic, see B. E. Collins and H. Guetzkon, *A Social Psychology of Group Processes for Decision-making* (New York: Wiley, 1964).

41. Isidor Chein, Stuart W. Cook, and John Harding, "The Field of Action Research," *American Psychologist* 3(1948), 43–50.

42. Kurt Lewin, "Education For Reality," in *A Dynamic Theory of Personality* (New York: McGraw-Hill, 1935), 175.

43. This study by F. Wiehe, "Die Grenzen des Ichs," is mentioned repeatedly in *A Dynamic Theory of Personality* (see especially the data given on 261–264). However, it is listed there as "in preparation." It seems doubtful that it was ever published, and I have been unable to find any manuscript.

44. Lewin, "Education For Reality," 171–179.

45. Ibid., 176.

46. Roger Barker, Tamara Dembo, and Kurt Lewin, "Frustration and Regression: An Experiment with Young Children," *University of Iowa Studies of Child Welfare* 18(1941), No. 1, 211.

47. Kurt Lewin, "Time Perspective and Morale," in Goodwin Watson (Ed.), *Civilian Morale* (Boston: Houghton Mifflin, 1942).

48. Ibid., 68.

49. Chein, *The Science of Behavior and the Image of Man,* 295. I am giving a slight reinterpretation of his presentation.

50. Jerome D. Frank, "Experimental Studies of Personal Pressure and Resistance," *Journal of General Psychology* 30(1944), 23–64.

51. Martin T. Orne, "On the Social Psychology of the Psychological Experiment," *American Psychologist* 17(1962), 776–783.

52. Stanley Milgram, "Behavioral Study of Obedience," *Journal of Abnormal Social Psychology* 67(1963), 371–378 (Bobbs-Merrill reprint P-521).

53. Philip G. Zimbardo, "The Psychological Power and Pathology of Imprisonment," *Catalogue of Selected Documents in Psychology* 3(Spring, 1973), 45.

54. Kurt Lewin, "Vectors, Cognitive Processes, and Mr. Tolman's Criticism," *Journal of General Psychology* 8(1933), 318–345, 331.

55. Karl Duncker, "On Problem-solving," *Psychol. Monogr.* 58(1945), No. 5.

56. Frank, "Experimental Studies of Personal Pressure and Resistance."

57. Max Wertheimer, "A Story of Three Days," in Ruth Nandon Anshen (Ed.), *Freedom: Its Meaning* (New York: Harcourt Brace, 1940).

58. Carlos Castaneda, *Journey to Ixtlan* (New York: Simon and Schuster, 1972); and *Tales of Power* (New York: Simon and Schuster, 1974).

INDEX